# The Destiny of Modern Societies

# Studies in Critical Social Sciences Book Series

Haymarket Books is proud to be working with Brill Academic Publishers (http://www.brill.nl) to republish the Studied in Critical Social Sciences book series, edited by David Fasenfest, in paperback editions. Current titles in this series are:

*The Destiny of Modern Societies: The Calvinist Predestination of a New Society*
Milan Zafirovski

*Dialectic of Solidarity: Labor, Antisemitism, and the Frankfurt School*
Mark P. Worrell

*Engaging Social Justice: Critical Studies of Twenty-First Century Social Transformation*
Edited by David Fasenfest

*The Future of Religion: Toward a Reconciled Society*
Edited by Michael R. Ott

*Globalization and the Environment*
Edited by Andrew Jorgenson and Edward Kick

*Hybrid Identities: Theoretical and Empirical Examinations*
Edited by Keri E. Iyall Smith and Patricia Leavy

*Imperialism, Neoliberalism and Social Struggles in Latin America*
Edited by Richard A. Dello Buono and José Bell Lara

*Liberal Modernity and Its Adversaries: Freedom, Liberalism and Anti-Liberalism in the Twenty-first Century*
Milan Zafirovski

*Marx, Critical Theory, and Religion: A Critique of Rational Choice*
Edited by Warren S. Goldstein

*Marx's Scientific Dialectics: A Methodological Treatise for a New Century*
Paul Paolucci

*Race and Ethnicity: Across Time, Space, and Discipline*
Rodney D. Coates

*Social Change, Resistance, and Social Practice*
Edited by Richard Dello Buono and David Fasenfest

*Transforming Globalization: Challenges and Opportunities in the Post 9/11 Era*
Edited by Bruce Podobnik and Thomas

Series Editor: David Fasenfest, Wayne State University

Editorial Board: Chris Chase-Dunn, University of California-Riverside; G. William Domhoff, University of California-Santa Cruz; Colette Fagan, Manchester University; Matha Gimenez, University of Colorado, Boulder; Heidi Gottfried, Wayne State University; Karin Gottschall, University of Bremen; Bob Jessop, Lancaster University; Rhonda Levine, Colgate University, Jacqueline O'Reilly, University of Brighton; Mary Romero, Arizona State University; Chizuko Ueno, University of Tokyo

# The Destiny of Modern Societies

## The Calvinist Predestination of a New Society

Milan Zafirovski

HAYMARKET
BOOKS
Chicago, Illinois

First published in 2009 by Brill

Copyright 2009 by Koninklijke Brill NV, Leiden, The Netherlands.
Koninklijke Brill NV incorporates the imprints Brill, Hotei Publishing,
IDC Publishers, Martinus Nijhoff Publishers and VSP.

This edition published in 2011 by Haymarket Books

Haymarket Books
PO Box 180165
Chicago, Illinois, 60618
773-583-7884
info@haymarketbooks.org
www.haymarketbooks.org

ISSN 978-1-60846-125-7

In the U.S. through Consortium Book Sales and Distribution, www.cbsd.com
In Canada through Publishers Group Canada, www.pgcbooks.ca
In the UK, Turnaround Publisher Services, www.turnaround-uk.com
In Australia, Palgrave Macmillan, www.palgravemacmillan.com.au
All other countries, Publishers Group Worldwide, www.pgw.com

Printed in Canada

Published with the generous support of Lannan Foundation
and the Wallace Global Fund.

Library of Congress Cataloging-in-Publication Data is available.

10 9 8 7 6 5 4 3 2 1

CONTENTS

Introduction ................................................. 1

I. America's Destiny and Calvinism ........................... 7
The "First New Nation" and European Calvinism ............... 7
    Calvinism via Puritanism ................................ 10
Calvinism—The Genesis and "Destiny" of America? ............ 13
Calvinist Predestination via the Puritan "Destiny" of America .... 19
    "All in the Extended Calvinist Family" ................... 26
The Nature and Scope of the Calvinist "Predestination" of the
    "New Nation" ............................................ 29
    From Total Mastery to "Holistic Destiny" ................. 29
    "Holism" in Societal Predestination: Varieties ........... 31
Appendix: America's "Destiny" and Tocqueville, Weber,
    and Marx ................................................ 36

II. America's Calvinist "Destiny" Identified and Specified .... 41
What is America's Calvinist "Destiny"? ...................... 41
    Calvinism Retrieved from the (Theocratic) "Golden Past" .... 41
    Calvinist Theocracy—America's "Destiny"? ................. 48
    Calvinist "Destiny" of Tocqueville's America ............. 50
Bibliocracy from the Genesis to the Destiny ................. 57
    Theocratic "Paradise Lost and Found" ..................... 57
    The Calvinist Theocratic Genesis and Evolution ........... 60
    The Calvinist Theocratic Destiny and Heritage ............ 66
The Calvinist Design and System of Theocracy Reconsidered .... 70
    Calvinist Theocracy as "Divinely Ordained" ............... 71
    Calvinist Theocracy and Despotism via Puritan
        Theocratic Tyranny .................................. 78
From Calvinist Theocracy to the Moralistic "Tyranny of
    Puritanism" to "Moral Fascism" ........................... 84
    Calvinism, Puritanism, and Moral Fascism ................. 84
Calvinist Theocracy as Total Society ........................ 90
    Calvinist Theocracy as a Total Social System: Theocratic
        Subsystems .......................................... 90
    From Total Mastery of the World to a Totalitarian
        Social System ....................................... 96

III. Economic System of Calvinist Theocracy ................. 101
A Theocratic Master-Servant Economy....................... 101
   From the Mastery of Society to a Master-Servant Economy
      and Back................................................ 101
   Calvinist Vision and Reality of a Master-Servant
      Economy................................................ 104
   Theocratic Economic Logic and Structure ................ 109
   A Master-Servant Economy versus the Weberian Elective
      Affinity of Calvinism and Capitalism................... 114
   The Master-Servant Economy—America's Calvinist
      Economic "Destiny"?.................................. 120
Elements and Subtypes of the Calvinist Pure Master-Servant
   Economy.................................................. 122
The Calvinist Slave Economy.................................. 124
   Pure Calvinist Theocracy and Economic Slavery........... 124
   The Calvinist "Rational Choice": Extermination
      or Enslavement?...................................... 129
   Composite Economic Slavery ........................... 132
Calvinist Feudal Servitude................................... 136
   Calvinist Theocracy and Feudalism ...................... 137
   Calvinist Feudalism Déjà Vu............................. 140
   Calvinist Neo-Feudalism ............................... 142
   Calvinist New Bibliocracy and Neo-Feudalism ............ 145
The Calvinist Caste System ................................. 147
   Calvinist Theocracy and the Caste Economy .............. 147
   Calvinist Caste Exclusion versus Total Extermination....... 149
   Forms and Meanings of the Calvinist Caste System......... 153
Elements of the Calvinist Diluted Master-Servant Economy ..... 156
   Diluted Calvinist Theocracy and the Master-Servant
      Economy.............................................. 157
   Attributes of the Calvinist Diluted Master-Servant
      Economy.............................................. 159
Calvinist Predatory Capitalism ............................. 163
   From Rapacious Theocracy to Predatory Capitalism—and
      Back.................................................. 165
   "Mafia Capitalism" ..................................... 167
   The Calvinist Spirit cum "Ghost" of Capitalism ........... 171
   Calvinist Master-Servant Capitalism: Specification......... 176
   Economic "Autocracy" versus Democracy ................ 177
   "One-Party" Economic System ......................... 180
   Extreme Economic Anti-Egalitarianism .................. 181

Extreme Economic Anti-Humanism .................... 186
"Free Enterprise" Epilogue: Anti-Labor Economy—
    America's Calvinist Economic "Destiny"? ............. 192

IV. Political System of Calvinist Theocracy .................. 193
Theocratic Polity ............................................ 193
Theocratic Polity: Formal Terms............................. 198
    Legal-Institutional Fusion between Politics and Religion.... 199
    Legal-Institutional Fusion of Secular and Sacred Powers .... 206
    Subverted Institutional Separation of Sacred and Secular
        Power................................................. 209
Theocratic Polity: Substantive Terms ......................... 213
    Factual Societal Fusion between Religion and Politics ...... 213
    Factual Societal Fusion of Sacred and Secular Power ....... 221
    Diluted Societal Differentiation between Religion and
        Politics.............................................. 224
Theocratic cum Anti-Liberal Polity ........................... 234
    Calvinist Political Anti-Liberalism versus Democracy ...... 235
    From the 16th Century French Calvinist Synod
        to 21st Century American Evangelicalism.............. 244
Theocratic Polity as a Non-Democratic Government .......... 249
    From Fundamentalist Anti-Liberalism to Theocratic
        Totalitarianism....................................... 252
    "Godly Politics" versus Liberal-Secular Democracy ........ 257
    Specific Calvinist Subversions of Liberal-Secular
        Democracy............................................ 260
Theocratic Aristocracy ...................................... 260
    From the Aristocracy of Heaven to the Aristocracy of
        Society............................................... 260
Theocratic Oligarchy......................................... 266
    The (Predestination) Doctrine of "Heavenly" Oligarchy..... 267
    The Sociological "Law" of Calvinism and Political
        Oligarchy ............................................ 275
    Theocratic Plutocracy.................................... 284
    Political and Social Closure and Exclusion ............... 289
    Appendix: Catholic and Neo-Calvinist Theocratic
        Tendencies ........................................... 296

V. Civil Society of Calvinist Theocracy....................... 297
Puritan Moralistic Tyranny .................................. 297
Rediscovering and Redefining Moral Fascism ................. 303

Syndromes of Puritan Moral Fascism . . . . . . . . . . . . . . . . . . . . . . . . 311
    Denial and Suppression of Individual Moral Freedom . . . . . . 311
    Equation of Pleasures, Sins, and Crimes . . . . . . . . . . . . . . . . . . 319
    Anti-Humanism . . . . . . . . . . . . . . . . . . . . . . . . . . . . . . . . . . . . . . 323
    Coercive Imposition of Puritanical Morality. . . . . . . . . . . . . . . 332
    "Draconianism". . . . . . . . . . . . . . . . . . . . . . . . . . . . . . . . . . . . . . 340
    Sadism and Masochism . . . . . . . . . . . . . . . . . . . . . . . . . . . . . . . 358
The Legal-Institutional Mechanism of Puritan
    Moral Fascism . . . . . . . . . . . . . . . . . . . . . . . . . . . . . . . . . . . . . . 362
    The Vice-Police State. . . . . . . . . . . . . . . . . . . . . . . . . . . . . . . . . 362
    Puritan and Islamic Vice-Police States Compared . . . . . . . . . . 369
From a Free Private Sphere to a Coercive
    Monastic Order . . . . . . . . . . . . . . . . . . . . . . . . . . . . . . . . . . . . . 384
Global Moral Fascism—Pan-American "Manifest Destiny"? . . . . . 390

VI. Cultural System of Calvinist Bibliocracy . . . . . . . . . . . . . . . . . . 397
Theocratic Culture. . . . . . . . . . . . . . . . . . . . . . . . . . . . . . . . . . . . . . . 397
    Culture as Theocratic Religion . . . . . . . . . . . . . . . . . . . . . . . . . 397
    Anti-Aesthetic Culture . . . . . . . . . . . . . . . . . . . . . . . . . . . . . . . . 400
    Anti-Rationalistic Culture . . . . . . . . . . . . . . . . . . . . . . . . . . . . . 402
    Secular Culture versus Theocratic Religion. . . . . . . . . . . . . . . 404
The Puritan "Culture of Death"? . . . . . . . . . . . . . . . . . . . . . . . . . . . 410
    Indicators ("Symptoms") of the Puritan "Culture of
    Death" . . . . . . . . . . . . . . . . . . . . . . . . . . . . . . . . . . . . . . . . . . . . 412
The Adverse Fate of Aesthetic Culture in Calvinist Theocracy. . . . 424
    The Anti-Renaissance and Anti-Humanism . . . . . . . . . . . . . . 424
    The Anti-Renaissance and Anti-Humanism Initiated . . . . . . . 428
    The Anti-Renaissance Generalized and Perpetuated . . . . . . . . 433
    Indicators of Puritan Anti-Artistic Antagonism. . . . . . . . . . . . 436
The Adverse Fate of Intellectual Culture in Calvinist
    Theocracy . . . . . . . . . . . . . . . . . . . . . . . . . . . . . . . . . . . . . . . . . . 441
    The Counter-Enlightenment . . . . . . . . . . . . . . . . . . . . . . . . . . . 441
    The Counter-Enlightenment as the Dark Middle Ages
    Déjà Vu . . . . . . . . . . . . . . . . . . . . . . . . . . . . . . . . . . . . . . . . . . . . 445
    Counter-Enlightenment in Religious and Cultural
    Intolerance . . . . . . . . . . . . . . . . . . . . . . . . . . . . . . . . . . . . . . . . . 453
    Counter-Enlightenment in Intolerance in Comparative
    Perspective . . . . . . . . . . . . . . . . . . . . . . . . . . . . . . . . . . . . . . . . . 460
    Instances of Religious Tolerance and Freedom in Calvinist
    Societies—Despite Calvinism . . . . . . . . . . . . . . . . . . . . . . . . . . 465

Counter-Enlightenment in Cultural Anti-Rationalism...... 471
　　Counter-Enlightenment in Anti-Scientific Nihilism........ 485

VII. Calvinism Reconsidered............................... 497
Reconsidering Calvinism..................................... 497
　　From Calvinism to Puritanism and Back................. 498
Calvinism's Genesis Revisited............................... 504
The Dual Story of Calvinism: From an Abysmal Failure in the
　　"Old World" to a Fateful Triumph in the "New Nation"....... 509
　　Summary of Calvinism's Path: The Birth, Decline,
　　　　and Rebirth........................................ 521
The Spirit and Heritage of Calvinism Reconsidered............ 525
　　"What is in the Name" (of Calvinism)?.................... 526
　　Orthodox, Conservative Protestantism................... 526
　　Extreme, Radical Protestantism......................... 537
　　Disciplinarian, Repressive, and Hyper-Ascetic
　　　　Protestantism...................................... 546
　　Calvinism Reinvented and Reinforced: Reenter
　　　　Puritanism......................................... 558
Appendix: "Differences" between Calvinism
　　and Puritanism Revisited................................ 562

VIII. Conclusions.......................................... 575
"Destinies" of Human Societies.............................. 575
The "Wealth and Destiny of Nations"......................... 585
The Calvinist-Capitalist Elective Affinity in the "New Nation":
　　Theocratic Capitalism?.................................. 591
The Supreme Historical Irony? The Calvinist "French
　　Connection" to America.................................. 594

References................................................ 601
Index..................................................... 615

# INTRODUCTION

Do societies or nations have a destiny or fate? And if yes, what primarily determines and predicts such a societal destiny or national fate? Early French sociologist Alexis de Tocqueville,[1] among others, provides an explicit answer to the first question and an implicit one to the second in his *Democracy in America*. Tocqueville specifically observes and predicts that the "destiny" of America is "embodied" in the first Puritans and that Americans are a "puritanical people". Most US, especially conservative, sociologists and other social scientists concur with and celebrate this observation and prediction of Puritanism as American society's present and future or legacy, just as its genesis and "golden past". In the above statement, Tocqueville hence affirmatively and explicitly answers the question of national "destiny" with respect to the "first new nation." He also implicitly identifies certain social, specifically cultural, forces, like a historically founding and dominant religion, operating as the prime determinant and predictor of this "destiny."

Tocqueville hence performs two important contributions to sociological analysis. First, he introduces the concept of "destiny" to considering modern societies, in particular America, thus as potentially applicable to sociological and other scientific analysis. He therefore proposes and understands the concept in a scientific or empirical form and meaning. In turn, Tocqueville does not use the concept in the theological or transcendental sense such as Providential "manifest destiny", "Divinely Ordained" fate and mission, God's "chosen people" and rulers with "Divine Rights", as assumed in American Puritanism and religious conservatism in general. Second, he identifies and predicts America's "destiny" as embedded in Puritanism (the "first Puritans") in an historical and empirical sense of the Puritan present, future, or heritage of American society. And, he implicitly distinguishes this sense from the theological, transcendental meaning of the "Divine" predestination of

---

[1] Following the standard citation practice for classical and early modern social philosophers (e.g., Plato, Aristotle, Machiavelli, Hobbes, Hume, Kant, Hegel, Voltaire, Montesquieu, etc.), references for Tocqueville and other "dead" sociologists and economists are not provided for reasons of space and economy of exposition. This is done assuming that their works are well-known to readers and a "public domain" after 75 years of their original publication.

the "new nation" as the "chosen people" replacing the "old" European nations with equivalent claims to Providential "favor" and "choice."

If Tocqueville's statement is generalized, it implies that the "destinies" of societies, including Europe in his time and later, are primarily (though not exclusively) determined and predicted by religious and related cultural, as distinguished from secular, factors. In short, they are conditioned by what Weber calls ideal or spiritual rather than material or economic values and interests. Tocqueville emphasizes that Americans constitute "at the same time" a Puritan *and* capitalist society, a "puritanical people" and a "commercial nation". He thus seemingly suggests that America forms a capitalist society in spite, rather than because (as in Weberian accounts), of being a Puritan-religious nation. This implies a dis-affinity or disjuncture, rather than a Weberian "elective affinity" or close association, between capitalism and Puritanism, a market economy and religion in general.

Coincidentally (or not), Adam Smith wrote his *Wealth of Nations* almost a century before Tocqueville's *Democracy in America*. In this context, Smith implied that the "destiny" of societies was primarily determined by their wealth or economic factors. The same holds true of Marx (as evident in *Capital*) and most classical, neo-classical, and contemporary economists. For instance, Schumpeter presents an account of industrial capitalism, via its constant technological and economic revolution ("creative destruction") as the prime mover, as the major determinant of the "destiny" or nature of modern societies, particularly of political democracy.

Yet, Tocqueville's statement also entails a relevant sociological omission. This is placing American and other Puritanism in a larger comparative and historical framework. Specifically, this is the global transcontinental network and "extended family" of European Calvinism or the "Reformed Church", which identifies and characterizes the first Puritans as English-American Calvinists. Tocqueville certainly knew and implied this framework, but just did not state it and elaborate on it explicitly. Moreover, living in and coming from the very homeland of Calvinism (France), he perhaps assumed that the original Calvinist framework or extant "family" of the first Puritans in America was commonly known, thus axiomatic or redundant, not needed to be stated. This may be a justified omission, but remains a missing link for the purpose of a comparative sociological analysis of the evolution and "destiny" or heritage of Western Calvinist-Puritan and other societies, in particular America.

The present work develops Tocqueville's contributions and addresses his omission. First, it applies the concept of destiny to considering modern societies or nations, in particular America as arguably a hypermodern society or a "new nation". It adopts the concept in a sociological, empirical sense of societies' present and future or heritage, as distinguished from the theological, transcendental meaning of their providential predestination as "chosen" nations. Second, this work elaborates on America's societal "destiny" embedded in Puritanism as a concrete historical and empirical phenomenon, namely a specific type of religion, morality, ideology, and culture. Alternatively, it abstracts from America's theological or "manifest destiny" determined by what Weber calls the absolutely transcendental "God of Calvinism", including Puritanism. Third, it situates Puritanism and America's societal "destiny" in the global framework of Calvinism and Western society, respectively, since post-Reformation times through the early 21st century.

Hence, the main argument of this work is that the "destiny", like the genesis, of America is essentially embedded in and predicted by Calvinism, specifically via Puritanism as its English-American offspring and substantive equivalent. To extend Tocqueville's insight, the "destiny" of America is "embodied" ultimately in early Calvinists, immediately in the first Puritans as what Weber and other analysts (Kloppenberg 1998; McLaughlin 1996; Mises 1966) call Anglo-Saxon Calvinist, as distinguished from non-Calvinist, Protestants. Alternatively, the "destiny", like the genesis, of America is embedded in and predicted by Puritanism in the sense of American Calvinism and inscribed in the first Puritans as early Calvinists in the "new nation". Negatively, that the "destiny" of America is "embodied" in the first Puritans and determined by Puritanism, while not incorrect, is not a complete proposition, and cannot be fully understood and explained unless considering Calvinists as their theological parents and Calvinism as its creator.

In a sense, America's description as Tocqueville-Weber's "Puritan Nation" does not do justice completely to its history and social reality unless it is specified as also "Calvinist society". This is in fact a sociologically more complete and historically more accurate designation, given that American Puritanism arose and functioned as essentially Calvinism transplanted from the "old" into the "new world" via England (and Scotland). There is hardly a sensible way, means, and reason to avoid, escape, or ignore Calvinism in a sociological analysis of America's genesis, evolution or functioning, and "destiny", simply its past, present, and future. As an auxiliary point, Tocqueville omits or downplays certain countervailing non-Puritan and thus non-Calvinist social, religious and secular, forces and influences, no matter how weak, atypical, and secondary in relation to Calvinist Puritanism and other sectarian Protestantism (Lipset 1996), in America. Notably, these non-Puritan forces comprise Jefferson-Madison's Enlightenment-based liberal, secular, democratic, egalitarian, and rationalist ideals and institutions (Archer 2001; Patell 2001).

And, Calvinism itself was originally the French version of Protestantism or the Protestant Reformation, founded and embodied by Jean (*not* John, as in the English translations) Calvin (Elwood 1999) born and raised in early 16th century France, in a small and obscure town near Paris, while living in exile later in his life, mostly in the French-speaking Swiss town of Geneva. This point of origin gives an ironic and perhaps, for most Americans, unexpected, mysterious, and undesirable, twist to America's "destiny" determined by none than "foreign" and "old" European Calvinism and Calvinists, notably Calvin as a "Frenchman"[2] (Mansbach 2006), via celebrated "all-American" and "new" Puritanism and Puritans like Winthrop et al. Apparently, even Tocqueville himself, the "patron saint" (Putnam 2000) of American political conservatism or communitarianism, in his classic, celebrated sociological and historical analysis of America omits or does not explicitly present an evident fact of major significance. This is that America's "destiny", like genesis, turns out to be effectively inscribed in early Calvinists born in his native France via their English-American theological and ideological "children" renamed as the first Puritans, perhaps assuming that this equivalence was commonly known, and thus axiomatic.

The above holds true, with certain exceptions, of most sociological analyses of America and England in relation to Puritanism and sectarian, fundamentalist Protestantism overall (Lipset 1996; Munch 2001), including Weber, Parsons, and contemporary sociologists. And, they entail such an omission perhaps for identical or similar reasons to Tocqueville's. Presumably, "every schoolboy knows" (Bateson 1979) of the Calvinist-Puritan equivalence or tautological identity, Puritanism equals Calvinism and conversely, just as Weber implies and Sombart explicitly states. Yet, "not every schoolboy", particularly in America,

---

[2] Mansbach (2006:111) remarks that "Calvin [as] a Frenchman blended easily in francophone Geneva."

seems to know of—and some US analysts deny or downplay (Hartz 1963)—the Calvinist-Puritan sociological equivalence, thus that its "destiny" is embodied in early European Calvinists as Tocqueville's first Puritans. For instance, probably not everyone is aware that the established Congregational Church in New England and generally Puritanism in colonial and post-revolutionary America was "Calvinist" (Baldwin 2006; Davis 2005; Foerster 1962; German 1995). Notably, "not every schoolboy" perhaps knows of the "austere Calvinism" (Kloppenberg 1998) of John Winthrop, the supreme Puritan master (Munch 2001) and role model for US religious and political conservatives like Reagan et al. (Dunn and Woodard 1996; Seaton 2006). Moreover, it appears that "Calvinism" or "Puritanism" as a term is less used—actually substituted by its branches or proxies like "Presbyterianism", "Methodism", and "Baptism"—by Americans than are "Lutheranism", "Episcopalism", and "Protestantism." In this sense, "Calvinism", including even "Puritanism," has become what Weber and Germans call *caput mortuum* ("clinically dead") as a name in America. Yet, it remains its "destiny" in the sense of America's present, likely future, or main heritage, as a social force in different forms and names such as sectarian and fundamentalist or evangelical Protestantism. Simply, Calvinist "deeds, not words" are relevant in considering Calvinism's role in America's "destiny", just as genesis.

Whatever the reasons and explanations, America's Calvinist "destiny" is "missing in action" or not fully established, revealed, and thus under-analyzed in the current sociological and other literature since Tocqueville, with some exceptions cited later. It is the objective and task of this work to more completely retrieve, reveal, and account for this Calvinist "destiny", just as genesis, of America, largely omitted or implicit in Tocqueville's and other sociological works. Alternatively, it takes account of certain secondary, atypical (Archer 2001) non-Calvinist or non-Puritan countervailing societal forces and ideas in American history and society like Jefferson's Enlightenment-based liberalism, secularism, egalitarianism, and rationalism (Patell 2001).

In sum, this introduction reintroduces and applies the concept of destiny or fate[3] (Bendix 1984) in its sociological version of societal

---

[3] A work of Weberian sociologist Bendix is entitled *Force, Fate and Freedom* with reference to modern developed as well as under-developed societies and heterodox economist Hirschman (1993) uses the expression the "Fate of the German Democratic Republic" during the late 1980s in the evident meaning of what Weber calls "adverse fate".

predestination (more precisely, co-determination or path-dependence) to analyzing contemporary Western societies or nations, specifically America. The remainder of the work reconsiders and develops Tocqueville's identification and prediction of America's "destiny" as incarnated in the first Puritans. In particular, the work addresses his and other sociologists' implied omission of or insufficient attention to the broader and antecedent Calvinist framework and parentage of Puritanism as America's genesis and destiny. This yields the main thesis and "rediscovery" of Calvinism as America's essential, underlying "destiny" as well as its genesis via Puritanism as the manifest expression and different name of Calvin's old-world creation in a new, promised land. Hence, to better understand or make sense of America's Puritan *cum* Calvinist "destiny" requires understanding more fully and reconsidering the "fate" or logic of Calvinism itself and consequently Puritanism.

CHAPTER ONE

## AMERICA'S DESTINY AND CALVINISM

*The "First New Nation" and European Calvinism*

Calvinism operates as America's social "destiny" in Tocqueville's sense in virtue of being its destination, present, and future, or main legacy, just as its historical genesis or point of origin. This is consistently and clearly distinguished from its presumed theological "manifest destiny" and "Divinely ordained" mission in the world. Hence, America's assumed social "destiny", like its genesis, in Calvinism implies a sociological, scientific conception, and has strictly empirical relevance and meaning, by positing and demonstrating that it is a Calvinist nation or society. And, a "Calvinist nation" is distinguished from "God's chosen people" as a theological construct or article of faith impossible, just as Calvinism's doctrine of individual salvation and damnation as the "double decree" by Divinity (predestination), to validate or "falsify" by science.

Science, sociology in particular, cannot prove or disprove that America or, as early Dutch Calvinists and English Puritans claimed, Holland and England is the "new Israel" or "Jerusalem" and a "chosen nation"—simply, it does not and cannot "know". It cannot provide a proof or disproof that the new or any nation is the "Divinely chosen" instrument for establishing God's "Kingdom on Earth" and realizing "Providential design" (Bendix 1984), just as whether certain individuals have the "certainty" of salvation, so an "obligation to sanctification" (Frijhoff 2002).

In this connection, some US Puritan admirers (Dunn and Woodard 1996) claim that the American Puritans attributed their origins "not to England, but to Moses", citing the Old Testament Israel as the "source of inspiration for the 'New Jerusalem' in Massachusetts." This remark fails to mention that their predecessors, Dutch and other Calvinists had also defined 16th century Holland and any Calvinist nation as the "new Israel" or "new Jerusalem". Consequently, this implies a sort of zero-sum game. If all Calvinist-Puritan societies, from Calvin's France and Swiss Geneva through Holland, in part Prussia, England and Scotland, to America, claim to be the "New Jerusalem" and by implication

"One Nation Indivisible under God" (or some variation thereof), then none is or can be. By definition, the "New Jerusalem" or "One Nation Indivisible under [the Calvinist] God" in the strict sense is just one—is it Calvin's France or Swiss Geneva, Holland, Prussia, England, Scotland, *or* America? And, within America itself, is it arch-Calvinist New England (in particular, Massachusetts) *or* the neo-Calvinist Southern and other "Bible Belt" and/or the "Wild West"? The claim to the "New Jerusalem" or "One Nation Indivisible under the God of Calvinism" is thus a Calvinist-Puritan variation on the perennial theme of God's "chosen people" as a zero-sum game and eventually the source and rationale of the Hobbesian universal war of religion between societies making such mutually exclusive and irreconcilable claims.

And, virtually all societies and groups have made and make such claims to Divine choice, spanning from the smallest primitive tribes (as in anthropological accounts) to the largest ancient and modern civilizations and empires, including the Chinese, Indian, Egyptian, Greek, Roman, Ottoman, Spanish, Dutch, British, French, Russian, German-Austrian, and American (Giddens 1984; Steinmetz 2005). If all nations or peoples claim to be "One Nation Indivisible under God" or the Divinely "chosen people", then none is, for the latter is precisely only one, a paradigmatic "impossibility theorem." Presumably, this problem can be "solved" only via religious wars as what Simmel[1] calls (collective) "ordeal by combat" as the mechanism of proving by "fighting and winning" mutually exclusive claims ("who is right"), thus making brute military might legal right. Hence, the problem is "solved" by means of a permanent crusade or jihad (Turner 2002) and the elimination of "ungodly" or "infidel" nations, a moment that US "reborn," like Islamic, fundamentalists overlook or "forget" by continuing and expanding these old Puritan claims to Divine choice and "holy" wars on the "evil" world.

However, crucially social science cannot either adopt or reject Calvinism's mix of dual collective and theological individual claims or arguments of predestination (Frijhoff 2002), but explores only whether and to what degree America, like Holland and England, is a Calvinist society or a "Puritan nation" in the sense of Tocqueville. In sum, while

---

[1] Simmel remarks that the German (Holy Roman) Emperor Otto the Great "decrees that a legal question must be decided through ordeal by combat [i.e.,] fighting and winning."

it does not and cannot really "know" the Divine predestination of individuals and nations as a non-empirical ("non-testable") issue, sociology can contribute to knowing and understanding the second, Calvinism's determining or conditioning of America and other societies, as the empirical ("testable") matter.

In Calvinism's terms, this implies the Calvinist "predestination" of America in the sense of societal over-determination (Alexander 1998; Munch 2001) and historical path-dependence (Inglehart and Baker 2000). It implies Calvinism's enduring and self-perpetuating function, heritage (Kloppenberg 1998), deep impact, and triumph (German 1995) in American society, but not transcendental determinism of America by the Calvinist God via Divine-style "manifest destiny". In this sense, social structure and change in America, like other Western and non-Western societies, are over-determined or path-dependent, as sociological research shows. They are primarily determined by or dependant on its "broad cultural heritage" (Inglehart and Baker 2000; Inglehart 2004; Lipset 1996; Munch 2001), specifically its Calvinist or Protestant legacy[2] as a historical-empirical factor with "traditional dominance and prestige" (Jenness 2004). In turn, social structures and changes in America and other societies are *not* considered with respect to what Weber calls the "God of Calvinism" or Protestantism, as the absolutely transcendental and thus non-empirical and non-demonstrable or (as Pascal implies) "non-falsifiable" determinant.

Calvinism's societal predestination of America, by analogy to its "destiny", means that the latter is essentially a Calvinist society by the 21st century (Munch 2001), as has been during most of its history (Lipset 1996) since the early 17th century. It signifies that it is the "promised land" of Calvinism *cum* Puritanism, not just, as usually described, a "Protestant nation." Thus, US conservatives imply and, as typical, celebrate America's Calvinist genesis or foundation and by implication "destiny" or future and heritage. In this view, America's founding institutions and values were primarily "influenced" by Calvinism and the Protestant Reformation rather than by secularism and liberalism, including the liberal-secular Enlightenment as a countervailing, "un-American" movement and set of ideals (Dunn and Woodard 1996).

---

[2] Inglehart and Baker (2000:19) observe that global social-cultural change is "path dependent" in the sense of depending on "the broad cultural heritage of a society", including its "Protestant" legacy, while not distinguishing Calvinism or Puritanism from the other branches of Protestantism.

Other conservative analysts register and glorify the "triumph of Calvinism" (and capitalism) over liberalism and secularism, including the Enlightenment, in America, particularly pre- and post-revolutionary New England (German 1995). Further, even some liberal analysts identify and extol the "Calvinist heritage" of America, though interwoven with or juxtaposed to the "virtues" of countervailing Jeffersonian Enlightenment-inspired liberalism, egalitarianism, secularism, and rationalism (Kloppenberg 1998; also, Byrne 1997).

In sum, it is imperative to distinguish America's two "destinies". The first is its societal "destiny" determined or predestination by Calvinism as a specific type of religious, moral, ideological, and cultural heritage and factor. The second is its "manifest destiny" determined or theological predestination by the "God of Calvinism" and thus transcendental causes. One cannot emphasize this distinction enough, insofar as most Americans appear to understand the first as the *second*, as "manifest destiny" or Providential "predestination" a la the "chosen" nation with a claimed Divine mission and right to "save" and rule, including destroy, the "evil", "corrupt," and "ungodly" world. US religious-cultural conservatives, including conservative analysts (Dunn and Woodard 1996; Lipset and Marks 2000), are especially prone to reduce America's societal to theological "manifest destiny" as Divinely Ordained "special mission" in "saving" the world.

*Calvinism via Puritanism*

First and foremost, Calvinism functions as America's societal destiny or predestination through Puritanism. It also does via Puritanism's various survivals, revivals, or generalizations in what Weber describes as "sectarian Protestantism" as the predominant and most prestigious religious force in American history and society from the 17th to the 21st century (Jenness 2004; Lipset 1996; Munch 2001). Calvinism operates as America's "destiny" not directly, immediately, or manifestly, but rather indirectly, ultimately, or almost invisibly by the agency of Puritanism. The Calvinist sociological—not theological by the "God of Calvinism"—predestination of American society thus functions through Puritan social over-determination, path-dependence, or cultural heritage (Inglehart and Baker 2000), deep impact, and triumph (German 1995) in that America historically has been and remains "religiously determined" by Puritanism (Munch 2001). Simply, Calvinism has done and continues to do its "job" in America by ways, means, and virtue of "all-American" Puritanism. Conversely, Puritanism as the "agent" did and does for Calvinism as the "principal" what Calvin et al. aimed but eventually failed to attain in most of Europe, including France, Germany, and England, with local and partial exceptions (Geneva, Holland, Scotland).

In this sense, it is via Puritanism that Calvinism has realized in the "new nation" what ultimately eluded Calvin's heirs in the "old world." This is to attain the Calvinist, as in Weber-Parsons' almost celebratory accounts, total mastery of the world, thus to become the "master" and "destiny" of, to rule and "predestine", human society. In essence, as founded and embodied by Calvin, original Calvinism proved to be ultimately a sort of failure, "abortive" (Heller 1986), or discredited, despite certain temporary and partial successes (parts of France, Geneva, Holland, Prussia, Scotland, England, etc.). Yet, its Anglo-Saxon derivative, Puritanism turned out to be a triumphant "winner-takes-all" or "over-achiever" within what Weber identifies as the global, transnational Calvinist system or "extended family". Calvinism eventually proved, as Weber would put it, *caput mortuum* (literally "death's head"), and not only because of Calvin's death, in most of the "old Europe," notably his homeland France. Yet, it "resurrected from the dead," as did religious conservatism (Dunn and Woodard 1996), thus proved "undying", ever-reborn, and "ever-green" and triumphant (German 1995), in the "first new nation." Predictably, Calvinism did and does so through its own English-American offspring renamed "Puritanism" and Puritan-incited sectarian and evangelical recurring revivals or awakenings as "permanent revolutions" in the "new nation" thus rendered older than the "old Europe," from the 17th to the 21st century.

The crucial point is that European Calvinism is America's "destiny" in the specific form and sense of English-American Puritanism. The Calvinist societal predestination of the "new nation" specifically functions as its Puritan over-determination or primary co-determination. Arguably, America's founding and enduring social institutions and values were more impacted by Calvinism than by non-Calvinist countervailing forces like the Enlightenment and generally liberalism and secularism, in spite or perhaps because of Jefferson, Madison, Franklin, Paine, and their followers. Calvinist factors operated through Puritanism as the "dominant political and intellectual force" in the "new nation" during the 17th–18th centuries (Dunn and Woodard 1996) and even the early and mid 19th century (Baldwin 2006; Clemens 2007; German 1995). They did and still do, given that Puritanism has substantively, as distinguished from formally, continued and remained a dominant social force in America since, through a myriad of survivals or revivals in sectarian and evangelical Protestantism, up to the 21st century (Lipset 1996; Mansbach 2006; Munch 2001). In short, if America's was primarily "Calvinist heritage", the latter translated into and functioned as the Puritan legacy[3] (Mansbach 2006).

Alternatively, American Puritanism as represented and embodied by Winthrop and other early Puritans reportedly "stamped" America with a "set of conservative values", such as respect for and maintenance of the "established order", political "leadership by the favored few" (aristocracy or oligarchy?), and the like[4] (Dunn and Woodard 1996; Seaton 2006). This societal conservatism precisely originated in and defined French Calvinism as a proto-conservative or anti-liberal exemplar in social-political terms, combined with theological or religious radicalism, notably extreme and revolutionary anti-Catholicism in France and beyond (Heller 1986; Sorkin 2005), and in part anti-Lutheranism, as in Germany (Nischan 1994). Arguably, America's social institutions, norms, and values were "influenced" by the Puritan Revolution in England of the 1640s–60s more than the 1789 secular Enlightenment-related (and perhaps directly inspired) Revolution in France (Dunn and Woodard 1996). If this argument is valid, these structures were more shaped by the Calvinist "Second", contrasted with the Lutheran "First", Reformation or the "Reformed Church" than by what Weber and Mannheim describe as revolutionary ("utopian") and rationalistic liberalism and modernism, simply liberal modernity, superseding traditionalism, specifically medievalism. A foremost "proof" or paradigmatic instance is what analysts identify as Winthrop's "austere

---

[3] In a cognate vigorous analysis and argument, Mansbach (2006:113) remarks that "Calvinism would then make its way to the New World with the Puritans. Its legacy continues to motivate many US evangelicals in their efforts to infuse politics and government with religion".

[4] Like most US religious (Protestant) conservatives, Dunn and Woodard (1996:84) claim that Puritanism "also gave the nation institutions like a written constitution, regular elections, and the secret ballot, and principles like the work ethic, the federalist principle, and the separation of church and state." And, then they conclude that America's "national institutions and values were influenced by Calvinism" more than any other factors, thus effectively equating Puritanism or using the concept interchangeably with it. Also, Seaton (2006:197) approvingly cites the statement (of Wilson McWilliams) that "Winthrop's "influence, like the religious tradition in general, lies in its effects on the ideas and guilts of Americans more than the conduct of American life. [Thus] The duty to establish the best city, short of which no failure is adequate or excusable: is that not the definition of the American dream?"

Calvinism"[5] (Kloppenberg 1998), the prime Puritan exemplar, master, and glorified hero or role model in America, notably conservatism (Gould 1996; Seaton 2006).

When Tocqueville identified and predicted the social "destiny" of America as embodied in the first Puritans and determined by Puritanism, he objectively implicated early Calvinists or original Calvinism in this "fate" of the "new nation". Recall, what he did not explicitly mention but certainly, like Weber, knew was that these first Puritans were the theological "children" and members of an "extended family" of Calvinists, for example Winthrop et al. as the true disciples of Calvin (Davis 2005). And, this is what "Winthrop's austere Calvinism" precisely signifies. Generally, Tocqueville implied that Puritanism in America was a Calvinist offspring, simply "American Calvinism" (German 1995). Further, Tocqueville certainly knew but did not state that Winthrop et al.'s strict Calvinism had originated and initially centered nowhere than in his native France. Also, he definitely knew that Calvinism had expanded from France to Europe, including Switzerland (Geneva, etc.), Holland and Germany (Prussia), as well as subsequently England (and Scotland) and America by reinventing, reinvigorating, and renaming itself as "Puritanism". This French (Paris) point of origin or connection of Winthrop's Calvinism in America yields a historical irony or coincidence hardly mentioned or explicated even by the "young Frenchman" (Lipset and Marks 2000) in his classical account of the first Puritans as embodying its "destiny", just as its pre-revolutionary genesis.

*Calvinism—The Genesis and "Destiny" of America?*

The preceding yields the seemingly surprising, and for most Americans astonishing, inference or argument. This is that the "old" European—and at that French—Calvinism operates as both the genesis or foundation and the "destiny" or principal heritage of the "first new" or the "youngest" nation (Lipset 1996) among Western and other modern nations. In Durkheim's words, both the genesis and functioning or evolution of America's prevalent values, norms, and institutions are rooted in Calvinism originating in France, although in addition to and

---

[5] Kloppenberg (1998:13) identifies the "distance separating Winthrop's austere Calvinism from [President] Clinton's rather less stringent standard of propriety."

connection with, as well as counteraction by, other social and economic determinants in a multiple co-determination. In turn, the latter are considered control or residual variables for the purpose of this analysis by analogy to Weber's analytical treatment of the non-Calvinist, non-religious factors of the rise of modern Western capitalism assumed to be in an "elective affinity" with Calvinism.

Alternatively, Calvinism functions as the process of societal predestination of America, in particular the "determination" of its religious evolution (Alexander 1983), specifically from early Puritanism to contemporary sectarian and evangelical Protestantism. Notably, this religious development proceeds from New England's "Biblical Commonwealth" (Munch 2001) to the Southern and Northern "Bible Belt" (Bauman 1997; Mencken 1982; Putnam 2000) as historical cases of what Weber identifies as Calvinist "Biblical theocracy" or "Bibliocracy". Further, some analysts argue that, in post-Reformation Europe, including England, and above all America the "values of freedom and liberty" were associated with Calvinism and its theological doctrines such as predestination or religious transcendence and human sin (Means 1966). In particular, in a similar view reflecting Weber's observations,[6] it was primarily owing to its "Calvinist heritage", combined with its peculiar historical conjunctures, that America presented individuals with the chance of active participation in "small-scale, egalitarian" community organizations nourishing "democratic values and institutions" (Kloppenberg 1998).

In retrospect, after Tocqueville's implicit "Puritan" identification or prediction, Weber almost explicitly identifies and predicts America's societal "destiny" in or "predestination" by original *Calvinism*, not merely or superficially Puritanism as its derivation and manifestation in a different geographic and historical setting. Thus, he observes that the "very striking" behavioral differences between Germans and Anglo-Americans have their origins in the "lesser degree of ascetic penetration of life" by Lutheranism in Germany, "as distinguished from Calvinism" and its more extensive and intensive asceticism (also, Akerlof 2007) in England and America.

In a more nuanced differentiation within the extended Calvinist "family" ("within-group" variation), Weber might add that Calvinism

---

[6] According to Kloppenberg (1998:90), Weber developed the America's "Calvinist heritage" argument "at length" in *The Protestant Ethic and the Spirit of Capitalism*.

attained such "ascetic penetration of life" or mastery of the world primarily and enduringly in America, secondarily and temporarily in England. This holds true in view of Calvinism's near-complete triumph (German 1995) and permanent legacy through Puritanism (Johnson 2003; Mansbach 2006) in the "new nation" by comparison with England (and in part Scotland) and continental Europe. Conversely, it did so in a lesser degree or duration in England, due to the initially triumphant, yet ultimately failed Calvinist *cum* Puritan Revolution (Gorski 2000), like what Weber calls the "abortive" rule of Cromwell's "Parliament of Saints", thus its eventual military defeat and societal discredit. Consequently, Calvinism in the form of Puritanism has been more "tempered" (Munch 2001) by countervailing religious and other social forces like Anglicanism and liberalism in Great Britain than in America. In the latter, these countervailing forces have been, if not absent, weaker and stigmatized, such as Jefferson's[7] "ungodly" Enlightenment, secularism, and liberalism (Baldwin 2006; German 1995), in relation to Great Britain and Europe. As a secondary point, Weber might add that Lutheranism retained its original designation, attributes, and significance in Germany and Europe overall, especially its northern parts like Scandinavia, except for England where it was readapted and mixed with Catholicism to yield "Anglicanism". In turn, Calvinism was renamed and reinvented, specifically reinforced, embellished, and extended, as "Puritanism" in Great Britain, including both England and Scotland ("Presbyterianism"), and especially America.

Also, recent sociological and historical studies corroborate the argument that European Calvinism is America's "destiny" or "genesis and functioning" and evoke Weber's observations. For instance, this is evident or implicit in the quoted neo-Weberian identification of America's "Calvinist heritage", starting with Winthrop's "austere Calvinism" (Kloppenberg 1998). Also, a sociological analysis, critical of the "Weberian theoretical tradition"[8] of the Calvinist-capitalist "elective affinity",

---

[7] German (1995:994) observes that in the aftermath of the American Revolution some prominent neo-Calvinists in New England (New Divinity representative Nathanael Emmons) "compared Thomas Jefferson to the wicked king Jeroboam." Also, Baldwin (2006:108) refers to Calvinists' accusations and fears of Jefferson for seeking to "overturn" New England's political institutions, specifically its Puritan theocracy via the Congregational Church.

[8] McLaughlin (1996:249) objects that the "Weberian theoretical tradition ignores Luther's and Calvin's [citing Erich Fromm] 'emphasis on the fundamental evilness and powerlessness of men'".

observes that eventually Calvinism fulfilled the "same sociological function" in Anglo-Saxon societies (McLaughlin 1996), primarily America and secondarily England, just as Lutheranism originally (and fascism later) did in Germany and Northern Europe. In a sense, to observe such a functional equivalence is to suggest that Calvinism functioned as America's and partially England's (and more Scotland's) "destiny" to the same extent that Lutheranism did as that of Germany and Scandinavia, and, for that matter, Catholicism for Italy and Spain, Islam for Iran, Saudi Arabia, Turkey (in part), and other Muslim societies. Recall, the "predestination" of these societies is understood in the historical-empirical sense of what comparative sociological analyses identify as their persistent "path-dependence" on a religious and generally spiritual or cultural heritage and tradition (Inglehart and Baker 2000; Inglehart 2004; Munch 2001).

One can add that Calvinism performed such a "sociological function" in America in the "new" form and under the changed name of "all-American" Puritanism (despite the continued coexistence of "Calvinist" *and* "Puritan" denominations and sects), in contrast to Lutheranism (and Catholicism) that was not reinvented, reinvigorated, and renamed in the same way or degree in the "new nation" (despite some US "evangelical" Lutherans). This curious moment indicates that Calvinism was virtually the only branch of Protestantism and Christianity that did not fully retain its original French name in America, instead becoming "Puritanism." (This does not count Anglicanism as, in Comte's, Weber's, and other sociological views, substantively the English proxy of Lutheranism mixed with Catholicism, and renamed "Episcopalism" in the US South.) French Calvinism was thus replaced in America by Anglo-Saxon "Puritanism" as a name, while continuing to coexist in "Calvinist" or "Congregational" alongside "Puritan" denominations in a formal distinction or confusion, but in substantive theological equivalence or agreement.

As a supreme irony, by the early 21st century some "Calvinist" denominations still exist, though not many US "born again" religious conservatives officially call themselves "Calvinists" and "Puritans." Yet, no "Puritan" denominations in the proper sense formally exist in America and elsewhere, as in Switzerland, Holland, and England. Apparently, "Calvinist" has outlasted "Puritan," which is a validation of Calvinism as the original and Puritanism as the derivative, thus of America's Calvinist, not merely Puritan, "destiny". Sill, the fact that "Puritanism" or "Calvinism" is *caput mortuum* as a name in America and beyond does not mean its death as a substantive heritage. Rather, it is "live and well", as indicated by the revival and continuing hegemony of Puritan-inspired Protestantism in modern America, like during most of its history from the 18th century Great Awakenings to the fundamentalist resurgence of the 1980s–2000s.

Alternatively, "Puritanism" directly and manifestly allowed Calvinism to fulfill the above "sociological function" in America, as well as to a lesser extent and temporarily in England (though more extensively and enduringly in Scotland). In terms of agency theory (Kiser 1999), "Puritanism" in America, just as England (and Scotland), essentially acted as the loyal agent or efficient instrument of Calvinism as the principal or "master" in an extended Calvinist "family". This is just a legalistic or rational-choice way to express what various sociological and historical analyses, from Hume to Weber and later times, identify as English-American Puritanism's basic, yet often obscured or neglected, ideological and theological loyalty and substantive equivalence to European Calvinism (Munch 1981; Sprunger 1982).

The above indicates that the shared unshakeable belief in being the "true" and "only" "Reformed Church", thus "Christian" religion, effectively neutralized virtually any geographical, national, or cultural ("Anglo-Saxon" versus "European") differences between Puritanism and Calvinism, including the personal divergences of Puritans and Calvinists (German 1995). And, this pattern persists in US fundamentalist Protestantism, for its adherents proclaim, above all, their allegiance, love, and sacrifice via "holy" war to Weber's "God of Calvinism", then to the "nation", third, their families, and lastly, if ever, other human beings. They are simply Calvinist "Christians" first, "Americans" second, fathers, mothers, and children third, and humans last or not at all as a sort of humanistic nuisance, distraction from God, or a luxury they cannot "afford". This reflects the typical scale of values or priorities in Calvinism and in extension fundamentalist Protestantism in a descending order: above all, God, religion, and church, including "holy" culture-military wars or crusades; then nationalism *cum* patriotism; "family values"; and lastly humanism, rather abhorrence for its secular form, thus anti-humanism eventuating in inhumanity.

At this juncture, historical research intimates that French Calvinism temporarily became the "destiny" or "master" of England. It registers that in England Calvinists renamed as Puritans dethroned and killed a monarch, transiently abolishing the monarchy (Elwood 1999) through the initially victorious, yet ultimately failed Calvinist Revolution and rule establishing the "Holy Commonwealth" and its "Parliament of Saints" of the 1640s–60s. Within what was to become Great Britain (in 1707) Calvinism had already, prior to England, reached through certain ("Presbyterian") derivatives such a position of dominance in Scotland, as Hume, Comte, Weber, Pareto, and other sociologists suggest, just as, in its pure form and initial name, in Geneva and Holland. Thus, like in Geneva and Holland before, in Scotland Calvinism almost expressly upon its arrival established itself as the "predominant religion" (Sprunger 1982), albeit in a changed form and name of "Presbyterianism" (a Calvinist term anyway, as Weber suggests).

And, if Calvinists almost destroyed or captured the political system, as well as the prior Anglican Church order, in England (plus *a fortiori* Scotland), they vastly out-performed these acts and out-did themselves in New England and America as a whole. As hinted, they did so by establishing and sustaining for two centuries (the 1630s–1830s), a Calvinist-based social system officially designated as the "Biblical Commonwealth" in New England initially. Such a "Biblical Commonwealth" was subsequently extended or designed, through a myriad of endemic religious, almost invariably Calvinist or evangelical, revivals, to America from the 18th to the 21st century (Munch 2001; Stivers 1994). A paradigmatic instance is Calvinism's expansion of its "Biblical Commonwealth" to and its transformation of the Episcopalian South, via the evangelical "Great Awakenings" during the 18th–19th centuries, into what Mencken's (1982) perhaps first described and deplored, and Southern evangelicals adulate as a "Bible Belt" (Boles 1999). In an almost equivalent pattern, Calvinism then expanded to and eventually succeeded during the mid and late 19th century to transform the newly conquered (from Mexico) "western territories" (Clemens 2007) into yet another "Biblical Commonwealth" planted on a "Wild West" society and culture, a mix paradigmatically exemplified in such states as Texas, Oklahoma, Kansas, etc. In turn, New England's "Biblical Commonwealth" was, and the Southern and Western Bible Belt" is, the special case of Weber's "Biblical theocracy" or "Bibliocracy" that Calvinism appropriated from medievalism and its "Christian Republic" (Nischan 1994) as the original and perennial ideal. The Puritan "Biblical Commonwealth" was established and perpetuated for exactly two centuries, after Calvin's Geneva theocratic model of "godly society" (*civitas Dei*) with Church dominating State (Frijhoff 2002; Mansbach 2006), just as the fundamentalist "Bible Belt" is attempted to reestablish or designed déjà vu.

## Calvinist Predestination via the Puritan "Destiny" of America

As indicated, Calvinism functions as America's "destiny" through its derivative Puritanism and Puritan-rooted survivals, revivals, or generalizations in sectarian, fundamentalist Protestantism as the dominant and most prestigious religious-cultural force in American history and society, up to the late 20th and early 21st centuries (Jenness 2004). The Calvinist societal predestination of America thus operates via the Puritan over-determination of the "new nation" or the latter's path-dependence on Puritanism and sectarian Protestantism generally (Inglehart and Baker 2000).

If arguably in America, like other Western Protestant societies, the major social values and institutions like freedom and democracy are founded on Calvinism, notably its theological doctrines of predestination or God's absolute transcendence and human sin (Dunn and Woodard 1996; German 1995; Means 1966), the latter operated as such a basis precisely via their Puritan derivation and implementation. In turn, on theoretical-logical and historical-empirical grounds it is difficult to see how the Calvinist doctrine of "human sin", just as non-universal predestination or Divine absolute transcendence, expressing anti-humanism can form the basis for America's and Western values and institutions of freedom and democracy as the expression and product of humanism, specifically its liberal-secular version.

Conceivably, the Calvinist and Christian or other (including Islamic) dogma of human "sin" and "deprivation", despite its underlying anti-humanism, may not be mutually exclusive with and opposite to human liberty, including democracy. Yet, in history and reality it has almost invariably been, even ultimately destructive to liberty and democracy. This is because evidently theological or ideological anti-humanism like the inhumane dogma of human "sin" and severe punishment (including death) for sins-as-crimes, does not or can not result in social-institutional humanism. At most, it transforms or subverts human liberty and democracy into the moralistic and oppressive "republic of virtue and the virtuous" such as, alongside Plato's Sparta (Infantino 2003) as the Calvinist and Puritan ideal (Garrard 2003), Calvin's Geneva, Winthrop's "Biblical Community", Cromwell's "Holy Commonwealth", and the "Bible Belt" and the "Wild West" eliminating the sinful, "infidels", and other "witches". In a way, whenever and wherever fully implemented, the Calvinist dogma of sin-as-crime and punishment (as Weber and Pareto imply) converted human society into an overarching monastic or Spartan order, a sort of "Salem with and ultimately without witches", thus an open prison, starting with Calvin's Geneva and ending with the "reborn" neo-Puritan "Bible Belt". Alternatively, the Western values and institutions of liberty have been established and maintained *not* because, but rather in spite and opposition of Calvinism, including Puritanism, particularly its inhumane doctrines of human sin-punishment and anti-universal, exclusive predestination *cum* election of a few versus damnation of most humans.

Against this background, America's Calvinist heritage or determination has expressed and renamed itself as the Puritan legacy, influence, or impression[9] (Seaton 2006). This is what Tocqueville implies predicting the "destiny" of America as incarnated in the first Puritans as Anglo-Saxon Calvinists, thus determined by Puritanism as early English-American Calvinism (German 1995). He finds that the ideas and values of the first Puritan colonial fathers impressed "very deep traces on the minds of their descendants." He cites the "extreme regularity of habits," notably the "great strictness of morals that are observable" in the "new nation" that he visited during the 1830s. Tocqueville infers that Americans are a "puritanical people" and "at the same time" a "commercial nation" or capitalist society dominated by "tradesmen and capitalists," dissociating "Puritanism" and "capitalism" as mutually incompatible or unrelated rather than, as in Weber's framework, connecting them. Evidently, Tocqueville's America of the past, present, and future is a "Puritan nation" and thus by implication a Calvinist, just as capitalist, society. Yet, in his context capitalism seems to be independent of and even in a tension and contradiction with (Munch 2001), rather than (as in Weberian-Parsonian accounts) grounded in and linked to (German 1995), Puritanism, thus Calvinism and religion overall.

Thus, a recent comparative-historical sociological analysis (Munch 2001) identifies and emphasizes both elements diagnosed or anticipated by Tocqueville. First, America is observed to remain by the late 20th and early 21st century a Puritan-determined and in that sense

---

[9] In a celebratory mode, Seaton (2006:197) states that while internal and external factors "led inexorably to Puritanism's demise" in New England, "Puritan thought and its once-upon-a-time reality also left a permanent legacy in the American psyche." Particularly "Winthrop's influence, like the religious tradition in general, lies in its effects on the ideas and guilts [sic] of Americans more than the conduct of American life" (Seaton 2006:197).

Calvinist-predestined society. Second, certain contradiction and tensions are found to persist or resurface between Puritanism and capitalism, religion and the market economy, in contemporary America. The analysis registers that in historical and contemporary America, the Puritan-based religion is effectively diffused into "all spheres of society," with the result that "myth and reality" become interpenetrating and even almost indistinguishable from each other. In particular, Puritanism has reportedly reached the status of the "carrier of modern normative culture" in the "new nation" that is without a parallel and comparison with other Western societies, including Great Britain. In this view, ushering in the 21st century, American society's "special characteristic" is that its political, cultural, and economic institutions remain more completely and vigorously determined and "penetrated" by Puritan-rooted "binding morality" yet "generalized" beyond Puritanism, than are European societies, including Great Britain. The analysis observes that the above has reproduced a society of "incomparable contradictions", including that between capitalism and a Puritan-rooted religion and morality, just as fierce political struggles for power and communal associations, all of them carried to the "extreme" (Munch 2001). In this account, the most salient contradiction is that contemporary America constitutes a society that is "simultaneously" both "unusually" materialist and "religiously determined" (and "politically molded" and "communally structured") specifically hyper-capitalist and over-Puritan, "individualistic and conformist" alike. Notably, the observation "religiously determined" about Puritanism as the primary determinant confirms or evokes Tocqueville's view of America's "destiny" as incarnated in the early Puritans (just as the term "simultaneously" does his expression "at the same time").

In sum, Calvinism reaffirms and reappears in the shape of Puritanism as the "destiny" or heritage, just as the genesis and functioning, of Tocqueville's America by reproducing the latter as a "puritanical people." Calvinism functions as the prime mover of the "new nation", operating separately from and incompatibly with capitalism or a market economy as another implied factor recreating America as a "commercial nation". Alternatively, the Puritan (though not the capitalist or "commercial") over-determination or legacy is the specific form, mechanism, or instrument of the Calvinist predestination or heritage (Mansbach 2006) of America in Tocqueville's influential and widely celebrated account. Also, echoing Tocqueville, US early sociologist Edward Ross states that America is a "lineal descendent" of Puritanism and implicitly Calvinism, and the latter ("Protestantism") and democracy "have worked together."

In addition, Tocqueville's contemporary Comte implies that America's "destiny", like its genesis, is determined by Calvinism and Protestantism overall. Comte states that the American Revolution "was as purely Protestant"—apparently signifying Calvinist or Puritan distinguished from Lutheran or Anglican—as some previous revolutions in Europe, specifically Holland and England (and Scotland). In his view, "in its origin, it was a reproduction of the Dutch revolution, and in its final realization it carried out the English which it realizes as far as Protestantism will allow".

While apparently not differing Protestantism's various branches and thus not specifying the concrete Protestant origin and effects of these religious revolutions, Comte evidently refers by the "Dutch revolution" to what Weber calls the "ecclesiastic revolution of the strict Calvinists in the Netherlands during the 1580s." Namely, Comte refers to the Calvinist disciplinary (Gorski 2003; also, Clemens 2007) or theocratic revolution as the result of which Calvinism established itself as the "predominant religion" (Sprunger 1982) and the state "true" and "only" Reformed Church (Hsia and Nierop 2002). Similarly, by "the English" Comte probably has in mind the Puritan Revolution of 1640s also installing Calvinism *cum* Puritanism as an official religion or "true" state church in England (like Scotland before) and enabling Calvinists to temporarily abolish the existing political and religious powers and institutions such as the monarchy and the Anglican Church (Elwood 1999; Goldstone 1986; Gorski 2000). Yet, unlike that in Holland (and Scotland), the English Calvinist revolution eventually proved, as Weber implies, an "abortive" revolutionary episode. This is a moment neglected in Marxian and other sociological accounts of the English Puritan Revolution as a case of successful "liberal" or "bourgeois" revolutions that, in Marx's words, conquered free market competition in 17th century England (also, Moore 1993).

In turn, Jefferson, Madison, Franklin, Paine, and other US founders or early liberals and secularists would likely disagree with Comte's sociological account of the American Revolution as "purely Protestant" and thus religious. Specifically, they would dispute his classification of the American in the same category as Dutch Calvinist and English-Scottish Puritan disciplinary revolutions (Clemens 2007; Gorski 2003; Loveman 2005), rather than, as in alternative accounts, a liberal-secular revolution premised on Enlightenment-based ideals and values,[10] at least as the "supporting rationale" (Byrne 1997; Patell 2001).

Comte would reply that at the time of the American Revolution two thirds of Americans were Calvinists as Puritans (Dunn and Woodard 1996) and even more Protestants (including also Anglicans, Lutherans, Quakers, etc.). Calvinism's demographic super-majority and consequently its religious-political predominance rendered Jefferson and other liberals-secularists (condemned as "atheists") and Enlightenment-inspired liberals a relatively small and "atypical" (Archer 2001) minority and countervailing force in those and subsequent times. In addition, Jefferson, Madison, and their followers, as moderate non-Calvinist Protestants, were a small and declining, due to the evangelical Great Awakenings, minority in Protestantism in relation to "strict", "austere", and "stodgy orthodox" Calvinists (Gould 1996) as American theocratic and fundamentalist Puritans. For instance, Franklin relinquished his father's Calvinism because of its being "inimical to morality" (Byrne 1997), and New England's post-revolutionary Calvinist orthodoxy attacked Jefferson and other Enlightenment-inspired figures as "wicked" (Baldwin 2006; German 1995). In spite or rather because of his non-Jeffersonian reinterpretation of the American Revolution as "purely Protestant" or Calvinist, Comte implies that Calvinism functioned via Puritanism both as the genesis and evolution or "destiny" of America in the strict sense of an independent nation or institutional founding, just as in the meaning of its colonial origin in Tocqueville's first Puritans (Seaton 2006). And, Comte has been partly vindicated by the subsequent conservative and other descriptions of the American Revolution

---

[10] Patell (2001:195) notes that in 1763 pre-revolutionary Philadelphia was the "heart of the American Enlightenment where the Declaration of Independence would be signed a little less than thirteen years later." Moreover, Byrne (1997:48) suggests that "the country where those with Enlightenment sympathies achieved greatest political success with the least violence was the United States." He adds that "many of the major figures of the American Revolution and its aftermath—most prominently Benjamin Franklin (1706–90), Thomas Paine (1737–1809) and Thomas Jefferson (1743–1826), all three of whom spent considerable time in France—were men deeply involved in the spirit and thinking of the age of Enlightenment]" (Byrne 1997:48). In this view, "in America the leading Enlightenment thinkers were themselves part of the establishment" in contrast to France (Byrne 1997:49). A cited example is Jefferson becoming both President of the American Philosophical Society and of the Union. Compare the Enlightenment philosopher-President Jefferson (also, Phelps 2007) with Winthrop's self-declared admirers and subsequent "born again" evangelical US Presidents like Reagan and his own disciples in the early 21st century.

24                         CHAPTER ONE

as Protestant-based and linked, notably as a "political expression of the religious revivals of the Great Awakening"[11] (Dunn and Woodard 1996; also, Byrne 1997; German 1995; Kloppenberg 1998; Seaton 2006) of evangelical Protestantism.

Also, Weber suggests the idea of Calvinist-as-Puritan "destiny", over-determination, or path-dependence of America, and in part England. For example, he observes that, as the "most important practical ideal" of Puritanism, "quiet self-control" and "cool reserve" distinguish the "best type of English or American gentleman today" from his European, including German, counterparts. Conversely, he also makes an almost amusing, if not ethnocentric or nationalist, comparison to the effect that "the typical German quality often called good nature or naturalness contrasts strongly, even in the facial expressions of people, with the effects of that thorough destruction of the spontaneity of the *natural status* in the Anglo-American atmosphere, which Germans are accustomed to judge unfavourably as narrowness, unfreeness, and inner constraint."

As indicated, Weber finds the origin of such "very striking" differences in character and behavior between Germans (and implicitly Scandinavians) and Anglo-Americans in Lutheranism and Calvinism as their respective religious bases and in that sense national "destinies" or primary determinants. His observation is to be qualified for "English gentlemen" if England's dominant or official religion remains Lutheran-like (though not identical) Anglicanism, and not Calvinist Puritanism, unlike 17th century and later Scotland dominated by the latter (Berry 1997; Sprunger 1982). He traces these national differences to the "lesser degree of ascetic penetration of life in Lutheranism as distinguished from Calvinism", thus in Lutheran Germany (and Scandinavia) compared to Puritan England (and Scotland) and America. Weber adds almost amusingly[12] that "the antipathy of every spontaneous child of

---

[11] Echoing Comte, Kloppenberg (1998:23–4) suggests the "connection" between the Calvinist-inspired Great Awakenings and the subsequent American Revolution. Specifically, in this view, during the American Revolution "Puritan millennialism in the north, and Baptist evangelicalism in the south, could join forces with more secular forms of radicalism. Through participation in symbolic communal activities, colonists were able to put aside their differences and unite—however briefly—against the British" (Kloppenberg 1998:28). Alternatively, Byrne (1997:49) suggests that while the "American desire for independence from British colonial rule found a supporting rationale in many Enlightenment ideals", still the American Revolution "owed comparatively little to those ideals".

[12] For sympathetic critics, it is amusing to describe Germans as "spontaneous children of nature" or claim that "good nature or naturalness" is the "typical German

nature to everything ascetic is expressed in those feelings" in Lutheranism and thus (Lutheran) Germans with their "good nature or naturalness" in contrast to hyper-ascetic Calvinism and hence Puritan "Anglo-Americans". Weber's Germans are "spontaneous children of nature" simply because they are or related to non-ascetic Lutherans. Conversely, "Anglo-Americans" show "narrowness, unfreeness, and inner constraint" because of being or linked with hyper-ascetic (Akerlof 2007), "austere", and "stodgy Orthodox Calvinists" (Gould 1996) *cum* Puritans, except for English-American Anglicans as, in Weber's view, less ascetic and more moderate.

This is another way to restate that Calvinism through Puritanism becomes the "destiny" or the primary determinant and heritage of America, while by implication Lutheranism being that of Germany and Scandinavia, at the level of individual attitudes and actions. At this juncture, Calvinism predestines America in social-psychological terms via Puritanism's over-determining of the celebrated "American character and way", just as Lutheranism apparently does Weber's glorified "typical German quality." And it does, if not literally as predestination or determinism, then in the sense of what sociological analyses identify as religious determination (Munch 2001) and path-dependence, or general cultural heritage (Inglehart and Baker 2000; Mansbach 2006).

In sum, Calvinism through Puritanism acts as both the birth and the "heart and soul", the past, present and future, the origin and heritage of America. In this sense, Calvinism is through Puritanism, as the latter is often described, (the source of) Americanism (Gelernter 2005; Lipset 1996), particularly the "American character and way" (Seaton 2006), nativism (Merton 1939), or nationalism (Calhoun 1993; Friedland 2001), including what Pareto identifies as jingoism. And, conversely, if America represents a "lineal descendent" of Puritanism and *John* Winthrop et al., it is one of the latter's theological parent, Calvinism and *Jean* Calvin as "the most influential of the Protestant reformers"

---

quality", given the exactly opposite experiences, perceptions, or stereotypes in Europe, including Germany itself. (A sympathetic joke is that his description is fully justified in view of Germany's *Oktober Fest* or world-famous beer tradition, production, and consumption, and related expressions of German "spontaneous" and "good nature".) For others, such descriptions may be nationalistic, thus pernicious in light of Nazi and pre-Nazi German, primarily conservative, patterns of conduct. Thus, Pareto observed and predicted that German conservatism, and in part via a social contagion liberalism, "preaches militarism, war and extermination against the enemies of Germany and also against those who, though not her enemies, refuse to be her slaves".

(following Luther), who was born and raised, trained in theology and civil law in, of all places and times, late medieval Catholic France (Mansbach 2006).

*"All in the Extended Calvinist Family"*

To return to Tocqueville, while not stating explicitly he likely knew that his first Puritans in America had been the theological or intellectual "children" and in that sense members of an extended Calvinist "family" or global brotherhood (Sprunger 1982). Notably, he was probably aware that the theological and sociological name of the supreme Puritan master and role model, Winthrop had been precisely "austere Calvinism." And, as a peculiar historical and geographical curiosity or irony, he likely knew, though did not say, that these "all-American" Puritans were theologically part of a Calvinist "family" that was originally as French as, say, "French fries" (or wine and cheese). Recall Calvinism had its origin and first home nowhere else than in his native France as its own Protestant, specifically Calvinist Reformation (Morck, Wolfenzon, and Yeung 2005) during the early 16th century (Heller 1986). Also, remember Calvinism expanded via its disciplinary revolutions (Gorski 2003; Loveman 2005; Sprunger 1982) subsequently beyond France into especially Switzerland (Geneva) and Holland, in part Germany (Prussia), then also Scotland (Berry 1997) and England (Dahrendorf 1959; Elwood 1999), and eventually America (Dunn and Woodard 1996; Kloppenberg 1998; Mansbach 2006; Means 1966). Curiously, this is what that none than Marx also knew or implied when referring to the "Puritans of New England" as "those sober virtuosi of Protestantism", thus implicitly Calvinism as the paradigmatic instance of Protestant ascetic and moralistic sobriety. The same can be said of Weber, Sombart, Tawney, Parsons, Merton, and other sociologists usually treating "Puritan" as (part of) "Calvinist", and conversely the second as comprising the first as its integral element.

To fill the void or redress the omission Tocqueville unwittingly left in his diagnosis or prophecy of America's Puritan "destiny", it is instructive to recall that Weber typically does not substantively distinguish between but uses "Calvinism" and "Puritanism" interchangeably, as do Sombart and most other prominent analysts since Hume, Comte, and Mill. And when/if Weber occasionally distinguishes them he considers Calvinism to be the origin and global framework of "Puritanism" as its derivative and integral element, as indicated by his distinction between the first as "church" and the second as its internal sect or Calvinist sectarianism (also, Munch 1981). The equivalence is indicated by expressions like "Calvinism and [its] Puritan sects".[13] Moreover, Sombart goes further establishing a sort of tautological or mathematical identity of "Puritanism = Calvinism" and conversely, "Calvinism = Puritanism" in the *general* sense of moralizing purism.

Weber's substantive equivalence or Sombart's tautological identity of "Calvinism" and "Puritanism" is striking and inadmissible for some US sociologists or historians (e.g., Hartz[14] 1963) extolling the Puritan sources of American liberty and democracy. It is also, if a sort of perfect precision is needed in historical and geographical, though perhaps not theological and, most importantly, sociological, terms. Thus, Calvinism is more precisely defined, described, and considered as the second, 16th century Protestant Reformation or Reformed Church in continental Europe (France, Geneva, Holland, in part Germany) in contrast to Puritanism as mostly the 17th–18th century Calvinist derivation, extension, and revolution in Great Britain and America (some other formal or potential "differences" between the two are identified and reexamined later on).

Still, as Weber and even more Sombart suggests, this equivalence of "Calvinism" and "Puritanism" in the sense of that between an original and a derivative, respectively, is plausible and admissible in sociological, even if not completely precise in historical, terms. Calvinism was in

---

[13] Weber uses the expression "Calvinism and other Puritan sects", but "Calvinism and its Puritan sects" (or "Puritan and other Calvinist sects") is more consistent with his treatment of Calvinism as "church" and Puritanism as its sectarian derivative or "sect". It is also suggested by Munch's (1981) expression "Puritan sects and denominations" within Calvinism.

[14] Hartz (1963:369) contends that "fragmentation would detach Puritanism from the European past, would elevate it to the rank of a national absolute, [yet] in secular terms: the movement of Locke from the Old World ["the depravations of Europe"] to the New, not quite the movement of Calvin." Also, Kloppenberg (1998:25) suggests that the "sober Puritanism of Locke" (distinguished from the "stark individualism of Hobbes") was at the root of a "liberal tradition" in Great Britain and America. Yet, given Locke's Puritan-rooted illiberal religious intolerance of Catholics and non-believers (Champion 1999) and underlying Calvinism (Mitchell 1995) overall, other analysts would nominate Hume for that position (Berry 1997). By contrast, Means (1966:377) suggests that in America as well as post-Reformation Europe the "values of freedom and liberty [were] related to the Calvinist doctrines of religious transcendence and human sin." Yet, it is admitted that the "Reformation did not immediately lead to a state of toleration and liberty [but rather] many cases of [Calvinist] intolerance and bigotry", including those committed to the point of murder by Calvin himself (Means 1966:37).

a substantive sense 16th century European—and of all peoples and countries, French—proto-Puritanism in the general form and meaning of what Keynes might call moral and religious (and economic or financial) purism within Protestantism and the Reformation. It was "pure", more specifically Protestant, asceticism or austerity, including strict, almost (Gorski 2003; Tawney 1962) military and inquisitorial discipline, control, constraint, and repression. Alternatively, Puritanism was substantively a sort of specific, 17th and 18th century English-American "new" Calvinism, or reinvented, reinforced, and renamed Calvinist, distinguished from and opposed to Lutheran and Anglican, Protestantism (Davis 2005). At least, Puritanism is thus considered and described for the purpose of the present analysis. At this point, it is sufficient to redefine and consider Calvinism as, in Sombart's words, "only" original Puritanism *cum* purism in Europe, and Puritanism as "just" derivative, transposed, and renamed Calvinism in England and America.

To revisit Tocqueville, his first Puritans, including their supreme master Winthrop, were early "strict", "austere", and "stodgy orthodox" Calvinists, thus America's "destiny" proved to be effectively incarnated in the second through their manifestations and representations in the first. Conversely, these Puritans by their manifest over-determination of the "new nation" acted as the efficient agents of Calvinists as the principals and their latent societal predestination of America. In turn, both acted as predestined Divine tools and representatives, notably chosen masters of the "reprobate" ("damned") and "sinful", with claimed medieval-style Divine rights to the Weberian total mastery of the world, sociologically and geographically alike.

In terms of principal-agency theory in a proper legal-formal sense, early Calvinists as the "principals" were precisely responsible for the genesis and "destiny" of America, and not strictly speaking the first Puritans as their "agents" or "representatives" in the new world, thus legally-formally lacking such responsibility. This is just a legal analogy or metaphor and thus legalistic hyperbole not to be taken at face value. It can still illustrate and emphasize such a Calvinist-Puritan substantive equivalence, thus the "French-American connection", even if by dubious legalism or formalism and similar analogies. It is a legalistic way of saying that Tocqueville's first Puritans like Winthrop et al. were the theological or ideological "children" and members of the "extended family" of Calvin born and raised in France, and Puritanism was part of the global network of European Calvinism. It just restates legalistically that America's Puritan "destiny" or over-determination, like its genesis or (first) founding, reveals itself beneath the surface as its Calvinist "force and fate" (Bendix 1984) or societal predestination. This yields a disclaimer that agency-principal and other legal and related rational-choice analogies, metaphors, or concepts while occasionally useful cannot, in virtue of often being formalistic or simplistic, substitute for and greatly illuminate a substantive sociological analysis of this and most other subjects.

### *The Nature and Scope of the Calvinist "Predestination" of the "New Nation"*

#### *From Total Mastery to "Holistic Destiny"*

The Calvinist societal predestination via the Puritan over-determination of America is, first and foremost, a "holistic" or total design, process, and outcome. By assumption and in reality alike, the nature and scope of America's Calvinist predestination or "destiny" is holistic or integral in accordance with the very nature and operation of Calvinism. Namely, Calvinism is the religious design and social system of total, absolute mastery of the world or human society, like nature, rather than (as in Weber's account) passive "adaptation" or "mere accommodation" assumed to be characteristic for non-Calvinist or non-Protestant religions, including traditional Catholicism. Alternatively, Calvinism's ideally or proximately absolute mastery, via Puritanism's conquest and rule, of the new world *cum* American society and nature ("wilderness") generates, explains, and predicts the holistic nature and scope of America's Calvinist "destiny" or predestination. This is important to emphasize, because in order to better understand, explain, and predict the holistic character and scope of America's Calvinist "destiny" presupposes taking account of Calvinism's original and persistent design ("dream") and institutional practice of total mastery of the societal and physical world.

In essence, Calvinism, including Puritanism, is either the total mastery, rule, domination of the world, including society and nature, or is not "Calvinism" or "Puritanism" in the strict sense, as Hume, Comte, Mill, Weber, and contemporary sociologists (Munch 2001) suggest. For Calvinism, including Puritanism, non-total, partial, or incomplete mastery of society is (as Weber may put it) an impossible inner contradiction or self-negation, a sort of "impossibility theorem" (Arrow 1950), simply "does not make sense". At most, it represents the "second best" prudent option a la a Machiavellian tactic adopted when the optimum of total societal rule or domination is not attainable temporarily or otherwise, and dispensed with if this maximum can be attained.

As elaborated, such a totality was the prime mover of the rise and expansion of Calvinism as the self-defined Second, "true" Protestant Reformation in France (Elwood 1999; Heller 1986) and beyond, including Geneva, Holland, and even Lutheran Germany (Nischan 1994). Early Calvinism did so on explicit or implied grounds that the First Reformation or Lutheranism failed to attain what it, as Comte and Weber suggest (also, Munch 1981), had promised. This is the total ascetic mastery or reign over the "sinful world" and human sinners by religious virtuosi and saints forming the "pure church". As known, initially the Protestant Reformation aimed at substituting a more complete and intense "ethical penetration" of society (Munch 1981) for what it had perceived and condemned as too "lax" and "imperceptible" traditional Christian moral control, namely what Weber calls the "very human Catholic cycle of sin, repentance, atonement, release, followed by renewed sin." And, through its claimed Second and final, "true" Protestant Reformation, Calvinism aimed and occasionally succeeded to replace or intensify Lutheranism's supposedly incomplete or unwilling ascetic mastery of society, thus to complete or restore the First Reformation, in addition and connection to its vehement anti-Catholic ideas and practices. This was witnessed in Calvinism's attempted, yet failed, Calvinization of no less than *Lutheran* Germany (Nischan 1994), just as of Catholic France, also abortive, and of Geneva and notably Holland, successful in both cases.

As a consequence of its "holism" in the methodical mastering of the social world, the Calvinist, including Puritan, "destiny" or predestination of a society under its mastery is likely to be equivalently holistic. With local (Geneva) and diminishing exceptions (Holland and Great Britain, minus Scotland), no Western society has been and remains more manifestly, intensively, systematically, and enduringly under Calvinist-as-Puritan holistic mastery or reign than America during most of its history, as Tocqueville, Weber, and contemporary sociologists (Munch 2001) suggest. This especially holds true of New England during its "Biblical Commonwealth" and the South and the "Wild West" turned into a "Bible Belt" through the evangelical Great Awakenings (especially the Second of the 1800s) and other ever-recurring Calvinist revivals (Clemens 2007). Consequently, such mastery endows America's Calvinist predestination through Puritan over-determination with an equivalent quality or tendency of societal holism or totality. And, this is what Tocqueville's description of America as a Calvinist society in the form of a Puritan nation comprising the economy, polity, civil life, and culture signifies. Alternatively, it means that America is not just a Calvinist-Puritan economy (capitalism) or polity, civil society, and culture, but *all* of the above in reciprocal relation and reinforcement, epitomizing holism or totality.

## *"Holism" in Societal Predestination: Varieties*

The preceding anticipates the specific forms and meanings of America's holistic "destiny" embedded in Calvinism, or Calvinist "holism" in its societal predestination. One form and meaning is systemic or sociological holism. This is in the sense that America's Calvinist "destiny" in its scope encompasses society as a whole, as a total social system, with the economy, polity, civil society, and culture as its constituents or subsystems. In short, it is holistic in its being societal, including economic, political, civil, and cultural, "destiny" and predestination. Conversely, it is not merely any one of these elements taken separately, namely not just economic, political, civil, and cultural "destiny" and predestination, as its particular interrelated dimensions.

While seemingly self-evident, this systemic holism needs to be emphasized because of its actual or potential reductions and conflations, especially economic reductionism or determinism. Economic reductionism posits or implies that America's Puritan "destiny" is only or primarily a capitalist economy[15] (Friedman and Friedman 1982), as distinguished from and not necessarily determining a democratic polity (Binmore 2001), plus a free civil society and a humane culture. Economic reductionism is also in part implicit in Calvinism's assumed "elective affinity" with modern industrial capitalism, but not explicitly,

---

[15] Friedman and Friedman (1982:108) state that Puritans, just as more moderate once-Calvinist Quakers, emigrated to the new world "because they could accumulate the funds to do so in the market" despite their non-economic "disabilities imposed on them". However, Weber suggests the opposite in his observation that the Southern states of America "were founded by large capitalists for business motives, while the New England colonies were founded by preachers and seminary graduates with the help of small citizen, craftsmen and yeomen, for religious reasons". In this sense, Anglicans were economic "pilgrims", and Calvinist Puritans "religious entrepreneurs", and since the first had preceded the second by almost two decades they more deserve to be called

as least within Weber's framework, with liberal-secular democracy, civil society, and culture as non-economic societal realms. As implied, this systemic holism overcoming economic reductionism in social predestination is the outcome of Calvinism's pursued holistic mastery or integral rule of the world in a sociological sense of what Durkheim and Parsons call total society.

Another form and meaning of America's Calvinist holistic "destiny" is its geographic holism in the sense of being initially situated in the "new nation" and eventually expanded to the world as a whole. Thus, it is holistic in being not only American or national, but global, transnational "destiny" extending by "word and sword" (or "stick and carrot") Calvinist "American" values and institutions beyond the "Puritan Nation". Simply, America's Calvinist "destiny" is geographically holistic in encompassing not only Winthrop's "shining city upon a hill" driven by "austere Calvinism" or alternatively "Salem with witches" (Putnam 2000). It is also through its global expansion by Puritan-style "holy" wars, militarism, and imperialism (Steinmetz 2005), or the neo-conservative (Reaganite) "empire of liberty" driven by nativism or religious nationalism (Friedland 2001) *cum* Americanism originating in and championed by Puritanism (Lipset 1996; Munch 2001). By analogy, this geographic holism in social predestination is the outcome of the Calvinist holistic mastery of the world in a geographical sense of both America as a territorial state and other "liberated" states by and within this new empire for "good", while (as US "born again" Puritan or evangelical Presidents put it) only the "stars" being the limit. A self-evident reduced geographic holism is that America's Calvinist "destiny" or heritage spans as a reality or command all of its regions, North and South, "red" and "blue" states, with secondary variations, as initiated and realized by the Great Awakenings and other pandemic Puritan-inspired revivals and social contagions, including the evangelical revival and contagion of the 1980–2000s.

Another form and meaning of the Calvinist holistic "destiny" of America is its historical holism in the sense of encompassing virtually

---

the "Pilgrims" in the general sense of founders. Also, Gould (1996:30) remarks that Puritans "emigrated, not for the advantage of trade, but for religion, and the enjoyment of liberty of conscience" as they understood it, namely only for themselves and usually denied to non-Puritans and especially non-Christians (Native Americans, etc.) condemned, branded and persecuted as "heathen" (Davis 2005; Fehler 2005; Harley 1996).

its entire history, ranging from the very birth of the "new nation" to its further evolution, and present and likely its foreseeable future. For instance, this is what Tocqueville implies when observing that the "destiny" of America during the early 19th century was embodied, and predicting that it will continue to be in the future, in the first Puritans, thus in its Calvinist genesis. This "destiny" has been invariably embedded in Calvinism as Puritanism, initially during the colonial period (17th–18th century New England), subsequently in post-revolutionary times (notably the 19th century South) through the Great Awakenings as Calvinist contagions, and spanning into the early 21st century and likely beyond ("Bible Belt" or "red" states) via another evangelical revival or neo-Calvinist religious contagion.

Specifically, in the spirit of Tocqueville's insight, America's Calvinist "destiny" follows its equivalent genesis in the 17th century, and remains historically holistic or integral. It does in the sense of an essential continuity and unbroken sequence from the Calvinist dominated 18th century (e.g., the Great Awakenings) through the early and mid 19th century, including his visit and identification of Americans as a "puritanical people", to the late 20th and early 21st centuries punctuated by Calvinism's another rebirth via reborn evangelicalism. This is suggested by the observations of the dominance of Calvinist sectarian Protestantism, particularly Puritanism, in American history and society, in a continuous line, with certain minor disruptions, from the 17th to the 21st century (Lipset 1996; Munch 2001). This historical holism of America's Calvinist "destiny" does not signify or predict that it is or will be, as US evangelicals claim or dream, eternal as a non-sociological, non-empirical theological proposition. Rather, this means only that it has been historically operative and observed during a specific time period and likely to operate in a foreseeable, yet not necessarily infinite, future. By analogy, this historical holism in social predestination is the outcome of Calvinism's inherently holistic mastery of the world in temporal terms, namely of past, present and future worlds or societies and humans.

An additional form and meaning of America's Calvinist holistic "destiny" is what can be described a la Weber as methodical or "methodological" holism. The latter is understood in the sense of comprising virtually all possible methods, techniques, and procedures, from spiritual to military ones, for attaining and sustaining the Calvinist total mastery of the world in sociological, geographic, and historical meanings alike. In Weber's words, America's "destiny" is holistic in that

Calvinism's "methodical mastering" of the "sinful" world, including others and oneself, thus implicitly sadism-masochism (Adorno 2001; McLaughlin 1996), invents and uses any available effective methods and means in the manner of Machiavellianism. These range from the "doctrine of sanctification" and other "spiritualism" to violence, militancy, and militarism like aggressive "holy" wars against the "evil" and "ungodly" world.

In this sense, the methodical holism of America's Calvinist "destiny" is manifested in pursuing, first, spiritual, yet often violent, culture or temperance wars (Bell 2002; Wagner 1997) against domestic "witches" or "enemies", ranging from moral sinners and social non-conformists to political dissenters and liberal secularists, agnostics, and religious non-believers as supremely "un-American" (Edgell, Gerteis and Hartmann 2006). Second, it is expressed in methodically conducting offensive "preemptive" and permanent military wars on the "corrupt", "ungodly," and "evil" world to be saved from itself by destroying it via the Calvinist "sword" of moral purity, godliness, and goodness of the "Puritan nation" (Holton 1987; Turner 2002). Negatively, America's Calvinist "destiny" is holistic in "methodological" or technical terms in that virtually *no* methods or techniques are discarded and ruled out ("off the table") so long as they prove to be effective in the service of attaining and sustaining certain purposes and higher causes. And, the foremost and constant of these purposes is the total domination over the "sinful world" both in a sociological and geographic sense, of American and global society, by Puritan saints-masters in the new face of "born again" US Calvinist-rooted evangelicals as the true, sole "Christians".

The preceding form of America's Calvinist holistic "destiny" constitutes Machiavellian and generally utilitarian holism extolled by Parsonian sociologists (Mayway 1984). Simply, as US Puritan-inspired neo-conservatives say, "whatever it takes" will be applied or "anything goes" to fulfill their "American dream" (Merton 1968) as they understand and pursue it. In this context, their dream, as Comte prophetically implied long ago for Calvinism, is the Calvinist total mastery of society, mixed with exorbitant wealth reproducing the "top-heavy" plutocracy (Wolff 2002). Alternatively, in the process of fulfilling their "American dream" of theocratic dominance and plutocratic wealth, US "reborn" Calvinists tend to make life for most humans a "nightmare" (Beck 2000) or what Tawney (1962) calls living "hell in this world" to describe Puritanism's inhumane, "non-Christian" treatment of non-Puritans. In Mannheim's words, what makes this Calvinist "destiny" technical, Machiavellian holism is that Calvinism-Puritanism, like conservatism overall, is the holistic "technique of domination" or Machiavellianism adopting any effective techniques to attain its ends that "justify the means" (Simon 1976). By analogy, this "methodological" *qua* Machiavellian holism in social predestination is the predictable outcome of the Calvinist holistic mastery of the world by any efficient methods, means, and procedures.

Some other forms and meaning of America's Calvinist holistic "destiny" encompass the following. An additional form and meaning of America's Calvinist holistic "destiny" is that it is both individual and group, private and public. In turn, this form is implicit in Calvinist systemic holism in social predestination. Specifically, individual-private destiny is implied in civil society and culture, the group-public in the polity in accordance with the dichotomy between the cultural or civic sphere and the state, while both forms are implied in the economy. A related form and meaning of America's Calvinist holistic "destiny" is in its being both formal, including legal, and informal or substantive, notably institutional and non-institutional, codified and diffuse alike. Likewise, this form is implicit in Calvinist systemic holism. Formal and institutional "destiny" is implied in the economy and polity, the informal and non-institutional in civil society and culture, also in accordance with the conventional dichotomy (Parsons' AGIL model) between economic-political institutions and the civic sphere (his societal community) or the life-world (Alexander 2001; Habermas 2001). Still another form and meaning of America's Calvinist holistic "destiny" is being both material and ideal or spiritual in Weber's words, sensate and ideational or idealistic in Sorokin's. As before, this form is implied in Calvinist systemic holism, the material-sensate "destiny" in the economy, the ideal-spiritual in culture and civil society, and both in the polity. (These forms of America's Calvinist holistic "destiny" are summarized in Table 1.1.)

The present study focuses on the social-systemic holism, or the sociological form and meaning of America's Calvinist holistic "destiny", in conjunction with the others listed above. For that aim, the study first identifies and considers the type of total social system or society that specifically and essentially constitutes, reproduces, or reflects America's Calvinist "destiny". It then disaggregates this total social system into its constitutive components or subsystems as the specific dimensions, mechanisms, or reflections of the Calvinist "destiny" of the "new nation".

Table 1.1. Forms and meanings of America's holistic Calvinist "destiny"

Systemic holism
  total social system
    economy
    polity
    civil society
    culture
Geographic holism
  the "new nation"—all US, "red" and "blue" states
  the "empire of liberty"—the entire world
Historical holism
  from the 17–18th to the 21st century and beyond
"Methodological" holism
  "spiritualism"—culture and temperance wars in America
  militancy—military offensive "holy" war or crusade against "evil" and "infidels" in the world
Other holisms
  individual and group, private and public
  formal and informal, institutional and non-institutional
  material and ideal

## *Appendix: America's "Destiny" and Tocqueville, Weber, and Marx*

In an alternative Weberian interpretation of Tocqueville, America is a "commercial nation" or capitalist society precisely because it is a "puritanical people" in accordance with the assumed "intimate connection" or "elective affinity" between ascetic Protestantism like Calvinism and the "spirit of capitalism" in general.[16] In Tocqueville's words, this means that America's capitalist, economic "destiny" is also embodied in the first Puritans, and thus determined by Puritanism. At this point, the Weberian grounding of the genesis of American and other Western, primarily Anglo-Saxon, capitalism in Calvinism becomes a special case of Tocqueville's identification or prediction of America's "destiny" in the early Puritans. Conversely, America's Puritan "destiny" logically and empirically involves its economic "fate" as a special case in Puritanism, though Tocqueville does not explicitly state and explicate such a possibility.

---

[16] For instance, in a Weberian vein German (1995:969) contends that pre-revolutionary America such as late 18th century Connecticut and the rest of New England witnessed both the "triumph of Calvinism and capitalism", thus Biblical theocracy and free enterprise, "God and Mammon" or "Money" alike (Friedland 2002; Munch 2001).

However, such Weberian interpretations of Tocqueville's insight may be dubious, as especially suggested by his seeming disassociation of "puritanical" and "commercial" or capitalist, the economic and the religious, as mutually incompatible, though co-existing. If they are acceptable, America's capitalist "fate" in Puritanism can be subsumed under its general national or societal "destiny" embodied in Tocqueville's first Puritans, as Weber suggests or intimates.

By contrast, a Marxian, economic interpretation of Tocqueville's statement may propose that America is a "puritanical people" precisely because it is a "commercial nation" or capitalist society in accordance with the assumed determination of Protestantism, including Puritanism, by capitalism, and generally religion and culture as the "superstructure" by the economy as the base. This effects a reversal of Tocqueville's thesis implying that America's "destiny" is embodied in the first *capitalists* rather than Tocqueville's Puritans, thus determined by capitalism, and not by Puritanism assumed to be just its religious expression ("epiphenomenon"). Reflecting economic determinism, this is an assumption in a sense common to most economists, from Smith and his *Wealth of Nations* to Friedman's *Capitalism and Freedom*; as Marx may put it, the first Puritans and other Protestants were above all *capitalists* rather than conversely. Simplistically, in Marxian and other economic accounts, they were Calvinists or Puritans because of being capitalists in the first place, not, as Weber suggests, "capitalist" due to their "Calvinist" or "Puritan" origins.

Curiously, this is what some staunchly anti-Marxian US economists (Friedman) imply by observing that the Puritans (and Quakers) emigrated to the new world because of the possibility of capital accumulation (Friedman and Friedman 1982). If so, this describes these Puritans as Marx's capitalists first and foremost, rather than Tocqueville's "pious adventurers" or Sorokin's "ideational" creatures migrating to and founding, as Weber suggests, America (New England) "for religious reasons", not "for business motives". While converging with Marx, let alone Smith and neo-classical economists, on economic determinism, this is contrary to Tocqueville's and Weber's prediction of America's "destiny" embedded in Puritanism, thus religious or spiritual factors. At least in Tocqueville's account of America's Puritan "destiny", both Marxian and anti-Marxian economic determinism, especially (as in the second case) market absolutism (Hodgson 1999), is incongruent, at most complementary as part of a multifactor framework or multivariate model involving both Weber's ideal and material values and interests, culture and economy.

Of course, the Calvinist societal predestination of America is to be understood and taken as operating in interaction and reciprocal reinforcement with, or conversely, counteracted by, other non-Calvinist and generally non-religious social determinants. It proceeds as what Weber calls co-determination within a complex process of multi-determination, rather than as single determination or mono-causation. Within a multiple co-determination, Calvinism is assumed to act as the prime determinant leading to a sort of over-determination (Alexander 1998), and non-Calvinist factors as secondary determinants analogously implying under-determination. Thus, Tocqueville by describing America as "at the same time" a Puritan and capitalist (or commercial) society suggests two *independent* determinants, the first being Puritanism or religion, the second capitalism or a market economy. Moreover, he implies that "puritanical" and "commercial", thus religious and capitalist, are mutually incompatible or contradictory while coexisting. He follows the traditional opposition or tension in virtually all religions and societies between (as Weber and Sorokin) note, piety and wealth, "God and Mammon", ideal and material, spiritual and economic values generally. In a way, Tocqueville's description of America as simultaneously a "puritanical people" and a "commercial nation", implying the most Puritan *and* the most capitalist, religious and materialist, society is perhaps intended to express a paradox, tension, or contradiction of Puritanism and capitalism (Grossman 2006; Munch 2001).

In turn, within a Weberian framework, the birth of American and other Western modern capitalism is a dependent variable of—or in "intimate connection" with—Calvinism, including Puritanism as the explanatory, and thus ultimately subsumed under the latter as the primary co-determinant or "destiny" of America. In statistical terms, the high, almost perfect (near 1) intercorrelation of (the rise of) modern capitalism and Calvinism or Puritanism, as the dependent and explanatory variables respectively, requires retaining the second variable in and removing the first from the multifactor model ("multivariate regression") in a Weberian framework, in contrast to that of Tocqueville operating with both. The present work centers on Tocqueville's diagnosis of "puritanical people" or Calvinism considered to be the primary variable, and treats (controls for) a "commercial nation" or capitalism as the secondary (or residual) in his implied two-factor framework of co-determination of America.

In short, Tocqueville implies that America is a capitalist society or "commercial nation" in spite, rather than because, of being a Puritan and thus Calvinist one. By contrast, in Weber's framework, America is a capitalist society precisely because it is a Puritan nation, as exemplified by Franklin's Calvinist "spirit of capitalism". Marx occasionally implies exactly the opposite: America, as well as Holland and England, is a Puritan or Protestant nation overall due to being a capitalist society. In Weber-Sorokin's terms, Tocqueville implies that America is a materialistic, "sensate" (Lane 2000) society in spite, not because of, even in certain tensions and contradictions with, being an idealistic ("ideational") or spiritualistic culture.

Curiously, even in a general Weberian framework (*Economy and Society*), Tocqueville's implied conventional position seems more congruent. This holds true insofar as, as Weber (and Sorokin) suggests, the pursuit of material ("sensate") interests is not necessarily connected with, but typically mitigated and counteracted by seeking ideal ("ideational") values, in a certain trade-off or opportunity-cost relationship. This is indicated by his distinction between instrumental- and value-rational action, or formal and substantive rationality, pursuing such ends, respectively.

It is also suggested by the identification of various frictions and contradictions between America as the most capitalist-materialistic *and* the most or even sole Puritan-religious modern Western society[17] (Munch 2001). This also applies to the finding that today's US "born again" fundamentalists subordinate the "goal of material gain" to idealistic, cultural ends, even evincing "anti-materialist orientations" (Darnell and Sherkat 1997). After all, the revival and dominance of Protestant fundamentalism (Baptism and allied sects, etc.) in America over the 1980s–2000s was (also) driven by "spiritualism" (Wuthnow 1998) and anti-materialism (Lane 2000), though not anti-capitalism (e.g., the pro-capitalist "Christian Coalition"), just as by anti-secularism, anti-rationalism or anti-scientism, and anti-liberalism (Bauman 2001; Bell 2002; Munch 2001).

In sum, it seems more plausible to say that America was and remains a capitalist society in spite, as Tocqueville does, rather than, as Weber and Parsons do, because, of being the Puritan and thus Calvinist "new nation" (*pace* the "Protestant ethic" thesis of American capitalism). Still, this is a secondary issue for the present purpose of positing and demonstrating that Calvinism via Puritanism constitutes its holistic societal "destiny." The latter is a sociological, thus (as Pareto implies) broader and more complex, matter than the relatively narrow and simple problem of capitalism as an economic structure, with the former comprising the latter and other, including *non*-capitalist, types of economy, as its particular case.

---

[17] Such frictions and contradictions between capitalism and the heritage of Puritanism in America are evident within the modern Republican Party, as indicated by the internal tensions or conflicts between modern capitalists and "reborn" neo-Calvinist culture warriors, with the latter usually prevailing since the 1980s through the 2000s.

CHAPTER TWO

## AMERICA'S CALVINIST "DESTINY" IDENTIFIED AND SPECIFIED

*What is America's Calvinist "Destiny"?*

The preceding has argued and established that Calvinism is through Puritanism the "destiny" or heritage, just as the genesis or (first) founding, of America but has not specified the nature of such Calvinist societal predestination via the Puritan determination of the "new nation". One wonders what America's Calvinist "destiny" specifically entails. The issue is what constitutes the single most crucial and enduring dimension of America's Calvinist "destiny" understood as a holistic design, (predestination) process, and outcome. In order to better address this issue it is instructive to retrieve and reconsider the original and continuing aim, nature, and operation of Calvinism, including its offspring Puritanism.

*Calvinism Retrieved from the (Theocratic) "Golden Past"*

First and foremost, Calvinism, including Puritanism, essentially originates, functions, and remains by the 21st century as the theological design and, whenever and wherever established, the social system of religious fundamentalism, notably theocracy. Calvinism and consequently Puritanism is fundamentalist and theocratic Protestantism, or more so than such other Protestant branches as Lutheranism and Anglicanism. In short, it constitutes the axiomatic or paradigmatic Protestant variety of religious fundamentalism and societal theocracy. More specifically, original Calvinism, including derivative Puritanism, is evangelical and bibliocratic Protestantism, or Protestant evangelicalism in the sense of Biblicism (Coffey 1998) and Bibliocracy, as the concrete forms and dimensions of "Christian" fundamentalism and theocracy, respectively.

Notably, Calvinism historically originated and operated as the evangelical and theocratic movement and revolution or the Second Protestant Reformation first in France and then beyond under Calvin's leadership[1] (Heller 1986). Consequently, it did as the theological design and the institutional practice of fundamentalist theocracy in the evangelical form of Bibliocracy, a "Bible Community" or "Biblical Commonwealth," as in England and New England.

This was indicated by early French Calvinism's striking but indicative and even prophetic conclusion and implied prescription at a Calvinist Synod nearby, "of all places", Paris in 1559. This was that the "evangelical religion" and thus Bibliocracy as a society could only be instituted through the "extermination of papists, parlementaires and nobility"[2] (Heller 1986) and other "infidels", notably "libertines" as precursors of modern liberals. Conversely, conceivably such extermination of non-evangelicals and all "infidels", thus establishment of the "true" evangelical religion and morality, could be successfully realized "only in a theocracy" (Tawney 1962). And, Calvin and other French Calvinists, including those attending the Paris Synod, were evidently aware of the necessity of theocracy as the necessary condition or effective means of attaining that end, by attempting to *first* establish theocratic rule, while immediately afterwards methodically conducting the "extermination" of these "infidels". This awareness apparently continues in their successors or proxies like US "reborn" Calvinist evangelicals, notably Baptist and related sects aiming to (as a Southern Baptist pastor stated during the 2000s) "persecute" and make the "ungodly" "perish" in America. And, their establishing Biblical theocracy (the "Bible Belt") in America becomes the necessary condition or the ultimate and effective means and path, simply the "best" formula of attaining that aim, the "water-proof guarantee" for total success.

Notably, setting the pattern, mood, or "method in the madness" (Mansbach 2006), Calvin in Geneva, after failing in his native France, established an evangelical religion and theocracy (Byrne 1997). He and his disciples did so in the form of the monistic model of the medievalist *civitas Dei* in which Church is dominant over State and all society (Frijhoff 2002) through some form of extermination or persecution of non-evangelicals and dissenters (Servetus, libertines, etc.), as "infidels." Conversely, Calvin et al. could conduct the extermination or persecution

---

[1] Heller (1986:114) finds that the "attribution of faith to God rather than man was of course common to all the evangelicals of Calvin's generation."

[2] Heller (1986:237) refers to the conclusion of the Calvinist synod at Chalons-sur-la-Saone, France, during the late 16th century.

of non-evangelicals and dissenters and establish the true "evangelical" religion only in a theocracy, specifically Bibliocracy. This indicates a sort of "virtuous circle" in original Calvinism embodied by Calvin in 16th century France and Geneva, as in neo-Calvinist evangelicalism (Baptism, etc.) incarnated by "reborn" fundamentalists in 21st century America. First, original Calvinism could and neo-Calvinist evangelicalism can conceivably establish the "true" evangelical religion and Biblical theocracy *cum* the "Bible Community" primarily through the methodical extermination or persecution of "infidels" and the "ungodly," notably early libertines and modern liberals respectively, subjected to the Calvinist (Baptist) "godly" command of "perish" and "persecute". Second, Calvinism could and can methodically conduct such extermination and persecution of "ungodly" libertines and liberals primarily within a Biblical theocracy after the image of the "Bible Garden" and thus the established "true" evangelical religion.

Calvin's creation and rule of an evangelical and theocratic Geneva and his method or design of extermination and persecution of "infidels" have become an ideal or model followed by Calvinism in Europe and through Puritanism in England and America. For instance, following Calvin's Geneva evangelical model of theocracy, Calvinism was imposed on politics and society in Holland by establishing the Reformed Church as a "real State Church", overtly revealing and forcibly fulfilling its "theocratic desires"[3] (Frijhoff 2002). Calvinism was the Divine design and the social system of evangelical theocracy and religious fundamentalism, with its rule in Geneva and Holland originally establishing a "model of theocratic governance" (Mansbach 2006).

Thus, Weber identifies and emphasizes what he describes as Calvinist theocracies or state churches in Europe like France, Geneva, and Holland, as well as, via Puritanism, England and America, specifically New England. Notably, he remarks that Calvinism considered what he calls Biblical theocracy ("in the Presbyterian form") to be "divinely ordained". Weber adds that, however, Calvinism was able to create such a theocracy "only for a limited time and only in local areas", like the Huguenot-ruled parts of France ("incompletely"), Geneva, the Netherlands, and longer and more extensively New England.

---

[3] Frijhoff (2002:52) adds that in Holland under the Calvinist Church "the state, which had to ensure the best conditions for the effective sanctification of the people of Saints, was at its service". Also, Prak (2002:159) registers the "self-conscious exclusiveness of the Calvinist Church in Holland".

As a curious omission, Weber does not mention what he does on other occasions, namely England's Biblical theocracy designated as a "Holly Commonwealth" established and ruled by Cromwell's "Parliament of Saints," as well as Scotland's earlier and longer "Presbyterian" version. Weber makes this omission in view of what he describes as the "Parliament of Saints" eventually "abortive" rule and consequently the failed Puritan Revolution of the 1640s–60s (Goldstone 1986; Gorski 2000) in contrast to the victory of Puritanism and thus the "triumph of Calvinism" (German 1995) in America.[4] In short, he identifies the "well-known" and "strict Bibliocracy" of Calvinism, as the Biblical, evangelical version of "Christian" theocracy. Weber particularly finds that certain Calvinist groups or proxies in Europe such as the "first Baptist communities" in Switzerland and Germany practiced the "strictest Bibliocracy" by adopting the "life of the first generations of Christians as a model", and conceived the "Biblical way of life" with "radicalism" comparable to monastic medievalism. Yet, by contrast to the latter, Calvinism, including Baptism, wanted and tried to expand the medieval monastery to all society designed as and converted into a monastic order and thus a sort of open super-prison for those transgressing its rules, by forcing humans to live like monks-saints or proxy prisoners for their entire life.

The above implies that Calvinism, including Puritanism, designed and established not any theocracy but specifically a primitive "Biblical theocracy" or "strict Bibliocracy", as defined and distinguished from what Comte would denote as a modernized, "more advanced" theocracy. Moreover, Comte suggests that Calvinism and Protestantism as a whole displayed an "exclusive predilection for the primitive church" and even a "more injurious enthusiasm for the Hebrew theocracy" dreaming about its "restoration". He adds that it reproduced the "old Greek notion of a kind of metaphysical theocracy" in the shape or rather face, in Protestant minds, of a "reign of Saints"[5] as originally witnessed in French Calvinism as the self-proclaimed "community of

---

[4] Also, when referring to the Calvinist theocracy in New England, Weber effectively equates American Puritanism, not even mentioned, with Calvinism.

[5] Comte's statement apparently refers to Plato's Sparta (also, Garrard 2003; Infantino 2003) and Calvinist-Puritan theocracies ("Holy Commonwealths") and theocrats in England (Cromwell) and America (Winthrop), respectively. Overall, Comte's insights are potentially instructive, because he was among the first sociologists to systematically explore what he calls the "theocratic order" and the "theological age" overall in relation to liberal-democratic and secular modernity or the "positive age".

the saints" (Mentzer 2007). Comte apparently refers to Calvinist Puritanism in England, specifically Cromwell's "Parliament of Saints" or what Hume describes as Puritan "Divines" establishing and ruling the "Holy Commonwealth" as their substitute for the "unholy" monarchy and the Anglican Church as the prior sociopolitical and religious order, respectively (Elwood 1999).

In Sorokin's (1970) terms, Calvinism and consequently Puritanism was the theological design and social system of "pure" or "perfect", as contrasted with "diluted" or "imperfect", "Christian" theocracy. To that extent, Calvinism, especially Puritanism, revealed some sort of theocratic and other primordialism (Smelser 1997) or primitivism and pre-modern traditionalism (Goldstone 1986; Gorski 2000), and even what Hume and Comte identify as barbarism. It did in the specific predictable "holy" form of Biblical primeval fundamentalism, simply evangelicalism *qua* "Biblicism, primitivism, and restorationism" (Coffey 1998). Comte observes that Calvinism and Protestantism in general not only attempted to return to the "period of the primitive Church," but imposed or offered the "most barbarous and dangerous part of the Scriptures," the "Hebrew antiquity", as well as the "Hebrew Bible" and its admitted mix of the "acceptability of genocidal campaigns" with the "pursuit of justice" (Angel 1994). Calvinism, notably Puritanism, as he puts it, tended toward longing for or dreaming about restoring the "early Christian times" as the "golden past" or "paradise lost" due to "infidels" like "papists", libertines, and others to be exterminated or persecuted for their role in the loss of Eden and implicitly "original sin."

In general, Calvinist theocratic primitivism or fundamentalism in the specific form of evangelicalism (Heller 1986) consisted in attempting to restore or dreaming about restoring what Simmel describes as the "primitive identity" of religion and politics through a "godly" polity and all society (Zaret 1989). This was epitomized by the Calvinist-as-Puritan "dream of the godly community" (German 1995) in colonial and post-revolutionary America, first New England and subsequently the South (Boles 1999) and the "Wild West" (Clemens 2007), and beyond via a "holy" war or crusade against the "ungodly" world (Turner 2002). For example, in his classical historical account of the "spectre" of Puritanism (Seed 2005), Hume registers early Puritans' "intemperate use of authorities" from Scripture, particularly the Old Testament. Also, he notices that they were induced by a "more unreasonable obstinacy" in the English Parliament in which they attained a majority at first and then ascendance over and ultimately the "destruction of the church and monarchy" during the late 16th and mid 17th century, respectively (Elwood 1999). Moreover, he describes these Puritans (e.g., Presbyterian preachers) as "full of barbarism and of ignorance", in particular their self-proclaimed "Lord of the Domain" Cromwell as a "barbarian". Notably, following French-European Calvinists, English-American Puritans, as Hume observes, claimed to represent the "only pure church" and stipulated that their tenets and practices be "established by law", while no alternatives being "tolerated", effectively claiming and seeking, just as eventually establishing in old and New England, legal theocracy (Stivers 1994).

In sum, Calvinism, including Puritanism, designed and whenever and wherever possible, as in 16th century Geneva and Holland and 17th century England, Scotland, and New England, instituted fundamentalist theocracy in the invariant form of strict Bibliocracy. The latter was by assumption premised on theocratic evangelicalism established by the methodical extermination and persecution of non-evangelicals and other "infidels," just as conversely, "exterminate" and persecute" of these could and can be optimally conducted primarily in an evangelical theocracy. Calvinism did the above through the primitive institutional "merger" of religion and politics, sacred and secular power, church and state (Dahrendorf 1979; Dombrowski 2001). Hence, it recreated from the medieval "golden past" what even Puritan John Locke, despite his intolerant (Champion 1999; Fitzpatrick 1999), albeit "muted" (Mitchell 1995), Calvinism, considered a non-entity or impossibility, the "Christian Commonwealth" (Zaret 1989) as "Christ's Kingdom on Earth" (Tawney 1962). Notably, following and escalating Calvinism, Puritanism engaged in systematic "sectarian attempts" at applying Calvinist doctrines to politics by creating a "Holy Commonwealth" (Zaret 1989; also, Gorski 2000) as the design and designation of theocracy or a sacred tyranny by Puritan self-proclaimed "divines" both perplexing and bemusing Hume.

Consequently, Calvinism, including Puritanism, attempted and frequently succeeded to perpetuate or revive and reinforce rather than, as often assumed, abolish or mitigate ("liberalize") the medieval theocracy as an exemplar and sequel of Comte's primitive Bibliocracy. Of course, it did so in a "new" Calvinist form and meaning replacing the old (Catholic, Orthodox) Christian and even other Protestant (Lutheran and Anglican) forms. Thus, Tawney (1962) concedes that Puritanism and generally Calvinism reproduced and even intensified the "medieval idea of a Church-civilization" with respect to not only "doctrinal purity" but also "social righteousness", a society that constituted "Church and State in one", thus axiomatic theocracy. In this account, the Calvinist-Puritan, as, for that matter, Catholic, Islamic, and other religious, design and endeavor of translating morality in society into an "objective discipline" was logical and/or feasible "only in a theocracy", more specifically its evangelical form or Comte-Weber's primitive Bibliocracy. As observed, what was "characteristic of early Calvinism", notably Puritanism, was its adoption and realization of the medieval "idea of a moral code" as defined and enacted by Church (and premised on Scripture) via theocracy and the general conception that "every department" of human life was subjected and dissolved to, as its servant, the "same all-encompassing arch of religion" (Tawney 1962; also, Mentzer 2007; VanDrunen 2006).

For example, Calvinism attempted to reestablish and reinvigorate in a "new", Calvinist form the medieval theocracy designated as the *respublica Christiana*, yet converted in a "system of independent principalities and states" (Nischan 1994), in none than Lutheran Germany. One can add that it did but not so successfully as in other regions like Calvin's Geneva, Holland, and, via Puritanism, England, Scotland, and New England. In another example, while triumphant, the medievalist "theocratic ambitions" of Calvinism, officially established as the only true Reformed Church in Holland over the late 16th century, were in a "permanent tension" with the "secular political reason" of public institutions and officials (Frijhoff 2002). As a clear syndrome of its theocratic ambitions, Calvinism in Holland attempted to force its own "true" beliefs and values on the "society as a whole", starting with the anti-Catholic "Calvinist coup" (Utrecht in 1586) ushering in the "ensuing years of militant Calvinist rule" (Pollmann 2002) via a medieval-style or Calvin's Geneva theocracy (Byrne 1997). Furthermore, early Holland's official "Calvinist theocracy" was experienced and described in "tones of dark foreboding" (Kaplan 2002), thus evoking, if not restoring, the Dark Middle Ages, including the Catholic Inquisition.[6]

---

[6] Kaplan (2002:13) comments that "for opponents, the Calvinist Church "merely replaced the old Spanish Inquisition with a new Genevan one [by] violent efforts to suppress Catholicism" and even other Protestantism (Lutheranism) in Holland and elsewhere. Similarly, Frijhoff (2002:27) observes that Calvinism "was a publicly recognised Church with its rights and privileges [while other confessions were] condemned either to a secondary role or even to near-secret worship".

## Calvinist Theocracy—America's "Destiny"?

The preceding apparently provides or implies an answer to the question of America's Calvinist "destiny" or societal predestination via the Puritan over-determination of the "new nation". It is essentially Calvinist theocracy as a theological design and a social system. Calvinist theocracy is understood in the sense of what Weber and other sociologists (Dahrendorf 1979) call the alliance or merger between secular political and sacred "hierocratic" power, state and church, generally politics and religion,[7] premised on and sanctified by fundamentalism as evangelicalism. Hence, America's Calvinist "destiny" means that the "new nation" is predestined and designed to be the most theocratic or theocentric, fundamentalist or evangelical, and religious or "godly" society in Christendom (Lipset 1996) and the Western world (Inglehart 2004; Munch 2001). Alternatively, if the "new nation" has been or will become such a society, this is primarily due to Calvinism via Puritanism, as the paradigmatic exemplar of Protestant "Christian" theocracy, fundamentalism *qua* evangelicalism, and "godly" community.

Hence, America's Calvinist-as-Puritan "destiny" or social predestination is specifically a fundamentalist *cum* evangelical, thus, as Comte suggests, primitive and original theocratic form termed by Weber Biblical theocracy or Bibliocracy. By assumption, the latter is, in Sorokin's (1970) words, "pure", distinguished from diluted, "Christian," including Protestant, theocracy. It is the expression of what Comte calls the "primitive church" in Christianity and the realization of the "most barbarous and dangerous" part of Scripture, including, in its establishment and enforcement as legal theocracy, the application of, as Tocqueville puts it, the "legislation of rude and half-civilized" people.[8] Pure, primitive "Christian" as evangelical theocracy or Bibliocracy thus constitutes the specific and principal form or facet of the Calvinist "destiny" of America. It is the initial and final point, beginning and end, gestation and consummation of the Calvinist predestination, via

---

[7] Weber adds that in general, "the alliance between political and hierocratic power reached two high points in the Occident": first, the Holy Roman Empire, second Calvinist theocracy, plus, in "caesaro-papist" forms, the Lutheran and Anglican Reformation and the Counter-Reformation in Spain and France.

[8] Tocqueville adds that the first American Puritans applied the "legislation of a rude and half-civilized people" such that the "punishment of death was never more frequently prescribed by statute [and] there was scarcely a sin which was not subject to magisterial censure" as in New England under Puritanism.

the Puritan over-determination, of the "new nation". It is both the theological design and the societal or institutional outcome of Calvinism through Puritanism and its religious, moral, ideological, and cultural heritage and triumph in America. In sum, America's Calvinist-as-Puritan "destiny" directly or indirectly, explicitly or implicitly, immediately or ultimately revolves around or moves toward evangelical theocracy as its essence, epitome, and symbol. Virtually everything begins with and ends in evangelical theocracy within the context of America's Calvinist-as-Puritan "destiny", just as generally in Calvinism and Puritanism.

The above therefore yields a two-step specification of America's Calvinist "destiny" or societal predestination. This Calvinist societal predestination is, first and foremost, theocracy. Second, it is the evangelical and thus fundamentalist or primitive form of theocracy that Weber named Bibliocracy as a pure, original type of "Christian", specifically Protestant, theocracies. Simply, America's Calvinist-as-Puritan "destiny" is not just any theocracy, but, to use Comte-Weber-Sorokin's terms, a primitive, Biblical, or pure "Christian", as distinguished from "more advanced", non-evangelical, or diluted, theocratic type. This is important to emphasize because even observing or assuming that America's Calvinist "destiny" is theocracy is not specific and precise enough without specifying its concrete design and system, given the various designs and systems of theocracies, and thus actual or potential theocratic variations, within Christianity, including Protestantism, and beyond. In sum, the specific answer to the question about the nature of America's Calvinist-as-Puritan "destiny" is primitive evangelical, pure "Christian" theocracy, simply Bibliocracy. The latter is both an original theological design or, as Comte[9] puts it, the dream of a "godly" society *and* an ultimate aggregate societal outcome or institutional structure.

In passing, a case of "more advanced" and non-evangelical or pseudo-Biblical, yet pure theocracy in America is the theocratic system of Mormonism, as almost totally implemented in Utah. Hence, what distinguishes Mormon-controlled Utah from the Southern "Bible Belt", and irritates the latter's would-be-theocrats is only the specific design

---

[9] Comte observes that Calvinism and Protestantism as a whole shows the "exclusive predilection for the primitive church and [even] its more injurious enthusiasm for the Hebrew theocracy [and] dreamed about [its] restoration."

or form of theocracy, "more advanced" and not strictly Biblical in the first, primitive and evangelical, in the second case. At this juncture, Southern theocrats' irritation and intolerance for Mormonism is at the same time irrational and "rationalized". It is irrational because Mormon-ruled Utah is a more total, purer, and implemented experiment in "Christian" theocracy than even the "Bible Belt" so far, and "rationalized" because this oasis of Mormonism is seemingly non-evangelical or not strictly "Biblical". In the context of Calvinism, Mormonism is substantively Calvinist in virtue of its system and design of "pure" still Christian *theocracy*, yet non-Calvinist due to the latter being *less* "primitive" and evangelical or Biblical in contrast to the Southern "Bible Belt" as almost completely neo-Calvinist in Weber's sense.

## Calvinist "Destiny" of Tocqueville's America

Given his prediction of America's Calvinist-as-Puritan "destiny", the above question is initially and primarily posed for Tocqueville. What is the Calvinist-as-Puritan "destiny" of Tocqueville's America, or why his Americans are a "puritanical people"? In a broad interpretation, he intimates theocracy but does not explicitly state it, thus only implies an answer along the above lines. He suggests that America's Calvinist "destiny" consists in that the ideas and practices of the first Puritan colonial "fathers" bequeathed "very deep traces on the minds of their descendants", epitomized by the "great strictness of morals", conjoined with the "extreme regularity of habits", as observed in the "new nation" that he visited half a century after the Revolution.

This implication is plausible since Calvinist evangelical—and perhaps any Christian or non-Christian, including Islamic and Hindu—theocracy, notably what Weber and Ross identify as the "tyranny" of Puritanism", is precisely defined and typified in moral terms by the "great strictness of morals", as well as the "extreme regularity of habits". And, Calvinism originated and functioned as what Weber calls "strict" and even "iron" (Tawney 1962) Protestantism, thus Calvinists did as the "hotter sort" of Protestants (Gorski 2000), in moral and other societal terms. In turn, Puritanism inherited and further "reinvented" and intensified this pattern of Calvinist strictness and Puritans became ever-more neo-Calvinists in Weber's meaning (also, Gorski 2003; Hiemstra 2005), simply (to paraphrase a US comedy) "strict, stricter, strictest" (if not "dumb, dumber, dumbest" on the account of what many Americans call Puritan "dumb laws").

If this is correct, Tocqueville implies (as does Weber) that Americans are a "puritanical people" and thus a "Calvinist nation" because of their "great strictness of morals" inherited from "strict" and "gloomy" Calvinism through ever "stricter, strictest" and "gloomier" Puritanism. The Calvinist-as-Puritan "destiny" of Tocqueville's America thus turns out to be moralistic, ascetic Biblical theocracy through Weber's "unexampled tyranny" of Puritanism as axiomatic theocratic moralism or moral absolutism (Munch 2001) and purism (yet "pure hypocrisy") in Calvinism and Protestantism.

At any rate, Tocqueville can be credited for implying that America's Calvinist-as-Puritan "destiny" primarily consists in moralistic theocracy—and to that extent moral proto-fascism as elaborated later—by identifying the "great strictness of morals" in the "new nation". In the latter, incidentally or not, New England's (Massachusetts') theocratic Calvinist Congregational Church (Foerster 1962) of Puritanism had been "disestablished" during the 1830s[10] (Dayton 1999; Gould 1996). It was thus "gone with the wind" after two centuries of being established and enforced as an official "true" and "only" Reformed religion and more half a century following the secular American Revolution (Baldwin 2006; German 1995), just around the time of his visit.[11]

In sum, Tocqueville infers that America's Puritan "destiny" as well as genesis consists in that most Americans are of "strictly Puritanical origin" and act accordingly, thus with the "great strictness of morals." He therefore suggests that these Puritan origins over-determine (Munch 2001) and predict such strict morality and conduct in America. He implies, like Comte, that the "great strictness of morals" is by design the defining ethical attribute or outcome of Calvinist-Puritan and other theocracy as the reign of saints or, in Hume's words, self-designated divines,[12] as Weber and Ross explicitly indicate by identifying the

---

[10] Gould (1996:9–10) remarks that religious disestablishment or the abolition of theocracy in America, primarily under the impetus of Enlightenment-inspired liberals like Jefferson et al. commenced in his own Virginia in 1786 and ended by its "final eradication in Massachusetts in 1833." In turn, Dayton (1999:41) suggests that Calvinism's "disestablishment would not occur in Massachusetts until 1815, and religious tests for office-holding would persist in the US long after the passage of Thomas Jefferson's landmark 1786 Act for Establishing Religious Freedom."

[11] New Hampshire's Senate started disestablishing the Congregational church in the state with a bill submitted in 1817 (Baldwin 2006:108).

[12] Hume recounts that "in 1643, the parliament had summoned an assembly at Westminster, consisting of one hundred and twenty-one divines and thirty laymen,

"tyranny" of Puritanism as paradigmatic moralistic absolutism. To that extent, the "great strictness of morals" is an attribute or outcome of what is presently described and reconsidered as moral fascism as the ultimate elimination of individual liberty in morality and privacy. More textual support is present in Tocqueville's work for his implied specification of America's Calvinist-as-Puritan "destiny" (and genesis) in terms of primarily and specifically moralistic theocracy,[13] but this is not imperative at this juncture.

The above confirms and illustrates that America's Calvinist-as-Puritan "destiny" either directly or indirectly, as in Tocqueville's case of the "great strictness of morals", substantively revolves around or moves toward primitive Biblical theocracy. Simply, it initially designs itself as and eventually crystallizes into Bibliocracy. Alternatively, primarily in an evangelical, pure "Christian" theocracy, in virtue of being the original and perennial design (or eternal dream) and outcome of Calvinism and Puritanism, can America's Calvinist "destiny" be completely realized and revealed, and conversely, incompletely so in non-evangelical, diluted theocracies.

In sociological terms, Calvinist evangelical theocracy is not merely what Comte denotes "theocratic government" or an official "true" and only Reformed, yet, in his words, "primitive", "Christian" church. This applies either when and where such theocracy is actually established, as in New England's "Biblical Commonwealth" from the 17th–19th centuries, or partly so, designed, and "dreamed" of, as in the Southern and other "Bible Belt" in contemporary America. Rather, Calvinist evangelical theocracy is, in Comte's words, a complete "theocratic order" of society, including its economy, polity, civil life, and culture. It is what

---

celebrated in their party for piety and learning [and] a new directory for worship was established suitably to the spirit of the Puritans." He apparently refers to Cromwell's "Parliament of Saints".

[13] Tocqueville implies Biblical legal theocracy when observing that Puritan legislators (e.g., of Connecticut) "begin with the penal laws, and, strange to say, they borrow their provisions from the text of Holy Writ. "Whosoever shall worship any other God than the Lord shall surely be put to death"." He adds that "this is followed by ten or twelve enactments of the same kind, copied verbatim from [it]—Blasphemy, sorcery, adultery, and rape were punished with death; an outrage offered by a son to his parents was to be expiated by the same penalty." Notably he comments that he Puritan "legislator, entirely forgetting the great principles of religious toleration that he had himself demanded in Europe, makes attendance on divine service compulsory, and goes so far as to visit with severe punishment, and even with death, Christians who chose to worship God according to a ritual differing from his own."

Durkheim, Pareto, and Parsons call a total social system with its economic, political, civic, and cultural subsystems, notably a totalistic (Eisenstadt 1965) or totalitarian (Stivers 1994) society. This theocratic totality is self-indicated by the Calvinist design and designation of Biblical theocracy as "Christ's Kingdom on Earth" (Tawney 1962), notably the "Puritan dream of the godly community" (German 1995) or a "faith-based" society in America (Munch 2001; Turner 2002), not only a church-state, theocratic government and polity.

Theocracy, specifically Bibliocracy, is the theological design and the societal outcome of the Calvinist total mastery of the world in sociological and geographic terms. Conversely, for Calvinists, including Puritans, their mastery of the world "thou shall" establish or culminate in theocracy ultimately, with intermediate stages or tactical compromises a la Machiavelli like the legal separation or disestablishment of church and state in America, especially when themselves are deprived of theocratic rule or "non-established". It was shown by the conduct of Puritan sects like Presbyterians, Baptists, and Methodists in the officially Episcopalian South and during their Great Awakenings, and even New England under established, admittedly petrified Calvinism[14] (Baldwin 2006). Short of evangelical theocracy, the Calvinist mastery of the social and physical world is an "unfinished business", "job not completely done", and has no meaning or "makes no sense". It is so in relation to its masters' quest for the "higher" meanings of human life ultimately sacrificed to "greater than life and humans" supra- and anti-human causes, notably the merciless "God of Calvinism", Providential design, and "harsh" religious dogmas (Fourcade and Healy 2007) of predestination and original sin.

---

[14] Baldwin (2006) observes that early Methodists advocated the legal separation of church and state in late 18th and early 19th century New England, specifically disestablishing Calvinism as an established and petrified religion via the Congregational Church, just as they did, alongside Baptists and other Puritan sects, in the South against official Anglicanism. This observation invites two remarks. First, these Puritan sects and Calvinism overall did and do demand the legal separation of church and state or disestablishment of religion *only* when and because they were and are themselves *not* dominant or "non-established" yet, as in the Episcopalian South and in part (Methodists and Baptists) in New England. Second, they tend to abolish or undermine such separation and "establish" themselves as the only "true" religion and church whenever and wherever, as J. S. Mill suggests, becoming "sufficiently powerful" or dominant, as precisely admittedly happened in the South (Boles 1999) and the "Wild West" following Puritan or Calvinist-inspired Great Awakenings (German 1995) and their ramifications (Clemens 2007).

This point is instructive to emphasize for it helps to realize, explain, and even predict that America's Calvinist-as-Puritan "destiny," like genesis, has been, seems to be, and likely will be not only the resulting mastery of the world, sociologically and geographically. Rather, "destiny" is more accurately considered and described as Weber's Biblical theocracy that is the manifest and eternal providential design of Calvinism, the point of origin and destination, the first and last principle, simply the "alpha and omega" of its mastery of the social world or human society in America and, via interlinked "holy" wars and religious missions, globally. And, the Calvinist world mastery is to be understood sociologically in the form (in Weberian accounts) of modern advanced capitalism as its unintended celebrated aggregate outcome, *and* geographically via Americanism, militarism, offensive "holy" war, and the resulting "empire of liberty" as another glorified effect, "manifest destiny" leading to the "salvation" via destruction of the "evil" world.

In a way, Calvinism may, as Weber implies declaring the Calvinist roots of the modern capitalist economy "dead", under certain social conditions and historical conjunctures "divorce" itself, as in part via "born again" evangelicalism in America, from its "marriage" (for liberalism, cf., Dahrendorf 1979) with advanced, mature capitalism (Habermas 2001). Conversely, advanced global capitalism in its liberal-secular democratic version would no longer necessitate Calvinism as its putative initial religious basis and support. Thus, sociological observations suggest that the revival of Calvinism via "born again" evangelicalism in America during the 1980s–2000s, with some exceptions (the "God and free market" Christian Coalition), developed partly in adverse reaction to materialism or "Mammon", including consumerism, as well as secularism, liberalism, and rationalism, thus implicitly, if not openly, to capitalism and markets (Darnell and Sherkat 1997; Lane 2000; Wuthnow 1998). Alternatively, it did in opposition to the supposed decline of spiritualism, "godliness", and moral values (Bell 2002; Wagner 1997) since the 1960s. Further, Calvinism may even "divorce" or temporarily separate itself from its more solid and harmonious "marriage" with militarism, imperialism, and aggressive wars, via nationalistic isolationism and its ethnocentric depreciation or ignorance of the world beyond the Puritan "shining city upon a hill", just as totally separating from and opposing liberal-secular democracy defined as "evil" and its eternal "enemy". Yet, it may hardly ever, though with disguises or tactical Machiavellian adjustments, relinquish its original design and supreme end of Biblical theocracy via Puritanism, at least in America, while being effectively *caput mortuum* or in a terminal condition, vegetative state in Europe, including even Calvinist Holland and once Puritan England.

In Comte's words, Calvinism and consequently Puritanism might "forget" virtually all of its dreams that it had had from its birth in Calvin's France, but hardly ever the master dream of primitive Bibliocracy, as indicated by its persistent theocratic design and recreation of America, from the 17th to the early 21st century, as a "Bible Community". Simply, the Calvinist-as-Puritan "dream of the godly community" in America (German 1995), as a sort of theocratic substitute for disdained liberal hope (Lemert 1999), may, like the latter, never die or is likely to "die hard", being the "last stand" of Calvinism through Puritanism. In short, Calvinism is either the system and design of Biblical theocracy as a society *or* is not really "Calvinism" as known from its birth, life history, and current reality or legacy, as is Puritanism.

Hence, if Calvinism via Puritanism continues to be America's "destiny" by social over-determination or self-perpetuating cultural legacy (Inglehart and Baker 2000), American Puritan-rooted exceptionalism will remain, as sociological analyses (Inglehart 2004) indicate, primarily evangelical theocracy and religious fundamentalism. And, the latter will function, as it does presently, in a mixture or coexistence, yet tension or contradiction (Lipset 1996; Munch 2001), with liberal-democratic capitalism. However, it will/does in perfect, dream-like concord with aggressive nationalism, militarism, imperialism, and offensive "holy" wars against the "ungodly" and "evil" to form a theocratic-militaristic "dream team" bent on saving the world through the judgment-day "delirium of annihilation" *cum* Calvinist salvation (Adorno 2001). At this point, suffices it to specify America's Calvinist "destiny" as evangelical theocracy or Bibliocracy after the model, image, or dream of a "Biblical Garden" as "paradise lost and found" on the Earth.

In general, virtually everything in America's Calvinist-as-Puritan "destiny" in the sense of social over-determination, historical path-dependence, heritage, and exceptionalism originally revolves around or eventually moves toward Biblical theocracy. This is indicated by the term the "Bible Garden" as the providential design, if not already established social system, of the "new nation". Simply, "it is (almost) all about" Weber's Bibliocracy, rather than or just secondarily, as he and Tocqueville partly imply and most ordinary Americans say, "about money" and wealth. Of course, this holds true unless money or wealth, like science and advanced technology, serves as the instrument or intermediate step to Calvinist theocracy (the sign of Divine grace, election), as it does in his account of the "formation" and "expansion" of modern capitalism in an "elective affinity" with Calvinism. First and foremost, the theocratic design or dream of a "godly" society (German 1995; Wuthnow 1998) is what is crucial when reconsidering America's Calvinist-as-Puritan "destiny." Negatively, it is not capitalism and materialism (Darnell and Sherkat 1997), or just secondarily in coexistence, yet reciprocal tension, friction, and contradiction (Munch 2001) with theocracy, yielding "theocratic capitalism" or "capitalist theocracy", let alone Jeffersonian liberty, equality, and justice "for all", including liberal-secular democracy as the anti-theocratic antidote. At least, this is what the present work wishes to argue and demonstrate.

To paraphrase a nominally neo-Calvinist US President—yet hardly "puritanical" and with "less stringent standard of propriety" than Winthrop's "austere Calvinism" (Kloppenberg 1998)—from the region, the evangelical design and social system of the "Bible Belt" operates as America's Calvinist "destiny." It does so in the form and sense of main heritage, historical path-dependence and triumph, and celebrated exceptionalism within contemporary Western society. Negatively, Jefferson's liberal-secular, individualistic democratic ideals and institutions do *not* function as such "destiny," thus American exceptionalism within Western society, contrary to ethnocentric preconceptions (Lipset and Marks 2000). For example, Tocqueville's diagnosis of the "great strictness of morals" as expressing America's Puritan "destiny" and Americans as a "puritanical people" implicates Calvinist theocracy. The latter forms the societal framework and the religious rationale of strict morality and resulting moral repression eliminating individual liberty, dignity, and eventually, via the death penalty for sins-crimes and "holy" offensive wars, human life. It does so in virtue of Calvinist theocracy being instituted and functioning as the reign of Hume's divines or Comte's saints as moralistic virtuosi or methodical perfectionists (yet, as it turns out, paradigmatic hypocrites) in morality, notably via Ross-Weber's "tyranny" of Puritanism as exemplary moral absolutism or moralistic purism.

To summarize, Tocqueville's America's "destiny" embedded in Calvinism via Puritanism is for the present purpose most properly or conveniently specified and analyzed as evangelical theocracy or Bibliocracy. Second, this theocracy is a total social system or society encompassing and implicating virtually all the other elements of its "destiny" and originating as the primary end and ultimate outcome of the Calvinist total mastery of the world. Overall, the Calvinist sociological, as distinguished from theological, predestination of the "new nation" via the Puritan over-determination is, first, theocratic in nature, second, holistic in scope, a systemic design, process, and outcome through total societal mastery by saints-masters. The following elaborates on America's Calvinist-as-Puritan "destiny" as evangelical theocracy and considers the latter as a total social system with its specific economic, political, civic and cultural systems, and as the outcome of Calvinism's realized or attempted totalistic mastery of the world in both sociological and geographic terms.

## Bibliocracy from the Genesis to the Destiny

### Theocratic "Paradise Lost and Found"

Calvinism, specifically its evangelical theocracy, constitutes the "destiny" or cardinal heritage of America because of being, through Puritanism, notably Puritan Bibliocracy, its genesis or point of origin. It does in a pattern of Calvinist "iron consistency", continuity, or path-dependence in American history, as Tocqueville, Weber, and other sociologists imply (Munch 2001; Symonds and Pudsey 2006). For example, the neo-Calvinist fundamentalist "Bible Belt" is designed by its designers and rulers as the "destiny" or future of America, because the Calvinist-as-Puritan "Biblical Commonwealth" was its genesis, as in New England and beyond—a "golden past" and "paradise lost to be found" or revived. Simply, both are the systems and designs of Bibliocracy.

In terms of *dramatis personae*, "Bible Belt" would-be theocrats or masters, including Reaganite "born again" evangelical "rigid extremists" (Blomberg and Harrington 2000), are the self-proclaimed "destiny" or the future faces of America. And, they are such precisely because Winthrop et al. as paradigmatic aristocratic and austere Calvinist theocrats (Bremer 1995; Gould 1996; Munch 2001) were America's genesis or glorified founders, heroes, and models (Seaton 2006). Now, this is so in conventional accounts considering the first Puritans, as Tocqueville does, the "fathers" or "Pilgrims", though non-Puritans like Anglicans (not to mention Columbus, Amerigo Vespucci, and Catholics) had historically preceded them in American settlement and historically deserved more this pioneering or founding status and name in the general sense. Thus, US Puritan apologists claim that the "first white Americans" were the "Pilgrim Puritans" as "hardy forebears", Puritanism was "here first" and well as had "truths" ignored or obscured by liberalism (Seaton 2006; also, Dunn and Woodard 1996). This is indicative of the conservative pro-Puritan, anti-Anglican, and near-racist, specifically anti-Catholic, interpretation of America's settlement or discovery. It denies or overlooks that, first, Anglicans (let alone Catholic Columbus et al.) preceded the "Pilgrim Puritans" in the new world by almost two decades, second, these non-Puritan groups, especially the "Papists", were "white Americans" and even "Americans" at all. Such denials simply "forget" who was that "Americans" were named after in the first place, thus effectively the "first white American", yet a non-Puritan, "Papist" one (Amerigo Vespucci).

Admittedly, "reborn" US religious conservatives, especially (though not solely) in the "Bible Belt", self-consciously stand in and continue the celebrated tradition of Tocqueville's first Puritans (Dunn and Woodard 1996). A predictable exemplar is that US neo-conservatives (e.g., Reagan et al.) display public admiration for and covertly attempt to resurrect Winthrop's Puritan theocracy (Munch 2001) from the dead past as the "shining city upon a hill". In turn, reflecting his "austere Calvinism", Winthrop's Puritan "shining city upon a hill" was an almost word-by-word replica of the antecedent Calvinist "community of the Saved" as "the city on the mountain" and the "hub of society" in Holland (Frijhoff 2002), as well as in France and Geneva before, both expressions using Biblical words. This reaffirms that early American Puritanism, beginning with Winthrop and his glorified 1630s address aboard the *Arabella* flotilla of ships (Gould 1996; Kloppenberg 1998), lacked sociologically significant or substantive originality and novelty in this and other respects compared to Calvinism, apart from making the latter even more extreme. Instead, Puritanism was and remains, via "born again" evangelicalism, near-totally dependent ("parasitic") on and an uncreative "child" of Calvinism as its theological and ideological parent.

Alternatively, America's genesis or "paradise lost" in the form of Calvinist evangelical theocracy generates, inspires, and predicts its equivalent "destiny" or future, at least its heritage, memory, or dream. For instance, New England's "Biblical Commonwealth" does so with respect to the Southern and in extension middle, Western, and all-American "Bible Belt", and Winthrop et al. do in relation to Reagan et al. and US "reborn" extremist evangelicals. Reagan's famous "I am one of you" proclamation to US neo-Calvinist evangelicals is indicative in this respect, albeit it may be dismissed as a Machiavellian conservative electoral slogan and political tactic by the master "communicator" (a Calvinist Presbyterian). This proclamation and public admiration for Winthrop's theocratic ideals and practices indicate striking Calvinist continuities in America, spanning from the "Biblical Commonwealth" as its theocratic genesis to the "Bible Belt" as its projected equivalent "destiny" ("genesis" refers to conventional accounts treating only the first Puritans, but not Anglicans who had actually preceded them in settlement, as the "Pilgrims").

Consequently, the linkage between America's genesis and "destiny", its past and future, in Calvinist evangelical theocracy is essentially consistent, unbroken, or continuous. This holds true despite certain mostly transient non-Calvinist interruptions, exceptions, and countervailing forces or "nuisances" and "outliers," primarily Jeffersonian Enlightenment-based (Patell 2001) liberal-secular, egalitarian, and humanist "atypical" (Archer 2001) ideas, values, and institutions. It is at least indicated by the apparent connection, continuity, or affinity between New England's arch-Calvinist "Biblical Commonwealth" and the Southern neo-Calvinist (largely Baptist) "Bible Belt" (Hinson 1997). Specifically, the latter is evidently path-dependent on and even explicitly inspired by the former (Boles 1999), as respectively represented and incarnated by Winthrop et al. and Reaganite "born again" evangelicals (Seaton 2006).

In sum, the Calvinist theocratic connection is revealed by the continuity and sequence between Winthrop's "austere Calvinism" and Reaganites' moralistic, theocentric neo-Calvinism. The latter is conceptualized and analyzed as moral fascism in this work, and yet self-rationalized and propagated into society as "godly" and "all-American" anti-liberalism. In general, America's Calvinist theocratic genesis in reality—though it does not necessarily in theory—predicts its equivalent "destiny" in the sense of main heritage (Kloppenberg 1998), deep impact and triumph (German 1995), and path-dependence (Inglehart and Baker 2000). It does with some intervening variations and countervailing, especially Enlightenment-rooted, forces like Jefferson, Madison, (post-Calvinist), Franklin, and their disciples (Byrne 1997). Then, to better understand and predict America's Calvinist-as-Puritan "destiny" of evangelical theocracy after the image of a "Biblical Garden", it is useful to reconsider and have in mind its theocratic genesis *cum* the "golden past" and "paradise lost" in Calvinism through Puritanism.

## The Calvinist Theocratic Genesis and Evolution

As implied, Calvinist theocracy and Calvinism overall operated as the genesis or point of origin of America through New England's 17th century Puritan "Biblical Commonwealth" and thus Puritanism in general. In terms of *dramatis personae*, Calvin as the master proto-theocrat in Geneva (Byrne 1997; Mansbach 2006) and "principal" acted so via Winthrop-plus consummate celebrated theocrats as his theological "children" and loyal "agents" driven by and intensifying original "austere Calvinism" originating in France and spreading beyond to Europe and America.

And, Calvinism's evangelical theocracy has continued to function or to be nostalgically (almost tearfully) remembered as a sort of "golden past" in America, in view of the remarkable and even unparalleled, as compared with England, official obstinacy and longevity of the Puritan "Biblical Commonwealth" of two centuries. A more accurate term for Calvinist theocracy in this respect is perhaps "paradise lost". This is so, given its eventual legal demise through the formal disestablishment of Winthrop's Congregational Calvinist Church during the 1830s (Gould 1996), including Massachusetts in 1815 (Dayton 1999). As known, the latter was disestablished in the aftermath of and mostly consequent to the impact of Jefferson-Madison's Enlightenment-based secular and liberal ideas (Baldwin 2006; Byrne 1997; German 1995; Gould 1996) and activities repudiating the original Puritan theocratic vision and creation of America as no less (or more) than "Christian Sparta"[15] (Kloppenberg 1998). Recall Puritan Franklin rejected this Calvinist theocracy in that he virtually renounced his father's strict Calvinism by experiencing, like many contemporaries, its anti-humanistic rejection or devaluation of Christian "good works" in favor of predestination regardless of human merit as "inimical to morality"[16] (Byrne 1997).

Yet, this officially "dead" Calvinist theocracy was also attempted to revive and expand through various Puritan-incited religious revivals

---

[15] Kloppenberg (1998:32) observes that "Madison and his allies repudiated the [Puritan] ideal of a "Christian Sparta" and embraced commercial agriculture and economic growth as the salvation of the American republic."

[16] Byrne (1997:48) adds that "Franklin was for a while a deist, but eventually he settled for a sort of benign and skeptical indifference in religious matters".

beyond New England[17] originally, as Hume put it, "planted entirely by the Puritans," most dramatically via the Great Awakenings of the 1740s–1800s to virtually all America. In particular, it was expanded to the old Episcopalian South, as well as the "Wild West" (Clemens 2007), turned into another "Biblical Garden" dominated by evangelical sects and similar cults (Baptists, Methodists, Mormons, etc.). In light of these never-ending religious revivals and the "new" South and the "Wild West", and in extension or by design all America (Bauman 1997; Cochran 2001) *cum* the "Bible Belt", Calvinist evangelical theocracy is better described after the image of "paradise lost and found". Specifically, it was "lost" by the non-Calvinist "ungodly" Jefferson (and Madison), the post-Calvinist Franklin, and their liberal-secular disciples and allies during the age of Enlightenment and post-revolutionary times. Yet, it was "found" by "born again" neo-Calvinist evangelicals, spanning from the Great Awakenings largely inspired by Calvinism (German 1995) during the 18th–19th centuries to the new fundamentalist revival of the 1980s–2000s (Smith 2000). In Durkheim's words, Calvinist theocracy functioned as both the genesis and evolution, creation and development of America, specifically in New England until the American secular Revolution, namely Jefferson-Madison's rendition. And, it has continued to do so, in slightly modified forms, in the South and beyond (the "Wild West", etc.) since the Great Awakenings and ironically the Revolution (in its wake Anglicanism was construed, attacked, and displaced as "foreign" or "British" by its Puritan sectarian adversaries) and its aftermath.

First and foremost, the old "Biblical Commonwealth" as America's, minimally New England's, genesis and evolution, or "paradise lost and found," as in the South *cum* the "Bible Belt", represented Calvinist evangelical theocracy in a sort of Puritan representation and agency. While by now self-evident and clear, this is instructive to emphasize and keep in mind. For the standard description of New England's "Biblical Commonwealth", just as the Southern "Bible Belt", as "Protestant" or "Puritan" is overly general or superficial, lacking sufficient precision and depth. It is so unless one "rediscovers" its underlying Calvinist

---

[17] Hume adds that New England before the "commencement of the [English] civil wars, it is supposed to have contained twenty-five thousand souls." Also, he remarks that "all the settlements in America, except New England, which had been planted entirely by the Puritans, adhered to the royal party, even after the settlement of the republic" in England during 1640, citing Virginia.

roots or links and nature, notably Winthrop et al.'s "austere Calvinism". It is also so unless reconsidering the historical moment that theocratic and repressively and ascetically "iron" Protestantism was axiomatically Calvinism (in contrast to Lutheranism) and Puritanism was its offspring or "agent" in America and England. It was Calvinism, not any or Protestantism as a whole (e.g., Lutheranism), that effectively established, and thus realized its design of, Biblical theocracy in America through its Puritan offspring or "agent", at least in New England[18] (Davis 2005) in contrast to the old South and other initially non- and less Calvinist regions. In retrospect, this is what Weber explicitly states and J. S. Mill implies, and also subsequent sociological and historical analyses suggest.

Recall, Weber observes that Calvinism was able to establish evangelical theocracy "only for a limited time and only in local areas" in Europe and America. Alongside some sections of France (curiously not mentioned by Weber) controlled by Calvinist Huguenots (Mentzer 2007), French-speaking Geneva, and Holland during the 16th century, and temporarily England (plus more enduringly Scotland) in the mid 17th century, these local areas included especially and lastingly New England via its official "Biblical Commonwealth". Thus, what Weber identifies as the evangelical "theocracy of New England" encompassed a local area within both colonial and revolutionary (Davis 2005; German 1995), even early post-revolutionary Jeffersonian (Baldwin 2006), America, well into the mid 19th century (Fehler 2005). To add, the underlying design and ultimate outcome of recurring Calvinist revivals in America such as the Great Awakenings was precisely to geographically expand the evangelical theocracy from the local area of New England to the entire "new nation", notably the old Anglican South, designed as and to be eventually converted into a "Biblical Garden" by these movements (Archer 2001; Boles 1999).

Also, Weber might add New England's Puritan theocracy lasted more than just "for a limited time" and proved the longest lasting theocratic society within Calvinism. It did given its remarkable longevity of two

---

[18] This was in sharp contrast to the "old" South originally founded, as known, even before Tocqueville's Puritan fathers or Pilgrims, and dominated by Anglicanism as the official church (Dombrowski 2001), but falling short, at least in Weber's view, of true Biblical or ascetic theocracy. And, this shortcoming evidently provided the impetus and rationale for the anti-Anglican, as well as anti-liberal, Great Awakenings resulting in or projecting the Southern "Bible Belt" (Boles 1999) as America's model and future or fate.

centuries compared with other Calvinist evangelical theocracies, in particular those more transient in France, England, and eventually Holland (with the secondary or partial exceptions of Geneva and Scotland). Moreover, upon visiting and witnessing first-hand various theocratic vestiges or revivals in America, he could plausibly change the expression "for a limited time" into "for an unlimited time" in respect of the Calvinist theocracy in New England and America overall. This is so given the transmission of New England's theocracy via the Great Awakenings from—and after or precisely *because* of its official disestablishment in the 1830s—this local area to, thus self-perpetuation in, the nation as a whole, minimally the South turned into a "Bible Garden", up to the early 21st century. To that extent, this signifies that Calvinist theocracy *substantively* lasted infinitely or, as US "reborn" evangelicals expect, "forever" in America, namely during the entire American history of about four centuries (also, Munch 2001). If anything, on the account of surpassing both Weber's "limited time" and "local areas" of the Calvinist theocracies in Europe and England, New England's and in extension Southern Puritan theocracy demonstrated that American Puritanism was really hyper-Calvinism and its adherents like Winthrop et al. super-Calvinists in theocratic terms, a kind of "over-achievers" achieving what Calvin and his disciples, including Cromwell and his "Divines", could only dream about.

In this respect, New England's "Biblical Commonwealth" and thus (in conventional pro-Puritan accounts) America's "genesis" was not just "Protestant" or even superficially "Puritan" but rather specifically and profoundly "Calvinist". Similarly, Weber observes that Calvinism's theocratic rule was first established in Geneva—and even before in France's Calvinist-controlled parts—and Scotland during the 16th century and in ("large parts" of) the Netherlands, New England, and lastly ("for a time") England at the turn of the 16th and 17th centuries (the 1640s–60). Notably, he notes that such Calvinist theocratic rule in these societies became no less than the most absolute and repressive theocracy or hierocracy in existence and imagination, the "most absolutely unbearable form of ecclesiastical control of the individual which could possibly exist".

Curiously, in these observations, like Comte and Sombart, Weber does not even mention Puritanism in reference to New England (and England and Europe), in an apparent substantive equivalence or tautological identity with Calvinism, perhaps surprising those American readers wondering as to "what happened" to the first Puritans or

"Pilgrims" in his picture of America's pre-revolutionary founding or genesis. But, like Tocqueville, he certainly knew and implied that precisely through Puritanism as its Anglo-Saxon derivative or "agent" Calvinism could establish and maintain its Biblical theocracy in New England for two centuries and attempt to expand and perpetuate it into all America, minimally the South, for additional two centuries, up to the 2000s. Calvinists did so via the first Puritans as their theocratic children or "agents" in the "new nation". In a substantive sense, Calvin et al. could do so via Winthrop and his "austere Calvinism" and other Calvinist Puritans (Davis 2005; Mansbach 2006) in colonial and modern America alike.

In turn, anticipating Weber, J. S. Mill implies that the Puritan "Biblical Commonwealths" in both England and America were oppressive Calvinist evangelical theocracies. Mill does so by observing that wherever "sufficiently powerful", as in New England and Great Britain during its "Holy Commonwealth", Puritans engaged in repressive activities, including the suppression of the secular arts and "amusements", that were motivated by the "religious and moral sentiments of the stricter Calvinists" (including Methodists), designated as "intrusively pious members" of society. Like Weber, Mill in his observation apparently equates "Puritans" with "Calvinists", and conversely, as do explicitly or implicitly his own precursors Hume and Comte.

Further, New England's Puritan "Biblical Commonwealth" was established and operated as not just an exemplary Calvinist and thus European Bibliocracy, though with various nativist embellishments and disguises attacking the "vices of Europe" (Gould 1996). It was also the most total or absolute and among the longest, as is or likely will be, in consequence or extension, the neo-Puritan "Bible Belt" as the heir apparent. A sociological analysis identifies and describes New England's Puritanism and thus its Bibliocracy as the "most totalitarian" form of Calvinism and by implication Protestantism (and perhaps Christianity) and so Calvinist and implicitly Protestant (if not all Christian) theocracy (Stivers 1994), respectively. In this account, Calvinism via Puritanism in America sought and rapidly succeeded to institute "legal theocracy" by redefining most of its code of law and Draconian punishment "almost word for word from the Old Testament" (Stivers 1994). In a similar account, though officially extolled as a "Body of Liberties" and designated as a Republic, New England's "Bible Commonwealth" was an ultra-totalitarian Calvinist Biblical, including patriarchal, theocracy modeled after the "Old Testament patriarchs" (Gould 1996) as "role models". Alternatively, a sociological analysis identifies and describes this Puritan creation as the least mitigated Calvinist and thus Protestant theocracy. The reason is that American Puritanism has been more resistant to tempering of its moral absolutism by non-Calvinist or non-Puritan countervailing religious and social forces like Anglicanism and liberalism than has its English variant in later times (Munch 2001).

To that extent, America's Puritan genesis, or "golden past" and "paradise lost", is not just a Calvinist evangelical theocracy. Also, it is, positively, the most totalitarian, and negatively, the least tempered theocracy in the extended family of Calvinism and in extension Protestantism. Arguably, its Calvinist creation, as Tocqueville and in part Weber imply, generates and predicts, through path-dependence or a historical continuity, impact, triumph, and heritage, America's destiny or future. To that extent, the latter can probably be predicted and described in almost equivalent terms ("more of the same" or the "more things change … "), as elaborated later. At this point, suffices it to propose that America's Puritan Bibliocracy and thus genesis was not simply Calvinist, but, so to speak, "hyper-Calvinist" in the sense of American Puritanism as the most totalitarian and the least tempered Calvinism.

In addition to and conjunction with its unrivaled totalitarianism or moral absolutism, this Puritan Bibliocracy belonged among the longest and the most persisting Calvinist Biblical and implicitly Protestant and Christian theocracies or state churches in modern societies and times, within post-Reformation Western society. By spanning for no less than two full centuries (the 1630s–1830s), it was longer than any Calvinist-as-Puritan theocracy in Anglo-American settings like England under Cromwell's rule and Scotland during Presbyterianism as the official religion. Within the global framework of Calvinism, it was one of the longest and most persisting Biblical theocracies, alongside its prior versions and models in, abstracting from France's Calvinist-ruled sections, Calvin's Geneva (from the 1530s) and Holland (from the 1580s). Further, when/if considering its actual or attempted revival and extension in America, notably the South, in the form of a "Bible Belt" even after its official death or "disestablishment" in the 1830s, it turns out to be the longest Calvinist and in extension Protestant theocracy.[19]

---

[19] This perhaps excludes England's official Anglican Church and Scandinavian countries' Lutheran Churches if deemed to have a formally theocratic status, but not many sociological analysts would consider or describe these states and societies as "theocracies" unlike early New England and the "Bible Belt" but rather exemplary secular and even "post-Christian" (Inglehart 2004) democracies.

At least, it does so with respect to the design or dream of Calvinist and Protestant theocracy in substantive sociological, as distinguished from formal, terms. For example, the Dutch version of Calvinist theocracy, as the major "competitor", is *caput mortuum*, as indicated by modern Holland's evolution in a non- or pseudo-Calvinist or liberal-secular direction[20] (Tubergen, Grotenhuis and Ultee 2005).

Less controversially, even in formal terms of an official beginning and end, the Puritan Bibliocracy remains the second longest major Calvinist and implicitly Protestant theocracy, after or along with that of Holland (viewing Calvin's prototypical theocratic governance in Geneva as local limited to the Swiss city or canton and the "dead past" long ago, despite certain residues). Moreover, abstracting from that in Holland, it was officially perhaps the second longest official and major theocracy among Western Christian societies after the Vatican Church State as both the defined enemy and the covert model or historical precedent of Calvinist theocracies (Stivers 1994) and Calvinism as the most strident anti-Catholicism within Protestantism (Hsia and Nierop 2002; Nischan 1994). On this account, by analogy to its Puritan genesis or founding, America's evolution, its "golden past" or "paradise lost and found", is not simply Calvinist theocracy. It is a "long, longer" and (among) the longest and the most persisting or tenacious, via the "Bible Belt", within the global system of Calvinism and the extended family of Calvinists.

*The Calvinist Theocratic Destiny and Heritage*

As indicated, Calvinist evangelical theocracy and Calvinism in general also acts as the theocratic destiny or heritage of America through its system or design of the "Bible Belt" (Bauman 1997; Boles 1999; Gould 1996) as the heir apparent, ultimate revival, or self-perpetuating vestige of the 17th century "Biblical Commonwealth" *qua* "paradise lost to

---

[20] According to Tubergen et al. (2005:800), in today's Netherlands, "there are two main Protestant (both Calvinist) denominations: Reformed Protestant, which is the main Protestant denomination in the Netherlands, and Rereformed Protestant, which refers to all smaller denominations and churches that seceded from the Reformed Protestant Church from the year 1834 onward. Reformed Protestants are more liberal than the Rereformed Protestants." These Calvinist denominations merged with the Lutheran Church in the 2000s. Ironically, Dutch Catholics reestablished themselves as the largest single religious group for the first time since the 16th century and the Calvinist 1580 anti-Catholic revolution whereby Calvinism via "disciplined, militant minorities" seized political power (Gorski 2003).

be found". Alternatively, to identity and predict, as US "born again" evangelicals do, the "Bible Belt" as the present and future of "Christian" America, at least the South and other ultra-religious ("red") regions, is identifying and predicting the new nation's "destiny" or crucial heritage of Calvinist evangelical theocracy. This holds true just as the "Biblical Commonwealth" represented the revealed act and symbol of the creation or "golden past" of America (Seaton 2006), minimally New England.

Calvinist evangelical theocracy is not only, as usually supposed, the historical point of origin and "golden past". It is also, which is somewhat neglected or downplayed by the claims to libertarian and democratic "American exceptionalism" (Lipset and Marks 2000), the apparent present and projected "bright" future or destination, of America. It is in an essentially unbroken line or historical continuity from the 17th to the 21st century, from New England's arch-Puritan "Biblical Commonwealth" to the Southern and other "red-state" neo-Puritan "Bible Belt." Such a remarkable and perhaps unparalleled, among Protestant and other Western societies, continuity and consistency in Bibliocracy expresses and documents the Calvinist theocratic predestination of the "new nation" via the Puritan over-determination or path-dependence of America as a "Biblical Garden" or a new Eden (Gould 1996). As such, Calvinist Bibliocracy in America *cum* the "Biblical Garden" is what Weber would call a supreme abomination of, extreme aberration from, and hyper-primitive anachronism, just as the global "laughing stock" (Hill 2002, Wagner 1997), within modern liberal-secular democracy and civil society (Inglehart 2004; Munch 2001).

Alternatively, the American "Bible Belt" is difficult and even impossible to comprehend and explain as a social phenomenon until and unless it is considered and placed in a comparative and historical framework of Calvinism, consequently Puritanism. Predictably, the evangelical or "Bible Belt" does not make much sociological sense without reconsidering the Calvinist original theological design and historical system (e.g., in France, Geneva, Holland, Prussia) of Biblical theocracy through the persecution and extermination of non-evangelicals and other "infidels." This more specifically holds true of the "Bible Belt" in relation to the Puritan variant of Calvinist Bibliocracy in the form of New England's "Biblical Commonwealth" (or "Christian Sparta"). The latter is the acknowledged model of the "Bible Belt", just as is Puritanism that of "reborn" religious fundamentalism (Dunn and Woodard 1996). It is experienced and glorified as "paradise lost", only "disestablished" owing to "ungodly" liberals and secularists like Jefferson, Madison, Franklin, Paine, and their heirs in the 19th century (Gould 1996; Kloppenberg 1998). Presumably, it would have still existed ("forever") if such countervailing "wicked" (German 1995) forces were non-existent or destroyed for the glory of the omnipotent and merciless God of Calvinism.

At this juncture, recall Calvinism could establish, through Puritanism, Biblical theocracy "only" in New England, alongside Geneva and Holland, and later attempted and succeeded to expand it, as by the Great Awakenings, beyond this Puritan heaven, notably to the "awaken" South (Boles 1999) and the "Wild West" (Clemens 2007). Consequently, Calvinism solely perpetuated this Bibliocracy indefinitely in most of America through the present or future, the factual or designed, neo-Puritan "Bible Belt." At this point, the latter, far from being an "all-American" native creation, is no more than the old Calvinist Biblical theocracy such as Calvin's France as an unfulfilled dream and Geneva as a totally realized design, not to mention post-Calvin's Holland under theocratic Calvinism, déjà vu. More specifically, it is the revival from the "golden past" of the New England's "Biblical Commonwealth", and in that sense theocratic "paradise lost and found" either in reality or in design and dreams. In sum, America's reality or vision as the "Bible Belt", just as its Puritan origin and past as the "Biblical Commonwealth", is probably best understood and explained in terms of Calvinist evangelical theocracy starting with Calvin's model-theocratic design in France and rule in Geneva (Byrne 1997; Mansbach 2006).

Hence, to say that the "Bible Belt" is the present and future of America is implying that Calvinist evangelical theocracy or Calvinism overall is its "destiny" or heritage via "born again" fundamentalism, just as it was its genesis or "golden past" through theocratic Puritanism and its "Biblical Commonwealth". Observing or predicting that America has or will likely become more a "Bible Belt" than a liberal-secular society (Munch 2001), as during the 1980s–2000s, implies that the Calvinist theocratic predestination of America, far from ending or weakening, continues unmitigated and even escalates and intensifies. And, it does so via, as always, the Puritan over-determination in the form of "born again" evangelical, sectarian predominance déjà vu (Lipset 1996). This is implied in the observation of American democracy and politics "heading South", by being placed in and thus subverted, if not eliminated yet, by the "shadow of Dixie" (Cochran 2001; also, Amenta and Halfmann 2000). And, this "shadow" is essentially theocratic, thus non-democratic and anti-liberal, notably the counter-Enlightenment (Byrne 1997), fervently opposing and attacking the ideal and reality of modern liberal-secular and pluralist society (Munch 2001).

In consequence, America has become or approached a sort of Calvinist Bibliocracy[21] déjà vu. It has via the ever-increasing political and cultural dominance and expansion of the "Bible Belt" ("red states", electoral and other political influence, culture wars, etc.), and thus another Southern and Western Puritan-inspired Great Awakening. Hence, the 21st century "Bible Belt" as ("Christian') America's divinely designed "fate" or "bright" future, like the 17th century "Biblical Commonwealth" as its genesis and "golden" past, is not, as often supposed, something random and transient. Rather, it is systematic and perennial when placed and analyzed within the comparative-historical context of Calvinism or the extended family of Calvinists. It is the "good old" Calvinist Biblical theocracy in consistent action and perpetual motion, or in eternal design and dream, yet in the new or "youngest" nation rather than in the old and despised world. While from the prism of liberal-secular democracy and civil society, such Bibliocracy déjà vu looks as a proof and syndrome of social "madness", notably of absolute power acting and making the world "mad" (Bourdieu 2000), it forms a system, pattern, or "method in the madness" (Smith 2000) within Calvinism's perennial evangelical theocracy *cum* a "Biblical Garden".

In sum, theocracy operates as the Calvinist "destiny" or heritage of America through neo-Puritan, "born again" Bibliocracy informally named a "Bible Belt", just as it did as its genesis or "golden past" via its proto-Puritan version officially designated the "Biblical

---

[21] For example, even the usually conservative *Economist* following the 2004 Presidential elections lamented that "now, it seems, the conservative rural red-neck Calvinist vote has captured America", suggesting Calvinism's survival in evangelicalism. Also, according to *New York Times*, a "fundamentalist Christian revival was in revolt against the traditions of the Enlightenment, on which the country is based". No doubt, this revolt and outcome would have pleased Calvin and Winthrop et al. ("I told you so"), while Jefferson, Madison, and other key American figures and symbols of the Enlightenment may have wondered about the return of the Dark Middle Ages to America (Berman 2000) once again, after Puritan and fundamentalist witch and "monkey trials". And, in the next elections "conservative rural red-neck Calvinist" or evangelical forces tried exactly the same by preferring overwhelmingly the anti-liberal candidate(s), though failed this time, a rare failure of neo-Calvinist evangelicalism since the 1980s mostly due to the severe financial and economic crisis apparently overshadowing its wining card of "social issues."

Commonwealth". Simply, the commandment and design of America "forever", just as in conception or creation, as a "Biblical Garden" and thus Bibliocracy déjà vu, is its Calvinist-as-Puritan "destiny", as was its genesis. Incidentally, since the "Biblical Garden" was a term used by Tocqueville's first Puritans as their vision of America (Gould 1996), US religious neo-conservatives may well prefer it to the "Bible Belt" invented anyway by critics (Mencken 1982) or "evil enemies" (Baltzell 1979), although also adopted and extolled by Southern and other "reborn" evangelicals (Boles 1999).

Revisiting and reconsidering Calvinism and its design and social system of evangelical theocracy is useful to better understand, explain, or simply makes sense of what is seemingly incomprehensible and senseless, or exceptional and transient. This is a "Biblical Garden" reality or design, thus a theocratic and fundamentalist "deviant case" (Inglehart 2004), a kind of island, within the ocean of Western and global liberal-secular democracy, civil society, and culture. It is primarily Calvinism as, through Puritanism, its predominant and triumphant cultural heritage (Dunn and Woodard 1996; German 1995; Inglehart and Baker 2000; Kloppenberg 1998; Lipset 1996; Munch 2001) that can explain and resolve America's deviation or exceptionalism in this respect. Otherwise, this exceptionalism remains a sort of mystery and best kept secret within modern Western society, if not an utterly incomprehensible Shakespearean "American tragedy" in Dreiser's sense mixed with elements of a "laughing stock" comedy (Hill 2002; Wagner 1997). Specifically, Calvinist theocracy, with its seeds in Calvin's France and prototypical realization in his second home Geneva, explains and predicts the "Bible Belt" as America's reality and future destination, just as it did the "Biblical Commonwealth" as its first beginning and "paradise lost".

## *The Calvinist Design and System of Theocracy Reconsidered*

As indicated, Calvinism originated and functioned essentially as the theological design and the social-institutional system of what Weber describes as Biblical theocracy or Bibliocracy. On this account, Calvinism constitutes theocratic, as well as, in conjunction and mutual reinforcement, ascetic and fundamentalist or evangelical Protestantism, a sort of paradigm, pattern, and method of Protestant theocracy *cum* Bibliocracy and of fundamentalism *qua* evangelicalism. In a way, if

Calvinism by any chance was not named and known after Calvin but instead according to its true substantive character and pattern of action, its sociological (and theological) name and surname might have been Reformed "theocratic Biblicism" or "Biblical theocracy"[22] (Mansbach 2006). In short, Biblical theocracy is the first and final principle, beginning and end, dream and reality, a sort of obsession and life, Divine design and creation, in Calvinism and its derivative Puritanism.

*Calvinist Theocracy as "Divinely Ordained"*

Recall Weber registers that Calvinism and consequently its Anglo-American transplant or agent Puritanism considered Biblical theocracy, in "the Presbyterian form", to be Divinely ordained. (In passing, this form probably explains why Calvinism expanded to and established a Biblical theocracy in Scotland during the 17th century under the name of "Presbyterianism", just as it did, more transiently, in England while being renamed "Puritanism", though "Presbyterian" is usually seen as part or facet of "Puritan.") Predictably, Calvin initiated this Providential definition and sanctification of Calvinist theocracy and thus the inverse of liberal-secular democracy, though he was hardly original in this respect, for the medieval Catholic *respublica Christiana* (Nischan 1994) had been defined and sanctified in these terms long ago.

A historical study finds that Calvin believed in the "inviolability" of the existing societal system and individual Christians' obligation to subordinate, thus implicitly sacrifice themselves, to the "divinely ordained" social-political order (Heller 1986). The latter was by Divine design and eventually in reality an evangelical theocracy in a Calvinist rendition, with Calvin himself as God's supreme divinely ordained ruler, as precisely happened during his life ("only") in Geneva. Furthermore, in Calvin's view, such a "divinely ordained" social-political order is *not* a system of freedom and humanity, but the polar opposite. It is inexorably the social system of repression as God's decreed punishment that humankind has to suffer in this world for committing—and still being under—original sin, and because humans shall be ruled, in virtue of being "incapable" of self-governance, by a few self-proclaimed

---

[22] Mansbach (2006:110) notices that Calvinism instituted "theocratic practices based on a literal reading of scripture." In particular, Calvin "believed that political and religious authority flowed from scripture", displaying his "fundamentalist reliance on the literal word of the Bible" (Mansbach 2006:110).

Calvinist divines (Heller 1986) or saints (Mentzer 2007). Evidently, Calvinism designed, established, and sanctified primitive theocracy as the "godly" mechanism for repression of the sinful via their totalitarian mastery by Calvin et al. as self-assigned saints establishing the "Calvinist form of theocratic government" (Byrne 1997).

In short, for Calvin and Calvinism as a whole, both the social system ("secular order") in the form of totalitarian theocracy as the antithesis of liberal-secular democracy *and* its Calvinist masters are "ordained by God". This indicates that only a theocratic social system, specifically medieval-style theocracy, is "divinely ordained" for Calvin and Calvinism, and not its opposite, liberal-secular democracy and society instead condemned, attacked, and destroyed or perverted as "ungodly" and "evil". This is witnessed by what Weber calls neo-Calvinism (also, Hiemstra 2005) in the form of revived fundamentalist Protestantism, especially in America, with its anti-liberal and anti-democratic antagonism and "holy" culture and military wars (Bell 2002; Turner 2002) against modern liberal-secular, pluralist, and pacifist or peaceful[23] society (Munch 2001).

Notably, since, as Weber observes, Calvinism could institute a Biblical theocracy "only" locally and for limited periods, citing New England, besides Calvin's Geneva, 16th century Holland and Cromwell's England (as well as Presbyterian Scotland), Puritanism effectively acted as the Calvinist theocratic "agent" or "representative" in Anglo-American societies. In a more precise specification, Weber's statement would be that in its original form Calvinism was able to establish theocracy only for a limited time and in Geneva and Holland, and in part France (via the Huguenots) and Germany (Prussia's court). And, in its derivative form or changed name as Puritanism, Calvinism was able to do so in Great Britain and America, officially and initially New England, substantively and subsequently in the "awaken" ("deep") South, and then in part the "Wild West" (Texas, Oklahoma, Kansas, Arizona, etc.).

---

[23] According to the Global Peace Index (constructed by the Economist Intelligence Unit in 2008), America has been the least peaceful or pacifist society among Western societies during the 2000s, primarily on the account of Puritan-style culture and military wars on "evil" groups and societies (e.g., Iraq, etc.). Moreover, it ranks America 97th out of 140 societies in terms of peaceful interactions within society (implicitly) due to the neo-Puritan or fundamentalist gun culture, and toward other societies because of "preemptive" wars, thus among the most violent (domestically) and bellicose (globally) countries in the world.

The point is evidently that Calvinism, regardless of its form and geographic and social environments, from the 16th century France, Geneva, and Holland to 17th century old and New England to 21st century America, invariably attempted and often succeeded to establish Biblical theocracy or Bibliocracy virtually by any effective means. As typical, it all started with Calvin's persecuting and even, by his control of the judiciary, murdering of his theological opponents and former friends or allies (e.g., Servetus) and libertines. Calvin hence set the model or precedent (Mansbach 2006) for his descendents or disciples and their corresponding practices, in particular American Puritans and evangelicals, with their notorious "witch-monkey" trials and perpetual anti-liberal culture or temperance wars extending into the 21st century. In a remarkable theocratic "iron consistency", continuity, or path-dependence, Biblical theocracy was Calvin's obsession or dream, yet failing to materialize in his native France but only locally in French-speaking Geneva.

And, the dream remained the same for Calvin's Puritan theological heirs apparent, from Cromwell and Winthrop to Reagan ("I am one of you") and other US "reborn" fundamentalists. Thus, anticipating Weber, Hume identified this Calvinist theocratic obsession in early English and in extension American Puritans. He does in his quoted observation about their claims to be the "only pure church" and that their tenets and practices must be "established by law", with no others being "tolerated". This observation is the diagnosis of a manifest intention of and claim to Puritan theocracy self-defined by official church monopoly, legal coercion, and religious and other intolerance.[24] Predictably, Puritans attempted to validate their claims and realize their aims by effectively establishing themselves as the "only pure church" by law, thus legal theocracy, while tolerating no other churches, as in England (and Scotland) temporarily and New England enduringly, just as did

---

[24] In light of such Puritan tendencies toward coercive, legal theocracy, Hume comments that "it may be questioned, therefore, whether the administration at this time could with propriety deserve the appellation of persecutors with regard to the Puritans" in England before the Revolution. At this juncture, he invokes Lord Bacon's view that "no toleration could with safety be given to sectaries." Apparently, this is a classic statement and implied resolution of the problem of tolerance for the intolerant, ever-recurring in various forms, including fascists and neo-fascists in Europe and beyond, including America, and American, Islamic, and other theocratic fundamentalists. Thus, fascists act as modern functional equivalents of Puritans by making identical claims to possess the "only true" ideology, more (Italian, Spanish, Polish and other Catholic) or less (the Nazis) theocratic or religiously grounded.

previously original Calvinists in Geneva, Holland, and partly Germany. For instance, they did in 17th century New England via the legally established Congregational Church as the only "true", admittedly oppressive, and intolerant Reformed Church (Baldwin 2006), and thus Calvinist legal theocracy (Stivers 1994), just as did their Calvinist forebears and models in 16th century Geneva and Holland. On this account, Winthrop et al. with their "austere Calvinism" were the true and legitimate theocratic and theological "children" of Calvin, and their Congregational Church was truly the "Calvinist"[25] (Baldwin 2006; Davis 2005; Fehler 2005; Foerster 1962) one, or rather a Puritan sect in the new position of near-absolute political power.

In particular, Weber suggests that within the extended family or cousins of Calvinism in Reformation Europe early Baptism especially regarded and reestablished Biblical theocracy as Divinely ordained. He observes that early Baptist sects, notably their leaders, in Europe pursued and produced the "strictest Bibliocracy" embracing the "life of the first generations of Christians as a model" conjoined with "strict avoidance" of the social world in the meaning of "all not strictly necessary intercourse with worldly people" and even being "ruthlessly radical in their rejection of worldliness." He cites the "first Swiss and South German Baptists" on the account of their conceiving and practicing the "Biblical way of life" with radicalism akin to that of medieval monasticism (Saint Francis), revealing radical "Baptist evangelicalism" (Kloppenberg 1998).

Overall, he considers Baptism to be Calvinist sectarianism and asceticism by describing it as "one of the most typical sects" within Calvinism and thus Puritanism, even "one of the largest Protestant denominations in the world", arising in and spanning from Europe to America. Weber observes that Baptism "everywhere and in principle" created sects rather than churches and this sectarianism was equally propitious to the "intensity" of Baptist asceticism, including moralism, as was to that of Calvinism overall as a church or hierocratic institution. In his view, Baptism's "strict morality" and asceticism in reality followed on the "path prepared" by Calvinism and its ethical system that effectively submerged the ethic for humans into the ethic for the priesthood through eliminating the conventional and Christian distinction

---

[25] Foerster (1962:26) uses the expression the "Congregational (Calvinist)" church, thus suggesting a virtual identity between American Puritanism and Calvinism.

between the two ethics (Munch 1981). This redefines Baptism as a theocratic, sectarian, and extremely moralistic species of Calvinism or Puritanism, thus hyper-Calvinism in moral terms, though devoid of the Calvinist theological core like the dogma of predestination, and endowed with what Weber[26] calls non-Calvinist hyper-emotionalism expressed in "hysterical conditions" (akin to Methodism).

In retrospect, these observations are mostly impertinent or outdated for Europe, including Germany, Scandinavia, and in part Switzerland, in which theocratic and fundamentalist Baptism and Calvinism generally has since become *caput mortuum* in relation to secularism or liberalism, notably the Enlightenment and its legacy (Byrne 1997), as well as non-Calvinist Protestantism like Lutheranism. However, they are relevant and almost prophetic for contemporary America. They are relevant because, first, Baptism has since become the ever-growing and even largest and perhaps dominant Calvinist-Puritan and thus Protestant and—in the Baptist explicit or implicit exclusionary, sectarian, anti-Catholic, and anti-Orthodox, redefinition of Christianity— "Christian" denomination[27] in America (Hout, Greeley, and Wilde 2001). This is demonstrated by the expansion and dominance of "Baptist evangelicalism" in the US South (Kloppenberg 1998) and beyond through and following the Great Awakenings.

Second, Calvinist-Baptist evangelicalism has operated, especially since the second Awakening of the 1800s, as the driving force behind the social reality and/or the theological design of America, in particular the "awaken" South, as the "Bible Belt" and in that sense its Calvinist "destiny" in Biblical theocracy. Apparently, not much has substantively changed in Baptism in respect of radical evangelicalism, particularly

---

[26] Weber adds that Baptism (e.g., Barclay's doctrine of rebirth) was the "equivalent in practice of the Calvinistic doctrine, and was certainly developed under the influence of the Calvinistic asceticism, which surrounded the Baptist sects in England and the Netherlands." Also, he implies that Baptism was a sort of hyper-Calvinism in moral terms in stating that Baptists sought "complete conquest of the power of sin" and condemned the "godlessness" of the "natural man" (as "purely a creature of the flesh") "almost even more harshly than" did Calvinists.

[27] For example, the "Southern Baptist Convention" with about 20 million members has become the largest Protestant denomination in America as a whole, not just the South, by the 2000s. Generally, Hout et al. (2001:469) find that the Southern Baptist Convention and other fundamentalist or conservative denominations (e.g., the Assemblies of God, the Pentecostal and Holiness churches) and sects outside of mainline Protestantism "have grown both in absolute numbers and as a share of the Protestant population over this time" since the 1970s to reach no less than 60 percent of US Protestants during the 1990s–2000s.

CHAPTER TWO

Biblical theocracy, spanning from the "strictest Bibliocracy" of the first Baptist sects existing within or related to the extended family of Calvinism in Europe to the "Bible Belt" of "born again" Baptists in America, especially the post-bellum South and Midwest.

On this account, while nominally "presumed dead" as a name, the old Calvinism, thus Puritanism, substantively "lives on" in and continues to act as America's theocratic "destiny" through Baptism as the Calvinist original subtype or ally, as both in Europe and Puritan New England (Dayton 1999), and its "Bible Belt" system and design. In a way, Calvin's original and in extension Winthrop's derived Calvinist obsession with and initial successes in evangelical theocracy are self-perpetuated or reenacted through the Baptist "Bible Belt" and evangelicalism in America centuries later. Alternatively, the Baptist-driven "Bible Belt" is the "most qualified" candidate for a "new" 21st century Calvinist Biblical theocracy, thus fulfilling Calvin-Winthrop's old obsession déjà vu.

Hence, theocratic and evangelical neo-Calvinist Baptism, along with cognate or allied evangelical sects and cults, is the concrete form and the most prominent and visible factor and symbol of America's "destiny" in Calvinist Bibliocracy and Calvinism. For example, observers register with alarm or concern that "conservative rural red-neck Calvinist" forces have captured and in that sense politically predestined or over-determined America signaling its "destiny" in Calvinism, as in most political processes during the 1980s–2000s starting with "godly" Reagan's (re)election largely thanks to evangelical "brothers in arms." And, these observations primarily refer to Baptists and Baptist-allied fundamentalists, sects, and cults. In this sense, Baptist and allied "red-neck" evangelicals with their political dominance or growing influence in the post-bellum South and increasingly beyond are the "new" faces and symbols of America's "destiny" in Calvin-Winthrop's evangelical theocracy.

Conversely, if Calvin and his theological child Winthrop ever again, after New England's Puritan theocracy, either literally by a miracle of their God of Calvinism or substantively became America's "destiny" or future, they would primarily through these neo-Calvinists as neo-Puritan Baptists. The latter act as the best and the most consistent or obstinate agents in perpetuating and realizing déjà vu Calvin-Winthrop's original theocratic obsession through, as did their Calvinist role models, persecution and extermination of "ungodly", "un-American" groups, as exemplified by the "persecute" and make non-evangelicals "perish" commandment of some "godly" and "only true Christian" Southern Baptist pastors. In essence, just as did Winthrop's Puritanism, Baptism in America, especially the South, continues to operate as theocratic, including in effect or in intent persecutory, if not conceivably exterminatory, as well as sectarian, rigidly moralistic, and austere neo-Calvinism, thus as the theological design and institutional practice of evangelical theocracy. This is indicated by the observed "resurgence of Calvinistic doctrine" within the major Baptist and Protestant denomination[28] in the South and America or the "Calvinizing" of Southern and other American Baptists (Hinson 1997) since the 1980s and before.

And, the ever-growing social influence of Southern Baptism reborn in the "cradle of Calvinism" (Hinson 1997), as of related evangelical sects and cults, epitomizes an over-arching religious and political trend in modern America. This is the rebirth, expansion, and renewed dominance of religious fundamentalism (Emerson and Hartman 2006), notably neo-Calvinist evangelicalism (Smith 2000), and its ultra-conservative, notably theocratic "political agenda"[29] (Hout and Fischer 2002), and of strident, intolerant, and militant religiosity (Greeley and Hout 1999) generally in contemporary America.

No doubt, Baptism in modern America displays a remarkable consistence, continuity, and persistence with respect to the Calvinist design and social system of Biblical theocracy, including apparently persecution and conceivably extermination as the effective ultimate means and path to this supreme "godly" end. Moreover, it does so perhaps more than any other subtype or proxy of Calvinism, including its original French, Dutch, and German types eventually forced or induced to relinquish or mitigate their theocratic obsessions, designs, or practices (Hsia and Nierop 2002; Nischan 1994; Tubergen et al. 2005). In particular, it

---

[28] Hinson (1997) registers a "resurgence of Calvinistic doctrine", including the dogma of predestination, renamed "unconditional election", within the Southern Baptist Convention, the largest Protestant denomination in America, "largely from within conservative ranks" since the 1980s.

[29] Hout and Fischer (2002:165–66) observe that during the 1990s many Americans "who had weak attachments to religion and either moderate or liberal political views found themselves at odds with the conservative political agenda of the Christian Right and reacted by renouncing their weak attachment to organized religion." Further, they predict that "if the identification of religious affiliation with political conservatism strengthens, then liberals' alienation from organized religion may become, as it has in many other nations, fully institutionalized" (Hout and Fischer 2002:189).

does so even more than subsequent English Puritanism tamed or moderated in moral and religious absolutism by Anglicanism and liberalism (Munch 2001). Such consistency implies that the "strictest Bibliocracy" of the first Baptists in 16th century Europe in a way continues and expands in, thus ultimately explains and predicts, the Baptist "Bible Belt" in 21st century America. This reveals a striking, perhaps for most Americans unexpected European-American continuity or path-dependence from Switzerland or Germany to the "awaken" South.

In general, American, especially Southern (Hinson 1997), Baptism in theocratic and other substantive terms is the most credible successor or closest proxy of Calvinism or Puritanism in America and beyond. In a way, what was Calvinism in 16th century Europe or Puritanism in 17th century old and New England has become "Baptism" in 21st century America with in respect to Biblical theocracy and fundamentalism, as well as most other respects, including sectarianism, asceticism, moral absolutism, radicalism, militarism, nationalism, xenophobia, anti-humanism, and the like. In sum, in a sociological sense US Baptism is a sort of neo-Calvinism or neo-Puritanism, despite certain non-Calvinist traits in theological and psychological terms like non- or modified predestination and hyper-emotionalism to the point of what Weber calls "hysterical" emotions and actions.

### Calvinist Theocracy and Despotism via Puritan Theocratic Tyranny

As implied, the specific form and operation, *modus vivendi* and *operandi* of Calvinism's Biblical theocracy or theocratic despotism in non-European societal and geographic settings like America and England was what Weber calls the "unexampled tyranny" of Puritanism. Consequently, if Biblical theocracy is America's Calvinist "destiny" or heritage, just as its genesis or creation, it can or will be in the way of Puritan theocratic tyranny. In short, the Calvinist theocratic-despotic predestination of America acts via the Puritan tyrannical over-determination of the "new nation".

If Calvinism could, as Weber suggests, establish and maintain its Biblical theocracy and thus theocratic despotism "only" in America and temporarily England (alongside, in its initial shape, Geneva and Holland), it did in the derived form of the religious and political tyranny of Puritanism as its English-American derivative and "agent". Hence, Calvinism could realize its essential aim, in contrast to Lutheranism, and the typical element of theocracy like the "radical elimination" of the distinction between the ethics for priests and for laymen (Munch 1981), only in America and England (and Scotland). It did so through Calvinism's sectarian extensions in "Puritan sects and denominations" (Munch 1981) in these societies, just as, via its original forms, in Geneva, Holland, and partly Germany before. In short, it could attain its theocratic "reciprocal penetration of religious ethics and the world" (Munch 1981) in America through Puritanism's moralistic tyranny. In this sense, Calvinism with its theocracy and despotism overall in Europe generates and predicts the tyranny of Puritanism in America, from New England to the "awaken" South (Boles 1999) and the "godly" Calvinized "Wild West" like Texas, etc. (Clemens 2007).

Conversely, this implies a sort of "impossibility theorem" for Calvinism. Its evangelical theocracy or despotism overall is impossible or difficult to transplant from the old and despised world of Europe to, or to reestablish in, non-European settings like the "new nation" of America unless through the agency of the theocratic tyranny of Puritanism. The latter was a profoundly Calvinist, yet supposedly novel "all-American" religion and church or rather sect embodied and dominated by Winthrop et al. as supremely "good guys" (Gould 1996), in particular perennial conservative role models (Dunn and Woodard 1996; Seaton 2006). The old Calvinist theocracy and despotism in general was transplanted to and sustained in the "new nation" through various "all-American" embellishments, renames, and disguises of the theocratic tyranny of Puritanism like the "Biblical Garden", Winthrop's "shining city upon a hill" and "Christian Sparta", and "manifest destiny" (Gould 1996), just as via "sweetened" (Beck 2000) or "apple-pie" religious authoritarianism overall (Wagner 1997).

In this way, Calvinist despotic theocracy and Calvinism as a whole operates as America's "destiny", just as it became its colonial genesis, courtesy of what Hume,[30] Mill, Weber, and other analysts identify as

---

[30] The Puritan reputation for hypocrisy is so legendary, as in Dickens' novels, etc., that it has in a way survived Puritanism and Puritans as a name "gone with the wind", but still it may be instructive to recall Hume's classical insights. For example, he refers to "Puritanical pretensions to a free and independent constitution" and cites the following observation by Sir John Lambe: Puritans "to the world they seemed to be such as would not swear, whore, or be drunk; out they would lie, cozen, and deceive; that they would frequently hear two sermons a day, and repeat them too, and that some, times they would fast all day long." If, like Tocqueville and Weber, he visited America and witnessed their behavior, Hume might have added that this observation describes how many, if not most, "born again" Puritan-inspired fundamentalists behave in America, especially in the "Bible Belt".

Puritanism's "pure" and "vigorous hypocrisy" (Bremer 1995; Heckathorn 1990) in this respect. For Puritans escaped the "old" Europe, including England, presumably because of its theocratic despotism or tyranny. At this juncture, Puritanism reemerges, operates, and reappears as hypocritical, and in that sense dishonest Calvinism, and thus Puritans act as Calvinist hypocrites, though early Calvinists were far from being fully devoid of hypocrisy or dishonesty (Mansbach 2006), in spite of Calvin's famously methodical, dedicated, and heroic asceticism by self-imposed austerity or masochistic deprivation (Heller 1986; also, Fromm 1941). At this point, if some things never change and something is "pure" within Puritanism and its evangelical revivals in America, it is primarily what Weber calls "pure hypocrisy", along and yet in axiomatic contradiction with moralistic repression and theocracy.

Alternatively, the tyranny of Puritanism, including its "pure hypocrisy", operated as the form, manifestation, and instrument of Calvinist theocratic despotism in such non-European societal settings as America and in part Great Britain. Consequently, if Puritanism and thus by Weberian implication its theocratic and hypocritical tyranny is the "destiny" of Tocqueville's America, then this expresses and implements its predestination by Calvinism and its evangelical theocracy. Simply, beneath and behind the tyranny and hypocrisy of Puritanism as the prevalent American religious and cultural heritage (Munch 2001) lies what Weber identifies as Calvinism with its despotism and despotic theocracy in particular, thus America's Calvinist "destiny". As Weber's expression suggests, in virtue of being religious and consequently moralistic or morally hypocritical, just as political-economic, the tyranny of Puritanism, like of any religion and sect, was effectively a Calvinist theocracy as Bibliocracy. Hence, this Puritan tyranny was initially implemented or manifested in the New England's "Biblical Commonwealth" and subsequently self-perpetuated or revived, via the Great Awakenings, in the Southern "Bible Belt" and beyond.

At this juncture, Calvinism's despotic theocracy and Puritanism's tyranny function as functionally equivalent, with the second as the American transplant or product and the first as the European seed or producer. It is a theocratic or tyrannical expression of Weber's and Sombart's substantive equivalence and axiomatic identity of Calvinism and Puritanism as the "principal" and the "agent", respectively. The theocratic tyranny of Puritanism in America and transiently England is thus fully understood and explained only when placed in the context of Calvinism's theocracy and despotism as its historical point of origin and global framework. This implies that understanding America's "destiny" or main heritage in, as Weber, Tocqueville, and Ross imply, theocratic and generally tyrannical Puritanism requires taking into account despotic Calvinism and its theocracy as a sort of "holy" tyranny (Heller 1986) and "godly" society starting with Calvin's Geneva as medieval-style *civitas Dei* or a theocratic city-state (Byrne 1997).

Further, Weber's word "unexampled" suggests that the tyranny of Puritanism, properly understood as an Anglo-Saxon Calvinist subtype, was unrivaled and unprecedented even within the global framework or extended family of otherwise tyrannical or despotic Calvinism and in extension Protestantism. In particular, Weber and other sociologists (Munch 2001; Stivers 1994) suggest that it was the tyranny of American Puritanism that was "unexampled" by identifying the "theocracy of New England" as the most despotic or totalitarian Calvinist theocratic rule. In this sense, New England's Puritan tyranny or theocracy was not just Calvinist but ultra-Calvinist. It was so by carrying Calvin's theocratic system and model of *civitas Dei* with Church as State[31] (Frijhoff 2002) to its ultimate societal limits, just as geographically from France and Geneva to America.

Thus, following Hume, J. S. Mill remarks that American Puritanism commands that all humans must subordinate or conform to the "idea of a Christian commonwealth", as conceived and imposed by the early Puritans in New England, if the Puritan or similar theocratic religion ever succeeds in recovering its "lost ground". At this point, recall even Puritan Locke, with his "muted Calvinism" and recommended intolerance for non-Christians and Catholics as well as ordinary non-believers (Champion 1999; Fitzpatrick 1999), hardly ever embraced the "idea of a Christian commonwealth" as by implication a repressive theocracy (Zaret 1989). In turn, Weber explicitly describes this creation of Puritanism as the "theocracy of New England" defined by "an aristocratic rule by the ecclesiastically qualified" through its sectarian capture of or alliance with secular political power, just as "Cromwell's "Parliament of Saints" in England.

The above demonstrates that with respect to theocratic tyranny or despotism as the prime design, attribute, or outcome of Calvinism,

---

[31] Frijhoff (2002:48) comments that the Calvinist "new idea of a Church for the Saved was like the dogma that was taking shape (the predestination of a limited number of chosen people) and like the disciplinary practice which preferred a small perfect community easy to control".

Puritanism reinvents itself and functions as a sort of American hyper-Calvinism. Hence, Tocqueville's first and later Puritans act as super-Calvinists, (or, as they claim, "super-men") with self-assigned Divine rights to master, including to "save" by persecuting, torturing, and killing, "inferior", "ungodly", "sinful," or "corrupt" humans. It indicates that American Puritanism is just Calvinism gone "mad" or "wild" (Habermas 2001) in virtue of its pursuit and exercise of absolute societal power (Bourdieu 2000) in the "new nation". Consequently, American Puritans and their evangelical descendents are Calvinists turned into Keynes' "madmen in authority" due to their pursuing and exercising of what they attempted but eventually failed to achieve in the old world, including Great Britain. This is their total mastery or absolute power in the "new nation", initially New England and subsequently the "awaken" South and "Wild West." They extend Calvin's local tyranny, including the persecution and execution of "infidels" and libertines, in a total societal Calvinist Leviathan by culture-political wars (Bell 2002; Hout and Fischer 2002) and other aggressive, exclusionary practices against non-believers, secularists, and liberals in early and modern America (Edgell et al. 2006).

Further, US neo-Calvinist "born again" evangelicals seek to expand beyond America both tyrannies to create a sort of global evangelical Leviathan. The latter assumes the form of a spurious or hypocritical neo-conservative (Reaganite) "empire of liberty" effectively destroying or perverting human freedom and eventually life, but fulfilling and universalizing America's "manifest destiny" through religious nationalism, imperialism, militarism, and a constant "holy" war against the "ungodly" and "evil" world (Steinmetz 2005). This seems like the apparent and initial happy-ending Hollywood or Reagan style (Johnson 2003), yet on closer inspection works as, or is likely to become, profound and ultimate theocratic totalitarian madness, consequent to and predicted by absolute power-as-corruption (Bourdieu 2000). The latter holds true, if, as Comte and Spencer imply for offensive wars within primitive or barbarian military society,[32] such a "preemptive" war tends to ultimately result in the "delirium of annihilation" as Calvinist salvation (Adorno 2001), "unconditional election" (Hinson 1997) of a few evangelicals (e.g., Baptists and related sectarians) and damnation of

---

[32] Comte registers the "primitive tendency of mankind to a military life" in contrast to the "repugnance of modern society to a military life."

other humans. Particularly, it does so by using ever-more "high-tech" weapons of mass destruction, including new generations of nuclear arms[33] that US "born again" evangelicals and neo-conservatives (e.g., Goldwater, Reagan, and other "evangelical" Presidents) constantly threaten to use against "evil enemies" (Schelling 2006).

And, the outcome of the "delirium of annihilation" perfectly fits the model of "Puritan millennialism" (Kloppenberg 1998) or judgment-day nihilism by violent global destruction and self-destruction, as prefigured or advocated by evangelical doomsday sects and cults in America. Hence, it is an outcome in the form and image of Armageddon and its MAD, mutually assured destruction, nuclear (Habermas 2001; Schelling 2006) "happy-end" promised by Goldwater, Reagan, and other evangelical or neo-conservative "rigid extremists" (Blomberg and Harrington 2000). MAD becomes the fitting abbreviation for the "mad" world (Bourdieu 2000) or societal madness of Puritanism and its "reborn" evangelicalism due to near-absolute power within society and a total "holy" war against other societies. After all, MAD is what the Biblical metaphor of and warning about the "double-edged sword" admonishes and predicts. Yet, "reborn" Puritan-rooted evangelicalism almost invariably ignores and violates this Biblical admonition about the self-destructiveness of offensive wars in the image of a self-destructive "sword." Notably, this holds true of Southern Baptism as the most warlike or bellicose, imperialist ("missionary"[34]), and nationalistic, including xenophobic, branch of Protestantism and the "Christian" faith in modern America[35] (Friedland 2002). And, to that extent, Baptist and

---

[33] Schelling (2006:937) comments that as "advertising a continued dependence on nuclear weapons, i.e., a US readiness to use them, a US need for new nuclear capabilities (and new nuclear tests)—let alone ever using them against an enemy—has to be weighed against the corrosive effect on a nearly universal attitude that has been cultivated through universal abstinence of 60 years." Also, Schelling (2006:937) deplores that the neo-conservative US Senate "rejected" (in 1999) of the Comprehensive Test Ban Treaty, while "nearly 200 nations ratifying the CTBT" with its "potential to enhance the nearly universal revulsion against nuclear weapons". Perhaps nothing more dramatically and eventually lethally and self-destructively than this rejection epitomizes and demonstrates Puritan-rooted militarism and bellicosity as well as the disdain for international rules and institutions like the U.N. in American neo-conservatism, including conservative-dominated Congress during recent times (until 2007).

[34] Hinson (1997) praises the "Southern Baptist Convention" as becoming "one of the greatest missionary-sending agencies in history" and as "rocked in the cradle of Calvinism."

[35] Friedland (2002:387–8) remarks that "America's Christian right has been resolutely nationalist", namely that "most "fundamentalist" Christians in America are religious

other evangelicalism or Protestant sectarianism in America acts as anything but evangelical or Biblical and truly Christian.

### *From Calvinist Theocracy to the Moralistic "Tyranny of Puritanism" to "Moral Fascism"*

The Calvinist-as-Puritan "destiny" of Tocqueville's America proves to be moralistic theocracy through the tyranny of Puritanism as axiomatically theocratic moral absolutism (Munch 2001), sectarianism, and totalitarianism (Stivers 1994) in Calvinism and Protestantism overall.

### *Calvinism, Puritanism, and Moral Fascism*

On this account, Tocqueville's Calvinist-as-Puritan "destiny" of America ultimately and, likely for most readers, shockingly reveals itself as a sort of moral fascism. The latter is defined by what he identifies as the "great strictness of morals" and puritanical, ascetic moralistic tyranny, or the denial and suppression of individual liberty, choice, and responsibility in morality and all private life. Austere or extremely ascetic Calvinist theocracy, notably the moralistic tyranny of Puritanism, as what Hume and Comte call the reign of divines or saints functions as or prefigures moral proto-fascism before fascism. Conversely, fascism is typically, with secondary "secular", "ungodly" variations in Nazism, theocratic, "godly", and morally and otherwise absolutistic.

At first glance, moral fascism as America's Calvinist-as-Puritan "destiny" appears to be an ironic, unexpected, and, for most Americans, "outrageous", "shocking", and "dead wrong" thought and twist to be elaborated later on. Before dismissing it, at this point suffices it to state that moral fascism is implied in the observation that through its derivative or "agent" Puritanism, Calvinism fulfilled the identical "sociological function" for Anglo-Saxon societies (McLaughlin 1996) such as America and partly England, as did fascism in interwar Europe, notably Nazism in Germany. In sum, moral fascism is understood as the

---

nationalists [who] make politics into a religious obligation". As a predictable symbol, Sothern Baptists churches—rather sects in Weber's sense—usually display an American flag in front of their buildings, symbolizing their nationalist fusion of religion and nation, and implicitly their theocratic merger or de-differentiation between church and state. This makes one wonder how these self-declared "true and only" Christian denominations can reconcile this nationalist fusion with original Christianity's disassociation from any nation or its trans-national character.

substantive equivalent or ultimate outcome of Calvinist theocracy and ascetic Calvinism, especially of Puritan moralistic-theocratic tyranny.

If this work has any theoretical originality or empirical "discovery", then it is that moral fascism thus understood ultimately constitutes and epitomizes the "destiny" of Tocqueville's America as emanating in the first Puritans a la Winthrop et al. as austere, orthodox Calvinists. This may not be novel, and thus merely a "rediscovery" in Merton's (1968) sense, in relation to Tocqueville's and Weber's diagnoses of the Calvinist-Puritan "great strictness of morals" and the "unexampled tyranny" of Puritanism in America, as the substantive equivalents or defining traits of moral fascism in the sense of moralistic oppression. At least, it is original in relation to those works contending that America's and Western values of religious, political, and other freedom were associated with Calvinism and its main theological and moral doctrines like predestination, Divine absolute transcendence, human sin and depravity, etc. (Davis 2005; Dunn and Woodard 1996; Means 1966). In particular, this work differs from Weber's implied or the neo-Weberian explicit view that precisely because of its "Calvinist heritage" in America "democratic values and institutions" were cultivated and expanded through individuals' participation in "small-scale, egalitarian" community organizations (Kloppenberg 1998). To wit, moral fascism constitutes, first and non-controversially, the paradigmatic antithesis and the supreme destruction of freedom in individual morality and all private life. Second and seemingly controversially, it represents the equivalent or product of Calvinist ascetic theocracy, most notably of Puritan moralistic tyranny. Consequently, these libertarian-democratic values and institutions in America and other Western societies are indeed *disassociated* from rather than linked to Calvinism and its child Puritanism, thus established and maintained in spite, *not* because, of Calvinists-as-Puritans themselves

Hence, if Calvinist theocracy and despotism in general establishes itself and operates in America and other non-European environments through Puritanism's moralistic tyranny, then the latter does by means of conservative moral fascism. In short, Calvinist theocracy is the creator or basis of the tyranny of Puritanism, and the latter one of moral fascism in Puritan societies. Just as Calvinist ascetic theocracy in virtue of being tyrannical in America functions as or produces and grounds Puritan theocratic tyranny, so the latter does, because of its being extremely moralizing or morally absolutistic, moral fascism. In essence, Calvinism's theocracy and despotism overall generates, predicts, and rationalizes Puritan tyranny, while Puritanism's extreme moralism or moralistic absolutism does neo-conservative moral fascism. Calvinism thus effectively produces, predicts, and sanctifies, as a "godly" society, moral fascism in America indirectly and almost invisibly via Puritanism and its moralistic tyranny and absolutism. By analogy, it does directly and visibly, minus Puritan "vigorous hypocrisy", in Protestant Europe, including partly Calvinist Germany (Prussia). This path is what sociological and other analyses suggest or imply (Adorno 2001; Fromm 1941; Gorski 2003; Grossman 2006; Mansbach 2006; McLaughlin 1996). When such an analysis observes that Calvinism fulfilled the "same sociological function" for Anglo-Saxon societies (McLaughlin 1996) primarily America and secondarily England, as fascism did in Europe, notably Nazism in Germany, this is, first and foremost, that of moral, as distinguished from, yet eventually merged with political, fascism. And, such a function is in the form and sense of Puritan *moralistic* tyranny and absolutism, a sort of fascist "functionalism".

Predictably, the preceding primarily holds true of New England's proto-Calvinist, Puritan "Biblical Commonwealth" and the neo-Calvinist, "reborn" evangelical Southern "Bible Belt". If the tyranny of Puritanism" and thus Calvinism operated as or produced moralistic proto-fascism and absolutism in early America and in part England, then its "Bible Belt" revival does moral neo-fascism or moralizing authoritarianism. Evidently, Calvinist theocracy, from the 17th century "Biblical Commonwealth" to the 21st century "Bible Belt", generates, perpetuates, and predicts moral fascism in America via the theocratic and moralistic tyranny of Puritanism. In particular, if the "Bible Belt" is what is or designed to be precisely because of being defined by the theocratic and moralistic tyranny of Puritanism under various embellishments, then the latter objectively or eventually reproduces and predicts moral fascism as the ultimate suppression and perversion of individual freedom in morality and private life overall. Simply, as Weber implies, the "Bible Belt" and any Calvinist Bibliocracy invariably functions as, or cannot be and produce anything than, the moralistic tyranny of Puritanism and consequently moral fascism in the broad sense. In sum, the path from theocratic Calvinism via hyper-moralistic or absolutist Puritanism to moral and perhaps political fascism or totalitarianism is shorter, though roundabout and tortuous, than US and other "born again" Calvinist-Puritan fundamentalists would admit or realize.

As a corollary, the above yields a curious, perhaps for most Americans unexpected and hidden historical-geographical trajectory or path-dependence, notably sociological continuity. It can be represented as follows:
Calvinism's ascetic theocracy and despotism in France (designed, partly instituted), Geneva and Holland (established), Germany (attempted) → Calvinist Puritanism's theocratic and moralistic tyranny in England, Scotland, and New England → neo-conservative moral fascism in modern America, especially the Southern, mid-Western, and Northern "Bible Belt" and the "Wild West".

Alternatively, just as the moralistic tyranny of Puritanism expressed and implemented the "good old" Calvinist theocracy and despotism in the "new nation", so moral fascism does Puritan tyrannical moralism and absolutism in contemporary America, notably the "Bible Belt". In short, just as Puritan tyranny was the ultimate outcome of despotic Calvinism in past English-American societies, so is moral fascism one of moralistic Puritanism in modern America. Moral fascism in the latter invariably emerges and operates as or mirrors a sort of reenacted or resurrected Puritan moralistic tyranny from what Mannheim calls the "dead past". In extension, moral fascism cum Puritan tyranny in Anglo-Saxon societies functions as or reflects Calvinist ascetic despotism yet *caput mortuum* in Europe (France, Holland, Germany), just as it does theocratic Catholicism in Catholic countries (Italy, Spain, Portugal, Poland, Latin America) and fundamentalist Islam in Iran, Saudi Arabia, and similar Islamic theocracies. *Prima facie*, moral fascism in contemporary America is axiomatically the eventual outcome or even the substantive equivalent of moralistic, tyrannical Puritanism and in extension of ascetic Calvinism. Generally, in virtually all societies and times, it is the outcome or equivalent of extreme religious (Catholic, Orthodox Christian, Protestant, Islamic, Hindu) conservatism, as its creator or "sacred" basis and justification.

And, since the moralistic tyranny of Puritanism is just the "agency" or manifestation of Calvinist theocracy and despotism as the "principal" or basis in America, moral fascism in this and other Puritan settings such as England is ultimately grounded in and predicted, as is that in Calvinist societies proper like Geneva, Holland, and in part Prussia, by Calvinism. By analogy, moral fascism in Catholic societies like interwar Italy and Spain and post-communist Poland is grounded in and predicted by theocratic Catholicism, just as fundamentalist Islam grounds and predicts its analogues in Islamic theocracies like

Iran and Saudi Arabia. In sum, moral fascism, while near-universally "godly" or religious, thus conservative or reactionary, is invariably the expression of the "nervousness and fanaticism of Calvinist godliness" (Walzer 1963) in America and England (and Scotland) via Puritan moralistic absolutism, obsession, and repression.

In particular, moral fascism in America is grounded in, sanctified by, and realizes the original Calvinist dogma of human evilness, depravity, sin, and Divine predestination by the agency of Puritan moralistic tyranny over "evil", "corrupt", "sinful", and "ungodly" humans. In Weber's words, moral fascism in Puritan, as distinguished from non-Puritan (including Lutheran, Anglican, Catholic, Orthodox Christian, and Islamic), environments is Calvinism in action and realization, with its harsh (Fourcade and Healy 2007) and extremely inhumane doctrines of the corruption of humans and Divine absolute transcendence or predestination. By assumption, it is so via Puritanism and its moralistic absolutism and suppression of individual freedom in morality and all private life. In fact, there is no such thing as private life or privacy, just as "free lunch", in Puritanism and Calvinism overall (Mansbach 2006; Stivers 1994; Walzer 1963; Zaret 1989), like in fundamentalist Islam and Hinduism (Archer 2001; Turner 2002). This is exemplified by the "Bible Belt" and Iranian Islamic theocracy both belonging to the proto-totalitarian "solutions" to the supposed "agony" and "burden" of individual choice, liberty, and privacy (Bauman 1997).

If the preceding is correct, then it yields an ironic twist and even "shocking" inference. This is that Calvinism, specifically its evangelical theocracy, turns out to be America's theocratic "destiny" immediately or directly through the tyranny of Puritanism, and ultimately or indirectly via neo-conservative, "born again" fundamentalist moral fascism. If Calvinist ascetic theocracy intrinsically harbors or eventually generates through the moralistic tyranny of Puritanism moral fascism, then the latter, rather than "liberty" or "democratic values and institutions", has the "last word" and "laugh" as America's Calvinist-as-Puritan "destiny" or legacy (Mansbach 2006).

The above leads to a series of successive propositions or first approximations. These are, first, Calvinism is America's "destiny" or main heritage through Puritanism. Second, America's Calvinist "destiny" or heritage consists in evangelical theocracy or Bibliocracy. Third, Calvinist theocracy is America's "destiny" in the form of Puritanism's theocratic and moralistic tyranny. Fourth, Puritanism's theocratic-moralistic tyranny self-perpetuates and operates as America's "destiny" via neo-conservative moral fascism or moralistic authoritarianism. Fifth, moral fascism operates as the totalitarian suppression and subversion of individual freedom in morality by coercive imposition, including irrational laws and Draconian punishments for immoral acts or sins-crimes. Lastly, as a corollary, Calvinism-as-Puritanism operates as America's "destiny" in the form of moral fascism sanctified as fundamentalist theocracy or the "Biblical Garden."

At the minimum, moral fascism is the particular moralistic and (anti) civic dimension of America's "destiny" in Calvinist theocracy as a total social system composed of certain types of economy, polity, civil society, and culture as its subsystems. At least, the "destiny" of American civil society as the realm of moral and other individual liberties and a subsystem of this system consists in theologically, Calvinist-rooted and institutionally, Puritan-enforced moral fascism. This is in part suggested or anticipated by the observations about civil society as well as political democracy, economy, and culture, in contemporary America being placed under, thus subverted by, the moralistic, intolerant, and under-democratic "shadow of Dixie", or "heading" (Cochran 2001) the Southern "Bible Belt" as the proto-totalitarian "solution" to individual moral and other liberty. This work considers moral fascism a specific, destructive type of civil society integral to Calvinist theocracy as a total social system, also comprising corresponding economic, political, and cultural systems, thus "just" America's moralistic "destiny" or future prospect and heritage in Calvinism via Puritanism.

In turn, the expression moral fascism does not mean that fascism is "moral", albeit most fascists, including the Nazis, made and still make such claims to superior "morality", especially in relation to what they attack as "immoral" or "amoral", "degenerate", and "corrupt" liberalism and liberals, including liberal-secular democracy and civil society. "Moral" and any fascism is what Weber (despite his possible *Verstehen* for his German countrymen) would call abomination of any system of social ethics, including the Christian "Golden Rule" (somewhat "egocentric" for Habermas 2001), let alone the primeval ethic of brotherliness (Symonds and Pudsey 2006) and Enlightenment liberal-secular universalistic morality considering all humans within Kant's "kingdom of ends". Expressions like "moralistic fascism" or "morally absolutist fascism" are evidently more adequate and precise to convey the nature and effects of "moral fascism". Still, "moral fascism" is retained for the sake of simplicity and convenience by analogy to "civil war", "religious wars", "culture wars", etc. So, if one wonders what is "moral" or "ethical" about "moral fascism", this can be answered by analogy to what is "civil" about "civil war", truly "religious" or "holy" about "religious wars", "cultural" about "culture wars," and the like.

## Calvinist Theocracy as Total Society

From a sociological stance, perhaps like most other (Catholic, Orthodox Christian, Protestant, Islamic, Hindu, etc.) theocracies, Calvinist-Puritan evangelical theocracy or Bibliocracy is more than just a political system, a type of polity and state or government. Rather, it extends beyond to encompass society, including also the economy, the civil sphere, and culture. Calvinist theocracy is not merely the design and reality of a theocratic polity, church-state. It is a society as a whole, incorporating economic, civil and cultural life as well, as epitomized by the "Puritan dream of the godly community" (German 1995), not merely of "faith-based" government. More precisely, perhaps like most other theocracies, it is the rule or control not only of politics or government but of the entire society. It is what Weber calls the "domination over the sinful world" by the "pure church" through its religious virtuosi or saints as masters with Divine Rights, as putative God's agents or Hume's divines, to rule and dominate, including punish and kill to "save", humans.

## Calvinist Theocracy as a Total Social System: Theocratic Subsystems

As noted, in terms of systems theory, Calvinist evangelical theocracy is what Durkheim, Pareto, and Parsons would call a total social system, and Sorokin a "super-system", with its respective theocratic entwined economic, political, civic, and cultural elements or subsystems. In Pareto's words, Calvinist theocracy is a complex "sociological system" of which the economy, including Weberian Calvinist capitalism, politics, the civic sphere, and culture, are "particular cases."[36] Notably, as a "sociological system" it is more complex than the economy, thus capitalism as its integral element or unintended outcome, as well as the polity, the civil realm, and culture as its respective political, civic, and cultural subsystems (Arrow 1994). In Pareto's words, the principal

---

[36] Pareto specifically remarks that the equilibrium states of the economic system are "particular cases of the general states of the sociological system".

reason why Calvinist theocracy as a "sociological system" is "much more complicated" than the economy (capitalism) is that the former involves both rational and irrational elements, or "logical and non-logical actions" driven by material interests and residues (sentiments) and derivations (rationalizations of non-rational action) respectively, and the latter does only or mostly the first. This is another way to state that Calvinism's evangelical theocracy is more complex, because it is what Durkheim and Parsons (1951) elaborating on Pareto denote a total society involving both rational and non-rational factors and incorporating the economy, polity, civil society, and culture as its four integral and interconnected elements or subsystems.

In terms of Parsons' (1967) own Pareto-inspired AGIL scheme, Calvinist theocracy as a total social system has four "logically independent functional requirements", such as adaptation, integration, goal-attainment, and latent-pattern-maintenance. These imperatives are fulfilled by a "plurality of subsystems" in interaction like a theocratic economy, polity, societal community or civil society, and culture, respectively (Alexander 1998; Smelser 1997). Applying the AGIL scheme, Calvinism's evangelical theocracy can be represented accordingly, though this is likely *not* what Parsons et al. would do. It is not given the Parsonian implied equivalence or link of Calvinism, notably American Puritanism and its New England's Puritan Bibliocracy (though not so called), with both democratic capitalism *and* political democracy and a free civil society and culture, thus with the inverse of their theocratic and overall authoritarian forms.

Hence, Calvinist theocracy's functional imperatives are adaptation (A), goal-attainment (G), integration (I), and latent-pattern-maintenance (L) each performed by one of its partial social systems, its *theocratic* economy (including capitalism and pre-capitalism), polity, civil society, and culture, respectively (Figure 2.1). This application of the AGIL scheme to Calvinist theocracy adopts Parsons' four functional imperatives and respective subsystems but conceives the latter as equivalent, namely theocratic and thus authoritarian. It entails a substantial departure from the Parsonian implied equation of Calvinist Puritanism with secular and liberal-democratic capitalism, politics, civil society, and culture. In this sense, the application proceeds in the letter but not in the spirit of Parsons' AGIL model and functionalism, being a formal rather than a substantive one.

Hence, in this representation, Calvinist theocracy, like perhaps most others, is not just, as usually represented and conceived, a theocratic

| | | | |
|---|---|---|---|
| A | THEOCRATIC ECONOMY/ CAPITALISM | G | THEOCRATIC POLITY/ STATE |
| I | THEOCRATIC CIVIL SOCIETY/ COMMUNITY | L | THEOCRATIC CULTURE |

Figure 2.1. Calvinist theocracy as a total social system with four functional imperatives and subsystems.

political system or church-state. It also involves a theocratic economy or (as in Weber's account) capitalism, theocratic civil society, and theocratic culture, thus being theocratic society as a whole. The representation is consistent and does justice to what Weber describes as the "iron consistency" of Calvinism, including, in Hume's words, the "obstinacy" of Puritanism. It is because Calvinist theocracy as a total social system consistently or logically and obstinately incorporates or creates an equivalent "plurality of subsystems", such as *theocratic* economic (capitalist or pre-capitalist), political, civil, and cultural systems. Simply, a theocratic social system is composed of identical subsystems, including such an economy, in particular capitalism as the specific, but not exclusive, economic system of Calvinist theocracy.

Alternatively, representing and conceiving some but not all—say, polity and culture, yet not economy and civil society or conversely—subsystems of Calvinist theocracy as theocratic is inconsistent or logically contradictory. Consequently, it does not do justice to Calvinism's "iron consistency," including Puritanism's "obstinacy". In a sense, this is what Parsons et al., if not Weber, implicitly do. They do so by typically representing and conceiving the Calvinist-Puritan economy (capitalism), polity, and civil society as democratic and secular (Mayway 1984), and thus non-theocratic, while admitting or hinting that its culture might contain certain theocratic or predominant religious elements, like the Bible as the "only common culture" (Bloom 1988) in American history and society. Imagine an AGIL scheme of Calvinist theocracy as a total social system with a *non*-theocratic, democratic economy and polity but a theocratic civil society and culture, or some other combinations thereof, thus its logical consistency or empirical validity (close to zero). In a certain amplification of, if not deviation from, Weber who does not equate "capitalist" and "democratic" (Binmore 2001), Parsons et al. tend to conceive and extol Calvinist capitalism as invariably democratic and libertarian. Predictably, they focus on and celebrate especially its Puritan American version as the culmination of social evolution or the "end of history" in, as critics object, an ethnocentric and even "ridiculous" manner[37] (Giddens 1984).

At this juncture, the AGIL scheme as modified and applied above ironically exposes Parsons et al.'s inconsistency or contradiction in failing to do justice to the "iron consistency" of Calvinism and its theocracy. Notably, it does the Parsonian contradiction or omission that a non-theocratic economic system like democratic secular capitalism is axiomatically inconsistent with and contradictory to a *theocratic* social system such as Calvinist theocracy.

Instead, the modified AGIL scheme indicates and predicts that the "iron consistency" of Calvinism logically and, more importantly, empirically necessitates that its theocracy as a total social system have an equivalent theocratic economic system and logic, including capitalism (as well as feudalism or slavery), just as political, civil, and cultural systems. For example, the scheme implicitly reflects the historical fact that New England's Puritan theocracy had basically a theocratic economic system and logic, including slavery, a feudal aristocracy, or ruling caste, and authoritarian capitalism, in that it was reportedly "merciless" (Tawney 1962) to complete freedom in the economy (German 1995), just as liberty in the polity, civil society, and culture (Baldwin 2006). In this sense, the four theocratic systems in the AGIL scheme express and predict "mercilessness" to the composite of economic, political, civil, and cultural liberties within Calvinist-Puritan (and any) theocracy.

Alternatively, the AGIL scheme implies that if its economic system is conceived, as implied in Parsons' Weberian framework, as non-theocratic or secular democratic capitalism, Calvinist theocracy effectively ceases to be a theocratic *total* social system. Instead, it is reduced, if ever, to one of Parsons' *partial* social systems such as church-state or religiously dominated ("Bible") culture, and thus loses its intrinsic "iron consistency" and totalistic "soul" of universal oppression. If so, Parsons et al. would have to reconcile Calvinist democratic capitalism with the theocratic state like New England's Puritan theocracy to reestablish some modicum of the "iron consistency" of Calvinism, including Puritanism. Yet, as Tawney (1962) and other analyses (German 1995) show, the economic system of New England's Puritan theocracy was

---

[37] Giddens (1984:273-4) objects that "Parsons's view that half a million years of human history culminate in the social and political system of the United States would be more than faintly ridiculous if it did not conform quite neatly to his particular 'world-growth' story".

hardly democratic or libertarian capitalism, as its masters were "merciless" not only to political, civil and cultural liberties but also to unrestricted economic freedom ("license").

The rest of the work applies and elaborates the AGIL scheme to Calvinist theocracy with the above qualifications in relation to Parsons' original version. To summarize the previous and anticipate the following, it, first, conceives Calvinist theocracy as a total social system or societal super-system in the sense of Durkheim, Pareto, Sorokin, and Parsons. Second, the following disaggregates and analyzes this total system into four analytically independent and empirically interconnected equivalent social systems. These are a *theocratic* economy, polity, civil society, and culture all existing and functioning within such a theocracy as a total societal system.[38]

This sociological totality or holism may be more or less common to most theocracies and religions in history and present. Yet, it is, first and foremost, even paradigmatically characteristic of Calvinist Biblical theocracy as a total social system and Calvinism as the blueprint or "dream" of totalistic or absolute mastery of society. Calvinist Bibliocracy is an instance of Sorokin's pure theocracy and in this sense a total or integral societal system to be distinguished from "diluted" theocracies as partial or not fully integrated social systems, specifically governments, confined (as Simmel implies) to politics and not encompassing or controlling the economy, civil society, and culture. It is thus a case of Sorokin's social "ideational" or "non-sensate" super-system that comprises theocratic economic, political, civil, and cultural subsystems or realms as its integral and interconnected elements. In this way, Calvinist theocracy is sociologically "holistic" tending to completion or perfection by encompassing and controlling all society, not just its government.

In turn, Calvinist Bibliocracy is "holistic" in virtue of being the ultimate, theocratic form and creation or the theological design of the Calvinist total mastery of the world. As a sort of what some analysts describe as "chiefdom consciousness" pervading institutional arrangements[39] (Angel 1994), the Calvinist total or absolute mastery of society

---

[38] Still, the concept of "functional imperatives" is not explicitly used as being of questionable usefulness to the present purpose and debatable overall, as admitted by Merton (1968) and neo-functionalists (Alexander 1998).

[39] In general, Angel (1994:347) singles out the "damage that chiefdom consciousness has perpetrated in rippling through our social institutions and entrenching ego-consciousness" in Western and Eastern societies alike.

generates and predicts Biblical theocracy as a total social system, and conversely the latter exercises and perpetuates such rule. In this sense, it is paradigmatically or axiomatically (by design) a total theocratic social system, and conversely, this mastery of the world inherently or ultimately functions via and regenerates an integral theocracy. In Sorokin's words, it is a social super-system because of Calvinism being the theological design and methodical practice of total mastery of society and nature, including the persecution and extermination of non-Calvinists and other "infidels." Conversely, such total mastery, including the persecution and extermination of non-Calvinist "infidels", is possible and efficient only in a Calvinist theocracy (Tawney 1962) as a societal super-system in the image, if not form, of Hobbes' Leviathan. And, Hobbes' metaphor seems appropriate given his treatment of religions, Gods, spirits, and demons as the mere products of human "fancies" and imagination.

Just as the Calvinist mastery of the world inherently (logically) tends to be, or eventually becomes, total or absolute, so does Biblical theocracy as its theocratic form, product, or design. Simply, just as Calvinism's mastery of the world, Calvinist theocracy is either a total social system, not just a polity and government, in the image of Hobbes' Leviathan—or not *Calvinist* theocracy at all. Recall, New England's Puritan theocracy was "merciless" or at least "not very compassionate" to all social, including political, moral, and religious, and in part economic, liberties and thus a total societal system or a society as a whole. Negatively, it was not only a theocratic polity or state as just one of its integral elements or subsystems.

In passing, as known, Weber implies that certain exceptions to this theocratic totality or holism are "other-worldly" religions and theocracies that adopt passive "adaptation" or "mere accommodation" to the social and natural world rather than its mastery in contrast to "innerworldly" Calvinism. Hence, he includes among these exceptions pre-Calvinist world religions and theocracies mostly in the Orient, as well as traditional Catholicism. As also known, Weber uses this dichotomy between passive adaptation to and active mastery of the world to explain the absence and rise of modern capitalism in non-Calvinist and Calvinist societies respectively over post-Reformation times. If so, it turns out that theocratic totality through the total mastery of the world pursued by Calvinism eventually explains the birth of modern capitalism, and conversely, in the Weberian framework, as he implies by recognizing Calvinist "despotism" and Puritan "tyranny" (but does not elaborate). Notably, this theocratic genesis endows modern capitalism with equivalent, thus authoritarian, rather than liberal-democratic or secular attributes. To wit, Calvinist totality in theocracy either in theological design or in social reality explains theocratic, thus authoritarian, not secular and liberal-democratic (including welfare), capitalism, namely a master-servant economic system. This is a manifest moment within Weber's framework of the Calvinist-capitalist "elective affinity" or "intimate connection". Yet, it seems overlooked in the Weberian literature, especially Puritan Parsons et al. concurring with an economistic conflation a la Mises-Hayek of "capitalism" and "democracy", economic freedom and non-economic liberty, "free market enterprise" and free civil society, as even some economists admit (Binmore 2001).

*From Total Mastery of the World to a Totalitarian Social System*

As a corollary of its sociological holism and Calvinism's total mastery of the world, Calvinist Bibliocracy typically tends to be a totalitarian social system or society, including, but not limited to, its polity. Thus, sociological analyses suggest that Calvinist Bibliocracy is a totalitarian social system in virtue and in the sense of Calvinism seeking and attaining "totalistic" rule and control of society, including both its economy and polity (Eisenstadt 1965). In this account, Calvinism's (as well as Lutheranism's) "original political impulse" and eventual practice was "totalistic" through constraining "autonomous activities in both the economic and the political field" rather than, as supposed by Parsons et al., liberal-democratic, (also politically) individualistic, and even secular. Arguably, Calvinism's total mastery of the world manifested itself and eventuated in a totalistic restriction of freedom or totalitarian domination over the "sinful" and "ungodly" by Weber's Calvinist religious virtuosi *cum* Divine masters-theocrats in the face of Hume's Puritan divines.

Alternatively, Calvinism's "totalistic" domination over and ultimately destruction of the "sinful world", including the extermination of "infidels", could and can be implemented, as Weber and other sociologists (Munch 2001; Tawney 1962) suggest, only within theocracy or hierocracy as the "godly" form of totalitarianism. It could and can in that sense only in moral-religious fascism, including, as Pareto and other analysts imply, the fascist-like mix of sadism and masochism through "tormenting" others and themselves because of actual or potential sins and vices defined and harshly punished as crimes (Adorno 2001; Fromm 1941; Mansbach 2006).

Notably, if original Calvinist theocracy was totalitarian due to Calvinism as totalistic, then its Puritan derivatives predictably reinvented and reinforced such theocratic totalitarianism owing to Puritanism's reinvention and reinforcement of this initial totality. As noticed, what Weber and other sociologists (Munch 2001; Tawney 1962) identify as the Puritan evangelical theocracy or the "Bible Commonwealth" of New England or Massachusetts was reportedly the "most totalitarian" Calvinist theocratic system due to American Puritanism being precisely such a supreme type of Calvinism[40] (Stivers 1994). On this account, this Puritan Bibliocracy was a sort of hyper-Calvinist theocracy and American Puritanism super-Calvinism in a variation on the pattern of converts becoming "more Catholic than the Pope" (Lipset 1955) in this case Winthrop et al. being more Calvinist than Calvin himself in theocratic and austere Calvinism.

And, this is perhaps the only or main sociologically substantive, to be distinguished from formal, theological or psychological, difference between "all-American" Puritan and European Calvinist theocracies, Puritanism and Calvinism. If anything, the American-Puritan derivative or disciple surpassed the European-Calvinist original or theological master in respect of theocratic totalitarianism and/or totalistic mastery of the "sinful world." This is thus a difference that contradicts the conventional and ethnocentric view of the first as liberal-democratic compared to the second and all religions, including Catholicism, Lutheranism, and Anglicanism, in Europe.

From another angle, this is no substantive or pertinent difference, because it is the matter of pseudo-statistical "degrees of unfreedom" rather than of substance of illiberty. It is equivalent or analogous to the difference between Nazism as the most totalitarian fascism compared with other, non-German (Italian, Spanish, etc.) inter- and post-war fascisms. Thus, New England's Puritan Bibliocracy was the old-world Calvinist theocracy, conceived in France and instituted in Geneva and Holland, just becoming ever-more totalitarian in the "new nation", as is, with prudent qualifications, its putative revival through

---

[40] According to Stivers (1994:18–23), in America Puritanism "was the most totalitarian form of Calvinism, [which] not satisfied with a minimalistic morality, searched for a rigorous moral discipline."

the Southern and other "Bible Belt". This remarkable theocratic intensification and subsequent escalation, as via the Great Awakenings, was primarily due to the virtual absence or weakness of countervailing non-Calvinist, anti-Puritan social forces, at least in pre- and post-Jeffersonian America (Archer 2001; Davis 2005; German 1995), and perhaps geographic isolation and the physical environment (if not, as Montesquieu and economist Jevons might half-amusingly suggest, "weather" and "sunspots").

Alternatively, this was the result of Calvinism's near-absolute power and consequently, if Acton is correct, equivalent corruption by, as Pareto implies and predicts, its "gross abuses" in America compared to Europe (France, Holland, Germany) and England where it, including Puritanism, was more tempered by such forces (Munch 2001). In short, these are secondary differences in intensity of totalitarianism or "degrees of unfreedom" between the European and American forms of Calvinist theocracy. At any rate, Calvinist theocracy constituted a "totalistic" despotic social system both in its original form in Europe (Geneva, Holland) and its derivative, Puritan version in England and America from the 16th–17th centuries. And, it still remains by the 21st century in a renewed, embellished form as another, neo-Calvinist "Biblical Garden" in the US South and beyond (the Midwest, the "Wild West", and parts of the North).

In sum, Calvinist theocracy in America is a total, in particular "totalistic" social system or society constituted of four integral elements or equivalent partial and intertwined social systems, in an application of Parsons' AGIL model. The first element is a "totalistic" economic system in the form of a theocratic economy, including pre-capitalism and capitalism. In this respect, the economic system and logic of Calvinist theocracy is a sort of master-servant and generally authoritarian or repressive and anti-egalitarian economy. The second element is a "totalistic" political system in the form of a theocratic state and polity, formally or substantively. In this respect, the political system of Calvinist theocracy is an anti-liberal and non-democratic government.

The third element is a "totalistic" civil society through the theocratic destruction or domination of the civic sphere (Parsons' societal community) or the life-world. In this sense, the civil or rather uncivil system of Calvinist theocracy is what Weber identifies as the moralistic tyranny of Puritanism in private life and in that sense moral fascism. The fourth element is a "totalistic" cultural system in the form of theocratic culture and notably religion. Alternatively, the cultural or rather

# AMERICA'S CALVINIST "DESTINY" IDENTIFIED AND SPECIFIED

| | | | |
|---|---|---|---|
| A | MASTER-SERVANT ECONOMY (PRE-CAPITALISM AND CAPITALISM) | G | ANTI-LIBERAL AND NON-DEMOCRATIC GOVERNMENT (CHURCH-STATE) |
| I | MORAL FASCISM IN PRIVATE LIFE (MORALISTIC TYRANNY OF PURITANISM) | L | DARK MIDDLE AGES DÉJÀ VU (DESTRUCTION OF SECULAR CULTURE) |

These four social subsystems of Calvinist theocracy are redefined and reconsidered in this order.

Figure 2.2. Calvinist theocracy in America as a total and "totalistic" social system with four subsystems.

anti-cultural system of Calvinist theocracy is the theocratic substitution or dominance of secular human culture in the model and image of the Dark Middle Ages déjà vu. The above yields the corresponding modified representation of America's Calvinist theocracy as a total social system (Figure 2.2).

CHAPTER THREE

# ECONOMIC SYSTEM OF CALVINIST THEOCRACY

## A Theocratic Master-Servant Economy

The economic system of Calvinist evangelical theocracy is by assumption and/or in reality a theocratic economy, including both its pre-capitalist and capitalist forms. In turn, a theocratic, either pre-capitalist or capitalist, economy is also a paradigmatic exemplar of what can be described as a master-servant economic system in the form and sense of Calvinist theocrats or divines claiming to be or acting as masters, and others being their servants or subjects. In this sense, the economic subsystem and logic of Calvinist theocracy as a total or totalitarian social system is a master-servant *cum* theocratic economy. While certainly not all master-servant economies are theocratic or religiously sanctified, but also non-theocratic or non-religious (as in Nazism and communism), the opposite is invariably true for the economic system and logic of Calvinist and perhaps any similar theocracy. Universally, the Calvinist and other comparable (e.g., Islamic, Hindu) theocratic economy is an axiomatic (by design) master-servant and thus authoritarian or totalitarian and in that sense anti-egalitarian and exclusionary economic system.

## From the Mastery of Society to a Master-Servant Economy and Back

In economic terms, Calvinist theocracy consistently proceeds from the mastery of the social world to a master-servant economy, thus from societal to economic masters, and conversely. Calvinism's aimed total mastery of society and nature, as a species of "chiefdom consciousness" (Angel 1994), logically or eventually comprises the economy, thus resulting in a master-servant economic system as the constituent component of this societal rule and sanctified as Providential Design (Bendix 1984). Simply, Calvinist theocratic masters, political and military "chiefs" seek and typically succeed to become so in the economy also, making others their economic servants.

Negatively, it seems illogical and unrealistic to assume or expect that the Calvinist total mastery (or "chiefdom consciousness") of the social-physical world, by comprising the economy and technology as well, does not entail or generate a master-servant economic system, either pre-capitalism (slavery, feudalism, patrimonialism, caste) or capitalism. And, it would be irrational for Calvinism not to do so in respect of fully attaining its supreme aim. Alternatively, it is also illogical to assume or predict that Calvinism instead comprises or results in a liberal-democratic and secular economic system, notably modern capitalism in the form and sense of liberalism in the economy. Economic liberalism is *prima facie* deeply incompatible with the Calvinist total, specifically theocratic, mastery of the world. In essence, Calvinism's mastery of society, and thus theocracy as a total social system without a master-servant, and conversely with a liberal-democratic, secular economic, as well as political, civic, and cultural, subsystem, is incomplete or partial. Hence, it is "non-Calvinist" and what Weber calls an "impossible contradiction."

Simply, Calvinists, rather their charismatic (or not) leaders a la Calvin et al. (Heller 1986; Sorkin 2005; VanDrunen 2006), act as or aim to become masters of the world in a sociological, just as eventually geographic, sense, thus incorporating by assumption or in reality the economy. In short, they behave as or claim to be Divinely ordained rulers in the economy and society alike, including the polity, the civil sphere, and culture. Hence, they transform the economy, including both pre-capitalism and capitalism, into an equivalent economic system. This is the system in which Calvinist "godly" theocrats or divines act as pre-destined, "chosen" masters with Divine rights to rule and other "ungodly" humans are reduced to servants or subjects with their equally Providential destiny of serfdom or subjection owing to their damnation by the God of Calvinism.

By transforming the economy, including modern capitalism, into a master-servant system and sanctifying this transformation, like their theocracy overall, as Divinely ordained, Calvinists apply the foundational Calvinist doctrine of predestination. Specifically, they apply what Weber calls God's everlasting "double decree"[1] of salvation and

---

[1] Weber adds that Calvinist predestination "is a "belief of virtuosi, who alone can accept the thought of the everlasting "double decree." But as this doctrine continued to flow into the routine of everyday living and into the religion of the masses, its gloomy severeness became more and more intolerable. Finally, all that remained of it in Occidental ascetic Protestantism was a remains (*caput mortuum*), the contribution which this doctrine of grace made to the rational capitalistic orientation."

damnation, election and reprobation to the economy, just as society. Predictably, they claim to be and act as economic and total societal masters on the grounds that they are "saved" or "elected," and other humans are their servants or subjects (including "witches" in pact with the "devil", to be exorcised for their own "good") due to being "damned" or "reprobate", by the double predestination of the God of Calvinism. In this sense, Calvinist theocrats are or would be the masters of the economy and all society, because they are putative God's agents or representatives with equivalent Divine rights, belonging to, in Weber's words, the "aristocracy of predestined salvation". Thus, Puritanism in England and New England claimed to be "God's vice regent" (Zaret 1989) with the equivalent Divine right by its "chosen" theocrats to total mastery in society, including logically or ultimately the economy.

Hence, their mastery of the economy is a particular integral element and function of what Hume and Comte call the total societal reign of Calvinist-Puritan divines or saints respectively, or, in Marx-Weber's words, "sober" religious virtuosi Calvin, Cromwell, and Winthrop et al. In turn, this is a certain variation on the theme that, as leading sociologically minded contemporary economists recognize, the "conception of the *good economy*" is part of and conditional on the "conception of the *good life*"[2] (Phelps 2007) in society (not beyond). For instance, from the 1540s Calvin was able to "master" the Protestant Reformation in France and in the process to translate it into the "basis of an effective religious and political movement" (Heller 1986). Further, perhaps more than as a metaphor, these Calvinist saints (Mentzer 2007) were dual economic as well as religious-political masters, thus a sort of God's "double agents" or regents. They were the masters of other humans and of themselves alike through what Weber calls the "methodical mastering" of others' and one's own "conduct of life" in economy and society.[3]

---

[2] Economist Phelps (2007:555) acknowledges that "it is axiomatic that one's conception of the *good economy* depends upon one's conception of the *good life*." As a case in point, he remarks that "for John Calvin, the good life consisted of hard work and wealth accumulation" in sharp contrast to what Weber calls "joy of living" (*vitalism*) proposed by Enlightenment figures like Voltaire and Jefferson as well as later philosophers, James and Bergson (Phelps 2007:555).

[3] Pareto implies that such Calvinist and any "methodical mastering" (patho) logically or eventually results in and sanctifies what he calls as "tormenting" the "ungodly" and oneself alike and in that sense what other sociologists identify as a mix of sadism-masochism (Adorno 2001; Fromm 1941). After all, what defines Calvinist and any saints or ascetics is precisely Weber's identified "methodical mastering of one's own

Negatively, the economy, including modern Weberian capitalism, cannot fully escape and avoid Calvinist saints as the actual or would-be masters of all society, consequently their theocratic and generally totalitarian rule. In consequence, the economy, including capitalism, is ultimately transformed (if it is liberal-democratic) into, or self-perpetuated (if otherwise) as, a theocratic master-servant, and thus a repressive and anti-egalitarian, economic system. In sum, the observation that Calvinist theocrats, from Calvin et al. through Cromwell and Winthrop to "Bible Belt" fundamentalists, tend to act as predestined masters ("saved") and make all others ("damned") their servants or subjects in the economy (and society) justifies conceiving the latter as a proxy master-servant and thus unfree, unequal, and unjust economic (and social) system.

*Calvinist Vision and Reality of a Master-Servant Economy*

In economic terms, Calvinist theocracy and Calvinism in general is the vision and reality of a theocratic master-servant economy. Predictably, Calvin and original Calvinism provides the original theological design and "proof" of a theocratic master-servant economy as an economic subsystem and logic of Calvinist theocracy as a total social system, thus also Divinely ordained. As his theological writings as well as political practices in France and Geneva testify, he posited and, whenever feasible, instituted a master-servant economy in the form of a theocratic, "godly" economic system, with Calvinist theocrats like himself as masters and others as their servants or obedient subordinates subjected to methodical material and universal mastering, repression, and deprivation (e.g., poverty, extreme inequality, denial of charity or assistance, etc.).

For instance, Weber refers to Calvin's "much-quoted statement that only when the people [i.e.,] the mass of laborers and craftsmen, were poor did they remain obedient to God." Some contemporary analysts echo Weber showing that Calvin advocated obedience to "established secular authority", just as insisted on submission to the "new ministerial order" (Heller 1986), to feudalism and despotism and to the Calvinist

---

conduct of life" and in extension of that of others. Thus, Weber remarks that the "distinctive goal" of inner-worldly asceticism, epitomized by "ascetic Protestantism" or Calvinism, "always remains the conscious, methodical mastering of one's own conduct of life."

theocracy or church. Also, a sociological analysis (Grossman 2006) suggests that Calvinism was instrumental in keeping the masses "obedient" to the new theocratic order by its "irrational presuppositions" of "predestined salvation" via deep faith as well as total submission to rulers for the "glory of God". Weber adds that in this respect Puritanism was "quite in the spirit of the old Calvinism" in which humans "only" work and obey their Puritan masters "because and so long as they are poor". In general, he notes that Calvin and early Calvinism sanctified the "unequal distribution" of worldly goods as a "special dispensation of Divine Providence", just as poverty was condemned, as in Puritanism (Baxter), as "a symptom of sinful slothfulness", yet necessary for obedience to God and his self-proclaimed agents, thus religiously virtuous and instrumental in theocracy (in a seeming tension or contradiction).

Particularly, Weber identifies the "analogy" between the unjust (after "human standards") positive predestination or election of only a few ("a small proportion of men" being "chosen for eternal grace") and the "equally unjust" divinely ordained wealth distribution as "too obvious" to be avoided in Calvinism, including Puritanism. *Prima facie*, this implies an analogy and perhaps substantive identity between what can be described as theological-Divine and economic-societal oligarchy or aristocracy in Calvinism. The first is associated with the doctrine of predestination and the second with the Calvinist master-servant economy and society, as both are oligarchic or aristocratic. As Calvinism's doctrine of predestination is the dogma of "heavenly" (Zaret 1989) oligarchy or spiritual-religious aristocracy (Clark 1999), the Calvinist economy is an oligarchic and thus master-servant economic system, both privileging only a few versus most humans.

At this juncture, the Calvinist master-servant or oligarchic economy seems an economic version and realization of the theological doctrine of predestination of "heavenly" oligarchy, thus its masters as wealthy oligarchs (plutocrats) are the materialist variants of spiritual aristocrats. Weber's analogy implies that Calvin and Calvinism, like Luther and Lutheranism, furnished a medieval-style sanctification or rationalization—or a societal theodicy or sociodicy (Bourdieu 1998)—of sharp and perpetual economic inequality or anti-egalitarianism in feudalism. To that extent, Calvinism sanctified a master-servant economy substantively defined and typified by unjust (not solely unequal), yet in its theocratic version, Divinely ordained wealth distribution. Weber specifically notices that Calvinism, including Puritanism, embraced and further developed the "providential interpretation" of the economic system from medievalist scholasticism, citing Saint Aquinas's sanctification of class divisions and wealth inequalities in feudalism as a "direct consequence of the divine scheme of things."

Just as did Aquinas and other medieval scholastics, Calvin posited that the economic and all social system is God's "ordained" and consequently that differences in both wealth and social status and power ("station") are "inevitable" (Heller 1986). Following Calvin and by implication Aquinas, the supreme American Calvinist-as-Puritan Winthrop proclaimed (in his glorified 1630 address aboard *Arabella*) in virtually identical words the "divinely ordained and irremediable" condition of human society, in which some "must be rich" and "high and eminent in power and dignity", and all others "poor", "mean" and "in subjection" (Gould 1996; Kloppenberg 1998). Evidently, Winthrop inherited, along with his overarching "austere Calvinism", its and implicitly medievalist vision and reality of a theocratic master-servant economy as its economic logic and system, acting as the true heir of Calvin. Alternatively, this confirms that Calvinist total societal theocracy or "austere Calvinism" in both the old and new world, Geneva and New England, was effectively Weber's "impossible contradiction" without such a Divinely ordained master-servant economy in which differences in wealth and status are "inevitable" and some must be "high and eminent" in power and dignity and all others "in subjection". In short, a theocratic society was an "impossibility theorem" (Arrow 1950) without a master-servant economy, just as conversely.

Calvin's and in extension Calvinism's, including American Puritanism's, economic ideal was basically a pre-modern master-servant economy or feudalism, rather than modern, notably liberal-democratic, capitalism (Eisenstadt 1965; Grossman 2006; Heller 1986; Walzer 1963). This holds true in conjunction with the fact that the Calvinist political model or dream was the medieval Biblical theocracy a la the *respublica Christiana* (Nischan 1994), not liberal-secular democracy. At most, assuming that Weber is correct in his thesis of an elective affinity (yet see Alexander 1998; Cohen 1980; Collins 1997; Delacroix and Nielsen 2001; Grossman 2006; Hirschman 1977), Calvin's and generally Calvinist unintended aggregate outcome has been modern, yet authoritarian and theocratic, rather than liberal-democratic and secular, capitalism. In this sense, the outcome of Calvinism has been a "goodly" version of what economists and sociologists identify as capitalist dictatorship (Habermas 2001; McMurtry 1999; Pryor 2002; Schutz

2001), thus effectively a modernized or "capitalized" master-servant economic system. Recall that Weber does not necessarily or explicitly equate or connect Calvinist-based modern capitalism with liberal-secular democracy and civil society[4] (Aron 1998), and even some US "libertarian" and other economists[5] (Friedman and Friedman 1982; also, Binmore 2001) admit that capitalist economies historically have not been always democratic, but often combined with authoritarian or totalitarian political and social institutions. Further, by the "iron cage" metaphor of capitalist society and its "instrumental rationality" (Martin 1998) and the diagnosis of human "disenchantment" Weber implies that Calvinist capitalism may lead to an "enslaved humanity" deprived of the highest human values and to a "disenchanted world"[6] (Aron 1998).

At any event, Calvin's and in extension the Calvinist-Puritan economic system has been either by design (Merton's manifest function) or in effect (latent function) a sort of theocratic master-servant economy. The latter has ranged from pre-modern despotic feudalism or serfdom in Europe to modern authoritarian—repressive, oligarchic, and anti-egalitarian—capitalism, just as slavery before, in America (Pryor 2002). Calvin's is the paradigmatic vision and reality of conservation, rigidity, or petrifaction in the economy and society in the image of what Mises (1950) calls the "peace of the cemetery" in economic and societal terms. It is in view of the fact that the nature, operation, and outcome of a master-servant, either pre-capitalist or capitalist,

---

[4] Aron (1998:302) comments that "Weber had recognized that rationalization [capitalism] did not guarantee the triumph" of "liberal values" and thus liberal-secular political democracy and civil society. Overall, according to Aron (1998: xviii), the "continuity between Marx and Max Weber and between [the latter] and Parsons is obvious."

[5] US "libertarian" economist Milton Friedman admits that "history suggests only that capitalism is a necessary condition for political freedom. Clearly it is not a sufficient condition. Fascist Italy and Fascist Spain, Germany at various times in the last seventy years, Japan before World Wars I and II, tsarist Russia in the decades before World War I—are all societies that cannot conceivably be described as politically free. Yet, in each, private enterprise was the dominant form of economic organization. It is therefore clearly possible to have economic arrangements that are fundamentally capitalist and political arrangements that are not free" (Friedman and Friedman (1982:10). Similarly, Binmore (2001:229) recognizes that capitalism "does not need libertarian political institutions to flourish", citing the "totalitarian regimes operating before the Second World War in Germany and Japan" as largely capitalist economies.

[6] Aron (1998:301) adds that Weber "was too much of a Marxist [i.e.] too pessimistic in his interpretation of modern society", specifically Calvinist capitalism.

economy, are inherently conservative, rigid, or petrified, as well as Calvin's strict and essentially reactionary societal conservatism or traditionalism, essentially retrogressive medievalism.

Thus, historical research shows that in early 16th century France Calvin's strategy was two-fold: first, reassuring the monarchy and feudal rulers (seigneurs or notables) of the "essential conservatism" of his societal aims, second, undertaking "radical reform" in the religious domain (Heller 1986). Alternatively, Calvin's feudal master-servant economy, as indicated by the "lack of capitalists" (Simon 1995) or secondary pseudo-capitalist embryos in 17th–18th century France, was the economic dimension of the medieval-style Calvinist theocracy's "peace of the cemetery" in the sense of a "holistic" and eternal, God-decreed theocratic condition of society as a whole. In sum, the design and reality of a feudal-style master-servant economy, just as a medieval-type theocracy, epitomize Calvin's and overall Calvinist-Puritan medievalism or traditionalism. Thus, it does (in Comte's words) retrograde economic and political conservatism, or anti-liberalism and anti-modernism versus democratic capitalism and liberal-secular democracy and society.

To illustrate the above, a historical study suggests that the willing submission of the early Calvinist movement and bourgeoisie to the feudal nobility or aristocracy did not really disturb Calvin. Rather, it was completely in accord with Calvin's beliefs in the "inviolability" of the social order and the duty of individual Christians to submit themselves to the "divinely ordained" sociopolitical order (Heller 1986), first in France and then Geneva during the mid 16th century. By implication, this social order comprised an aristocratic or oligarchic master-servant economy in conjunction with a theocratic polity, thus feudalism economically and despotism politically. Further, in this account, while making "certain concessions", rather than contributions and direct links, to a nascent capitalist economy, Calvinism's economic or class bases did not "fit exactly" capitalism in virtue of appealing primarily not to capitalists but to small artisans, who in their attitudes were "violently hostile to capitalist control and subordination" (Heller 1986). The study infers that original Calvinism turned out to be an "abortive" bourgeois revolution or movement in France for its economic vision or system, far from expressing Weberian modern industrial capitalism, was "only partially" distinguishable from feudalism as an exemplar of a pre-capitalist master-servant economy or serfdom, and thus economically "immature"[7] (Heller 1986). Even if, as Weber and Parsons would suggest, it was fully distinguishable from feudalism, it was still authoritarian, notably theocratic and oligarchic, as opposed to liberal-democratic and secular, post-feudalism and capitalism and to that extent just another type of master-servant economy. Hence, in both cases a master-servant economy, feudal or medieval in the first case, capitalist or post-medieval in the second, was the economic system and ideal of Calvinism, thus its Biblical theocracy either as a reestablished social order or an eternal Providential Design and dream.

*Theocratic Economic Logic and Structure*

The preceding points to the intrinsic economic logic and structure of Calvinist and perhaps any other Christian and non-Christian, including Islamic and Hindu, theocracies. It indicates that the master-servant economy was and remains the logical and integral element, what Schumpeter may call the "inner" economic logic, of Calvinist and other theocracy, as elaborated below. This may be the iron economic "law" of any theocracy in general, not just its Calvinist type; and yet, Calvinism, and consequently Puritanism, is invariably theocratic and thus confirms the "rule".

Calvinist theocracy as a Divinely ordained total social system logically and historically requires and incorporates an equivalent economic subsystem as its creation and constituent, as perhaps do most, including Catholic, Islamic, and Hindu, theocracies. This is in principle and reality a theocratic and to that extent a master-servant economy as Divinely ordained as well. In this "Divine ordinance" Calvinist saints-theocrats become economic masters and other humans are reduced to servants either in the strict or broad sense, from pure slaves to "only" subjects or subordinates in Winthrop's meaning of "subjection" or "mean" condition. In short, it is God's *economic* Kingdom on Earth with a few "godly", "preordained" saints-masters ruling "ungodly", "damned" humans-servants. Calvinist (and perhaps any) theocracy reproduces,

---

[7] Heller (1986:258) adds that this "economic weakness expressed itself politically in the subordination of the Calvinist movement in France to the ambitions of a party among the aristocracy". In this account, even though small artisans established the anti-feudal (or proto-capitalist) "character of early French Calvinism alongside Puritan sectarianism" in England (Heller 1986:243–55), the eventual outcome was its subordination to the aristocracy and to that extent feudal forces and ideas.

explains, and predicts a theocratic and thus master-servant economy as its economic creation and element. Notably, in Weber's terms Calvinism's spiritual "aristocracy of predestined salvation" and/or "heavenly" (Zaret 1989) oligarchy acts as or claims to be the Divinely "elected" economic and total societal aristocratic or oligarchic master. In conjunction with or by analogy to these claims, those societies under Calvinism and Puritanism tend to claim to be God's "chosen" people or nation, including, as in the case of the Calvinist Netherlands, the "new Israel" (Frijhoff 2002) or, as with Puritan New England, the "new Jerusalem" (Dunn and Woodard 1996), a consistent and perpetual pattern observed from Calvin's Geneva and Holland to England and America, and a sacred rationale for wars of extermination against other peoples or nations as "ungodly."

While not all master-servant economies are Calvinist, including Puritan, thus theocratic or religiously based, but also secular or non-religious (e.g., fascist, communist, etc.), the opposite is essentially true. Namely, a Calvinist-Puritan, like other theocratic (e.g., purely Islamic, Hindu), just as an aristocratic, oligarchic and plutocratic, economy is invariably or ultimately a master-servant economic system. It is in virtue of the fact that its "spiritual" theocrats, analogously to aristocrats, oligarchs, or plutocrats, act as or claim to be economic masters and make all others Calvin's medieval-like servants or at most Winthrop's subjects. At least, Calvinism, including Puritanism, does not contradict and depart from but confirms and exemplifies—as do medieval Catholicism and fundamentalist Islam for comparison—the sociological rule or historical pattern. This is that a theocratic economy is universally a master-servant, repressive, and in that sense an anti-egalitarian one, just as theocracy as a total social system tends to reproduce or incorporate an equivalent economic logic and subsystem for its logical "closure" and empirical completion.

Conversely, a theocratic master-servant, thus authoritarian and anti-egalitarian, economy is in essence the only type of economic system created or designed by, integral to, or compatible with Calvinist and other theocracy as Providential design and a total social system. As noted, this economy comprise both traditional pre-capitalist (slave, feudal, patrimonial) and, as in Weber's framework, modern capitalist economies. In short, a theocratic master-servant economy is the economic logic, "body and soul" of Calvinist theocracy and of Calvinism in general. Hence, to assume or expect that Calvinist or any other theocracy would create and incorporate a different, *non*-theocratic and thus non-authoritarian, or liberal-democratic and secular type of economic system is not only apparently a logical non sequitur or inner contradiction. It is also, and more importantly, historically and empirically unfounded, as shown below. On this account, Calvinist *cum* Puritan Bibliocracy as America's "destiny" is, contrary to the claims to exceptionalism, not an exception to what, paraphrasing Michels' conception of oligarchy, can be posited as the "iron law" or sociological generalization of "who says theocracy says a master-servant economy."

Further, Bibliocracy is a paradigmatic confirmation or epitome and even intensification of the sociological rule that theocracy as a total social system generates and predicts a theocratic, thus master-servant economy, as its economic logic and subsystem. As elaborated later, Calvinist theocracies have been economically more or less typically master-servant economies, initially in the pure form of slavery and feudal serfdom, subsequently in diluted forms such as authoritarian, oligarchic, and anti-egalitarian economic systems. This is exemplified by the historical sequence and continuity from Calvin's Geneva and partly Holland via Cromwell's "Holy Commonwealth" and Winthrop's "Biblical Commonwealth" to the fundamentalist "Bible Belt". To wit, the inner economic logic and reality of Calvinist theocracy as the economy of theocratic, "predestined" "godly" masters and "ungodly" servants has been realized and confirmed in the past and present. In this sense, a theocratic master-servant economy is systemic ("built-in") and perennial, rather than random or exceptional and transient, within Calvinist Bibliocracy like those listed above.

Alternatively, a non-theocratic, free or liberal-democratic, including secular, as well as egalitarian and inclusive economic system is both a logical non sequitur and an empirical non-entity or rarity in Calvinist and other theocracy, as are liberty or liberalism, political democracy, societal egalitarianism, and universal inclusion within Calvinism generally, including Puritanism, and cognate theocratic religions (e.g., fundamentalist Islam). This holds true notably of liberal-democratic, secular, and egalitarian or welfare, as opposed to conservative-authoritarian, "godly" and anti-egalitarian "unfettered" or anti-welfare, capitalism (Esping-Andersen 1994; Pryor 2002; Trigilia 2002). This is an economic system contradictory to and incompatible with Calvinist and other (Islamic) theocracy, in spite or because of Weber's capitalist elective affinity of Calvinism.

In essence, liberal-democratic and egalitarian capitalism and Calvinist theocracy, just as liberalism, secularism, and secular egalitarianism and humanism versus Calvinism as a whole, including Puritanism (Munch 2001; Walzer 1963; Zaret 1989), are in principle and in reality profoundly different, incompatible, and mutually exclusive or contradictory. Simply, they are as divergent or opposite as are liberal humanist optimism or hope and conservative anti-human "original sin" pessimism or transcendental "heaven" (Lemert 1999). It is a difference epitomized in that between Hume-Kant-Jefferson's free, secular "pursuit of happiness" within human society and Calvin-Cromwell-Winthrop's theocratic bliss beyond the social world and their systematic subjection and eventual sacrifice of humans to the admittedly, as Weber implies, *not* so humane, compassionate or understanding, and even downright anti-human and anti-egalitarian[8] (Reiland 2006), God of Calvinism, or to his self-proclaimed agents *cum* economic and societal masters.

The ideal of liberal-democratic, egalitarian, and inclusive capitalism, just as liberalism, egalitarianism, universalism and humanism overall, as originated in and championed by the secular and anti-theocratic Enlightenment, is the polar opposite of what Weber describes as the absolutely transcendental and anti-universalistic God of Calvinism[9] (Bremer 1995). So are the former's representatives or precursors, Hume, Kant, Montesquieu, Voltaire, Condorcet, Smith, Saint Simon, Jefferson, Franklin, Madison, Comte, or Spencer[10] (and in part Locke, the supposed founder of modern liberalism) to self-proclaimed Divine agents and Calvinist-Puritan theocrats such as Calvin, Cromwell, and Winthrop (Dombrowski 2001; Zaret 1989). For instance, like Calvin before and Cromwell after, Winthrop was admittedly far from being a liberal

---

[8] Reiland (2006:47) comments and asks: "All this [in the economy] had been choreographed for all of us beforehand, predestined, so that God's favorites get the diamonds and the kid doing the panning dies at age twelve. Choreographed by what kind of God?" The answer is apparently contained in the question.

[9] Bremer (1995:225) suggests that "pushed to its logical extreme, the Enlightenment would later become a philosophical movement totally antithetical to the Calvinist world view that lay at the core of New England Puritanism. But in the early 18th century, in England and in the colonies, many were attracted to the philosophers" claim to have discovered natural laws, their optimistic view of man, and their skepticism toward all orthodoxies."

[10] This is due to Locke's "muted Calvinism" (Mitchell 1995), notably his endorsing and even prescribing Puritanism's intolerance to non-Christians or non-believers and even Catholics in England and beyond. For instance, Champion (1999:24) observes that "for Locke there were limits to tolerable opinion. Atheism and popery were beyond the pale" and comments that "so even for Locke, still studied as a founder of modern liberalism, the defense of conscience was ultimately rooted in a conception of the duty to pious conviction, rather than the logical rights of free expression [i.e.] the free ex pression of a Christian conscience, rather that the rights of free expression."

and (thus) democrat in virtue of regarding social hierarchy as "fixed" (and religious truth as revealed and absolute), and alternatively equality and dissent as "intolerable" (Kloppenberg 1998). And what Weber and Parsons et al. identify and emphasize or extol as the "elective affinity" or "intimate connection" of modern capitalism with Calvinism turns out, as intimated, on close inspection to be one of an authoritarian, specifically theocratic and oligarchic, and anti-egalitarian capitalist, thus master-servant economy, with Calvinist theocracy as a total and totalitarian social system.

Counterfactually, it could not and cannot be otherwise, as Weber intimates and Pareto and other sociologists (Inglehart 2004) indirectly imply.[11] Namely, Calvinist theocracy would lose or self-deny its inner economic logic and structure if it were to establish liberal-democratic, secular and egalitarian capitalism instead of a theocratic, capitalist or pre-capitalist (slave, feudal, patrimonial), master-servant economy. Equally, Calvinism would lost its "soul" if, by a miracle or self-denigration, it embraced liberalism, democracy, secularism, and egalitarianism rather than rigid conservatism, despotism, fundamentalism, and anti-egalitarianism. For instance, to contend that Calvinist theocracies (with the partial exception of Holland yet due to countervailing non-Calvinist forces) would and did do so is both a logical non sequitur and an historical fallacy, in a sequence comprising Calvin's medievalist *respublica Christiana* in Geneva, Cromwell's "Holy Commonwealth" in England, Winthrop's "Biblical Commonwealth" in New England as well as its revival through the "Bible Belt" in the "awaken" South and "Wild West". This contention or expectation is substantively analogous to contending or expecting that, say, Islamic theocracies in Iran and Saudi Arabia would entail or embrace liberal-democratic or secular, as opposed to theocratic or religiously-based (Davis and Robinson 2006; Kuran 2004), capitalism as their inner economic logic and system (Van Dyke 1995). Simply, the empirical plausibility or probability of such

---

[11] As an example of analogous, but not identical, counter-factual prediction, Pareto predicts that during the 18th century "had the French nobility living on income, and that part of the French bourgeoisie which was in the same situation, not succumbed to the lure of [liberal] humanitarian sentiments [the Enlightenment], they would not have prepared the ground for the Revolution that was to be their undoing." More directly related to the present matter, Inglehart (2004:8) also counter-factually hypothesizes that if Calvinism or ascetic Protestantism "had occurred two centuries earlier, it might have died out" with respect to its Weberian "intimate connection" with modern capitalism.

contentions or expectations is near zero, as witnessed in a sequence from Calvin's Geneva to Puritan America and the "Bible Belt" in relation to the long line of past and present Islamic theocracies (Mansbach 2006). In sum, the inverse of a theocratic master-servant economy, such as economic liberalism or democratic, egalitarian, "welfare", and secular capitalism is a liberal hope, dream, or utopia (Kloppenberg 1998). Conversely, it is condemned as "ungodly" and "evil" in Calvinist theocratic "heaven" as America's "destiny" or heritage and future celebrated by US religious conservatives (Dunn and Woodard 1996; Lemert 1999; Seaton 2006).

In general, a theocratic, oligarchic, anti-egalitarian or anti-welfare, and in that sense master-servant economy is the inner economic logic, while a liberal-democratic, secular, and egalitarian or welfare version is the non-logic (alien body) and non-entity, of Calvinist-as-Puritan theocracy and Calvinism or Puritanism overall. Simply, the true economic "name" of Calvinist theocracy is a master-servant, including capitalist, economy, and its corresponding misnomer or non sequitur is liberal-democratic capitalism, just as liberalism as a whole. This is important to emphasize in light of the conventional wisdom, albeit increasingly disputed or qualified, linking or attributing modern capitalism to Calvinism and thus its theocracy. This attribution results in an illogical and historically spurious link of economic and political liberalism (Kloppenberg 1998) with Calvinist theocratic anti- or pre-liberalism (Dombrowski 2001), of a liberal economy and political democracy with paradigmatic totalitarian theocracy! (Munch 2001; Stivers 1994).

*A Master-Servant Economy versus the Weberian Elective Affinity of Calvinism and Capitalism*

The preceding apparently reopens the question of whether and how the design and reality of a Calvinist master-servant capitalist (or non-capitalist) economy affects the Weberian assumed "elective affinity" or "intimate connection" between Calvinism and capitalism. While apparently unavoidable, this issue is secondary importance to the present aim, so a few remarks will suffice.

First, one can wonder how to reconcile a Calvinist master-servant economy with Weber's celebrated, yet disputed (Alexander 1998; Collins 1997) thesis of an affinity between Calvinism and modern capitalism. Presumably, the thesis is still plausible even after a myriad of revisions, critiques, and direct rejections[12] (Grossman 2006), as a "beloved myth" (Delacroix and Nielsen 2001) in Protestant societies and the literature, from Sombart to contemporary sociologists and economists, to the point of accumulating what Merton (1968) calls a "library of criticism" of Weber's work. On this charitable assumption, the solution is positing or realizing that Calvinist capitalism is essentially a master-servant or authoritarian and anti-egalitarian rather than liberal-democratic economic system, as Weber implies by his "iron cage" metaphor[13] (Aron 1998).

By design and in reality in Calvinism, including Puritanism, capitalism is a theocratic "godly" and to that extent a master-servant capitalist economy, with Calvinist-Puritan saints and theocrats as predestined masters and others as their servants or subjects in Winthrop's sense, as well as forced monks (Munch 1981; Zaret 1989). Alternatively, Calvinist capitalism is far from being, contrary what is usually supposed by Parsons et al., a liberal-democratic or "voluntaristic" (Mayway 1984), including secular, economic system. By substantive identity or analogy, the same holds true of fundamentalist Islam as, in Weber's view, a sort of substantive substitute or proxy of Calvinism, including Puritanism, in the Orient (Mansbach 2006). Like its Calvinist variant, also by design and in reality, Islamic capitalism, if any, is theocratic and in that sense a master-servant and generally authoritarian, repressive economic system (Kuran 2004), despite some egalitarian ideas of "economic justice" and charity (Davis and Robinson 2006).

After all, if for Calvinism, as Calvin et al. did and do proclaim, evangelical theocracy as a total societal system is Divinely preordained, Calvinist capitalism must logically and empirically conform with this

---

[12] Grossman (2006:205) states that Calvinism "had nothing at all to do with the origin and development of capitalism [for] its emergence [was] much further back than Calvinism and the Reformation. [It] did not form a *necessary precondition* for the *origins* of capitalism [as] capitalism emerged two centuries earlier in Italy without any help from religious irrationalism [viz.] Calvinism!". He rejects Weber's account ("petit bourgeois ideology") of "emergent capitalism" as "children's storybook idyll" on the grounds that "brutal, direct violence was the chief means used for compelling people to work" (Grossman 2006:206). Grossman (2006:212) infers that "renunciation, obedience, submission, are rewarded because they smooth the way to other-worldly salvation [which] is visible spirit of capitalism, not only of [Calvinism] but of every religion aimed at the domestication of the masses."

[13] Aron (1998:302) comments that in Weber, "a philosophy of struggle and power of Marxist and Nietzschean inspiration is combined with a vision of universal history leading to a disenchanted world [modern capitalism] and an enslaved humanity stripped of its highest virtues."

Providential Design as its economic logic and element. Hence, this capitalism originates, operates, and remains as a theocratic and thus master-servant economy in the above sense. In essence, Calvinist, like Islamic, capitalism is intrinsically a master-servant economic system in Calvin-Winthrop's sense of respective domination and subjection, because of its being *theocratic* or "godly", as is Puritan politics (Zaret 1989), a moment that Weber registered but not explicated and emphasized. And, Calvinist (and Islamic) capitalism is inherently or eventually theocratic because Calvinism (and Islam), including Puritanism, is the inherent and persistent theological design and societal system of theocracy.

The preceding redefines accordingly the historical transmutation of Calvinistic theology into the "spirit of capitalism" (Kaufman 2004), or the "Calvinist Reformation" into capitalist entrepreneurship (Morck et al. 2005). This was essentially or ultimately the transmutation of Calvinism and its theocracy as a total social system or design into an equivalent economic logic and subsystem, a theocratic master-servant capitalist economy. And, as hinted, it could not and likely cannot be otherwise both logically and empirically, namely transforming Calvinist, just as Islamic and other, theology and theocracy into secular and liberal-democratic capitalism as an economic system and liberalism overall. This is not only a logical non sequitur but also and more importantly an empirical or historical non-fact or rarity. Virtually all Calvinist-derived and, by comparison, Islamic capitalism has been a theocratic and in that sense master-servant economic system, from Calvin's Geneva and (in part) Holland to Cromwell's old England and Winthrop's New England and the Southern "Bible Belt" (and Iran). Simply, if Calvin conceived the doctrine of theocracy and his disciples "made" capitalism[14] (Kaufman 2004), then consequently the latter was a theocratic, master-servant economic system, thus a polar antithesis of a liberal-democratic and egalitarian or welfare capitalism, let alone political liberalism, secularism, and democracy. In systems terms, recall within Calvinism and consequently Puritanism, capitalism is the subsystem of

---

[14] Echoing Weber Kaufman (2004:340) remarks that "Calvinist Christians constructed a new repertoire of economic action out of their struggles with "salvation anxiety" and so by implication as the effect or part of their creation of Biblical theocracy as "Divinely ordained" or "God's Kingdom on Earth". Also, Morck et al. (2005) interpret Weber as proposing that the Calvinist Reformation "by emphasizing individual accountability, fostered a cultural shift that favored entrepreneurs over old-money elites."

Calvinist totalitarian Bibliocracy as a total social system, and in that sense a theocratic master-servant and generally authoritarian and anti-egalitarian economy. For instance, some economists identify and describe Calvinist capitalism in America during neo-conservatism a la Reaganism as an authoritarian, notably repressive and oligarchic, and even mafia-like (Pryor 2002), and to that extent a master-servant economic as well as political system, economy and state alike.

Conversely, Calvinist theocracy as a totalitarian social system, yet without a theocratic master-servant economy or capitalism as an equivalent and integral economic system, but with its liberal-democratic, notably secular, form, is a logical non sequitur and historical nonentity. Hence, to recognize and even celebrate, as most US Puritan-inspired religious conservatives do, that Calvinism reestablishes or redesigns theocracy as Divinely ordained, as in New England, and then to consider Calvinist capitalism to be a libertarian, democratic rather than a theocratic master-servant economy is logically contradictory and historically incorrect. Simply, Calvinist, like Catholic or Islamic, totalitarian theocracy and theocratic or authoritarian capitalism, and thus a master-servant economy, go logically and historically "hand in hand" as the whole and the part, as total sacred and partial material power. Alternatively, such theocracy and a liberal-democratic, notably secular, economic as well as political system eventually "part ways".

At this juncture, the Weberian elective affinity operates and reappears as that between Calvinism, including Puritanism,[15] and the "spirit" ("ghost"?) of *authoritarian*, as distinguished from liberal-democratic, capitalism. It does through the "inner relationship" between Calvinist theocracy as a Divine design or a total social system—and in extension the inhuman or harsh theological doctrine of predestination[16] (Fourcade and Healy 2007)—and a theocratic, master-servant capitalist economy as its equivalent economic product, logic, and subsystem. A historical exemplar is pre- and post-revolutionary America (e.g., 18th century New England) involving a fusion of Calvinist theocratic

---

[15] Thus, Weber observes that "Puritanism accepted the routinization of the economic cosmos, which, with the whole world, it devalued as creatural and depraved", and, one can add, consequently subjected to its mastery.

[16] Fourcade and Healy (2007:295) comment that "Weber was careful to show that the rational search for profit he observed among the protocapitalist Calvinists did not follow logically from their religious worldview. Rather, their actions made psychological sense as a way to relieve the salvational anxiety their harsh religious doctrines tended to produce."

theology and official theocracy (the established Congregational Church) with capitalism. Thus, in a historical account, Calvinist evangelical theology, including revivalism propelling the Great Awakenings, notably theocratic "ecclesiastical power", and "capitalist enterprise" or "acquisitive capitalist behavior," though "distinguishable" in principle, were in reality "indivisible", deriving from the "common ground" of austere Calvinism, in pre-revolutionary New England (German 1995). Hence, the registered and celebrated "triumph" of both Calvinism and capitalism in New England was effectively the joint victory of Calvinist theocracy and a capitalist *cum* theocratic master-servant and thus authoritarian economy, as its equivalent economic logic and system.[17] Conversely, it was not the triumph of Calvinism *and* liberal-democratic or secular capitalism and democracy, but their disjuncture and conflict, as indicated by the Calvinist (e.g., "New Divinity") theocrats' and theologians' attacks on "wicked" Jefferson for his liberalism, democracy, and secularism (German 1995; also, Baldwin 2006).

Consequently, Calvinist authoritarian capitalism functions as the particular form or substantive equivalent of a theocratic, master-servant economic system among contemporary capitalist societies, in particular America. This is what precisely is suggested or can be taken to suggest by the observation of American capitalism during religious and other neo-conservatism as further moving in the direction of an authoritarian economic and political system, notably an oligarchic and repressive economy and state alike conducting the ever-increasing Puritan-style repression of the population (Pryor 2002), notably labor and its collective organizations. In sum, considering a master-servant, capitalist or pre-capitalist, economy to be the economic logic and system of Calvinist theocracy as society is not contradictory to or contradicted by, but consistent with Weber's assumed elective affinity between *theocratic* Calvinism and modern *authoritarian* capitalism. And, if it is, it is impertinent for the present purpose, as is his assumption overall.

For, even if Calvinism, including Puritanism, did actually or could conceivable lead to, as in Parsons' and implicitly Schumpeter's framework, liberal-democratic capitalism as well as political liberalism, what

---

[17] German (1995:969:70) adds that, first, though Calvinism "could be enlisted *against* capitalism", they both triumphed in New England, and second, that Calvinism "buttressed" capitalism by "Calvinist theologians", not (as Weber assumed) by "psychological sanctions" of a belief in predestination.

Weber calls Calvinistic theocracies ("state churches") did not and could not by assumption. Instead, they resulted in and involved as their economic logic and system a theocratic and thus master-servant capitalist economy. This in particular holds of what Weber identifies as the Puritan "theocracy of New England". Significantly, he uses the term "theocracy" in the form of "Bibliocracy", not "democracy" or even "republic", thus implies an equivalent, theocratic type of capitalism or economy (Munch 2001). This chapter focuses on the economic system or type of capitalism of Calvinist theocracy rather than Calvinism in general, though, given that the latter is inherently theocratic, no substantive difference is found in this respect.

Overall, the previous literature hardly ever asks "what kind of capitalism" in its affinity or connection with Calvinism as a redundant question with a self-evident answer. Presumably, it is, as Parsons suggests, "liberal-democratic" capitalism in an apparent "libertarian" (or Mises-Hayek's) and generally economistic conflation between capitalism and democracy as economic and political systems, though Weber is more sophisticated or qualified and circumspect. In fact, Weber implies that as Biblical theocracy is Divinely ordained in Calvinism, so is consequently a theocratic economy or capitalism as its economic logic and system. And, if Parsonian "liberal-democratic" capitalism, just as liberalism overall, was established and sustained in America and other Calvinist-Puritan societies it was *not* because but rather in spite of and even opposition by theocratic Calvinism or Puritanism, as Weber and other sociologists (Munch 2001; Walzer 1963; Zaret 1989) imply and shown in this work. To put this statement in comparative perspective, if there exists Catholic or Islamic capitalism, like secular democracy, in its respective societies, this is not because but in spite and opposition of Catholicism or Islam, respectively. Curiously, while US Calvinist neo-conservatives and perhaps most Americans agree with and actually contend this, they refuse to apply the same logic and historical evidence to the relationship of American democratic capitalism or democracy to Calvinism. Moreover, Calvinism, notably Puritanism, has been the main (not the only) social force against liberal-secular society, including democratic capitalism, and in favor of its opposite, thus an undemocratic economic system, in America and beyond. This is logical or expected given Weber's "Divinely ordained" Calvinist theocracy, of which a theocratic and so master-servant economy, specifically authoritarian and anti-egalitarian capitalism, is an intrinsic logic and system.

*The Master-Servant Economy—America's Calvinist Economic "Destiny"?*

The above yields the seemingly dubious and even startling or outrageous inference. The master-servant economy operates as America's economic "destiny" or heritage in Calvinism through the agency of Puritanism. It suggests that a theocratic, thus master-servant or authoritarian, economy in the vision and sense of Calvin and Winthrop, including (but not limited to) its capitalist form, turns out to be America's Calvinist-as-Puritan economic "destiny". It is in the form and meaning of Calvin's style unequal and unjust economic distribution as the "special dispensation of Divine Providence" and Winthrop's command that "some must be rich and some poor, some high and eminent in power and dignity; others mean and in subjection" as the "divinely ordained and irremediable" condition of human society. Since a theocratic master-servant, either pre-capitalist or capitalist, economy constitutes the inner economic logic, creation, and subsystem of Biblical (or any) theocracy as a total social system and America's Calvinist "destiny", it is a consequent dimension of this predestination of the "new nation" by Calvinism via the agency of Puritanism.

As indicated, a theocratic Calvinist (and other) master-servant economy provides the paradigmatic exemplar of an unfree, unequal, and unjust economic system. It is thus what Weber might call the abomination of Jefferson-Madison's liberal-democratic, secular, egalitarian and fairness ideals of America as a society of liberty, equality, and justice "for all." These ideals are evidently destroyed or perverted by Calvin's Providential illiberal, unequal, and unjust economic distribution and by Winthrop's equally Divinely ordained wealth, "high" power and dignity for a few "elect", with poverty, indignity, and subjection for most humans. Economically, Calvinism is hence an axiomatic model of a sort of predestined illiberty, inequality and injustice[18] in the economy: economic repression, anti-egalitarianism, and inequity or unfairness (Reiland 2006).

---

[18] Reiland (2006:46) comments that in the Calvinist "theological blame game", "none of the calamities in this man's life come as a surprise, or as anything approaching real injustice. It's all scriptural, in full accordance with the Bible and God's will. Damnation deservedly comes to those who do bad things—damnation first in [this world], and then by way of disease, and then in the eternal sense. [Yet], those who aren't bad will inherit the Earth, including the best cars and houses, and then eternal bliss."

In its prevalent (but not sole) capitalist form in America, the Calvinist master-servant economy is theocratic and thus unfree, antidemocratic, unequal, including anti-welfare, and unjust, opposed to liberal-secular or free, democratic, egalitarian or welfare, and fair, capitalism. In essence, it is a sort of capitalist dictatorship (Pryor 2002) in the form of Hobbesian anarchy via unrestrained "free market enterprise" for Calvinist theocrats as "heavenly" preordained and "godly" economic masters, yet Leviathan or tyrannical oppression of the rest of the population (Wolff 2002) enforcing Calvinism's mastery or domination of the "sinful world." And, while not every master-servant economy in America, like elsewhere, is Calvinist *cum* Puritan in origin and character but also non-Calvinist (including Anglican as in the "old South"), the inverse is almost invariably true. The Calvinist inner economic logic and system in America, through the practice or design of Bibliocracy as a total social system, invariably or axiomatically has been a master-servant economy. It has thus been a polar opposite of liberty, equality, and justice, in particular, what Ross terms an antidote (or poison) of liberal-democratic, secular, egalitarian and inclusive capitalism, as witnessed in Puritan New (and old) England's defunct "Biblical Commonwealth", and its revival as "paradise lost", the Southern "Bible Garden" and beyond[19] (Reiland 2006).

Two general types and meanings of the Calvinist and Puritan theocratic master-servant economy in America and elsewhere can be identified and distinguished. The first type is a pure, primitive, or original master-servant economy. This type constitutes the inner economic logic and subsystem of Calvinist pure, primitive, or original theocracy (Sorokin 1970) as a total social system. The second type and meaning is analogously a diluted, derivative, or modern master-servant economy. By analogy, this type represents the inner economic logic and subsystem of Calvinist diluted and derivative, more precisely modern *cum* updated theocracy, yet remaining "pure" or primitive in the sense of Bibliocracy, thus understood. These two types of a Calvinist-Puritan

---

[19] Reiland (2006:47) relates the personal experience of being taught in mandatory chapel sermons at an American Calvinist college "Calvin's doctrine of predestination, the idea that God decreed, beforehand, the salvation of some and the damnation of others. It's the kind of doctrine that makes people anxious about whether they're stuck from day one in the bad crowd or the good one. To get some reassurance, this led people who believed this stuff to go full blast in achieving economic success, thinking that God signifies his favor by giving the best cars [etc.] to the elect. In short, the fat cats are God's people, hence "the Protestant ethic and the spirit of capitalism."

Table 3.1.  Types of Calvinist master-servant economy

---

I. Pure, primitive, original Calvinist-Puritan master-servant economy
   economic slavery
   feudal servitude
   caste system
II. Diluted, derivative, modern Calvinist-Puritan master-servant economy
   authoritarian, anti-egalitarian economic system
   predatory capitalism
   mafia capitalism ("Enronism")
   economic power monopoly

---

master-servant economy, with their respective subtypes (Table 3.1), are considered in this order next.

### Elements and Subtypes of the Calvinist Pure Master-Servant Economy

First and foremost, as noted, a pure and primitive theocratic master-servant economy is the economic logic, creation, and system of Calvinist theocracy with its equivalent attributes of purity and primitivism. As in general terms, while not every pure and primitive master-servant, either pre-capitalist or capitalist, economy is Calvinist, including Puritan, in origin and character, the inner economic logic and system of pure and primitive theocracy in Calvinism, particularly Puritanism, invariably and axiomatically is. In essence, pure and primitive Calvinist, like other totalitarian (notably Islamic), theocracy as a total social system or Providential Design logically and empirically necessitates, recreates, and comprises a pure and primitive theocratic, master-servant economy as its intrinsic economic logic and complement or subsystem. Simply, purist totalitarian Calvinist theocratic rulers tend to be, in order to fully "self-actualize" a la Maslow themselves, pure and total economic masters, while equivalently reducing all other humans to, to use Winthrop's word, "mean" servants or subjects, including slaves as their ultimate emanations. Alternatively, pure Calvinist and other theocracy as a Durkheimian total society is illogical and incomplete without an equivalent, theocratic master-servant economy, and totalitarian Calvinist and any theocrats and theologians cannot fully "express" themselves unless they also become total economic masters or plutocrats, as witnessed in 18th century New England (German 1995). The above then yields a sort of "iron law" a la Michels or Weberian sociological generalization that Calvinist pure or primitive and other theocracy entails or generates and thus predicts a pure and primitive theocratic master-servant economy as its inner economic logic and system.

Historically, a pure, primitive theocratic and thus master-servant economy has been the economic system of the Calvinist original, primitive, or early theocracy in Europe, Great Britain, and America from the 16th to the 19th century and, in certain (e.g., feudal) vestiges, beyond. Instances include the economic systems of such Calvinist-Puritan theocracies as Calvin's Geneva during the 16th century, in part Holland from the 16th to the 18th century, Cromwell's England and Scotland over the mid 17th century, Winthrop et al.'s New England from the 17th to the 19th century, as well as the South following the evangelical Great Awakenings of the 1740s–1800s. The economic systems of all these Calvinist theocracies can basically be considered or described as purely or primitively theocratic, thus master-servant economies, either manifestly, as in New England and the US South, or latently, as in France, Geneva, Holland, England, and Scotland. Specifically, these Calvinist economic systems were, first, theocratic slave-based economies as exemplified by New England under Puritan theocracy (Dayton 1999), as well as the South after, just as before, the Great Awakenings. Second, they were theocratic feudal serfdoms, as during original Calvinism (Heller 1986) in France. Third, they were theocratic or despotic, still feudal-rooted capitalisms, as during Calvinism's subsequent expansion to Geneva, Holland, England, Scotland, and America (Elwood 1999; Frijhoff 2002; Orren 1991). In turn, (if) these capitalist systems were tempered or even transformed in liberal-democratic, including secular, capitalism and liberalism (it was) primarily by countervailing non-Calvinist forces, such as Lutheranism (Germany, Scandinavia), Anglicanism (England), and, above all, the Enlightenment (particularly France, in part Jeffersonian America). This was epitomized by Holland's striking economic as well as political and cultural liberalization, with the "sin city" of Amsterdam as the epitome or symbol, in spite of and opposition by Calvinism as its "only true" Reformed Church (Hsia and Nierop 2002), primarily because of the Enlightenment (Kaplan 2002) and liberalism (Tubergen et al. 2005).

The preceding anticipates the subdivision of a Calvinist and other pure and primitive master-servant economy into economic slavery and feudal serfdom, as elaborated below. In general, a pure, primitive

Calvinist and other theocratic master-servant economy comprises at least three elements or subtypes: a slave-economy or economic slavery proper, feudalism in the sense of feudal servitude or bondage, and caste or an extremely closed system, considered next.

*The Calvinist Slave Economy*

A slave-economy or economic slavery proper represents the ultimate, extreme form of pure and primitive Calvinist and other theocratic, master-servant economies. In a strict or formal sense, economic slavery is different from, specifically more primitive, extreme, and absolute, than, the master-servant economy in the narrow form or meaning of feudal bondage as an historically later development, as witnessed in medieval Europe. In this sense, it is defined by what Simmel calls the "extreme of absolute inner hostility" subjecting humans to "mechanical appropriation" by others, or treating them, in Tönnies' words, as "inanimate tools" as the "very essence" of slavery. For broader substantive purposes, the present work classifies economic slavery thus understood under a pure master-servant economy as a general category, alongside feudal serfdom and caste.

*Pure Calvinist Theocracy and Economic Slavery*

By analogy to and in a specification of the above, while not all slave economies in America and beyond have been Calvinist-Puritan (but also, for example, Catholic and Anglican, as in South America and the US South, respectively), the inverse is also true. Namely, the inner economic logic and system of Calvinism, notably its pure, evangelical theocracy, is invariably, alongside feudal serfdom, slavery as the pure or primitive master-servant economy. Analogously, the Calvinist-Puritan purest and the most primitive or fundamentalist theocracy as a total social system for its completion logically entails or necessitates and effectively creates and comprises as its integral economic element slavery as the purest master-servant economy and supreme primitivism in this respect.

In a way, Calvinist purism and primitivism or fundamentalism in theocracy and religion overall cause and predict those in the economy through a slave-based economic system, in a seeming joint return to the theocratic and predatory "fundamentals", pre-liberal, pre-democratic, and pre-capitalist priors versus liberal modernity, including democratic and secular capitalism. In short, in a pure Calvinist theocracy, humans are treated as slaves or Winthrop's "mean" subjects to Divinely predestined masters rather than as "free individuals" (Lemieux 1997). Recall, not just Marx, but Weber implies by his "iron cage" image that Calvinist capitalism leads to an "enslaved humanity" deprived of its "highest virtues" (Aron 1998), even if he understands "enslaved" in a substantive, minimalist sense of what his contemporary Tönnies[20] calls "domination or mastery" as the proxy or "corollary" of slavery rather than in a formal-legal and literal meaning.

The preceding yields a specification of the "iron law" or sociological generalization about Calvinism and other theocratic religion in relation to a pure master-servant economy. This is that Calvinist and any pure, primitive or fundamentalist theocracy entails or generates, thus predicts a slave economy as its proper economic logic and system of primitivism. For example, Comte[21] intimates this observing that Calvinism ("Protestantism") tends to establish and provide "excuse" for slavery on the ground of "civilizing the enslaved." He likely refers to or evokes American Puritanism's supposed Divine mission of bringing "civilization" to, via conquest of, the "new world" (New England) and its "wilderness" embodied in the "wild" as well as "ungodly" Native Americans (Munch 2001). It thus refers to what contemporary research describes as "Puritan expansionism" via a "holy" war on and enslaving the "ungodly" such as Native Americans, a practice self-rationalized by its Calvinist agents as the process of "civilization" (Gould 1996).

As indicated, historically a master-slave economy has been the economic system of the Calvinist *cum* Puritan original, primitive, or early theocracy in America from the 17th to the 19th century. It has been specifically one of New England's early and long Puritan theocracy during the 1630s–1830s, as well as of the US South turned into a puritanical "Bible Belt" following the Great Awakenings as the expressions

---

[20] Tönnies adds that "all non-capitalists within [capitalism] are either themselves like inanimate tools—the very essence of slavery or they are legally nonentities. In his view, "slaves may be seen as "persons", as free conscious beings with their own power to make choices, exchange goods and form contracts." Hence, he infers that "out-and-out slavery is by no means legally incompatible" with modern capitalism (*Gesellschaft*) in contrast to "formal slavery" in Rome as a "rather apathetic and ineffectual matter."

[21] Comte elaborates that Calvinist Protestantism overall "leaves entire impunity to private oppression [except for] a few temporal rules generally framed and always applied by the oppressors themselves."

and expansions of Calvinist revivalism[22] (German 1995). An initial exemplar of a Calvinist pure and primitive theocratic master-servant economy was New England's Puritan slave or pseudo-slave economy, overlooked or downplayed and even denied by most US analysts and Americans compared to the slavery system initially established by Anglicanism in the "old South."

However, historical[23] and sociological analyses suggest that the economic system of New England's Puritan theocracy was actually a slave-based and generally master-servant economy, at least at some geographic and historical points (e.g., New Haven during the 17th–18th centuries, cf., Dayton 1999). It was also in respect of the relations between Puritans as the ruling religious and political group, or their theocratic and aristocratic leaders a la Winthrop et al. (Munch 2001) as predestined totalitarian economic and societal masters, and other groups, especially "ungodly" Native Americans ("heathen"), as their slaves or "mean" servants subjected to their theocratic Divinely ordained mastery to the point of "godly" persecution and extermination via "holy" wars as well as witch-trials. For example, a historical study suggests that New England's Puritan "self-contained" economy was based on the shared labor of slaves, for example, "Indian slaves, a few Negroes" and indentured servants (Foerster 1962). Further, it indicates that the early American Puritans revealed and practiced, as "particularly lucrative", a sort of spirit of capitalism (trade) "in slaves", starting from Africa via the West Indies to the Southern plantations and to, of all commodities, alcohol like rum (Foerster 1962). Another historical study specifically registers "enslaved Africans" and by implication Native Americans in Puritan ruled New England (e.g., New Haven) over the 17th century (Dayton 1999).

---

[22] To do justice to it, Puritanism in the Southern "Bible Belt" did not create, as it did in New England's "Biblical Commonwealth", but rather inherited, perpetuated and largely sanctified, with some abolitionist exceptions, a slave economy initially established and dominated by Anglicanism (Dombrowski 2001). In this sense, a slave economy was American Puritanism's economic logic or system at least as much as was of Anglicanism in the South and the Caribbean as well as Catholicism in South America, contrary to its standard claim to exceptionalism or nativism in this and other respects.

[23] The overlooking and even denying of New England's Puritan slave economy compared with the emphasis on and recognition of the originally Anglican slavery system in the US South is the "flip side" of considering Tocqueville's first Puritans, as he does, America's "Fathers" or "Pilgrims" (Seaton 2006), but not or less the early Anglicans actually preceding them in immigration and settlement for about 20 years (1607 vs. the 1620s), not to mention Catholic ("Papist") Columbus et al. and Amerigo Vespucci.

On this account, New England's Puritan economic system was in part a slave and thus master-servant economy, even if it institutionally or forcibly rendered slaves "just" a specific racial and religious category like "ungodly" Native Americans, and not others like the other (a few or minority) Christians, just as the Anglican Southern system of slavery did another single group. The Puritan, just as the antebellum Southern plantation, profitable slave economy or spirit of capitalism in slaves was only or primarily feasible and viable within an official Calvinist and other totalitarian theocracy in the form of the established Congregational Church (Dombrowski 2001), while unfeasible and unviable with "democratic political institutions" (Acemoglu 2005).

In turn, this "lucrative" slavery was part and parcel of the perhaps best kept secret in the history of American Puritanism (the Pilgrims), if not America overall. This is what a sociological analysis describes as Puritanism's "expulsion" of Native Americans from their lands, the "oppression" and the "destruction of their culture" couched and rationalized as "civilizing the wilderness" (Munch 2001). A historical study also suggests that for Puritans, the "guiding hand of Providence", "civilization", and especially the "emergent ideology of Manifest Destiny" of the new nation commanded the "disappearance of Native Americans" (Gould 1996). This command was a sort of optimum or maximum in religious as well as racial terms, and their enslavement the second best "rational choice" in an economic sense. In this account, Puritanism appropriated and exploited the Enlightenment's ideals of "progress", "reason", and "civilization" to "justify" its war against and the resulting enslavement, displacement, and ultimately near-extermination of the "ungodly" and "savage" nations like Indians (Gould 1996; also, Bremer 1995; Byrne 1997).

Given the sacred ideology of "Manifest Destiny" commanding the "disappearance" of Native Americans via what Simmel calls a lawless war of extermination or methodical murder, for these and other "ungodly" groups slavery or servitude, as well as their displacement, was effectively the "best" that they could hope for under the Puritan theocratic "hum of civilization". It was so insofar as, as he remarks, enslaving, instead of exterminating, imprisoned enemies generates a "sociological condition and thus its own attenuation". Alternatively, enslaving rather than, or combined with, exterminating imprisoned Native American enemies was a sort of "consolation prize" for Puritans in light of their ideology of "Manifest Destiny" and their practice of total "holy" war of extermination against the "ungodly", including non-Christians ("heathen") and Christian non-Puritans (Catholics) and even Puritan dissenters (Quakers, in part Baptists). Hence, such Puritan extermination as well as enslavement or subjection of "ungodly" and "savage" nations was by assumption and in reality primarily driven and sanctified by a mix of "holy" and national causes as represented in the notion of America's "manifest destiny".

These Puritan practices also perhaps secondarily were driven by the Calvinist "spirit of capitalism" through making profits on such "godly" activities, as none than its foremost critic Marx suggests in an overlooked, by Weber and others, yet indicative observation in this respect. Thus, in a typically, Veblenian sarcastic manner, Marx comments that "those sober virtuosi of Protestantism, the Puritans of New England, in 1703, by decrees of their assembly set a premium of £40 on every Indian scalp and every captured red-skin."[24] If so, then such actions graphically indicate that for early American Puritanism even slavery, just as milder feudal serfdom or what Winthrop calls subjection, was only the second-best "rational choice" compared to the profitable extermination of "infidels" as the Pareto-like economic optimum or maximum, just as was/is, as Weber and other analysts (Mansbach 2006) suggest, to militant Islam although presumably less driven by such material interests (Davis and Robinson 2006; Kuran 2004). It thus reaffirms that American Puritanism was the functional equivalent of Islam in terms of militancy, expansionism, and extermination or genocide via a total "holy" war, crusades and jihads, respectively (Turner 2002). Thus, "those sober virtuosi of Protestantism" were, while enemies in theological terms, "brothers in arms" with Islamic warriors in theocracy and the systematic murder or subjugation of "infidels." Yet, Marx, like most economists, including those staunchly anti-Marxian (Friedman and Friedman 1982), overlooks or downplays that the Puritan extermination of Native Americans was only secondarily driven by profit motives and primarily by religious factors a la America's "manifest destiny" or "Divine mission" as "godly" society, as were, if Tocqueville, Weber, and other analysts are correct, the pilgrim Puritans in founding New England.[25]

---

[24] Marx adds also sarcastically that the Puritans of New England by decrees of their assembly set "in 1720 a premium of £100 on every scalp; in 1744, after Massachusetts-Bay had proclaimed a certain tribe as rebels, the following prices: for a male scalp of 12 years and upwards £100 (new currency), for a male prisoner £105, for women and children prisoners £50, for scalps of women and children £50."

[25] Recall Weber suggests that Puritans founded New England for "religious motives" in contrast to Anglicans creating the Southern states for "business motives".

## The Calvinist "Rational Choice": Extermination or Enslavement?

The preceding implies that New England's Puritan masters faced a kind of "godly" variation on the classical economic alternative of Schumpeter's capitalist entrepreneurs (produce or buy for maximal profit)—exterminating *or* enslaving "ungodly" Native Americans as more "profitable". And, seemingly they solved this entrepreneurial problem by choosing the first course of rational action, thus revealing and materializing their Calvinist spirit of capitalism. Critics may comment that on this account, Weber's supposedly peaceful and Schumpeter's non-imperialist Calvinist spirit of capitalism, embodied by benevolent and generous Franklin (Byrne 1997), turned out to be a sort of capitalist "ghost"[26] of profitable murder, militancy, and expansionism in Puritan New England and in extension America. Cynics may add that by exterminating rather than enslaving Native Americans, New England's Puritans were perfect "rational choice" economic actors in realizing, perhaps the first in America, that slavery was less profitable or economically efficient, as well as what Smith and Ricardo may call more "trouble", "risk", and "inconvenience," than its alternatives, including the extermination or methodical mass murder of "infidels" for the "glory of God." They did so in stark contrast to Anglicans "irrationally" preferring economic slavery to the war of extermination of "infidels" in the old (Episcopalian) South.

In turn, this dual combination of primary "godly" and secondary economic imperatives commanding or preferring the extermination over the enslavement of the "ungodly" perhaps helps explain or shed light on why a slave economy was less comprehensive, prominent, and even invisible in Puritan New England than in the Anglican old South, and not, as usually assumed, "abolitionist" Puritanism as a putative explanation versus slavery-prone Anglicanism. Alternatively, if the Anglican Southern system of slavery was the only real slave economy, as commonly assumed (yet cf., Dayton 1999), in antebellum America, then a reason might have been that, in contrast to Puritanism, Anglicanism considered the extermination or methodical murder of imprisoned enemies and others both less "Christian" or human— namely, all humans as "equally valued by God" (Lucas 2000)—*and* less profitable than their enslavement. Recall, the latter is Simmel's "sociological condition and its own "attenuation", including even what

---

[26] In fact, Weber comments that in modern capitalism the Calvinist "idea of duty in one's calling prowls about in our lives like the ghost of dead religious beliefs."

some sociologists identify as some degree of slave economic mobility, as in Virginia (Budros 2004). Consequently, Anglicanism largely refrained from such extermination on either religious or economic grounds in favor of an ultimately inefficient and self-defeating system of slavery, while Puritanism adopted both as the optimum and the "second-best" option, respectively. Apart from economic considerations, emphasized by Weber and other sociologists, Anglicanism in the South and elsewhere (the Caribbean) instituted a slave economy rather than practiced systematic extermination. This was because it was by assumption ("British", "foreign" religion as construed and attacked by Puritanism following the Revolution) or in reality less actuated by the ideology of America's Manifest Destiny" postulating disappearance of "ungodly" and "savage" nations. In general, the likely reason for such a difference consisted in that Anglicanism, like Lutheranism, was, as Weber implies, less fundamentalist (despite some "evangelical" Anglicans or Lutherans), theocratic, ascetic, and anti-human (though not necessarily less racist) than was Puritanism and Calvinism as a whole[27] (Akerlof 2007). To avert misunderstanding, the aim is not to somehow justify what cannot be justified even by Simmel's sociological logic, the Anglican system of slavery in the old South versus the Puritan combination of primary extermination and secondary enslavement in New England. It is to pursue Simmel's logic that enslavement is a "sociological condition and thus its own attenuation" and in that sense "lesser evil" in terms of human life than extermination practiced as the optimum, combined with slavery as the "second best", by Puritanism. A fortiori, this holds true of enslavement in relation to a mix of extermination and slavery as created by Puritanism. Yet, it is striking that the sociological and historical literature, while justifiably emphasizing the Anglican system of slavery in the old South, de-emphasizes, if not neglects, the Puritan practice of extermination of the "ungodly", let alone "invisible" slave economy, in New England. At least, the above is "food for thought" to those wondering why and how Puritanism linked and preferred extermination to economic slavery as secondary, while Anglicanism[28] largely opted for a slave-type economy.

---

[27] Akerlof (2007:15) comments that "Weber describes Calvinists as aspiring to be 'worldly ascetics.'"

[28] At least, Anglicanism's extermination of Native Americans in the South and adjacent regions was secondary to the enslavement of Africans, while Puritanism exhibited an exactly opposite pattern preferring the first method to the second (of course, mostly in regard with Indian tribes).

In so doing, predictably American Puritanism reinvented and reinforced Calvinism with its explicit or implicit original commandment that the extermination of the "ungodly" via an equivalent, exterminating "holy" war is the God-decreed optimum or maximum, while anything else, including slavery or servitude, is the second-best "rational choice" or a "consolation prize." To better understand it, Puritanism's attempted, though not fully realized disappearance—if not genocide seemingly implementing the Bible's "genocidal instructions"[29] (Angel 1994)—of Native "heathen" Americans as the supposed realization of America's "manifest destiny" needs to be placed in the global comparative-historical framework of Calvinism. Consider that original Calvinism at the Calvinist synod near Paris, France in the 1550s concluded and prescribed that evangelicalism could be instituted only by means of "extermination" of various religious and non-religious groups, including Papists, *parliementaires*, libertines, nobility, etc. (Heller 1986). If so, then anything short of (war of) extermination or Puritan methodical murder is the "best" could happen to these "ungodly" non-evangelicals, including "heathen" Native Americans and internal "witches" (e.g., Quakers) in New England, just as perhaps to secularists and liberals, notably non-believers or agnostics (Edgell et al. 2006), in evangelical "Christian" America" (Smith 2000), at least the "Bible Belt". "Anything" ranges from slavery, subjection, and displacement in the first case to exclusion, marginalization, and discrimination in the second.

Moreover, what original Calvinism concluded and commanded but largely failed to realize in France and the rest of Europe, with the local and partial exceptions of Geneva and Holland, it did, through Puritanism, in New, as well as old England. This is the extermination of non-Calvinists by Calvinist powers such as Irish and other "Papists" by Cromwell's Puritan army and Native Americans by Winthrop's descendents. Puritanism operated as hyper-Calvinism and its masters acted as super- or over-achieving Calvinists on the account of the war and practice of extermination of the "ungodly" as the optimum or maximum *cum* profitable premium, and their enslavement or displacement as merely the second-best option or "consolation prize."

Likely, the Calvinist original conclusion and commandment that "thou shall" establish evangelicalism solely by the extermination (as the

---

[29] Angel (1994:342) suggests that the Hebrew Bible presents "genocidal instructions" and takes for granted the "acceptability of genocidal campaigns".

132    CHAPTER THREE

optimum) or the enslavement (as the "second best" option) of non-evangelicals operated as the prime mover of Puritanism's "contribution" to the disappearance of Native Americans. And, it self-perpetuates, with predictable mitigations and embellishments like exclusion (Edgell et al. 2006) and "saving" people from their "mistakes" (Terchek 1997), in Protestant fundamentalism in America. Recall Winthrop et al.'s Puritanism was "austere Calvinism" originated in Europe and transplanted into New England, thus including the Calvinist original command of extermination of the "ungodly" in the function of establishing the "true and only" religion. Most important to the matter under discussion, such an imperative and the corresponding practices made a slave economy a sort of secondary economic by-product or even inconvenience and nuisance, at least in New England under Puritanism and its attempted realization of America's "manifest destiny" through the "disappearance" of Native Americans.

*Composite Economic Slavery*

In intra-regional terms, New England's Puritan slave economy, while less comprehensive and almost invisible, due to being the secondary option compared with the extermination of potential slaves as the "godly" optimum, was even more consistently and intensively a theocratic master-serfdom economic system than was the Southern, initially Anglican, slavery system in America. While the second system was solely based on racial and not religious grounds, and to that extent racist but non-theocratic or secular (yet not necessarily more "humane" or "civilized"), the first was founded both on race and religion, and consequently racist and theocratic alike, thus even more total or totalitarian. While the Southern, non-Calvinist slavery system transformed into slaves only certain supposedly "inferior" races, New England's Puritan slave economy did both "uncivilized" *and* "ungodly" racial groups, specifically Native Americans enslaved not only because of their different race, but also, even more, of their differing "ungodly" Pagan or, in the Puritan redefinition of them and all pre- and non-Christians as the "heathen", no religion at all[30] (German 1995; Munch 2001). Hence,

---

[30] For instance, German (1995) cites the following statement of a New England prominent Puritan (Dyer): "Had not our forefathers had this spirit of emigration," America would have remained a "wild and uncultivated desert thinly populated with artless savages" [and instead] "invite the natives" to a "true knowledge of God".

Puritanism apparently adopted and implemented in the new world the belief of the Dark Middle Ages, alongside that in the existence of witches as the devil's emanations, that non-Christians like pagans *cum* "heathen" were savages "interesting as curiosities and useful as slaves", yet "undeserving of the Christian dispensation" (Byrne 1997).

In this sense, the Puritan theocratic economic system was a double or composite, almost perfect slave-economy, not just slavery but doubly or perfectly so. It hence made non-Puritans, at least Native Americans, slaves not only because of their "inferior" race but even more of their "ungodly" or "false" religion and culture. Apparently, the early American Puritans aimed at and to some extent attained "purity" and "perfection" in economic slavery or Winthrop's subjection, as in theocratic rule and totalitarian domination over the "sinful world". What is a sociologically significant and remarkable, yet overlooked difference, between the two, Puritan and non-Puritan, forms of economic slavery proper in past America is Puritanism's composite or juxtaposition. In contrast to its arch enemies like Catholicism in South America and Anglicanism in the old South, Puritanism in New England juxtaposed theocratic—at least "Christian" equated with "Calvinist" or "Protestant" versus "non-Christian" or "pagan"—religion to biological race and "inferiority" as the foundation and rationalization of a master-slave economy.

Notably, the above difference indicates that New England's Puritan slave economy was in fact the most theocratic and thus totalitarian master-serfdom economic system in antebellum America, and in extension post-medieval Europe where slavery had been officially abolished and replaced by feudal serfdom as its actual or supposed mitigation and relaxation. This then made American Puritanism, just as less theocratic and less ascetic Anglicanism, and in consequence the new nation primitive, anachronistic, and degenerate in relation to the despised "old world", including ancient Rome[31] (Temin 2006) and its slavery system, as indicated by the European Enlightenment's theories about "degeneracy in the New World" (Gould 1996). At this juncture, its double, racist-theocratic, slave economy rendered American Puritanism the most primitive, anachronistic, and degenerate, just as its theocracy

---

[31] Temin (2006:141–2) finds that the manumission rate (freeing slaves) in the early Roman Empire was 10% of slaves for a period of five years and only 0.2% in the US South during the 1850s. Moreover, Temin (2006:142) suggests that Roman slavery "conformed to the open model" of slave society "in sharp contrast to American slavery" as the opposite.

made it the most tyrannical or totalitarian, Calvinism in economic terms. It was so given that even in Calvinist ruled regions like France (partly and temporarily), Holland (almost totally), and Switzerland and Prussia (locally), as well as Puritan England, slavery had been long before abolished and replaced by the milder feudal serfdom and later on, as Simmel implies, despotic capitalism or a "money economy".

By assumption and in reality New England's slave economy was such because its larger societal framework and creator, New England's Puritan Bibliocracy as a total social system was the "most totalitarian" Calvinist theocracy and American Puritanism a sort of super-Calvinism or Calvinism "out of control", more theocratic and thus Calvinistic than Calvin et al. In short, such a total or totalitarian theocratic social system incorporated and sanctified a slave economy as its economic logic and subsystem with the equivalent traits of totality or totalitarianism. And, like any pure theocracy this Puritan form axiomatically had to juxtapose religion to race—only used by the original Southern non-Puritan non- or less theocratic slavery system—as another basis and even supreme God-given justification of a slave economy thereby made actually or potentially more composite, totalitarian, or "perfect". Generally, while lesser in scope and visibility, New England's Puritan slave economy was more totalitarian or "perfect" in the sense of combining race and religion as the grounds for recreating humans as "masters and slaves" or Winthrop's rulers and subjects than the non-Puritan Southern slavery system. This was because American Puritanism, following on and reinforcing Calvinism, was both racist, nativist (Merton 1939) or nationalist (Friedland 2001) *and* theocratic, religiously fundamentalist and intolerant, morally absolutist and extremely ascetic, while Anglicanism, like Lutheranism, was not the second or more moderate in this respect, as Weber and other sociologists suggest (Munch 2001).

And, in the post-Anglican South as the "Bible Belt", Puritanism adopted, reinvented, and solidified an existing non-Puritan slavery system though based solely on race (but not religion as that in early New England), through and following the Great Awakenings, especially the Second in the wake of the American Revolution (the 1800s). For instance, Spencer points to the "holding of slaves by [Southern] ministers of religion in America", including implicitly both non-Puritan (Anglican) and Puritan slave-holders. In addition, Puritanism and its ramifications (e.g., Southern Baptism) typically and fervently sanctified, with some minor exceptions of "abolitionism," the Southern slave system that it inherited from Anglicanism as Providential Design. Thus,

Mises (1950) remarks that most of Protestantism, including by implication Puritanism, "supported the slave-economy of American plantations", as exemplified by the "wily proslavery "priesthood"" (Clark 1999). Furthermore, Puritan evangelicals (e.g., Southern Baptists) became the foremost defenders of the system of slavery in the old South as, like Biblical theocracy, Divinely ordained, thus exhibiting the old pattern for converts claiming to be "greater Catholics" than the Pope as a parable, specifically more Calvinist than Calvin.

In turn, both New England's proto-Puritan and Southern neo-Puritan (and Anglican) slave economies were inconsistent or impossible along with "democratic political institutions" (Acemoglu 2005). Conversely, they were both solely or mostly consistent with or possible in Calvinist and other totalitarian theocracy like the old and new "Biblical Commonwealths", respectively. In sum, both Puritan ruled New England and the South following the Great Awakenings were essentially defined by the "twin inhumane institutions of Calvinism and slavery" (Clark 1999), thus a Calvinist theocracy and a master-servant economy.

In comparative-historical terms, American Puritanism was perhaps the only form of Protestantism, if not Christianity overall, that established slavery on the religious basis of "godly" versus "ungodly" in post-Reformation times, alongside, expansionist Islam via, for example, the Ottoman Turkish empire (Kuran 2004). Hence, Puritanism and Islam (as Weber implies) instituted, maintained, and sanctified slavery or subjugation, just as extermination or genocide by a "holy" war against "infidels", crusade in the first case, and jihad in the second (Gorski 2000; Turner 2002). On the account of its religiously grounded slavery as well as its extermination of "infidels" (Native Americans, etc.), American Puritanism, like Calvinism as a whole, was from the beginning the "Christian" substantive substitute or proxy for militant Islam (Mansbach 2006), just as for arch-ascetic Sparta before (Kloppenberg 1998). And, in a striking continuity or path-dependence (Inglehart 2004), Puritanism over-determined or prefigured the observed functional equivalence of modern Puritan America, notably the evangelical "Bible Belt" (Bauman 1997), with Iranian and other Islamic theocracy in many respects. These include "slave-like" (Wacquant 2002) economic settings (coerced prison labor, suppressed unions), just as Draconian legal institutions like a vice-police state, executions for sins and/or crimes, and culture or temperance wars and warriors (Friedland 2002; Jacobs, Carmichael and Kent 2005).

At this juncture, in Puritanism and Islam slavery or subjugation functioned, as in Puritan New England and the Ottoman Islamic Empire (e.g. the mass killing of Armenians and other Christians in the former Byzantine), as the "second best" option in relation to extermination or genocide as the optimum or maximum with its, as US militant neo-conservatives put it, "take no prisoners" logic and "method in the madness". This consequently made post-slavery feudal serfdom the distant "third best", not to mention a diluted master-servant economy in which labor is legally free, as a sort of luxury, in both Puritanism and Islam. It perhaps helped explain why American Puritanism, first, started with or preferred the extermination of the "ungodly" to their enslavement or subjugation, as did, in Weber's account, militant Islam, second, as a secondary option, established slavery, even if this had been abolished in the old Europe long ago, rather than feudal serfdom (Winthrop's *mixt aristocracie*) as a third alternative adopted, in various "new world" disguises, when the first two were impossible or imprudent. Moreover, on the account of preferring slavery (for Native Americans, at least) to feudalism as its evolutionary "milder" sequel Puritanism was even more anachronistic or primitive, brutal and anti-human than militant Islam commonly considered a feudal economic system (Kuran 2004). In turn, this economic primitivism was part of Puritanism's Calvinist vision and reality (e.g., Salem, etc.) of America as primitive "Christian Sparta" (Garrard 2003; Kloppenberg 1998).

### *Calvinist Feudal Servitude*

Another subtype and element of a pure Calvinist theocratic master-servant economy is feudal servitude, serfdom, or bondage, used interchangeably, simply feudalism historically succeeding and substantively attenuating economic slavery as the primitive type. Such a historical pattern holds true of Europe and the rest of the world (Russia, Turkey, Japan) in contrast to America and some other former colonies (Brazil, the Caribbean) where the sequence has been different and even opposite, with slavery succeeding (though not mitigating) or "skipping" feudal servitude as the stage of a master-servant economy in the Anglican South and Puritan New England during antebellum times. At any rate, feudal servitude is the paradigmatic exemplar of a master-servant economy, even its axiomatic form and proper meaning, if masters or lords and servants or serfs as non-slaves in a strict sense are characteristic for feudalism in contrast to slave-holders and slaves populating a more primitive or antecedent slave-economy.

*Calvinist Theocracy and Feudalism*

Despite, in Weber's view, "opposing all concessions to feudal 'wastefulness'" by Calvinism or ascetic Protestantism, Calvinist theocracy's economic logic or system is essentially a feudal-style master-servant economy. It is at least as the second best "rational choice" if and when slavery as the Pareto-optimum or maximum—abstracting from the Calvinist extermination of "infidels" as a non-economic category even when profitable, as was for American Puritans—has become the dead past impossible to retrieve and economically unfeasible, non-profitable, or just inefficient. In short, it is a medieval, estate-based economic and societal order in which the Calvinist-Puritan "aristocracy of predestined salvation"[32] acts as one, or the oligarchy, of the economy and society. Thus, Calvinism, including Puritanism, like religious conservatism overall, is observed to reveal a "curious preference for social collectivities" (Dahrendorf 1979), including, and conjoined with medieval church and patriarchal family (Gould 1996), hierarchical feudal estates like aristocracy, clergy, and peasantry, as well as the bourgeoisie (Collins 2000) originating as an integral element of a feudal society based on the "estate principle" (Habermas 1989; also, Grossman 2006).

First and foremost, recall Calvin's original economic vision and system turned out to be essentially feudal or medievalist in character, at least closer to despotic feudalism than modern liberal-secular, as distinguished from illiberal or theocratic, capitalism (Grossman 2006; Heller 1986), as were, with certain secondary modifications, those of his Puritan disciples in old and New England like Cromwell and Winthrop. For example, it is instructive to remember that New England's theocracy by Winthrop et al. (Munch 2001) was "merciless" (Tawney 1962) not only to political and civil, including moral-religious, liberties. It was also so to unrestrained individual economic freedom seen as a threat ("Mammon") to the "Puritan dream of the godly community" (German 1995) and defining what US "libertarian" economists and neo-conservatives celebrate as laissez-faire, "unfettered" capitalism

---

[32] Weber adds that "in no other religion was the pride of the aristocracy of predestined salvation so closely associated with the person of a vocation and with the idea that success in rationalized activity demonstrates god's blessing as in Puritanism".

(Fishback 1998). To that extent, it was more feudal and thus medievalist than capitalist in economic terms, just as axiomatically totalitarian rather than liberal-democratic politically and socially. Notably, its supreme master's, Winthrop's vision and reality of the economy, polity, and society overall was what he called *mixt aristocracie* (Bremer 1995) and even, in Weber words, "hereditary nobility", or aristocratic theocracy. In that sense, it was fundamentally feudal and medievalist rather than, as usually assumed, capitalist, let alone liberal-democratic, secular, and egalitarian. Recall, far from being an early liberal or egalitarian, Winthrop was the exact opposite, considering feudal-style and other economic-social hierarchy "fixed" and "ideas of equality and dissent intolerable" (Kloppenberg 1998). Yet, he could not have been otherwise because his sociological "heart and soul" was "austere Calvinism". Overall, Tocqueville's first American Puritans accepted and perpetuated economic and social inequality or hierarchy, thus coercion and oppression "as a natural part of God's plan" (Kloppenberg 1998).

After all, Calvin et al., including Winthrop, like Luther and their counter-Reformation Catholic adversaries, still lived in feudalism and medievalism overall (the 16th–17th century), at least in Smith's, Marx's, in part Weber's, Schumpeter's, and other prominent economic and sociological accounts of modern capitalism ushered in by the 18th century Industrial Revolution. Despite their attributed Weberian charismatic powers (Heller 1986) or strong leadership (e.g., about Winthrop, cf., Munch 2001), and visionary ideas, they evidently sanctified the late feudal economic and political system as Divinely ordained, and thus could not transcend it by modern capitalism[33] (Grossman 2006; Walzer 1963), let alone liberal-secular democracy, civil society, and culture (Zaret 1989). For instance, what Spencer remarks about Luther holds true also and perhaps more of his contemporaries or successors like Calvin et al. (Sorkin 2005) and subsequent Calvinist Puritans such as Cromwell and Winthrop. In Spencer's words, "to those living in the feudal times, so unquestionable seemed the duty of serfs to obey their lords, that Luther (no doubt acting conscientiously) urged the barons to vengeance on the rebellious peasants, calling on all who could

---

[33] Walzer (1963:63) finds what he calls the "basic incompatibility of Puritanism with both liberalism and capitalism". In particular, he suggests that the "effort to establish a Holy Commonwealth (to universalize the tension and repression) is rendered inexplicable once liberalism and capitalism are read" into Puritanism (Walzer 1963:68).

"to stab them, out them down, and dash their brains out", as if they were mad dogs", as well as forces helping destroy the old social and economic order (also, Markoff 1997).

Moreover, as noted, Winthrop and other Puritan theocrats converted or redesigned, when not exterminating for Divine glory, obedient feudal serfs into subhuman slaves in New England (Native Americans) and then, via the Calvinist-propelled theocentric Great Awakenings (German 1995), inherited and perpetuated or sanctified economic slavery in the antebellum South. Such a conversion, just as the extermination as the sociological and even economic Pareto-optimum, of potential servants into actual slaves reveals a striking and unparalleled, yet denied or neglected by overly patriotic US analysts (Lipset and Marks 2000) and others, evolutionary retrogression or involution from feudal serfdom to slavery in America rather than conversely, as happened in Europe and beyond. To that extent, it is this evolutionary regression into despotic pre-capitalism, instead of the "quantum leap" to liberal-democratic capitalism, that turns out to be true original, Puritan-rooted, American exceptionalism in economic terms.

The above highlights what Comte detects or implies as Calvinism's and in particular American Puritanism's remarkable retrograde, anachronistic, degenerate (Gould 1996), even ultimately—*pace* Weber and Parsons—irrational[34] (Grossman 2006), character and effects in economic as well as political, civic, and cultural terms. It indicates that, contrary to theirs and their descendants' claims to novelty and exceptionality, Tocqueville's first Calvinist Puritans effectively made the "new", "exceptional" nation" (Lipset 1996) even older, so less exceptional economically than the despised "old world" left behind in the search for a "promised land". They did so by reestablishing what had been the dead past in Europe for long (at least ten centuries), a slave economy, and thus the purest, harshest, and the most irrational master-serfdom economic system. In conjunction, politically they reinstituted the most totalitarian medievalist or primitive (fundamentalist), anti-rationalist or superstitious Calvinist theocracy (e.g., persisting beliefs in witches and witch-trials, cf., Byrne 1997; Harley 1996).

---

[34] Grossman (2006:211) suggests that that, like all religion (including Lutheranism), Calvinism is a form of "religious irrationalism" in virtue of being an "instrument for distracting the masses from the struggle for a rational structuring of their fate in life– an instrument of mass domestication."

## Calvinist Feudalism Déjà Vu

Since, to cite Pareto, slave economies, like elites or aristocracies and dictatorships, "do not last" forever, their version in New England formally or substantively ended due to or coinciding with the disestablishment of its pure Puritan theocracy, primarily attributed to "wicked" Jefferson et al. (Baldwin 2006; German 1995), in favor of secular democracy over the 1830s. This is implied in the moment that slavery was impossible to coexist with "democratic political institutions," just as it ended via a civil war in the post-bellum South. Following the formal termination of its slave economy, Puritanism or sectarian Protestantism far from relegating its master-servant economic logic and system to the dead past continued to search and seemingly found what economists may call an imperfect substitute, reaffirming its Calvinist "iron consistency" or "obstinacy." Namely, it substituted the slave economy with a sort of feudal-style master-servant economic system or what analysts call "belated feudalism" (Orren 1991) evoking, if not retrieving, that of medieval Europe, with capitalist embellishments and rationalizations, and existing within the nominal or official setting of "unfettered" capitalism.

Like that of original Calvinism, American Puritanism's "second-best" economic system is feudal-like serfdom, with "all-American" "free enterprise" and political (authoritarian) "apple-pie" sweetening (Beck 2000; Wagner 1997). It is whenever a true slave-economy as the Pareto-optimum or economic maximum (abstracting from exterminating the "ungodly" enslaved) is impossible, inexpedient, and unprofitable or inefficient to reestablish from the primitive past, as in America since the 1860s. At this juncture, surprisingly, if not "shockingly", Weber's Calvinist capitalism reemerges and operates in America as the "new" feudalism or feudal patrimonialism (Cohen 2003) and to that extent a theocratic master-servant economy rather than, as commonly supposed, a liberal-democratic secular capitalist economic system, elaborated next. Moreover, this is what Weber himself in part implies by observing that "everywhere the casing of the new serfdom is ready", implicitly in the new form of his capitalist "iron cage" (Aron 1998) as a sort of "neofeudalism" in its "triumphal advance",[35] defined by oligarchic rule (Binmore 2001).

---

[35] Binmore (2001:230) adds that new forms of feudalism "have emerged in modern times". In this view, a neo-feudal economy and society is one "in which the same oligarchs rule all the time" (Binmore 2001:229).

Further, some of Weber's American contemporaries (Ghent 1902) explicitly rediscover and describe Calvinist capitalism in America as what is called "Benevolent Feudalism" and in that sense an anti-liberal, non-democratic, anti-egalitarian, and anachronistic economic, political and social system. In this view, late 19th century American capitalism turned out to be feudalism defined by a "baronial regime", mixing the "rapacity of the masters" with the "blindness" of laborers, combined with "almost pure paternalism" or "enlightened absolutism" against the "democratic spirit and will", and represented and ruled by the notorious capitalist robber barons. Contemporary analysts also observe that during the early 20th century what US "libertarian" economists identify and glorify as "unfettered capitalism" (Fishback 1998) after the model or image of Hobbesian economic anarchism actually operated or appeared as benevolent feudalism threatening "individual autonomy" in America by analogy to conservative authoritarianism (e.g., Bismarck's authoritarian "welfare state") in Germany (Kloppenberg 1998).

At this juncture, the term "robber barons", like "baronial regime", appears particularly symptomatic of the feudal and medievalist origin, character, or effects of Calvinist capitalism in America, and perhaps, as Pareto[36] suggests, of Calvinism and even Protestantism overall. After all, as Weber remarks, the US capitalist robber barons "always wanted to live like feudal lords", which is perhaps why they have been described and even publicly or secretly admired as such by many Americans[37] (Merton 1968). In general, the reality or concept of "Benevolent Feudalism" perpetuates and exemplifies in America what is often called "enlightened" feudal or post-feudal despotism and despots in Europe. In turn, it anticipates or resembles what sociologists describe as Puritan-rooted moral "friendly fascism" (Gross 1980; also, Bonefeld 2002; McCleary 2002) in modern America, notably the evangelical "Bible Belt" and its extensions, as discussed later.

---

[36] Pareto states that the Protestant Reformation involved the "emergence of the robber barons" (e.g. Sickingen and Hutten) or a "revolutionary knighthood". Apparently, he uses the term "robber barons" in the literal sense of actual violent robbery in contrast to its largely metaphorical meaning in American capitalism.

[37] Referring to Veblen, Merton (1968:195) notices that "the history of the great American fortunes is threaded with strains toward institutionally dubious innovation as is attested by many tributes to the Robber Barons." Notably, he comments that Americans" "reluctant admiration" for the robber barons as " "shrewd, smart and successful" men is a product of a cultural structure in which the sacrosanct goal [of success] virtually consecrates the means" a la Machiavelli (Merton 1968:196).

Also, following and elaborating on this early rediscovery, some contemporary historical analysts identify and describe capitalism in America during the late 19th and early 20th centuries as "belated feudalism" (Orren 1991), just as, implicitly, in England[38] (Ingram and Clay 2000). In this historical account, as a "vestige of a feudal past" providing capitalists with the "leverage of state authority" for subjugating laborers, the English common law of "masters and servants" defined labor in America, like in England during its laissez-faire capitalism (Steinfeld 2001), as unfree and lying at the "foundation of capitalist development and industrialism" (Orren 1994). In consequence, American capital-labor relations were in their "essential character feudal" during the 19th and early 20th century until the New Deal and its economic liberalism (also, Allan 1991). The study infers that pre-New Deal anti-labor laws solidified and rationalized a "structure of domination" preexisting "time out of mind" to the effect that even during the 1930s economic and other liberalism did not really displace repressive capitalism (Orren 1991), thus indirectly, given its legal basis in the English common law of masters and servants, belated feudalism. In sum, these historical observations document and confirm what US conservative sociologists (Dunn and Woodard 1996; Nisbet 1966) otherwise extol. This is that European and American religious conservatism, including Calvinism and Puritanism (like Catholicism), rediscovers feudalism as the "model" of the conservative design of the "good society" and its "bequeathed" economic and social-political order as "absolute reality," thus evidently "priceless" heritage.[39]

*Calvinist Neo-Feudalism*

By analogy, the Calvinist-rooted neo-conservative economic system in modern America can be considered or described as a sort of new master-servant, a neo-feudal economy and society, thus "benevolent feudalism" déjà vu, as some sociological and economic observations suggest (Beck 2000; Bourdieu 1998; Cohen 2003). If the proto-Calvinist

---

[38] Ingram and Clay (2000) note that in early pre-industrial England "feudal rules persisted". Also, Steinfeld (2001:82) remarks that "in the most advanced capitalism of the 19th century [England], wage labor, was, by modern standards, unfree labor".

[39] Thus, Nisbet (1952) admits and extols alike that American and European religious conservatism in general considers feudal arrangements like medieval estates, notably aristocracy, conjoined with church and theocratic state, as the "absolute reality" of an economic, political, and social order "bequeathed" by feudalism.

economy in historical America was, as the above suggests, legally or substantively "belated feudalism" (Orren 1991) rather than liberal-democratic capitalism or economic liberalism until the early 20th century, then its neo-Calvinist or neo-conservative sequel is by analogy neo-feudalism (Beck 2000; Binmore 2001; Bourdieu 1998) or neo-patrimonialism (Cohen 2003) ruled by Veblen-Weber's new "robber barons". At the minimum, it is so, if not formally or legally, by name and law, then substantively, in nature, operation, or effect. Recall Winthrop's "shining city upon the hill" was an economically self-perpetuated and English-imported feudalism in the form of what Weber identifies as feudal-style hereditary nobility or *mixt aristocracie* (Bremer 1995), in which a few "must" be rich, "high and eminent" in power and dignity and most poor, mean and in "subjection." Also, Puritan-inspired Reaganism is in economic terms a sort of capitalistic, plutocratic neo-feudalism (Binmore 2001) and new patrimonialism (Cohen 2003), or feudal and patrimonial *cum* oligarchic and repressive capitalism (Pryor 2002; Schutz 2001). To that extent, a master-servant feudal-like economy is what economically, just as the medievalist evangelical theocracy sociologically/totally, connects, through the 19th century robber barons, Winthrop and Reagan et al., New England's 17th century "Biblical Commonwealth" and the 21st century "Bible Belt." Most notably, it inspires, as they solemnly proclaim, the latter and most US Protestant conservatives (Dunn and Woodard 1996).

Crucially, the neo-Calvinist economic system in America turns out to be a neo-feudal, thus a master-servant economy in virtue of being authoritarian, repressive, oligarchic, and anti-egalitarian in particular (Pryor 2002), given that the defining attributes of neo-feudalism are authoritarianism, coercion, sharp religiously sanctified inequality, or oligarchy (Binmore 2001). Specifically, it represents repressive, oligarchic, theocentric (Wall 1998), and anti-egalitarian, as opposed to liberal-democratic, secular, and egalitarian, and in that sense neo-feudal and neo-patrimonial capitalism, thus a sort of capitalist dictatorship or the "factory of authoritarianism." Negatively, it is far from being Smith's "system of natural liberty" in the economy and beyond (Buchanan 1991). On this account, not only until the New Deal period (Orren 1991), but even by the early 21st century in neo-Puritan America, economic and other liberalism as axiomatic anti-feudalism has not really replaced feudal-rooted capitalism and its capital-labor as master-servant relations, thus "belated feudalism" or neo-feudalism and its servitude, at least in the fanatically anti-labor or anti-union "Bible Belt".

In Weber's words, the neo-Puritan economy operates as a neo-feudal master-servant economic system in substantive terms like authoritarianism, including repression, oligarchy, anti-secularism, and anti-egalitarianism, even if not in a formal sense on the premise that neo-conservative capitalism is not formally or overtly "feudalism" proper.

For example, some sociologists observe that American and other neo-conservatism as a form of (counter) revolution assumes an "unprecedented form" in that by contrast to its early forms it moves from invoking an "idealized past, through exaltation of soil and blood" or the "archaic themes of the old agricultural mythologies" to appealing instead to "progress, reason and science [e.g. economics]" (Bourdieu 1998). In this account, if neo-conservatism in America and beyond has been capable of deceiving or "brain-washing" most Americans by the equation "conservative = good" ("liberal = bad"), this is because of its retaining "nothing of the old Black Forest pastoral of the conservative revolutionaries [fascists] of the 1930s" and wearing "all the signs of modernity". Arguably, what typifies conservative revolutions like the Nazi Revolution in Germany of the 1930s and "those of Thatcher, Reagan [etc.]" is that they aim at and operate as "restorations", primarily of feudalism and medievalism against liberal-democratic capitalism and liberalism. Moreover, the observed opposition between dominant and subjected economic groups in neo-conservative American capitalism is described as "rather like that between masters and slaves" in the old European feudalism, and by implication between Winthrop et al. as predestined rulers driven by repressive Calvinism and their equally predetermined subjects in New England's medieval-like *mixt aristocracie*. In this view, notably by social neo-Darwinism (the Chicago School of Economics) neo-conservatism in America reinvents and celebrates a new ruling class with "all the properties of a nobility in the medieval sense" owing ever-increasing wealth and power to expertise and superior intelligence as a presumed "gift from Heaven" (Bourdieu 1998).

Also, other sociologists consider and describe contemporary Calvinist capitalism as a new feudal or service society in America (Beck 2000). Similarly, some economists (Cohen 2003) identify the advent of what is called the "new patrimonial capitalism" primarily in America, and secondarily in Europe. The new, capitalist patrimonialism is defined as an economic system that is defined or marked by the "revenge" of capitalists (shareholders) over laborers or wage earners (Cohen 2003), thus a novel master-servant economy in which, predictably, the first act as proxy masters, the second as servants or their proxies, namely Winthrop-Reagan's subjects.

*Calvinist New Bibliocracy and Neo-Feudalism*

Minimally, if not that of America as a whole during neo-conservatism, the economic system of the new Southern "Bible Belt" is a neo-feudal master-servant economy, just as was that of its perennial model New England's "Biblical Commonwealth". At the minimum, this is indicated and symbolized by the legal and political status of near-servitude, at most what Weber may call the pariah position of organized labor or union organization outlawed or restricted and obstructed as "evil" and "ungodly" in what is supposed to be the supreme implementation of the "Biblical Garden" governed by the Golden Rule (Habermas 2001) and Sorokin's (1970) "Christian love".

Moreover, the "Bible Belt" has become a heaven for feudal-style theocratic capitalist masters epitomized by Weber-Veblen's Baptist and other Calvinist robber barons and their sequels, just as, in conjunction, the "paradise" of Puritan moralistic tyranny and moral fascism. Alternatively, the region has become a kind of "hell" or "purgatory" for workers, including those employed in state agencies, such as primary, secondary and higher education, in which they are denied the basic globally recognized liberty and right of collective organization and bargaining in most Southern states (with rare exceptions like Florida), thus effectively reduced to "cheap" and subservient or powerless labor (e.g., public schools and universities in Alabama, Texas, etc.). In comparative terms, this adverse treatment of labor collective organization in the South and beyond in America is virtually unknown in modern Western and other (e.g., Eastern European) economies, and only found in third-world dictatorships, from Singapore and China to Iran and Saudi Arabia, precisely defined by such economic repression mixed with political oppression. On this economic dimension, like on non-economic dimensions, the "Bible Belt" locates itself outside of the modern Western economy and democracy and comes closer to or resembles more non-Western theocratic and other dictatorships like Iran, Singapore, and China (Bauman 1997).

Just as democracy and politics, the economy is contemporary America has been observed "heading South" not only geographically by industrial relocation from the North due to "cheap" and subservient labor. It has also sociologically in the sense of Southern anti-labor, anti-union, anti-welfare and anti-egalitarian, economic institutions and practices being expanded beyond the "Dixieland". The US economy, like politics, has been placed in the neo-feudal master-servant or anti-labor and generally repressive, theocratic, anti-egalitarian, and oligarchic "shadow of Dixie" (Cochran 2001). On the account of this expansion, the "Bible Belt" may shape America's economic system after its own neo-feudal anti-labor, oligarchic ("good old boys"), plutocratic or mafia-capitalist Enron-like and theocratic "godly" image. And, it has in fact done in recent times via, for example, Wal-Mart's notorious "antiunion labor practices"[40] (Basker 2007) spreading as a sort of social contagion or epidemics to the American economy.

In particular, the economic system of the Southern "Bible Belt" and consequently, if this "Dixie" shadow continues to be widely cast on it, America as a whole seems a neo-feudal master-servant economy. It does so at least in the concrete sense and form of oligarchy and the "new" aristocracy embodied by, alongside the legendary "robber barons", proverbial "good old boys" networks, including their latest manifestations in Enronism (Desai 2005) and other crony or mafia-style capitalism (Pryor 2002), plus the celebrity status system[41] (Kurzman et al. 2007). Thus, some analysts identify and predict capitalism in America under neo-conservatism as an oligarchic economic as well as political system (Pryor 2002) ruled by a narrow group, thus in a substantive, distinguished from legal, sense a neo-feudal master-servant economy of the same repressive oligarchs (Binmore 2001) and of the repressed populace. This yields a variation on Michels' "iron" sociological law and historical pattern in the sense that Calvinist theocracy reproduces and predicts oligarchy in the economy and beyond, thus a master-servant

---

[40] Basker (2007:185) suggests that "if the retail sector is relatively nonunionized, Wal-Mart is an extreme example: there are no unionized Wal-Mart stores in North America. After meat packers in a Texas Wal-Mart Supercenter voted to unionize in 2000, Wal-Mart switched to prepackaged beef and closed down its meat-packing departments in several states. In 2005, Wal-Mart closed a store in Quebec whose workers had voted to unionize." Basker (2007:185) infers that "Wal-Mart's antiunion stance has changed practices throughout the retail sector", notably through its "negative effect on retail wages."

[41] For Kurzman et al. (2007:347), in America "by the late 20th century, members of the high-status group had come to expect obsequious deference, exact significant financial tribute, and lay claim to legal privilege, as aristocratic and caste elites did in earlier centuries. But the new status system was different. It was born out of capitalism and mass media, and its dynamics reflected the conditions of the modern era. This system is called celebrity."

feudal economic system. Overall, the above confirms that the economic system of a Calvinist, in this case neo-Puritan and presently regional (Southern) or potentially national and global, Biblical theocracy as a total social system and providential design is a feudal master-servant economy, alongside slavery (and profitable extermination) as the Pareto-like optimum or maximum.

## The Calvinist Caste System

Still another related form or element of a pure and primitive Calvinist-Puritan master-servant economy is a caste system usually typifying or overlapping with feudal servitude in European and other societies (India), just as with economic slavery in America and elsewhere. Feudalism, as the dominant economic-political order (*ancien regime*) of Europe spanning into the 17th and 18th centuries was a "well-ordered caste" or estate society, while liberalism, including the French Revolution, eliminated these "social structures and lack of individual freedom" (Garry 1992).

### Calvinist Theocracy and the Caste Economy

The pure, primitive Calvinist master-servant economy is a sort of caste, thus closed economic, system in the sense of Calvinists or rather their theocrats forming a narrow and exclusive ruling group, a master caste against the rest of society as servant groups or subjugated, excluded, and segregated castes. In Weber's terms, both economically and socially, Calvinist theocracy is a caste system by means of "monopolistic closure" of economic opportunities or life chances, as well as "monopolization of social power and honor". It is thus a closed and rigid economy and society alike, in which, like in the feudal estate order, the dominant group wields superior and stable material and non-material resources (Collins 1975). Like religious-political conservatism in general, Calvinism, including Puritanism, involves what Michels calls a "clique cherishing an aristocratic exclusivism at once by instinct and by conviction," as revealed in the "conservative spirit of the old master-caste."

Sociological observations identify or intimate the Calvinist caste economic and social system as a particular type or element of a theocratic master-servant economy and society. For example, Comte observes that Protestantism, including Calvinism, "has nowhere, and least of all in England shown itself averse to the spirit of caste, which it has even attempted to restore". Also, Weber implicitly defines Calvinist capitalism in America, specifically in the post-bellum evangelical South, as the caste-like system in virtue of the observed "monopolization" of wealth, as well as political power and honor,[42] the "monopolistic closure" of economic and other social opportunities or life chances by certain "positively privileged" religious and ethnic groups (e.g., Mencken's ruling Baptists/Methodists) as preordained masters versus the "negatively privileged" or excluded, including non-believing others (Edgell et al. 2006), as their servants or subjects.

On this account, Calvinist-Puritan theocracy, from 16th century Geneva to the 21st century "Bible Belt" represents an economy and society that is, in Mannheim's words, "organized along the lines of closed castes or ranks", as exemplified by Calvin's theocrats and Southern oligarchs ("good old boys"), respectively, against all others as their servants or subjects. To that extent, it substantively constitutes and functions as a caste-based economic and social system overall. In such a socioeconomic system, Calvinist religious leaders and theologians a la Calvin, Cromwell, Winthrop and his "Bible Belt" descendents become, in Mannheim's view, a ruling or influential caste, as precisely happened in Puritan-ruled New England during from the 17th to the early 19th century[43] (German 1995), just like magicians, Brahmans, and medieval clergy before. And, if the "nearest approach to an absolutely rigid society" is a caste-society (Sorokin 1959; also, Lehmann 1995), then this characterizes accordingly a Calvinist or Puritan social-economic system.[44]

---

[42] Weber observes that in America, notably the post-bellum the South, the racial "abhorrence on the part of the Whites is socially determined by the previously sketched tendency toward the monopolization of social power and honor", while adding "pure" anthropological types are often a secondary consequence of such closure", citing racially homogenous sects *cum* castes in India.

[43] German (1995:971–88) finds that during the late 18th century New England's prominent Calvinist theologians (the "New Divinity") "embraced ecclesiastical power the better to promote the "peculiar doctrines" of Calvinism" and in the process reportedly "abused their power by pursuing their private interest at public expense" to become a part of plutocracy (e.g. "wealthy ministers in Connecticut").

[44] Also, Nisbet (1970:210) remarks that "of all forms of status aggregate in society, caste is the most rigorous and encompassing of human behavior." However, he and other conservative US sociologists somewhat ethnocentrically associate the caste system, like feudalism (e.g. Lipset and Marks 2000), with non-Puritan religions or non-American settings (e.g. Hinduism, India, Europe, etc.) but not with American Puritanism and religious conservatism overall.

The latter is defined by the "monopolization" of economic and all other life chances by Weber's Calvinist virtuosi and Hume's Puritan divines or saints as predestined theocratic masters or "godly" oligarchs ("only a few") in the economy and society. Negatively, it is defined by their "monopolistic closure" of such life chances for others, especially religious (and ethnic) outsiders condemned as "infidels" as well as actual non-believers, all equated with enemies and subjected to "holy" war and extermination as the Pareto-like optimum and, when unfeasible or imprudent, as Winthrop commands, master-caste subjection as the second-best "rational choice". Recall, this was exemplified by Cromwell's "holy" wars against "infidels" (Goldstone 1986; Gorski 2000), including what Simmel calls the "cruel suppression" of Irish Catholics and other "Papists", in England, those by Calvin in Geneva (Mansbach 2006), Winthrop et al. in New England (Gould 1996), and their heirs via culture and temperance wars (Bell 2002; Hout and Fischer 2002), in modern America, notably the "Dixieland" and its equivalents (Mormon-ruled Utah, etc.).

*Calvinist Caste Exclusion versus Total Extermination*

Minimally, the Calvinist-Puritan economy and society is a caste-like, master-servant economic and social system in virtue of, if not complete closure like slavery or even feudal servitude, its methodical exclusion and discrimination against out-groups. Notably, these out-groups include non-Calvinists or "non-Protestants" (especially Catholics condemned as "Papists"), and non-believers or agnostics, as observed in historical and contemporary America, especially the "Bible Belt", primarily due to predominant fundamentalism (Edgell et al. 2006). Yet, skeptics or cynics may object that, by analogy to slavery in Simmel's sociological logic but substantively different ("better"?), such caste-type exclusion and discrimination is the objective maximum that can happen to these out-groups, notably "infidels", the best that they can realistically expect and hope for in such an economic and social system.

This holds true given that the Calvinist-Puritan, just as Islamic, original imperative and ultimate outcome is the extermination of "infidels" as the optimum via "holy" war, crusade and jihad, with anything else, including their subjugation or conversion, being the second-best option or at most merci to them. For example, this was the maximum to happen and the best to hope for to Servetus (yet eventually killed) and various other heretics and libertines in Calvin's theocratic Geneva

(Mansbach 2006). The same applies to Catholics and in part Lutherans in Holland under official Calvinism (Hsia and Nierop 2002), to Irish and other "Papists" (typically massacred or at least banished) and many Anglicans in England during, in Hume's account, the barbarian rule of Cromwell and other "divines" (Gorski 2000), and to Native Americans, Quakers, and "witches" in New England under its tyrannical Puritan theocracy (Munch 2001). It also does to liberals, secularists, atheists, or agnostics in the "Bible Belt" and "red" America overall under "reborn" evangelicalism, just as before (Edgell et al. 2006). Simply, in Puritan "Salem with witches", as an historical event (Harley 1996) and a sociological metaphor (Putnam 2000) alike, their and infidels' "best bet" is mere survival even if through caste-style exclusion, subjection, and discrimination as a "piece of cake" compared with their methodical exorcism (burning at the stake and execution). In sum, as Schumpeter would put it, "live and let live", even as outcasts or what Weber calls pariahs, as well as slaves and feudal servants, is the "best deal" that "witches" and "infidels" can expect and likely get from a Calvinist *cum* Puritan theocracy. For instance, this is the maximum to expect or hope for from witch-trials and executions in Puritan America and the Leviathan-style death-penalty and penal system in the post-bellum "Bible Belt" (Texas, Florida, Oklahoma, Georgia, etc.).

At this juncture, "Salem with witches", in which the latter or infidels are *not* exorcised or exterminated (burned or executed) through witch- and monkey-trials (Boles 1999), but "only" excluded, persecuted, or expelled (e.g., Quakers), and discriminated against is both the historical case and sociological micro-model of a Puritan caste, master-servant economic and social system in America, spanning from the 17th century "Biblical Commonwealth" to the 21st century "Bible Belt". To return to the point of origin, by analogy Calvin's Geneva as a local *civitas Dei* (Frijhoff 2002) in which Servetus and other heretics are *not* killed for their blasphemy but "just" excluded, expelled, and discriminated against is the original Calvinist caste economic and social system. It served as a model or precedent, alongside the medieval theocracy and its Inquisition, for "Salem with witches" and other Puritan creations and practices, including "Monkey Trials", in America. And yet, "infidels" and dissenters, like "witches" at Puritan Salem (Harley 1996), in Calvin's model theocracy usually were executed for the glory of the God of Calvinism. This consequently renders the caste economy, like slavery and subjugation, a second-best rational option as well as a "consolation prize", if not nuisance and inconvenience, compared to the ideally profitable extermination of the "ungodly" (e.g., Native Americans) or the exorcism of "witches" (thus their "master", the devil), as the efficient Pareto-optimum within Calvinist, just as Islamic, theocracy, via a crusade/jihad as their respective "holy" and total wars against "infidels" (Turner 2002).

The above may be instructive to emphasize, because (or if) the intrinsic economic and general sociological logic and outcome of a Calvinist and other totalitarian, especially Islamic, theocracy is pure and simple. This is the preferably profitable extermination of "infidels", both other religious out-groups and non-believers, *cum* "enemies." And, their subjection or conversion via a caste system and a slave economy is merely a complement and secondary option, as Weber and other analysts (Mansbach 2006) specifically register or imply for evangelical Calvinism and fundamentalist Islam. At this juncture, contrary to Weber, however, the true Calvinist spirit of capitalism may well have been incarnated not in Franklin's secular, generous, and pacifist post-Calvinist (Byrne 1997) ideas and practices like "time is money" and (appearance of) "honesty is the best policy" but instead in his Calvinistic figuratively grandfathers' theocratic "godly", yet lucrative extermination as well as the subjugation of Native Americans as the "ungodly" heathen. Still, this serendipitous and likely controversial "rediscovery" is consistent with the assumption and reality that the economic logic and system of a Calvinist theocracy is a theocratic economy defined by the combined "rational" or methodical extermination and the caste-type (and slave or feudal-style) subjugation and exclusion of "infidels", "heretics", "witches", and "enemies." This was witnessed almost invariably, from Calvin's Geneva and Holland under the official Reformed Church to Cromwell's England and Winthrop's New England and to the "Bible Belt". In short, it is fully congruent with the "iron consistency" of Calvinism as the paradigmatic theocratic design and social system through a total "holy" war of extermination combined with subjugation.

At this juncture, Simmel's dilemma between enslavement and extermination assumes the form of a "rational choice" or "cost-benefit calculation" as to which course of (anti)human action is more profitable. Namely, is it exterminating "infidels" and exorcising "witches" via holy wars *or* excluding and discriminating against them by a caste (or slave) economic system?, as another variation on the entrepreneurial "producing or buying" option. In respect of a caste system, this is the only or major "rational choice" and "decision problem" that Puritan theocratic masters need to make and resolve. Tocqueville's first Puritans apparently opted for the exterminating option as the more profitable, and their descendents in the "Bible Belt" and beyond for that of exclusion, while not entirely relinquishing or "forgetting" the first, as indicated by their "holy" war against the "evil" world and their domestic use of the death penalty for sins-crimes. This reveals a remarkable continuity or path from the Puritans' hyper-rational profit-making on the Calvinist extermination of the "ungodly" for the higher cause of the "true" evangelical religion to executions and other Draconian punishments like life imprisonment for sins and minor crimes ("three strikes" laws) by a Puritan-rooted neo-conservative growingly private death penalty and prison system maximizing profits in modern America. Simply, Puritan theocratic masters and their descendents, to paraphrase Weber, "make money" out of humans and their legal misery or misfortune, including illness, life and death. Thus, humans, to cite the notorious "Wild West" persistent expression and practice, are "wanted dead or alive" for their Puritan or evangelical masters' maximal profit. And, this is perhaps the true spirit *cum* ghost of capitalism in American Calvinism or Puritanism and its evangelical revivals in the "Wild West" (Clemens 2007), just as in the Southern "Bible Belt."

In sum, exclusion or "monopolistic closure" after the model and image of Calvin's Geneva with Servetus-like heretics and "Salem with witches" *not* exterminated or exorcised but "only" expelled, excluded, or "negatively privileged" defines the Puritan economic and social system in America in terms of caste-like subjection, as well as feudal-style servitude. Yet, since they typically or ideally are exterminated or exorcised, preferably profitably so, the caste system of exclusion and subjection, like slavery, effectively functions as the secondary economic option and mechanism, compared with the extermination of "infidels", including the death penalty for the sinful, as the optimum, within Calvinist-Puritan, just as Islamic, theocracy. In accordance with the "iron consistency" of Calvinism and the "obstinacy" of Puritanism, the secondary status of the caste economic system is only consistent or logical. Calvinist Bibliocracy, like Islamic theocracies, is after all "godly" *theocracy* as a total-itarian social system that can be established and perpetuated primarily via Simmel's "holy" war of extermination, and secondarily by a caste economy and other forms of subjugation like slavery and serfdom. Alternatively, by design it is not, contrary to Parsons' conflation or link of Puritan theocracy with, liberal-secular democracy and civil society. This is because, like most theocracies, Calvinist theocracy, from late-medieval Geneva to modern America, is the vestige or revival of the pre-liberal and pre-democratic Dark Middle Ages, including, as Weber and Tawney suggest, their Inquisition. Negatively, it is not, contrary to what Parsons and other analysts (Kloppenberg 1998; Mayway 1984; Sorkin 2005) suggest, the correlate of or the prelude to the Enlightenment and its liberal-democratic ideals.

*Forms and Meanings of the Calvinist Caste System*

Broadly understood as the exclusion and subjection of outsiders, notably "infidels" incorporating both religious out-groups and genuine non-believers, the Calvinist caste system in the economy and society assumes a number of different forms and meanings. First, the Calvinist economy is a caste system thus understood in a formal-legal way and sense, simply "by law", as especially evident in the past, specifically from early 16th century Europe to mid 20th century America. Using the criterion of legal exclusion and subjection of or discrimination against "infidels" and other out-groups in the economy and all society, most Calvinist-Puritan economies in history more or less functioned, qualified, or appeared as caste systems. On this basis, original examples include Calvin's Geneva and Holland under official Calvinism on the account of their strict legal exclusion and subjection of or discrimination against other religious out-groups such as Catholics and in part Lutherans, as well as secularists, libertines, and actual non-believers (Kaplan 2002). Derivative and subsequent instances involve England (and Scotland) during Cromwell's rule also in virtue of the institutional persecution *cum* crusade against Irish and other Catholics and partly Anglicans, let alone genuine non-believers (Goldstone 1986; Gorski 2000). A related instance is Puritan ruled New England owing to a mix of "all of the above" exclusionary grounds, practices, and targets, non-Calvinist and non-Protestant, Christian and non-Christian, conjoined with the exclusion, subjection, or worse of "ungodly" and "savage" Native Americans (Munch 2001).

The probably last legal form and meaning of a Calvinist caste system was the segregation economy and society officially established in the post bellum South (Boles 1999) dominated by revived Puritanism (Presbyterianism, Baptism, Methodism) displacing Anglicanism through the Great Awakenings and following the American Revolution. As known, it was self-perpetuated into the 1960s by various "separate but equal" judicial rationalizations. On this account, while the Southern slave economy was a sort of mixed Anglican originally and Puritan subsequently system, the post-bellum caste-like segregation regime was largely (although not solely) that of Puritan-rooted fundamentalism or conservatism. The latter was its main enforcer and defender, through both spiritual and violent means, including support for lynching (Messner, Baller and Zevenbergen. 2005) and related vigilante violence (Jacobs et al. 2005) against religious and racial out-groups, just as the exclusion of actual non-believers and agnostics (Edgell et al. 2006).

Alternatively, "born again" evangelicalism was and remains by the 21st century the major (though not the only) religious and social force opposing and subverting on "godly" grounds the abolition of the segregation and thus caste system in the South and America, seemingly more so than it did abolishing slavery a century and half ago. In a way, "abolitionism" with respect to this post-bellum caste (Jim Crow) system is in Calvinist evangelicalism, if not absent, even weaker than it was with regard to the antebellum slave economy and society. In a way, this is indicated by the dramatic, even "schizophrenic" (Amenta and Halfmann 2000; Cochran 2001; Hill 2002), split and conversion of the evangelical South from "Democratic" into "Republican" in political terms, just as conversely during post-bellum times. And, sociological observations indicate that this schizophrenic split of a collective personality in the South has occurred primarily because of the first political party's imputed "vice" of supporting, and the second's "virtue" of opposing, the civil rights movement and political and, notably, cultural liberalization since the 1960s through the 2000s (Brooks 2000; Brooks and Manza 1997). In particular, the two major political parties' perceived divergent or opposites stances on cultural liberalization and secularization promoting social liberties and choices (private choice in family formation and control, consensual sexuality, alcohol use) have persisted, perhaps more than those on race-based civil and political rights, as the principal single factor of such a curious sociological "schizophrenia" from "Democratic" for a century to "Republican" for several decades in the South through the 2000s. And, it is this "schizophrenic" split and conversion from "Democratic" now condemned as liberal-secular to "Republican" embraced as conservative and "godly" redefines and reaffirms this region as a "Bible Belt", and only secondarily and even in part diminishingly as the epicenter of racism.

Yet, in spite of such opposition and occasional attempts at reversal by fundamentalist forces, the Puritan caste system of segregation is in formal-legal terms the "dead past" or "gone with the wind" in the South and thus America. In comparative-historical terms, it is striking that this Puritan system was legally abolished in America even after its Hindu version in India (the 1940s) as the oldest, proto-typical, and best known caste economy, and generally was the last to be so (minus the apartheid in South Africa ending in the 1990s). This evokes Hume's prophetic diagnosis of the "unreasonable obstinacy" of Puritanism; and, no species of the latter has been more obstinate, absolutist (Munch 2001), and self-righteous or unrepentant than the American.

Second, by analogy the Calvinist economy is a caste system in a substantive, as different from legal, form and meaning. It is in the shape and sense of substantive or effective, although not necessarily formal or legal, exclusion and subjection of and discrimination against "infidels" in both meanings and other outsiders in the economy and society. And, as Weber suggests on general grounds, the abolition of a Calvinist and other caste system in its formal-legal form while a necessary is not a sufficient condition of eliminating it in a substantive or actual sense, as the post-segregation South at least in part shows, just as, for that matter, India after the outlawing of castes during the 1940s. This holds true at least on the account of what sociological analysts identify as the continuing factual and institutional exclusion of and discrimination or bias against certain religious or rather non-religious groups like non-believers or true "infidels" as supremely "un-American" (not to mention some minority racial groups) in the Southern "Bible Belt" and other parts of America even after the legal abolition of the above type of caste system (Edgell et al. 2006). On this account, the caste socioeconomic system in the South has substantively self-perpetuated from being race- to religiously-based and sanctified by the admittedly methodical exclusion or intolerance of religious and non-believing out-groups, thus a sort of "method in the madness" (Smith 2000). More specifically, the system has maintained and expanded the religious basis and rationalization, while relinquishing or tempering the racial type. For the exclusion and discrimination against "infidels", both non-evangelicals or non-Protestants (Catholics) and non-believers, have been its constant fixture since post-bellum times and even the Great Awakenings.

At this juncture, cynics or skeptics might comment that Puritanism's caste economic and social system in the sense of systematic exclusion, subjection, or intolerance of out-groups in America is "dead in a formal, racial sense, yet long live the Puritan caste system in substantive, religious and other terms." For instance, these other terms include economic exclusion or sharp and growing segregation and inequality, with some analysts observing that US current wealth and income trends generate "something very like a caste society" (Perrucci and Wysong 2008; Wolff 2002), though the caste system is officially "gone with the wind" even in the post-1960s South. If anything, proverbial Southern "good old boys" in the sociological sense of "godly" exclusionary, effectively the same oligarchs (Binmore 2001), or theocratic plutocrats act as the "living proofs" and symbols of such substantively "die hard" Puritan-rooted caste socioeconomic system in the South and beyond, just as do, *ceteris paribus*, their counterparts in India. Overall, the above indicates that the Calvinist, like other (including Indian) caste socioeconomic system is in substantive forms and meanings more complex and enduring than in its legal form and sense.

Also, as intimated, the Calvinist and other economy is a caste system in virtue of being economic slavery. In this connection, a slave economy functions and appears as a pure, primitive or original, and extreme or ultimate caste system, as exemplified by slavery in the US South. The same applies to the Calvinist economy as feudal servitude, although feudalism and its estates in Europe are usually distinguished, as relatively less rigid and closed, from the caste system and castes proper like those in India. By analogy, as noticed, what Weber identifies as segregation[45] can be considered and described as a diluted, derivative, and contemporary or "milder" caste economic and social system, as exemplified in the post-bellum South and embodied and ruled by Southern "good old boys" either formally, as until the 1960s, or substantively, as in later times.

*Elements of the Calvinist Diluted Master-Servant Economy*

By analogy, a diluted, derivative, or modern master-servant economy forms the economic logic, creation, and system of a Calvinist corresponding, that is, adapted and contemporary evangelical (and in that sense *still* primitive or fundamentalist), theocracy.

---

[45] In apparent reference to the US post-bellum South, Weber remarks that "a status segregation grown into a caste differs in its structure from a mere ethnic segregation: the caste structure transforms the horizontal and unconnected coexistence of ethnically segregated groups into a vertical social system of super and subordination".

## Diluted Calvinist Theocracy and the Master-Servant Economy

A pure and primitive master-servant economy, including slavery, feudal servitude, and caste (racial segregation), may be the "dead past" and "gone with the wind, yet, its diluted, derivative, or modernized version is "well and alive" as an economic reality or future prospect of Calvinist theocracy in America, at least the "Bible Belt", as are pure and diluted theocracies, respectively. In Michels' words, the "spirit of the old master-caste" or servant economy is "dead, long live the ghost of the new, diluted master-servant economy" in the Puritan "new, exceptional nation", and because pure and diluted Calvinist theocracies as its societal determinant or framework are dead and "born again", respectively. Notably, some observations suggest that a diluted master-caste or servant economy logically and empirically persists and even expands from the South to most of America thus placed in the "shadow of Dixie" (Cochran 2001). It does so as the inner economic logic and subsystem of a diluted Calvinist evangelical (thus still primitive) theocracy as a total social system or theological design in the image of a Southern "Biblical Garden", just as a pure or old master-servant economy did in relation to corresponding theocracies. Alternatively, a diluted master-servant economy will only be "gone with the wind", as in the anti-labor South, when Puritan Bibliocracy in this image is disestablished, if ever, just as its old, pure prototypes (e.g., the enslavement and profitable extermination of Native Americans, etc.) only ended when ancient theocracies had been de-invented, as in the Jeffersonian secular disestablishment of New England's theocratic Puritanism as the official Calvinist Church.

Historically, the Calvinist or religiously-grounded conservative diluted master-servant economy has hence followed on the demise and discredit or mitigation of its pure forms such as slavery, in part "benevolent" or "belated feudalism", and the caste system (racial segregation) in America since the second half of the 19th and the mid 20th century. Thus, a diluted master-servant economy, though in its various embellishments and disguises, seems the prevalent, expanding, and intensifying economic reality of America dominated by "reborn" Puritan evangelicalism in the early 21st century, just as its pure, primitive form did from the 17th to the mid 20th century.

Regionally, as expected, the Calvinist diluted master-servant economy is primarily, albeit not only, present or designed in the Southern "Bible Belt" (and other "red-state" regions), as its theocratic basis, framework, and "godly" sanctification. Also predictably, as observed, such a Calvinist model has expanded to most of America by placing its economic and political system in the anti-liberal, under-democratic, anti-secular, and anti-egalitarian, including anti-labor or anti-union, "shadow of Dixie", with both the economy and democracy subjected to increasing Southern dominance or influence, almost literally "heading South" (Cochran 2001). In this sense, the aggregate outcome of such an expansion has been the "Southernization" of the American economy and politics (Heale 1998; also, Carter 1996) through a Calvinist-rooted economic and political system. This is a sort of theocratic capitalism or capitalist theocracy after the theocratic-capitalist model of Puritan New England (German 1995) and embodied by neo-Puritan sects (the Christian Coalition, etc.) mixing "God" with free enterprise" and greed, implicitly "Mammon".

At this juncture, the above Southern expansion can be described as the modern economic, as well as joint political and religious, equivalent and reenactment of the 18th century Calvinist Great Awakenings, yet in the opposite direction, from South to North, including proto-Puritan New England itself—as if its theocracy and its partial slave economy were never established and then disestablished—and beyond. This appears to be a striking regional and historical American grotesque irony and even, as some analysts (Bauman 1997; Cochran 2001; Hill 2002) admonish, a potential tragedy and dangerous reversal in economical as well as political, social, and cultural terms. While the "old" racist South may have lost the civil war about slavery, the "new" illiberal "Bible Belt" (with other "red" regions) has reignited, reinforced, and even triumphed (so far) with vengeance in its economic, just as ideological, religious, temperance, or cultural, wars against its liberal, secular, democratic, and egalitarian adversaries ("blue" states). This Southern revenge has contributed to and augured a renewed master-servant economy and generally a déjà vu theocratic social system in modern America. In economic as well as social terms, the "new" persistently and even increasingly theocratic South is thus ever-more Puritan and in extension Calvinist in the sense of a master-servant economy than America's home of Puritanism, New England in the period since the official demise and replacement of its theocracy by Jeffersonian liberal-secular democracy during the 1830s.

The preceding confirms that regionally in America, just globally, Calvinist theocracy, pure or diluted, as a total social system and theological design ultimately generates, sanctifies, and predicts an equivalent master-servant economy respectively, as its inner economic logic and subsystem. Conversely, the demise of the former results in and predicts the absence or weakness of the latter. Apparently, the "rebirth" of the "Bible Belt" and generally "born again" Puritan fundamentalism relates to the first outcome, and the official "death" of New England's "Biblical Commonwealth" and primitive Puritanism overall to the second.

*Attributes of the Calvinist Diluted Master-Servant Economy*

The defining attributes of a Calvinist diluted master-servant economy are specified as follows. In a general definition, a Calvinist and other diluted or modernized master-servant economy is an authoritarian or repressive, oligarchic, and anti-egalitarian economic system. In this system, the "new" masters and servants replace but are substantively equivalent with the old, including feudal lords and serfs, privileged and excluded castes, if not slave-owners and slaves (Bourdieu 1998). In consequence, a diluted contemporary master-servant economy of adapted Calvinist theocracy as a total social system in America is an authoritarian and anti-egalitarian, particularly repressive and oligarchic or plutocratic, economic system. The latter is in turn conjoined with and maintained by an equivalent political regime (Pryor 2002), notably an ever-growing policing state (Bourdieu 1998; Wacquant 2002) with the Puritan-style vice-police as its "body and soul" especially in the "Bible Belt". In short, a diluted master-servant economy is (ruled by) plutocracy or "moneyed" oligarchy in Calvinist diluted theocracy as its "godly" basis and rationale, just as its pure form was theocratic slavery, aristocracy, and a caste system.

In a concrete, operational definition, a Calvinist diluted or modernized master-servant economy is a pro-capital and anti-labor economic system, with the new capitalist masters and labor servants substituting for but substantively equivalent to the old, in particular feudal lords and serfs, if not slave-owners and slaves. The Puritan diluted, modern master-servant economy in America is an exemplary pro-capital and anti-labor capitalist economic system (Fligstein 2001; Myles 1994) in the sense of Hobbesian Anarchy or unrestrained freedom, figuratively and even literally "license to kill" for capital, and yet Leviathan or tyrannical oppression for labor and the population as a whole (Pryor 2002). Conversely, what renders a pro-capital, anti-labor capitalist economic system a diluted master-servant economy is predictably antagonistic, aggressive, and exclusionary "anti-labor" rather or more than preferential "pro-capital" ideas, institutions, and policies. This holds true since (if) conceivably modern democratic economies and societies can be both pro-capital and pro-labor in a sort of balancing act, specifically proximate institutional equilibrium or compromise, including basic state neutrality and equal legal treatment, defining the American "New Deal" and its ensuing postwar social contract, and especially European welfare capitalism and liberal democracy (Beck 2000; Esping-Andersen 1994; Habermas 2001).

At this point, the Calvinist diluted, modern master-servant economy through a "new" pro-capital, anti-labor economic system originates, operates, and continues as the result of failure of balance, notably of institutional equilibrium or compromise, including state neutrality and equal legal treatment, of capital and labor in America under neoconservatism. Alternatively, it does so as the product of an institutional imbalance or asymmetry, in particular state non-neutrality and preferential or unequal legal treatment, of capital and labor. It thus reflects systemic bias defining structural inequity, including judicial unfairness, just as some degree of legalized immaturity, if not infantile childishness in Weber's sense.[46] If, as "libertarian" economists like Mises, Hayek or Friedman insist, equal legal treatment or "equality before the law", as the only egalitarian form they admit, defines justice or equity in general, then what they celebrate as superior "unfettered" capitalism in America in virtue of preferentially treating capital versus labor is the paradigmatic exemplar of injustice or inequity and to that extent a pro-capitalist master-servant economy.

Thus, a sociological analysis suggests that, for instance, the US (federal) government "always" operates in the function of preserving and promoting large capitalist corporations, while other governments do or may conduct policies instead "protecting other social groups" (Fligstein 2001). Generally, in this account, the US system of institutional rules and market exchange marks a "victory for capitalist firms" (Fligstein 2001) over labor and its collective organization, if any. In comparative terms, this victory is in sharp contrast with and salient deviation from virtually all affluent economies, including Western Europe and Japan, which lack such a sharp institutional imbalance or asymmetry in favor

---

[46] Weber cites the expression the "childlikeness of religious feeling".

of capital against labor[47] and to that extent do not operate and qualify as master-servant economies in the way Calvinist capitalism in America does. Thus, since labor is "much less protected" from economic crises and changes in the America than other Western economies, the US government proceeds on the apparent anti-labor injunction or rational expectation that "all-American" workers shall endure the "brunt of market crises more systematically" (Fligstein 2001) than their non-American counterparts, let alone their capitalist masters.[48] In a striking comparative contrast, this analysis registers that while in America economic crises result in appeals for "deregulation" favoring capital and reducing labor (and government) "influence" as the solution, as epitomized by Reaganomics, in France state officials are instead urged to act in the "public interest" (Fligstein 2001). In sum, at least on the account of the low and further reducing influence and structural power of labor in relation to capital as well as its typical ally (federal and state) government, Calvinist capitalism in America self-perpetuates, functions, or qualifies as a diluted, modern master-servant economy, including "belated feudalism", in contrast to and deviation from Western capitalist economies.

The Calvinist diluted modernized master-servant economy in America thus constitutes an economic system in which capital or plutocracy is the substantive (albeit not necessarily formal) equivalent of pre-capitalist masters or lords, and, alternatively, labor one of feudal servants and Weber's "negatively privileged" castes (pariahs), even if not of pre-feudal slaves. This gives an ironic twist to what Mises and Hayek et al. predicted for supposedly non-religious "socialism" (summarily equated or conflated with "communism") but overlooked or denied for theocratic capitalism or capitalist theocracy like Puritan-ruled New England and its "Bible Belt" revival. Such a diluted modernized

---

[47] Fligstein (2001:57) suggests that, for example, Japan is "a case where capitalists and state officials share control over the policy domains of the economy", while the Scandinavian welfare states are the "real societies closest to the ideal type of dominance of workers with the assistance of state actors". Also, he observes that the German system is a "political compromise between capital and labor although in many domains labor [has] the upper hand", while the French system is an "interesting hybrid [with] the strongest control by state actors in any of the OECD countries" (Fligstein 2001:58).

[48] This was dramatically witnessed in the governmental preferential treatment of airline and other industries in contrast to their employees in the aftermath of September 11, 2001, as if only corporations were adverse affected by the terrorist attacks and deserved assistance, as was also, with some qualifications, during the housing and financial crisis in the fall of 2008.

master-servant economy is the Calvinist "road to serfdom" (Boettke 1995) in America, with capital emerging as the new master and labor reduced to its servant, thus capitalists and workers as, in Tönnies' view, modern-day proxy masters and servants (and even slaves), respectively. Such a "road to serfdom" and to that extent, as Hayek would suggest, economic "hell", is axiomatically within Calvinist evangelical theocracy paved by theocratic "godly" and thus "good intensions". Second, it is a historical déjà vu through reviving or evoking "belated feudalism" and/or the religiously based caste system characteristic of Puritan-rooted evangelicalism, even if not a slave economy proper, from the "dead past" of America.

First, recall New-Deal economic and political liberalism replaced "belated feudalism" *cum* "unfettered capitalism" through what Keynes and even Popper diagnosed as the "end of laissez-faire." In turn, the new Puritan or neo-conservative economic system systematically and vehemently attacks and even reverses the New Deal or F. D. Roosevelt's legacy via anti-labor, anti-welfare, and other anti-egalitarian ideas, institutions and practices. In doing so, this system effectively aims and even succeeds to resurrect from the dead past "belated feudalism" in the face of Weber's capitalist robber barons wanting to "live like feudal lords," as well as Winthrop et al. No wonder, Reagan et al. through their evangelical ("voodoo") Reaganomics, politics, and culture wars publicly exhibit more admiration for and inspiration from these "robber barons" and Winthrop and thus his new feudal-style *mixt aristocracie* or "heavenly" oligarchy than for FDR and his post-feudal economic liberalism and egalitarianism, so liberal-democratic and egalitarian capitalism. Negatively, the New-Deal otherwise minimal version of a welfare state has been the object of intense detestation, systematic attack, and *un*-creative destruction as "big government" by this and other forms of American neo-conservatism. This inverted Schumpeterian destruction is "uncreative" because it is not followed by the creation of really new economic institutions. It entails a return to old, once "presumed dead" pre-liberal, even feudal, and thus pre-democratic institutions, contrary to Schumpeter's expectation of creative destruction as the dynamic process of simultaneously destroying the old and creating new structures in the economy and society, thus the "dramatic mechanism of economic progress" (Fischer 2003). Yet, it is fully consistent with Veblen's early diagnosis of American and other religious-political conservatism as not capable or willing of "creation" and only of conservation or restoration.

Second, the Calvinist diluted and modernized master-servant economy is axiomatically a "godly" road to serfdom. It is in that it resurrects from the "dead past", or rather perpetuates, the old "undying" religiously grounded caste system characteristic of Puritan-rooted evangelicalism via the economic as well as political, civic, and cultural exclusion and mistreatment of religious non-believers (Edgell et al. 2006). It does so especially in the Southern "Bible Belt" and its "red" state equivalents in the "Wild West" or "Middle America" (e.g., Utah as even a less diluted or purer, virtually official, theocracy in which non-Mormons are effectively pariahs or second-class citizens, than even the South). It further expands beyond to encompass some Northern states (e.g., Idaho, Montana, Nebraska, the Dakotas, Wyoming, etc.) also pervaded by theocratic fundamentalism (including "Christian" terrorist militia), thus substantively, as distinguished from geographically, part of this Southern and "Wild-West" Calvinist "Biblical Garden".

The Calvinist diluted modernized capitalist master-servant economy in America hence becomes and operates as authoritarian, notably repressive, oligarchic and partly theocratic, and anti-egalitarian rather than liberal-democratic, secular, and egalitarian capitalism. Negatively, it is, like all "born again" Puritanism, the polar antithesis of and virulent attack against a "liberal and pluralist" economic and social system (Munch 2001). This recasts a new light on Weber's Calvinist-capitalist affinity in America, as elsewhere and before, including Holland and old and New England. Namely, it is an affinity between a fundamentalist, theocratic religion and an illiberal, undemocratic economy, substantively (though not formally) equivalent to that between Islamic fundamentalism or theocracy and an economic system in those societies under its rule (Davis and Robinson 2006; Kuran 2004). Negatively, it is not an affinity, as in Parsons' implied view, between Calvinist individualistic theology (individuals' "immediacy to God") and modern democratic capitalism (Mayway 1984), let alone liberal-secular democracy and civil society.

### Calvinist Predatory Capitalism

Furthermore, some sociological and economic observations suggest that the Calvinist diluted or capitalist master-servant economy in America becomes and operates as a sort of what Veblen would call predatory or rapacious, "wild" or "untamed", and primitive, distinguished from non-violent, civilized, tamed, or mature (Beck 2000;

Habermas 2001), capitalism. It does so both within society or America in the form of what some economists (Pryor 2002) call mafia capitalism and many Americans see as a rapacious ("rip-off") economy *and* against other "ungodly" societies subjected to predation or plunder, exploitation, and subjugation via the "holy" war of extermination against "infidels" in the high service of a new "empire of liberty" (Steinmetz 2005). In this respect, the Calvinist capitalist master-servant economy in America effectively operates or appears as, to paraphrase Spencer and Durkheim, not as simple or single but "doubly-compounded", endogenous and exogenous, and thus composite predatory, rapacious capitalism. Recall, Calvinist capitalism in America in the form of benevolent or belated feudalism was characterized by the "rapacity of the masters." In general, predatory capitalism, Calvinist or other, can be defined in terms of what Pareto calls "rapacity and greed for the goods of others" by means of "unlawful appropriations" and "major usurpations" of the wealth of a society. In short, Calvinist and other predatory capitalism (or economy) is typified by what Veblen calls the "transition from peace to predation", including war, via the "cumulative growth of predatory aptitudes, habits, and traditions."

A sort of "operational definition" or lay description of Calvinist predatory capitalism in America is what many Americans call a "rip-off" economy as the economic system of systematic and widespread fraud, scum, and crude or subtle forms of plunder or predation (especially in the "Wild West" like Texas and Oklahoma). This description is exemplified in many Americans saying that "all" that US businesses, small and big, "want from you is your money, no matter what" or "whatever it takes", including some form of plunder or fraud as a sort of semicivilized (or "Americanized") variant of violent barbarian predation. In particular, the conservative-reproduced health system qualifies as an exemplar or syndrome of Calvinist predatory or mafia capitalism or the "rip-off" economy in America, alongside, say, the credit-card industry often identified as the "main reason" (White 2007) for the rise of personal bankruptcy in recent times (until a 2005 neo-conservative law). In a sense, this health system, like the credit-card industry, operates or appears as the "method in the madness" of predation or plunder on the account of its (e.g., pharmaceutical companies") exorbitant profits and prices, yet inefficiency (to the point of waste) and inequity, compared with, for example, Canada, and other Western economies. As some economists suggest, US ruling groups if "could set aside their innate pride in matters of health care, they might on this point learn a useful lesson or two from the experience of other nations" (Reinhardt 2000:82). In short, the health system in America functions or looks as a sort of institutionalized or legalized criminal enterprise or mafia-like extortion. And, the neo-conservative vehement, almost fanatical, opposition to and systematic obstruction of a universal health-care system in America, as functioning in virtually all modern capitalist economies, is what Durkheim might call a pathological or morbid ("life and dead") expression of Calvinist, notably Puritan, anti-universalism, anti-egalitarianism and exclusion.

*From Rapacious Theocracy to Predatory Capitalism—and Back*

In retrospect, predatory capitalism is a (patho) logical or ultimate outcome consummating and expressing the "normal pathology" (Gouldner 1970) of Calvinism, notably American Puritanism. In particular, this holds true of predatory capitalism in relation to Calvinist-Puritan theocracy as the social system or Providential design of economic and other predation or rapacity[49] (McCann 2000) via, like Islam, the joined extermination and subjugation of "infidels" by "holy" culture and military wars, crusades and jihads, respectively (Turner 2002). Thus, a historical analysis pinpoints "rapacious implications" in American Puritanism, notably "Puritan expansionism" and its "rhetoric of Manifest Destiny" (Gould 1996) that it attributed to the "new nation" after the Revolution, or the "promised land" it supposedly discovered, just as original Calvinism endowed with such a Divine election those European societies it ruled like Holland and in part England.

Essentially, a predatory or rapacious Puritan theocracy as a total social system inherently entails and sanctifies, and ultimately generates and predicts, an equivalent economic logic and subsystem, a moment that Weber implied but did not explicate or emphasize enough. The above then recasts his "elective affinity" of Calvinism and modern capitalism accordingly. It is thus an affinity between predation or rapacity, that is, conjoined extermination, subjugation and plunder, in society via "holy" war *and* in the economy through physical and symbolic violence (Bourdieu 1988; Hallett 2003; Loveman 2005). To invert Clausewitz's famous definition of war, Calvinist predatory or rapacious

---

[49] McCann (2000:12) identifies "rapacity and terror" as the result of an " "omniscient and omnipresent" system of enforcement that denies personal freedom" in Mormon-ruled Utah.

capitalism in America is the "continuation" of the Puritan "holy wars" of extermination and subjection after the formula of Winthrop et al., or simply predation, of the "ungodly" by identical or other means, just as, as he may suggest, conversely, coming full circle. While not all predatory capitalist and non-capitalist economies are Calvinist-Puritan in origin, nature, and effect, but also non-Calvinist (including Catholic, Islamic, and fascist), the opposite is almost invariably true. The economic logic, system, or outcome of Calvinism and its theocracy as a total social system is ultimately predation or rapacity in the economy by the "holy" war of combined extermination, subjugation or plunder, and exploitation of "infidels" in society.

Consequently, predatory capitalism in America is functionally equivalent or closer, if not returning, to early or late feudalism as the exemplary system of economic and other predation and, as Comte, Spencer, Weber, and other analysts stress, militarist society overall rather than to a liberal-democratic capitalist economy. In Comte-Spencer's words, it is a resurrected theocratic and militarist system defined and ruled by what has come to be known as the "military industrial complex" rather than a secular "positive" and pacifist industrial economy and society. Calvinist and other predatory capitalism in America and elsewhere is, by definition, an economic system characterized by Hobbesian anarchy and the "license to kill"—figuratively[50] (Desai 2005) and even literally (e.g., of strikers in the past and workers by lack of work safety continuously)—for capitalist plutocrats as masters, and yet Leviathan or tyrannical oppression for American laborers reduced to servants déjà vu and the subjected population as Winthrop's ideal (Schutz[51] 2001).

In this sense, when analysts identify or predict Hobbesian economic anarchy enjoyed by the "godly" capitalist oligarchy, yet combined with the growing "repression of the population" (Pryor 2002) in America, they imply a sort of Puritan predatory capitalism as both anarchic or wild *and* tyrannical, controlling or violent. On this account, such an

---

[50] Desai (2005:190) observes that American capitalism and government "allows managers to characterize income differently depending on the audience [and so] legitimizes earnings manipulation and permits managers a certain license that may mark the onset" of a cascade, by manipulating a la Machiavelli high-tech information systems for their private gains.

[51] Schutz (2001:162) suggests that American and other capitalist economies "constitute societies that are just as hierarchical as those based on other economic systems [e.g.], Soviet-style central planning, feudalism, and ancient slave-based systems."

economic system operates as the reenactment of the Hobbesian state of nature (Munch 1994) of universal inter-personal, inter-group, and inter-societal, war, violence, and plunder after the image of the jungle. It specifically does in the self-perpetuated celebrated national form of "Wild West" capitalism and politics (Hill 2002), as embodied by proverbial "cowboy capitalists" or Enron-style capitalist entrepreneurs (Desai 2005) and "shoot first, then ask questions" (Schuparra 1998) domestically coercive and globally warlike or bellicose "godly" politicians, including "born again" evangelical Presidents.

*"Mafia Capitalism"*

A particular form and symbol of the Calvinist predatory capitalist economy is what some US economists identify or predict as reemerging or impending "mafia capitalism" in America (Pryor 2002) under neoconservative economic, political and culture "regressive" dominance during the 1980s–2000s (Schutz 2001). If so, then the Calvinist capitalist economy can be considered and described as "predatory" or "rapacious" at least in the form and meaning of "mafia capitalism". Simply, if one does not know or see predatory capitalism in modern America under Puritan-rooted neo-conservatism, "mafia capitalism" may provide at least partial "proof in the pudding." While not all predatory capitalism is "mafia capitalism", the latter by definition is an exemplar or proxy of the former. Like the predatory capitalist and non-capitalist economy in general, mafia (also called crony[52]) capitalism represents a paradigmatic case of master-servant or hierarchical, oligarchic, anti-egalitarian, repressive, and coercive economic-social system. If this is correct, mafia capitalism helps answer the question of whether a Calvinist diluted (if not pure) master-servant, including predatory, capitalist economy does or will exist in America. So, if one does not yet know to define and detect such an economic system, "you know it when you see it" as mafia capitalism. The latter is recently exemplified and symbolized by Enron-type predatory as well as manipulative business ideas and practices or simply Enronism reportedly widespread and growing in the modern American economy[53] to the

---

[52] Also, some US politicians used the term "crony capitalism" identified as the underlying source of the housing and financial (banking) crisis of in the fall of 2008.
[53] According to Desai (2005:172), such instance of corporate predation or manipulation (malfeasance) during the 2000s as Enron, Tyco and even Xerox are or "part of a

point of becoming its "normal pathology" rather than an isolated, "black sheep" deviation (Desai 2005). By analogy, if one does not know and see "mafia capitalism", Enronism thus understood can provide some "food for thought".[54]

In retrospect, cynics or politically incorrect commentators and comics may remark that American Puritanism has "specialized" within Smith-Durkheim's societal division of labor or work specialization in the reproduction of mafia capitalism since at least Prohibition and its amoral and intelligent (Merton 1968; Simon 1976) "unwanted children" Al Capone and other mafias during the 1920s–30s. Specifically, it has done so in its reproduction as an unintended outcome or latent function. This was witnessed in Prohibition and its various vestiges and replays since its formal ending ("dry" Southern states, the increased federal legal age limit for alcohol use), and its expansions or proxies in the new or ever-recurring temperance and culture wars (the war on drugs, birth control, sexual sins).

Also, American Puritanism has "specialized" in the reproduction of this pathological economic system as an intended effect or manifest function. This has been witnessed or apparent in recent mafia capitalism, at least Enronism as the system, method, and symbol of predatory and manipulative "godly" profit-making linking the theocratic "Bible Belt" and the anarchic "Wild West" (Texas, etc.) and via a social contagion beyond (Desai 2005). Relatedly, Puritanism has profitably "specialized" in reproducing mafia and predatory capitalism in America either as an illegal and non-institutional *or* "perfectly legal" and institutional—until a certain threshold of official and public tolerance, credulity, or even admiration—economic system. Predictably, the first was

---

larger dynamic" and "representative of larger trends in the deteriorating quality and reliability of corporate profit reports" in modern American capitalism during neoconservatism. For instance, in his view each of these instances is the "paradigmatic example of some kind of abuse: Enron as an example of fraudulently reported earnings, Tyco as an example of managerial theft, and Xerox as an example of subtle manipulations to reach targets" (Desai 2005:176). Desai (2005:186–9) reaches the conclusion that "a secular change in the nature of profit reporting, particularly amongst large firms, is at the center of the degradation of corporate profits, rather than a transitory failure of governance mechanisms" and so "something more widespread is happening with respect to the reliability" of profits "easily gamed by financial engineers" in American capitalism.

[54] Even the free-market *Economist* comments that "most US Presidents surround themselves with a regional mafia," with Reagan and his "Californians" as a cited case in point.

exemplified by Prohibition or the "amoral intelligence" (Merton 1968) of Al Capone and his mafia, as well as drug "free market" entrepreneurs (Friedman 1997) and mafias, and the second by Enronism and the "blissful ignorance" (Wacquant 2002) and violence of "red-neck" or "cowboy" capitalists.

The preceding implies a historical trajectory or path-dependence spanning from Calvinist theocratic to oligarchic, repressive and predatory, notably mafia, capitalism in the way or image of Enronism, thus a master-servant economy déjà vu. If the above observations are correct, then the Calvinist master-servant economy in America tends to eventuate in mafia capitalism as a sort of modernized version of a predatory economy and the axiomatic case of an oligarchic or closed, violent, and authoritarian economic system. At this juncture, the latest epitome or symbol of the Calvinist master-servant economy in America, especially the Southwest, represents Enronism as the "paradigmatic example" (Desai 2005) of mafia and generally predatory capitalism. If so, then mafia capitalism, combined with and actually defined by Hobbesian anarchy for capital and ever-increasing authoritarian control and repression of labor and all of Winthrop's subjected populace, may, as Veblen actually predicted and Merton implied, become the Calvinist economy "destiny" of America, minimally the anti-labor South and the "Wild West" (Alabama, Texas, Oklahoma, Utah, etc.). This recasts Weber's affinity of Calvinism and the modern capitalist economy in an "intimate connection" of Calvinist theocracy with mafia or predatory theocratic capitalism as total societal and partial economic systems in America.[55] And, this was witnessed or prefigured by the link of neo-Calvinism (the "New Divinity") and abuses of political power in the service of "pecuniary interests" in 18th century New England (German 1995).

Apparently, mafia and generally predatory capitalism may ultimately reemerge as the economic logic and system of Calvinist-Puritan theocracy as a total social system in America. No wonder, Enronism as the paradigmatic instance and emblem of mafia capitalism primarily (although not solely) emerged and operated in the Southwestern "Bible

---

[55] Weber did and would perhaps not use the term "mafia capitalism" in connection with Calvinism, but still his Calvinist capitalism is by assumption and in his description essentially theocratic and to that extent authoritarian, i.e. illiberal and non-democratic, including predatory. And "mafia capitalism" is just a consummate instance of the latter.

Belt" (Texas, etc.) as Weber's Calvinist (Baptist) Bibliocracy déjà vu. To be sure, not all mafia capitalism in America and elsewhere (e.g., Italy, Poland, Russia, China, South America, etc.) is Calvinist in its religious origin and connotation but also non-Calvinist (Catholic, Orthodox Christian, non-Christian). Yet, sociologically through its invariant theocracy and economically via its inner theocratic, master-servant economy, Calvinism, including Puritanism (psychologically due to its "pure hypocrisy"), intrinsically entails and ultimately generates mafia capitalism as its economic logic and system.

In Merton's terms, mafia capitalism arises and operates as a manifest or latent function, or an intended or unintended outcome, of Calvinist theocracy and its equivalent, master-servant economy in America. Mafia capitalism as the manifest function is demonstrated by what Weber and Veblen identify as the Calvinist robber-barons (e.g., Baptist "captains of industry"), not only apparently emulated by their reincarnations in "Bible-Belt" and "Wild-West" Enronism. They are, as Merton observes, secretly admired because of their attaining the all-important success-goal, the "American Dream" even if through methodical robbery and (as Dickens put it) plunder for the "glory" of and "ordained" by the God of Calvinism, by most Americans. Mafia capitalism as the latent function is evidenced by what Merton calls Al Capone's "amoral intelligence" and organized crime or mafia produced by Puritanical Prohibition (Simon 1976) and reproduced by the neo-Puritan war on drugs and a panoply of other temperance and culture wars against sins and vices *cum* crimes in America under "reborn" fundamentalism (Bell 2002; Wagner 1997). In this way, Calvinist evangelical theocracy in America generates and predicts two aggregate economic outcomes. The first outcome is institutionalized mafia capitalism in the form of "institutionalized corruption" (Linton 2001) or predation, as epitomized by Enronism as a generalized, via social contagion, "free enterprise" pattern rather than an isolated case (Desai 2005)—and eventually state terrorism or moral fascism via a vice-police state—as the manifest function. The second outcome is illegal organized crime exemplified by alcohol, drug, prostitution, and other vice-mafias or criminal organizations (Merton 1968), and analogously and in reaction, counter-state terrorism ultimately ("Christian" fundamentalist terrorist militia, etc.), as the latent function.

Now, one can object, as US conservatives or economic "libertarians" do, that mafia-style practices and institutionalized or non-institutionalized corruption are found in all capitalist (and more non-capitalist) economies, and so are not something peculiar to American capitalism ("what's the big deal"?). These objections are, first, dubious, second, self-contradictory. They are dubious in overlooking or denying that mafia-style practices and corruption are more pervasive in American capitalism than in most other capitalist economies, as indicated by research (Pryor 2002) and various comparative surveys or estimates. Second, they are self-contradictory in contradicting American economic and other celebrated exceptionalism, namely the claim to America, including its economy, as the "pure", "virtuous" and "uncorrupted" nation by comparison with the "corruption" and "vices" of the "old" Europe and all other societies.

*The Calvinist Spirit cum "Ghost" of Capitalism*

The preceding implies that the neo-Puritan predatory, including mafia-style, capitalist economy in America is the pathological mutation of Weber's Calvinist spirit of capitalism into, in a play of words, what he and especially Tönnies[56] might call the "ghost of capitalism" in the substantive sense of economic (plus political and cultural) predation, plunder or rapacity, including mafia-style business ideas, practices, and outcomes. By analogy to what Weber calls the "ghost of dead religious beliefs", the "ghost of capitalism" would express the death or degenerate, Frankenstein-like (Friedman and Friedman 1982) transmutation of the normal Calvinist spirit of capitalism as incarnated by Franklin in his post-Calvinist benevolent, generous, or secular phase (Byrne 1997).

Hence, at least mafia capitalism, in particular its quasi-institutionalized exemplar and symbol such as "godly" Enronism in the "Bible-Belt", reveals the Calvinist spirit *cum* "ghost" of capitalism. Just as during the late 19th and early 20th century what Weber calls the Calvinist spirit and structure of modern capitalism in America reportedly functioned or appeared as the "ghost" and regime of a feudal master-servant economy or "belated feudalism" (Orren 1991), by the 21 century it does as what some US "libertarian" economists (Friedman and Friedman 1982) call (in reference to government, notably a welfare state) Frankenstein (or perhaps "Dracula"?) in terms of economic and other predation and

---

[56] Tönnies states that "spirit as a special entity exists in the world of ghosts" in reference with a "Messianic hope [for community] based on the "spirit" alone".

inhumanity. In short, Puritan predatory, in particular mafia, capitalism exemplified or symbolized by Enronism, in America expresses the Calvinist spirit of capitalism (Dahrendorf 1959) turned "ghost" or "mad", "gone wild" (Habermas 2001).

Instances of the "ghost", "madness", and "wildness" of Calvinist capitalism in America abound, historically spanning from the 17th to the 21st century, and geographically from New England's "Biblical Commonwealth" to the Southern "Bible Belt", while fluctuating between deadly seriousness and grotesque, usually in a tragic-comic mix after the image of "dumb laws". One "classic" instance has been mentioned, Tocqueville-Marx-Weber's Puritan "sober virtuosi" of Calvinism in New England undertaking capitalist profit-making on American Indians (their scalps) priced by a menu of different prices depending on the "quality and profitability of the product". If anything, at least such a curious historical episode, yet usually overlooked even by Weber in his celebrated account of an affinity, transforms the Calvinist spirit of capitalism in this Puritan profitable experimental application to Native Americans into "ghost" or "mad" (unless one claims, as Tocqueville's Puritans did and their evangelical heirs do, that this profit-making on the "ungodly" and "savage" was historically necessary, legitimate, and "civilizing"). At least to those Native Americans, like other "heathen" or "pagans"[57] (Fehler 2005), to be cured of their "ungodliness" by profitably exterminating them ("only good when dead"), the Calvinist spirit of capitalism really operated and appeared as a "ghost", (Friedman's) mixed proto-capitalist or late-feudal and government Frankenstein.

Another classic, less lethal instance has also been mentioned: early American Puritans' capitalist profit-making on trading slaves (Dayton 1999), "stirred and shaken" with trade in rum to form a "particularly lucrative" and tragic-comic cocktail (Foerster 1962). Even if abstracting from the first instance, the profitable hunting of the native "heathen", as though it never actually happened, as extreme and atypical "extra" Puritan profit-making, at least this historical case made the Calvinist spirit of capitalism appear as the "ghost" or "mad" to its objects subjected to "godly" profitable, although eventually inefficient, enslavement and "free market enterprise". Curiously, Weber notes that "there were

---

[57] Fehler (2005) cites the description by the 19th century American "orthodox Calvinist clergy" of Aristotle as "the most pious of all the heathen" and, following them, himself describes him as a "pagan philosopher."

complaints over the strong greed for profits of the New Englanders as early as 1632", yet does not mention the above two instances of the spirit of capitalism turned "ghost" or "gone wild". But even the expression the "strong greed for profits" contains such an implication, since (if) the implied Biblical commandment "thou shall not be greedy" is maintained as a sin even within Puritanism and Calvinism generally, so its violation implies abnormality and in that sense the Calvinist spirit *cum* pathological "ghost" of capitalism. In short, the Calvinist spirit of capitalism becomes a sort of "ghost" even within Calvinism if "Mammon", apparently revealed in the "strong greed for profits", replaces or competes with rather than as commanded, serves and glorifies "God". In fact, the glorification of "Mammon" (Bellamy 1999) reflects the very Calvinist spirit of capitalism turned into a "ghost" by escaping from, to use Weber's expression, the "iron cage" of Calvinism's capitalist theocracy or theocratic capitalism, and then acting independent.

Yet another, more benevolent and grotesque instance, also implied, is predictably the "good old" Benjamin Franklin described by Weber as one of the "great men of Puritanism", with his "strict Calvinistic father", and considered to be the embodiment of the spirit of capitalism. Yet, Weber himself implies that the spirit of capitalism turned into a sort of "ghost" or "mad", though a benevolent or grotesque one, even in Franklin. This is due to Franklin's identified profitable—the appearance of "honesty is the best policy"—"pure hypocrisy" and utilitarianism, including Machiavellianism, as none than Parsons suggests for Puritanism in that it reduces humans to the means of "one's own ends", just as of "the purposes of God". And if not Franklin himself as a supremely "good guy" and hero in American history and memory (Gould 1996), yet eventually moving away from his Calvinist heritage in favor of Enlightenment-based ideas and during his Paris life[58] (Byrne 1997), then this holds true for most American Puritans.

In particular, it applies to those Puritans, as perceived by German and other European observers cited by Weber, who by making "money out of men" effectively transformed the spirit of capitalism in a capitalist "ghost" in virtue of this evident profitable Machiavellianism and for

---

[58] Byrne (1997:48) remarks that during his eleven years (before the French Revolution) as the American ambassador to Paris "he quickly moved away from the Calvinism in which he was raised, thinking (like many of his contemporaries) that its rejection of good works was inimical to morality", being for a while a deist, "but eventually he settled for a sort of benign and skeptical indifference in religious matters".

those thus treated. Perhaps only Sorokin's (1970) actors actuated by unconditional "Christian love" and Homans' (1961) "true Christians" would consent to being used as the means for others' profit and related ends, thus would not experience the Calvinist spirit of capitalism as a "ghost", even if applied to them by Franklin et al. as the supreme exemplar of "goodness" and initially "godliness". Yet, even these putative saints or angels would, especially if overused for such extraneous materialist and other ends, perhaps at some point say, as Americans do, "enough is enough" and eventually see the light (or rather darkness) in being subjected to the Calvinist spirit *cum* "ghost" of capitalism. This precisely happened in 18th century New England in which many condemned neo-Calvinist theologians *cum* capitalists ("New Lights") for abusing their power by promoting their "private interest at public expense" (German 1995). Yet, as experience shows and the proverb goes, most, even supremely pious humans by definition or in reality are "no angels" (Somers 1998), but instead "flesh-and-blood" creatures (Bowles 1998) consequently condemned or distrusted as "corrupt" by Calvinism, notably American Puritanism.

By analogy, "neo-classic" and/or contemporary instances and symptoms of the Calvinist spirit of capitalism turned "ghost", "mad", or "wild" in America are even more numerous. They also mix elements of Puritan tragic deadliness or morbid seriousness, inherited from what Weber calls Calvinist "terrible seriousness" (the doctrine of predestination), with grotesque and perhaps that kind of comedy that makes and keeps American Puritanism and its economy and society the "laughing stock" of the world (Hill 2002; Wagner 1997) for long, up to the 21st century. Because even enumerating such instances would require a separate chapter, if not another book, at this juncture suffice it to mention only a few of them. A general instance or rather pattern is what can be considered the typical sociological and often historical evolution, sequence, or trajectory from Calvinist capitalist and other "virtues" to "vices", from normalcy to "normal pathology".

In Merton's framework, this is the sequence and path from Franklin's benign Calvinist "time is money" spirit of capitalism to the American dream construed as (in James's words) the "bitch goddess" of monetary success and to social anomie, ultimately deviance, including violent and other crime, as the illegitimate, yet efficient means, in the absence of or limited legitimate avenues, to attain that "sacrosanct" end. In his words, "a cardinal American virtue" like ambition reproduces or aggravates a "cardinal American vice", deviant conduct (Merton 1968). In this account, such an outcome is primarily (though not solely) attributed to the money-success spirit of Calvinist capitalism. The latter thus effectively mutates into a "ghost" in the sense of acting as an extant source and rationalization of deviance and crime in the function of a supreme end to be attained, as Merton puts it, "by any means whatsoever," justifying any efficient instruments and tactics (Simon 1976) a la, as Pareto also implies, Machiavellianism. In a way, the Calvinist spirit of capitalism turns into a "ghost" or "mad" in accordance with the general pattern that, as Merton comments, "all virtues can easily become vices by merely being carried out to excess". Simply, it does because it tends to "overdo" and "overreach" in following and applying Franklin's "time is money" maxim and related Calvinist profit-making or proto-capitalist principles.

A concrete instance or pattern of the Calvinist spirit of capitalism thus understood is the expanding private prison industry in America, especially (not solely) in the "Bible Belt" and the "Wild West" (Texas, California, etc.), under "reborn" religious and political neo-conservatism. Predictably, the latter, including conservative or "libertarian" economics, promotes and extols the private prison industry on economic efficiency grounds, thus as expressing the "true spirit" of American capitalism, as well as the Calvinist-capitalist "Bible Belt" (like Alabama, Texas, etc.). However, its victims, notably, those two thirds of nearly 2.5 million prisoners punished for drug-war "crimes" (Becky and Western 2004) and other moral offenses, especially sexual sins, as well as many (to be) executed innocent persons, likely experience such a system in exactly opposite terms. Simply, they experience its putative Calvinist spirit of capitalism run "wild" as a capitalist "ghost" or "madness" of profit-making not just, as Weber's early German observers noted, "out of men" outsmarted or "ripped-off" in free market transactions, but also from humans' ultimate misery and death, namely incarceration and execution for sins-crimes. This is likely in view of the reported economic, legal, and medical horrors[59]—so surreal as if coming from

---

[59] For instance, according to reports, in 2006 almost 70 inmates, mostly elderly, died in the California's growingly private prison system because of no or poor medical care, despite the US Supreme Court ruling (in 1976) that prisoners "have a constitutional right to health care". Similar and even more disturbing or even horrifying cases are reported for many, especially the "Bible Belt", states, notably Texas as the perennial US and Western leader in both executions and prisoner death from "natural" causes. For instance, a Texas county (sic) grand jury "indicted" one of "private prison companies running the federal detention centers" "on a murder charge in the death of a prisoner

Hollywood-style horror movies—combined with the growing profits, of the Puritan private prison and death penalty system in America. For those two-plus millions of Americans confined in and thousands executed, respectively, by the private neo-conservative prison and death penalty system as the "fastest growing industry" in America in recent decades, the real face and image of the Calvinist spirit of capitalism is a "ghost" (citing a horror movie). Specifically, it is Friedman's government Frankenstein compounded with and intensified by—what he, like other "libertarian" economists since Mises and Hayek, denies or overlooks—a "free-enterprise" equivalent literally maximizing profits on what Churchill may call human "blood and tears" (execution and imprisonment). In turn, both components of the penal system reproduce and are being reproduced alike by an ever-expanding police state, notably the Puritan vice police in the "Bible Belt", as discussed later.

*Calvinist Master-Servant Capitalism: Specification*

The definition and decomposition of the Calvinist diluted, capitalist master-servant economy in America is further specified and qualified by what Weber would call a contrasting formal and substantive specification. First, modern Calvinist capitalism in America is *not* considered a master-servant economic system in formal or legal terms, for legally capitalists or plutocrats are not masters and laborers or the masses no servants, let alone slaves, but formally or legally "free and rational choosers" (Buchanan 1991), unlike their pre-capitalist antecedents. Thus, to describe American capitalists and laborers, except for certain economic groups (sweat-shop workers and prisoners coerced into slave-like work settings), as their Western counterparts sometimes do, as "masters" and "slaves" or "servants", respectively, in capitalism is inaccurate or exaggerated, a hyperbole or metaphor in a formal-legal sense.

Second, in substantive or sociological terms Calvinist capitalism in America functions or appears as a master-servant economic system. It does in the sense and form of pro-capital and notably anti-labor ideas, institutions, and practices, and consequently capital's near-complete

---

days before his release [by allowing] other inmates to beat [him] to death with padlocks stuffed into socks." And, to add insult to injury some neo-conservative federal officials (Attorney General) reportedly (as a local official accused) stopped an investigation into "abuses at one of the privately-run prisons."

institutional dominance or asymmetrical structural power over labor in an equivalent state of subjection or weakness (Fligstein 2001). Simply, while not the matter of law, as in its pure forms in slavery, feudal servitude, and the caste system, it does in virtue of factual capital-labor drastic and even growing, as during the 1980s–2000s, power asymmetry in the economy and all society. If so, the description "masters" and "servants" or "slaves" for most American capitalists and workers, respectively, in Calvinist capitalism may not be inaccurate or exaggerated, thus more than a hyperbole or metaphor in a substantive sociological sense, namely, the first's proximately absolute power or total domination and the second's almost complete subjection or subordination (Dahrendorf 1959). Generally, the defining element or the eventual outcome of absolute power or total domination is transforming the economy and society into a master-servant, if not slave-style, economic and social system, making the world arbitrary or "mad" (Bourdieu 2000). To say that the Calvinist economy is not truly a master-servant system in formal but only in substantive terms means that it is not a pure and strict but diluted and tempered one, in accordance with and premised on the distinction between pure or primitive and diluted or contemporary theocracy in Calvinism. In retrospect, such a pro-capital and anti-labor economic system fulfills Winthrop's and in extension Calvin's commandment that some are "high" in wealth, power and dignity, and others "mean" and "in subjection" as Divinely ordained.

*Economic "Autocracy" versus Democracy*

Consequently, the Calvinist diluted, capitalist master-servant economy in America is a sort of "democracy free zone." Instead, it is a sort of factual or metaphorical "autocracy" in the sense of near-complete dominance by a single agent over the economic system, with almost no relevant countervailing forces or balancing influences defining democratic processes and institutions. In particular, the modern Calvinist capitalist economy in America is a diluted master-servant one on the account of its lack of or weak industrial democracy as the system of reciprocal economic freedoms and rights and countervailing powers, owing to its anti-labor, pro-capital institutions. The anti labor, pro-capital capitalist economy in the US since Reaganism (and before) and in part the UK, as during Thatcherism (Fligstein 2001; Myles 1994), intrinsically proscribes and eventually eliminates economic democracy thus understood as a metaphorical taboo and actual inefficiency or nuisance, respectively. It does by denying and eliminating basic labor liberties and rights (union organization, collective bargaining, management co-participation, etc.), while affording and extolling virtually unlimited freedom to capital or plutocracy. And, this is the true substance and meaning of what US conservative or "libertarian" economists (Buchanan 1991; Friedman and Friedman 1982; Fishback 1998) extol as "unfettered capitalism" in America. It is Leviathan-style control and oppression of labor, Hobbesian anarchy or unrestricted freedom for capital to the point of, figuratively or literally, "license to kill" in the image, if not the model, of the "Wild West" (e.g., Texas, Oklahoma) ruled by metaphorically "big guys with big guns" (Hill 2002; Munch 1994) *cum* power and wealth, and in the substantive sense of classic robber-baron and "neo-classic" Enron-style practices (Desai 2005).

Furthermore, in comparative terms, various data and estimates indicate that the modern Calvinist economy in America entails the minimal and weakest degree of economic democracy, just as its polity has one of the lowest indexes of political democracy as discussed later (Bollen 1990), among contemporary Western economies (Flanagan 1999; Nickell 1997). For instance, this comparative minimalism in economic democracy is exemplified by the lowest index of labor standards, actually no standards at all (0), the lowest level of employment protection (1), the weakest capital-labor coordination in wage formation (1), as well as the least active government engagement or labor market policies (3) in America's economy. Notably, the latter features the lowest indexes of union coverage (1) and density (1), indicating the "strength of organized labor" (Amenta and Halfmann 2000) in general and to that extent its comparatively unrivaled weakness or minimal countervailing positional power (Perrone 1984; Wallace, Griffin, and Rubin 1989) in relation to capital. These indicators yield the lowest aggregate index of economic democracy (7) for America's economy among contemporary Western economies (ranging from 17 and 18 for Australia and the UK to 88 for Sweden, see Table 3.2). In addition, America has the lowest or even virtually no labor coparticipation in management or decision making (e.g., through work councils) as both a factor of economic efficiency, including profitability (Hodgson 1999), and of democratization in the economy and beyond (Giddens 1998), yet apparently a sort of non-entity or taboo in American Calvinist capitalism. On the account of such remarkable lack or weakness of economic democracy, this type of capitalism in America operates after the model or presents the image of the "Wild West" or Hobbesian state of nature (Hill 2002;

Table 3.2. Indexes of economic democracy in advanced economies, 1989–94

|  | Index of economic democracy |
|---|---|
| Australia | 17.2 |
| Austria | 37.3 |
| Belgium | 42.6 |
| Canada | 15.9 |
| Denmark | 26.3 |
| Finland | 39.6 |
| France | 34.8 |
| Germany | 53.7 |
| Ireland | 31.1 |
| Italy | 44.3 |
| Japan | 18.3 |
| Netherlands | 26.9 |
| New Zealand | 16.8 |
| Norway | 38.7 |
| Portugal | 46.8 |
| Spain | 36.7 |
| Sweden | 88.3 |
| Switzerland | 21.2 |
| UK | 18.4 |
| US | 7.0 |

Estimates based on Flanagan (1999); and Nickell (1997).

Munch 1994) ruled by predatory cowboys *cum* capitalists Enron-style, as well as third-world capitalist dictatorships like Singapore and Chile under military rule before, rather than of modern Western economies.

In consequence, this lack of or weak economic democracy makes the Calvinist anti-labor, pro-capital economy in America a form of illiberal, undemocratic rather than, as usually claimed or supposed, liberal-democratic capitalism, thus some kind of diluted and modernized capitalist dictatorship, as portrayed in unorthodox economic analyses (Hodgson 1999; McMurtry 1999; Pryor 2002; Schutz 2001). At the minimum, this holds true of the post bellum evangelical US South that looks closer to third-world capitalist dictatorships (e.g., Singapore) than to Western liberal-democratic capitalist societies. Primarily, this is because of the initial absence or ultimate suppression of economic democracy in the South via anti-labor laws and practices outlawing or limiting basic labor liberties and rights in private and public (e.g., education) sectors (Amenta et al. 2001; Cochran 2001; Lipset 1955) and favoring capital and "corporate hegemony" (Berman 2000). Moreover, a sociological analysis suggests that American capitalism is among Western societies the "purest case" of a modern economy and society in which capitalist elites have the institutional power to harness the "policy domains of the state for their own interest" (Fligstein 2001). To that extent, it functions as the "purest" type of anti- or quasi-democratic capitalism within contemporary Western society, while converging with third-world capitalist dictatorships.

*"One-Party" Economic System*

These anti-labor, pro-capital institutions and practices in America, especially (but not limited to) the neo-Calvinist South, transforms what is supposed to be and extolled as a freely competitive or pluralist economy into an almost exact opposite, at least for one major economic agent (labor), in a functional equivalence or analogy with the one-party political system. By virtue of anti-labor institutions and practice and the consequent lack or weakness of industrial democracy, Calvinist capitalism in America, at least in the "Bible Belt", becomes a substantive economic equivalent or analogue of a one-party political system and in that sense effectively (capitalist) dictatorship in the economy (Hodgson 1999; McMurtry 1999; Pryor 2002; Schutz 2001). For example, its anti-labor and pro-capital preferences, agencies, and practices are functionally equivalent to, say, the US government officially or effectively favoring and institutionalizing only a single political (Republican or Democratic) party and establishing a one-party American polity, thus more than just an analogy. In particular, outlawing and systematically obstructing labor organization or unions and collective bargaining in America, notably the vehemently anti-union South, is hardly different from the stance of economic democracy or freedom than doing the same with respect to a major political (Republican or Democratic) party. This practice exemplifies an egregious case of unequal legal treatment, sanctified on "godly" religious, notably theocratic grounds like labor or unions condemned as "ungodly" and thus "un-American" in the "Bible Belt".

In particular, the preceding implies a functional equivalence or at least analogy between economic power monopoly in Calvinist capitalism and political duopoly in American politics. In both cases, the aim or outcome is what Weber calls "monopolistic closure" or "monopolization" of wealth, power, and status and in that sense economic (not necessarily market monopolies in the strict sense) and societal monopoly as the antithesis or subversion of freedom and democracy in the economy and society. With respect to capital-labor relative power, the modern Calvinist economy in America is effectively economic monopoly—as well as oligopoly in terms of market structure proper (Pryor 2002)—just as the American polity is usually considered, by analogy to duopolistic markets, political duopoly or a two-party regime (Hill 2002; Schutz 2001). In this sense, Calvinist capitalism seems even more monopolistic or less competitive in broad capital-labor, as distinguished from strictly market, terms and to that extent less open, pluralistic, and democratic than the polity that is at least formally duopolistic with an equal legal treatment of both major political parties.

And, as noted, such effective and even often, as in the South, legal power monopoly in the economy is the antithesis or perversion of industrial democracy, just as market monopolies and oligopolies are so in relation to free competition and economic freedom overall, and political monopoly and even perhaps duopoly relative to democracy and pluralism. In economic terms, capital's almost complete and even recently increasing dominance over labor represents what economists call the maximum "index of the degree of monopoly power" (Lerner 1955) in the "free market" economy, or alternatively the minimal, near-zero level of industrial democracy. In sum, the reality or design of the modern Calvinist capitalist economy in America is economic democracy as a taboo or non-entity—zero or minimal labor liberties, rights, and countervailing power or influence, from worker organization to collective bargaining to coparticipation.

*Extreme Economic Anti-Egalitarianism*

As hinted above, the modern Calvinist capitalist economy in America is a diluted master-servant also on the account of its extreme anti-egalitarianism or sharp economic inequalities perpetuating or evoking and almost functionally equivalent to those in feudal serfdom and the caste system, if not even slavery. Simply, it is so because it reproduces and sanctifies master-servant economic inequality, extreme wealth, and privilege for Calvinist capitalist masters and material insecurity and even deprivation for most (of course, not all) workers (Wolff 2002), including comparatively pervasive and persisting poverty (Smeeding 2006).

Calvinist capitalism is a master-servant economy in that it sharply and increasingly in recent times separates, as some economists put it, the super-wealthy "top heavy" one percent (or less) owning almost half of America's wealth from the rest of the American population (Wolff 2002), thus not only the abjectly poor underclass (about 15–20 percent) but also "prosperous" middle classes that have fulfilled their American dream of material success. As known, Calvinist capitalism in America is the Western capitalist economy persistently reproducing the greatest economic, both wealth and income (Wolff 2002; Keister and Moller 2000; Alderson and Nielsen 2002), inequality in general and the highest poverty in particular, including that for children. As regards the latter, US poverty rates have been for long and remain by the early 21st century "at or near the top of the range" by comparison with those of other Western countries (Smeeding 2006). In this account, a major reason for this Western "leadership" in poverty is that the US government expends "by far the smallest share of its resources" on antipoverty programs such as income transfers (Smeeding 2006), thus expressing the anti-egalitarian paradox or puzzle of "high inequality yet low redistribution" (Benabou 2000) in the economy and polity, respectively.

Hence, at least in relative, cross-national terms, modern Calvinist capitalism in America qualifies or appears as a master-servant economy on the account of these evidently unparalleled levels of economic equality and poverty among Western *capitalist* economies ushering in the 21st century. Particularly, a singular "proof" or syndrome of such a capitalist master-servant economy is the large and ever-growing gap between average executive compensations and worker wages in America (from 20 times in the 1960s to 700–1000 times during the 2000s) (Bebchuk and Fried 2003). And, this gap, like wealth inequality overall, has almost reached or evoked the differences between masters and servants in feudal serfdom and the caste system, at least the robber barons versus workers in pre-New Deal capitalism as "belated feudalism". In sum, Calvinist capitalism in America reproduces and rationalizes, by social neo-Darwinism a la merit (Bourdieu 1998), master-servant style gaps in wealth and income between the new robber barons *cum* Enron-like entrepreneurs or executives (Desai 2005) and their workers[60] (Bebchuk and Fried 2003).

---

[60] Bebchuk and Fried (2003:73) remark that "average director compensation in the 200 largest US corporations was $152,626 in 2001 [while] in the notorious Enron case, the directors were each paid $380,000 annually."

Overall, the point is that modern Calvinist capitalism is a diluted master-servant economy not merely because of its wealth and income inequalities per se found in any known economy. Rather, it is because of their extreme and ever-growing, as during the 1980s–2000s, proportions similar to or reminiscent of those in feudalism and the caste system, if not even slavery. In short, it is because of its economic hyper anti-egalitarianism, not just its weak egalitarianism in itself. No doubt, it is often difficult or controversial to specify substantively or quantitatively what level of economic inequality—or, as Americans would say, when "enough is enough"—indicates an instance or proxy of a modern master-servant economy and in consequence of an equivalent anti-egalitarian and authoritarian or repressive polity (Acemoglu 2005; Benabou 2000; Lee 2005; Putterman, Roemer and Silvestre 1998; Pryor 2002), as well as political corruption (You and Khagram 2005). Still, a substantive indicator, criterion, or proxy can be, as economists suggest, identified in that those economic arrangements reproducing "a very unequal distribution of income and wealth" tend to be compatible with a "similarly unequal distribution of political power" and ultimately with "dictatorships and other repressive regimes"[61] (Acemoglu 2005). This implies that economic inequality indicates or approximates a master-servant economy only when it is substantively extreme such as "a very unequal distribution of income and wealth" and also corresponds to political anti-egalitarianism in the form of comparable unequal power and eventually dictatorship or repression. Namely, when Calvinist capitalism is, as typically, both extremely non-egalitarian *and* intertwined with political repression, as in the form of a joint oligarchic economy and state (Pryor 2002), it effectively functions as a master-servant economy. And, then simply "enough is enough" even for most Americans largely supportive or tolerant of large economic inequalities regarded and justified as "just deserts".

Also, certain quantitative measures can specify what level of economic inequality—or what "a very unequal distribution of income and wealth" precisely is—indicates or approximates a master-servant economy and in extension an anti-egalitarian, repressive polity. For example, the share of the top one percent of the population in the total wealth can serve as an indicator or estimate in this respect. More specifically, if

---

[61] Acemoglu (2005:1041) suggests that "those with political power would be greatly tempted to use their power to redistribute income and change the economic institutions in line with their interests."

the "top heavy" one percent of the US population owns nearly half of the total and even more of financial wealth during the 2000s (Wolff 2002), this can serve as an indicator or proxy of the rebirth of Calvinist master-servant capitalism, just as relatedly political anti-egalitarianism and repression as well as religious fundamentalism, in America. For strikingly this figure is exactly identical to the respective share of pre-New Deal robber barons during "belated feudalism" of the 1920s and also comparable or similar to that of feudal landlords in the US South and medieval Europe, with one percent of the population also owning about half of the total wealth and/or income of a society (Lenski 1984). In retrospect, some sociologists admonish that such increasing wealth inequality in America during the 1980s–2000s serves to reaffirm and reinforce the "continuing relevance of Tocqueville's fears about the emergence of a new [feudal-style] aristocracy" (Goldberg 2001) in the non-feudal "new nation".

Also, the Gini index of income inequality can analogously be used for the above purpose, though it is more problematic because there is no conventional or convenient threshold or cut-off short of the extreme and unrealistic point of 1 indicating total expropriation by a single person or group, as is the 1/50 percent combination in wealth inequality. Some other measures of income inequality can serve as indicators or proxies of Calvinist master-servant capitalism, indirectly political anti-egalitarianism and repression, in America, such as the share of the top decile and percentile (10 and 1 percent) of the US population. For instance, an economic study finds that the income share of the US top decile revolved around 40–45 percent in interwar times, then declined "substantially to just above" 30 percent during World War II and remained "flat" at 31–32 percent until the 1970s (Piketty and Saez 2006). Notably, following postwar stability the top decile income share in America has grown "dramatically" during the last three decades to the point of currently reaching a level near to that of prewar times. The exactly identical trend has been observed in the income share of the top one percentile of the US population during the 20th and early 21st century, from 18 percent before WW I to "only" 8 percent during the 1960s–70s, and then "back" to 17 percent by 2000[62] (Piketty and Saez

---

[62] Piketty and Saez (2006:203) add that the increase in the top (0.1 percent) income share during the last 25 years "is largest in the US" by contrast to, for example, France and Japan with no noticeable increases with the effect that income concentration "is much lower" in these countries. In their account, overall "while top income shares have

2006). The above indicates another déjà vu: like wealth inequality, these income inequalities mean precisely "back" to pre-WW I "robber barons" capitalism or "belated feudalism", and in that sense a proxy return to a master-servant economy.

In another example, the gap between average executive compensation and US worker wages multiplies so fast and much (e.g., from 20 to 700–1000) that it, notably the first, becomes an agency problem (Bebchuk and Fried 2003) in the sense of almost arbitrary corporate power,[63] combined with "camouflage", and determination. To that extent, it can also provide an indicator or proxy of the return of Calvinist master-servant capitalism and in extension political repression. In this account, the recent dramatic "surge in top compensation" in America derives from the "increased ability" of corporate executives to determine their "own pay" and collect rents to the point of "enormous" salaries (Weisbach 2007) or "pay without performance" (Bebchuk and Fried 2003) at the "expense" of shareholders (Piketty and Saez 2006) and especially workers. To that extent, corporate executives effectively behave as the new feudal-style masters (Beck 2000; Bourdieu 1998) or neo-feudal oligarchs (Binmore 2001), and what Keynes identified as capitalist rentiers (while proposing their "euthanasia").

In retrospect, the above tendencies within modern Calvinist capitalism are predictable or unsurprising given that, as noted, Calvinism, including Puritanism, was a theocratic blueprint, system, and defense of extreme anti-egalitarianism in the economy and society, or

---

remained fairly stable in continental European countries or Japan over the past three decades, they have increased enormously in the United States and other English-speaking countries" (Piketty and Saez (2006:204). Also, Piketty and Saez (2006:204) add that many countries like France, the US and Japan "grew fastest in the postwar decades when income concentration was at its lowest", indicating a positive link between economic growth and equality.

[63] Bebchuk and Fried (2003:72) argue that "managerial power and rent extraction are likely to have an important influence on the design of compensation arrangements" in the modern American economy. Arguably, in the latter corporate "executives have substantial influence over their own pay" to the effect that "the greater is managers" power [and camouflage], the greater is their ability to extract rents" (Bebchuk and Fried 2003:75). To exemplify the disjuncture between company performance and executive pay, for example, Countrywide incurred losses in the magnitude of billions of dollars and its stock lost 80 percent of its value in 2007, and yet its CEO was paid about $2 million salary and $20 million in stock awards (while selling $121 million in stock). And, this is not an isolated example, but a generalized pattern or "method in the madness" in contemporary American "unfettered" capitalism.

master-servant economic and social inequality since Calvin. Recall, Weber registers that Calvin and in extension Calvinism established (as in Geneva and beyond) and defended the "unjust, but equally divinely ordained, distribution of wealth". Thus, for Calvin economic and social-political inequalities, or differences in wealth and in station, are "inevitable" (Heller 1986) on primarily Divine grounds. On this account, original Calvinism operated as what Weber and other sociologists would call the theodicy (Bourdieu 1998), or theological sanctification, of economic inequality and injustice, and in extension political repression, as Providential Design. By analogy, derivative Calvinism via American neo-conservatism acts, in addition, as the sociodicy or sociological rationalization of material inequality and privilege (and poverty), as "meritorious" or "deserved" by social neo-Darwinism as a déjà vu variation on the old "survival of the fittest" theme (Bourdieu 1998).

*Extreme Economic Anti-Humanism*

Also, the modern Calvinist-Puritan economy in America is a diluted master-servant on the account of its extreme economic anti-humanism in general, or alternatively its lacking of basic humanity or human decency, including compassion and charity. Indicators or symptoms of such economic anti-humanism include the following: comparatively longest work hours and shortest or no (paid) vacations, strict anti-welfare institutions and policies, and the like.

As known, in American Calvinist capitalism workers are forced by a mix of personal economic and (often) coercive business imperatives to work the longest hours among developed Western economies during the 1980s–2000s. On this account, American workers appear as or are perceived by their Western counterparts as equivalents or proxies of modern-day happy slaves or servants after the model of Winthrop's subjects or in the image of Huxley's "Brave New World", though this is not a correct description in formal-legal, as distinguished from substantive, terms. For example, in Europeans' perceptions, Americans tend to "overwork themselves" to an extent that "not much point in continuing to live" remains, even "if not exactly to death" (Manent 1998). As a particular facet of this overwork as a necessity made a kind of virtue, in American Calvinist capitalism workers, as also known, are given the shortest paid vacation (10–15 days), usually half as long as those (20–30 or more days), among other developed Western economies[64] during recent times, just as before. Thus, economists observe that in vacations when America and Europe are compared, the first ranks "among the poorest European countries" like Portugal and Italy, such that in terms of the "enjoyment of life", Americans look "worse off" or "poorer" than most other Western societies (Scitovsky 1972). In this view, "less good vacation amenities" in America are also, at least partly, explained by US puritanical authorities' intolerance or lower tolerance for citizens' "taking risks for pleasure" (Scitovsky 1972). If anything, the longest work hours and the shortest vacation time make modern Calvinist capitalism in America function or look as a new, diluted master-servant economy, specifically "belated feudalism" déjà vu, since the latter was precisely defined by such attributes (feudal masters, like slave owners, extend in direct or indirect ways the length of the labor of their servants and give them no paid vacations).

Hence, what is called a "joyless" capitalist economy (Scitovsky 1972) in contemporary America is the aggregate outcome of the longest work hours, the shortest vacation time, and related elements such as anti-labor and anti-union practices, "downsizing," job insecurity, company intrusive surveillance and mistreatment, diminishing job satisfaction or socializing, etc. In a way, a Calvinist economy is intrinsically "joyless" and thus "lifeless" given that Calvinism, especially Puritanism, like medieval monasticism and asceticism, as Pareto notes, proscribes and severely punishes pleasure and/or joy as forbidden sin and consequently crime, and discounts or suppresses human emotions. Simply, American Puritan saints-masters command that "thou shall not have joy or pleasure" in the economy and all human life. Instead humans are subjected to, as Pareto puts it, constant tormenting or pain, thus a blend of sadism and masochism (Adorno 2001; McLaughlin 1996; Mencken 1982), for the glory of the God of Calvinism, mixed with the full realization of America's "manifest destiny" via "holy" wars against "ungodly" societies. At this juncture, the Puritan socioeconomic system in America operates as what analysts describe as the "natural Puritanism of a 'pain economy'" (Calhoun 1925) instituted, imposed, and sanctified

---

[64] In addition to having longer paid vacations (between three weeks in Great Britain and five weeks in Germany, France, Holland, and Scandinavia), workers in most Western European economies receive an additional, 13th "monthly" salary (around Christmas), which is a sort of dream or utopia for their US counterparts, and virtually unknown in American anti-labor Calvinist capitalism.

on grounds of Divine Glory and transcendental supra-human "pleasure" or "caprice".

Alternatively, Weber's God of Calvinism and Puritanism is the only one assumed and justified to have any pleasures and joys, whatever they may be, while humans can only expect and experience grief and pain, inflicted on them by Calvinist masters for the high purpose of Divine "pleasure" or Glory, in a Puritan economy and society. Ultimately, then Puritan "godly" sadism-masochism in the above sense, including what analysts detect as the "sadistic intolerance of cultural otherness" (Bauman 2000), and thus anti-humanism overall reproduces, rationalizes, and predicts a "joyless" or "painful" and basically inhumane capitalist economy in contemporary America. Representing what critics (Mencken 1982) describe as the "haunting fear that someone, somewhere, may be happy" and joyful, notably has pleasure, Calvinist Puritanism (re) makes America as a "joyless" and inhumane economic and social space. Specifically, this is a "joyless" capitalist economy of sadistic "pain" solely or mostly for workers and the masses as a whole subjected to ever-increasing control, repression (Pryor 2002), and sadistic abuse (imprisonment, torture, and executions for sins, including drug-war crimes and strikes). Yet, it is not for their capitalist masters, excluding sadistic-masochistic characters, secretly indulging in the very kind of joys and pleasures (including sexual vices and sins) that Puritanism forbids to others and harshly punishes, thus hypocritically couched and rationalized in the best Puritan pattern and tradition of hypocrisy. Hence, a "joyless" economy of sadistic pain, primarily for labor, makes modern Calvinist capitalism in America a diluted master-servant economy, in particular "belated feudalism" after the model or image of medieval-like rational monasteries (Collins 1997), as in the latter servants or monks are by default proscribed from any having any joy or pleasure.

Also, in comparative terms, it is remarkable, if not incredible, that, for example, US federal (and most state) employees are legally prohibited from going on strikes, virtually alone among advanced Western and other (including Eastern European) economies and democracies. Thus, federal employee strikes are legally permitted collective actions and routine occurrences in Western (and even Eastern) European capitalist economies, including France and Germany, in stark contrast to America under neo-conservatism, with Reaganism setting the model with its anti-labor or anti-union policies during the 1980s (viz. the suppression of the strike of aid-controllers). For example, mass national strikes as those routinely observed in France or Germany during the

2000s have been rendered by religious and political neo-conservatism an "impossibility theorem" or "forbidden apple" and taboo in modern America. At least on the account of being denied by the anti-labor conservative government such elemental, globally recognized (a reason in itself for their denial as "un-American") labor liberties and rights, US federal and most state workers perhaps feel or appear as sort of modern "happy or not so happy slaves" to their Western counterparts.

In addition to and conjunction with the longest work hours, the shortest vacation, labor oppression, and a "joyless" economy overall, Calvinist extreme economic anti-humanism is manifested in strict anti-welfare and generally anti-egalitarian, as distinguished from welfare and egalitarian, capitalism. Anti-welfare capitalism is operationally or simplistically defined or symbolized by that, as US conservative economists (e.g., Friedman) like to state, "there is no such thing as free lunch" in this economic system. Of course, they claim that this statement is a universal economic truth. This is trivially true in the formal accounting sense of costs or prices, but not in substantive sociological terms, as it is valid only or primarily for anti-welfare, yet not for welfare, capitalism, and generally for a master-servant Calvinist or other, and not a liberal-democratic and egalitarian, economy. In Weber's words, these US economists conflate the formal and substantive rationality of economic action, in this case the cost-benefit calculation of "free lunch" and the ultimate social values (equality, justice, morality, charity, etc.) associated with this and other goods and activities. Thus, if there is no such thing as "free lunch", it is solely or primarily in Calvinist anti-welfare capitalism and hence a Puritan master-servant economic system due to its lack of or weak charity, compassion, and humanity overall, or alternatively, its sharp wealth inequality, brutality, and general inhumanity as Divinely ordained.

Conversely, contrary to the above claim to timeless and societal universality, there *is* such thing as "free lunch" despite its costs or price in a formal accounting sense, especially for those who objectively and urgently need it (the poor, children, elderly, etc.) in welfare capitalism and generally a liberal-democratic and egalitarian economy. This holds true precisely in virtue of the latter's charity, compassion, understanding, tolerance, and humanity as a whole, as well as its lesser wealth and income inequalities. After all, this is the basic character or meaning of welfare capitalism and an egalitarian economy generally—redistribution of "free" goods and services (including food, health case, education, housing, and money income) to those in dire need (Korpi and Palme 1998). Alternatively, the logic of Calvinist anti-welfare capitalism in America and an anti-egalitarian economy generally is the exact opposite. This is the denial or restriction of such "free" redistribution on Divine as well as political grounds, for the purpose of sacred and secular powers, expressing transcendental and other anti-humanism. It is the logic or rather the illogical paradox of "high inequality yet low redistribution" characterizing unequal, plutocratic (Benabou 2000) or oligarchic (Binmore 2001) and (relatedly) rigid or closed societies[65] (Breen and Jonsson 2005; Erikson and Goldthorpe 2002; Solon 2002).

In retrospect, Calvinism, notably Puritanism, from its beginning was in economic terms the design and system of an anti-welfare or anti-charity economy and society. In the latter, its theocratic masters inflict the rest of the population with material and spiritual deprivation and oppression, including poverty, and deny or restrict them assistance or relief through welfare or charity, for the glory of and obedience, ultimately sacrifice to, God as well as political authority. For example, recall Weber cites what he calls Calvin's "much-quoted statement that only when the people, i.e. the mass of laborers and craftsmen, were poor did they remain obedient to God." He adds that "in the spirit of the old Calvinism the people only work [and obey] because and so long as they are poor [weak]".[66] In particular, he registers that "one of the most notable economic effects of Calvinism was its destruction of the traditional forms of charity [alms-giving]".

Also, he observes that, following Calvinism, in England as well as America "the Puritan battle-cry was: "Giving alms is no charity" in

---

[65] Solon (2002:63–4) reports that anti-egalitarian capitalism in America is, contrary to received views, "less mobile" than its Scandinavian egalitarian or welfare versions in Sweden, Denmark, and Finland, i.e. that these (plus Canada) "are more mobile societies than is the United States", just as Great Britain during anti-welfare Thatcherism. Notably, he suggests that the differences between America and, for example, Sweden in "both inequality and intergenerational mobility may be related" (Solon 2002:65) in the sense of the first adversely affecting the second (Bjorkland and Janti 1997). Breen and Jonsson (2005:232–3) summarize the comparative research on economic mobility by commenting that American capitalism is observed to be "noticeably more rigid than the countries with which it has been compared (mostly the Nordic countries)."

[66] Weber adds that "Calvinism put an end to all this, and especially to any benevolent attitude toward the beggar. For Calvinism held that the inscrutable God possessed good reasons for having distributed the gifts of fortune unequally. It never ceased to stress the notion that a person proved oneself exclusively in one's vocational work. [So] begging was explicitly stigmatized as a violation of the commandment to love one's neighbor [i.e.] the person from whom the beggar solicits. Charity becomes an impersonal operation of poor-relief for the greater glory of God".

contrast or even deliberate opposition to the Christian medieval ethics of "good works through giving alms" and the "Anglican social ethic" of the Stuarts that "was very close to this attitude". In his account, Puritanism was the enthusiastic participant "in the severe English Poor Relief Legislation which fundamentally changed the situation" during the 17th century and later. Also, contemporary analysts register and emphasize that Puritanism in England and America is emptied of the values of *caritas* and *compassion* which are in the "lineage of the welfare state" (Tiryakian 2002). Others suggest that Calvinism was "different" from other Protestantism and Catholicism not (only) by its work ethic but rather its "willingness and ability" to impose its ethical code with a "vengeance" (Hudson and Coukos 2005:4), notably in America as well as England through Puritanism. In this account, the "harsh moral tenor" and even "Draconian" restrictions of welfare institutions and policies in England and America are "rooted" in Calvinism via Puritanism which explains why "hostility to public aid" is a specifically English-American attribute that other Protestant societies do not share.

In sum, such anti-welfare ideas, institutions and practices render Calvinist capitalism in America and to a lesser extent, given the defeat and discredit of Puritanism, in England a diluted master-servant economy, in particular "belated feudalism" characterized by lack of institutional forms of welfare assistance or charity (in spite or because of feudal masters' occasional alms to their servants). Moreover, Calvinist anti-welfare capitalism in America is even harsher or more "Draconian" and thus inhumane than European feudalism in virtue of what Weber identifies as the latter's medieval ethics of "good works through giving alms", which Calvinism, notably Puritanism, vehemently attacked and eventually eliminated as "ungodly", reversing the "scale of traditional Christian values" (Tawney 1962), notably compassion and tolerance. In this sense, contrary to its claims to being truly, only "Christian", Calvinist-Puritan anti-welfare capitalism in America reverses and thus ultimately destroys this scale of true Christian values. In short, like Calvinism and Puritanism, this type of capitalism has the major problem of a "budget deficit" of what Marx sarcastically calls and Sorokin (1970) extols as "Christian love".

At this juncture, Calvinist-Puritan anti-welfare capitalism in America is an economic logic and system of Bibliocracy but without original Biblical values, notably love, compassion, and tolerance for others, including those materially deprived, let alone infidels or foreigners. In particular, anti-welfare capitalism in the South as the emerging regional champion in attacking and destroying the otherwise minimal welfare state in America is a sort of capitalist "Bible Belt" (as promoted or symbolized by the theocratic-capitalist "Christian Coalition" albeit in seeming decomposition while writing these lines). Yet, it somehow lost or "forgot" the true spirit and message of the Bible (if so interpreted), that is, Christian love, caritas, compassion, and tolerance for others reversed by the "sadistic intolerance" and even hatred of otherness (e.g., hate crimes).

*"Free Enterprise" Epilogue: Anti-Labor Economy—America's Calvinist Economic "Destiny"?*

To summarize, as a corollary of the preceding, an anti-labor and pro-capital authoritarian, as (charitably interpreted) a diluted, not pure, master-servant, economy is the contemporary and/or prospective economic logic, creation, and subsystem of Calvinist theocracy as a total social system in America. Consequently, it forms the economic dimension of America's "destiny" in Calvinist theocracy. An anti-labor, pro-capital and in consequence anti-egalitarian, unfair, and repressive economy is America's Calvinist economic present and likely "destiny" or future in the sense of Leviathan or repression, subjection, and injustice for labor, and Hobbesian Anarchy or license, domination, and "justice" for capital after the image, if not model, of the "Wild West".

And, since or if such an economy tends to ultimately culminate in institutionalized, yet predictably hypocritical Puritan-style, predatory, mafia capitalism a la Enronism, the latter may prove, as Veblen expected and Merton implied, the Calvinist economic "destiny" of America. Placed in a Weberian sociological framework, this thus leaves intact Weber's affinity between Calvinism and American capitalism. However, it recasts the latter as explicitly non- or at most quasi-democratic, notably oligarchic and repressive (and hypocritical) in the form or image of generalized predatory, mafia-style Enronism, though it was already, by being rooted in Calvinist theocracy, implicitly a theocratic, and thus illiberal or authoritarian economy in his own account. In any scenario, America's Calvinist economic "destiny" or heritage remains a diluted master-servant economy, either in the "mild", covert and "acceptable" form of an anti-labor, pro-capital oligarchic economy juxtaposing labor repression and capital anarchy or in the intense, overt, and dubious, criminal yet legal, face of predatory, mafia capitalism, as analysts predict (Pryor 2002).

CHAPTER FOUR

POLITICAL SYSTEM OF CALVINIST THEOCRACY

*Theocratic Polity*

As indicated, the political system of Calvinist, like any, theocracy is by assumption a theocratic polity, including a church-state. At this juncture, Calvinist theocracy is considered both a partial political *and* a total societal system, a polity and society alike. In the narrow sense it is a political system in itself, a theocratic polity or government, in particular an overt, formal and/or covert, substantive variation of a state-church. For example, Weber refers to Calvinistic theocracies *cum* legally established and substantively dominant "state churches" in Europe and America. These theocracies include that of Holland in the form of the "only true" Reformed Church, of England through the "Parliament of Saints" or "Divines", and notably the "theocracy of New England" by means of the established Calvinist Congregational Church during the 17th–19th century (Baldwin 2006; Bremer 1995).

In general, the above is a conventional conception of theocracy, Calvinist or other, in the strict political sense, by analogy to aristocracy, oligarchy, bureaucracy, plutocracy, technocracy, democracy, autocracy, and related concepts. In a holistic sociological sense, as conceived in the present work, Calvinist theocracy constitutes a total social system or society, incorporating its intertwined theocratic economic, political, civic, and cultural systems, including a state-church, as its integral elements or subsystems. In terms of Calvinism, specifically Puritanism, it is the theocratic design and reality of a "godly" society or community, including, but not limited to, "godly politics" (Zaret 1989) as its integral part. A historical exemplar is the "Puritan dream of the godly community" (German 1995) in America, a dream originally fulfilled in New England and subsequently expanded or perpetuated ("dream on") in the "Bible Belt" and beyond.

In holistic sociological terms, the political system of Calvinist theocracy thus understood is defined by equivalent theocratic and to that extent anti-liberal and non-democratic attributes and outcomes, as are its other entwined partial systems, the economy, civil society, and culture. Hence, the type of polity inherent to Calvinist and other theocracy as a social system or society is an anti-liberal and non-democratic, or authoritarian and even totalitarian, *qua* theocratic state or government, yielding the antithesis of liberal-secular democracy. This renders an anti-liberal and non-democratic polity, or the inverse of liberal-secular democracy, in the form of a theocratic or theocentric (Wall 1998) government the political dimension of America's Calvinist-as-Puritan "destiny". In this sense, what Weber's contemporary Ross, in reference to Puritanism, denotes as the "antidote" (rather poison) of liberal-secular democracy turns out to be America's Calvinist political "destiny." This is what Ross implies by stating that America is a "lineal descendent" of Puritanism, and thereby liberal-secular democracy produces "its own antidote" in the form of the latter, in spite or because of that the two "have worked together".

The Calvinist polity in America, at least in Puritan ruled New England in the past and the evangelical "Bible Belt" in prospect, has been or is likely to be anti-liberal, non-democratic, thus the "antidote" of liberal-secular democracy, precisely because of the inner logic of Calvinism. Calvinism originated, functioned, and remained as the paradigmatic species of extreme political anti-liberalism and consequently (other things equal) totalitarianism (Dahrendorf 1979), fulfilling through Puritanism in Anglo-Saxon societies the same "sociological function" that fascism did in Germany (Adorno 2001; Fromm 1941; McLaughlin 1996). Calvinism was and remains via neo-Calvinist evangelicalism in America, what Weber implies as "strict" anti-liberalism and hence totalitarianism, revealing its "iron" anti-liberal and "totalistic" (Eisenstadt 1965) consistency, including theocratic "totalitarian monism" (Dahrendorf 1959) or absolutism (Habermas 2001).

In essence, Calvinism, in particular Puritanism, was strict and consistent anti-liberalism and totalitarianism on the account of its establishment and defense of a despotic or tyrannical political and social system on "higher" Divine grounds. In short, a Calvinist-Puritan polity and society was anti-liberal and totalitarian because it was "Divinely ordained" despotism or tyranny in the form of theocratic "godly" politics and community. Thus, Weber suggests that Calvinism's "ecclesiastical regimentation", in particular that by "Calvinistic state churches" in Europe and America, was "excessively despotic" in political as well as religious and social terms to the point of almost amounting to an "inquisition." For example, Calvin stipulated that, so to speak, "thou shall" suffer in complete submission "even tyranny" on the grounds of its being "ordained by God." His stipulation was premised on the despotic commandment that humans must be "held in check" by any means and "at all costs" (Heller 1986) and times, because of their "fundamental evilness" (Fromm 1941; McLaughlin 1996) attributed to "original sin" carried to its ultimate, tyrannical and anti-human consequences. Consequently, a major tenet of political liberalism and modern democracy like popular sovereignty had "no place" in Calvin's political and theological doctrines (Heller 1986; Mansbach 2006) and those of his disciples[1] in Geneva (Sorkin 2005) and America a la Winthrop (Bremer 1995) pervaded by "austere Calvinism" (Kloppenberg 1998).

Generally, a sociological study suggests that the "original political impulse" of Calvinism (like Lutheranism) and consequently of Puritanism was totalitarian or "totalistic" by constraining "autonomous activities" in politics, just as in the economy, rather than in a liberal-democratic direction (Eisenstadt 1965). Another analysis also implies that Calvinism was associated with the "strengthening of the authoritarian state"—rather or more than was Lutheranism—and not, as often assumed, with "democratic constitutional principles" and "commitment to freedom and human rights" (Nischan 1994) in Europe and beyond, including America via Puritanism.

In particular, Calvinism, including Puritanism, was essentially a type of revived and even reinforced medievalist anti- or pre-liberalism and totalitarianism or despotism. As noted, it was particularly enamored with intensifying, expanding, or "purifying" the illiberal, despotic Biblical theocracy of the Dark Middle Ages such as the *respublica Christiana* as the Divine design in an attempt at recreating a "purer" medieval social order rather than superseding it (Eisenstadt 1965). Calvinism originally reestablished and "purified" this medieval theocracy in Calvin's Geneva as a "godly society" (*civitas Dei*) becoming a "model of theocratic governance" (Mansbach 2006). Subsequently, it extended its model theocracy to Holland and in part Germany by means of the "only true" Reformed Church, then, via Puritanism, to England (and Scotland) and New England made "Biblical Commonwealths,"

---

[1] In a laudatory study, Sorkin (2005:299) recognizes that Calvin's main successor Jacob Vernet, alongside Beza (VanDrunen 2006), in Geneva revealed a "republican preference for hierarchy over democratic participation", that is, "order", "submission" and "subordination" over popular "sovereignty", and even the "profound abhorrence of democracy and liberty."

subsequently to the US South and the "Wild West" reawaken by the Calvinist Great Awakenings as the "Bible Belt," and to all America eventually after the Puritan undying "dream of the godly community". Minimally, Calvinism, including Puritanism, like other religious conservatism, was, in Mannheim's (1967) words, a pre-liberal and thus pre-democratic or authoritarian political "mind" (ideology) and system, as distinguished from and opposed to its liberal and democratic version. Typically, it originated and functioned as an anti-liberal and hence totalitarian political ideology and system, as a (patho) logical extension and reinforcement of this primitive pre-liberalism and authoritarianism in accordance with a kind of inner pre-liberal and authoritarian logic of metastasis or escalation.

Sociological analyses indicate that the Calvinist theological and political revolution (and the prior Lutheran Reformation) originally, far from being a "modernizing" movement, sought to reestablish a "'purer' medieval socio-political and religious order" (Eisenstadt 1965), specifically a more disciplinarian, repressive, and ascetic society (Gorski 2003; Loveman 2005). Calvinism, notably Puritanism, often did so in a remarkable sociological consistency and continuity or an historical sequence. This continuity spans from Calvin's reestablishing a medieval political order in Geneva (Byrne 1997), and Holland under Calvinist medieval-style theocratic rule (Kaplan 2002) to England during Cromwell's medievalist "Holy Commonwealth" (Goldstone 1991) and New England as Winthrop's *mixt aristocracie* (Bremer 1995) and to America as a whole[2] (Orren 1991), particularly the South following the evangelical-driven Great Awakenings (Boles 1999).

By analogy to medieval despotism as its point of origin or ideal-inspiration, Calvinism, including Puritanism, was substantively a sort of proto-typical, prefigured, or anticipated fascist anti-liberalism and totalitarianism as its destination or outcome. In short, it was proto-fascism, fascism in "Divine" conception or gestation before modern fascism, including Nazism. In this sense, Calvinists, notably Puritans, acted as arch-fascists or prefigured modern fascists, just as, conversely, the latter as well as communists (Walzer[3] 1963) are their "secular"

---

[2] Orren (1991) observes that 19th century Puritan America was a society in which workers and citizens lived in a "divided political world" in the sense that party politics was "liberal" and the court system "at its foundation, medieval".

[3] Walzer (1963:86) suggests that also an "analogy" is "worth pursuing" between Calvinism or Puritanism with communism, just as with fascism. In this view, the "first

counterparts. For example, some sociologists object that Weberian sociological theory neglects Calvinism's (and Lutheranism's) "emphasis on the fundamental evilness and powerlessness of men" versus Divine power and thus its link with modern fascism, in which human life must be sacrificed to "higher" powers as well, like the "leader of the racial community" (Fromm 1941; also, Mansbach 2006; McLaughlin 1996). In this critique, such sacrifices to supra-human powers eventually assumed the mix of sadism and masochism, as the extreme form of anti-humanism or inhumanity and thus immorality, such as a "sado-masochistic character structure" in Calvinism and fascism (Nazism).

If this view is correct, then at least on the account of this sadistic-masochistic sacrifice of "evil" and "powerless" humans to supra-human Divine causes, Calvinism, including Puritanism, functioned as proto-fascism. For fascism is precisely defined in psycho-sociological terms by the mixture of sadism and masochism defining a fascist-as-authoritarian personality (Adorno 2001). While certainly not all sadism and masochism is Calvinist-Puritan and even fascist, but also non-Calvinist or non-religious and non-fascist, the opposite is almost invariably true for Calvinism, including Puritanism. Calvinism, notably Puritanism, is typically sadistic-masochistic due to its human sacrifices to supra- and anti-human purposes like Divine Design and Glory and a "holy" war against the "ungodly", combined with "patriotic" offensive wars on the "evil world". Such sadistic-masochistic practices started with Calvin et al.'s projected extermination (Heller 1986; Mansbach 2006) of non-Calvinists or non-evangelicals in France, Holland, and Europe generally and continued, via Puritanism, in Cromwell-Winthrop's crusades against "infidels" (Goldstone 1986; Gorski 2000; Munch 2001). They resumed and culminated in neo-Calvinist evangelical culture wars against non-believers (Edgell et al. 2006), secularists, and liberals in America and a "preemptive" and permanent imperial (Steinmetz 2005) war on the "evil" world over the 2000s.

Generally, in this account, what was originally French Calvinism reportedly performed the identical anti-liberal, totalitarian, and consequently anti-human "sociological function" in, of all places and

---

triumph" of both communism and Puritanism, was "over the impulse of "disorganization" in [their] own midst [and also] over one of the first impulses toward freedom" (Walzer 1963:86). In particular, just as Puritanism "vigorously attacked Renaissance experimentation in dress and in all the arts of self-decoration [so Lenin was] preaching with all the energy of a secular Calvinist against free love [as] "bourgeois" [and] "decay" (Walzer 1963:86).

peoples, non-French, Anglo-Saxon societies (McLaughlin 1996) via Puritanism as did fascism in Germany and other European countries. In turn, Calvinism's mixture of "godly" sadism and masochism intrinsically entails or eventually metastasizes in anti-human, ultimately judgment-day, nihilism via a global self-destructive (likely nuclear) "holy" war on "evil" (e.g., the "axis of evil", Russia, China) with a likely MAD outcome (Habermas 2001; Schelling 2006). To that extent, this Calvinist sadistic-masochistic-nihilistic mixture is a social-psychological or psycho-analytical component of its "sociological function" through Puritanism in Anglo-Saxon societies, notably America as the "only remaining" (Baudrillard 1999) Puritan and consequently, in some accounts, the most "sadistic" (Bauman 2000) and bellicose (Tiryakian 2002) modern Western society. This yields the inference that Calvinism and Protestantism in general was not, as commonly assumed, associated with "political freedoms and economic progress", but rather (or more) with fascism, including Nazism, and thus totalitarianism (McLaughlin 1996).

The Calvinist, including Puritan, political and generally social system is theocratic in, to use Weber's words, formal-legal and/or substantive sociological terms, as elaborated next. To wit, it is formally theocratic in virtue of the legal or institutional fusion of religion and politics in general, church and state in particular. It is substantively theocratic on the account of the societal or factual fusion between religion and politics and society overall, sacred and secular powers and realms. Since the political system of a Calvinist and any theocracy as a society is axiomatically theocratic government or church-state, it may seem tautologically, thus redundantly to redefine and elaborate on it in formal and substantive and other terms. Still, it is instructive and necessary to specify and analyze the concrete forms and meanings as well as the factors and effects of such a theocratic political system within the context and in relation to the other partial social systems of Calvinist theocracy as Sorokin's societal super-system, as done next. The ensuing thus focuses on the theocratic polity as a particular, political element of Calvinist *cum* total societal theocracy.

### *Theocratic Polity: Formal Terms*

In general, the legal and overall institutional fusion of politics and religion, secular or political and sacred or religious institutions and spheres defines, identifies, or signifies a Calvinist and other theocratic polity in formal terms. Negatively, a theocratic polity is defined, identified, or signified by the non-existent or degenerated formal differentiation between religion and politics, including the legal separation of church and state. In particular, what formally defines, identifies, or signifies such a polity is the legal and generally institutional fusion of certain, *ruling* political and religious groups, secular and sacred powers, simply state and church. Conversely, a reversed, subverted, or countered legal-institutional, including constitutional, separation of politics and religion, particularly secular and sacred power or church and state, defines, identifies, or signifies a Calvinist theocratic polity in formal terms. These three formal definitions, types, and meanings of a Calvinist theocratic sociopolitical system are considered in this order next.

*Legal-Institutional Fusion between Politics and Religion*

Generally, the Calvinist, including Puritan, political and social system is theocratic in formal terms by virtue of a legal-institutional fusion or official "merger" between politics and religion (Dahrendorf 1979; Dombrowski 2001), or secular and sacred institutions, powers, and spheres. In short, the Calvinist polity is theocratic due to what Simmel describes as the formal "primitive identity" between religious and political group-affiliation typical of ancient and pre-democratic societies (e.g., China). Such a formal, as well as substantive, "primitive identity" or legal merger between religion and politics has typified virtually all Calvinist ruled societies, from Calvin's Geneva as a local *civitas Dei* and Holland under official Calvinism through Great Britain and New England during their Puritan "Holy Commonwealths" to, in part, America, specifically the South and the "Wild West" turned into a "Bible Belt", since the neo-Calvinist Great Awakenings and the consequent evangelical and sectarian predominance (Lipset 1996). On this account, they were simply legal or institutional theocracies. New England's Puritan "Biblical Commonwealth" was a paradigmatic prototype (Munch 2001), as well as a persisting model or inspiration for the Southwestern and ultimately American "Bible Belt" (Dunn and Woodard 1996) as its attempted revival from the "dead" and its geographic transmission, though seemingly a less manifestly or overtly legalistic and more diluted, disguised type.

In manifestly or more often latently (almost invisibly) legal ways, the "primitive identity" of religion and politics has been perpetuated, albeit through various "secular" embellishments and disguises, in the Calvinist-as-Puritan political system in America, up to the 21st century.

This is especially evident in the legal and other institutional exclusion of and discrimination against non-Puritan and other "infidels" in the sense of non-believers in religious terms or non-religious outgroups. These are condemned, stigmatized, and excluded as more "un-American" than any others, a sort of perpetual "witches", in American politics and society (Edgell et al. 2006), most zealously (not only) in the "Bible Belt" and its theocratic equivalents (e.g., Mormon-ruled Utah).

On a national level, such exclusions of the "ungodly" involve the federal government's official enforcement and defense of the belief in the "existence of Divinity" as the "law of the land" and the "best kept secret" until violated. They also include related legal norms, sanctions, and institutional practices, as enacted by a conservative Congress during postwar times, from McCarthyism ("one nation under God", "we trust in God") to neo-conservatism, such as public proclamations of "strong faith in God" or "godliness" by presidential candidates, presidents, and other politicians. For instance, ushering in the 21st century in the substantively same way that Puritanism did the 17th or 18th century, neo-conservative Congress reportedly attempted to make the law of the "land of freedom" the near-theocratic commandment that all political subjects and institutions must proclaim and rest on, respectively, "acknowledgment of God as the sovereign source of law, liberty or government"—or else. The latter sanctions involve the exclusion and discrimination, if not worse (imprisonment, etc.), against the "ungodly" in politics, democracy, and power, civil society and culture, as a variation on the sacred Puritan exorcism of "witches".

Notably, as well-known and politically incorrect comedians may comment, a monkey given a typewriter or computer is, to paraphrase British economist Alfred Marshall, more likely to type Shakespeare's collected works than an "infidel" truly non-believing, agnostic, and secular or even moderately religious American to become President (with the 2008 Presidential election confirming rather than, as it might seem, contradicting the rule[4]). This is perhaps the single most manifest

---

[4] For instance, an evangelical ("megachurch") pastor gave the "closing prayer" at the 2008 Democratic National Convention and reportedly "prayed" with President-Elect by phone (sic!) before the latter's victory speech. Overall, this President-Elect, while perceived and attacked as more liberal, including pacifist and cosmopolitan, as "un-American" than most US presidents since Jefferson, persistently emphasized, or forced to do so by a neo-Puritan "godly" political system, his "Christian faith", even more than did his conservative opponent. Moreover, he has been long the member of

and salient "proof" or syndrome of a self-perpetuating Calvinist theocratic or at least theocentric political system in America. Or, as some contemporary economists put it, perhaps "a blindfolded chimpanzee" playing with the *Wall Street Journal* would "choose" an investment portfolio that may perform as one selected by an expert (Malkiel 2003) before a secular, let alone agnostic or non-believing, American is elected President. In a similar parable ("practical joke"), chimpanzees and other monkeys, like humans, are more likely to be subject to anti-evolutionary "Monkey Trials" in the sense of anti-scientific and anti-liberal culture, temperance wars in the "Bible Belt" and beyond than a competent, visionary, and otherwise ideal, yet "only" moderately religious, let alone non-religious, American lacking solemn (preferably tearful) proclamation of "faith in God" (Bell 2002) to become President (and Vice-President). For instance, Jefferson, as well as perhaps Madison, Franklin and Paine, would have virtually zero-chances of being (re) elected Presidents during the 2000s (including even that of 2008 electing a "godly" candidate). Recall, Jefferson et al. were the paradigmatic cases and symbols of American Enlightenment-based liberalism and secularism (Byrne 1997) transcending the Puritan theocratic ideal of America as "Christian Sparta" (Kloppenberg 1998) and condemned as "wicked", "ungodly," or "atheist" by Puritan arch-conservatives (German 1995; Gould 1996) in post-revolutionary times.

The period of renewed conservative political dominance since the 1980s (like most of American history) has witnessed presidential elections as Schumpeter-like "free competition" in proclamations of "faith in God" and "godly politics" as the "best" or necessary[5] qualification for

---

a denomination descending from New England's Puritanism. This confirms that what Jefferson tried to make the Puritan "dead past" of the 17th century, the religious test for political office, at least Presidency, is still "well and alive" in American politics, notably Presidential elections, during the early 21st century, contradicting or making ridicule of the legal separation of church and state. Generally, it affirms that the "primitive identity" of religion and politics persists in America, including its major political parties, as does even more what Weber witnessed and described as the "annoying ceremonial" of prayer at virtually all political occasions, from the Supreme Court, Congress, and government meetings to party conventions and other public events.

[5] For example, according to a Pew Research Center poll in 2007, seven of ten Americans "believe it is important for a President to have strong religious beliefs" and hence would not vote for someone moderately religious, let alone a non-believer, agnostic, or secularist. In turn, the *Economist* (November 2007) comments that the American "born again" evangelical President "begins each day on his knees and each cabinet meeting with a prayer", thus by implication emulating his Islamic counterpart in Iran or the Catholic Pope.

the highest political office in America and the world as if, as often described, candidates were running for President as a Puritan "pastor-in-chief" rather than a "commander in chief." Perhaps a better description is that they act as if they competed for a Puritan "pastor-in-chief", with some of US Presidents and would-be-Presidents literally being ordained neo-Puritan (e.g., Baptist) ministers, as seen in the Presidential campaigns of the 1970s and 2000s, respectively. And, then this elected "pastor-in-chief" becomes quasi-automatically "commander in chief", which is a sort of microscopic, operational definition of Calvinist and other Protestant theocracy. Such a near-equivalence perpetuates Simmel's identified "primitive identity" of religion and politics with chief priests being political rulers. Evidently, despite the "disestablishment" of New England's Calvinist theocracy in the early 19th century, "religious tests" for Presidency and other types of political office have persisted in America "long after the passage" of Jefferson's "landmark" *Act for Establishing Religious Freedom* of 1786 and the "epistemological skepticism" by this and other "Enlightenment thinkers" (Dayton 1999), two centuries later. If anything, these persisting religious "faith in God" tests for Presidency define the Puritan-based political system in America as diluted, proximate, if not pure, true, theocracy long after Jefferson's anti-theocratic efforts. Comparatively, they redefine it as a theocentric deviation from modern Western democracies that have dispensed with such religious tests, except in part from Great Britain (with its Anglican or anti-Catholic test for the monarch, but not for the executive power or prime minister).

The above "impossibility theorem" with respect to Jeffersonian secular and moderately or reasonably, as distinguished from fanatically, religious Presidents and candidates is essentially what some sociological observations suggest or imply. For illustration, in an observation, during the 2000 Presidential elections the winner-President self-declared to be a "born-again Protestant" whose life had been radically altered by what Pareto may call the "God of Christianity" (or rather Calvinism) as his "favorite philosopher", and the losing candidate proclaimed exactly the same (Bell 2002). This yields the inference that "nothing" of sorts has ever happened in such previous American political campaigns. Strikingly, the last statement indicates that in spite or rather because of Jefferson-Madison's "wicked" and "ungodly" liberalism and secularism, the Calvinist political system in America has actually become more, not less, theocentric or non-secular since their (post-revolutionary) times, as during the 1980s–2000s punctuated by another evangelical "awakening" and Presidents, and dominated by religious and political neo-conservatism overall.

In comparative-historical terms, it is even more likely that the Vatican Church will elect, in Pareto's words, "popes more concerned with terrestrial than with celestial interests", or what Sorokin (1970) ironically calls "sensate", non-ascetic popes, as actually witnessed in its history (almost 20 percent in his estimates), than electing non-believing, agnostic, secular, or moderately religious Presidents in America's Calvinist polity. Alternatively, it is likely that those "reborn" Americans seeking to become US Presidents will attempt to "prove", through public (ideally tearful) proclamations and what Weber identifies as the Puritan (Baptist-Methodist) "hysterical" and "most terrible ecstasies"[6] of "faith", to be even more "godly" or "Christian" than prospective popes, either "sensate" or ascetic. In so doing, they will present the "proof" of being figuratively "bigger Catholics than the Pope" (Lipset 1955), substantively "greater Calvinists that Calvin."

As the cited observation indicates, this was precisely witnessed during recent Presidential elections, commencing with Reagan's (re)election as self-proclaimed "born again" evangelical ("I am one of you" evangelicals) and perhaps climaxing with those of 2000–2004 (Bell 2002) compared to previous times (Manza and Brooks 1997). In this context, the likelihood of electing a non-religious or secular, religiously indifferent, and even moderately religious President after the Enlightenment model of Jefferson in America in the present and foreseeable future is equal to that of the election of a non-Catholic one in postcommunist Poland or a non-Islamic one in theocratic Iran—virtually zero (with the Presidential elections of 2008 seemingly contradicting but actually by continuing the "God and faith" test for Presidency confirming this rule). Further, it is more likely to witness a moderately religious (as also called) President even in Iran under Islamic theocracy ("republic") than in contemporary America during the "rebirth" of Puritan evangelicalism and political conservatism. This actually happened in Iran during the early 2000s electing a President widely

---

[6] Specifically, Weber remarks that in early Baptism, waiting for the word of God, "might result in hysterical conditions". Also, he observes that Puritan Methodism assumed a "strongly emotional character, especially in America. The attainment of repentance under certain circumstances involved an emotional struggle of such intensity as to lead to the most terrible ecstasies, which in America often took place in a public meeting."

seen as a religious moderate, even "liberal" or "secular" mitigating and partly counteracting its theocracy, thus indirectly less theocentric or conservative than his neo-conservative US counterparts like Reagan-style "evangelical Presidents" and other "rigid extremists" (Blomberg and Harrington 2000).

On this account, at the start of the 21st century the Calvinist-as-Puritan political system in America actually reveals itself as the most rigidly and obstinately theocratic or theocentric polity not only among modern Western democracies, except for post-communist and hyper-Catholic Poland and in part Ireland (Byrne 1997; Inglehart 2004). It is also globally, only contested by or comparable to Iran, Saudi Arabia, and other Islamic theocracies, as comparative sociological analyses imply (Inglehart and Baker 2000; Inglehart 2004). In a sense, virtually no sociopolitical system in the Western and democratic world (except for Poland) and beyond (excluding Iran, Saudi Arabia, and other Islamic theocracies) so zealously upholds and rigidly enforces the proto-theocratic commandment of "God and faith" Presidents and other rulers (e.g., parliaments) and "godly" politics, as the supreme religious test for political office, than does the Puritan-based polity in modern America, climaxing during the 2000s. In this respect, Puritan "godly" politics in America operates or qualifies as the last remaining theocratic polity and to that extent political "primitivism" (Baudrillard 1999) in Simmel's sense, within Western liberal-secular democracy (alongside the Vatican Church and Poland). Alternatively, it does as a substantive analogue to Islamic theocracies or third-world ultra-religious states also using "godly" tests (Inglehart 2004).

At regional levels, these exclusions of "infidels", secular, and even moderately religious persons and groups from politics, democracy, and power by the Puritan-rooted political system in America are even more numerous, explicit, and categorical. Predictably, this especially (but not solely) holds for the Southern "Bible Belt" and other super-conservative or extremely anti-liberal, "hot-red" states like Utah, Montana, Idaho, Oklahoma, Nebraska, etc. (sincere apologies to those regions not mentioned, for it is difficult to find a major non-conservative or truly liberal US state during the 1980s–2000s, as California was in the 1960s–70s). These exclusionary and thus theocratic practices incorporate in particular laws and practices outlawing and institutionally excluding or discriminating against "infidels"—atheists, agnostics, deists, secularists, liberals, non-evangelicals, non-Protestants, non-Christians, etc.—with respect to participation in political power (running for local and state office), as well as culture and civil society (Edgell et al. 2006). Simply, the law or at least the institutional and societal expectation is that "infidels" thus defined "need not apply" for political office or public service, as is persistently witnessed in the "Bible Belt" (e.g., Alabama, Tennessee, Florida, Mississippi, Virginia, Georgia, Oklahoma, Texas, etc.) and beyond. This confirms that a theocratic political system remains a more enduring ideal and legacy, thus "destiny", of the "Bible Belt"—as, after all, the very term, indicates—than the racist. It thus endures more strongly and longer than slavery and racial segregation and discrimination, though theocratic evangelicalism and racism, including vigilante violence (lynching, etc.), have historically been intertwined in the "Bible Belt" (Jacobs et al. 2005; Messner et al. 2005).

In sum, on the account of such legal and other institutional overt or covert exclusion and discrimination, the US Federal government, including Presidency, Congress, and the Supreme Court, is latently theocentric or theological in Comte's sense rather than constitutionally secular or "positive". On this account, the neo-Puritan "Bible-Belt" and other "red" states are manifestly theocratic in the sense of Simmel's "primitive identity" of religion and politics. In passing, Mormon Utah qualifies even more than the evangelical "deep South" as legal reconstituted theocracy (Gould 1996; Weisbrod 1999) in America in virtue of maintaining the formal as well as substantive "primitive identity" of religion and politics,[7] including the pseudo-legal and other institutional exclusion of non-Mormons, let alone non-believers and secularists from political power and life, yielding a "nightmare" (McCann 2000) experience for these out-groups.

In comparative terms, due to the legal-institutional exclusion and discrimination against the "ungodly" as supremely "un-American", the

---

[7] In a way, Utah's constitutional provision that "there shall be no union of church and state, nor shall any church dominate the state or interfere with its functions" (Weisbrod 1999:136)—given that it is precisely the exact opposite that defines this state—is not worth the paper on which it was written in 1894, or a sort of cruel joke and even "nightmarish world" (Gould 1996) for non-Mormons as well as genuine non-believers like atheists or agnostics. Of course, as Weisbrod (1999:146) comments, "even in Utah" during modern times, certain religious group, or in this case sect or cult, "cannot control its environment in the way that was possible" in the 19th century and before. Yet, admittedly the Mormon "church" aims at or tends to "overlapping and penetrating the state in the form of religious ideas in the consciousness of individual voters or religious affiliations of state officials" (Weisbrod 1999:146). In short, Weisbrod (1999:147) infers that the state of Utah, after gaining statehood within the US federal system, is the "reconstitution of a theocracy".

US Puritan-rooted government at all levels is, as Pareto implied by diagnosing its perennial tendency for coercively enforcing "morality by law", resembles more the Vatican Church and Islamic and other third-world theocracies than modern Western liberal-secular democracies, including its neighbor Canada. Notably, in this respect the evangelical "Bible Belt" (and Mormon Utah) is closer to theocratic Iran and Saudi Arabia or at most theocentric Poland than to once-Calvinist Holland, Lutheran Sweden, or Anglican England.

*Legal-Institutional Fusion of Secular and Sacred Powers*

In particular, the Calvinist-Puritan political and social system is a theocratic polity and society in formal terms in virtue of the legal-institutional fusion of specific, ruling political and religious groups, secular and sacred powers or authorities. Simply, it is formally theocratic through the official "marriage" of church and state by means of positive, as distinguished from natural, law and institutions. Negatively, it is so in virtue of a non-existent legal separation between church and state, and religion and politics overall. As hinted above, this was historically witnessed in Calvin's Geneva, Holland under the official and "only true" Reformed Church, then England's during Cromwell's Government of "Divines" (the "Parliament of Saints"), and New England under the officially established Calvinist Congregational Church from the 1630s–1830s, and partly the Southern "Bible Belt" by design via the Great Awakenings or in effect ("Monkey Trials") and its equivalents (Utah during its existence). Generally, all these were sociopolitical systems in which church and state are, so to speak, one "indivisible under God" (Tawney 1962) in accordance with the medieval theocratic design and order of "godly" politics and society (the *respublica Christiana*) adopted and reinforced by Calvinism, including Puritanism (Zaret 1989).

In particular, Puritanism predictably acted as sectarian Calvinism with respect to the legal separation of sacred and secular power, church and state. It did so by demanding and advocating such separation for reasons of strategic dominance or sheer survival while a sect in what Comte and Weber describe as "fanatical opposition" to existing non-Puritan authorities and institutions, as in Anglican England and the Episcopalian South. Yet, Puritanism merged sacred and secular powers whenever and wherever established as governing power. This precisely happened after the English Puritan Revolution of the 1640s and its delayed reflex or extension in America, the evangelical and theocentric or anti-liberal Great Awakenings during the 1740s–1800s as the manifestations of Calvinist revivalism (German 1995). As Weber implies, like any "pure sect", Puritanism *cum* sectarian Calvinism must for its own survival demand, advocate, and even extol (Sprunger 1982) the legal "separation" of church and state, religious "tolerance", and "freedom of conscience". Yet, what he partly neglects, Puritanism does the exact opposite once established in governance by formally as well as substantively merging what it precisely wanted separated, church and state, and eliminating or perverting what it extolled as liberty and tolerance before.

Old and New England's "Biblical Commonwealths" as Calvinist legal theocracies are the past testimonies to such merger of church and state virtually whenever and wherever Puritanism assumes political power from non-Puritan forces, and the "Bible Belt" as their attempted revival or vestige is the present and prospective testimony in this respect. Thus, none than sympathetic Tocqueville deplores the new world's Puritan godly legislator for "entirely forgetting the great principles of religious toleration that he had himself demanded in Europe", specifically Anglican England, and making "attendance on divine service compulsory, and goes so far as to visit with severe punishment, and even with death, Christians who chose to worship God according to a ritual differing from his own". Tocqueville adds that Puritan legislators do so in accordance with New England's cited law "Whosoever shall worship any other God than the Lord shall surely be put to death". A number of contemporary sociological and historical analyses largely confirm or echo Tocqueville's implied diagnosis of New England's Puritan legal theocracy, thus established Calvinism, and its resulting elimination or intolerance of political and religious freedoms[8] (Davis 2005; also, Baldwin 2006; Fehler 2005; German 1995; Harley 1996; Munch 2001; Stivers 1994).

In comparative terms, Weber registers that religious tolerance and implicitly freedom and pluralism across post-Reformation Protestant

---

[8] In an otherwise laudatory study, Davis (2005:350) admits that New England's ruling Puritans (e.g., Ames) "identified civil magistrates as divine ministers charged with the maintenance of order [so] divine law obligates them to obey the laws of human government". This is essentially a description of legal theocracy, as is the observation that for Puritans the "jurisdictional boundaries of ministers and magistrates overlap significantly", citing Ames" view that "the chief care of the magistrate ought to be that he promote true religion and repress impiety" (Davis 2005:351–52).

and other Christian societies actually "was least strong" in none than those countries and regions "dominated by Puritanism" like "Puritan old or New England." He might add that Puritanism had demanded and extolled them while *not* being dominant but instead in "fanatical opposition" to "ungodly" non-Puritan powers and institutions. In particular, this dual pattern of conduct was observed in New England under Puritanism. Thus, the latter moved from its "vociferous defense of liberty" against "British authoritarianism" and Anglicanism to its own "ecclesiastical tyranny" once established in power,[9] as during the period following the American Revolution (Baldwin 2006), just as before ever since Winthrop et al.

Evidently, to paraphrase Lord Acton's "law", absolute domination or power "absolutely corrupted" Calvinist Puritans in old and New England to become and act as what Keynes calls "madmen in authority." They did so by denying to others and eliminating what they, as Hume classically observes and emphasizes, fanatically had demanded for themselves before, religious tolerance, pluralism, and freedom. Moreover, Weber's expression "least strong" with respect to religious toleration and freedom indicates that absolute power "corrupted" Puritans even more "absolutely" than other religious groups in a comparable condition of political domination, such as ruling Lutherans in Germany, Anglicans in England, and Catholics elsewhere in Europe, and even original Calvinists in France, Geneva, and Holland. In this, like virtually all other respects, Puritanism really functioned as "iron Protestantism" (Tawney 1962), notably hyper-Calvinism, and Puritans acted as the "hotter sort" of Protestants (Gorski 2000), specifically super-Calvinists.

In sum, while being in opposition and protest against non-Puritan religious and secular political powers and institutions Puritanism acts as a Calvinist "pure sect" sanctimoniously and ceremoniously demanding separation of church and state or religious and political freedom and tolerance. And yet when in power it acts instead as "church" or Weber's "hierocratic" institution, thus as true Calvinism. It does by

---

[9] For instance, Baldwin (2006:106) notes that the 1790s "were a time of "near paranoid cries for order and stability arising from the Federalist clergy" in New England, yet "contradicting the clergy's vociferous defense of liberty against British authoritarianism before and during the American Revolution". Then, in this view, early Methodists "turned the rhetoric of religious liberty and ecclesiastical tyranny on the established [Calvinist] clergy" in New England (Baldwin 2006:108).

legally merging church and state and unceremoniously denying and eliminating religious-political freedom and tolerance by its own "ecclesiastical tyranny", as witnessed in 17th–19th century New England and subsequently the US South following the Great Awakenings transforming it into a "Bible Belt". In turn, this is a dual pattern that Puritanism and in extension Calvinism shares with fundamentalist Islam (Mansbach 2006), as well as fascism, including Nazism (minus legal or formal theocracy). They all demand religious-political freedom and tolerance, including separation of church and state, or "democracy" while not in power only to deny and destroy everything they demanded once established in dominance by their tyranny.

*Subverted Institutional Separation of Sacred and Secular Power*

Alternatively, the Calvinist political system is a theocratic polity in formal terms on the account of the reversed, subverted, or attacked legal-institutional separation between sacred and secular power, church and state. As hinted, this has been witnessed in virtually all Calvinist and Puritan societies in which theocracy has been officially disestablished or diluted, from Holland to New England (e.g., after the 1830s) and most notably the Southern "Bible Belt" and other evangelical ("red") parts of America during the 1980s–2000s. At least, the theocratic design or designation of America as the "Bible Belt" is the axiomatic exemplar and symbol of the formal-legal separation of church and state being undermined or attacked and challenged through Puritan-style "godly" politics and "holy" culture and military aggressive wars, and consequently or likely reversed or subverted. Analogously, New England's "Biblical Commonwealth" was such an instance of their institutional fusion via ruling Puritanism *cum* the established Calvinist Congregational Church self-perpetuated almost into the mid 19th century, more than half a century after the American admittedly secular Revolution[10] (Baldwin 2006; German 1995).

---

[10] Baldwin (2006:96) registers that Calvinist State establishments "persisted in New England well into the 19th century". In particular, he notices that the 1780 Massachusetts Constitution "mandated the support of "public Protestant teachers of piety, religion, and morality" (Baldwin 2006:96). Also, German (1995:972) suggests that Calvinist orthodoxy and neo-Calvinist (the "New Light") revivalism, including "New Divinity" theology, "remained inseparable well into the 19th century" in New England. Admittedly, during the 18th and 19th centuries, New England's exponents of Calvinist revivalism (or the "New Divinity") "embraced ecclesiastical power the better to promote the 'peculiar doctrines" of Calvinism'" (German 1995:971).

Instances and proxies of such theocratic reversals or subversions and attacks against the constitutional separation between church and state in America under self-perpetuating or "die hard" Puritanism, abound, continuing and even expanding and intensifying during "born again" fundamentalism, notably in the "Bible Belt", over the 1980s–2000s. Some indicative legal cases of such subversions include the "one nation under God" official insertion in the US Pledge of Allegiance and the replacement of a secular Latin maxim (*pluribus unum*) by "in God we trust" on currency notes. Both "godly" measures were enacted during and in tacit connection with the "glorious" time of McCarthyism or proto-fascism[11] of the 1950s (Putnam 2000) and its creator paleo-conservatism general. US religious conservatives deny and most Americans appear to believe that these and similar measures are not really theocratic attacks on and subversions of the constitutional separation of church and state, but "democratic" and "all-American". Yet, the fact suggesting the exact opposite is that the US founders such as Jefferson, Franklin, and Madison, who substantively, in the sense of ideas and values, "wrote the American Constitution" (Binmore 2001), did not institute or endorse these and similar practices (e.g., official prayer), but opposed or suspected them as more or less theocratic. As a particular curiosity, even authoritarian arch-conservative (Dunn and Woodard 1996) Alexander Hamilton, as the first secretary of treasury, did not find it necessary or prudent to inscribe "in God we trust" on dollar notes, in passing an inscription unwittingly emulating or evoking medieval Islam's equivalent insignia "in the name of God, Most Beneficent, Most merciful" on Arab gold (Moisseroon 2002). The same can be said of the moment that these legal measures were enacted almost two centuries after the American Revolution in an apparent hyper-emotional over-reaction to the Cold War or a partial symptom of the mass hysteria of McCarthyism and religious conservatism generally, as in passing Weber anticipated observing "hysterical" neo-Puritan (Baptist) sectarianism in America.

In turn, some pseudo-legal, yet institutionalized instances in this respect encompass what Weber himself witnessed during his visit and described as an "annoying" ceremonial "for quite some time" in American "godly" politics and society. This was the "opening by prayer

---

[11] In Putnam's (2000:350) words, America during the 1950s was no less than "proto-fascist" (sic!) as well as "provincial, misogynist, racist" by comparison to the "enlightened, liberated" 1960s and even the 1990s.

of not only every session of the US Supreme Court but also of every Party Convention", and, to add, schools (legally until the 1960s) and virtually all political institutions and occasions, including Congress sessions (plus the "breakfast prayer"[12]), and public sports, musical, and similar cultural events. As before, US religious conservatives deny and most Americans appear to believe that these institutionalized rituals are not theocratic attacks on or subversions of the constitutional separation of church and state but "democratic" and "all-American." Yet, the Supreme Court's decision of the 1960s that prayer in public schools and by sociological (but not legal) implication other non-private, including political, settings is unconstitutional indicates the exact opposite.

At this juncture, one wonders if prayer in state schools is declared unconstitutional, then why it is not so in other public, notably political settings, including, as Weber observes, the Supreme Court itself and Congress. Seemingly, this is one of those characteristic contradictions or paradoxes of the Puritan-rooted legal-political system in America, analogous to or evoking the Supreme Court's "separate but equal" contradictory rulings prior to the 1950s and, even in some interpretations (e.g., school segregation), during the 2000s "déjà vu all over again". Moreover, the constitutional separation of church and state is methodically subverted in public schools by religious conservatives, as indicated by the penetration of fundamentalist and other churches and sects into and even their interference with most university campuses in America, a phenomenon largely unknown in Western democracies. On this account, from the stance of liberal-secular democracy and for those not belonging to these religious groups, the constitutional separation of church and state is not worth the paper on which it is written with respect to public schools, not to mention political institutions and practices like Congress and its practice of public prayers.

And, just as their earlier forms were enacted under the impetus of paleo-conservatism in open association or covert "flirt" with McCarthyism or proto-fascism, these theocentric laws and institutional practices are typically promulgated and enforced by religious neo-conservatism in overt or tacit collaboration with its product or ally

---

[12] As known, Jefferson was perhaps the only US President resisting the establishment of a national, federal "day of prayer", in contrast to a long sequence of his predecessors and successors, from George Washington, declaring "a day of prayer and thanksgiving", to the "born again" evangelical Presidents since Reagan over the 1980s–2000s.

neo-fascism (e.g., fundamentalist "Christian" neo-Nazi sects and cults), in the 1980s–2000s. In historical terms, hence history repeats itself, as a farce or not, in respect of theocratic subversions in postwar America. In comparative terms, in no contemporary Western society, with the exception of semi-theocratic, Vatican-linked post-communist Poland (see appendix), has the legal separation of church and state been under such systematic, obstinate, and intense attempts at its reversal or subversion and virulent attacks as in America, especially its "Bible Belt", during "born again" Puritan-rooted fundamentalism, just as before since the Calvinist Second Great Awakening of the 1800s.

These and a myriad of related theocentric, "faith-based" practices confirm what has been in a sense known or anticipated ever since both the official establishment and disestablishment of Puritanism and in extension Calvinism as the dominant religion and theocratic church, or rather sect in Weber's sense, in America (New England) during the 1630s and the 1830s, respectively. This is that, like Calvinism in Europe (Geneva, Holland) and elsewhere (Canada,[13] cf., Hiemstra 2005), Puritanism in America has never fully and genuinely, as distinguished from partially and tactically a la Machiavellianism, embraced or reconciled with the legal separation of religion and politics, church and state, in the American polity and society overall (Archer 2001; Munch 2001). And, probably Puritanism never will by its recurrent revivals via fundamentalism. At this juncture, the reasonable, proverbial "never say never" does not seem to apply to "born again" US theocratic and thus, from the angle of liberal-secular democracy, unreasonable or irrational Puritans (Dombrowski 2001), at least to "Bible Belt" (just as Islamic) fundamentalists, especially Southern neo-Calvinist Baptists (Hinson 1997), as their multiple "rebirth" into "godly" politics and life indicates. On this account, American Puritanism's political vision and system has always been and remains by the 21st century profoundly theocratic or theocentric (Wall 1998). It is couched in and sanctified by the never-ending dream (German 1995) and the institutional system of a medieval-style "godly" politics and society generally, while "sweetened" by "apple-pie" or "all-American" ethnocentric exceptionalism and authoritarianism (Beck 2000; Wagner 1997).

---

[13] Hiemstra (2005:153–4) finds that neo-Calvinists, moving from Holland to Canada during the 1950–60s, promoted their "idiosyncratic ideas of Christian schooling, politics, economics, and media" in deliberate opposition to "prevailing liberal and secular" ideas.

## Theocratic Polity: Substantive Terms

Generally, by analogy to its formal-legal version, the societal or factual fusion of religion and politics and all society, sacred and secular powers and realms, defines, identifies, or signifies a Calvinist and other theocratic polity in substantive, sociological terms. Negatively, it is defined and detected by the non-existent, degenerated, or blurred substantive "fission" or differentiation, as distinguished from the formal-legal separation, of religion and politics and society as a whole, sacred and secular life. Particularly, what substantively defines or detects it is the factual societal fusion of specific ruling religious and political groups, sacred and secular powers, or church and state. Alternatively, a diluted and blurred societal differentiation or "fission" between religion and polity, sacred and secular spheres, form the defining element or "diagnostic criterion" of a Calvinist theocratic polity in substantive, sociological terms. These substantive definitions and meanings of a Calvinist theocratic polity are considered as follows (Table 4.1).

## Factual Societal Fusion between Religion and Politics

In general, the Calvinist political and social system is theocratic in substantive sociological terms in virtue of the factual societal, as distinguished from formal, fusion or merger between religion and politics (Dahrendorf 1979; Dombrowski 2001), secular and sacred powers, institutions and realms. In Simmel's terms, the Calvinist political system is substantively theocratic in virtue of perpetuating the substantive societal, as well as legal, "primitive identity" of religion and politics characteristic of ancient pre-democratic societies. Alternatively, it is on the account of the non-existent factual differentiation or the existent

Table 4.1. Definitions, types and meanings of Calvinist theocratic polity

I. Formal definitions, types and meanings of Calvinist theocratic polity
 legal fusion of politics and religion,
 legal fusion of ruling political and religious groups, state and church
 reversed or attacked legal separation of church and state
II. Substantive definitions, types and meanings of Calvinist theocratic polity
 factual fusion of religion and politics/society
 factual fusion of ruling religious and political groups, church and state
 diluted or blurred differentiation between religion and polity/society

"de-differentiation" (Alexander 1998; Smelser 1997) between religion and polity and society, sacred and secular institutions and powers. In short, concerning the substantive relationship of religion and politics in a Calvinist polity the biological or sociological "fusion-fission" principle (Smelser 1997) operates mostly as fusion.

In essence, virtually all Calvinist, including Puritan, political and social systems have been typified by the substantive fusion or the de-differentiation between religion and politics and society as a whole. This is a remarkably continuous sociological pattern and historical sequence spanning from Calvin's Geneva to Holland under official Calvinism through England during the "Holy Commonwealth" and New England under the "Biblical Commonwealth" to America after the Great Awakenings to the Southern and other "Bible Belt" ushering in the 21st century. In Simmel's terms, all these societies have substantively perpetuated the primitive identity between religion and politics, sacred and secular realms. In turn, this identity has usually been combined, especially at earlier stages, with their formal merger. And, it has continued even after the usually prior legal or constitutional separation of church and state, as in Holland during the 18th century and New England and in America as a whole, notably the South, in the wake of the American Revolution[14] (Baldwin 2006; Fehler 2005; German 1995).

In particular, sociological analyses identify and emphasize a sort of factual fusion or lack of substantive "fission" between religion and polity and society in Puritan America during most of its history since the 17th century (Bell 2002; Lipset 1996; Munch 2001). Historically, this fusion proceeded either in conjunction with, as in colonial New England, or disjuncture from and even contradiction and opposition to, as in America, notably the South, after the Revolution, the formal separation of church and state. A predictable, though mostly historical, regional exemplar in America was early Puritan ruled New England

---

[14] Baldwin (2006:97) remarks that Calvinist state establishments and their theocratic principles, persisting in New England for long and supported by political conservatism like Federalism, "were under assault" after the American Revolution by the "voluntary principle" propounded by Jefferson et al. and some religious groups (early Methodists). In turn, German (1995:974) observes that political conservatism in the shape of the Federalist Party "protected the religious establishment" of Calvinism. Also, Fehler (2005:135) suggests that the orthodox Calvinist clergy in 19th century America was "eager to reestablish their influence that had largely diminished in the wake of the American Revolution."

typified by a lack of substantive differentiation between religion and politics (Munch 2001), initially and for long in association with the legal merger of (the Congregational) church and state, from the 17th–19th century. Subsequently, it was in the aftermath of, disjuncture from, and opposition to the constitutional separation of church and state with the official "disestablishment" of theocratic Puritanism during the 1830s, no less than half a century after the American Revolution and Constitution.

Notably, the official disestablishment of theocratic Puritanism, thus the legal separation of church and state did not appreciably weaken the societal fusion or produce immediately the substantive fission between religion and politics, as indicated by various events and instances in officially post-Puritan New England during the early 19th century. For example, a historical study (Hull 1999) cites two indicative events in Massachusetts during 1834, thus exactly one year (or two decades in Dayton 1999) after Puritanism's official disestablishment, and half a century following its (1780) reenactment by mandating yet again Calvinist ("Protestant") "piety, religion, and morality" (Baldwin 2006). First, the state's High Court reaffirmed its Puritan-era blasphemy law, and second, some religious dissenters (e.g., the *Boston Investigator* editor) were harshly punished (imprisoned) for violating the law through their public expression of a "lack of belief in prayer, miracles, and Christ." Hence, for these "infidels" the official disestablishment or the legal separation of church and state in this Puritan sanctuary was hardly worth the paper on which it had been written in 1833, just as medieval heretics experienced, while executed or punished by the "holy" Inquisition, in identical terms the Biblical promise of universal salvation by Pareto's Roman theocracy.

Conversely, what substantively weakened the long fusion between religion and politics, or the mandating of Calvinist "piety, religion, and morality", was the remarkable countervailing non-Calvinist process of liberalization, secularization, democratization, and religious pluralism[15] (Baldwin 2006; Fehler 2005), joined with demographic changes

---

[15] Baldwin (2006:119) notes that Calvinist "patterns of hierarchy, deference to authority [etc.] gave way to a more individualistic, egalitarian, and mobile society" in New England and America as a whole, though, one can add, with the implied exception of the "new" neo-Calvinist or evangelical South. Also, Fehler (2005:146) suggests that during the 19th century Calvinist orthodoxy in New England and America overall "was being challenged on many fronts—especially by liberalism and populism."

resulting in another numerically prevalent religion (Irish Catholicism). These processes transformed New England, including Massachusetts (plus Vermont, etc.), from the most theocratic or illiberal into the probably the most secular or liberal region of America by the 21st century. They did at the chagrin and dismay of "Bible Belt" and other Puritan-rooted fundamentalists (as mobilized in the 2004 Presidential elections to prevent an "ungodly" Massachusetts "elitist liberal" from becoming President).

At least, New England's striking transformation since the official demise of its Puritan theocracy (and non-Puritan immigration) typifies what Michels may term an "iron" sociological law or historical pattern. This is that liberal-secular democracy emerges and persists in Calvinist and Puritan societies in spite of and even in opposition by, and *not* because of, Calvinism and Puritanism. In comparative-historical terms, like New England, Holland is another, perhaps more salient exemplar confirming this "iron" law in virtue of undergoing an even more dramatic and visible transformation from an official Calvinist theocracy to what is commonly considered or perceived as a model liberal-secular, "permissive" Western European democracy (Kaplan 2002). Notably, this outcome happened not because but in spite of and in opposition by Calvinism since the late 16th century, including neo-Calvinism[16] (Hiemstra 2005; Tubergen et al. 2005) and its reflexes such as Calvinist-rooted or allied neo-fascism and xenophobic racism during the 2000s.

Another predictable and yet current or perhaps prospective regional exemplar in America succeeding and eventually surpassing proto-Puritan New England in the factual fusion or lack of substantive differentiation between religion and politics is the neo-Puritan, evangelical South turned into a "Bible Belt" via and following the fundamentalist Great Awakenings (especially the Second of the 1800s) expressing Calvinist revivalism. In contrast to New England from the 17th to the 19th century but like it since the 1830s, in the ante- and post-bellum ever-growingly Calvinist (Presbyterian, Methodist, Baptist) South,

---

[16] According to Hiemstra (2005:146), neo-Calvinism, a term Weber also used, resulted from the attempt by the 19th century Dutch Calvinists (Kuyper) to "update the Calvinist idea of God's sovereign care of creation in order to address a rapidly modernizing culture", that is, "to reform Calvinism when it appeared wrong or antiquated." In this account, these Calvinists "developed the idea of a pluriform public order in order to counter the hegemony of liberalism and secularism" within Dutch politics and society, including schools (Hiemstra 2005:160).

such a substantive fusion between religion and politics was dissociated from, and yet it contradicted and even opposed, just as followed after, the legal separation of church and state following the American Revolution, especially its Jeffersonian strands and outcomes[17] (Baldwin 2006). At this juncture, the original design of the "new" South and America as a whole as a "Bible Belt" was essentially a project of recreating the substantive fusion between religion and politics, in a new evangelical (e.g., anti-Episcopalian) form (Boles 1999). It contradicts, neutralizes, and eventually eliminates the legal separation of church and state as a liberal-secular "evil" and "ungodliness" (Jeffersonian "foreign atheism"), with the Great Awakenings acting as theocratic Calvinist revivalism (German 1995) and the efficient anti-secular, anti-rationalist instrument to realize such a Divine design (Foerster 1962). (On this account, the Great Awakenings, especially the second of the 1800s, functioned as Puritan-inspired movements and attempts to reestablish and reinforce the substantive fusion of religion and politics and to counteract and eventually eliminate the formal separation of church and state in America, as in the South during "foreign" and not "godly enough" Anglicanism.)

In this sense, following the Calvinist disciplinary and theocratic revolution in Europe (Gorski 2003; Loveman 2005), notably France, Holland, England, and partly Germany, these Puritan revolutions or revivals in America (especially the second Great Awakening of the 1800s) were really Schumpeter's style creative destructions, though in a form and sense opposite to that in liberal-democratic polity as well as modern capitalism. They were the creation of a substantive fusion between religion and politics, and the destruction of or attack on the formal separation of church and state. And yet, since such a creation was not really a political innovation or invention in Schumpeter's sense but rather the recreation of the medieval merger of religion and politics, sacred and secular power, in a *respublica Christiana* (Nischan 1994), they effectively functioned as counter-revolutions, including populist counter-offensives[18] (Fehler 2005; Foerster 1962). In sum, they

---

[17] Baldwin (2006:119) cites orthodox Calvinists" accusations and fears that the early Methodists "were going to join Jefferson to overturn [New England's] political institutions."

[18] Foerster (1962:26) remarks that the most "formidable opponent" to the Age of Reason or Enlightenment in America "was the counter-offensive of the Revivalist movement", specifically the Great Awakenings in revolt "against worldliness and skepticism". Moreover, Fehler (2005:145) proposes that orthodox Calvinism in New England

did as regressive restorations or revivals of the old structures from the "golden past" in a new formally secular, post-revolutionary polity and society, just as did Calvinist revolutions in Europe before.

In historical and regional terms, the South is the inverse (flip-side) of New England, not to mention Holland, with respect to the substantive fusion of religion and politics and thus the Calvinist theocratic polity. The "Southern story" is that of a reverse transformation or involution. It is one from the least theocratic (despite official Anglicanism), ascetic, evangelical, or "godly" American region (Gould 1996), which provided the impetus and rationale for the Puritan-driven Great Awakenings, to an exact opposite and thus anti-liberal, anti-secular, and under-democratic, even proto-totalitarian "Bible Belt" (Amenta, Bonastia and Caren 2001; Bauman 1997; Cochran 2001), from the late 18th to the early 21st century. In this sense, the new 21st century evangelical South appear as the historical mirror or reflex, just as the geographic extension and the historical vestige or revival, of 17th century New England's Puritan theocracy and in extension Calvin's 16th century Geneva and Holland under Calvinism's rule. No wonder, it is designed/designated as a "Bible Belt" emulating or mirroring the old dead "Biblical "Commonwealth" or "Garden".

On this account, the sociological, as distinguished from chronological, time of the "Bible Belt" and its societal, as different from geographical, space in the sense of a substantive fusion or de-differentiation between religion and politics, are not really the 21st century and contemporary Western and even American society. Rather, they are the 16th–17th centuries and Calvin's Geneva through Winthrop et al.'s theocratic New England and, consequently to Calvinist-Puritan implied medievalism, medieval times and their Biblical theocracy. Not surprisingly, it is often described as or compared with the New "Dark Ages" (Bauman 2001; Berman 2000). Simply, the "Bible Belt", as is often said,

---

"had lost ground" not only in encountering liberalism ("professionalism and materialism") but also "populist religious movements", notably by implication the Great Awakenings. However, German (1995:971–2) suggests that the Great Awakenings and in extension most "populist religious movements" in 18th and 19th century America were expressions of neo-Calvinist ("New Light") revivalism and instruments for promoting Calvinism's "peculiar doctrines". If so, the Great Awakenings actually operated as the means of Calvinism to "reestablish" and even expand beyond New England its diminished political and other influence following the American Revolution (Fehler 2005). At the minimum, while the "Calvinists no longer exerted an especially strong influence over their country, they could still demonstrate the importance of their role as moral legislators" (Fehler 2005:139), with the Great Awakenings, specifically the Second, serving as an effective instrument or path to that aim.

exists on a different sociological and historical planet than post-Puritan New England and related ("blue") regions in America, and a *fortiori* post-Calvinist Holland and other Western liberal-secular democracies (Inglehart 2004), excepting growingly theocentric as well as grotesque post-communist Poland under the persisting Vatican influence and impetus. As observed, in contemporary America secular urban Americans tend to distance themselves from the "Bible Belt" in virtue of the "backwardness of religious fundamentalism" (Gould 1996) as its defining element and rationale. This shows a tension of "country westerners or rural values" with "urban, liberal elites [i.e.,] cosmopolitan, yuppie class culture" (Eliasoph and Lichterman 2003).

Hence, primarily this region with the "backwardness of religious fundamentalism", as well as relatedly "rural values", remakes America what some sociological observers describe as the "last remaining primitive" society (Baudrillard 1999) and polity, or a salient "deviant case" (Inglehart and Baker 2000) among modern Western societies and democracies. Alternatively, the "Bible Belt", like Utah (Gould 1996; Weisbrod 1999), exists in the functionally equivalent or analogous, specifically proto-totalitarian, sociological time and space as Iran, Saudi Arabia, and other Islamic theocracies or societies (Bauman 1997; Friedland 2002; Mansbach 2006; Van Dyke 1995). Predictably, this holds true in virtue of the persistent substantive primitive identity of religion and politics, and related aspects and outcomes, including Draconian irrational ("dumb") laws, the massive and brutal Puritan vice-police state, executions for sins-crimes on primarily religious grounds, etc. (Jacobs et al. 2005).

As a corollary, Calvinism through the Puritan political and social system intrinsically or eventually tends to recreate and redesign America, like other societies under Calvinist rule, as a substantively theocratic and generally non-secular, thus anti-liberal and non-democratic polity and society in spite, or perhaps because, of a constitutionally secular state or government. Thus, early Calvinism directly recreated and perpetuated Geneva and Holland (and almost Prussia) as theocratic *cum* "godly" societies and indirectly through Puritanism old and New England and the rest of America, at least the Southern "Bible Belt".

The point of departure, model, or image for all these Calvinist, including Puritan, society-builders, was Calvin's original vision of France and its partial realization (only) in Geneva as *civitas Dei* or theocratic government (Byrne 1997). It was a "godly" polity and society from which the "ungodly" were (to be) exterminated, as the French Calvinist Synod concluded (Heller 1986) in the 16th century and happened to his critic Servetus and libertines for blasphemy, or, as "charity" or "merci" to them, imprisoned and banished. Yet, in Calvin's proto-theocracy these dissenters burned at the stake and beheaded for criticizing his "holy" theocratic doctrines could hope for "little mercy" (Mansbach 2006). In particular, Calvin's original *civitas Dei* defined by exterminating "ungodly" and "evil" non-Calvinists represented an evident model[19] (Mansbach 2006) or precedent for its Puritan theocracies in Great Britain (both England and Scotland) and America. For instance, it was the model for Cromwell's theocratic "Parliament of Saints" and Winthrop's theocracy (Munch 2001) premised on "austere Calvinism", including the profitable extermination of Native Americans and "Salem with witches" as unmitigated emanations of "ungodliness" and "evilness" following medieval superstitious or irrational beliefs (Byrne 1997).

It may be inaccurate or unfair to directly credit or blame as the case may be Calvin for what Hume, Weber, Simmel, and other sociologists and historians describe as Cromwell's power usurpation, tyranny, and even cruelty and barbarism, as well as Winthrop's descendants' profit-making predation of "ungodly" Indians and cruel and irrational witch- and monkey-trials (Boles 1999; Harley 1996). Still, Calvin's blueprint and system of medieval-style *civitas Dei* constituted the permanent ideal or venerable precedent for Calvinism, including American Puritanism from 17th century through the 18th–19th centuries Great Awakenings to the new "Bible Garden" ushering in the third millennium. A sociological analysis suggests that American Puritanism's "inheritors" like the evangelical movements of the (Second) Great Awakenings only reluctantly agreed with the formal separation of church and state, but persisted in their mission of "moral regeneration" and reestablishment of a "Godly society in America" (Archer 2001), as a typical designation and sanctification of Calvinist total societal

---

[19] Mansbach (2006:110–1) observes that in Geneva "Calvinist rule was first established as a model of theocratic governance" with the effect of the city becoming "widely known as the "Protestant Rome." In his account, Calvin "instituted his theocratic views with relish. He integrated the church with the civic government, ensuring that the clergy would play a key role in political decision-making and incorporating an austere morality into the law. The 12 elders selected from the city's councils formed a Consistory [as] the most important instrument for enforcing Calvinist norms" (Mansbach 2006:111). Mansbach (2006:113) infers that the "Calvinist theocracy was complete" and Geneva "solidified its role as a center of transnational Protestantism."

theocracy after the model and image of Calvin's medievalist *civitas Dei* in Geneva. As known, these movements eventually succeeded in reestablishing a Calvin- or Winthrop-style "Godly society", if not in America as a whole (yet), at least in the "deep" South. The latter was converted into a "Bible Belt" (Boles 1999) as a putative "Biblical Garden" déjà vu after New England, a theocratic polity and society, despite the formal separation—yet, increasingly degenerated, attacked, or questioned by "reborn" fundamentalists (Emerson and Hartman 2006)—of church and state.

As noticed, such a comparatively unparalleled success, first, places the region outside of the setting of Western liberal-secular democracy and modernity, in particular the Enlightenment and its legacy (Byrne 1997), including the American Jeffersonian variant, in which Calvin's *civitas Dei* is the *caput mortuum* (corpse) of the medieval theocracy and the Dark Middle Ages. Second, it conversely puts it in the category of proto-totalitarian (Bauman 1997) destructions of human liberty and democracy, specifically in the proximity of Iran under Islamic theocracy as its substantive equivalent or counterpart. Recall, this is exemplified by their functional equivalence in irrational laws and Draconian punishments like executions for sins-crimes and an intrusive, massive, and growing religious vice-police (Infantino 2003) state enforcing and inflicting them.

*Factual Societal Fusion of Sacred and Secular Power*

In particular, by analogy to its formal-legal version, the Calvinist-Puritan sociopolitical system in America is substantively theocratic in virtue of the factual societal fusion of certain, specifically ruling religious and political and other social groups, or sacred and secular powers. In Simmel's terms, the Calvinist polity in America tends to be substantively theocratic in the form or sense of a substantive primitive identity of religious and political affiliation specifically with dominant social groups, sacred and secular rulers or powers. Negatively, it is through the absence of a substantive differentiation or the existence of a factual de-differentiation between these ruling powers, either in connection and reciprocal reinforcement with the lack of formal separation of church and state, as at early and intermediate stages, or in contradiction with and opposition to it, as in subsequent and modern developments. In sum, a Calvinist polity and society is substantively theocratic in that its church and state powers are "one indivisible under

God" (Tawney 1962) factually or sociologically, even if they may or may not be necessarily so formally or legally.

In Comte's words, a Calvinist polity and society is substantively theocratic because it is designed and created as the effective—usually also, but not necessarily, legal—"reign of Saints" or what Marx and Weber call religious virtuosi. Hence, it is because Weber's Calvinist spiritual or religious aristocracy (Clark 1999) of predestination, predestined "heavenly" oligarchy (Zaret 1989) ultimately becomes substantively—as distinguished from, though often combined with, legally—political and societal aristocracy in Pareto-Michels-Mosca's sense. And, it does on the grounds of being God's a few elect and agents with medieval-style Divine Rights to rule. In short, this Calvinist spiritual aristocracy becomes or acts as a factual elite, an oligarchy, or ruling group, in politics and society, expanding from sacred into secular power[20] (Ashton 1965).

In this sense, the above tendency can be stated and generalized as Michels' style "iron" sociological law or historical pattern of an intrinsic link of (who says) Calvinist-Puritan "spiritual aristocracy" or religious oligarchic sainthood (also says) with a political elite or closed oligarchy. This is the pattern or tendency of Calvinist theological, sacred authorities eventually becoming theocratic political powers, of supreme theologians acting as master theocrats and oligarchs, as epitomized by Calvin himself (Mansbach 2006). The pattern was followed by his main disciples in Europe (Sorkin 2005) and via Puritanism in England (Gorski 2000; Zaret 1989) and America (Baldwin 2006; Davis 2005; German 1995).

In turn, the above is the Calvinist variation on the general pattern or theme that leading theologians or spiritual leaders in virtually all local and world religions typically seek to become, overtly or covertly, theocrats and political elites overall in their societies or theocracies, with exceptions such as what Weber calls mysticism and "other-worldly" asceticism and Sorokin passive ideationalism. This is what Mannheim suggests observing that in traditional societies theologians and similar groups (magicians) whose "special task is to provide an interpretation of the world" for society tend to become a ruling or separate caste, as exemplified by the medieval clergy. It indicates that Calvinism, including

---

[20] This is what Ashton (1965:583–4) suggests by citing the Puritan (Presbyterian) claim that "only the enlightened elect are capable of fighting against the sins and corruptions of the mass of humanity. Hence it is the divine will that they should be in a position of power over the unregenerate many".

"exceptional" American Puritanism, confirms rather than contradicts this common rule or pattern. Moreover, as Weber and other analysts suggest, Calvinism, including Puritanism, is, along with Islam (Mansbach 2006), the prime "proof" or paradigmatic exemplar of a long-standing tendency. This is factually fusing sacred and secular rule, theological and theocratic authority, spiritual and political aristocracy or oligarchy, ideal and material or "sensate", power to form "godly" politics and society.

As typical, Calvin provides a model or precedent for Calvinism, including Puritanism. He did by being effectively (and in part legally) both a supreme church and state power, a foremost theological and theocratic authority, a leading spiritual and political aristocrat or oligarch, the master theologian-theocrat in the *civitas Dei* that he established in Geneva during the early 16th century. In short, Calvin was, in Rousseau's words, a theologian who claimed his "superiority," thus the superior head of the "Calvinist form of theocratic government" (Byrne 1997; Mansbach 2006). In consequence, with rare exceptions actually confirming the rule (e.g., post-Calvinist Franklin), most of Weber's "great men" of Calvinism and Puritanism were Calvin-style mixtures of supreme sacred and secular rulers, theological and theocratic authorities, that is, spiritual and political aristocrats or oligarchs, simply master theologians-theocrats.

The above involves a continuous Calvinist trajectory. It spans from Calvin's Geneva (Vernet) (Sorkin 2005), through Holland under Calvinism and Great Britain during Puritanism, to colonial New England (Winthrop, Cotton, Ames) (Davis 2005; Harley 1996; Seaton 2006) and its post-revolutionary phase (the "New Divinity" theologians) (Baldwin 2006; Fehler 2005; German 1995) to the post-bellum or modern "Bible Belt" and its evangelical "entrepreneurs" (Bauman 1997) and its equivalents (Utah's "elders") (Gould 1996). In essence, with almost no major exceptions[21] (Vernet?, Ames?), most of the above

---

[21] For instance, Vernet alleged that his precursor in Geneva Calvin "was not, "the Pope of the Protestants"—this was but one more of Voltaire's well-turned but false phrases. Calvin merely 'taught, wrote, and preached'" (cited in Sorkin 2005:304), implying that Calvinist theologians, including himself, were not necessarily theocrats. Yet, even in a laudatory study, Sorkin (2005:304)) implies that Vernet was hardly just a theologian (adopting Arminianism) concerned only with heaven by registering his typical Calvinist "profound abhorrence of democracy and liberty" in favor of "eager embrace of subordination" and "patrician politics." How about New England's Puritan Ames as a putative exception to the Calvinist theologian-theocrat rule? Despite a partly

Calvinist and Puritan *dramatis personae* in Europe and America traversed what they construed as the Divinely ordained path from chief theologians to theocrats, spiritual aristocrats to political oligarchs, sacred to secular powers.

At least, this holds true of the two greatest or the best known single figures of English and American Puritanism, respectively, Cromwell and Winthrop. Thus, like Calvin in Geneva, after assuming political power, Cromwell proclaimed to be both a foremost sacred and secular power or authority, a master theologian-theocrat, as indicated by his self-designated double title of God's "agent" and "Lord of the Domain" on the Divine path of a self-declared "holy" war on "infidels" (Gorski 2000). Also, recall, driven by "austere Calvinism" Winthrop and his disciples (Cotton, Ames, the "New Divinity" theologians, etc.) declared themselves or acted in equivalent terms and titles, as both God's theological voices (Davis 2005; German 1995) *and* theocratic agents or "Divinely ordained" aristocratic masters (Baldwin 2006; Bremer 1995; Harley 1996). Winthrop et al. as Weber's paradigmatic "spiritual aristocracy" or oligarchy of predestination effectively became political *mixt aristocracie* (Bremer 1995) in the sense of a narrow ruling group and thus an aristocratic or oligarchic and theocratic type of polity and society defined by the "domination over the sinful world" by religious virtuosi or simply the "reign of Saints." In turn, Winthrop and by means of his "austere Calvinism" Calvin has been a perennial role model (Mansbach 2006) and inspiration for American Puritan-inspired fundamentalists and actual or would-be theocrats. The latter particularly (but not solely) comprise "Bible Belt" or "born again" evangelicals and other neo-conservatives (Reagan et al.) perpetuating the theocratic tradition of Puritanism (Dunn and Woodard 1996), especially its substantive and, whenever possible and prudent as in New England for long, legal primitive identity of religious and political powers.

### Diluted Societal Differentiation between Religion and Politics

Alternatively, the Calvinist-Puritan political system in America is substantively theocratic in virtue of a diluted and blurred societal

---

praising account, Davis (2005:352) implies a largely negative answer by citing Ames" view that "the care and knowledge of the things which are God's may well belong to the King." He also comments that Ames "is less interested here in respecting an inviolable sphere for belief than he is in advocating for civil government a certain preemptive authority in matters of religious purity" (Davis 2005:352), and to that extent theocratic governance after Calvin's model.

differentiation between religion and politics and society overall, or sacred and secular realms, institutions, and powers. At the minimum, even if not a complete de-differentiation or fusion, then a diluted and blurred substantive differentiation or fission between religion and polity and secular society overall has characterized Puritan America during most of its history, up to the early 21st century, as various sociological analyses indicate (Jepperson 2002; Lipset 1996; Munch 2001; Tiryakian 1975).

On the level of institutional politics this diluted and blurred substantive differentiation of religion and politics is manifested in what some sociologists identify as the tendency of the US government and polity overall for "godly" religious, including in consequence or by implication theocratic or theocentric, solutions to what are yet non-religious or secular political and social problems in America during most of its history, up to the 21st century (Jepperson 2002). Further, such solutions often combine a "blurring" substantive differentiation between religion and polity, religious and secular realms and institutions[22] (Tiryakian 1975), with, first, the legal merger of church and state, second, the subversion of and opposition to their constitutional separation.

The first combination by assumption and historically was typical of pure and primitive Calvinist theocracy in America and elsewhere, specifically 17th–19th century New England under Puritanism. It was singularly exemplified or symbolized by Salem's "Calvinist psychology and the diagnosis" of "witches" (Harley 1996) as a historical event and a sociological symbol for a theocratic or sectarian polity and society (Putnam 2000). It was also by related religious or rather theocratic solutions to political and social problems, including "ungodly" Native Americans and even some dissenting Protestant groups (Quakers, Anglicans) and other Christians (Catholics), in Winthrop's "shining city upon a hill", that is, to some "troubles" and "troublemakers" in the "Biblical Garden" or "paradise on Earth" (Gould 1996; Munch 2001).

The second combination is analogously typical of diluted or contemporary (still primitive in the sense of evangelical) Calvinist theocracy in America, at least the new South awaken from its long Episcopalian "ungodly" as well as non-ascetic "nightmare" by the Great

---

[22] Tiryakian (1975:18) registers that America Puritanism's "cardinal feature [is] a blurring of the differentiation between [religious and secular] life [i.e.,] sacred and profane activities and objects."

Awakenings and converted into a "Bible Belt" from the late 18th century to the early 21st century. By analogy, it is instantiated and symbolized by recurring "monkey trials" (Boles 1999) against secular "ungodly" science (including but not limited to evolutionary biology), knowledge, and education (Darnell and Sherkat 1997; Martin 2002) by Puritan fundamentalism (Archer 2001) in the "Bible Belt" and beyond in America, mostly its "red" states. It is also exemplified on a national level by Puritanical anti-alcohol Prohibition during the 1920s–30s (Friedman 1997; Simon 1976) and its various vestiges and replays like the increased federal legal limit for consumption (from 18 to 21 year, of course, the highest by far in the Western world) and "Bible Belt" and other "red" no-alcohol ("dry") regions (Merton 1968). Notably, it is in Prohibition's functional equivalent or analogue, the war on drugs (Reuter 2005) and other renewed culture and temperance wars (Bell 2002; Wagner 1997) through Draconian "tough on crime" and irrational (i.e., as Americans call them, "dumb") Puritan-inspired laws, institutions, and punishments.

Other instances and symbols incorporate some religious or theocentric solutions to poverty such as "faith-based" government charity institutions and practices (Chaves 1999), as well as "God and faith" elections and politics (Bell 2002) registered above and further discussed below. Generally, such manifestly or latently theocratic and other religious solutions to political and social problems so abound in American history and further multiply in modern America during "reborn" fundamentalism that it would require another chapter to even enumerate, let alone analyze in detail, them.

In comparative terms, Puritan America is the probably the only or major contemporary Western society that primarily relies on religious and consequently or implicitly theocratic and theocentric solutions to secular political and social problems, except for some relatively minor exceptions (e.g., post-communist Poland under the Vatican impetus). In turn, it is only emulated by or comparable in this respect with non-Western or third-world theocracies like Iran, Saudi Arabia, and other Islamic countries, which also primarily and even exclusively apply theocratic and other religious solutions to political and social, including economic, problems (Davis and Robinson 2006; Kuran 2004). This curious "elective affinity" (Turner 2002) and even functional equivalence (Jacobs et al. 2005) in some respects—notably, in the religiously grounded and sanctified death penalty and penal system—between Puritan America and theocratic Islamic societies like Iran and Saudi

Arabia indicates and confirms what has been implied and observed by Weber and other analysts (Friedland 2002; Inglehart 2004; Mansbach 2006; Van Dyke 1995).

First, as Weber and other early sociologists (e.g., W. Thomas[23]) suggest, it reaffirms that Calvinism, including American Puritanism, and Islam are substantive equivalents with respect to theocracy in the sense of a substantive fusion of religion and "godly" politics, just as the legal merger of church and state[24] (also, Mansbach 2006). Second, it suggests that what defines and typifies both Calvinist-Puritan and Islamic—and, for that matter, all—theocracies is applying primarily religious solutions to various non-religious political and other problems in society. Third, it confirms that on the account of its primary theocratic and religious solutions to secular political and social problems, Puritan "godly politics" remakes and maintains America closer to non-Western, third-world traditional, illiberal, non-secular, and authoritarian societies like Latin American Catholic and Islamic countries than to Western liberal-secular democracy at the start of the third millennium (Inglehart 2004; also, Byrne 1997). If so, this exception to or deviation from Western liberalism and secularism is true Puritan-rooted American exceptionalism and thus America's Calvinist "destiny" in political terms, rather than, as commonly claimed by US "born again" neo-conservatives and assumed by sociologists (Lipset and Marks 2000), "individualism", secular "democracy", and "freedom".

At this juncture, America's Calvinist political "destiny" reappears as historically Calvin's 16th century *civitas Dei* via Winthrop's 17th century "godly politics", comparatively or figuratively as 21st century "Iran" or "Saudi Arabia" in a non-Islamic "Christian" theocratic version. Admittedly, to US "born again" fundamentalists it may be inaccurate, inappropriate, or offensive to describe Puritan America as a "Calvinist Iran" in view of the latter classification under the "axis of evil". Yet, this description is used by analogy and inspired by Winthrop et al.'s (Samuel

---

[23] Weber's contemporary Thomas remarks almost a century ago that "Mohammedanism, Hebraism and Puritanism are instances of [religion] as the excellent carrier of suggestion [manipulation and as] associated with conservatism".

[24] Mansbach (2006:108) suggests that "Calvinism was a thoroughly fundamentalist rebellion against Rome that struck at the very idea of state sovereignty, pursued theocratic governance, and was carried forward by leaders as intolerant and fanatical as Osama bin Laden [etc.]". In his view, in particular both initially Islam and Calvinism later sanctioned a "militant polity" through the "search for converts" (Mansbach 2006:103).

Adams') design and creation of the "promised land" as "Christian Sparta" (Kloppenberg 1998), thus should be understood and treated accordingly. (Also, one wonders why, apart from short-term political reasons a la the "axis of evil", "Calvinist Iran" should be more inappropriate than "Christian Sparta" since both terms refer to non-Christian and non-Puritan societies and their respective religions, Islam and Paganism, respectively. For these very reasons, "Calvinist Saudi Arabia", for example, is a less inappropriate and offensive term for US religious and political conservatives, since the latter is a "friendly" country and "ally", but this moment does not make it less of a theocracy, thus an antithesis of Western liberal-secular democracy, just as is theocratic Iran.)

Notably, what is evident and incontrovertible from the prism of liberal-secular democracy is that virtually all these theocratic and religious Puritan solutions to America's ills are either by assumption or in reality problems on their right, even more serious and destructive to political liberty than those they claim or attempt to resolve. Recall, this was and is dramatically evidenced and symbolized by Puritan "Salem with witches", evangelical "Monkey Trials", puritanical Prohibition, the war on drugs, and other old and new temperance and culture wars. Simply, to paraphrase Mannheim and Keynes, they are the kind of solutions and remedies that cure the disease by killing the patient, as they literally did and do so, as Pareto notes, to keep people "healthy" (e.g., "thou shall drink no alcohol") or "save" humans and their souls from their moral "mistakes" (Terchek 1997). As Ross might put it, Puritan solutions purport to be an "antidote" to political and social ills but eventually act as a deadly "poison" of democracy and human freedom and ultimately life. Paradigmatic exemplars are the religiously sanctified death penalty system enacted by the federal government and most US states, notably the "Bible Belt", and "holy" wars of self-destruction against "ungodly" and "evil" societies.

In essence, for liberal-secular democracy, these solutions are ultimate anti-solutions in that they dilute or blur the substantive differentiation between religion and politics, and even degenerate or subvert the formal separation of church and state, as witnessed and perceived in "faith-based" government practices during the 2000s, let alone anti-science "Monkey Trials". They are so in virtue of destroying or degenerating democracy and all human freedom, choice, and life, and revealing the "dead past" or "Trojan horse" of theocracy, especially the theocratic Dark Middle Ages defined by theocratic and other religious "solutions" to political and social problems. As analysts observe, the "allure" of fundamentalist solutions in modern America, like in Islamic countries, is the promise of ending the "agony" of human choice by eliminating the "choice itself" (Bauman 2001). Predictably, the "evangelist churches of the Bible Belt" are especially identified as belonging, together, as also expected, with the "Islamic integrisme of ayatollahs" in Iran, to a "wider family" of proto-totalitarian alternatives to the imputed "burden" as well as "ungodliness" of human freedom (Bauman 1997; also, Van Dyke 1995).

In particular, as hinted, the diluted or blurring substantive differentiation between religion and politics has typically been observed during Presidential and virtually all elections and events in America, even increasingly so recently. Recollect, some sociologists observe that in the US Presidential elections during the early 21st century (e.g., 2000) all the candidates proclaimed to be "born-again" Protestants, usually evangelicals, or "Christians", whose lives had been changed "directly by Jesus Christ" as, in the words of a "reborn" puritanical President, their "favorite philosopher", while commenting that something like this has never been witnessed before in these political campaigns even in Puritan America (Bell 2002).

And, the latter comment suggests that the substantive differentiation between religion and politics in America during "reborn" Puritan evangelicalism has been further diluted and blurred, if not in part reversed, at the highest level and office by such proclamations of "godliness" rather than, as one might expect given the opposite experience of other Western democracies, promoted and increased during recent times, perhaps climaxing in the 2000s. One can add that both in the 2000 and especially the 2004 Presidential elections the winner was victorious largely (though not entirely) thanks to the publicly proclaimed and expressed "faith" and "godliness" or promises of "godly politics", including "God-told-me to be President" and conduct "holy" war on the "evil" world proclamations restating medieval-style Divine-right and crusade claims. Conversely, in both elections, manifestly (2004) or latently (2000), the despised "losers" were defeated mostly (not solely) because of their perceived lack or rather insufficient degree and proof of "faith" and "godliness", predictably, above all, in the "Bible Belt". As a supreme irony or historical rarity, yet a (patho) logical, predictable outcome of "reborn" evangelicalism, in the cited Presidential elections, the losing candidate lost as a "home boy" even his native "Bible-Belt" state and region apparently on the grounds of a "mortal sin" of insufficient "faith" and "godliness."

(The "loser" was self-described as "used to be the next President" given the electoral fiasco and the post-electoral drama and the Supreme Court's arbitrary determination of the Presidency. "Politically incorrect" comedians may comment that such an electoral outcome in the "Bible Belt" state of Tennessee in the 2000 Presidential election was in a way prefigured or predicted by its irrational "Monkey Trials" against and its state law prohibiting biological evolutionism during the 1920s. Perhaps, by punishing its "home boy" and the holder of no less than a "divinity study" master's degree for his perceived "insufficient faith" and "godliness", including implicitly evolution theory, this state reenacted and won again its "Monkey Trial" almost a century later. Even more ironic was the fact that the "loser" was a Southern Baptist, hence in theory "true" evangelical and an academic theologian, and the "winner" a Methodist, thus theoretically a "liberal" Protestant as well as somewhat overly "secular" or "non-ascetic" in personal morality and private "first" life. But, apparently the "Bible Belt", in particular the home boy's own state, "defined" the religious situation or "constructed" political reality in exactly opposite terms, exemplifying what Merton calls the "perversities" of such social definitions or constructions in accordance with the Thomas sociological theorem, "if men define situations as real, they are real in their consequences".)

In Schumpeter's terms, American Puritan-inspired politics has thus mutated from the free market-style secular competition for political power and influence into a sort of "beauty contest" in public proclamation and hyper-emotional (ideally tearful) expression or hysterical ecstasy of "true faith", "godliness", "belief in Almighty", or "godly politics", and stirred with super-patriotic Americanism. Such a mix forms an efficient Machiavellian formula to attain such ends, notably Presidency as the arguably climactic point of the American dream fulfilled. Evidently, this is the venerable and predictable pattern of US "born again" Puritanical Protestants or "Christians", including those Presidents (re)elected on "godly" grounds and with self-assigned Divine rights to rule and save *cum* destroy the world via permanent "holy" wars on "evil". Yet, in so doing they neglect or deny a basic fact of Western liberal-secular democracy and modernity in contrast to its illiberal and anti-secular, including theocratic, alternatives. The fact is that, first, the free *secular* competition for political power defines or typifies, at least in Schumpeter's reductive market-economic definition, modern Western liberal democracy. Second, the "God and faith" contest or "godly politics" defines substantively its antithesis and destruction, theocracy and its own proxies in third-world societies like Islamic, Catholic, and other traditional countries.

Perhaps, in a typical Orwellian double-thinking defying elemental logic, US "reborn" fundamentalists, including would-be theocrats-presidents with Divine rights, think, as it often seems, that the free and secular competition for political power may represent democracy in other Western societies but not in America as an exceptional "one nation indivisible under God" (Giddens 2000) or "godly", "faith-based" society, and, even more, conversely. Thus, they seem to think and leave the impression as though the "God and faith" contest and politics overall reflected theocracy and thus non-democracy in Iran and other "axis of evil" Islamic societies as well as the Vatican and "unfriendly" Catholic countries, but not in America itself, including the Southern "Bible Belt", due to its celebrated exceptionalism. Prima facie, such Orwellian double-thinking is the totalitarian destruction of human logic, reason, and eventually life (e.g., permanent offensive war on the "evil" world as "defense" spending and "peace"). It can only persist and convince as a form of "true lies" and self-deceptions through mass, constant, and intense political indoctrination (Myrdal 1953) and "brain-washing" manipulative propaganda[25] (Baudrillard 1999; Beiner 1992; Trey 1998), which, as Mannheim suggests, even its Puritan, just as Nazi, masters cease eventually to believe and instead revert to their usually efficient formula of "pure hypocrisy", notably the asymmetry of hypocritical moral rhetoric (Heckathorn 1990). Yet, by doing so these, like most theocrats and other totalitarian forces, overlook or negate what Spencer admonished long ago. This is that a democratic polity and society "cannot prosper by lies"[26]—though they would not publicly claim that

---

[25] Trey (1998:128) observes that the public ream in the US during the 1990s "was occluded by systematic imperatives that convened against critical perspectives" on the Gulf War and, one can add, even more on the second war against Iraq and terror generally. The US political system "seemed to learn a great deal more from Vietnam than did the opposition. In the "90s [and 2000s], the system is both more diffuse and more consolidated: diffuse in the sense that it has branched out, into the world, in ways that are difficult to track quickly; consolidated in the sense that internal pressure has been all but annulled" (Trey 1998:129).

[26] A leading US newspaper reported that a retired military official and a network television analyst said, after the revealed human rights violations by the US military at Guantanamo Bay's detention center for foreign terrorist suspects, the following: "It was them [the Pentagon and the administration) saying, "We need to stick our hands up your back and move your mouth for you." Another military analyst reporting about the war in Iraq also said "night and day I felt we'd been hosed" by the defense department and the US administration. The newspaper also found that the Pentagon described

America is an "exceptional nation" in this kind of prosperity—not to mention the proverb about the long-term effectiveness of lying politically (as Americans say, "you can't lie to all people all the time").

On this account, in historical terms most Presidential and other electoral processes in America under neo-conservatism during the late 20th and early 21st century resemble and evoke, if not replicate, Puritan "elections" in which the people's role admittedly was only to elect the most "godly" predestined saints-masters (Bremer 1995) in 17th century New England, with particularly Reagan et al. publicly emulating and admiring Winthrop as the model. In particular, the "born again" evangelical (including Reaganite) renditions of these and virtually all political processes and events in America are similar to or reminiscent of Winthrop's and Cromwell's "holy" wars against the "ungodly" as well as Calvin's war of extermination of non-evangelicals.

Recall that following Calvin's theocratic model of politics in France (yet a failure) and Geneva (success), Winthrop's and Cromwell's Puritan political campaigns amounted to "holy" wars or crusades against "infidels" (Goldstone 1986; Gorski 2000) in old and New England. And, US "reborn" fundamentalists proudly continue this tradition of Puritanism (Dunn and Woodard 1996). In general, as America ushers in the 21st century, its political system essentially continues and even expands through Presidential and other elections Puritan "godly politics" (Zaret 1989) from 17th century New England, and thereby Calvin's *civitas Dei* from 16th century Geneva as the point of origin. At this juncture, nothing or just little has substantively changed—or perhaps as Calvin and other French Calvinist theologians might put it, the "more things have changed, the more they have stayed the same"—from 16th century Geneva *civitas Dei*, and thus the medieval *respublica Christiana*, to 21st century evangelical America as a "faith-based" society via New England's "godly politics". In that sense, Calvin's *civitas Dei* reasserts or reappears as America's Calvinist political and even holistic, theocratic sociological "destiny" via Puritan "godly politics".

---

these network television military analysts as "message force multipliers" or "surrogates" for reliably delivering administration" themes and messages" to the American people "in the form of their own opinions." The newspaper concluded that "records and interviews show how the [US] administration has used its control over access and information in an effort to transform the analysts into a kind of media Trojan horse—an instrument intended to shape terrorism coverage from inside the major TV and radio networks."

In comparative terms, one can add that nothing like this godliness has ever been observed before (Bell 2002) and after in Presidential and equivalent elections and other political processes among contemporary post-war Western liberal-secular democracies, including post-conservative Great Britain. Proclaiming by key political agents to be "reborn" Protestants, especially Calvinist evangelicals, and "Christians" overall whose lives have been altered "directly by Jesus Christ" as their "favorite philosopher" remains the "only in America" phenomenon within modern Western liberal democracy and modernity (Inglehart 2004; Lipset 1996; Munch 2001). It is the evident legacy of Puritanism and its "godly politics" and in extension Calvinism and its design of *civitas Dei*. In a way, this is considered and perceived as an American religious oddity or exceptionality, which with its seeming grotesque as well as "vigorous hypocrisy" Puritan-style (Bremer 1995) is one of those multiple elements that remake America the "laughing stock" (Hill 2002; Wagner 1997) in the eyes of the Western world and beyond.

Yet, given what Weber and other analysts identify as the morbid, "terrible seriousness" or stodginess of Calvinism (Gould 1996), including its dogma of predestination, and hence of "born again" evangelicalism, this grotesque or comic exceptionality is typically mixed with tragic or serious elements. The mixture promises to make such exceptionalism a sort of Shakespearean or Dreiser's like American sociological tragedy in comparative terms. Sociologically, it is a tragedy in the sense of theocratic proto-totalitarian destruction of liberty and democracy by the design of a "Bible Belt" (Bauman 1997) and ultimately self-destruction via a global and permanent "holy" war against the "evil" world in accordance with Puritan judgment-day nihilism, annihilation *cum* Calvinist salvation (Adorno 2001). In a way, this exceptionalism may mutate from the "laughing stock" into "apocalypse now" or later, as heralded or adumbrated by the apocalyptic outcomes or scenarios of various fundamentalist sects and cults in America, especially (but not solely) in the "Bible Belt". If so, this would represent a fitting and predictable consummation of the Calvinist-Puritan implied commandment of "either a godly society or else existential nothingness" via self-destructive "holy" war against the "ungodly" at home and in the world. For illustration, a variation or vestige of this nihilistic commandment in contemporary America is that "reborn" Protestant fundamentalism commands a sort of "godly education or nothing" ultimatum in that it decrees that no education is "better" than secular schooling (Darnell and Sherkat 1997). In doing so, it seemingly perpetuates the "forbidden apple" explicit or implied treatment of secular human knowledge and reason versus Providential design and intelligence (Bendix 1984) in Puritanism, as well as medievalist Christianity overall.

Either grotesque or deadly serious—or rather both—comparatively this striking and ever-persisting American exceptionalism in the sense of a "faith-based" polity and society indicates that Calvinism with its design of a *civitas Dei* has succeeded in its political and generally societal predestination *only* in America via Puritanism and its "godly" politics and society. Conversely, it has failed in Europe, including even post-Calvinist Holland and once-Puritan England. In short, this suggests the political "triumph of Calvinism" (German 1995) America, and its defeat in most of Europe. In sum, it confirms that Calvinism has become the political and overall sociological "destiny" of a distant land and "new nation" solely or primarily, but not or less of its French home and the "old world". (Holland is a partial and rapidly diminishing or dramatically tempered Calvinist exception.)

### *Theocratic cum Anti-Liberal Polity*

By design and in reality, a Calvinist and other theocratic polity and society in America and elsewhere is anti-liberal, including anti-pluralist and anti-secular, in nature, operation, and effect. In this respect, it seems axiomatic and thus tautological to consider and describe it in anti-liberal terms. Yet, it may be instructive and necessary to do so, given what critical analysts identify as the "liberal mythology" (Gould 1996), the "naïve assumptions" (Coffey 1998), and "speculative explanations" (Zaret 1996) of the link of Calvinism, notably Puritanism, and liberty in America, including the post-Weberian, especially Parsonian, sociological literature. These mythologies and assumptions contend that a Calvinist theocratic polity, like New England's Puritan "Biblical Commonwealth" and the Southern neo-Puritan "Bible Belt", is "liberal", "pluralist," "secular", or "libertarian" and "democratic", minimally not anti-liberal, anti-pluralist, and anti-secular.

Thus, Parsons, if not explicitly states, often implies that his native New England under Puritanism was admittedly theocracy (even when not so described) with "iron collectivism" and "almost inquisitorial discipline" (Tawney 1962), yet exemplary liberal-secular, pluralist, and individualistic democracy, showing his complex and ambivalent, if not contradictory, treatment of his "Puritan heritage" (Alexander 1983). In general, he implicitly admits that Protestantism, specifically Puritanism, was actually or potentially theocratic by reducing polity, society, and all humans to the "purposes of God" (Parsons 1967) via "godly politics", as well as Machiavellian (others reduced to "one's own ends"). Yet, he extols it as the prime source of Western political liberalism and individualism in an invidious distinction from pre-Protestantism or Catholicism, as do his followers (Mayway 1984).

Even Tocqueville implicitly associates what he clearly identifies above as New England's Puritan legal repressive and deadly theocracy (while not using the term) with, or at least does not disassociate it from, what he, like Parsons, regards as liberal-secular, pluralist, egalitarian, and individualistic democracy, or political liberalism, pluralism, egalitarianism, and individualism, in America. In general, Tocqueville evidently identifies American Puritanism as theocratic and otherwise repressive ("oppressive laws" with the "striking marks of a narrow sectarian spirit") and yet considers it to correspond with the "most absolute democratic and republican theories" in the Western world, in a mixture or tension between theocracy (or oppression) and "democracy" (and perhaps "republic").

The above Parsonian "liberal mythology" of American Puritanism not only involves an evidently convoluted logic or anti-logic, thus a non sequitur—theocracy *cum* political liberalism, pluralism, secularism, and individualism, hence liberal, pluralist, secular, and individualistic democracy? It also entails the Orwellian-like double, ethnocentric reasoning of Puritan-rooted American exceptionalism as universal superiority and triumphalism (Bell 2002). "Theocratic" has always and everywhere been considered anti-liberal and thus non-democratic, including the old Europe and the Islamic world, but not in the Puritan "first new nation" (Lipset 1996) as the sole superior exception to the "iron" law of theocracy in the entire world from the 17th to the 21st century. The Orwellian anti-logic of Parsonian exceptionalism is that "non-American" Orthodox, Catholic, Islamic, even Anglican and Lutheran theocracies are unmitigated undemocratic "evil", but "all-American" Puritan theocracy *cum* a "faith-based" polity and society after the image of a "Biblical Garden" is a supreme democratic "good", utopia realized, a sort of "paradise on earth." Further, this Parsonian "liberal mythology" of Puritan theocracy is empirically contradicted, as shown below.

*Calvinist Political Anti-Liberalism versus Democracy*

Against the above background, it may not be completely tautological and redundant to restate and emphasize that a Calvinist-Puritan theocratic polity in America and beyond is an exemplary and even ultimate form of political anti-liberalism and anti-secularism, simply extremely anti-liberal and anti-secular. Alternatively, it is far from being, as in Parsons' conception, the origin and "heart and soul", through extolled theological individualism (the individual's "immediacy to God"), of what he patriotically celebrates as American liberal democracy (and capitalism) as a sort of end of societal evolution or history (Giddens 1984). Even such a preeminent sociological mind as Parsons was unable or unwilling to realize what many early and later sociologists clearly did and do. This is that it is not because, but precisely in spite and in opposition of Puritanism and in extension Calvinism that liberal-secular democracy, specifically its Jefferson-Madison's version, was established and sustained as a political system or an ideal in America. Simply, not Parsons' inherited Puritanism, but rather non-Puritanism, especially Jefferson's non- and anti-Calvinist Enlightenment[27] (Baldwin 2006; Bremer 1995; Gould 1996), is primarily functional to or instrumental ("smart") in liberal-secular democracy in America. Conversely, Puritanism is so for anti-liberal theocracy and authoritarianism overall (or, to paraphrase a US President, "stupid" in the sense of irrational "dumb" theocratic laws and primitive Draconian punishments for their violation), thus Ross' antidote-poison of liberal-secular democracy and human liberty in general.

In comparative terms, this Parsonian fallacy of "democratic" Puritanism is equivalent or analogous to contending or implying that liberal or secular democracy in Catholic and Islamic countries like France

---

[27] Bremer (1995:225) observes that the Enlightenment, especially its French version and by implication that of Jefferson and Franklin both residing in France for some time, developed as a "philosophical movement totally antithetical" to Calvinism and in consequence Puritanism in America. Still, in his views, "in the early 18th century, in England and in the colonies, many [Puritans] were attracted to the philosophers' claim to have discovered natural laws, their optimistic view of man, and their skepticism toward all orthodoxies" (Bremer 1995:225). However, Bremer (1995:225) concludes that generally in the "Anglo-American world the Enlightenment left its mark more particularly upon Anglicans" than on Puritans. Also, Gould (1996:29) registers the proliferation of "European Enlightenment theories about degeneracy in the New World" (Gould 1996:29), especially New England under Puritanism. In turn, some other analysts (Byrne 1997; Hartz 1963; Kloppenberg 1998) downplay this antithesis between the Enlightenment or liberalism and Puritanism or the Protestant religion in pre-revolutionary America by contrast to Europe, in favor of their affinity, particularly their collaboration during the American Revolution in facing the British Empire as the common enemy. Still, within the present context or for the purpose at hand, the first historical views are adopted as more sociologically consistent and empirically plausible.

or Italy and Turkey, has been established and sustained because, not in spite and opposition, of anti-liberal Catholicism and fundamentalist Islam respectively. This is precisely opposite to what most sociological and other analyses suggest (Burns 1990; Davis and Robinson 2006; Dombrowski 2001; Kuran 2004; Mansbach 2006). Negatively, the fallacy is analogous to negating or overlooking that the connection of liberal or secular democracy to anti-liberal Catholicism in France or Italy, and to fundamentalist Islam in Turkey (and Hinduism in India) has been and remains accidental, just as theocratic Puritanism's links with democratic liberalism in England and America have been and remain "fortuitous" (Zaret 1989).

Of course, as implied above, the Parsonian answer and rationale is that Puritanism and in extension Calvinism and all Protestantism is, in virtue of its glorified theological individualism, different from, namely more liberal, individualistic, and democratic (Mayway 1984) than, both Catholicism (and Orthodox Christianity) and Islam and other world religions (e.g., Hinduism). In consequence, arguably Calvinism via Puritanism has produced and sustained such outcomes for democracy in America that are the exact opposites of those that these religions have generated in their respective societies, such as Catholic France or Italy and Islamic Turkey (and Hindu India). Such is the prevalent assumption in the US sociological and other literature (e.g., Lipset 1996; Lipset and Marks 2000) and common belief in American as well as other Protestant societies. Yet, it is both logically contradictory and empirically implausible, each in at least two respects.

It is logically contradictory, first, given that virtually all world religions have been and remain what Weber calls "religiously determined systems of life-regulation", notably of political and moral "restraint" (Bell 1977) and depreciation of humans for supra-human Divine or proxy causes, thus intrinsically or eventually repression, authoritarianism and anti-humanism in politics and society. This is what Michels may call an "iron" sociological law of world religions to the effect of "who says world religion says human restraint, depreciation, repression, and anti-humanism." At least, it forms a Weberian empirical generalization or historical pattern typifying world religions like Hinduism, Buddhism (in part), Judaism, Islam, and Christianity, and within it the Orthodox Church, Catholicism, and Protestantism, including Calvinism and Puritanism (with Confucianism as the only humanistic exception in Weber's account). To that extent, it is a self-contradiction or inconsistency to argue that the world religions of restraint like Catholicism, the Orthodox Church, Islam, and Hinduism reproduce anti-liberalism, anti-individualism, authoritarianism, and anti-humanism, while Protestantism only, notably Calvinism or Puritanism, miraculously regenerates democracy, individualism, liberty, and humanism! It is a non sequitur or does not make logical sense and consistency to allege that Catholicism, Islam, the Orthodox Church, and Hinduism undermine or destroy liberal-secular democracy in, say, France or Italy, Turkey, Russia, and India, while Protestantism, specifically Calvinism via Puritanism, does the exact opposite in America as a superior exception. For these world religions are the systems of political and other restraint, depreciation, and humiliation, thus ultimately of theocratic control and repression, of humans for what Parsons (1967) calls the supra-human "purposes of God" and in that sense anti-humanism. (This is a statement of fact beyond, to paraphrase Weber, "good and evil", not a value-judgment, for anti-humanism is judged as "good" in Calvinism or religious conservatism, just as is humanism in secularism or liberalism.)

Second, the Parsonian assumption of Calvinism and democracy is logically contradictory or inconsistent so long as all the world religions, Christian and non-Christian, rely on charismatic or traditional authority. Charisma, like tradition, is what Weber describes as the "authoritarian principle" of power legitimation and thus incompatible with liberal-secular democracy typified instead by legal-rational authority (Lenski 1994) as an ideal type (which means that elements of charisma and tradition are not absent, yet secondary). It is a clear contradiction or inconsistency to claim that Catholicism, Islam, the Christian Orthodox Church, and Hinduism are antithetical or destructive to liberal-secular democracy and all freedom in France or Italy, Turkey, Russia, and India, respectively, while Puritanism and in extension Calvinism or Protestantism is at the origin and heart of democratic politics and liberty in America. For all these religions involve an *authoritarian*, non- or at most pseudo-democratic political principle. If they do so, then they are all essentially antithetical to liberal-secular democracy and liberty, though in varying, statistical-like "degrees of unfreedom". And, Calvinism, including Puritanism, is a paradigmatic exemplar of this rule or historical pattern, rather an exception reproducing in America celebrated American exceptionalism in an oxymoron of "theocratic democracy" (and capitalism) or democratic (and capitalist) theocracy *cum* "faith-based" politics and "godly" society.

More importantly, the Parsonian sociological assumption linking Calvinism with liberal-secular democracy in America is empirically implausible also in two respects. First, it overlooks that theological individualism, expressed in individuals' "immediacy to God", in Puritanism and in extension Calvinism (and Protestantism overall) is not necessarily associated with, or does not represent a sufficient condition of, political or secular individualism in the sense of what Mannheim calls modern individualistic liberalism (also, Bird 1999), particularly the European Enlightenment. To that extent, Calvinist theological individualism is not linked with and does not predict liberal-secular democracy. What Parsons extols as the "immediacy of the individual soul to God inherent" in Calvinism is simply not enough for individual freedom in politics and society, thus democracy, just as the pre-Calvinist Christian doctrine of "equality of souls" does not render "all Christians political democrats" and social egalitarians (Linton 2001). Thus, what Weber detects as "Calvinistic state churches" in Europe and America, including the Puritan "theocracy of New England", were premised on such theological individualism. Yet, they functioned as exemplary anti-liberal, anti-individualistic[28] (Tiryakian 1975), and thus non-democratic political systems permeated by what Tawney (1962) identifies as "iron collectivism" and nearly "inquisitorial discipline", as do their modern vestiges like the "Bible Belt" and its equivalents (e.g., Utah). For instance, New Haven's Puritan legal-penal system admittedly shared more of the "continental inquisitorial approach" than of English common law (Dayton 1999).

Second, the Parsonian assumption overlooks what Weber and contemporary sociologists identify as an affinity (Friedland 2001; Mansbach 2006; Turner 2002; Van Dyke 1995) or, to use Parsons' term, convergence, of Puritanism and Calvinism in general with Islam. Specifically, this is an affinity in political anti-liberalism, anti-secularism, anti-humanism, and anti-individualism or collectivism, including aggressive religious nationalism, imperialism, militarism, and "holy" wars (crusades and jihads, respectively) against "infidels", including religious out-groups and non-believers or secularists. Moreover, such an affinity sometimes becomes a sort of functional Puritan-Islamic equivalence in various respects, including a religiously founded and rationalized

---

[28] Tiryakian (1975:24) remarks that "radical individualism is alien" to American Puritanism.

Draconian "tough" on sin-crime penal system of execution and incarceration (Jacobs et al. 2005). At the minimum, the Puritan-Islamic affinity is exemplified by that between the neo-Puritan "Bible Belt" and Iranian theocracy identified as near-equivalent proto-totalitarian destructions of liberal-secular democracy and human liberty and eventually life, as via the shared fundamentalist grounded and sanctified death penalty system *and* "holy" wars alike (Bauman 1997).

In essence, Calvinist politics in America is intrinsically a theological, "godly" antithesis and ultimately a theocratic, totalitarian destruction of political liberalism and pluralism, liberal-secular and pluralist democracy, just as of civil society and culture with equivalent properties (cultural diversity or multiculturalism). A sociological analysis observes and emphasizes that Puritan-rooted fundamentalism in contemporary America systematically and sanctimoniously acts "against the reality of a liberal and pluralist" polity and society (Munch 2001) ushering in the 21st century. Historically, this is a consistent pattern or "method in the madness" (Smith 2000), because Puritanism has attempted to prevent the creation of such a society at least since its acting as the anti-Enlightenment (Nisbet 1966) versus the Jeffersonian Enlightenment and liberalism in the 19th century and later (Archer 2001; Patell 2001).

In so doing, "born again" US fundamentalists do not "rediscover America" (or "reinvent the wheel"), but perpetuate a long-standing tradition of Calvinist-Puritan anti-liberalism, anti-pluralism, and anti-secularism, just as anti-rationalism, anti-egalitarianism, anti-pacifism, anti-universalism, etc. Hence, when US conservatives (Dunn and Woodard 1996; also, Seaton 2006) extol contemporary American Protestant conservatism for methodically and proudly standing in the tradition of Puritanism, they primarily refer to and glorify Puritan and in extension Calvinist anti-liberalism, anti-pluralism, and anti-secularism, just as anti-rationalism, anti-egalitarianism, anti-pacifism, anti-universalism, anti-humanism, etc. Evidently, to better understand why and how "reborn" American fundamentalism opposes liberal-pluralist democracy with its universal political liberties in the "land of freedom", remember that Calvinism, including Puritanism, constituted a paradigmatic case of political anti-liberalism, anti-pluralism, and authoritarianism rather than (in the Puritan "liberal mythology") of liberalism and pluralism in polity and society.

First and foremost, Calvinism, including Puritanism originated as medieval-based and inspired pre-liberalism, particularly the pre-Enlightenment. This holds true assuming, as Spencer, Durkheim, Weber, Mannheim, and other sociologists suggest, that liberalism, in particular the Enlightenment, did not exist during medievalism—as the "Dark Middle Ages" indicates—and prior to the Calvinist Revolution and the Protestant Reformation. Consequently, Calvinism arose as what Mannheim calls a medievalist or traditionalist "pre-democratic, authoritarian" political ideology ("mind") and system not only on the formal account of its birth *still* within despotic medievalism (the early 16th century). More importantly, it did because of its substantive ideas, institutions, and practices designing, establishing, or defending medieval-style "godly" tyranny. Recall that Calvin decreed that people must submit to, in total obedience, "even tyranny" on the grounds of its being "ordained by God", thus to pre-liberal and pre-democratic medieval-style "godly" theocracy in the anti-humanistic belief that "ungodly" humans shall be "held in check" by all means and "at all costs" and times (Heller 1986).

In turn, Calvin's decree and resulting "model of theocratic governance" (Mansbach 2006) has persisted and expanded as an ideal and inspiration in subsequent Calvinism by establishing tyrannical and larger theocracies (Holland), including English-American Puritanism and its, in Weber's words, "unexampled tyranny," as in Great Britain briefly and New England for long. In particular, this theological decree in a way prefigured and inspired what can be considered the single ultimate, violent act, and syndrome of theocratic pre- and anti-liberalism, thus a pre- and non-democratic mind and practice, in original French Calvinism. This was the conclusion of the Calvinist synod held in late 16th century France that the "evangelical religion" was impossible to establish without the "extermination" of non-evangelicals or non-Calvinists ("Papists", libertines or *parlementaires*, etc.), with such "incitement" resulting in various acts of "godly" violence such as (attempted) murders of Catholic priests and attacks on aristocrats' castles (Heller 1986).

Overall, original Calvinism in Europe, from France and Geneva to Holland and Germany, was pre- and anti-liberal in that it denied to non-Calvinists those very political, religious, civil and other liberties that it had strongly demanded and appropriated for itself before. For example, historical research suggests that in Holland's supposedly liberal and pluralist early Calvinism, the Calvinist self-proclaimed love for freedom when deprived of political power did not develop or translate into "liberality", the willingness and readiness for granting others the freedom one demanded for oneself, citing the way the Dutch Calvinists treated their colonies[29] (Kaplan 2002). And, Puritanism originally was in consequence pre-liberal Calvinism transferred from Europe to and "reborn" and renamed in England and America during, as Hume suggests, the late 16th (the 1560s) and early 17th century (the 1620s–30s), respectively (Elwood 1999).

Second, Calvinism and consequently Puritanism subsequently expanded and functioned as anti-liberalism, including the counter-Enlightenment, despite some spurious mitigations like Geneva's "enlightened" (yet effectively anti-Enlightenment) Calvinist orthodoxy (Sorkin 2005). Predictably, it did in adverse reaction to the emergence of liberalism, notably the Enlightenment, during post-medieval times (17th–18th centuries) and has since, as elaborated later. For example, a particular brand and revival of Calvinism, specifically English Puritanism, called "Methodism" arose, as Mill and Weber imply, in adverse explicit or implicit reaction to the Enlightenment and liberalism overall during the late 18th century. It initially functioned as a sort of methodical anti-Enlightenment, in spite of some imputed links to Jeffersonian secularism (Baldwin 2006), while gradually tempering this anti-liberalism since to develop in "liberal" or moderate and mainline Protestantism in America (Hout et al. 2001; Martin 2002).

Generally, Calvinism, in particular Puritanism, was consistent political anti-liberalism, including anti-pluralism, as the negative (flip-side) of its theocratic politics to the point of what Weber might call anti-liberal "iron consistency". If, as he remarks, in post-Luther Lutheranism the "dominant interest" is the battle against political and cultural liberalism, just as rationalism, then this holds true a fortiori of both early and later Calvinism, notably American Puritanism and its perpetual evangelical revivals, up to the early 21st century. Significantly, he suggests that even more than orthodox Catholicism and early Lutheranism, when and if "strong enough" politically Calvinism (including Baptism) did not recognize but instead denied and violated the freedom of conscience for non-Calvinists. In a way, Calvin, even more than, as Weber implies, Luther, was a proto-typical Protestant "reformed" anti-liberal, including an anti-pluralist, anti-secularist, and anti-humanist, as the obverse side of a medieval-style theocrat and arch-conservative

---

[29] Kaplan (2002:18) comments that one "might well have cited the Reformation as another example".

(Mansbach 2006). This holds good not just because of Calvin's murdering of his critics (Servetus), but also his theological doctrines, notably the predestination doctrine experienced by these dissenters and rejected by non-Calvinists as "morally repugnant" (Ozment 1980) or, as by Franklin, "inimical to morality" (Byrne 1997), due to its inhumanity, and their realization through various theocratic activities and institutions in Geneva. And, Calvin's doctrines and practices further propelled and motivated his followers in Europe and beyond into anti-liberalism and anti-humanism. For example, apparently following Calvin's writings and actions in Geneva, in Germany orthodox Calvinists (e.g., those dominating the synod of Dort 1619) were "determined" to eliminate or stifle "all liberal views" (Nischan 1994). Such suppression of "liberal" theological and political ideas at the start of or in the prelude to liberalism was a logical, though seemingly non-violent, sequel of the previous Calvinist synod in France recommending the "extermination" of non-Calvinists and potential liberals in gestation as libertines for the "sacred" cause of establishing Calvinism as the true and only evangelical, "Christian" religion.

In sum, Calvinism, including Puritanism, was born as medievalist pre-liberalism and pre-Enlightenment when no "liberalism" or "Enlightenment" in the modern sense existed (the 16th century). And, it operated as post-medieval anti-liberalism, notably the counter-Enlightenment, in facing and resisting modern liberalism, including the Enlightenment during and since the 17th–19th centuries. Consequently, it was simply pre-democratic or authoritarian in Mannheim's sense before and anti-democratic after the advent of liberal democracy and modernity. Either way, Calvinism, including Puritanism, was far from being the source of "liberalism", including the "Enlightenment", thus modern "democracy", which contradicts the Calvinist "liberal mythology" in America (Coffey 1998; Gould 1996) and in part Europe (Nischan 1994).

As noted, Calvinism and consequently Puritanism represented a paradigmatic exemplar of theocratic political anti-pluralism as a particular dimension of anti-liberalism. By analogy to anti-liberalism, it originated as medieval-based political as well as theological, religious and moral pre-pluralism or absolutism when real pluralism or tolerance in politics and religion was non-existent or not yet institutionally recognized in the sense of modern pluralistic liberalism. (A partial exception was the Edict of Nantes institutionalizing Calvinism alongside Catholicism during late 16th century France yet revoked later, cf., Heller 1986; Mentzer 2007.) Subsequently, Calvinism and consequently Puritanism functioned as consistent anti-pluralism or anti-relativism in politics and religion in opposition or tension to the existence and institutional recognition of political and social pluralism, tolerance, and relativism, as during and since the 17th–19th century. Analogously, adumbrated or inspired by Calvin's theological commandments, the single ultimate (violent) act or syndrome of theocratic pre- or even anti-pluralism in original Calvinism was the 16th century French Calvinist Synod's conclusion[30] and prescription that evangelicalism could only established by the "extermination" of non-Calvinists, including Catholics and libertines as proto-liberals for their "mortal sin" of advocating religious liberty, pluralism, and tolerance. On the accounts of both pre- and anti-pluralism epitomizing pre- and anti-liberalism respectively, Calvinism, including Puritanism, was essentially political and other social absolutism or monism and to that extent actually or potentially totalitarianism as a monistic system (Dahrendorf 1959; Habermas 2001; Infantino 2003; Mises 1966). And via American "born again" fundamentalism as the new evangelical religion déjà vu in contemporary America, it substantively continues to be so by the early 21st century, as elaborated next.

## From the 16th Century French Calvinist Synod to 21st Century American Evangelicalism

The above then places contemporary American Puritan-inspired fundamentalism and its attacks against the "reality of a liberal and pluralist" polity and society in proper, comparative-historical perspective. In particular, it places "reborn" Protestant evangelicalism in 21st century America within the context of the 16th century French Calvinist Synod and its conclusion and implied prescription that the "evangelical religion" in France and beyond could only established by the "extermination" of non-evangelicals.

At the minimum, this indicates an equivalence or continuity between French Calvinism and American evangelicalism over a span of five

---

[30] The "extermination" conclusion of the Calvinist Synod was in turn perhaps a major implied cause or rationale for the revocation by the monarchy of the "Edict of Nantes" institutionalizing religious and political pluralism or tolerance by legalizing Calvinism and its coexistence with Catholicism (Heller 1986; Nischan 1994; Mentzer 2007).

centuries in the end pursued, even if not, charitably interpreted, in the means employed for attaining it. The shared end is reestablishing evangelicalism as the "only true" religion, a theocratic polity and society. The means is either extermination (the first case) of or more "spiritual" instruments like culture wars (the second) against the "ungodly", including non-evangelical Christians, non-Christians, and non-believers or secularists. US "born again" Puritan fundamentalists may have replaced the primitive method of Calvinist extermination, as attempted or proposed, alongside Calvin and Cromwell, by their role models Winthrop et al. against Native Americans and other "infidels" and "witches" (Gould 1996; Munch 2001), with less violent or ultimate means like exclusion (Edgell et al. 2006), subjugation, and "softer", symbolic violence against the "ungodly" via culture wars. Yet, they have retained the original, supreme end of Calvinism to be the official and only political and societal master, thus its design of Biblical theocracy. For instance, through the evangelical Great Awakenings as "spiritual" wars or "emotional explosions", in the late 18th and early 19th century Presbyterians, Methodists, Baptists, and other Calvinist groups or allies succeeded in establishing Protestant evangelicalism as the "dominant religion of America" (Foerster 1962), including both the South (Boles 1999) and the "Wild West" (Clemens 2007). And, Protestant evangelicalism or sectarianism has maintained and even expanded and reinforced its dominance ever since, through the late 20th and early 21st centuries (Lipset 1996; Munch 2001).

Yet, as the proclamation indicates and Weber implies, in Calvinism, notably American Puritanism (just as Islam), the extermination of "infidels" via "holy" wars has historically been, at least until the 20th century, the ideal, preferable, or "final" solution, and their subjugation, conversion, or exclusion only the "second best" when and if the first was impossible or onerous to realize for various reasons, as in present times. In short, the first is a sort of Pareto-optimum or maximum, and the second a suboptimum or minimum when the first cannot be reached. Hence, various categories of "infidels" in America and beyond can discount extermination as unrealistic in American Puritanism (like Islam) only at their own peril. They cannot do this discounting with impunity, at least eventually and under certain conditions like political crises, intensified culture wars, and especially a permanent "holy" war on the "evil" and "ungodly world. Simply, it seems plausible and prudent to "never say never" when it comes to the Calvinist-Puritan (as well as the Islamic) extermination of "infidels" via total warfare not constrained by "legal conventions"[31] (Mansbach 2006), crusade and jihad respectively. For extermination is "inborn" and strategic to, or long-term end of, Calvinism, including Puritanism, from Calvin and the cited Calvinist synod, just as is, in Weber's implied and other sociological views (Turner 2002; Van Dyke 1995), to fundamentalist Islam. Conversely, anything else or short of this optimum, including political subjugation, conversion, and exclusion, is just the second-best "public rational choice", tactical Machiavellian adjustment, or short-term objective in their shared crusade-style or jihadic politics resulting in "holy" war, with all, in Mises' words, the "horrors of religious crusades and wars".[32]

In Clausewitz's terms, Simmel's war of extermination defined as "warfare unrestrained by legal conventions" (Mansbach 2006) is the ultimate continuation and the optimal outcome of Puritan crusade-style (and Islamic jihadic) politics by other means, with subjugation, conversion, and exclusion operating as intermediate instruments and "second-best" outcomes in this process. On this basis, Calvin's and the Calvinist synod's commandment for extermination of "infidels" as the only or the most effective method to reestablish the true "evangelical religion" is not just a historical artifact or perversity, a ghost from the "dead past", as is not, for that matter, the Islamic jihad injunction even when nominally renounced or suspended, temporarily or tactically. Rather, it connects directly or indirectly original Calvinism with "born again" American evangelicalism and its vociferous attacks against liberal-pluralist democracy and modernity. Predictably, it does so via contemporary American evangelicalism's model, early Puritanism and its implementation of the Calvinist command on various "ungodly" groups and "witches", including, alongside "Papists" as the standard target since the 16th century, non-Christians (Native Americans) and even some moderate and pacifist Protestants (Quakers, etc.). Hence, the experienced or perceived evangelical "method in the madness" (Smith 2000) of anti-liberalism in 21st century America is best grasped

---

[31] Mansbach (2006:106) suggests that generally Europe's Protestant Reformation "brought about various forms of Christian fundamentalism, efforts to establish theocratic rule, and a host of willing martyrs—also characteristics of contemporary jihadist movements."

[32] Mises generally comments that "nothing could be less compatible with true religion than the ruthless persecution of dissenters and the horrors of religious crusades and wars", which is exactly what Calvinism has invariably practiced in Europe and, via Puritanism, Great Britain and America.

or revealed when linked with 16th century French Calvinism's commandment of methodical extermination of non-evangelical "infidels" by means of total political mastery or absolute power, thus making the world "mad" (Bourdieu 2000). Contemporary evangelicalism attempts to realize the Calvinist commandment with Hume's diagnosed Puritan "unreasonable obstinacy" and the ultra-conservative "politics of unreason" overall (Lipset and Raab 1978).

In general, seemingly incomprehensible American evangelicalism and its anti-liberalism, including anti-pluralism or absolutism, can only be understood completely and thus demystified from its celebrated mystical exceptionality if placed within a comparative-historical perspective. This is why its adherents, like all other theocrats and totalitarians, avoid and even condemn such comparisons and visits in Western history as "un-American". First, comparatively, contrary to its adherents' claim, anti-liberalism is not really as "all-American" as the apple-pie and "Puritan", but also "European" and "Calvinist" (as well as Catholic, not to mention Islamic), given that pre- and anti-liberal Calvinism originated in Europe and then "fathered" Puritanism. This thus holds true specifically of such various dimensions of anti-liberalism as anti-pluralism or absolutism, and anti-secularism, as well as anti-rationalism (anti-scientism), anti-egalitarianism, economic and political, anti-pacifism, anti-universalism, and anti-cosmopolitanism (Beck 2002).

Conversely, the ideal of a liberal, secular, and pluralist polity and society, thus political and societal liberalism, secularism and pluralism, is far from being, as US "reborn" evangelical neo-conservatives (Reaganites) claim, "un-American" and "European" in the standard pejorative and xenophobic sense of the "old decadent" foreign Europe and its "vices". It is rather both or (as Weber suggests) "Western" overall, as exemplified and embodied by Montesquieu, Voltaire, Hume, and Kant in the "old world" and by Jefferson, Franklin, Madison, and Paine in the "new nation". To that extent, "born again" US Puritan-inspired fundamentalists cannot plausibly claim any comparative exceptionalism, thus ostensive "superiority" in anti-liberalism, including anti-pluralism or absolutism, through attacking and eventually destroying a liberal-pluralist polity and society or liberalism as "un-American", within the hidden or "forgotten" extended family of European Calvinism and in extension traditional Christianity like official Catholicism. In sum, they are ever-more anti-liberal heirs apparent of Calvin and other Calvinists, if not of what they condemn as the "anti-Christ" popes with their "papal struggles" against liberalism

(Burns 1990), via Winthrop et al. as illiberal and theocratic role models (Bremer 1995; Munch 2001).

Second, in historical terms, contemporary American Puritan-inspired fundamentalism's attack against the "reality of a liberal and pluralist" polity and society or anti-liberalism is not really "new". This contradict the opposite claims expressed in the term religious and political "neo-conservatism" versus the "old", "outdated" liberalism and previous or paleo-conservatism. Such attacks are historically déjà vu replicating or continuing those by Calvinism in Europe and by Puritanism in England and America against the nascent liberal-secular democracy and modernity, including the Enlightenment, during and since the 18th century. On this account, US "born again" fundamentalists at the start of the 21st century act in the substantively identical or analogous way their Calvinist-Puritan role models and predecessors did during the 18th and 19th century as well as their condemned Catholic adversaries ("Papists") in medieval times. For virulent and systematic anti-liberalism is their common bond and denominator. This remarkable continuity and tenacity reaffirms what Hume identified as Puritan "unreasonable obstinacy" in attacking existing political and religious institutions—in England's case, Anglicanism and even Catholicism and the Monarchy—and Weber did as Calvinist "iron consistency" in asceticism and social control. If anything, Calvinism showed "iron consistency" in anti-liberalism in adverse reaction (and selection) to modern liberalism and secularism, and Puritanism did "unreasonable obstinacy" in attacking and destroying liberal-secular sociopolitical institutions.

Hence, contemporary American evangelicalism perpetuates and even expands beyond the "Bible Belt" and America, and intensifies ("hardens") such Puritan "unreasonable obstinacy" and Calvinist "iron consistency" in anti-liberalism. It does through the arch and neo-conservative "politics of unreason" (Lipset and Raab 1978), including domestic anti-liberal culture wars and a global "holy" war on the "ungodly" and "evil" world. "Born again" US evangelicals pretend that they engage in an epic, unprecedented crusade-like war on "ungodly" and "un-American" liberal democracy and modernity as supreme "evil" and the "work of Satan" to be destroyed once and for all, as if history in America and the world were to begin with them. Yet, the above shows that this is the typical self-delusion of crusaders or "holy" warriors sustained by and due to "blissful ignorance" (Wacquant 2002). It indicates that they, like their Catholic and Islamic enemies-allies (e.g., in the

Vatican, Poland, Iran, etc.), reenact what was a "mindless" (Habermas 2001) and eventually lost battle by medieval and post-medieval religious orthodoxy, including (alongside official Catholicism) Calvinism in Europe and Puritanism in Anglo-American settings, against liberal-secular democracy and modernity, in particular the Enlightenment and its legacy.

Calvinism, like traditional Catholicism (Burns 1990), might have largely lost this anti-liberal battle in Europe, including even modern Holland and Germany, not to mention France, and through Puritanism in Great Britain. Yet, its "all-American" evangelical survival or revival continues this anti-liberal war with remarkable but predictable tenacity and evident success in heroic disregard or blissful oblivion of the past history of failures in the Calvinist and papal (as well as Islamic) "holy" wars against modern liberalism. At this juncture, as medieval scholastics might say, there is "nothing new under the sun" of Calvinism, including American Puritanism, just as official Catholicism, in respect of anti-liberalism as a systematic "godly" antagonism to liberal democracy and society.

## *Theocratic Polity as a Non-Democratic Government*

As the aforesaid intimates, both by design and in reality, a Calvinist, like any other, theocratic polity or state in America and elsewhere is non-democratic or authoritarian, even totalitarian. What has been said about a Calvinist theocratic polity in relation to political anti-liberalism holds true of it relative to non-democracy in the sense of authoritarianism, including totalitarianism. Calvinist, like any other, theocracy is axiomatically and thus tautologically non-democracy or authoritarianism, including totalitarianism. Still, this needs to be conceptually reestablished and reiterated in light of the above liberal-democratic mythology and the "naïve assumptions" and "speculative explanations" of Puritanism *cum* liberty and democracy in America, including the Parsonian sociological literature evoking Tocqueville's celebrated analysis. Parsons establishes and celebrates the historical continuity and affinity between what he implicitly admits as the early Puritan theocracy or theocratic Puritanism and explicitly identifies and extols as subsequent and modern American democracy and liberty, democratic liberalism and individualism, as do his followers (Mayway 1984). Hence, he develops or evokes Tocqueville's historical association, or lack of disassociation, between New England's legal repressive (deadly) Puritan theocracy and liberal political "democracy in America" as a whole.

A "solution" to this problem or contradiction is to simply negate that New England's polity was a Puritan theocracy in the form of the official Calvinist Congregational Church at all but instead to argue that it was an exemplary democracy, more precisely, a democratic republic, as Parsonians would do (Mayway 1984). Yet, this "solution" contradicts Parsons' own "most influential" sociologist Weber who precisely identified, described, and even emphasized New England under Puritanism as a pure Calvinist theocracy, as do other analysts (e.g., Baltzell 1979; Dombrowski 2001; Gould 1996; Munch 2001; Stivers 1994; Tawney 1962; Zaret 1989), even those celebratory or sympathetic (Bremer 1995; German 1995). After all, Parsons' 19th century ancestors probably knew that if New England's "Biblical Commonwealth" was not a theocracy, or its established Congregational Church not really theocratic, an instance of Weber's Calvinist state churches, it would and should *not* have been officially "disestablished", as actually was, during the 1830s. Simply, there would have been nothing to "disestablish" (Baldwin 2006).

Alongside such logical arguments, salient historical facts, as exemplified and symbolized by "Salem with witches" (Harley 1996; Putnam 2000), make it unnecessary or superfluous to argue and substantiate the existence of New England's Calvinist-as-Puritan theocracy. This is well-established in the sociological and historical literature, except for Parsonians and apologists (Seaton 2006), and even in American and other Western societies, including Great Britain. To consider and describe New England, like America overall, notably the Southern "Bible Garden", as both a Biblical "theocracy" or *mixt aristocracie* and a representative "democracy", as Parsons implies, is not a model of logic and, more importantly, of sociological realism. It is so given that the two types of polity are commonly considered and in reality have been as opposite as, literally for US Puritans, theological "heaven" and liberal-democratic "hell" or hope (Lemert 1999). In short, the outcome of this dual treatment is a sort of theocratic, thus totalitarian or authoritarian "democracy" (Brouwer 1998), "democratic" theocracy and totalitarianism in general, as an inner contradiction and empirical impossibility, at least in the long run.

Now, the dual description "theocracy" and "republic" while logically contradictory—the rule of self-assigned divines versus the people's election of their rulers?—is not unusual. It is so given that Calvinist (and Muslim) theocracies have often been designated as "republics", from Calvin's Geneva to Holland under Calvinism to Cromwell's England and Winthrop's New England to the "Bible Belt" (and the "Islamic Republic of Iran"). However, these theocratic "republics" have been by design the antithesis and in reality resulted in the destruction of political democracies in their societies, in a dramatic self-negation of the dubious equation, as prevalent in America due to Puritan anti-monarchic bias, of "republic" and "democracy". The above does not, of course, mean that a non-Puritan and other, including Anglican, monarchy is necessarily democracy. Overall, the point is that neither monarchy nor republic is the necessary, let alone sufficient, condition of liberal-secular democracy, and conversely, none is necessarily an anti-liberal and anti-democratic factor. Yet, both a *theocratic* monarchy and a republic are the antithesis and destruction of democracy, as exemplified by Catholic monarchic and Calvinist-Puritan republican, just as Islamic monarchic-republican, theocracies, respectively. Simply, it is not enough to declare a political system "republic" or "monarchy" and then to claim that it is "democracy" or "free", "undemocratic" or "unfree", respectively, as did Calvin and his heirs in Geneva's Republic and ruling Calvinists in Holland's Dutch Republic, notably anti-monarchic Puritans, from Cromwell and Winthrop to US neo-conservatives (and Iranian fundamentalists).

Against this background, it is also useful and indispensable to restate and reiterate that the Calvinist theocratic polity *cum* fundamentalist "godly" politics, even if "republic" versus disdained monarchy, in America has invariably been and is likely to be the axiomatic antithesis and the factual destruction of political democracy, just as of liberalism overall. In comparative and historical terms, it has been so everywhere else and virtually at all times within the global system or extended family of Calvinism, from Calvin's Geneva and Holland under the official "Reformed Church" to old and New England during Puritanism and the "new" South dominated by evangelicalism, from the 16th to the early 21st century. At this juncture, Puritan America has not been an "exceptional nation" in respect of this evidently "iron" sociological law, historical pattern, or negative equivalence ("common sense"?) "who says Calvinist and any theocracy and fundamentalism, says non- democracy and anti-liberalism". This thus contradicts the standard ethnocentric claim to democratic and individualistic exceptionalism (Lipset and Marks 2000) in spite or because of manifestly and sanctimoniously theocratic and fundamentalist, yet celebrated Puritanism as its genesis and destiny, "heart and soul".

Rather, liberal-secular democracy in America has ever been established and sustained, at least during the Jeffersonian era, the "New Deal", and postwar years (until the 1980s–2000s), not because but rather in spite and methodical opposition of New England's Puritan theocracy and theocratic and fundamentalist Puritanism. This is demonstrated by such non-Puritan democratic founders or classical liberals-democrats as Jefferson, Madison, and their followers, then post-Calvinists like Franklin relinquishing Calvinism as "inimical to morality" and humanity overall. Recall, New England's Puritan theocracy through the Calvinist Congregational Church and thus Puritanism generally effectively resisted the American Revolution's and Constitution's secular principles, notably Jefferson-Madison's principle of separation of church and state, for more than a half century by self-perpetuating itself (Baldwin 2006). It even in a way aimed to expand to all America, as via the Great Awakenings implementing Calvinist revivalism (German 1995), until 1833 when it was finally "disestablished" as "paradise lost" (Seaton 2006).

This is what Tocqueville occasionally implies, especially in his observations about New England's Puritan legal theocracy ("whosoever shall worship any other God than the Lord shall surely be put to death", "fantastic and oppressive laws" induced by a "sectarian spirit", etc.), albeit in tension with his other insights into Puritanism (as corresponding with the "most absolute democratic and republican theories"). Yet, unlike Franklin effectively relinquishing his father's Calvinism as amoral or inhumane, Parsons seemingly was not ready or willing to face directly, let alone relinquish his admittedly dual, Janus-faced Calvinist-as-Puritan heritage (Alexander 1983). Recall, this was the heritage of, first, extolled manifest theological individualism (individuals' "immediacy to God"), second, regretted underlying political anti-liberalism, anti-individualism, and anti-secularism (humans reduced to the means to "purposes of God"), plus Machiavellianism or utilitarianism (to "one's own ends"), and thus non-democracy, repression, and un-freedom.

*From Fundamentalist Anti-Liberalism to Theocratic Totalitarianism*

Crucially, as implied, a Calvinist and other theocratic polity in America and beyond tend to be non-democratic and unfree primarily because it is deeply anti-liberal, including anti-secular and anti-pluralist. Conversely, non-theocratic political systems in this and other Western societies are democratic and free for the primary reason of being liberal, particularly secular (not necessarily atheistic) in the sense of Mannheim's rationalistic liberalism (not anti-religious communism and Nazism as "less godly" than other fascism). Like in other theocratic world religions (e.g., official Catholicism, the Orthodox Church, fundamentalist Islam and Hinduism, orthodox Judaism), within Calvinism, particularly Puritanism, a non-democratic, authoritarian, including totalitarian, sociopolitical system is ultimately reproduced, explained, and sanctified by anti-liberalism. This includes anti-secularism *cum* "godly" politics and society after the model of Calvin's *civitas Dei* in Geneva (Mansbach 2006) and in extension his own ideal, medieval theocracy (the *respublica Christiana*). At this point, sociopolitical anti-liberalism, including anti-secularism, operates as both the necessary and sufficient condition of non-democracy and ultimately totalitarianism in Calvinism, including American Puritanism. It also does in other theocratic religions and anti-liberal ideologies like conservatism, fascism, including Nazism, and communism (except for official atheism or lack of religiosity).

Alternatively, liberalism, including secularism and pluralism, functions as the antidote of non-democracy and totalitarianism. In turn, it does as the necessary and sufficient condition of democracy and freedom overall (Dahrendorf 1979) as a general rule, and yet only hypothetically within Calvinism and consequently Puritanism, as the paradigmatic and persistent exemplar of negative anti-liberalism and anti-secularism or, positively, rigid and reactionary conservatism. Hence, conceivably a Calvinist polity in America and beyond could become in part democratic or non-authoritarian primarily to the extent that its "godly" politics and Calvinism, in particular Puritanism, is liberalized, including secularized. Yet to liberalize, especially secularize, what is paradigmatic (Protestant) anti-liberalism and anti-secularism is an ultimate inner contradiction and factual euthanasia (by analogy to Keynes' reference to that of capitalist rentiers). And, this is what happened to Calvinism, merged with, or moderated and counterbalanced by Lutheranism (and Catholicism), as well as supplanted or neutralized by the Enlightenment in contemporary Holland (Kaplan 2002; Tubergen et al. 2005). It also happened to Puritanism, re-blended with or tempered and counteracted by Anglicanism in post-Puritan Great Britain (Munch 2001).

The above signifies the *caput mortuum* diagnosis of Calvinism, including Puritanism, as has been known since the 16th–17th century as a term—hardly ever used in Europe, Great Britain, and America, substituted by the European "Reformed Church" and American "evangelicalism" —and, more importantly, as an idea or heritage declining in the old world. Yet, it signifies its self-perpetuation or even resurgence in the new nation, especially its "Bible Garden" (Hinson 1997). In a sense, the liberalizing or secularizing of Calvinism, notably American Puritanism, especially from *within*, as different from outside sources such as Lutheranism and Anglicanism, not to mention liberalism, including secularism and pluralism, is a logical non sequitur or an empirical impossibility. It is substantively equivalent to liberalizing official Catholicism (the Vatican Church) and fundamentalist Islam, as well as fascism (Nazism). In short, this internal liberal evolution is typically impossible—Weber's "impossible contradiction"—or exceedingly difficult in Calvinism and all theocratic world religions, or never realistically possible in fascism.

The above helps explain or highlight why Calvinism, especially American Puritanism, has typically resisted any substantive liberalizing, including tempering of its political and moral absolutism (Munch 2001), and consequently democratizing, until and unless forced or induced by countervailing religious and social forces. The latter precisely has happened to Calvinism in contemporary Holland owing to a conjunction of Lutheranism and the Enlightenment (Kaplan 2002) and, in the form of Puritanism, in Great Britain due to that of Anglicanism with Hume's liberalism and secularism. Yet, this outcome has not occurred in America, notably the South (as the "Bible Belt" indicates), in spite or perhaps because of Jeffersonian countervailing atypical ideas and forces (Archer 2001; Pattel 2001). Recall, American Puritanism effectively continues its original and intrinsic anti-liberalism, including anti-secularism and anti-pluralism, via "born again" evangelicalism and its attacks on the reality or prospect of modern liberal-secular and pluralist democracy and society in America by culture wars and even beyond through a "holy" war on the "evil" world. And when Calvinism has discontinued or weakened its resistance and "mindless" counterattack against the process of liberalization and secularization, notably the Enlightenment as its liberal-secular and anti-theocratic nemesis or antithesis (Bremer 1995), it has effectively ceased to exist and operate as a relevant political, social, and cultural force. This was witnessed in contemporary Holland as the exemplar of a rapidly "liberalizing authoritarian [theocratic] state" (Almeida 2003), and even, via Puritanism, has become practically an extinct species, as in modern Great Britain.

At this juncture, while "presumed dead" or discredited at home, Calvinism's and thus Puritanism's "last stand" or war against liberalism and democracy enfolds precisely in America via modern evangelicalism and its attacks on and its attempted destruction of a liberal-secular and pluralist polity and society, just as that of the long "papal struggles with liberalism" (Burns 1990) does in the Vatican's persistent anti-liberalism. In this sense, US "reborn" evangelicals act as the *last* Calvinist "holy warriors" or Puritan crusaders against liberal-secular democracy and modernity via domestic anti-liberal culture wars and a global permanent war on the "evil" world. Thus, their anti-liberal culture (and "not-so-cultural") wars in America are the "last stand" in the Calvinist-as-Puritan (and Catholic, Islamic, Hindu, and other religious) battles against liberalism, in particular secularism and pluralism (diversity), thus liberal-secular and pluralist democracy. Their global "holy" war is the "die hard" phase of the crusade against "infidels" in Calvinism and Puritanism (as well as Catholicism and, in the form of jihad, Islam).

On the account of its remarkable and self-perpetuating anti-liberal antagonism, modern American evangelicalism operates as supremely consistent and heroic Calvinism, consequently obstinate Puritanism. US "born again" fundamentalists are true modern Calvinist heroes, last to or never desert the "holy" war against liberal-secular democracy, even after virtually all other Calvinists, including those in Holland (Tubergen et al. 2005) and Great Britain (Munch 2001), have deserted the theocratic "house" of anti-liberalism, non-democracy, and pain *cum* pleasure (in the sense of Puritanism's cited "economy of pain"), thus become extinct as one knows them or forced to change beyond recognition. They are the genuine, specific "living proofs" and faces of America's political "destiny" embedded in or "predestination" by Calvinism "presume dead" in its old home yet "well and alive" in the new nation via Puritanism, thus of American Calvinist *cum* anti-liberal and non-democratic or theocratic exceptionalism. Therefore, they redefine and reproduce America's glorified exceptionalism and exceptional "destiny" as Calvinist and anti-liberal and (thus) non-democratic, specifically theocratic and fundamentalist (Mansbach 2006), rather than, as usually assumed (Lipset and Marks 2000), "libertarian", "individualistic", and "democratic" self-contradicted by the anti-liberalism of Calvinism via American Puritanism.

Hence, anti-liberalism, including anti-secularism and anti-pluralism, reproduces, predicts, and, in virtue of being "Divinely ordained" or "Godly", sanctifies non-democracy. It thus does political and other un-freedom in society, ultimately the destruction of human life—as via the death penalty system and global self-destructive wars, both religiously sanctified—in Calvinism, especially American Puritanism. It follows that a Calvinist theocratic polity is intrinsically anti-liberal, including anti-secular and anti-pluralist or absolutist, consequently non-democratic or authoritarian and even totalitarian.

While self-evident within liberal-secular and pluralist democracy, it is instructive to emphasize that non-democracy, including totalitarianism, is a systemic and constant tendency and outcome of an anti-liberal Calvinist, notably Puritan, political system. Conversely, it is not, as often supposed, a "random walk" and "cheap talk", an accidental, transient theocratic social contagion not to be taken seriously. For example, this is how the US "Bible Belt" is often perceived by American liberalism in analogy to the perception of Nazism or fascism similarly underestimated by liberals as a sort of temporary totalitarian virus or temptation (Cohen 2003) in interwar Europe. It is also useful to do so because US "reborn" evangelicals and political neo-conservatives like Reaganite "rigid extremists" (Blomberg and Harrington 2000) have succeeded in most Americans' minds to disconnect liberalism as "un-American," "foreign" from democracy and liberty as a whole and to connect it with the virtual opposite like "big government" defined by a "tax and spend" welfare state. This is indicated by the negative meaning of "liberal" as a proxy new "witch" or political stigma in America, a la "big-spending" liberals (Binmore 2001), like "libertines" in medievalism. The preceding is American conservatism's typical ethnocentric misconstruction and Orwellian deception because modern Scandinavian and other welfare states are invariably "smaller" and admittedly (Samuelson cited in Tilman 2001) "freer" governments than the neo-conservative anti-welfare police-warfare state, combining pervasive Puritan-rooted vice police with the military industrial complex, after the image of Leviathan in America.

In essence, the Calvinist and any other theocratic (Catholic and Islamic) political system is intrinsically or ultimately totalitarianism, primarily because Calvinism, particularly Puritanism (like official Catholicism and fundamentalist Islam) is quintessential theocratic anti-liberalism. Hence, a consideration of Calvinist, notably Puritan, anti-democratic tendencies and outcomes is only sensible, serious, and complete when fully taking account of this anti-liberal antagonism. Conversely, it is difficult or impossible to completely understand and explain, simply to make sense of, why Calvinism, in particular American Puritanism, attacks, undermines, and eventually eliminates democracy if not reconsidering, to use Weber-Hume's words, the "iron consistency" and "unreasonable obstinacy" of Calvinist-Puritan political anti-liberalism. By analogy, the same holds for official Catholicism or the Vatican Church (Burns 1990) and a fortiori fundamentalist Islam (Mansbach 2006). In both cases anti-liberalism explains and predicts their anti-democratic ideas, practices, and institutions, just as does in Calvinism, including Puritanism.

Thus, a Calvinist, like any other, theocratic state and polity represents a religious, "holy" instance of what sociological analyses identify as "illiberal, authoritarian states" (Fung 2003) as the polar opposites and destructions of liberal democracies. In essence, Calvinist and related theocratic states are "authoritarian" or totalitarian primarily because they are "illiberal" or anti-liberal, and conversely, their authoritarianism or totalitarianism reproduces and reinforces their "godly" anti-liberalism, coming full circle. By contrast, their opposites are non-authoritarian or democratic states primarily because they are liberal. Simply, the causal arrow typically goes from "anti-liberalism" to "authoritarianism" or "totalitarianism"—and back—in such theocratic as well as fascist states, just as from "liberalism" to "democracy" in their democratic alternatives. This evidently contradicts US "born again" fundamentalists' disassociation of anti-liberalism from authoritarianism and their association of liberalism as "un-American" and "ungodly" with non- or quasi-democratic outcomes like "big" government or a "tax-and-spend" welfare state. In this sense, in Calvinism and related theocratic religion, authoritarian or totalitarian states are the "positive" obverse of anti-liberal political systems as the (photographic) "negative", just as is totalitarianism, including fascism, of anti-liberalism overall (Dahrendorf 1979; Habermas 2001).

### "Godly Politics" versus Liberal-Secular Democracy

In general, a Calvinist polity is non-democratic, including totalitarian, on the account of its attack on, subversion, and eventual elimination of liberal-secular democracy or political liberalism and ultimately human freedom and life as a whole on the ground of "godly" politics and society a la Calvin's *civitas Dei* and his Puritan ramifications in Winthrop et al.

For Calvinist "godly" politics in America and to a lesser extent Europe, in view of the terminal condition of Calvinism, including Puritanism (Great Britain), liberal-secular democracy is the supreme and unmitigated "evil", the "work of Satan", the foremost "public enemy", a sort of figurative chief "witch", thus the Devil's incarnate, from "Salem with witches" (Putnam 2000).

For illustration, US religious and political "reborn" conservatives condemn, attack, and seek to destroy liberal-secular, implicitly Jeffersonian, democracy in America and beyond for its imputed ungodliness, notably the "mortal sin" of promoting and protecting *human* liberty at the expense of supra-human causes. These causes involve the primacy of Deity, including Biblical revelation, truth and inerrancy, faith and piety, religiously determined strict moral virtues, and nationalistic patriotism (Deutsch and Soffer 1987; Dunn and Woodard 1996; Heineman 1998). Simply, "reborn" conservatives act so on the grounds that the "liberal democratic ideal" is too "libertarian" or, in an older word used by early Calvinists in Europe and Winthrop's Puritans in America (and Catholics), "libertine", as well as secular and humanistic, due to its "dedication to individual freedom" (Deutsch and Soffer 1987). Alternatively, they do in the belief that certain, as US evangelical "born again" Presidents and other politicians state, "greater than humans and life", religious values are "superior" to human secular liberties and rights (Dunn and Woodard 1996) thereby substantively downgraded to luxuries that America as the fulfilled Puritan dream of a "godly" polity and community cannot afford. Hence, they employ and mobilize (as during the Presidential elections of the 1980s-2000s) such anti-liberal grounds and forces and religious beliefs to establish, perpetuate, and rationalize Calvinist "godly" politics and society in the eventual form of a theocratic sociopolitical system. Predictably, such a system is exemplified and symbolized by the "Biblical Garden" design and reality in the "new" South and other "red" states, and operates as the "holy" antithesis and judgment-day destruction of the condemned morally "degenerate" (as also Nazism accused) liberal-secular democracy and modernity.

Counterfactually, if Calvin, notably his Puritan disciples like Winthrop et al. stamped by "austere Calvinism" lived during the early 21st century they, just as the medieval popes, would also likely condemn, attack, and seek to destroy modern-liberal democracy on the identical or similar grounds ("dedication to individual freedom") and in the same belief ("superior" religious values to human liberties and rights). And, they effectively did or prefigured during the 16th and 17th centuries. Recall, Winthrop substituted "democratical government" with *mixt aristocracie* or "godly" self-perpetuating oligarchy (Bremer 1995). At this point, Calvin's spirit—or (as Tönnies would imply) "ghost" from the stance of his murdered and mistreated theological dissenters and "libertines"—of "godly" theocratic (Mansbach 2006), thus totalitarian politics "lives on" as "undying", through Winthrop et al. as supreme role models, in US "reborn" religious-political conservatives, while effectively *caput mortuum* at home, France and Europe.

In turn, in spite or rather because of the growing reality or prospect of a liberal-secular democracy and society in Western and other countries (Inglehart 2004; Munch 2001), "reborn" US religious fundamentalist (to paraphrase Comte) "dream on" during the early 21st century to fulfill déjà vu what Calvin and Winthrop did in the 16th and 17th centuries, respectively. This is to reestablish Geneva's *civitas Dei* or New England's "Biblical Commonwealth" in America and via a global "holy" war the world. Moreover, they surpass Calvin's and Winthrop's creations and dreams by "dreaming" and even succeeding to extend what was merely local or regional "godly" politics to a national, "all-American" "faith-based", and perhaps ultimately, via such a religious-style crusade on the "evil" world, a global polity and society. They thus hope or even come close to fulfilling what their theocratic masters could only dreamed of in their small theocracies, that is, a societal or comprehensive evangelical theocracy as "God's Kingdom on Earth." And, by definition they identify and consequently attempt to destroy liberal-secular democracy as the main obstacle to their "road to paradise"—or "hell", as the case may be—of "godly" politics and society. This may provide Weber's *Verstehen* (understanding) or empathy for their "good" and "godly" intentions and meanings paving the path to theocratic heaven (Lemert 1999) by getting into their "beautiful minds" (as suggested by Smith 2000) or putting oneself in their "shoes".[33]

In comparative terms, the Calvinist-rooted political system in America tends to be less liberal and democratic, as well as less egalitarian or universalistic, than others, especially other Protestant (Lutheran and Anglican) states, in contemporary Western society. This is indicated by liberal-democratic indicators, including indexes of liberal and of consensual democracy, and estimates of political and other egalitarianism or universalism. Sociological calculations yield for US Puritan-rooted "godly politics" one of the lowest indexes of liberal

---

[33] Weber warns that in general understanding or empathy does not necessarily mean "pardoning" or sympathy.

Table 4.2. Calvinist subversions of liberal-secular democracy

Theocratic aristocracy
Theocratic oligarchy
Theocratic plutocracy
Political and social closure

political democracy (92) among contemporary Western societies (at or around 100) during recent decades (Bollen 1990; Bollen and Paxton 1998). Alternatively, virtually all other Protestant political systems (except for West Germany), as well as Catholic ones (minus France), are calculated to have higher liberal democracy indexes than that in America. In particular, analysts calculate that among Western democracies the US political system has the lowest index of consensual democracy indicated by the number of parliamentary parties or proportional representation in parliaments (Vergunst 1998). Also, comparative estimates yield the lowest degree of political and other egalitarianism or universalism and implicitly humanism, or the highest level of anti-egalitarianism or anti-universalism and anti-humanism, for this system among Western societies (Pampel 1998).

*Specific Calvinist Subversions of Liberal-Secular Democracy*

In particular, a Calvinist polity is a non-democratic, including totalitarian, political system on the account of its specific, interconnected and mutually reinforcing, subversions or eliminations of liberal-secular democracy. These are, first, theocratic aristocracy, second, theocratic oligarchy, third, theocratic plutocracy, and, fourth, as a corollary, political and social closure, reconsidered in this order next. To wit, a Calvinist political system is the antithesis of democracy in virtue of being (or ruled by) aristocracy, oligarchy, plutocracy, and consequently closure. Simply, it is non-democratic because it is aristocratic, oligarchic, plutocratic, and thus closed (Table 4.2).

### Theocratic Aristocracy

*From the Aristocracy of Heaven to the Aristocracy of Society*

First, a Calvinist polity is a non-democratic, including totalitarian, political system in virtue of constituting (or being ruled by) theocratic, "spiritual" aristocracy or aristocratic theocracy. And, if aristocracy in general, like theocracy, is, as Aristotle, Pareto, Mosca, and other social analysts suggest, the axiomatic elimination or subversion of democracy (and republic), then this a fortiori holds true of the aristocratic-theocratic form in relation to the democratic liberal-secular type.

As indicated, Calvinist "godly" politics tends to be aristocratic rule by what Hume calls divines, Comte saints, and Marx and Weber religious virtuosi, thus dominance by theocratic ("spiritual"), as distinguished from non-theocratic or secular, aristocrats or aristocratic theocrats. Recall, Hume portrays the Puritan political system, specifically the newly established Parliament of the 1640s, in England following the Calvinist Revolution as "consisting of one hundred and twenty-one divines" (plus "thirty laymen") and to that extent theocratic aristocracy or aristocratic theocracy. No wonder, English initially victorious Puritanism officially designed and designated the political system as the "Holy Commonwealth" ruled by Cromwell's "Parliament of Saints".

In turn, the latter was a subset of what Comte identifies, in apparent reference to Hume's Puritan "divines", as the "reign of Saints" in Calvinism as a whole (also, Mentzer 2007). Also, anticipating Weber, Marx implicitly characterizes New England's Puritan polity as aristocratic, as well as proto-capitalist profitable, rule by "those sober virtuosi" of Protestantism. Weber suggests that a Calvinist political system in general, by being founded on the implied aristocratic dogma of predestination, established or was ruled by the "spiritual aristocracy of the predestined saints of God within the world." This was in sharp contrast and methodical opposition to and replacing the "spiritual aristocracy of monks outside of and above the world" characteristic of pre-Calvinism, including medieval Christianity (Orthodox and Catholic Churches). Moreover, in his view, this Calvinist aristocratic system was, as one would expect given Calvin's theological dogma of predestination and theocratic practices in his local domain, Geneva, more divisive, exclusionary, or sectarian, just as ruthless, brutal, and inhumane as its medieval Christian and other non-Calvinist precedents. It was to the point of becoming the "hardest form of lovelessness and lack of brotherliness"[34] (also, Symonds and Pudsey 2006). He infers that

---

[34] Specifically, Weber states that "the organic pragmatism of [universal] salvation must consider the redemptory aristocracy of inner-worldly asceticism [as in Calvinism], with its rational depersonalisation of life orders, as the hardest form of lovelessness and lack of brotherliness". Further, he observes that "it was an aristocracy which, with its

Calvinism, though self-designated as the only "Reformed Church", substantively operated as or resembled a sect in virtue of its "aristocratic charismatic principle of predestination" as inherently sectarian and thus exclusionary in respect of "heaven" and, on such sacred grounds, in politics and society. Within the "extended family" of Calvinists, Weber cites Puritan theocrats as the exemplars of (the pride of) an "aristocracy of predestined salvation" and compares them with the pre-Calvinist Pharisees also described as "an aristocracy with respect to salvation" versus the "godless Jews".[35]

As hinted, various historical instances exemplify the Calvinist political system as (ruled by) theocratic "spiritual" aristocracy (or aristocratic theocracy), as opposed to liberal-secular democracy, spanning from original Calvinism in France and Geneva to Puritanism in old and New England and America overall. First and foremost, Calvin himself manifestly evinced or latently harbored aristocratic tendencies through both his theological doctrines and his theocratic practices in France and Geneva. Specifically, he did so by, first, the doctrine of predestination postulating a few "predestined" saints-rulers with Divine rights to rule the "eternally damned" majority of humans and thus sanctifying theocracy *cum* aristocracy (and conversely). Second, he did by the brutal suppression and exclusion, including the murdering, of the "ungodly". Weber implies that Calvin's dogma of predestination is essentially aristocratic or exclusionary and thus undemocratic or non-egalitarian theological predetermination, specifically the (s)election of a "spiritual" aristocracy as the "Divinely ordained" master, via salvation of "only a few" (Hume's 100-odd "divines"), and damnation of the "remainder of humanity" by the God of Calvinism. In a sense, Calvin represented the supreme emanation or prototype of Weber's Calvinist "spiritual aristocracy of the predestined saints of God within the world" dividing and ruling politics and all society with systematic "brutality" (Birnbaum 1953) and inhumanity overall (Mansbach 2006).

---

*indelible character,* was divided from the eternally damned remainder of humanity by a more impassable and in its invisibility more terrifying gulf, than separated the monk of the Middle Ages from the rest of the world about him, a gulf wvhich penetrated all social relations with its sharp brutality." Weber adds that in Calvinism, notably Puritanism, "this consciousness of divine grace of the elect and holy was accompanied by an attitude toward the sin of one's neighbour, not of sympathetic understanding based on consciousness of one's own weakness, but of hatred and contempt for him as an enemy of God bearing the signs of eternal damnation."

[35] Conversely, Weber characterizes the Jewish Pharisees as "Puritans" in an apparently pre-Calvinist or pre-Protestant and generally pre-Christian form and meaning.

Generally, during Calvin's and later times, Calvinism in France and beyond, including, through Puritanism, England, was essentially aristocratic and thus medievalist in virtue of being supported and eventually dominated by the feudal aristocracy or nobility in cooperation with and willing submission by the early bourgeoisie or middle classes (Heller 1986). For instance, Weber observes that it was "nobles" that led Calvinist French Huguenots and Scottish Calvinists "at the height of their great struggles" and the Puritan Revolution in England was "successful because of the cavalry provided by the rural gentry" (as a sort of pseudo- or would-be English aristocracy). In his view, initially the medieval French, Scottish, and English nobility played a "considerable role" in the rise and expansion of Calvinism, including Puritanism (though he adds that nobles "completely dropped out" from it or "stopped fighting" for it later). Historical research suggests that the above particularly holds true of original Calvinism in France in relation to the medieval aristocracy of the 16th century. In this account, French Calvinism's "deliberate policy" consisted in attracting "aristocratic support" (Heller 1986) and even in submitting to the dominance of the feudal aristocracy. In particular, the study shows that the feudal aristocracy eventually succeed to dominate Calvinism, for the Calvinist bourgeoisie exhibited willingness and even eagerness for subordinating itself to the nobility (Heller 1986). Notably, the study indicates that Calvinism's "subordination" to the aristocracy did not greatly bother Calvin because of its being in "complete accord" with his belief in the "inviolability" of the political system and the "duty" of individual Christians to submit themselves to the "Divinely ordained" social order, including medieval-style theocratic and murderous tyranny like Geneva under his rule (Heller 1986; also, Sorkin 2005).

And, what Calvin et al. failed to attain in France, turned out eventually to be their "not so sweet home", they attempted and succeeded to realize elsewhere by their expansion beyond. This included, initially Geneva locally, then Holland nationally, as well as, through their Puritan derivatives, England, Scotland, and America, from New England to the "awaken" South (e.g., Alabama and "Dixieland" overall as the "new sweet home"). Thus, they established (the rule of) theocratic, "spiritual" aristocracies or aristocratic theocracies through Calvinist state churches in Geneva during Calvin's exile from France, Holland, and in part Germany, as well as renamed as "Puritans" in Anglo-Saxon societies like Great Britain, New England, and the "new" US South.

In virtually all these instances, Calvin's Genevese model of a "godly" polity and society ruled by the "spiritual aristocracy" of Calvinist "predestined saints" represented an explicit, as in Holland and Germany, or implied, in old and New England, ideal of theocratic governance and a venerable precedent (Mansbach 2006). For example, Weber explains the "ecclesiastic revolution of the strict Calvinists" in the Netherlands of the 1580s in terms of their "aristocratic charismatic principle" as the underlying theological and political driving force. The principle was rooted in the dogma of predestination as the "double decree" of salvation or election of a few forming a "spiritual aristocracy" and eternal damnation or reprobation of most humans to be subjected to its total rule as "Divinely ordained." Another example involves Calvinist aristocratic theocracies in England and Scotland during the mid 17th century, exemplified by Cromwell's "Parliament of Saints" or Hume's one hundred-plus self-declared Puritan "divines". In this connection, Weber describes what he calls the "abortive rule by Cromwell's Parliament of Saints" and in extension the Puritan Revolution as the "greatest experiment" in Puritanism's typical "holy" merger or alliance with political power defining and resulting in Calvinist and other theocracies in general.

Notably, what Weber identifies as the "theocracy of New England" provides yet another exemplar of Calvinist, specifically Puritan, aristocratic theocracies or theocratic aristocracies. He suggests that, like in the "old world", Puritanism's merger or alliance with political power in New England resulted in "an aristocratic rule by the ecclesiastically qualified" like Winthrop et al. as self-declared "Divinely ordained" leaders (Munch 2001), thus an instance of aristocratic theocracies or theocratic aristocracies. Weber also registers that "under Winthrop's leadership" Massachusetts established an "upper house with a hereditary nobility" and hence theocratic ("ecclesiastically qualified") aristocracy. The latter incidentally self-negated the Puritan official political system or designation of "Republic" in which hereditary power is by definition a non sequitur, with the difference from the Anglican monarchy being that not the monarch, but "only" nobility was inherited via what Veblen calls the "inheritance of gentility". As noted, Winthrop designed and designated such an aristocratic polity or state as *mixt aristocracie* (Bremer 1995; Gould 1996), thus implicitly oligarchy, discussed latter.

It may be debatable if the latter was a true or pure aristocracy as in feudal Europe, and conservative US sociologists would answer negatively on the venerable, yet dubious, premise of America's non-aristocratic and non-feudal past (Lipset and Marks 2000; Nisbet 1966). Yet, Winthrop's *mixt aristocracie* was still medieval-style *aristocracy* even if diluted by or mixed with presumably democracy or republic, and actually, as Weber and other analysts suggest, merged with a Calvinist theocracy. First and foremost, this Puritan version of aristocracy, like any other, was non- or pseudo-democratic. To contend the opposite is not only a non sequitur or Orwellian "double thinking" in violation of elemental logic—"undemocratic" in feudal Europe, "democratic" in non-feudal America—but also historically incorrect. As sympathetic historical research admits, Winthrop et al. in New England effectively opposed the "concept of democratic government" by denying the "legitimacy of popular rule" in favor of *mixt aristocracie* with the people's part in elections being reduced to choosing a "ruling class" (Bremer 1995). And, since the latter invariably comprised mostly Hume's self-declared "divines", Comte's saints, or Marx-Weber's religious virtuosi "ecclesiastically qualified" and "Divinely predestined" to rule others, Winthrop's *mixt aristocracie* operated effectively as theocratic, "religious aristocracy"[36] (Clark 1999) or aristocratic theocracy (Baldwin 2006; German 1995; Harley 1996). In sum, either as general or specifically *theocratic* aristocracy, Winthrop's *mixt aristocracie*, thus New England's Puritan political system, was non-democratic or, assuming the non-existence of liberal-secular democracy during the early 17th century, pre-democratic in Mannheim's sense, just as anti- or pre-liberal overall as the underlying cause of its rejection and lack of democratic elements. In short, it was and remains, through its various vestiges in the original region or revivals beyond, especially the "Bible Garden", the "double jeopardy" to liberal-secular democracy and society.

Further, Winthrop's descendents in a sense attempted and even succeeded to expand his medieval-style theocratic aristocracy and his "austere Calvinism" overall to America as a whole, notably the South, as via the evangelical Great Awakenings expressive of Calvinist revivalism. These Calvinist revivals at this juncture operated as an attempt to awaken the entire new nation, in particular its "sleepy" and "not godly" enough Anglican South (Gould 1996), to the supreme virtues and godliness of the Puritan *mixt aristocracie* or aristocratic theocracy after the

---

[36] Clark (1999:70) observes that in antebellum America, the Calvinist orthodox priesthood was still described in terms of a "religious aristocracy".

model or image of Winthrop as "Divinely ordained". For example, Weber identifies theocratic as well as capitalist aristocracies and aristocrats in the post-bellum evangelical South by observing that the "new" dominant Southern Puritans like Baptist would-be theocrats and capitalists wanted to live "like feudal lords", just as did (not, as often assumed, unlike) their Episcopalian adversaries, as the term "robber barons" indicates. He registers that most "robber barons", thus would-be feudal lords or theocratic aristocrats in the post-bellum South were Calvinist Baptists (Hinson 1997) and other old and new Calvinists *cum* Puritans like Presbyterians and Methodists, respectively. At least on this account, the awaken South dominated by Puritanism—initially Presbyterianism, then Methodism, and eventually Baptism in a historical sequence (Boles 1999; Mencken 1982)—deposing Anglicanism as "ungodly" and "foreign", was in political terms (ruled by) theocratic aristocracy following the Great Awakenings (especially the Second) and continued to be in post-bellum times. And, it largely remained so, with minor modifications, by the early 21st century, as indicated by the revival déjà vu of the Puritan design-dream of America as a "holy" community (German 1995; Seaton 2006) *qua* another "Biblical Garden" (Gould 1996) in the 1980s–2000s.

## *Theocratic Oligarchy*

Second, a Calvinist polity in America is a non-democratic, including totalitarian, political system in virtue of constituting (and being ruled by) theocratic oligarchy or oligarchic theocracy, in conjunction and substantive equivalence with aristocracy. By analogy to, and perhaps even more than, aristocracy, if oligarchy is, as Michels, Pareto, Mosca, and other analysts since Aristotle suggest, also the axiomatic antithesis and elimination of democracy, then this a fortiori holds true of the oligarchic-theocratic form in relation to the democratic liberal-secular type. And, since (or if) oligarchy and oligarchs, as Aristotle implied and medieval nobles would claim, is and are, in particular when not of "noble" origin, just "ignoble", "non-honorable" or proxy aristocracy and aristocrats, what has been said of the first also mostly applies to the second, with some additional observations offered next.

By analogy to its definition in terms of aristocracy, a Calvinist polity is essentially an oligarchic rule or exclusionary domination by Hume's divines, Comte's saints, or Marx-Weber's religious virtuosi and in that sense (ruled by) theocratic oligarchy or oligarchic theocracy. While not all theocratic oligarchies and oligarchs, or oligarchic theocracy and theocrats, are Calvinist-Puritan in origin and effect but also non-Calvinist (including Catholic and Islamic), the converse is almost invariably true of Calvinism, including Puritanism. The Calvinist political system is almost universally a theocratic oligarchy or oligarchic theocracy, as is Calvinism as theology in virtue of its doctrine of predestination. Thus, Calvinism, including Puritanism, is oligarchic in a sociological sense and form as a sociopolitical principle and system, as well as in a theological-religious one as the theology and religion, of theocratic oligarchy. While the sociological sense is of primary importance in this context, it is instructive to recall that Calvinism originated as a sort of theological doctrine of theocratic, "godly" oligarchy by virtue of its doctrine of predestination.

*The (Predestination) Doctrine of "Heavenly" Oligarchy*

First and foremost, the Calvinist doctrine of predestination seems a paradigmatic or axiomatic theological dogma and sanctification of theocratic oligarchy in virtue of what Weber denotes the "double decree" by the God of Calvinism. As noted, this double decree is salvation or election of "only a few", and damnation or reprobation of most humans, and for reasons, as Calvin claimed, beyond human comprehension and intervention, including Christian "good works," as post-Calvinist Franklin and "Arminian" theologians[37] objected (Byrne 1997; Sorkin 2005). On this account, the doctrine of predestination defined and revealed early Calvinism as the theology and religion of "heavenly" (Zaret 1989) or spiritual oligarchy, and, as a corollary, what Weber calls a non-universalistic religion of salvation like Islam, yet in stark contrast and adverse reaction to original or traditional Christianity (Catholicism) as an "inwardly universalistic" one.[38] If there is such thing as

---

[37] Sorkin (2005:288) suggests that Arminian theology had softened the doctrines of predestination and the elect by introducing the role of free will and [hypothetically] the possibility of universal grace."

[38] Weber remarks that "the fact that] men are *differently qualified* in a religious way [standing] at the beginning of the history of religion had been dogmatized in the sharpest rationalist form in the "particularism of grace," embodied in the doctrine of predestination by the Calvinists" [versus the "inwardly universalist (Catholic) institution of grace". Also, he suggests that, in contrast to Christianity thus understood, Islam is not a true, universalistic religion of salvation in virtue of its theocratic oligarchy

a theological, as distinguished from, yet linked to Michels' sociological or political, design and practice of oligarchy, thus exclusionism or non-universalism, then it is the Calvinist doctrine of predestination. It is in virtue of what Weber identifies as its "particularism of grace" in consistent opposition to the original Christian (Orthodox/Catholic) "universalistic institution of grace," along with, as he implies, the Islamic non-universalistic dogma of predetermination.

In this respect, Calvin's doctrine of predestination can in sociological terms be deemed the theological version and sanctification of oligarchy. It is the theology of oligarchic exclusion, discrimination, and non-universalism or particularism in salvation or "heaven", and ultimately, on such "sacred" grounds, in politics and society or this world. It is a kind of religious ideology that postulates that only a few are "saved" or "qualified" for God's grace, hence it endows such "elected" Calvinist oligarchs with medieval-style Divine rights to rule, and most humans damned thus to be subjected to these masters and excluded from politics and society, or even persecuted and exterminated via "holy" wars. No wonder, Weber uses not only "particularism of grace" but "extreme inhumanity" to describe Calvin's doctrine of predestination, as well as non-Calvinists and some intra-Calvinist ("Arminian") dissenters rejected this theological dogma as "morally repugnant"[39] (Ozment 1980). Recall that none than Weber's epitome of the Calvinist spirit of capitalism, Franklin distanced himself from his father's Calvinism considering, just as many of his contemporaries, the Calvinist rejection, through the doctrine of predestination, of Christian-style good works to be "inimical to morality" (Byrne 1997). In particular, what Weber terms the "aristocratic charismatic principle of predestination" implies that this doctrine is substantively oligarchic and to that extent exclusionary and particularistic or non-universalistic and inhumane.

Curiously, while implicit in the "aristocratic charismatic principle of predestination" and its "particularism of grace" and "extreme inhumanity",

---

(composed of prophets) and militancy, including a "holy" war against "infidels" (jihad) subjected to extermination initially or subjugation and conversation subsequently. Alternatively, he implies that Islam is a non-universalistic, as opposed to universalistic, religion of salvation, thus identical or comparable to Calvinism and its anti-universalistic aristocratic or oligarchic doctrine of predestination dividing the "spiritual aristocracy" of salvation from the rest of humanity.

[39] Ozment (1980:368–9) gives the example of Jerome Bolsec who "publicly challenged Calvin's teaching on predestination, a doctrine [he], with many others, found morally repugnant. Banished from the city in 1551, he revenged himself in 1577 by publishing a biography of Calvin that charged him with greed, financial misconduct, and sexual aberration."

Weber, like his follower Michels, did not seem to identity and fully establish Calvin's doctrine of predestination and hence Calvinism as a theological exemplar of oligarchy. The step toward this identification was short given that Weber implied that Calvinism was paradigmatic non-universalism and exclusionism (or worse) within Protestantism, thus a deviation from Christianity as the universalistic religion of salvation, and alternatively, in a substantive identity with Islam as, in his view, non-universalistic in this sense. Presumably, Weber and Michels did not do so because this identification would be outside of the realm of sociology as a science. While the oligarchic and non-universalistic Calvinist doctrine of predestination belongs to the field of theology ("heaven") rather than of sociology (society), it is relevant in its social effects. Specifically, it is so long as it is used, as has consistently been by Calvin et al., to establish and sanctify theocratic oligarchy as secular power or a polity ruled by Weber's few predestined saints. The "double decree" of the God of Calvinism dividing humans into only a few "saved" or "elected" and most "damned" establishes and sanctifies the political division or duality of Calvinist masters and servants, "Divine" leaders and subjects.

Thus, in Weber's context the doctrine of predestination as the sacred dogma of oligarchy theologically predestines and sanctifies a Calvinist oligarchic political system or secular power.[40] And conversely, in Durkheim-Mannheim's framework of the sociology of knowledge, the first reflects and rationalizes the second once, as in Calvin's Geneva, or previously, like the medieval theocracy, established. Simply, the Calvinist "logic", from Calvin to his evangelical descendents (e.g., Southern Baptists) in America, seems to be, in a typical bumper-sticker form, "we only the few are saved, and most humans are damned, by the God of Calvinism, and hence predestined to totally master, including exclude, repress, murder, and exterminate, others for Divine Glory." Thus, in Calvinism total rule, exclusion, repression, murder, and extermination are perversely redefined as "good works" as Calvinists, notably Puritans, understand them,[41] or conversely such deeds are perverted

---

[40] Weber suggests that in general "the rational religious pragmatism of salvation, flowing from the nature of the images of God and of the world, have under certain conditions had far-reaching results for the fashioning of a practical way of life."

[41] This is partly implied in Weber's remarks that "whenever [Methodist] Wesley attacked the emphasis on works of his time, it was only to revive the old Puritan doctrine that works are not the cause, but only the means of knowing one's state of grace, and even this only when they are performed solely for the glory of God."

in the sense of "evil [as] distorted good" (Habermas 2001). While this was apparently the Calvinist reenactment and reclaim of medievalist rulers' Divine rights, it is even more theologically oligarchic and inhumane. It is so in that Calvin et al., unlike their Christian (Orthodox, Catholic) precursors, denied salvation to the most of humans, notably moral sinners, while monopolizing it for themselves. The latter is a paradigmatic instance of what Weber might call the "monopolistic closure" of universal life chances or equal opportunities, specifically those for salvation or grace in the world beyond as "heaven" (Lemert 1999), and on these "sacred" grounds in politics and society converted into "hell in this world" for most humans as "damned".

While in Weber's context, a Calvinist political system is oligarchic because the doctrine of predestination forms the theological dogma of "godly" oligarchy or "spiritual aristocracy", in Durkheim-Mannheim's framework of the sociology of knowledge it is exactly opposite. Within the sociology of knowledge, the doctrine of predestination is the theological dogma of oligarchy or aristocracy that expresses and rationalizes a pre-established Calvinist oligarchic or aristocratic sociopolitical system. In Durkheim's words, such theological, like other, classifications, reflect and justify those already existing in society, in accordance with that the "classification of things reproduces the classification of men". In Mannheim's terms, Calvin's ideology of the status quo in Geneva was the expression and justification of certain class and other social conditions (also, Heller 1986), specifically his oligarchic or aristocratic rule, in this town. In these terms, Calvin's dogma of predestination represented an ideological reflection and rationalization of the medieval oligarchy or aristocratic theocracy as his supreme ideal to be restored or purified in a "reformed" Calvinist church, initially in France and eventually in Geneva and beyond. In sum, while in the first context the doctrine of predestination leads to and sanctifies the Calvinist oligarchic political system as "Divinely ordained", in the second social conditions ground and thus demystify that dogma as the product and justification of a preexisting (Geneva) or predesigned (France) societal oligarchy, as well as the medieval theocracy to be remade "purer". In either case, Calvinism is oligarchic, first a theological doctrine, second, a sociopolitical system, of oligarchy.

On the account of its doctrine of predestination or Divine grace as a scarce spiritual good limited to only a few, Calvinism effectively transformed Christianity from Weber's universalistic and non-oligarchic religion of salvation into an oligarchic or "monopolistic", non-universalistic opposite. It effectively perverted originally salvationist Christianity into a *non*-salvation religion from the view of most humans, Christians (non-Calvinists, non-Protestants) and non-Christians. Alternatively, Calvinism converted Christianity into a substantive equivalent or proxy of Islam as the exemplar of oligarchic religions of salvation or rather of non-salvation. No wonder, Weber describes Calvinism, specifically Puritanism, as being, like Islam, "no longer a genuine religion of salvation" characterized by universal brotherliness because of its "particularized grace" and its "standpoint of unbrotherliness"[42] (also Symonds and Pudsey 2006).

To that extent, Calvinism, in particular Puritanism, ended Christianity as pre-Calvinists knew it as well as post-and non-Calvinists know it. As Simmel put it, "according to the Christian conception, the house of God has room for all", yet Calvinism, including Puritanism, reversed or perverted this universalism, just as Christianity's original set of ethical values (Tawney 1962). This means ending the kind of religion in which *all* humans are admittedly "equally valued by God" (Lucas 2000) and in that sense (qualified to be) "saved" in certain ways, notably by what Calvinism and its Puritanism dogmatically rejected, suspected, or perverted, as "good works". Calvinism thus became itself "morally repugnant" or "inimical to morality" not only to non-Calvinists like early libertines but also to some initial Calvinists like Servetus and Franklin (or "Arminians"). Of course, this holds true unless Calvinism, including Puritanism, redefined "good deeds" in the sense opposite to original Christianity and what Weber calls the primeval "ethic of brotherhood" or the ideal type of brotherliness (Symonds and Pudsey 2006), and thus effectively perverted them into their self-negation. This is the sense of "evil as distorted good" (Habermas 2001) through the exclusion, repression, persecution, and extermination of the "ungodly" for (in Parsons' words) the purposes and glory of God as the ultimate "good" and the "highest" cause.

In Weber's words, traditional Christianity (Catholicism) operated as a universal church, the organization for "administration of salvation" for all members, including sinners through what he describes—and Calvinism and the Protestant Reformation condemned and

---

[42] In Weber's view, following Calvinism, "Puritanism renounce[d] salvation as a goal attainable by man [i.e.,] by everybody [and] in favor of the groundless and always only particularized grace" and adds that the Puritan "standpoint of unbrotherliness was no longer a genuine "religion of salvation" [that] exaggerate[s] brotherliness".

attacked—as the "rule of the Catholic Church, 'punishing the heretic, but indulgent to the sinner'". In stark contrast and consistent opposition to this salvation universalism, while claiming to be the only and true "Reformed Church", Calvinism functioned as a theological oligarchy or market-like monopoly monopolizing this "life chance" or "equality of opportunity" for Calvinist masters and denying it to others. It thus substantively acted as a sect exerting, in Weber's view, the "most absolutely unbearable form of ecclesiastical control" of individuals that "could possibly exist".[43] By its pseudo-monopolistic dogma of predestination Calvinism developed as the most radical "Christian" negation of the original Christian universalistic tenet that all humans are "equally valued by God" ("brothers"), thus actually or potentially "saved" (subject to "good" deeds and intentions). In addition, it was the most radical religious denial of the liberal-secular principle of universalism that every human being is "equally worthy of consideration" (Dagger 1997).

What is sociologically most important, this theological pseudo-monopoly or oligopoly in "heaven" implied in the doctrine of predestination generated and sanctified oligarchy in politics and society via a Calvinist sociopolitical system. Conversely, the doctrine of predestination, like (as Mannheim and Durkheim suggest) ideology and religion overall, expressed and rationalized Michels' style oligarchy once established in "this world", as in Calvin's Geneva, Holland, and old and New England. Simply, to paraphrase Durkheim, the doctrine transformed oligarchy from what was initially a "profane", secular social fact or realm into a "sacred" or transcendental *cum* predestined one, specifically medieval-style theocratic, Calvinist or other, oligarchy. Remember Calvin's command that tyranny, by definition by a few oligarchs, in France and beyond "must" be suffered as "Divinely ordained" by all humans. This is what paradigmatically happened, in addition to France partially or transiently over Calvin's early years, in Geneva during his exile and once his oligarchic-theocratic governance was established (Mansbach 2006). It did virtually everywhere else Calvinism established oligarchy or proved dominant, from Holland (Frijhoff 2002) and England to New England. At this juncture, within Durkheim-Mannheim's sociology of knowledge, the doctrine of predestination

---

[43] At this juncture, Weber's distinction between Calvinism as "church" and Puritanism, including Baptism, as "sect" effectively evaporates.

effectively emerged as the "sacred" product or the ideological expression of either a preexisting or designed theocratic oligarchy (or aristocracy) as a sociopolitical system or ruling group, and medieval tyranny overall, initially in France and then Geneva and Holland, just as the means of perpetuation and sanctification of that "profane" order. A salient case in Anglo-American Calvinism was the Westminster Confession as Puritanism's official adoption of the doctrine of predestination following the victorious Puritan Revolution, notably the establishment of Cromwell's oligarchic "Parliament of Saints" made of Hume's 100-odd divines, in England, and subsequently in New England[44] (German 1995) in the aftermath of Winthrop's establishment of theocratic oligarchy in the form of *mixt aristocracie* (Bremer 1995).

The above seems useful to emphasize and reiterate because, while not a necessary or a sufficient condition of oligarchy in general, Calvin's doctrine of predestination is the theological equivalent as well as ground and justification of Calvinist, including Puritan, political oligarchy as a sociological phenomenon in Michels' sense. While certainly not all political oligarchies are grounded in and sanctified by the doctrine of predestination but also by similar or even different theological as well as non-religious doctrines[45] (e.g., Catholic Divine-rights theology, the Islamic dogma of predetermination, fascist and communist secular ideologies, etc.), the opposite is true. This doctrine is axiomatically oligarchic, thus exclusionary and non-universalistic, and hence is ultimately a Calvinist polity and society, a link that Weber apparently implied by his diagnosis of Puritan "particularized grace" and "unbrotherliness", though not fully established and explicated.

In sum, sociologically considered, the original Calvinist doctrine of predestination is the theological dogma of "heavenly" oligarchy, thus exclusionism in "heaven". Second, it renders and reveals Calvinism as an exclusionary, non-universalistic religious system, thus the opposite of what Weber calls a "genuine" religion of salvation. Third, as a corollary,

---

[44] German (1995:980) registers that the Westminster Confession reaffirming and even reinforcing Calvin's doctrine of predestination was "adopted by English Calvinists in 1643", exactly one year following their victorious Puritan revolution and establishing Cromwell's oligarchy in the face of the "Parliament of Saints." And, it was "endorsed by New England Congregationalists in the Cambridge Platform of 1648", less than two decades after the establishment of Winthrop's oligarchic rule or *mixed aristocracie* (Bremer 1995).

[45] For instance, Weber contrasts the "Calvinist belief in predestination" to the "Lutheran justification through faith" and the "Catholic doctrine of sacrament".

it makes Calvinism a deviation from or reversal of original Christianity as a universalistic, genuine salvation religion. Fourth, it makes Calvinism substantively equivalent to Islam as also a non-universalistic or non-genuine religion of salvation. Fifth, it theologically grounds and sustains a Calvinist oligarchic polity and society. And sixth, as a sacred dogma or ideology, it reflects and justifies a Calvinist oligarchic polity and society *once* established. Hence, to better understand the Puritan oligarchic political system in America it is instructive to consider that the dogma of predestination renders Calvinism, including Puritanism, the theology of "heavenly" oligarchy, thus a non-universalistic, exclusionary religion of salvation, unlike original Christianity, and like fundamentalist Islam.

The aforesaid of the oligarchic nature and effects of the doctrine of predestination holds true primarily of original Calvinism and Puritanism insofar as what Weber calls neo-Calvinism in Holland, for example, did not maintain the "pure doctrine of predestined grace" and neo-Puritanism like Baptism and Methodism even formally relinquished it. However, he remarks that the "doctrine was never completely eliminated from Calvinism; it only altered its form". Also, Weber may remark that, while formally relinquishing the doctrine of predestination, Baptism and Methodism in America, especially in the South, substantively act as his "predestined" oligarchy or aristocracy of salvation, thus political and societal domination.

In fact, this is what Weber implies by observing that in Methodism, the doctrine of and attempt to reach sanctification, or "the consciousness of perfection in the sense of freedom from sin", "finally guarantees the *certainty of salvation* and substitutes a serene confidence for the sullen worry of the Calvinist." On the account of the self-assigned certainty or confidence of salvation, thus domination in society, Methodism developed as hyper-Calvinism and Methodists (e.g., John Wesley) as super-Calvinists ("Calvin-plus"). This is also indicated by what Mencken (1982) deplores and religious conservatives (Boles 1999) celebrate as, sequentially or jointly, Presbyterian, Methodist, and notably Baptist growing dominance in the "Bible Belt" and beyond on the Calvinist grounds of their being preordained masters with proxy Divine Rights to rule America and the entire world. To that extent, Calvin's doctrine of predestination while officially "dead" in American "born again" evangelicalism (yet cf., Hinson 1997), can substantively help to understand the Puritan-rooted oligarchic political system in America, notably the "Bible Belt" dominated by Baptist, Methodist, Presbyterian, and other neo-Calvinist "good old boys".

*The Sociological "Law" of Calvinism and Political Oligarchy*

With these theological bases in mind, the above yields a variation on and application of Michels' sociological "iron law" of oligarchy specifically in relation to Calvinism, including Puritanism: "who says Calvinist and Puritan political organization, says oligarchy", thus theocratic exclusion, division, and oppression in politics and society. As hinted, a theological, secondary, version of this sociological statement is "who says Calvinist theology or the doctrine of predestination, says spiritual oligarchy" with respect to salvation, or monopolistic closure, exclusionism, and non-universalism concerning the world beyond, thus a sect or religious faction in Madison's sense. The oligarchic exclusion from salvation or heaven serves as the sacred rationale for making the life of those humans "damned" by the God of Calvinism a sort of "hell in this world" (Tawney 1962) through political oligarchy and repression, including, as Pareto and other sociologists (Adorno 2001; McLaughlin 1996) suggest, sadistic torment and extreme inhumanity. This is just another way to restate the link from theological to sociological oligarchy, from Calvin's doctrine of predestination to the Calvinist oligarchic polity and society—and back from the latter to the former, or perhaps originally in a causal path in accordance with the sociology of knowledge.

The following focuses on the sociological version of the "iron law" of political oligarchy in relation to Calvinism, while keeping in mind its theological variant as its "sacred" variant. If Michels' "iron law" of oligarchy has ever been a valid proposition in history and today, then it was and is especially (not only) for Calvinism, including Puritanism, and its political system in America in the present and a few European societies in the past. No wonder, some analysts identify the US polity under "reborn" religious-political conservatism as an exemplary oligarchic state, just as the economy as an oligopolistic economic system (Pryor 2002).

For instance, the lowest index of consensual democracy among Western democracies can be interpreted to, in part, indicate that the Puritan-based political system in America constitutes or approaches an oligarchy in general in virtue of a comparatively low number of parliamentary parties or proportional representation, implicitly less competition in politics (Vergunst 1998). Specifically, this holds true at least on the account of what some analysts identify and describe as "political duopoly"[46] (Schutz 2001) in America, as the opposite or reduction of competition in politics after the "winner-takes all" (Hill 2002; also, Frank and Cook 1995) model or image, by analogy to an equivalent market structure. In market terms, Puritan "godly" politics in America appears as less competitive or, alternatively, more monopolistic than does Calvinist capitalism, in the sense of not being even "political oligopoly" (three or more parliamentary and other major parties) in contrast to the US capitalist economy in most descriptions (Pryor 2002).

And, while not "political monopoly" in the formal sense of a number of parties, Puritan "godly" politics approaches or resembles a sort of ideological monopoly in substantive terms. In general, it does so on the account of a sort of persistent and growing, as during the 1980s–2000s, ideological pseudo-monopoly of higher or lower conservatism versus stigmatized and attacked "un-American" liberalism and other ideologies like socialism or social democracy that "never come and happened to America", as Sombart noted long ago and patriotically celebrated by US conservative sociologists (Lipset and Marks 2000). In particular, this holds true with respect to comparatively monolithic ("bipartisan") ideas on anti-welfare or slightly "regulated" unfettered capitalism, traditionalist Puritanical morality and religion, nationalistic, bellicose foreign policy, and militarism, including a global holy war on "evil", induced by ethnocentric Americanism as expressed in the common idea of America's "manifest destiny" (Inglehart 2004; Singh 2002).

At this juncture, its Parsonian defenders may retort that, while with the lowest index of consensual democracy and party competition, the US Puritan "faith-based" polity is blessed with what Parsons celebrates as the strongest ideological consensus on "basic values" among Western democracies. Yet, in accordance with Simmel's insight of what is a glorious ruler to some is instead a tyrant to others or the cure-poison parable, skeptics would object that Parsonian ideological consensus is

---

[46] Schutz (2001:169–70) suggests that "regressive changes" have occurred in the "last two decades of "conservative political dominance" in America and suggests that in the latter "a greater diversity of political parties is needed [instead] of a political oligopoly [duopoly] and the lack of alternative voices is stifling our public discussion of political issues and severely restricting our public policy choices at all levels of government."

functionally equivalent to or eventually results in Mises' "peace of the cemetery" or illusionary nirvana because of its monopolistic suppression and discouragement of dissent, as a major dimension of modern liberal democracy, as constantly witnessed in American history and society, from "Salem with witches" to "Monkey Trials" to McCarthyism to the "war on terror". To use another metaphor, it leads to a sort of "Salem *without* witches" (Putnam 2000) as "objective enemies" (Bähr 2002). Yet, since "witches" are defined by American Puritanism, replicating medievalist irrationalism or superstitions (Byrne 1997; Harley 1996), as the Devil's emanations ever-present and refusing to rationally exorcise themselves, this paradise on earth can only be reached by Puritan-style exorcism and a total war of extermination, thus acting as the ultimate way and means of Parsonian ideological "consensus" *cum* monopoly. To that extent, the strongest Parsonian ideological consensus *qua* monopoly of Puritan "godly politics" in America functions to maintain the lowest index of consensual democracy or party competition, thus an oligarchic or duopolistic "winner-takes all" political and economic system (Frank and Cook 1995; Pryor 2002), and in extension one of the lowest indexes of liberal democracy overall.

To be sure, Parsons does not recommend a war of extermination to reach his ideological consensus on "basic values", as admittedly his "most controversial proposition" (Smelser 1997), in America, as do US fundamentalists explicitly and some "libertarian" economists implicitly (e.g., Friedman and Friedman 1982). Yet, he naively or over-patriotically overlooked or denied that complete ideological consensus has been historically impossible to reach even by his Puritan ancestors; after all, if it were, no "Salem with witches", "Monkey Trials", and McCarthy's witch-hunts as realities or metaphors would have ever been existed or needed. In particular, while he correctly suggests that ideological consensus obtains on basic political values such as democracy or republic in America, he overlooks that it is not so with respect to its specific model and type—Winthrop's Puritan "godly politics" or conservative "faith-based" government *versus* Jefferson-Madison's liberal-secular state. To attain full ideological consensus on a Puritan-conservative version of democracy, or rather theocratic republic, would require another "Salem with witches", new "Monkey Trials" and McCarthy's witch-hunts. The same holds for Parsons' implied and extolled ideological consensus on the constitutional separation of church and state as an integral element of political democracy in America, though in reverse. He overlooks that such separation is compatible with and reached primarily in Jefferson-Madison's liberal-secular model but not in Puritan "godly politics" and its reenactment in a conservative "faith-based" government. This is indicated by the "faith-based" government's erosion of the church-state separation in the 1980s–2000s, as well as by the persistent attacks on the latter by Puritans and their fundamentalist heirs through various "Great" (and small) religious awakenings from the 18th to the 21st century.

In essence, Calvinism, notably American Puritanism, is, as hinted, the political system or ideological design of theocratic oligarchy or oligarchic theocracy primarily because it represents or resembles religious, specifically fundamentalist, sectarianism, or non-universalism in contrast to original Christian universalism (e.g., Catholic ecumenicalism). A Puritan state is oligarchic or factional political rule in Madison's sense because Calvinism acts or appears like, and Puritanism paradigmatically represents, a sect. Alternatively, religious sectarianism or non-universalism in Calvinism, notably Puritanism, like other sectarian or militant religion like Islam (Mansbach 2006), ultimately generates, rationalizes, and predicts theocratic oligarchy. That is, sect results in political faction, sectarians become oligarchs or factionalists. In essence, the Calvinist, especially Puritan, sectarian division into "saved" and "damned" through the dogma of predestination and the consequent exclusion and repression in theology and religion move toward oligarchy as the equivalent system of such elements in politics and all society. In Weber's words, the Calvinist spiritual, exclusive aristocracy of only a few by separating itself from the "eternally damned remainder" of society by a "impassable" and "terrifying gulf" leads to, or rather becomes itself, theocratic oligarchy excluding and subjugating the "ungodly" with "brutality" in sociopolitical life. Overall, what he calls Protestant sectarianism (also, Lipset 1996) in the form of Calvinism, notably Puritanism, ultimately eventuates in or is consistent with sectarian oligarchy and faction.

Theocratic oligarchy is then an intrinsic, systemic, and permanent rather than contingent, random, and transient tendency in Calvinism, especially Puritanism, as in other sectarian, non-universalistic, and militant world religions (e.g., Islam), simply "genetic" or built-in. Especially, Puritanism is either Calvinist sectarianism, exclusionism, and non-universalism, consequently politically oligarchic, exclusionary, and factional, or is not "Puritanism". In Calvinism, notably American Puritanism, sectarianism functions as the religious equivalent and source of oligarchy, and conversely, the second does as a political substitute and outcome of the first. In sum, oligarchy is political sectarianism via the exclusion and subjugation of out-groups, and sectarian politics a sort of oligarchic religious division, closure, and oppression within Puritanism.

The above offers a strong basis for the specification of Michels' "iron law" of oligarchy in terms of Calvinism, and its extended reformulation that "who says American Puritanism and its fundamentalist revivals says religious sectarianism, consequently theocratic oligarchy", thus division, exclusion, and oppression in polity and society. Notably, the preceding permits certain predictions or expectations concerning revived—once again since the Great Awakenings—American Puritan fundamentalism and its political system and ideological blueprint in relation to oligarchy. So long as, like original Puritanism, its revivalism continues to be sectarianism and non-universalism in religion, as it apparently does (Lipset 1996; Munch 2001), then it will likely reproduce or intensify theocratic oligarchy, factionalism, and exclusion in American politics and society, as it has done in the past and does in the present, especially in the Southern "Bible Belt". Conversely, "born again" Puritan sectarianism and absolutism in America is not likely to desist acting as politically oligarchic or exclusionary, factional, and generally anti-egalitarian, thus (as implied in Popper 1973), substantively (not legally) "criminal",[47] until and unless it is changed "beyond recognition" or tempered.

To place this too pessimistic or, as the case may be, optimistic expectation in perspective, it is instructive to recall that such change or tempering of sectarianism and thus reduced political oligarchy and exclusion is what has happened to Calvinism in Holland (Hsia and Nierop 2002; Tubergen et al. 2005) and Prussia (Nischan 1994), and to Puritanism in England (Munch 2001). This tempering was due to non-sectarian countervailing religious and other social forces, ranging from Lutheranism and Catholicism (in the first and second case) and Anglicanism (in the third) to, most strongly, secularism, rationalism, and liberalism overall (in all such cases). While all these countervailing forces, including secularism and liberalism, have been weaker, as compared to Puritanism, in America than Europe and Great Britain, also initially Calvinist Presbyterianism and Puritan Methodism (but not Baptism and related evangelicalism) have been moderated in their

---

[47] Popper (1973:236) states that in political life involving the "power of man over man", anti-equalitarianism "is just what I should call criminal".

original sectarianism and absolutism, thus in political oligarchy or exclusion. Consequently, they evolved in moderate, "liberal" or mainstream Protestantism (Hout et al. 2001; Martin 2002).

Given its past patterns and present tendencies, the above expectations about the persisting link between sectarian religion and sociopolitical oligarchic exclusion are especially (but not solely) likely for the "Bible Belt" and its "red" state extensions (e.g., Utah) in virtue of its being the creation, design, or true "heaven" of Calvinist sectarianism. It is consequently the exemplary system and region of theocratic oligarchy, as embodied and symbolized by proverbial "good [and godly] old boys" and their closed circles. While extrapolations from the past and present are always uncertain, what is a near-mathematical certainty or high statistical probability is that US "reborn" sectarians (e.g., Southern Baptists and other Protestant sects and cults like Mormons) will attempt to fulfill these oligarchic expectations in the absence or weakness of countervailing religious and political forces in the "Bible Garden" and other "red" regions, minimally Utah as the singular oasis or desert of theocratic oligarchy and the "nightmare world"[48] (McCann 2000).

As hinted, virtually all past and present Calvinist-Puritan political systems confirm and express rather than, as claimed by their masters and often assumed by others, contradict Michels' sociological "iron law" of oligarchy. Historical instances of Calvinist theocratic oligarchies and oligarchs thus abound, spanning geographically from Europe through England to America and historically from the 16th to the 21st century. As typical and expected, Calvin's exclusive rule in Geneva was a prototype of the Calvinist political system functioning as (and ruled by) theocratic oligarchy or oligarchic theocracy, as indicated by a myriad of practices, including the trials and executions of his critic Servetus

---

[48] McCann (2000:13) describes historical and contemporary Utah under Mormonism as a "nightmarish world" that is "outside the order of liberal society" primarily because of the subjugation and coercion of women by the "despotism of a patriarchal religious society" or "Mormon patriarchy". Such a narrow proto-feminist argument overlooks or denies that it was and is such a world, specifically totalitarian theocracy, to virtually everyone living in that region, except for Mormon patriarchal rulers ("elders"), regardless of gender, or most men and women alike, well as other ascribed attributes (race, ethnicity, nationality, age, etc.). For example, the Mormon past and in part present system of polygamy was and is detrimental and dehumanizing not only to women, but also, contrary to feminist arguments or nightmares, to most men unable to afford multiple or any wives versus their "leaders" or "elders" monopolizing through control, coercion, and outright predation such economic and social opportunities or life chances a la Weber.

and other libertines, and himself was an arch oligarch-theocrat, the role model, and hero for all others within Calvinism, including Puritanism (Mansbach 2006). In brief, theocratic oligarchy provided the sociological (Michels') substance and description to Calvin's *civitas Dei* as the theological content and designation of a Calvinist polity and society. The above holds true, with secondary qualifications, of subsequent Calvinist, including Puritan, political systems adopting and extending Calvin's *civitas Dei* as an ideal and consequently his theocratic oligarchy, from Holland and in part Germany to old and New England and the US "Bible Belt". For example, recall in Holland Calvinism adopted and expanded the Geneva model of the *civitas Dei*, in which Church dominates State (Frijhoff 2002), by becoming the "real State Church", thus effectively reestablished and extended Calvin's theocratic oligarchy from a local to a national level. Similarly, though less successfully, in Prussia Calvinism attempted to spread and implement the "Genevan creed" through total "Calvinization" undertaken by the "ruling elite" (at the Hohenzollern court), thus a political system of theocratic oligarchy (Nischan 1994).

Subsequently, Calvinism *cum* Puritanism in England deposed the monarchy and executed the king (Elwood 1999) to reestablish a "Holy Commonwealth" as a polity and society evidently after the model or image of Calvin's *civitas Dei* and ruled by theocratic oligarchy in the form and face of Cromwell's "Parliament of Saints" or "Divines". In a sense, Cromwell's "Parliament of Saints" provides the paradigmatic exemplar of theocratic oligarchy, and Hume's one hundred or so "Divines" are the prototypes of theocrats-oligarchs, within the extended family of Calvinism, notably Puritanism. Weber implies this by describing Cromwell's "Parliament of Saints" as the "greatest experiment" in the merger or alliance of Puritanism with political power, though what he calls the ultimately "abortive rule" of this Puritan theocratic oligarchy and Revolution made it really experimental. Another, more successful and enduring exemplar was New England's "Biblical Commonwealth" as the political and social system of (or ruled by) a *mixt aristocracie* embodied by Winthrop et al. Not only by assumption, but in reality the Puritan political system of *mixt aristocracie* was essentially or eventually evolved in theocratic oligarchy in accordance with Michels' "iron law" in virtue of the narrow circle of the "spiritual aristocracy of predestined saints" as only a few or small number of "Divinely ordained" rulers (Bremer 1995). This made Winthrop et al. quintessential theocrats-oligarchs or strong oligarchic leaders (Munch 2001). Admittedly,

Winthrop et al. practiced and advocated political "leadership by the favored few" (Dunn and Woodard 1996), thus effectively theocratic oligarchy or oligarchic theocracy.

Moreover, in purely stratification terms Winthrop's *mixt aristocracie* was actually more oligarchy than, as the term indicates, pure aristocracy proper. It was so given the largely non-aristocratic or middle-class origins and manners, yet aristocratic ambitions or emulations, of New England's early Puritans, from the stance of their Anglican adversaries, mostly belonging to the English nobility, in the Episcopalian South. Alternatively, the early Puritan theocratic oligarchy and oligarchs operated as the typical "all-American" form and faces of the "old", declaratively disdained, yet actually emulated or envied, European, including Calvinist, feudal aristocracy and aristocrats in the "new nation." This Puritan duality was in accordance with the "pure hypocrisy" of American Puritanism and its invidious distinction from aristocratic, monarchic Anglicanism, Catholicism, and even original, French Calvinism itself.

Still another historical and even the most persisting and manifest exemplar of Puritan theocratic oligarchy and theocrats-oligarchs in America and beyond involves the new South as a "Biblical Garden". The latter functions and qualifies as the political and social system of theocratic oligarchy or oligarchic theocracy in virtue of being ruled (Mencken 1982) or pervaded (Amenta and Halfmann 2000) by narrow and exclusionary "godly" circles, as exemplified and symbolized by persisting (mostly) evangelical "good old boys" networks. Sociological analyses suggest that a major reason why the US South remains persistently, even seemingly proudly "under-democratized" (Amenta et al. 2001; Cochran 2001) as well as anti-liberal overall is precisely such oligarchic "godly" rule or exclusionary dominance by these circles. Moreover, it is observed that this region (notably Texas) seeks and often succeeds to expand such "godly" oligarchic practices to America as a whole over the 1980s–2000s by placing American politics and society in the undemocratic, anti-secular, and anti-liberal "shadow of Dixie" (Cochran 2001). The outcome is American democracy "heading South" and thus subverted into a sort of theocratic oligarchy, just as the old South was ruled by a plantation (both Anglican and Puritan) oligarchy (Kloppenberg 1998).

In retrospect, this indicates that Winthrop's descendents effectively expanded, as through the Great Awakenings, the Puritan theocratic oligarchy as *mixt aristocracie* from New England to the South in the form and faces of evangelical "good old boys" (while deposing the Anglican landed aristocracy). It also indicates that at least the Southern "Bible Belt" tends or "promises" to recreate the American polity and society overall after the model or image of Winthrop's Puritan theocratic oligarchy ruling his "Biblical Commonwealth" as a "shining city upon of a hill", thus in extension Calvin's oligarchic *civitas Dei*. Further, recall analysts identify and describe the contemporary US polity (and economy) as an oligarchic political (and economic) system (Pryor 2002) primarily as the result of revived Puritan-rooted political and religious conservatism *cum* "neo-conservatism", notably Southern and other "reborn" evangelicalism.

In particular, remember that the US party system is commonly identified or designated as political duopoly (Schutz 2001) operating according to the pseudo-Hobbesian or "Wild West" "winner takes all" rule (Frank and Cook 1995; Hill 2002) by analogy to economic oligopoly or oligopolistic market structures, and in that sense not fully competitive, or oligarchic. Notably, in comparative terms, analysts imply that the Puritan "faith-based" political system in America is the most oligarchic, and in extension theocratic, fundamentalist, and religiously grounded (Lipset 1996; Munch 2001), among modern Western democracies. It is in virtue of its lowest index of consensual democracy, as indicated by the smallest number of parliamentary parties and non-existent or low proportional representation (Vergunst 1998).

In economic terms, its comparatively strongest or purest parliamentary party duopoly makes it most oligopolistic and thus politically oligarchic. In particular, Congress as well as state legislatures under recurring Puritan-inspired conservative predominance during the 1980s–2000s resemble more Cromwell's oligarchic "Parliament of Saints" in Hume's and Weber's description or Winthrop's "Divine" oligarchy than Parliaments and other equivalent political institutions in Western liberal-secular democracies. In a way, their Puritanical members, notably leaders, act or appear as Hume's one hundred self-proclaimed "Divines" (e.g., the US Senate) in Cromwell's "Parliament of Saints," or as Winthrop et al. as God-decreed and their perennial role models a la Reagan et al., and in extension Calvin as the overt or tacit original model in Geneva.

In sum, virtually all Calvinist political systems and rulers, from Calvin's Geneva through Holland under Calvinism to Cromwell's and Winthrop's "Holy Commonwealths" to the "Bible Garden", paradigmatically epitomize the "iron law" or historical pattern of theocratic oligarchy and Calvinism, including Puritanism. In respect of Calvinist theocratic oligarchy and theocrats-oligarchs at least, evidently not much has substantively changed, or, as French-born Calvin might put it, the "more things have changed, the more they stayed the same". This involves a historical continuity or sequence from Calvin's 16th century *civitas Dei* in France (as an ideal) and Geneva (as a reality), thus by implication medievalist "godly society", to the 21st century US "Bible Garden" dominated by "godly" and "good old boys".

*Theocratic Plutocracy*

Third, a Calvinist polity in America and beyond tends to be a non-democratic or authoritarian political system in virtue of representing (or being ruled by) theocratic plutocracy or plutocratic theocracy, in close association or even substantive identity with aristocracy and/or oligarchy. By analogy to aristocracy and oligarchy, if plutocracy, as Pareto and other analysts suggest, also the paradigmatic elimination or subversion of modern democracy, then this even more applies to the plutocratic-theocratic form relative to the democratic liberal-secular type. And, since plutocracy and plutocrats, as Weber, Veblen, and other analysts imply and medieval nobles would contend, is and are just "moneyed" aristocracy and aristocrats or oligarchy and oligarchs, thus economic masters discussed before, most of what stated about the first and the second, plus Calvinist rulers in the economy, can also be said of the third. Thus, only a few further remarks will suffice.

Generally, a Calvinist, notably Puritan, political system constitutes and operates as, in addition and interconnection to aristocracy and oligarchy, theocratic plutocracy or plutocratic theocracy in the sense of being reproduced and ruled by "godly" plutocrats or wealthy theocrats. In Weber's terms, it is the structure of political control and domination by a predestined spiritual *cum* economic aristocracy, or simply "Divinely ordained" and inspired theocrats-plutocrats.

As implied when considering the Calvinist master-servant economy, these theocrats-plutocrats historically comprised early ruling Calvinists in Europe, including Calvin himself in Geneva, and especially his theocratic-plutocratic disciples in Holland during the official rule of Calvinism (Hsia and Nierop 2002) and in England (and Scotland) via Puritanism (Gorski 2000). They also, as noted, included the Puritan "godly" wealthy owners and lucrative traders of Native-American and some African slaves and rum in 17th–19th century New England

(Dayton 1999). A paradigmatic exemplar of Calvinist theocrats-plutocrats is found in 18th century New England. For illustration, in 18th century New England (e.g., Connecticut), the major Calvinist theologians ("New Divinity" clergy) belonged to the top twenty-four "wealthy ministers" (German 1995). Admittedly, they were "not just" theologians and evangelists, but capitalist plutocrats benefiting from "a state-supported religious establishment" defining Calvinist theocracy (German 1995). In turn, these neo-Calvinist theologians and ministers ("New Lights") were "roundly condemned" by their critics or rivals ("Old Lights") for abusing their theocratic power in the service of their "pecuniary interests", including those as "speculators in western lands"[49], etc. (German 1995).

In addition, Calvinist theocrats-plutocrats comprised Southern evangelical (alongside Anglican) land and slave proprietors wanting to "live like feudal lords" and their successors, puritanical sectarian capitalist "robber barons", with their modern mutants or proxies. As regards these capitalist "robber barons" in the post-bellum South and beyond, recall that Weber registers that majority (of the "older generation" of American "promoters," "captains of industry," "multi-millionaires and "trust magnates") formally belonged to various Puritan sects, "especially to the Baptists", thus to Calvinist sectarianism. And, the neoclassic functional equivalents or proxies of these classic, proverbial sectarian "robber barons" comprise predictably "godly" mafia, including "cowboy" or Enron-style and Wal-Mart, capitalists (Desai 2005; Pryor 2002) in the persistently and even growingly Baptist-dominated "Bible Garden" and beyond. (This is exemplified by the once powerful "Christian coalition" created and dominated by Baptism and representing a mixed theocratic-capitalist design and practice of "God" and "free enterprise.")

In general, later-day US theocrats-plutocrats incorporate what economists identify as the "top heavy" (Wolff 2002) wealthy, mostly proclaiming, like their political equivalents, including Presidents, "God and faith", genuinely or (as Weber implies for the Baptist "robber-barons") hypocritically. At least, this applies to their fundamentalist elements seeking to recreate America as (ruled by) theocratic

---

[49] German (1995: 988) adds that their critics (Old Lights) showed how neo-Calvinist theologians and ministers (New Lights) "abused their power by pursuing their private interest at public expense".

plutocracy and so "faith-based" anti-liberal "democracy" and capitalism or capitalist "free enterprise" theocracy. Predictably, they do after the venerable model of New England's Calvinist theocrats-plutocrats met earlier and Weber's post-bellum Baptist "robber barons." They also do in the image of Enronism and the exemplar of "godly" Wal-Mart as the new economic pride and joy and symbol of the "Bible Belt", notably the pro-capital, anti-labor or anti-union repressive "shadow of Dixie" (Amenta and Halfmann 2000).

In comparative and historical terms, if most Western political systems or democracies have been and remain to certain degrees, or have elements of, what Pareto calls "demagogic" plutocracies or Michels' oligarchies, then the US Puritan polity or "democracy" has been and remains a theocratic, and not just, plutocracy. Thus, while these are solely or mostly plutocracies or oligarchies but not theocracies (with the exception of Holland under Calvinism and England during Cromwell), it is a composite of theocracy and plutocracy alike. This is what Winthrop's Puritan *mixt aristocracie* classically showed and the Southern evangelical mix of a "Bible Belt" and capitalism, the coalition of "God" and "free enterprise", neo-classically shows.

On this account, the Puritan political system poses a sort of double or triple jeopardy to, and inflicts a dual "demagogy" on, modern democracy. This jeopardy is not only a plutocratic or oligarchic one, identified by Pareto and Michels, but also a theocratic one, in contrast to non-Calvinist political systems even if, if they are correct, being plutocracies and oligarchies as well. In fact, this is what Pareto suggests prophetically rediscovering the US government's tendency to enforce Puritanical "morality by law", including prohibition of alcohol and other vices and sins, and the consequent "gross abuses" of "malignant" political power that are "not observable" in those, by implication non-Puritan, and yet plutocratic societies without such legal "restrictions". Hence, what contemporary sociologists (Munch 2001) identify as American Puritanism's still non-tempered moral absolutism helps to explain and predict the dual nature and operation of the US Puritan-based political system. This is the systemic duality of a composite theocratic (not just) plutocracy *cum* capitalist aristocracy after the model and image of New England's Calvinist theocrats-plutocrats, including double "demagogy" or hypocrisy, just as of the economy as theocentric ("godly") capitalism.

To that extent, what Weber also explicitly or even graphically identifies as, in his words, "naked plutocracy", embodied by the capitalist and sectarian (Baptist) "robber barons", in post-bellum America is so, by contrast to or more than in Europe, in a double meaning. First, as he explicitly suggests, it is "naked" in the economic sense of the capacity of mere money or wealth in America to "buy" political power or influence, even if not social honor. Second, it is "naked plutocracy" in the non-economic meaning of the proverbial, in this case theocratic, emperor with "no cloths", as he implies for the "godly" sectarian and evangelical (Baptist) "robber barons". Overall, it is in that capitalist plutocracy and plutocrats in America seek to become political oligarchy and oligarchs in Pareto-Michels' sense (Pryor 2002), just as functioning and acting as theocracy and theocrats *cum* "godly" capitalism and "faith-based" democracy and "God fearing" capitalists. Simply, Calvinist capitalists, with some "not so godly" exceptions, in America are not only plutocrats or oligarchs, as are their non-Calvinist, including Lutheran and Anglican (Munch 2001) and Catholic, counterparts. They are Puritanical theocrats, unlike the latter, and like those in other theocratic religions such as Islam (Davis and Robinson 2006; Mansbach 2006).

In sum, this is a major substantive difference between Weber's US Puritan (and, for that matter, Islamic) "naked" dual theocratic plutocracy, including "double demagogy", and Pareto's other Western "demagogic" plutocracies, a moment somewhat overlooked in the sociological and economic literature. Consequently, to state that the Calvinist political system in America is non-democratic in virtue of its theocratic plutocracy signifies that it is so not only, as Marxians or economists may suggest, because of being plutocratic or the "dictatorship" by the wealthy (Niggle 1998). It is also, what they overlook or downplay, because it is the design of "godly" politics or theocracy, thus a double (in Weber's words) materialistic and idealistic, jeopardy to liberal-secular democracy and eventually free-market capitalism (Hodgson 1999; Pryor 2002).

No doubt, not all Pareto's past and modern Western and other "demagogic" plutocracies and plutocrats are theocracies and theocrats but can also be secular or non-religious. However, Calvinist plutocracy, from Calvin's Geneva to Weber's and modern America, is as a political system and ruling class alike invariably theocracy *cum* "godly" politics and elites in accordance with Calvinism's original design and system of the medievalist *civitas Dei*. And conversely, Calvinist, including Puritan, theocracy as both a political system and a ruling class is almost invariably plutocracy, as epitomized by 17th–19th New England under Calvinism. This holds true even though not all theocracies are necessarily plutocracies, as in what Weber calls other-worldly ascetic and mystical religions (Buddhism, Hinduism, early Christianity, including the medieval Orthodox and Catholic Church, at least their monasticism, even early Lutheranism) and Sorokin (1970) identifies as passive ideational social-cultural systems.

In comparative-historical terms, Calvinism, including Puritanism, is probably the only or the principal form of Protestantism and Christianity overall with such a typical mix of theocracy and plutocracy, and even among world religions, excluding (as Weber implies) perhaps Islam and Judaism (e.g., the Pharisee elite as, in his words, "an aristocracy with respect to salvation which stood in contrast to the godless Jews"). At this juncture, Winthrop's *mixt aristocracie* substantively functioned or can be described as theocracy mixed with plutocracy, thus with economic aristocracy or materialistic oligarchy. Recall, Winthrop et al. and their descendents in 18th–19th century New England were "not just" theocrats and theologians or God's agents and ministers on Earth, but also a "wealthy" class and in that sense plutocrats, using their established theocratic power for private monetary benefits.

As intimated above, the reason for this theocratic-plutocratic mix is Calvinism's design and practice of total mastery of the world or complete domination over society rather than, as most economists might assume, its spirit of capitalism supposedly transforming ("secularizing") its "Divinely ordained" theocracy into a capitalist plutocracy and economy. After all, this "spirit" is just an economic facet or product of such political and societal mastery. Comparatively, such total mastery or absolute domination also explains Islam's comparable mixture of theocracy and plutocracy, embodied by wealthy theocrats or prophets, as identified by Weber (also, Davis and Robinson 2006), though he classifies Islamism in the category opposite to Calvinism, in religions acquiescing with passive "adaptation" or "mere accommodation" to the mundane world. Simply, most Calvinist, like Islamic, theocrats and theologians act as if they had the absolute imperative or "felt" the pressing need that they must, for logical closure and empirical completion of their rule, also become plutocrats or rich masters a la Puritan "wealthy ministers" in New England, rather than the opposite as in mystical asceticism or passive ideationalism (Buddhism, medieval Christian monasticism, etc.). In sum, they seek to blend the spiritual *and* economic aristocracy, as in Winthrop's *mixt aristocracie*, as (part of) the composite "God and Mammon", "faith and capitalism" (as in the "Bible Belt" and beyond), path toward the total mastery of society.

US conservatives would and do object that it is trivial and/or unfair to emphasize that America's Puritan-based political system or "democracy" is plutocracy (or oligarchy), because virtually all Western democracies and capitalist societies are Pareto's demagogic plutocracies, so "what is the big deal"? This objection overlooks or denies several key moments. First, America's political system or "democracy", as Pareto, Weber, Veblen, and Tocqueville imply, has been historically more plutocratic than other Western democracies since at least the robber-barons era, and even increasingly so during the 1980s–2000s period (Pryor 2002; Wolff 2002). Second, it is not only Weber's "naked plutocracy", but also a composite of the latter with theocracy, thus a dual degeneration of or double jeopardy to democracy, unlike other Western democracies as only or mostly Pareto's plutocracies. Third, such objections are self-defeating and self-contradictory by contradicting celebrated American exceptionalism, including the lack of "naked" plutocracy and oligarchy, compared to other Western societies. One wonders if Puritan America were not designed and supposed to be a totally different, "new nation", including non-plutocratic and non-oligarchic, as one of the major aims and rationales of its founding and celebration, compared to the old disdained, particularly plutocratic and oligarchic Europe (Lipset and Marks 2000).

*Political and Social Closure and Exclusion*

As a corollary of the preceding, a Calvinist polity in America and elsewhere is a non-democratic, including totalitarian, polity in virtue of constituting the system of political and social closure. It is a closed, as opposed to an open, polity and society (Popper 1973) due to its entwined complex of theocracy with aristocracy, oligarchy, and plutocracy. While not all closed and exclusionary states and societies have been Calvinist-Puritan but also non-Calvinist (including Catholic and Islamic), the inverse is almost invariably true of those of Calvinism, including Puritanism, as the theocratic design and system of political and other social closure. In Weber's terms, a Calvinist polity and society is typically closed and thus non-democratic in that it tends to "monopolistic closure" of life chances or "exclusiveness" of "social and economic opportunities to outsiders" through their "monopolization" by insiders or "monopolistic differentiation" between these and out-groups, notably non-Calvinists and actual non-believers. Predictably, within the extended family of Calvinism, this in particular holds true of Puritan "godly" politics and society in virtue of what also contemporary sociologists following Weber identify as "exclusionary" and non-brotherly Puritanism. In this view, Puritanism paradigmatically epitomizes the "exclusiveness" and non-brotherliness of the virtuosi sect versus the "democratic" impulses and "brotherliness" of the church[50] (Symonds and Pudsey 2006).

First and foremost, a Calvinist polity and society tends to be closed and exclusionary or non-universalistic, thus non-democratic, because it is theocracy and Calvinism overall, notably Puritanism, is theocratic, in reciprocal relation and reinforcement with its being a mix of "godly" aristocracy, oligarchy, and plutocracy. Hence, it seeks and attains political and social closure on primarily (though not only) religious grounds and by means of theocratic rule or "godly" politics. It does by closing itself to and excluding non-Calvinist or non-Puritan Christians (Catholics) and even Protestants (e.g., Quakers in New England, Anglicans in the "Bible Belt"), let alone non-Christian believers (Native Americans) and especially true non-believers, agnostics, secularists, and liberals. They are all condemned and excluded, or more, including, as in the past, persecuted and executed, as "heathen", "ungodly", "infidels", "witches", or "enemies", thus "un-American".

Sociological observations suggest that the Puritan-rooted political system or the religious and secular powers-that-be in America tended to exclude non-believers (viz., atheists, agnostics, secularists, liberals, etc.) not only from power and politics but also from civil society and culture during American history through the early 21st century (Edgell et al. 2006), most persistently and intensively in the "Bible Belt". What sociological analyses rarely, or deem it unnecessary to, mention and most Americans are unaware of is that Puritan "godly" politics in America thereby continues and expands an original and persistent institutional and non-institutional practice and tradition of closure and exclusion within the extended family and the *long durée* of Calvinism from Calvin's 16 century *civitas Dei* to the 21st century

---

[50] Referring to Weber, Symonds and Pudsey (2006:145) contrasts the "cosmic brotherliness" of original Christian ethics against "exclusionary Puritanism", stating that the ("organic") "social ethics" of traditional or medieval Christianity as well as Lutheranism "maintained a universal, ethical brotherliness" which Puritanism rejected. In general, building on Weber, they suggest that the "democratic impulses" of the church, as being universal with a "personal dimension to brotherliness", epitomized by Catholicism and Lutheranism, "are starkly opposed to the exclusiveness of the virtuosi sect", exemplified by Puritanism and its lack of "ethical brotherliness" (Symonds and Pudsey 2006:143).

"Bible Belt" through Cromwell's and Winthrop's "Biblical Commonwealths" of the 17th century. In this, like virtually all respects, American Puritanism by its theocracy does not "rediscover America" or "reinvent the wheel" of political and social closure, monopolization, and exclusion discovered or invented by original Calvinism and other theocratic religions, including medieval Catholicism and fundamentalist Islam. Rather, it only does, and expands and reinforces, what its sometimes forgotten European parent initially did through Calvin et al. and has subsequently done since.

As noticed, Calvin created and maintained his *civitas Dei* in 16th century Geneva as essentially closed and exclusionary "godly" polity and society by practicing political and social closure and exclusion, as well as persecutions and executions, against non-Calvinists (Catholics, etc.) and even some dissenting Calvinists (Servetus), not to mention libertines or secularists, all condemned and attacked as "infidels". He thus created a model or precedent to follow and build on for Calvinists of all societies and times (Mansbach 2006), from post-Calvin Geneva (Sorkin 2005) to modern America, at the minimum the "Bible Garden" (Hinson 1997). For example, what Calvin et al. attempted and succeeded only at a local level, his victorious heirs in Holland did at the national from the late 16th century through systematic political and social closure and exclusion, just as persecution, against non-Calvinists, especially Catholics and partly Lutherans (Frijhoff 2002; Kaplan 2002), though, unlike their supreme model in Geneva, they were more constrained and ultimately neutralized and discredited by countervailing forces such as secular authorities and the subsequent Enlightenment. Also, Calvinists attempted, yet failed, to establish and expand Calvin's closed and exclusionary *civitas Dei* in early 17th century Germany through their projected total "Calvinization" of this Lutheran (and Catholic) society (Nischan 1994).

And, what they had failed in Germany as well as France before, Calvinists *cum* Puritans succeeded in England at least temporarily. They did so by establishing their short-lived "Holy Commonwealth" characterized by religiously grounded and sanctified closure and exclusion against "infidels" (Irish Catholics and Anglicans) and ruled by the "Parliament of Saints" or Hume's self-designated one hundred or so "divines". Recall, Cromwell's political activities were effectively "holy" wars or crusades (Goldstone 1986; Gorski 2000) against non-Puritans *cum* "infidels." These were subjected to systematic closure and exclusion—yet as the "best" outcome they could expect compared to—cruel persecution and even extermination, especially of Irish Catholics and other "Papists" and in part Anglicans, as Hume, Weber, and Simmel imply. In general, historical research identifies Puritanism's "significant career" as the religious doctrine and political practice of "exclusion" (Ashton 1965) in England and in extension America.

Further, what Calvin achieved solely at a local city level, Calvinists just partially and transiently in Holland and minimally in Germany, and Cromwell eventually failed in England, Winthrop et al. realized nationally or regionally, almost completely and enduringly in America, initially New England and subsequently via the Great Awakenings beyond, notably the South. This is to establish a Calvinist-as-Puritan closed "godly" state and society (German 1995). They did through their "Biblical Commonwealth" as an essentially closed and exclusionary theocratic state and society (Gould 1996; Munch 2001). This was indicated by Winthrop's *mixt aristocracie* and exemplified or symbolized by "Salem with witches," as the microscopic exemplar (Harley 1996) and the symbol of sociopolitical closure, exclusion, and deadly oppression rooted in (as Tocqueville implies) Puritan-type religious sectarianism and fanaticism (alongside the profitable hunting of Native Americans). At least, Winthrop's *mixt aristocracie* and "Salem with witches" defined or qualified New England's Puritan political system as closed, exclusionary, persecutory, and brutal, not only with respect to "ungodly" non-Christian out-groups like pagans, but even Christian non-Puritans (e.g., Catholics, Quakers, etc., not many present or left anyway until the 1830s), simply both against foreign "infidels" and domestic "witches". Thus, reportedly "almost all Puritans" in 17th century New England advocated and implemented the "bloody tenet of persecution" (Coffey 1998; also, Harley 1996) against various "infidels" or out-groups.

In a way, Winthrop's was what Fiche might have called a "closed commercial-theocratic state". It was, first, closed to all kinds of "infidels", second, "commercial" in Weber's sense of the spirit or rather Tönnies' "ghost" of capitalism in the form of the Puritans' profit-making on "dead or alive" Native Americans" and their "lucrative" slave ownership and trade, and third "theocratic" in being ruled by the established Calvinist *cum* Congregational Church. Strikingly, Weber registers that under "Winthrop's leadership" New England's Puritan colony would permit the "settlement of gentlemen" in Massachusetts only on the condition of their adherence to the official church, and infers that the colony stayed "closed for the sake of Church discipline."

Weber might have added that historically the colony essentially remained a closed polity and society with respect to out-groups at least until the official "disestablishment" of Puritanism during the 1830s (Baldwin 2006) and even in part by the time of his visit (the 1900s), judging by his observations about US Puritan sects and their axiomatic continuing closure to and exclusion or distrust of religious outsiders. During his visit he observes that America continues to be the "major domicile" of Puritan—Baptist, Methodist, Presbyterian, and related—sects[51] in which, like in any sect, the "impact of exclusion" and the "intensity of indoctrination" is "much more effective" than any "authoritarian ecclesiastic discipline", including by implication Calvinism as an "hierocratic institution" or church. This hence indicates that American Puritanism was hyper-Calvinism and its members or leaders super-Calvinists in respect of political and societal closure and exclusion, just as indoctrination. Hence, Weber depicts American democracy as a "maze of highly exclusive" Puritan sects, associations and clubs that form the "center of the individual's social life", notably for what he calls the "naked plutocracy" and its "robber barons".

A second additional remark can be that Winthrop's followers attempted and remarkably succeeded to extend their "closed commercial-theocratic state" and society from New England to America overall, especially the "old" Anglican South, via the Great Awakenings, notably the second in the aftermath of the American Revolution. At this juncture, the Great Awakenings originated and operated, like most Calvinist revivals in America (German 1995) and beyond (Europe, England), as movements seeking to revive and expand the Puritan closed and exclusive polity and society, thus exclusionary Puritanism (Symonds and Pudsey 2006), to America, most dramatically and successfully in the old South turned into a new "Bible Garden" after the

---

[51] For example, Weber observes that in America during his visit "a person who wants to open a bank joins the Baptists or Methodists for everybody knows that baptism, respectively admission, is preceded by a strict examination which inquires about blemishes in her/his past conduct: frequenting an inn, sexual life, card-playing, making debts, other levities, insincerity, etc.; if the result of the inquiry is positive, creditworthiness is guaranteed, and in countries like the United States personal credit is almost unthinkable on any other basis." He adds that "a sect member of this kind is preferred in all responsible positions of the capitalist apparatus: as board member, director, promoter or foreman" and consequently "will soon gain an economic foothold in a way which is denied to the outsider." Also, Weber remarks that "the "Old Methodist confession in the weekly meetings of the small groups [was] set up for this purpose [ i.e.,] the intensity of indoctrination and the impact of exclusion".

model and image of New England's "Biblical Commonwealth." This casts doubt on the prevalent view and even glorification of these evangelical revivals as attempts at increasing political and social openness, including religious freedom, tolerance, and pluralism or competition. In essence, like virtually all Calvinist-Puritan revolutions and revivals before and after, they acted as "holy" wars to revive from the past political closure, monopolization, exclusion, as well as persecution and subjugation of all kinds of "infidels" (Catholics, Quakers, Anglicans, non-Christians, secularists, non-believers). And, they were sanctified, like their modern replays, as evangelical "crusades for Christ" and the Bible and a "godly society" to be purified from the "ungodly" (Archer 2001).

Hence, via these and a myriad of other fundamentalist revivals from the 18th to the 21st century, Puritanism effectively transformed the South from a system and region of political-social closure and exclusion (slavery) based on a single criterion (race) into one grounded on and sanctified by additional, "godly" grounds. This was witnessed by the post-bellum segregation and discrimination against racial *and* religious minorities, not to mention non-believers (Edgell et al. 2006), as well as those ideologically and politically "incorrect" in non-religious terms. To that extent, it further extended and compounded, rather than as usually assumed, abolished or mitigated, the old Southern closed and exclusionary polity and society, at least until the official end of segregation, discrimination, and exclusion in the 1960s. Simply, exclusionary Puritanism transformed the old racist, non-fundamentalist, and non-ascetic (Episcopalian) South into both the racist *and* fundamentalist and ascetic (Baptist-Methodist-Presbyterian) "Bible Garden" as the system or design of Biblical theocracy déjà vu. In this respect, this Bibliocracy originated and largely remains as a Southern closed polity and society in a dual form or sense. This is, first, racial-ethnic segregation, exclusion, and discrimination (or slavery), as at least until the 1960s, second, constant religiously and ideologically or politically based closure and exclusion, from post-bellum times to the early 21st century. At this point, the neo-Calvinist "Bible Garden" looks even more, doubly at least, closed and exclusionary than the "old", "sleepy, and "ungodly" non-Calvinist (Episcopalian) South prior to the Great Awakenings and the Civil War.

To that extent, the Southern "Bible Garden", like Puritan "godly" politics in America as a whole, has posed and still poses a double, not just single—as did the old Episcopalian South of slavery—racist *and* theocratic, "jeopardy" to political democracy in America, notably Jefferson-Madison's ideal of equality, liberty and justice "for all". If there is such thing as the Southern story and way (Boles 1999) or tragedy (Bauman 1997) of religion and politics alike, then this is probably the remarkable mutation of the old South of single racist closure and exploitation into the "Bible Garden" of compounded racist-theocratic, just as ideological or political segregation, exclusion and discrimination. And, judging from recent tendencies, the "Bible Garden" promises to become America's happy-end or, as the case may be, tragedy by putting American politics and society in the closed and exclusionary theocratic "shadow of Dixie" and consequently democracy "heading South" and converted in or approached diluted theocracy. And, it does so through its "godly" closure and exclusion, as well as its actual or advocated[52] persecution and execution via a fundamentalist-based death penalty and penal system, culture wars, and "holy" war on the "evil world". Predictably, such an outcome is a happy-ending and victory to Calvinist fundamentalism and its would-be theocrats and "holy warriors". Yet, it is a tragedy or ultimate defeat for liberal-secular democracy, at least its Jefferson-Madison's project, in America given that "Bible Belt" evangelicalism is found to belong, together with Iran's Islamic theocracy, to the proto-totalitarian "solutions" to the "evil" or "burden" of individual and political liberty (Bauman 1997).

In sum, what was Calvin's Geneva and Calvinist-ruled Holland in the early and late 16th century, Cromwell's "Holy" and notably Winthrop's "Biblical Commonwealth" during the 17th–19th centuries with respect to political-social theocratic closure and exclusion (and more) is the Southern "Bible Garden" or evangelical America overall in the early 21st century, just as before, since the Second Great Awakening of the 1800s. In short, the "Bible Belt", evangelical America in general, is the true heir or revival and extension of Calvin's *civitas Dei* from the old Europe's dead past in this respect via Winthrop et al. Generally, all these seemingly disparate historical instances exemplify Calvinist,

---

[52] For instance, a Southern Baptist pastor during the 2000s was reported to urge his "flock" to do, in an "imprecatory prayer", the following against some "ungodly" persons in America: "Persecute them. Let them be put to shame and perish and let [their] children be fatherless, and [their wives] widow[s]." If so, the rumors of the death of the Puritan-style actual or potential persecution of "infidels" by modern American fundamentalism, epitomized by Southern Baptism and allied Protestant sects or cults, are "grossly exaggerated" or just premature, unrealistic hopes.

including Puritan, "godly" politics and society as closed and exclusionary on religious and interrelated (racial, ethnic, ideological, political, cultural) grounds.

### Appendix: Catholic and Neo-Calvinist Theocratic Tendencies

For example, during the 2000s the Polish Catholic Parliament proclaimed Jesus Christ no less (or no more) than a "honorary king of Poland" and "held a special Mass to pray for rain during a drought", while two identical ultra-conservative twins becoming president and prime minister. No wonder, the Polish press has described this type of politics and period as political vaudeville or circus, a term also usually used to describe Puritan "godly" politics in America.

In global terms, such grotesque, just as not-so-comical, things among modern Western democracies can happen only or primarily in America, as when the governors and other officials, alongside religious figures, of some "Bible Belt" states like Alabama and Georgia also prayed "for rain" in the 2000s, and post-communist Poland self-defined by Puritanism and Catholicism, respectively. This grotesquely confirms Hume's classic warning about Puritan or other religious fanaticism or zealotry. As regards the curious practice of publicly praying "for rain" in the "Bible Belt", anthropologists (or comics) might suggest that US "reborn" evangelicals" (e.g., Southern Baptists) may want to perform what despised and almost exterminated pagan Indian groups in America have performed for centuries. This is what Merton 1968) calls a "rain dance" as perhaps a more effective instrument for producing, if not the desired meteorological outcome (manifest function), then integrative social effects (latent function). (An objection to this suggestion is that most Baptists, like their Puritan forebears and role models, "do not dance" and ban dancing.)

This grotesque example confirms how little, if at all, "reborn" Calvinist evangelicalism in America differs from what it despised and tried to eradicate as "ungodly", "heathen" religion with respect to religious superstition and irrationalism. In particular, it reflects evangelical anti-scientism. Most US "reborn" evangelicals vehemently attack the scientific theory and evidence of human-produced global warming as, like all other sciences, "ungodly," just as for the sake of protecting vested economic and political interests from consequent reforms. Yet, the predicted effects of such climate change include (also) long droughts thereby indirectly self-inflicted or aggravated by anti-science religious fundamentalism in a "holy alliance" with mafia or crony capitalism (Enron, Exxon, Wal-Mart). In turn, this self-infliction reaffirms Calvinist evangelical nihilism as self-destruction via either a global nuclear "holy" war with a MAD outcome or, as in this case, causing or exacerbating (minimally, dismissing) global warming—or else both.

CHAPTER FIVE

CIVIL SOCIETY OF CALVINIST THEOCRACY

*Puritan Moralistic Tyranny*

Calvinist theocracy's "civil society" constitutes the theocratic destruction or subversion and domination of the civic sphere, notably individual moral freedom and responsibility and private life. To that extent, civil society is effectively subjected to self-elimination or self-degeneration as an independent secular domain of individual, notably moral, liberty or autonomy and private life. Civil society or Parsons' "societal community" within Calvinist theocracy degenerates into what can be denoted religiously grounded and sanctified "moral fascism", thus becoming a non-entity, a sort of "uncivil society" (McCann 2000), epitomized by the Puritan theocratic "godly community" in New England (German 1995) and its "Bible Belt" revival (and Mormon Utah).

In essence, Calvinist theocracy transforms civil society from a free, humane "life-world" (Habermas 2001) into the world of unfreedom, inhumanity, and anti-life, ultimately of death through the religiously based and sanctified system of executions for "ungodly" acts (blasphemy and sins) and a global, permanent self-destructive "holy" war or crusade against "evil" societies. In Hobbes' words, civil society (the term he coined before Hegel) in Calvinist theocracy mutates from the secular realm of "human" life and politics into the sacred sphere of "divine politics" and the "kingdom of God." The latter is inhabited by human subjects, as he put it, "feigned to be animated, inhabited, or possessed" by "innumerable sorts of Gods" as the "creatures" of their "innumerable variety of Fancy", thus effectively vanquishing civil society as he conceived it.

More specifically, the civic subsystem of Calvinist theocracy as a total social system, including an equivalent civil society, alongside an economy, polity, and culture, is what Weber identifies as the moralistic "tyranny of Puritanism" as Anglo-Saxon Calvinism. Consequently or eventually, it is moral fascism in the broad sense of moralistic absolutism and authoritarianism or totalitarianism as the denial and destruction of individual liberty or choice and responsibility in morality and private life overall. At this juncture, moral fascism in Puritan societies, primarily America and in part England, originates and operates as the reenacted and readapted form of the moralistic tyranny of Puritanism and thus as the present and future (un)civil society or societal community of Calvinist theocracy after the image of a "Biblical Garden" as a holistic category.

Alternatively, Calvinist, especially Puritan, theocracy as a total social system generates, predicts, and incorporates moral fascism as its characteristic ethical logic and its civic subsystem, just as Calvinism and Puritanism entail or produce Bibliocracy. In this sense, Calvinism, notably Puritanism, eventually develops in or amounts to moral fascism thus understood through Puritan moralistic theocracy. For instance, recall that Comte characterizes Calvinism as the moralistic repressive "reign of Saints", and in that sense as the archetype or minimally anticipation of moral fascism precisely characterized by the fact that its leaders and most fascists act as or claim to be saints or purists in morality and ascetics. In doing so, Comte perhaps had in mind Calvinists in his France and beyond, with their "strong notion of election" and consequently their claimed formation of and belonging to the "community of the saints" (Mentzer 2007).

In particular, the above holds true of the Calvinist Anglo-Saxon derivative, Puritanism, as implicit in Hume's and Weber's observations about the English Puritan Parliament comprised of self-proclaimed one hundred-odd moralistic "divines" or "saints" exemplified by Cromwell et al. Also, J. S. Mill describes Calvinists and Puritans, including early Methodists, as "intrusively pious members of society" and in that sense moral arch-fascists. For what defines or typifies the latter is precisely their intrusion and control of others' individual morality, privacy, and life, notably the obsession with and severe punishment of human sins and vices. At this juncture, the "obsession with sin and vice" and their Draconian punishment, as observed for the old and ever-renewed moralistic "politics of Puritanism" in America (Wagner 1997), redefines US Puritans and their fundamentalist revivals as moral proto- and neo-fascists, respectively.

Significantly, Weber defines Calvinist Biblical theocracy in terms of ascetic mastery of or domination over the "sinful world" of "mundane affairs" by "religious virtuosi" forming the "pure" church or sect (Symonds and Pudsey 2006), as in Puritanism, with "authoritarian moral discipline" and in that sense moralistic tyranny or moralizing proto-fascism.[1] Moreover, recall that he describes the "rule of Calvinism" as the "most absolutely unbearable" and imaginable type of "ecclesiastical" control of individuals such that a "more intensive form" of the religious restraint and sanctioning of moral conduct "has perhaps never existed" and in that sense the supreme form of absolute moralistic repression precisely defining fascism in terms of morality.

Also, elaborating on or evoking Weber, contemporary sociological analyses suggest that, while the Protestant Reformation as a whole aimed at a "stronger ethical penetration of the world" against "too lax" Catholicism, only Calvinism in (implicitly) Holland and its Puritan sects in England and America fully realized that aim. They did so by the "radical elimination of any distinction" between the ethics of the priesthood and of laymen, in contrast with Lutheranism as well as Anglicanism (Munch 1981) as, in Weber's view, the least ascetic and moralistic branches of Protestantism.[2] At this juncture, the Calvinist-Puritan "radical elimination" of the distinction between these two ethics can be taken as the "proof" or syndrome of moral fascism, since (if) the latter is exactly characterized by ethical radicalism. This has been evidenced by Catholic-based fascism in interwar Italy, Spain, Portugal, Croatia, and other Vatican-supported countries and in post-communist Poland, as well as less "godly" but also moralistic Nazism, and neo-fascism in Europe and especially America (neo-Nazi "Christian" militia), just as various fascist substitutes or proxies in fundamentalist Islam like Iranian and Saudi hyper-moralistic theocracies.

Moreover, in this account Puritan sects and denominations in America "reinvented" and surpassed Calvinism in collective moral control and coercion over individuals through the "tight binding" of the latter to the group *cum* sect by means of its approval (Munch 1981) to a degree that was unprecedented even in the "extended" Calvinist family. This reaffirms that Puritanism has been, and remains via its evangelical revivals, hyper-Calvinism in the "new nation", and US Puritans have been "all-American" super-Calvinists ("super-men") with respect to sectarianism, anti-individualism, or "iron collectivism"

---

[1] Simmel also identifies theocratic or moralistic tendencies in Calvinism registering that unlike that in Catholicism, the Calvinist and other Protestant clergy "as a matter of principle is entirely enmeshed in civil life".

[2] Weber states that Calvinism and Puritanism or "the ascetic varieties of Protestantism have prevailed wherever the citizen was a social power, and the least ascetic churches of the Reformation, Anglicanism and Lutheranism, wherever the nobility or the princes had the upper hand."

(Tawney 1962), like other respects, in spite or perhaps because of Parsons' extolled Puritan theological individualism through individuals' "immediacy" to the God of Calvinism. Alternatively, it contradicts claimed and celebrated Puritan-American "universalistic", "individualist", and "libertarian" exceptionalism *cum* novelty, originality, and superiority in relation to the "old" and disdained Europe (Lipset and Marks 2000). Rather, it effectively reveals this exceptionalism as an exception or deviation in this and related terms like liberalism, secularism, and rationalism in modern Western and global society (Inglehart 2004).

In particular, Calvinism, including Puritanism, originated and functioned as moralistic despotism with medievalist roots and aims and to that extent as the prototype of moral fascism. As sociological analyses suggest, the Calvinist revolution in Europe and via, Puritan revolutions, in England and America, and even the Protestant Reformation as a whole, originally purported to reestablish a "purer" medievalist social and religious regime rather than being a "modernizing" movement (Eisenstadt 1965). This is what the term "Puritanism" signifying or claiming purity implies—a sort of "purism" in medieval-style or primitive "godly" politics, morality (austerity), and religion (fundamentalism), by being "purer" than any Christian religion and Christians had ever been during medievalism and before, a final return to the "pure church." At this juncture, Calvinism was, as Sombart put it, just "Puritanism" in the general sense of "purism" or "purity" in medievalist and generally primitive politics, religion, and morality, to be distinguished from its specific meaning as Calvinist sectarianism and moralist absolutism adopted in this work.

By implication, Calvinism, including Puritanism, via its revolutions especially attempted to reinstitute a purer, specifically more disciplinarian, ascetic, controlling, or coercive (Gorski 2003; Loveman 2005), medievalist moralistic theocracy *cum* a "godly" society (the *civitas Dei*). As noted, this is what precisely Calvin and his disciples attempted and failed in both France and Germany, while they succeeded to achieve in Geneva, Holland and, via Cromwell and Winthrop et al., in Great Britain and New England, respectively. In this respect, recall Weber's observation that the medieval-style theocratic "rule of Calvinism" was established in "the sixteenth century in Geneva and in Scotland, at the turn of the sixteenth and seventeenth centuries in large parts of the Netherlands, in the seventeenth in New England, and for a time in England itself". Of course, Calvinism established its theocratic rule in the last two cases (and Scotland) through the agency of Puritanism as its agent in Anglo-American societies. Notably, in early America local sectarian Puritanism reportedly subjected individuals to as strict "moral control" as that by the condemned centralized Roman Church, with the result of true individual liberty being "nonexistent" (Stivers 1994). In that sense, Puritanism in America functioned as a moralistic proto-fascism, just as had Calvinism in Europe before, and in extension its supreme enemy and rival, the Vatican church-state and its "holy" Inquisition during medieval times. If what precisely defines moral fascism is such moralistic control and repression of individuals by church or state (rather both) and the non-existence of individual moral and other civil liberty, then Puritanism substantively operated as or prefigured such a fascist force, as do its evangelicals revivals or survivals ("Christian" neo-Nazi movements, etc.) in America during the 21st century.

To that extent, Puritanism and in extension Calvinism, did not really rediscover America. It only substituted one type of medieval social order, notably moral control and repression for another—the Puritan-Calvinist for the Catholic-old Christian—and even perhaps, figuratively at least, of Inquisition, as Weber and Tawney suggest and "Salem with witches" in New England's "Biblical Commonwealth" and "Monkey Trials" in the "Bible Garden" indicate. For instance, New England's Puritan legal-penal code admittedly shared more of the medievalist "continental inquisitorial approach" than of English common law, acting on its sacred aim of eradicating and punishing "all sin" and demanding "repentance from the malefactor", through the "broad powers" of magistrates to eradicate "ungodliness"[3] (Dayton 1999). This reflected the fact that Puritanism was transplanted European Calvinism in contrast and opposition to Anglicanism. From Calvin's recreation of the *civitas Dei* in 16th century Geneva through the 17th century Puritan "Biblical Commonwealths" in old and New England to the evangelical "Bible Garden" in 21st century America, this "new" medievalist social order was even "purer", more moralizing,[4] in the form of what Hume calls "pretension", "cant and hypocrisy" that pervaded Puritanism,

---

[3] Dayton (1999:32) refers to New Haven as "the most Puritan of the New England colonies", in which, like in Massachusetts, "only men who were full church members could vote for civil magistrates or hold office."

[4] For instance, Simmel observes that a "corporal in Cromwell's [Puritan] army, who was well versed in the Bible, could deliver a moralizing sermon to his major".

restraining, and destructive of individual moral liberty, than the old Catholic or early Christian.

In this respect, such a remarkable "purity" or "perfection" in the moralistic medievalist control and repression of individuals objectively redefined and revealed Calvinism, especially American Puritanism, as prototypical or extant and proxy moral fascism before modern fascism. At this juncture, if American Puritanism was really, as it claimed, supreme purity or purism in austere morality and primitive religion and church (evangelicalism), as in "godly" politics, it was particularly in Calvinist moralizing fascism. If anything was "pure" or "purism" in "Puritanism", it was, apart from and yet mixed with what Weber calls Puritan "pure hypocrisy" (Bremer 1995), "pure" moral proto-fascism via the methodical moralistic suppression of individual freedom in morality and all private life on the ground of recreating a "purer" medieval-style "godly" society. Conversely, fascism (and communism) is typically moral purism and in that sense "Puritanism", and most fascists (and communists) act as moralistic purists, thus "Puritans", with secondary exceptions like seemingly less moralistic and "godly" Nazism than other fascist types or proxies (Italian, Spanish, Polish, and similar Catholic-based fascisms, Islamic and Hindu theocracies).

In short, Calvinism, especially Puritanism, tends to be proto-fascist in moral or civic, if not political, terms, just as fascism to be morally neo-Calvinist or neo-Puritan. This implies what Weber and Parsons may describe as an "elective affinity" or "convergence" between Calvinism, notably Puritanism, and fascism in the moralistic constraint and destruction of individual liberty in morality and private life, including sadistic cruelty, brutality, and inhumanity (Adorno 2001; Birnbaum 1953; McLaughlin 1996). In this sense, Calvinist theocracy as a holistic social system or design logically requires and invariably or eventually yields moral fascism as the destructive antithesis or degenerate type of civil society or life-world, and its proper uncivil and anti-life subsystem. The point is that moral fascism constitutes the systematic and permanent, rather than random and temporary, form that civil society or the life-world through a kind of self-destruction or self-degeneration assumes within Calvinist theocracy in America and elsewhere. It is therefore intrinsic (built-in), not extrinsic, to Calvinism, notably Puritanism as a paradigmatic theocratic, sectarian and moralistic religion. In sum, Puritan-grounded moral fascism in America functions as the reenacted moralistic tyranny of Puritanism and thus the antithesis of a free civil society or life-world, and the inherent logic and integral element of Calvinist theocracy as a holistic entity. Conversely, the moralistic tyranny of Puritanism perpetuates or revives itself, and thus Calvinist theocracy exemplifies or expresses itself, via Puritan moral fascism as the moralizing, "godly" destruction or perversion of liberal-secular civil society, notably individual freedom in morality.

*Rediscovering and Redefining Moral Fascism*

The preceding intimates the defining and constitutive elements of moral fascism. In general, it indicates that moral fascism is the specific authoritarian or rather totalitarian, thus degenerate and antithetical form of civil society or societal community in the sense of the autonomous private "life-world" (Habermas 2001) within Calvinist-as-Puritan theocracy in America and elsewhere. Hence, moral fascism is "fascism" in the realm of individual *moral* freedom, choice, and privacy defining civil society or the life-world. This is precisely what is "moral" about moral fascism, not as Puritan and other (Catholic and Islamic) theocrats claim, its "pure", "superior" morality or ethics. First and foremost, no fascism can be or has been considered "moral" in the sense of the liberal-secular ethics of modern civil society, notably the Kantian ethical system placing humans in the "kingdom of ends" (Habermas 2001), not the Machiavellian-utilitarian and religious field of efficient means to other aims, including Parsons' "purposes of God". In view of this ethics (as well as the Christian "golden rule"), the term "anti-moral" or "immoral" fascism is substantively more accurate and appropriate. Still, for conventional reasons and convenience, "moral fascism" is used in the above sense and by analogy to similar terms (e.g., moral-cultural wars, civil war). Positively, "moral fascism" is specifically used and understood as moralistic, moralizing fascism or fascist moralism to indicate and emphasize its contradiction with and degeneration of the liberal-secular (moderate and tolerant) ethics of modern civil society, even some Biblical ethical principles ("moralizing" or "moralism" as absolutist and intolerant versus "Let the one among you who is without sin be the first to throw a stone" on the sinner).

This reintroduces the concept of moral fascism redefined and understood as moralistic absolutism and tyranny or despotism, thus authoritarianism or totalitarianism as a "collapse of the distinction between the state and civil society" in its "classic definition" (Simon 1995). To use Schumpeter's description of modern capitalism, moral fascism operates as the process of "creative destruction" in civil society. It does through destroying human liberty and dignity and ultimately life in the realm of individual morality and privacy, and creating, more specifically restoring from the "golden past" or "paradise lost", unfreedom, humiliation[5] ("humility"), and death, as via the penal system and "holy" wars, in this sphere and the total social system overall. Hence, from the prism of a free civil society and liberal-secular democracy, instead it functions as the process of *un*creative, nihilistic destruction. It does so in that, in contrast to capitalism in Schumpeter's scenario, moral fascism ultimately destroys the "old" civic and political structures and symbols of liberty, choice, and privacy, a destruction rationalized as moralizing, "godly" anti-liberalism and conservatism, especially in America during the 1980s–2000s.

However, invariably moral fascism does not create substantively new social structures by instead restoring even the older institutions and signs of illiberty (Dahrendorf 1979), oppression, and inhumanity from Mannheim's "presumed dead" past. These restored structures specifically involve theocratic medievalism (New England's "Biblical Commonwealth", Europe's *respublica Christiana*) and despotic traditionalism generally. On this account, it is more accurately deemed and described as "anti-moral", "immoral", or "amoral" fascism. For the Schumpeterian inverted, nihilistic destruction of moral and all human freedom and ultimately life, and the recreation of unfreedom and death, is the supreme and ultimate act of immorality and inhumanity from the prism of a free civil society and liberal-secular democracy, notably Kantian ethics, as well as the Christian and any religious golden rule and what Weber identifies as the primeval social "ethic of brotherhood" (Symonds and Pudsey 2006). In essence, "moral" fascism is supremely immoral or amoral, because, as even conservative Hayek (1960) states in a Kantian vein (Caldwell 1997), moral virtue or ethic is meaningless and non-existent without universal liberty in morality[6] (Angel 1994), including freedom of choice between "virtue" and "vice" (Van Dyke 1995). In sum, moral fascism constitutes the total control and the tyrannical destruction or suppression of individual liberty and responsibility

---

[5] Simmel remarks that Puritan and any other asceticism involves the "pleasure of self-humiliation".

[6] Angel (1994:26) suggests that "if there is no possibility of free choice, then the sphere in which ethics and values are to arise suddenly disappears."

in morality and private life, simply moralistic dictatorship or totalitarianism religiously grounded.

And, probably no form of social control and tyranny or despotism is more moralistic than that of Calvinism, notably Puritanism as axiomatic moral absolutism *cum* purism (Munch 2001) or extreme moralism in Protestantism and Christianity (alongside in part monastic Catholicism) and even among world religions, together with probably Islam and Hinduism. As noted, while the Protestant Reformation as a whole attempted a stronger moral control ("ethical penetration") of society than had late medieval Catholicism, it was "only" Calvinism and its "Puritan sects and denominations" in Holland, England, and America that realized, in contrast to Lutheranism, the "radical elimination of any distinction" between the ethics for priests and for laymen (Munch 1981). Predictably, this elimination expressing moralizing Calvinism or "Calvinist moralism" (Murdock 2005) involved imposing the ethics of Hume-Comte's divines and saints or Marx-Weber's religious or sectarian virtuosi on humans forced into moral sanctification or "rebirth", as the initial step to or the key sign of moralistic theocratic tyranny, thus moral fascism as defined.

In particular, what Weber and Ross identify and describe as the tyranny of Puritanism, in virtue of the latter being self-designated supreme and paradigmatic Calvinist moral absolutism *cum* purism and perfectionism, was axiomatically and extremely moralistic. Moreover, Weber characterizes Puritan moralistic tyranny as no less than "unexampled" within Protestantism and even Christianity as a whole. Hence, Calvinist, notably Puritan, moralistic control and tyranny substantively functions as or prefigures moral fascism. If moral fascism constitutes the system and process of reproduction of unfreedom through the destruction of freedom or human agency (Barnes 2000) in individual morality, thus the polar opposite of a free civil society and liberal-secular democracy, then Puritan moralistic tyranny acts as its substantive equivalent or precursor.

In essence, moral fascism is the realization, expression (release), and rationalization of the fear, hatred, and disdain for individual liberty, choice, and responsibility, or human agency, in morality and private life. This is the kind of negativism pervasive in Calvinism, especially Puritanism, and various other theocratic, moralizing, and ascetic religions, including monastic Catholicism, Islam, and Hinduism. While not all forms of totalitarian social control or tyranny are moral fascism, but also non-moralistic, that of Calvinism, in particular Puritanism, invariably is, inhering to its moralistic absolutism or extremism couched and rationalized as ethical purism and perfectionism (Munch 2001; Wagner 1997). Further, even if not all types of fascism are entirely and explicitly moralistic (as in part shown by Nazism), the fascist type characteristic for Puritanism and Calvinism in general is necessarily and axiomatically so, given what has been observed as inherent, rigid, and uncompromising Puritan moral, just as political (Blomberg and Harrington 2000), absolutism or ethical extremism. Thus, what analysts identify and describe as "friendly fascism" (Bonefeld 2002; Gross 1980) in contemporary America (and "benevolent feudalism" before) is primarily Puritan and conservative overall in origin and operation or style and hence moralistic fascism or totalitarianism (and feudalism).

As a corollary of the preceding, moral fascism can be redefined and reconsidered in terms of destruction or subversion of private morality and life, or simply privacy. Thus, Puritan moral fascism is a social system which destroys or suppresses private morality, responsibility, and life subordinated and ultimately sacrificed to what Mannheim describes as a pre-determined "moral code" codified and coercively imposed by theocratic Puritanism and Calvinism overall (Munch 1981; Stivers 1994; Walzer 1963). In short, it is (un)civil society in which effectively there is no such thing as private morality and life, or simply privacy, just as no "free lunch" in a Calvinist master-servant, pro-capital/anti-labor capitalist economy. Practically, Puritan moral fascism is a type of moralistic, religiously based code and social structure that commands "thou shall do or shall not do this" in personal morality and private life to the greatest particulars. For instance, it commands to humans *what* beverages and foods (not) to drink and eat, medicines and other chemical substances (not) to use, books and other literature (not) to read and write, music, radio, and television programs (not) to listen to and watch, Internet content[7] (not) to search for, intimate

---

[7] For instance, during the 2000s the US neoconservative government is virtually the only one to prohibit Internet (online) gambling on, as typical, puritanical grounds, among modern Western democracies, including Japan. In turn, the European Union, Japan and Canada filed a complaint against the US government's ban on online gambling as an illegal restraint on "free trade" with the World Trade Organization (WTO). In 2007, the US government reportedly agreed to compensate these countries to settle the dispute within the WTO, while not revoking its ban on the "sin" of online gambling. Apparently, in the long-standing Puritan tradition, the US neoconservative government is more ready and willing to pay even "big" (ultimately taxpayers') money to compensate other governments for its illegal repressive actions rather than revoke or repent its prohibitions of such "sins" or vices".

behaviors and partners (not) to have, "what (not) to do" virtually everything else "under the sun".

And, far from making "practical jokes", Puritan moral fascism, especially in America, notably its "Bible Garden", condemns and punishes violations of these commandments typically with primitive Draconian harshness (Patell 2001), including mass long imprisonment ("three strikes" laws, etc.) and even actually or potentially the death penalty (e.g., drug "marketing"). These punishments are religiously grounded and sanctified in a fundamentalist severe, "tough on crime" system of incarceration and executions. Thus, Puritan, like all, moral fascism is "telling" humans what is good" and "bad" for them (Friedman and Friedman 1982) to do, or else, to the point of their physical sacrifice, as via executions and "holy" wars, for Divine "glory", or at least, in Parsons' words, their "usefulness" to the "purposes of God" as supposedly revealed to or miraculously deciphered by Calvinist theologians and theocrats since Calvin.

For illustration, it is almost unbelievable that Puritan moral fascism in America prohibits and severely punish the free use ("abuse") of prescription and even some "over the counter" medicine (e.g., pain medications) equated with and punished as illegal "drugs", dictating that "thou shall or shall not take this and that" in health care and private life. Alternatively, if anything, such interfering with not only individual moral freedom and privacy but also human health and life define these Puritan practices as instances and syndromes of moralistic fascism as well as anti-humanism. In comparative terms, among modern Western societies, no society so comprehensively prohibits or restricts and severely punishes the free use of legal medical (not to mention illegal harmful) drugs or medications than does Puritan moral fascism in America. At least, such prohibitions and restrictions on moralistic grounds—essentially, preventing humans from having "forbidden" and any pleasures or happiness even in protecting and improving their health—precisely indicates what is "fascist" about Puritan "moral fascism" in America, as Pareto and Mencken (1982) observed and would expect. Mencken (1982) defined American Puritanism as the "haunting fear that someone, somewhere, may be happy" as an "ungodly" human state.

Alternatively, Puritan moral fascism leaves almost nothing, with some minor elemental exceptions, to individual free agency, choice, and responsibility in private morality and life, and consequently of a free civil society and eventually liberal-secular democracy. Hence, humans are instead left with what Parsons et al. extol as their "immediacy to God" as a supreme reward and freedom. Rather, it is what Simmel calls a "compensatory substitute" for this loss of moral and other civil liberties, thus a kind of "consolation prize" or forced "game of solitary" in the form of what Weber identifies as "a feeling of unprecedented inner loneliness of the single individual" in Calvinism. In doing so, Puritan moral fascism effectively destroys or degenerates moral or civic individualism while recreating its theological-religious version a la Schumpeter. At this juncture, Parsons et al. seem able or wiling to identify only the second outcome, not the first, and failing to realize that what they celebrate as individuals' "immediacy to God" in Calvinism and Puritanism versus Catholicism is neither a necessary nor a sufficient condition of individual and political liberty. Also, they fail to recognize that such theological "immediacy" or individualism results in what Weber identified as the "feeling of unprecedented inner loneliness of the single individual". As regards the latter, Calvinism, notably Puritanism, evinces its "iron consistency" or "method in the madness", because the forced or induced "inner loneliness" of humans is the prerequisite *and* the instrument and outcome alike of tyranny or totalitarianism, as especially witnessed in Nazism (Adorno 2001; Arendt 1951, Bähr 2002; Fromm 1941).

Consequently, what Parsons et al. extol as individuals' "immediacy to God" exhibiting religious individualism in Calvinism, in particular Puritanism, may generate and sustain, via the "unprecedented inner loneliness" of the individual, tyrannical collectivism or totalitarianism in the form of Puritan moralizing fascism rather than, as they assume, political individualism and freedom, or democracy. In a proxy calculation of spiritual or symbolic (not economic) costs and benefits (Bourdieu 1988), the opportunity cost (trade-off) or price that individuals in a Puritan (un)civil society as "godly community" incur or pay for the benefit of promised heaven (Lemert 1999) through their "immediacy to God" is a sort of "hell in this world" (Tawney 1962) in the form of moral fascism. It is thus the loss of detested liberal hope (Lemert 1999) as an "ungodly" utopia, including "unprecedented inner loneliness".

In essence, Puritan moral fascism acts as the systematic commandment of considering and eventually converting humans into unfree sub-humans, thus denying and eliminating them as Kant's free, responsible, and mature agents in personal morality and civil society as a whole (Beck 2000; Bauman 2001; Habermas 2001). It does in that humans, except for Puritan masters or guardians, in moral fascism are denied and deprived of, or not to be entrusted with, individual moral liberty or choice, responsibility and maturity, even elemental (especially intimate) privacy. Instead, humans are subordinated and ultimately sacrificed to "higher" transcendental causes and forces a la the glory and purpose of Weber's God of Calvinism, in particular Puritanism.

In a way, Calvinist-as-Puritan, like any (notably Islamic), moralizing fascism constitutes a degenerate civic sphere after the model or image of civil society as a massive open prison and total domination premised on "the art of governing men"[8] (Foucault 1996). This is a civil society in which everyone, save for masters-saints, is actual or potential sinner *cum* criminal and thus prisoner, or (as Pareto and Weber imply) a coercive hyper-ascetic monastic order where humans are forced to be monks during their entire lives. In this sense, Puritan (and any) moral fascism is a sort of adapted slavery or bondage in the realm of individual morality and private life, with Calvinist (and other) saints acting as moralizing masters, and humans treated as "sinful" servants confined within an open and eventually a genuine prison. The latter is testified by the fact that most (two thirds) of nearly 2.5 millions of prisoners in America during the 2000s are immoral sinners, such as nonviolent drug users and other victims of temperance and culture wars, thus basically innocent prisoners of ethical conscience, under Puritan-inspired "reborn" conservatism. Analogously, moral fascism constitutes the realization and expression of the original Calvinist (Mansbach 2006), especially Puritan (Walzer 1963; Zaret 1989), theocratic fear, distrust, hatred, and eventual elimination of free private morality and life, simply moral liberty and privacy.

In general, moral fascism can be defined in terms of moral-religious conservatism as its invariant source and broader framework or extended family. In these terms, moral fascism is an extreme, ultimate creation, element, or version of moral-religious conservatism (Bendix 1984; Dahrendorf 1979; Moore 1993), Calvinist or other (Catholic, Islamic,

---

[8] In general, Foucault (1996:383–4) registers an "expansion into civil society" of the "art of governing men and the methods for doing it" from "monastic existence" during the time of and even prior to the Reformation.

Hindu, etc.). Hence, moral fascism is invariably conservative (Blinkhorn 2003), "right" moralistic totalitarianism (Giddens 1979; also, Plotke 2002). And, Calvinism, including Puritanism, is a paradigmatic exemplar of moral-religious as well as political and societal conservatism (Heller 1986) within Protestantism, as discussed later. In this sense, Calvinism, notably Puritanism, functions as or prefigures moral fascism precisely because it is paradigmatically strict moral-religious and other conservatism. Even if granting that not all types of moral-religious conservatism generate moral fascism, the Calvinist (like Islamic) type invariably does, consequent to the ethical radicalism or moralism of Calvinism, notably the moralistic "purism" or "perfectionism" of Puritanism (and Islam).

Conversely, fascism is a sort of puritanical in the sense of purist or austere, moralism or moralizing, just as Puritan moralistic absolutism operates as arch-fascism involving "holy terror" (Walzer 1963; Zaret 1989) and lethal violence due to the tendency or potential of any absolutist religion or ideology for being "deadly"[9] (Linton 2001). In a way, all fascism is moralistic, more (Catholic-based fascisms in Italy, Spain, Poland, etc.) or less (Nazism), as is communism[10] (Wallerstein and Zukin 1989), though also some (Soviet and Chinese) more than other (Eastern European, like Yugoslavian) communisms. However, it is American Puritan-rooted fascism (e.g., fundamentalist "Christian" neo-Nazism) that has become and remains the model or champion of moralizing among various fascisms, due to Puritanism being paradigmatic moral absolutism and "unexampled" moralistic tyranny within Calvinism and its inner moralism. Alternatively, Puritan moralistic absolutism or tyranny is axiomatic (by assumption) moral proto-fascism prior to and along with fascism proper like interwar Nazism and postwar neo-fascism, respectively.

---

[9] Linton (2001:5) observes that generally "employment of moral absolutes in political rhetoric will necessarily result in the use of violence against those whose moral and political allegiances differ from those of the dominant political group". Thus, Linton (2001:209) emphasizes the "terrible power of a language of moral politics, its capacity to bring power to those who defined themselves as "moral" and to destroy those deemed the enemies of virtue", as epitomized in Puritan and other moralistic tyranny or proto-fascism.

[10] Walzer (1963:86) remarks that just as Calvinism "vigorously attacked Renaissance experimentation in dress and in all the arts of self-decoration [so Lenin was] preaching with all the energy of a secular Calvinist against free love [as] 'bourgeois' [and] 'decay'."

## Syndromes of Puritan Moral Fascism

### Denial and Suppression of Individual Moral Freedom

An exact "proof" or pathological syndrome of Puritan moral fascism is denying and suppressing the individual freedom of choice between alternative courses of action, consequently of personal responsibility, in the sphere of morality. In short, it is "holy" war on and the elimination of the "evil" of individual moral freedom, the "agony of choice" in personal morality (Bauman 2001).

Like other fascisms, Puritan moral fascism is a sort of negativism or antagonism and ultimately nihilism against human liberty and eventually life, in particular individual freedom, choice, and responsibility in the realm of morality. It is negative or antagonistic and ultimately destructive to human liberty, notably the individual freedom of choice between morally right and wrong behavior, especially virtues and vices or sins, and thus personal agency and responsibility or maturity in the sphere of morality. Puritan moral fascism negates that human liberty comprises what Hayek's (1960) call the "freedom to act wrongly" in individual morality and private life, as the requirement of moral virtue or merit. Conversely, it denies that moral virtue is "meaningless" without such freedom thus denied and lost or restrained, the result of such loss being performing the "right thing for the wrong reasons" (Fitzpatrick 1999). It simply negates or overlooks that, as Montesquieu and other Enlightenment writers such as Kant and Hume suggested long ago, "only unconstrained acts can count as virtuous: actions performed out of fear of punishment or hope of reward are not meritorious" (Kenshur 1993). Alternatively, the Enlightenment was a "moralizing force" or "fundamentally ethical" (Fitzpatrick 1999), predicated on the concept of both private and public virtue (Linton 2001), primarily because it acted as a liberalizing or liberal-democratic movement, emphasizing the freedom and right of moral and religious conscience, and advocating tolerance in religion and civil society overall (Garrard 2003).

In so doing, like all moral fascism, its Puritan version destroys or subverts a free, liberal-secular civil society precisely defined by the individual freedom of choice between right and wrong action in ethical and related terms. A true or liberal-secular civil society thus becomes a non-entity or taboo ("forbidden apple") within the total social system of Calvinist theocracy in America due to Puritan moralistic tyranny methodically denying and destroying Montesquieu's "unconstrained acts" as "virtuous", or alternatively the "freedom to act wrongly", from the 17th to the 21st century. Puritanism thereby functions as or approaches and prefigures moral fascism.

As a special predictable facet of its negation and destruction of individual liberties with respect to morally right and wrong actions, Puritan moral fascism negates and eliminates the freedom of choice between "virtue and vice" (Van Dyke 1995), sinless conduct and sin. In its own terms, it denies to humans the freedom to choose between being "saints" and "sinners", and thus it abolishes what is seemingly a perennial, proverbial, or metaphorical moral dichotomy in virtually all known societies and times, including those Christian. It does so through (in Weber's words) the Calvinist, especially Puritan (e.g., Methodist), methodical doctrine and practice of, frequently sadistic-masochistic, sanctification that transforms society in a super-monastic order or massive open prison, and humans into permanent monks or potential "sinful" criminals ruled and severely punished for their sins equated with crimes by self-proclaimed saints-masters and Divine agents. Moreover, in so doing, Puritan moral fascism self-contradicts Calvinist putative evangelicalism, invidiously distinguished from non-evangelical pre-Calvinism like traditional Catholicism, specifically the Biblical tolerance or forgiveness of sins ("who has not sinned"), thus implicitly the freedom of choice between sinless conduct and sin, virtues and vices.

No wonder, not only non-Calvinists (Catholics, Lutherans, Anglicans), but many social analysts, including Hume, Comte, Weber, Tawney, and others imply that Calvinism, including Puritanism, is not, contrary to its opposite claims, truly (if at all) Christian, let alone liberal. So do even some disenchanted Calvinists like Franklin (and Servetus) experiencing it as "inimical to morality" (Byrne 1997) and in that sense effectively anti-Christian and anti-human. This is due to the Calvinist-Puritan observed reversal of traditional Christian moral values and sanctions, notably forgiveness for human sins and understanding and compassion replaced by intolerance, impatience, and inhumane punishment, including the death penalty, and to the predestination dogma reversing by its narrow "heavenly" oligarchy original Christianity as the universalistic religion of salvation "for all". Simply, there is no such thing as the freedom of choice between virtue and vice, "saints and sinners", in Puritan moral fascism as the (un)civil society of Calvinist theocracy in America, just as by analogy or substantive association "no free lunch" in its master-servant, anti-labor economy. In a way, as a sociological analysis suggests, Puritan moral fascism, like all sectarianism, aims to divide "saints and sinners" (Zaret 1989) and then punish the latter with Draconian severity, including death and minimally exclusion, thus actually denying them the freedom of choice between moral virtue and vice, sainthood and sin.

As implied, by negating and destroying the individual freedom of choice between virtue and vice or generally morally right and wrong actions, Puritan moral fascism denies and destroys personal agency and responsibility, thus human decision and maturity in the domain of morality. Conversely, the latter results in and reinforces the former. In other words, that humans possess a capability for "moral judgment" in the sense of differentiating between "good and bad" or "right and wrong" (Van Dyke 1995) is a non sequitur and equivalent to taboo in Puritan moral fascism. The latter instead attributes such moral capabilities only to supra-humans, specifically the God of Calvinism and his self-proclaimed agents with "Divine" rights to rule. Consequently, such supra-humans, specifically Calvinist-Puritan saints-masters, expropriate and monopolize this "Divine" capacity—like other life chances or economic and political opportunities—for moral judgment and chose for and impose on humans what is "good and bad, right and wrong."

In a sense, Calvinist saints-masters treat humans as immature adults in moral terms, thus effectively reduce them to sorts of permanent children in morality kept, as Tocqueville himself observed for New England's Puritan rulers, in the state of "perpetual childhood". These masters do so through self-perpetuating Puritan temperance wars against and obsessions with "vice and sin" (Wagner 1997), from "Salem with witches" through Prohibition to the war on drugs (plus "dry" Southern counties, the increased legal limit for alcohol consumption, etc.). Hence, like all theocrats and totalitarians in general (e.g., Nazis), they seek to remake human nature after the image of Puritan saints or angels. They attempt to transform humans *cum* "perpetual children" morally speaking into, as Weber and Pareto observe, monks for life. Alternatively, they convert humans into actual or potential criminals to be harshly sanctioned either for real or imagined sins and pleasures *cum* crimes, and constantly punished for "original sin" that they actually did not commit, thus via a sort of collective "eternal punishment"

(Schmidt 1996) and by association in their "utter depravity as the offspring of Adam and Eve"[11] (Byrne 1997). In sum, these Puritan saints-masters force and confine humans without their free consent into a super-monastery and/or a massive open prison, thus effectively reducing them to children or mental patients, and acting, as either original or "reborn" Puritans, as proto- or neo-fascists, respectively.

The Puritan, just as the fascist, denial and destruction of the human capability for a moral judgment between "good and bad", "right and wrong" is rooted in and explained by, and thus reflects, anti-humanism and (contrary to Weber-Parsons' rationalist accounts) anti-rationalism or religious irrationalism (Grossman 2006) in Calvinism, especially American Puritanism (Harley 1996). As Hume observed and sociologists suggest (Becker 1984; Goldstone 2000; Grossman 2006), this is manifested in the Puritan fear, hostility, or suspicion vis-à-vis *human* reason, rationality, progress, including secular science and learning, and humans as "sinful" and "evil" owing to their "original sin" in favor of and subordination and ultimate sacrifice to supra-human intelligence like Providential Design (Bendix 1984). On this account, such Puritan negativism and nihilism is anti-human and ethically irrational, just as anti-liberal. It is hence immoral in its own right ("non-Puritan" in a general meaning), for what Hayek calls moral merit or esteem, including complete "purity" or sainthood, is "meaningless" without freedom in morality. And, what defines and identifies moral fascism in general is the Puritan-style negativism and nihilism to the human capacity for judgment, agency, and responsibility in morality. This confirms that Puritanism invariably functioned as proto-fascism and still does, via "reborn" fundamentalism, as neo-fascism in ethical and related terms.

In general, Puritan moral fascism negates and eventually destroys individual agency and responsibility or decision-making, and maturity in morality for primarily anti- and supra-human and ethically irrational causes. It does so by sacrificing such human attributes and humans to the glory and purpose of the God of Calvinism, in reality to self-assigned Puritan "godly" agents or vice-regents (Zaret 1989) with Divine rights to rule and punish, including execute, them for their sins-as-crimes and in extension "original sin" subject to "eternal

---

[11] Byrne (1997:130) adds that for the Enlightenment "humanity was characterized by the dignity bestowed by reason and the doctrine of original sin was an affront to this dignity."

punishment" due to their "utter depravity". In short, Puritan moral fascism denies that humans (minus saints-masters) are free, active, responsible, or mature moral agents. It reduces them into immature adults or permanent children to be subjected to constant control, supervision, repression, and, if sinful or non-virtuous equated to criminal, Draconian punishment either effectively inflicted or on "stand-by" for their "original sin",[12] as contemporary Puritan apologists advocate (Seaton 2006). Consequently, like all fascism, its Puritan variant attacks and destroys civil society as an "association of equal, free, and accordingly responsible individuals" (Manent 1998).

And, this Puritan denial and suppression of individual free agency and responsibility in morality is the underlying factor and explanation of why a true, liberal civil society tends to be a non-entity or meaningless within Calvinist evangelical theocracy as the total social system in America, from New England's to the Southern "Bible Commonwealths". In a way, the reason for the death or impossibility of liberal civil society in a Calvinist (or any) theocracy is that Puritan moral fascism in America purports or claims to "save" humans from their own "moral mistakes" (Terchek 1997), especially immoral sins as defined by Puritanism and Calvinism overall with its moralism. In so doing, Puritan moral fascism assumes that humans are unable, incompetent, or immature to decide for themselves which of their actions are "moral mistakes", including sins, and which not. It hence denies them the freedom and capability of deciding between morally "wrong" and "right" conduct and taking the personal responsibility for such decisions. In the process, Puritan moral fascism ultimately destroys or perverts beyond recognition a free civil society in which moral virtue is only possible and meaningful through individual freedom and responsibility in morality, and even human life, as Pareto suggests in portraying US puritanical fanatical temperance (anti-alcoholic) movements as being "ready to kill a person only to keep him [sober]". Also, domestic critics like Mencken (1982) observe about American Puritanism that the "worst" government actually tends—or hypocritically claims—to be the "most moral"[13] or moralizing. This observation can serve as the

---

[12] For instance, Seaton (2006:197) approvingly restates the Calvinist-Puritan claims that "disobedience to God" by committing the original sin "had deeply distorting, debilitating, and damning consequences" on humanity.

[13] Mencken (1982:625) adds that a government "composed of cynics is often very tolerant and humane. But when fanatics are on top there is no limit to oppression", with

operational definition or diagnosis of Puritanism and its moralistic tyranny as moral fascism.

In short, Puritan, like other, moral fascism throws away with the dirty "bathwater of vice or sin" also the "baby" of individual moral and other social liberty, thus a free civil society. At this point, liberal-secular civil society in America becomes eventually the casualty or "collateral damage" of Puritan moral fascism as its nemesis. Notably, this holds true of a free civil society in relation to Puritan-style moralistic or temperance and culture anti- or pre-liberal wars during most of American history (Bell 2002; Lipset 1996; Wagner 1997) in a striking consistence and continuity from 17th century New England's "Biblical Commonwealth" and its witch-trials to the 20th–21st century "Bible Garden" and its "Monkey trials" in the substantive sense of theocratic attacks on individual liberty in morality and beyond. Contemporary US sociologists observe that what united "born again" Puritan-rooted religious conservatism in America during the 1980s-2000s (like before) was the "emphasis on the theme of moral decay", plus the imputed "role of liberalism" (Bell 2002) in this putative crisis of family and other social values.[14] Further, this view predicts "new wars of religion" in the future America predicted to remain "in trouble", if moral-cultural issues (abortion) resist to being "privatized", coupled with the "prospect of the continuing involvement" of religious conservatism or the "radical right" in politics[15] (Bell 2002).

To that extent, the "new wars of religion", morality, and culture will be the mechanisms through which Puritan moral fascism will operate, involve, and eventually dominate, and thus destroy liberal-secular civil society, in the future America, just as the old "holy" wars were in the past and are in the present. In Clausewitz's words, like any war, these

---

apparent reference to US Puritans or their heirs, notably what he calls Baptist and Methodist "barbarism" in the South that he perhaps the first described as a "Bible Belt".

[14] Bell (2002:484) comments that "what is troublesome is the politicization of moral and cultural issues, for by their very nature they are non-negotiable and serve to polarize society".

[15] Most US sociologists (also, Lipset 1996; Munch 2001) view anti-liberal Puritan-inspired culture wars in America as evident, persistent, and intense, though some contest them, particularly, those about abortion (e.g., Mouw and Sobel 2001). The first views are more acceptable, given the observed persistence and intensity of culture wars and self-declared "cultural warriors", notably (but not only) the methodical Puritan-style war against abortion within Congress, the Supreme Court, and state legislatures and outside of them (referenda, etc.) during the 1980s–2000s.

new moral-religious wars are the continuation of politics, in this case that of moral fascism, by "other means", physical and spiritual or symbolic violence. As observed, these "other means" include both illegal murders and legal executions of the "sinful", alike religiously grounded and sanctified. This is witnessed in the mixture of "godly" counter-state terrorism epitomized by "Christian" terrorist militia (Turk 2004), including lynching and other vigilante violence in the past and the present (Messner et al. 2005), with the fundamentalist-based and justified death penalty (Jacobs et al. 2005) and overall Draconian penal system in America during "reborn" fundamentalism, notably its "Bible Garden" (Texas, the "deep South"). For instance, like anti-liberal and anti-secular terrorists, state officials (prosecutors, judges, politicians) in this region (e.g., Texas) often advocate and justify the use of the death penalty for both nonviolent sins (some sexual offenses, drug trade) and violent crimes like murders on religious, specifically Biblical, grounds. They do so by citing for support certain passages of the Bible ("eye for eye", etc.) effectively remade the "law of the Dixieland" thus converted in a legal theocracy déjà vu following New England's "Biblical Commonwealth", just as do their Islamic enemies-equivalents by invoking the Koran. And, the predicted "continuing involvement" of religious neo-conservatism in politics is just another way to predict that Puritan moral fascism, as invariably "right-wing" or extreme conservative moralistic totalitarianism, will continue to be involved, to say the least, in the American polity and in extension civil society hence likely to be subverted, if not ultimately vanquished, at least in the "Bible Garden" (and Mormon-ruled Utah), as the realm of individual moral and other liberties.

Lastly, Puritan-rooted moral fascism in America involves not only the obsession with but also the reproduction of "vice and sin". Moreover, it is the probably the largest producer of vice, sin and thus "crime" in America through various practices and methods, including entrapment. In particular, the Puritan government or police state at all levels in America methodically entraps people with respect to sexual vices and sins, including prostitution, "public display of affection", the Internet indecent content and other pornography, and the like. For instance, none than one of "holier than thou" US puritanical neo-conservatives (a senator) was entrapped in an attempt at a sort of "public display of affection" by vice-police at an airport during the 2000s. His response "you shouldn't be out to entrap people" reveals Weber's "pure hypocrisy" of Puritanism, because this senator was among the strongest advocates of "tough on crime" temperance wars, including measures like police entrapment, against and Draconian punishments for sexual sins and vices, effectively moral fascism. More importantly, "you shouldn't be out to entrap people", notably his lawyer's comment that the senator's arrest in an undercover police operation "raises very serious constitutional questions", implies that this is *not* what a democratic government does or should do and how a free civil society operates. Conversely, it implies that this is precisely what defines moral fascism and a police state at a practical level or, what Americans call, as a "practical joke," yet usually "not so funny".[16] While liberal-secular democracy and civil society by assumption or in reality does not use entrapment and similar methods to reproduce sin and vice, what is fascist about Puritan moral fascism in America is precisely entrapping and thus making humans sinners-as-criminals. If anything, it is entrapment as a method of reproduction of "crime" that defines the (un)civil society of Calvinist Biblical theocracy in America as moral fascism and its government as the vice-police state. No wonder, Puritan America is virtually the sole or "leader" Western country, in which government *methodically* entraps humans into sins-as-crimes via vice-police, thus applying a "method of the madness" of reproduction of sinners-as-criminals, and beyond the West only emulated by Islamic theocracies like Iran in the global "entrapment contest."

This method of reproduction of sins and vices defined and punished as crimes confirms the following. First, Puritan moral fascism in America is anti-humanistic by reinventing humans as "evil" and "degenerate". Second, it reproduces rather than actually reduces sins, vice, crime and criminals, and thus is socially irrational. Third, it is also economically irrational in spending vast material and human resources on entrapment and related eventually inefficient methods of the vice-police state. Fourth, it is comparatively anomalous or deviant, as virtually no modern Western government and society does this. Fifth, it is a

---

[16] Even the conservative *Economist* sarcastically commented that such entrapment is "a strange way to stop terrorism". Also, it commented, with respect to the federal government's entrapment or spying on some persons (e.g., a Governor) in committing the moral sin of prostitution, that "resources that might have been spent on something more urgent, such as looking for terrorists. It went to the trouble of obtaining a federal wire-tap and examining thousands of e-mails." The magazine added that "all sorts of draconian punishments are now possible for [this moral sinner]", such as "a year in prison for violating a 1910 federal statute, the Mann act, which prohibits crossing state lines for 'immoral purposes'".

functional analogue of Islamic theocracy with its equivalent practices. Sixth, it is self-destructive, as witnessed by those "holier than thou" entrapped US conservatives (senators and governors) complaining "you shouldn't be out to entrap people". In short, it indicates that the 17th century "Puritan policeman", thus the moralistic tyranny or spirit ("ghost") of Puritanism, is still "live and well" in 21st century America.

*Equation of Pleasures, Sins, and Crimes*

Another, related "proof" or syndrome of Puritan moral fascism in America is the equation of human sins or moral vices, thus, as Pareto implies, implicitly pleasures, with crimes subjected to Draconian or cruel, inhumane punishment, hence anti-humanism in general considered separately. Puritan moral fascism in America equates human sinners with criminals and then punishes them accordingly, invariably with primitive, Draconian harshness, including mass and permanent or long imprisonment and even execution for sins, as witnessed during the new Puritanical war on drugs (non-violent drug offenses like the consumption and production or trade, respectively) and other diverse temperance wars ("three strikes" and other harsh or "dumb" laws).

Minimally, it is this sin-crime and sinners-criminals equivalence that defines and reveals Puritan (un)civil society and "godly" politics, including the legal-penal system, thus Calvinist theocracy, as moral fascism, just as that between ideological-political dissenters and criminals did and does political fascism, including Nazism (and communism). Even more minimally, the Draconian severity of punishment, notably executions, for sins, as witnessed in New England's and Southern "Bible Commonwealths", inflicted on human sinners does, just as the punishments for ideological and political offenses did Nazism and all fascism. What is "fascist" about Puritan moral fascism and Calvinist theocracy is at the minimum equating human sinners with criminals and punishing, to the point of executing, them in a Draconian manner in the same way political fascism like Nazism treated and punished/executed political-ideological dissenters (Bähr 2002).

Predictably, American Puritanism did not really "reinvent the wheel" and "rediscover the America" of an equation of human sins/sinners and indirectly pleasures with crimes/criminals. It only inherited and reinforced such an equivalence from Calvinism and in extension pre-Calvinist asceticism, including medieval Catholic and other Christian and non-Christian monasticism. By inventing the model for Puritanism as well as modern fascism (Fromm 1941; McLaughlin 1996), originally Calvinism established and performed a dual equation and reduction ("alchemy"). It did so by equating and reducing, first, human pleasures to sins or vices, thus (let us use a later term) Bentham's hedonists or epicureans to sinners, second, sins to crimes, hence sinners to criminals, subjected to corresponding, invariably severe, cruel, degrading and inhumane, punishments.

Such a double equation and harsh sanctions functioned as the expression and realization of Calvinist theological anti-humanism, notably Calvin's own extreme original-sin "Christian pessimism" (Heller 1986), emphasizing the supposed "fundamental evilness and powerlessness of men" (McLaughlin 1996). A historical study suggests that Calvin showed "heroic disdain for worldly matters" (Heller 1986) in a prototypical display of Calvinism's and hence Puritanism's condemnation, contempt, or suspicion of human pleasures as sins or (as Calvinist Rousseau put it) "destructive vices". Namely, Calvin was "supremely confident" of his self-righteousness and willing to abandon "everything", including "career, fortune, esteem" in his native France and to accept exile in Geneva for "conscience's sake" (Heller 1986). Furthermore, Calvin reportedly insisted that those who were "elected" had the "obligation and competence" for eliminating "sinfulness" and by implication pleasure, just as individual salvation was predestined by Deity and thus impossible to obtain "either by good works or priestly indulgence"[17] (Mansbach 2006).

Calvin hence provided a personal exemplar and true role model for subsequent Calvinism like his successors in Geneva[18] (e.g., Vernet) (Sorkin 2005) and beyond, including Puritanism, with respect to

---

[17] Mansbach (2006:110–1) adds that in 1536 "Geneva's city councils, as is often the practice of fundamentalists, imposed rigid austerity on citizens based on strict moral and religious norms, prohibiting gambling, heavy drinking, and blasphemy, outlawing the Catholic sacraments, and requiring church attendance", with the result of the "boundary between public and private affairs was largely erased". For illustration, in Calvin's Geneva "clothing and food were regulated, excommunications multiplied, the press was muted [etc.]" (Mansbach 2006:113).

[18] Sorkin (2005:292) remarks that Calvin's successor in Geneva, Vernet "the Pharisees' hypocritical morality [was] concerned with outward behavior" and that "Adam abused his liberty and became the original sinner; in turn, his sin became hereditary and plagued his progeny with a state of enduring corruption. Man's faculty of reason is intact and he is free to be moral, yet because of his corruption he needs faith in Jesus for expiation and grace."

treating worldly pleasures as sins (or "ungodly") and the latter as crimes, just as in other respects. For illustration, Pareto remarks that according to the moral code of Scottish Calvinism (the Presbyterian clergy), "all the natural affections, all the pleasures of society, all the pastimes, all the guy instincts of the human heart were so many sins" and consequently crimes. He adds that "long before, the monks had carried this kind of insanity [sic!] to the utmost limit" in that pleasure and sin or even crime in itself were "synonyms" in the medieval monastic order. Significantly, he remarks that long after monastic medievalism, they "still are [synonyms] to our modern ascetics". This implicitly refers to Calvinism, especially American Puritanism and its governmental enforcement of pure "morality by law" with consequent "gross abuses" of power, including its fanatical anti-alcoholic and other temperance movements climaxing in Prohibition and thus heralding the war on drugs (Hill 2002) and related ever-recurring or, unlike in most other Western societies, never-ending wars against "sin and vice" in America (Wagner 1997).

In general, Puritanism was just a sort of hyper-Calvinism, and Puritans were super-Calvinists in terms of a negative or suspicious attitude to worldly pleasures, including traditional amusements and sports in England, and social life, or secular civil society. Hume writes that the "thorough-paced Puritans were distinguishable by the sourness and austerity of their manners, and by their aversion to all pleasure and society." He remarks that "some encouragement and protection which the king and the bishops gave to [various] cheerful festivals of the common people, were the objects of like scandal to the Puritans", citing the non-Puritan objection "as if Christ had been a Puritan." Evoking Hume's comment, Mill explicitly provides a sort of liberal prescription or antidote to Puritanism and Calvinism. Mill states that "mind their own business" is "precisely what should be said to every government and every public, who have the pretension that no person shall enjoy any pleasure which they think wrong", citing the "Calvinists and Methodists" in England and America as "intrusively pious" groups entertaining and acting on such pretensions. At this juncture, the principle and practice of "mind your own business" is what "operationally" defines a liberal-secular or true civil society, and conversely the rejection and violation of the first produces and signifies the elimination or degeneration of the second.

Yet, what Mill and especially Hume implies is that there is no such thing as "mind your own business" or "do not intrude" in respect of others' pleasures or sins in a Calvinist, notably Puritan, theological and societal framework, hence no true civil society. This holds good given that especially Puritanism reportedly "never" showed respect for human privacy (Walzer 1963), thus liberty and dignity, in old and New England[19] (German 1995) and probably, judging by its evangelical revivals in America, never will. Hence, to expect that Calvinism, notably Puritanism, would adopt and apply the principle of "mind your own business" or "do not intrude" in this and other respects is expecting its own self-termination or dilution into an opposite to its nature of anti-privacy "instincts". This in part happened in modern Holland (Tubergen et al. 2005) and Europe overall, including England, but not in America (Munch 2001) by the early 21st century. In essence, Calvinism, especially Puritanism, is either the antithesis of "mind your own business" and "do not intrude" in other people's pleasures, thus sins, and lives, hence of a free civil society or is not "Calvinist" or "Puritan" at all. Simply, Schumpeter's and common-sense "live and let live" co-existential principle in moral and all terms is a logical non sequitur and empirical non-entity—there is no such thing—in Calvinist theocracy, notably Puritan methodical tyranny. This substantively redefines and reveals the latter as moralistic proto-fascism before modern fascism. Evidently, in Puritan moralizing fascism ethical anti-universalism and irrationalism versus moral universalism and rationalism in Kant's sense of universal free agency, or Jefferson's "liberty for all", in morality and civil society overall (Habermas 2001), is pervasive, as is anti-humanism.

In comparative-historical terms, Calvinism, notably Puritanism, on this account functions as the functional equivalent or analogue, in addition to Pareto's medieval Christian and other monasticism, of fundamentalist Islam. The latter is also characterized by rejecting the "mind your own business" or "do not intrude" liberal principle and equating pleasures, at least for the masses versus theocrats, with sins, and these to crimes subjected to Draconian punishments. No wonder, the "born again Puritan", evangelical "Bible Belt" is often identified as functionally

---

[19] German (1995:980) indicates that in late 18th and early 19th century New England, neo-Calvinist theologians and theocrats (the "New Divinity") "clearly preserved the essential Calvinist distinction between sinners and saints [by] defining all unregenerate action as sinful." In this view, "in demanding that the wicked, despite their moral inability, obey God's law", they (New Divinity preachers) "affirmed familiar and comforting absolute distinctions between right and wrong" (German 1995:983).

equivalent to Iran under Islamic theocracy in terms of their shared proto-totalitarian attacks on individual moral and other liberty, thus on the "mind your own business" principle. These shared practices include executions for non-violent sins (drug trade, some sexual offenses) or violent crimes, as well as mass long, and even permanent imprisonment for such and other comparatively minor offenses (possession of drugs, consensual sexuality, small theft) under "three strikes" and the old "dumb" laws.[20]

*Anti-Humanism*

A general "proof" or pathological syndrome of Puritan and other moral fascism in America and elsewhere is anti-humanism expressed *inter alia* in the equation of human pleasures with sins, and then the latter with crimes subjected to Draconian, including cruel and inhumane, punishment. While not all anti-humanism is fascist and Calvinist or generally religious in its origin, operation, and effects, Puritan, like other, moral fascism is precisely defined and typified by anti-humanistic ideas, institutions, and practices, including cruel, degrading, primitive, or inhumane punishments to the point of legally or illegally killing humans for sins defined as crimes.

In essence, Puritan moral fascism is "fascism" primarily because of its anti-humanism, including the cruel and other inhumane treatment of sinners. It is thus deeply immoral or amoral for humanity is axiomatically the essence or basis of morality as the Biblical "Golden Rule" and Kantian universalistic ethics (humans as ends) suggest, and conversely, inhumanity (e.g., cruelty) defines immorality at the basic existential level (Bauman 2001). Predictably, this anti-humanism, including cruel, degrading, primitive, and inhumane punishment like permanent imprisonment and executions for sins-crimes, derives from Calvinism, in particular Puritanism, as essentially anti-humanist Protestantism and Christianity generally. Calvinism, including Puritanism, was and remains via "born again" fundamentalism in America, the paradigmatic exemplar and major force of transcendental anti-humanism, including "gloom and doom" pessimism concerning humans a priori condemned or distrusted in virtue of "original sin" (Byrne 1997) as "natural born"

---

[20] For instance, the *Economist* suggests that the real and "bigger" question in modern Puritan America is that certain laws are "dumb," for example, whether the 1910 federal Mann Act "is an ass" (*sic*), not violations of these laws by moral sinners.

sinners, the descendants of Adam as the "original sinner" (Sorkin 2005), "degenerate", or "impure". Alternatively, it is the theological negation and theocratic destruction of liberal-secular humanism as "ungodly". Predictably, Calvinist, including Puritan, anti-humanism originated and was epitomized in Calvin's "emphasis on the fundamental evilness and powerlessness of men"[21] (Fromm 1941; McLaughlin 1996).

For instance, Comte identifies this Calvinist anti-humanism by observing that human emancipation has become "more repugnant" to established Calvinism (and Protestantism) and its Puritan sects than to the "most degenerate" official Catholicism. Moreover, Weber implies that Calvinism was anti-humanistic and inhumane in intra-Christian, not just secular, terms. He states that the "God of Calvinism", described as a "transcendental being, beyond the reach of human understanding," replaced the Christian "Father in heaven" (from the New Testament), "so human and understanding, who rejoices over the repentance of a sinner". In particular, he emphasizes that Calvin's God dispensed with the "very human Catholic cycle of sin, repentance, atonement, release, followed by renewed sin". Conversely, Calvinism rendered humans' "good works" basically "useless" as the "means of attaining salvation" and "meaningless in the face of God's unchangeable decree" and hence no individual "good" deeds could "compensate" for one's sins in stark contrast and systematic opposition to Catholicism and in extension original Christianity. He infers that in Calvinism life centers on "impersonal" supra-human ends, not human beings, to the effect that "humans exists for the sake of God" (also, Bendix 1977), not conversely, defining and expressing its transcendental anti-humanism and its repugnance for secular humanism. No wonder, one of Weber's "great men of Puritanism",[22] Calvinist-raised Franklin basically deserted Calvinism because he regarded its "rejection of good works", via the doctrine of predestination, as "inimical" to human morality (Byrne 1997; also, Mansbach 2006), and thus by implication to humanity, including, owing to its "unbrotherly consequences" (Schluchter 1981), to the "ethic of brotherhood".

---

[21] Fromm (1941:248) objects that "the Weberian theoretical tradition ignores Luther's and Calvin's "emphasis on the fundamental evilness and powerlessness of men" and thus Lutheran and Calvinist anti-humanism.

[22] Weber cites what he calls Milton's "well-known opinion" of the Calvinist doctrine of predestination: "Though I may be sent to Hell for it, such a God will never command my respect."

Elaborating on Weber, Tawney (1962) registers that Calvinism's, notably Puritanism's, code of moral values almost "exactly reversed" the original, conventional "scheme of Christian virtues" like compassion, understanding, caritas, patience, tolerance, and humanism. Tawney remarks that what actuated the typical Calvinist, especially Puritan, was not or less "compassion for his erring brethren" but rather "impatient indignation" for those who "sinned their mercies". In particular, subsequent historical research indicates that transcendental anti-humanism or the repugnance to secular humanism, through the "attribution of faith" to God rather than humans, was shared by "all the evangelicals of Calvin's generation" (Heller 1986) during the 16th century, as has been since, from his successors in Geneva (Sorkin 2005) to American evangelicalism. US "reborn", like "first born" European, evangelicals "abhor" secular humanism (Van Dyke 1995) as focused on humans rather than God, or simply as "ungodly" and (thus) "un-American".

As noted, Calvinist, like any other, transcendental anti-humanism intrinsically entails or ultimately eventuates in actual, "worldly" inhumanity, including brutality and cruelty to the point of methodical torture and systematic murder for the "glory of God", and on such divine grounds redefined as "good works" *cum* "evil as distorted good" (Habermas 2001). For instance, Calvin's strident "emphasis on the fundamental evilness and powerlessness of men", as an original or paradigmatic statement of Calvinist anti-humanism, harbored, resulted in, and predicted, as well as rationalized as righteous, his inhumane treatment, torture, and ultimately cruel murder of libertines and other critics and adversaries (e.g., Servetus). To use Clausewitz's definition of war, in Calvinism, notably Puritanism, inhumanity, including brutality and cruelty, is the "logical" continuation of transcendental anti-humanism by "other means" like death and other Draconian punishments for sins-crimes and the extermination of "infidels". Hence, Calvinist transcendental "godly" anti-humanism regenerates, sanctifies, and predicts inhumanity, including brutality, cruelty, torture, and murder, and these latter express ("load on") the former.

Weber notices that in Calvinism, especially Puritanism, transcendental anti-humanism, expressed in the idea of a "transcendental being" opposite to the Christian Father in heaven "so human and understanding", implied or reached what he calls "extreme inhumanity" attributed to the doctrine of predestination. Such inhumanity produced the "feeling of unprecedented inner loneliness of the single individual"²³ (Schluchter 1981) subjected to what Weber describes as the "strikingly frequent repetition, especially in the English Puritan literature, of warnings against any trust in the aid of friendship of men" in favor of "exclusive trust" in or, to use Parsons' term, "immediacy" to the God of Calvinism, who only "should be your confidant".²⁴ Calvinism, especially Puritanism, is simply inhuman in attacking the "sentiments of love and friendship" condemned as encroaching on the "service" that believers owe to God (Bendix 1965).

In Weber's words, the inhumanly "harsh doctrines" of the absolute transcendence of God or predestination and the "corruption of everything pertaining to the flesh" epitomizing Calvinist transcendental "godly" anti-humanism manifestly or latently generated "extreme inhumanity". In short, Calvinist anti-human theology, particularly its predestination dogma, as the "most extreme form" of exclusive trust in God, contained the seed and then produced the full-grown fruit of inhumanity. In particular, this inhumanity and in extension anti-humanism included what Weber identifies as Calvinist (Schluchter 1981), especially Puritan (Symonds and Pudsey 2006), un-brotherliness as the "abomination" of the ethic of brotherhood.²⁵ Such Calvinist un-brotherliness metastasizes into what he also detects as Puritans' "peculiar misanthropy" to the point of deep pathological hatred²⁶

---

²³ Elaborating on Weber, Schluchter (1981:172–74) remarks that (consistent) Calvinism produced the "inner loneliness of the individual and the treatment of 'brothers' as 'others'" and describes its religious ethic as a "monologic ethic of conviction with unbrotherly consequences."

²⁴ Weber adds that "even the amiable [Puritan] Baxter counsels deep distrust of even one's closest friend" and comments that "in striking contrast to Lutheranism, this attitude toward life was also connected with the quiet disappearance of the private confession, of which Calvin was suspicious only on account of its possible sacramental misinterpretation, from all the regions of fully developed Calvinism", notably old and New England or America.

²⁵ Symonds and Pudsey (2006:137) comment that "Weber identifies two major trends that place [Puritanism] in direct contrast with the ideal-type of genuine brotherliness." These are, first, that the "ideal of universalism stands in stark contrast to the idea of "brotherhood" found in sects of religious virtuosi, as early Protestantism, particularly in America, second, the "Puritan logic of abandonment of the personal, or ethical, aspect of the brotherly ethic of suffering" while for Weber ""personal" or "human" relations between people are the [very] place where an ethical dimension is possible" (Symonds and Pudsey 2006:137-8). In their view, in Puritanism, "there is no longer any regard for the person and [their] suffering; rather, such charity is aimed at promoting labor and the market. Brotherliness has become loveless" (Symonds and Pudsey 2006:139).

²⁶ Symonds and Pudsey (2006:139) register that in Puritanism "brotherly love" involves or rather degenerates into "elements of hatred when the ethical concern with

(Fromm 1941; Mansbach 2006; Symonds and Pudsey 2006) for humans, notably moral sinners as well as religious "infidels" and heretics or dissenters.

Further, note Weber's use of the word "extreme" to describe "inhumanity", in particular "unprecedented" in reference to individual "inner loneliness" in Calvinism, including Puritanism. It suggests that Calvinism, particularly Puritanism, was not just inhumane but extremely so, and it reproduced not mere "loneliness", but "unprecedented", while providing an extant precedent, if not a model (McLaughlin 1996), for that found in fascism, notably Nazism (Arendt 1951; Bähr 2002). In particular, Weber implies that Puritanism was the "most distant", thus the unparalleled aberration, from the ideal-type of the ethnic of brotherliness, in spite of the "variety of Puritan doctrines and practices" (Symonds and Pudsey 2006) within the family of Calvinism. Recall also his expression the "most absolutely unbearable form" of church control of individuals to describe Calvinist theocracy, in particular "unexampled" to characterize Puritanism's moralistic tyranny. At this point, in Calvinism, particularly Puritanism, theological, dogmatic anti-human extremism yields "extreme inhumanity." Notably, the Calvinist "most absolutely unbearable" theocracy and Puritan "unexampled" tyranny presuppose and reproduce the "unprecedented inner loneliness" and hatred of humans, prefiguring those in Nazism and other fascist totalitarianism.

In sum, in Weber's account, Calvinism, in particular Puritanism, is extremely inhumane, including hateful, cruel, and murderous to sinners and infidels, because it is theologically anti-human. It forces and maintains humans into the state of "unprecedented inner loneliness" (also) owing to Calvinist "most absolutely unbearable" theocracy and Puritan "unexampled" moralistic tyranny. He thus implies that such inhumanity renders Calvinism, including Puritanism, extreme Protestantism and Calvinist theocracy the "most absolutely unbearable" and Puritan moralistic tyranny "unexampled", including human loneliness "unprecedented".

Alternatively, inhumanity makes Puritanism and Calvinism a sort of, as Tawney suggests, near-exact reversal of original Christianity— and not just official Catholicism, as claimed by Calvinist and Puritan

---

the suffering of every person is replaced by the elect's sense of vocational labor and certainty of grace".

virulent anti-Catholicism—and its explicit or implicit humanism (assuming that his account is correct). In particular, this entails reversing the Biblical compassion, caritas, and forgiveness for sins ("who has not sinned") and what Sorokin extols as (and Marx sarcastically calls) "Christian" brotherly love turned into "Christian" hatred or misanthropy in Calvinism, especially American Puritanism (Symonds and Pudsey 2006) and its evangelical revivals. Weber might add that Puritanism and Calvinism generally due to its anti-humanism, notably its extreme inhumanity, un-brotherliness and pathological hatred, functioned as or prefigured, if the term was available, moral fascism as the axiomatic anti-humanist, inhumane destruction or perversion of individual moral liberty and civil society overall.

Also, Calvinism originated and functioned as moral fascism in theological terms on the account of its oligarchic doctrine of predestination, specifically the "double decree" of salvation of only a few acting as "heavenly" oligarchy (Zaret 1989) and damnation of most humans as its servants. Consequently, this doctrine was experienced and rejected by non-Calvinists and some Calvinist (Arminian) dissenters as "morally repugnant" (Ozment 1980; Sorkin 2005) and (as per Franklin) by its rejecting "good works" even "inimical" to morality (Byrne 1997). In such a form, Calvin's predestination dogma was a sort of theological equivalent of fascism's, including Nazism's, invariant ideology of oligarchy, and Calvinist predestined saints-masters were sacred analogues or precursors of fascist, notably Nazi, self-elected leaders (McLaughlin 1996). Both Calvinist saints and fascist leaders claimed and acted as if they were preordained to be a narrow master-caste in society and the world, with self-assigned rights to rule, including oppress and exterminate, others, in the first case owing to Divine election, in the second (also) the ideology of innate racial and other superiority.

Further, while Weber implied it, Simmel explicitly identifies cruelty as a sort of tangible, as distinguished from "intangibles" like loneliness or hatred, form of extreme inhumanity within Calvinism, specifically Puritanism. Simmel does this by registering the "cruel suppression of the Irish Catholics" in England by Cromwell's Puritans (and other Protestants), as did Hume in his classical historical study (Seed 2005). Also, contemporary sociologists identify and emphasize the "methodical, ruthless" brutality of Puritans (Birnbaum 1953), as an expected consequence of their misanthropy or hatred and un-brotherliness toward humans. At least due of its cruelty and brutality, thus, as Hume suggests, barbarity, against human sinners and "infidels", Puritanism and Calvinism in general effectively operated as or prefigured moral (and political) fascism as a self-evident cruel, brutal, and barbaric antithesis of a free civil society (and democracy). While surely not all forms and instruments of cruelty, brutality, and barbarity are Calvinist, including Puritan, in origin and effect, Calvinism, especially Puritanism, was typically—with secondary exceptions mostly due to countervailing forces—cruel, brutal, and thus substantively barbarian. In that sense, it acted as proto-typical or extant, minimally proxy, moral (and political) fascism.

For better understanding Puritan moral fascism and its anti-humanism and inhumanity, including cruel, primitive, and inhumane punishment (e.g., the death penalty) for sins-crimes, in America, it is helpful to retrieve the "original act" or classic model of extreme humanity, notably cruelty, brutality, and barbarism, in Calvinism and thus Puritanism. The "classic case" is Calvin et al.'s burning of Servetus (Means 1966; also, Dombrowski 2001) "at the stake" (Mansbach 2006) in 16th century Calvinist Geneva. According to historical records, Calvin et al. during their theocratic rule in Geneva (in 1553) were instrumental in the "burning of Servetus"—the inhumane and cruel or barbarian details of which evoke those of the medieval Catholic Inquisition—for theological heresy.[27] Recall, Calvin "wished to kill" Servetus (Dombrowski 2001) and eventually satisfied his "dead wish" for the "glory of God" in this and other cases involving dissenters and libertines. Apparently, this was not the "sad story of the death of kings", as the killed were just "lowly" heretics or libertines, but rather one of the rise of the new Divinely preordained rulers as Calvinist masters. In a sense, Calvin et al.'s burning of Servetus was an original act and provided a Calvinist, including Puritan, model (Mansbach 2006) for "saving" humans and their souls from moral and religious or theological "mistakes" (Terchek 1997) by simply killing them, effectively continuing or restoring the medievalist Inquisition.

Further, historical research indicates that Calvin not only "murdered" his enemies but never "repented" his crimes[28] (Fulton 1954).

---

[27] For illustration, Calvin reportedly stated that if Servetus comes to Geneva, "I shall never let him go out alive if my authority has weight" (cited in Schaff-Herzog 1977:371) and also during the latter's trial "I hope that the verdict will call for the death penalty" (Nigg 1962:328).

[28] Fulton (1954:35) adds that a year after the burning of Servetus (1554), Calvin "published a defense in which further insults were heaped upon his former adversary in most vindictive and intemperate language".

This suggests that Calvin's burning of Servetus at the stake (and executing other heretics or libertines) was not just a random murder. It was the original act and the Calvinist, including Puritan, model of self-righteous crime, or murderous self-righteousness. And, the act logically escalated in the mass extermination of the "ungodly", "witches", and sinners, as in England and New England, and perpetuated in also unrepentant or "sanctimonious" neo-conservatism (Bourdieu 1998), including moral fascism via the policing state, in America. In short, it was the act or model of "evil as distorted good", the type of murder or aggression that its perpetrators believe to be justified in perpetrating (Habermas 2001).

Certainly not all un-repented and self-righteous torture, murders, and other crimes against "enemies" like dissenters, "infidels", and moral sinners, thus not every "evil as distorted good", are Calvinist-Puritan, as witnessed by "not so godly" Nazism as a cited exemplar in this respect. Yet, the opposite is almost invariably true of Calvinism, including Puritanism. Since Calvin's murder of Servetus and other libertines or heretics in Geneva, Calvinism's murderous and related activities have virtually always been un-repented or sanctimonious, perpetrated with a supremely "good conscience." These activities were thus perversely or cynically redefined as "good works, notably sanctified as God-decreed "holy" wars on "infidels" or enemies. This Calvinist pattern of un-repentance in murder and other crimes was witnessed, in a Puritan form, in Cromwell's "cruel suppression" of Irish Catholics and in part Anglicans, in Winthrop et al.'s partial extermination of Native Americans and "witches", with most Puritan rulers in New England being unrepentant with respect to their witch-trials[29] (Harley 1996). For example, even after these witch-trials with their punishment by death proved patently unjust, cruel and inhumane, New England's ruling Puritans (Cotton Mather, Lieutenant-Governor Stoughton) remained unrepentant claiming that "justice being so far, executed

---

[29] Harley (1996) mentions New England's Lieutenant-Governor Stoughton during the Salem with-trials as "unrepentant". He also remarks that "self-image" of such key Puritan figures as the Mathers (father and son) as the "champions of [Calvinist] orthodoxy made it hard for them to recognize mistakes"; in particular, Cotton Mather "did not lose his belief in witchcraft" (Harley 1996). In turn, the *Economist* used (in reference to a governor's cited sin of prostitution sin) the expression "revisiting Salem" and commented that "American history is littered with examples of puritanism deranging the law, from the Salem witch trials onwards."

among us" and refusing to recognize their "mistakes", while still maintaining their irrational, medieval-rooted superstitious "belief in witchcraft" (Harley 1996). Also, New England's ruling Puritans reportedly acted "righteous in their policy of intolerance" against dissenters even within the "Puritan fold," let alone non-Puritans, during the 17th century, revealing their admittedly "inflated notion of their own, exclusive righteousness" (Dayton 1999).

The pattern is also evidenced and self-perpetuated in Puritan moral fascism's executions for sins and crimes and its "preemptive" war on the "evil" world in contemporary America. In this sense, from Calvin et al. to "born again" US fundamentalists, Calvinism and its derivative Puritanism originated, functioned, and remained as the system and design of "evil as distorted good". It thus did as prototypical moral fascism precisely (notably, Nazism) defined in these terms, as the type of systematic murder and aggressive war that the perpetrators believe or claim to be morally "justified" in perpetrating. Calvin et al.'s ultimate justification was the assumed "fundamental evilness and powerlessness" of humans in a "hereditary" condition of "enduring corruption" due to the "original sinner" (Sorkin 2005), simply theological anti-humanism. The latter eventuated in, predicted, and justified their cruel murder of Servetus and other dissenters and libertines, thus tangible, real-life inhumanity.

No wonder, in view of the burning of Servetus, the beheading of libertines, and other inhumane theocratic practices reminiscent of the Catholic Inquisition, Calvinist-ruled Geneva was described as the "Rome" in the sense of the "capital" of Protestantism (Saisselin 1992) or the "Protestant Rome" (Mansbach 2006). Calvin acted and was described as the "Protestant "Pope" of Geneva (Fritchman 1944), in spite (or because) of his vehement anti-Catholicism and fanatical anti-popery. In essence, this French-speaking city became the Calvinist model of a theocratic state and society (Byrne 1997; Mansbach 2006), thus a "dictatorial regime"[30] (Nigg 1962) with Calvin as the supreme theocrat or dictator *cum* "merely" theologian (as defended by his successors like Vernet, cf., Sorkin 2005). Another historical study concludes and predicts that Servetus' "ashes will cry out" against Calvin as

---

[30] Nigg (1962:326) points out that since the Geneva government was theocratic, it "became a matter of prestige—always the sore point for any dictatorial regime—for Calvin to assert his power in this respect. He was forced to push the condemnation of Servetus with all the means at his command".

long as their names remain "known in the world" (Nigg 1962). While the "two men", particularly Servetus, are hardly known in the "new world" today, their relation from theological friendship to enmity, and notably the outcome can shed a radically opposite light on what US analysts imply as effectively America's "destiny" in Calvin by connecting its values of freedom to his doctrines of "religious transcendence and human sin" (Means 1966; also, Dunn and Woodard 1996; Kloppenberg 1998; Seaton 2006). Simply, this makes Calvin less of a "good person" than is usually assumed in Calvinist societies, including America. Equally, their equivalent practices (e.g., the "holy" war of extermination of Native Americans, witch-trials) make his disciples adopting "austere Calvinism" like Winthrop et al. less than, as commonly viewed, quintessentially "good guys" (Gould 1996) and perennial "all-American" role models for US moral conservatives.

### Coercive Imposition of Puritanical Morality

Another exact "proof" or pathological syndrome of Puritan moral fascism in America consists of extremely moralistic and typically irrational laws legislating and enforcing morality. These laws attempt and perform the coercion and imposition of Puritan morality on civil society effectively eliminated or degenerated as the sphere of individual moral and other liberties and choices. What is fascist or totalitarian about Puritan moral fascism is thus legislating and coercing humans into "pure" morality, denying them moral freedom, choice, responsibility or maturity. This Puritan morality in reality typically eventuates in what Hume[31] and Weber detect as "pure hypocrisy" admittedly inherent to American Puritanism (Bremer 1995). The latter causes Puritans to act as exemplary hypocrites or Calvinist Pharisees defined by "hypocritical morality" that Calvin et al. (Vernet) nominally rejected[32] (Sorkin 2005). (Conversely, Weber denotes the original Jewish Pharisees as "Puritans" in a non- or pre-Calvinist shape and meaning.)

---

[31] Recall, Hume cites the observation that Puritans "to the world they seemed to be such as would not swear, whore, or be drunk", while in reality doing the opposite, namely "they would lie, cozen, and deceive." Hume also refers to "Puritanical pretensions to a free and independent constitution. In turn, Weber comments that "the impression of many Germans that the virtues professed by Americanism [Puritanism] are pure hypocrisy seems to have been confirmed by this striking case [Franklin]".

[32] Sorkin (2005:292) cites Vernet's view that the Pharisees' "hypocritical morality [was] concerned with outward behavior" to be substituted with the need of Calvinist "expiation and grace".

Puritan moral fascism in America self-proves and reveals itself, by analogy to the adage of the "emperor with no cloths," via its extremely moralistic, typically irrational or ineffective laws that legislate and enforce its pure, typically hypocritical, morality on civil society thereby destroyed or subverted. If anything, what defines Puritan and other proxy (Catholic, Islamic, or Hindu) moral fascism is the theological design and theocratic attempt to make humans "moral" even if and primarily by law, thus coercion. As noted, Pareto especially identifies and predicts American Puritanism's tendency to moral fascism by observing that the US typically puritanical government seeks to impose "morality by law" in apparent reference or prediction of Prohibition, also instigated by fanatical anti-alcoholic and other temperance Puritan movements, in the 1900s.

In particular, implicitly contradicting what Weber and Parsons extol as Calvinist-Puritan rationalism in economic and social terms alike, Pareto suggests that these attempts and laws are intrinsically or ultimately irrational in being destructive or subversive to free civil society as well as political democracy. Strikingly, he observes that, as the result of governmental attempts to impose "morality by law", America experiences "gross abuses" of "malignant" power, which are "not observable" in those societies with "no such restrictions." If so, Puritan moral fascism may perhaps recreate and impose its hypocritical morality and by implication "godliness" by law and government, yet in the process it grossly subverts and eventually destroys democracy and a free civil society as the casualty or "collateral damage" of moralistic legislation and state coercion.

To cite Mannheim and Keynes, Puritan moral fascism constitutes the kind of "splendid" surgery" and remedy that cures the disease of (supposed) immorality or moral crisis by killing the patient of a free civil society and democracy, eventually or conceivably Calvinist capitalism itself (Beck 2000). It thus commits the act of ultimate irrationality in social life (like medicine), including the legal system degenerated into a complex of irrational, extreme, anachronistic, self-destructive, and admittedly "biased"[33] (Hinchman 1984)—or, as many Americans

---

[33] Hinchman (1984:258) suggests that individual liberties and rights "are threatened by large private organizations or (as in this country) biased laws and institutions" referring to contemporary America. Dahrendorf (1979) implies that they are threatened both by private corporate and public or political power, notably conservative-authoritarian "law and order" slogans and institutions, in America and other modern societies.

describe them, "dumb"—laws and institutions subverting or threatening individual liberties, choices, and rights. For instance, American Puritanism vehemently attacked and exorcised the supposed "vices of Europe" (Gould 1996) via its witch-trials and similar "godly" and "virtuous" practices. And yet, in the process it transformed its "shining city upon a hill" into an admittedly dark and deadly "Salem with witches" (Putnam 2000), thus in the Ross' antidote of civil society and democracy.

In general, Pareto predicts that the deformation of a free civil society as well as "uses and abuses of power will be the greater, the more extensive the government's interference" in private life and personal morality by laws and coercion, a prediction grounded in his observations of Puritan moralistic "restrictions" in America making it the Western "leader" in such interference. And, it has perpetuated America as such a leader, as indicated by the striking, but not surprising, observation and admission that "born again" puritanical US moral-religious conservatives tend to be "much more aggressive in imposing their own morality" on the polity and civil society than their ideological allies[34] (Lipset 1996) in other modern Western societies. For instance, with the exception of their Catholic counterparts in the Vatican Church and Poland, as well as Islamic fundamentalists, US conservatives are the only ones that define and rationalize this denial the freedom of choice in the sphere of birth control as the "right to life" among Western and other societies, where it is a resolved matter or non-issue anyway. What is the freedom of choice in most Western societies has become "evil" and thus its elimination miraculously the "right to life" for US religious conservatives.[35] In turn, most "right to life" US conservatives apply on religious Biblical "eye-for-eye" grounds the death penalty for sins, including drug trade and abortion, and crimes in apparent, yet denied or overlooked, self-contradiction. In comparative terms, the fact that the opposition to private choice in human procreation *cum* the "right to life" has become and remains a major issue in American politics and

---

[34] Lipset's (1996:293) full statement is that 'social conservatives in [the US] are much more aggressive in imposing their own morality on the body politic with respect to issues like the right to life than their ideological compeers elsewhere', including Italy, France and Germany. What is indicative is that Lipset, as usual, over-patriotically adopts US social conservatives' denial of the freedom of choice with respect to birth control as the "right to life".

[35] If this was really the "right to life", one wonders why US conservatives did not change their birth-date certificates accordingly and become almost a year older.

society, while being a non-issue in most Western societies, except for hyper-Catholic and Vatican-influenced Poland (and Ireland), testifies to the unrivaled power of religious fundamentalism in America compared to Western Europe, and only rivaled by that of its Islamic version in Iran, Saudi Arabia, and other Muslim theocracies.

In addition, Pareto implies that such state interference and formal laws are irrational in being eventually ineffective in attaining their declared end of enforcing or inculcating morality on civil society, thus self-defeating, as dramatically witnessed in his time and since (and before). He would invoke the commonly admitted dismal failure of puritanical alcohol Prohibition to, via no less than a constitutional amendment, attain its initial goal (manifest function) of eradicating vice and sin and reestablishing virtue (sobriety). Yet it instead reproduce even more serious and numerous social pathologies (latent functions), notably diminished liberty[36] (Friedman 1997; Simon 1976), as well as organized violent crime and criminals embodied by Al Capone's Mafia and "amoral intelligence" (Merton 1968). This remarkable act almost, if it were not repealed, ended in "killing the patient" of individual liberty and thus a free civil society in America, while performing, like Mannheim's surgeon, a "splendid surgery" on the Constitution, for example, or, to paraphrase Keynes, curing the disease of vice and sin like alcoholism and its effects.

In comparative-historical terms, except for the "Puritan nation", it is unknown or atypical for any modern Western constitutional democracy during the 20th century (and before) to have prohibited alcohol and related sins by means of constitution, no less. Also, excepting the "dry" states of the "Bible Belt", virtually no contemporary Western country or region prohibits alcohol by law. If anything, such alcohol and related prohibitions make Puritanism and in extension Calvinism America's "destiny" on the level of everyday life, in this case the kind of food or beverages people will ("thou shall") consume.[37]

---

[36] Simon (1976:64) comments that by the Prohibition Amendment the "particular means used to attain this particular end had many consequences [on liberty] other than the specific end sought, and these had to be given their proper weight in considering the desirability of the means".

[37] As the *Economist* remarks, in America the "combination of legalism and puritanism invariably produces the same dismal results. It creates expensive government bureaucracies that seize on any excuse—rules relating to inter-state commerce are a particular favourite—to extend their powers to boss people about or spy on them. It throws up swivel-eyed zealots who pursue their manias with little sense of proportion

336                          CHAPTER FIVE

And, if Pareto lived during the 2000s he would have likely cited as another paradigmatic exemplar in enforcing "morality by law" Prohibition's sequel or proxy. This is the ineffective, repressive, and crime-generating "war on drugs" (Reuter 2005), and other new Puritan-style temperance or culture wars (Bell 2002; Wagner 1997) in America, not to mention no-alcohol "dry" zones in the Southern and Middle "Bible Garden" (Merton 1968) and beyond (Utah, etc.). A paradigmatic instance is the observed continuing failure of Puritan-style neoconservative "tough on crime" ("three-strikes") laws to reduce or control crime in US states like California and others (Erikson and Parent 2007; also, Akerlof 2002). Even a conservative US economist proposes that the enforcement and eventual repeal of Prohibition supply a "highly relevant body of data on possible effects" of the "most promising candidate for decriminalization" in modern American civil society and politics, the "prohibition of the consumption, purchase, or sale of a limited number of chemical substances" officially classified by ruling conservatism, as "illegal drugs" (Friedman 1997).

Moreover, this conservative economist provides some kind of operational definition or proximate diagnosis of Puritan moral fascism in America. He does so by the observation that "hardly" any American, except for its masters or guardians, "could not be convicted" of crimes as sins, if typically fanatical or over-zealous prosecutors, thus effectively persecutors, showed a "real effort", because "so many laws" exist regulating "so many activities" that virtually "none" of Americans know them "in full detail" (Friedman 1997). The observation unwittingly admits that even innocent Americans, and a fortiori non-Americans or foreigners, *could* be convicted of, including imprisoned and executed for, sins-crimes, if only Puritanical prosecutors-persecutors made "real" efforts or tried "hard", the American way. And, this has actually happened to many persons during "tough on crime" neo-conservatism in America. Notably, it applies to the "Bible Garden" (Texas[38]), with its

---

or decency." The magazine also suggests that this combination "ends by devouring its children," as with the case of a US governor *cum* fallen angel due to moral sins (prostitution) in an "endless line of self-righteous crusaders impaled on their own swords."

[38] For instance, following the DNA-based exoneration of yet another prisoner, after being convicted on 99 and serving 26 years in prison for the rape he did not commit, in Dallas in 2007, District Attorney admitted a "past culture of overly aggressive prosecutors seeking convictions at any cost" in Texas during the 1980s–2000. Also, the founder of the Innocence Project of Texas commented that "it is time we stop kidding ourselves in believing that what happened in Dallas is somehow unique. What happened in Dallas is common. This is Texas [*sic*]." Overall, according to the Innocence

religiously grounded and justified penal and death penalty system, as witnessed by DNA tests proving that innocent persons have been long imprisoned (some even for thirty years) and on death row for fabricated crimes, especially (alongside murders) sexual offenses (rapes, etc.). It is the kind of arbitrariness or absolute power that precisely defines and identifies Puritan and other moral-political fascism like Nazism, and generally state terrorism as unlawful official murder and violence, thus making the world "mad, arbitrary" (Bourdieu 2000). The Orwellian fantastic totalitarian scenario of convicting and even executing innocent people if only the US "godly" government makes a "real effort" is precisely what none than the foremost legal institution in America explicitly allowed in a surreal ruling allowing for "constitutionally correct" executions of such persons during the 1990s (Bauman 2001).

*Prima facie*, such and similar legal practices may seem incredible and pathological within contemporary Western civil society and democracy. Yet, they are logical, predictable outcomes of Puritan moral fascism and its "normal pathology" (Gouldner 1970) of imposition of morality by law and Draconian punishment for immorality, while couched in and rationalized as "tough on crime" neo-conservative laws and policies. They are the product and instrument of Puritan moral fascism's definition and implementation of conservative authoritarian "law and order" slogans (Dahrendorf 1979) as legal terrorism, including procedurally proper or "constitutionally correct"[39] (Bauman 2001) executions of innocent humans. Humans are thus sacrificed as potential sinners anyway, on the account of original sin supposedly perpetrated by their ancestors, at the altar of "get tough" policies and "holy" culture wars, simply "gone with the wind", especially by the fundamentalist

---

Project, "Texas leads the country in prisoners freed by DNA testing, releasing at least 30 wrongfully convicted inmates since 2001." Moreover, a defense attorney remarked that DNA exoneration cases "are the very tiniest tip of a gigantic iceberg of injustice in Texas' committed in and justified by the Puritan-style neo-conservative paranoia against human sin and vice *cum* a "tough on crime" war.

[39] Bauman (2001:43) remarks that "in 1992 in the infamous case of Herrera vs. Collins [Supreme Court] ruled that the accused may be innocent, but he could still be executed if his trial was properly conducted and constitutionally correct [sic!]". In turn, Angel (1994:20) comments that generally "if all we were interested in were increasing happiness, then one could conceive of a situation in which it would serve happiness to find an innocent person guilty". Yet, finding many innocent persons in America guilty and punishing, including executing, them for the glory of Weber's God of Calvinism or in the service of their "tough-on-crime" ideology and policy apparently makes US neo-conservatives or "reborn" fundamentalists really happy and "holier than thou".

grounded death-penalty and generally penal system in the "Bible Garden" and beyond, including the Federal Government. To be sure, the above ruling and its implications may seem as, and thus dismissed, as a fantasy and surreal. Yet, nothing is fantastic or unrealistic and impossible in Puritan and other moral fascism, like in Nazism. This is what the long history of Puritanism and in extension of Calvinism in America shows, from "Salem with witches" to the executions and other Draconian punishments of innocent persons during the 2000s. The history clearly indicates that Puritan moral fascism in America can be underestimated or, as US "born again" Presidents and other fundamentalists say, miscalculated only at one's own peril, or never with impunity, just as was Nazism with the well-known outcomes in interwar Europe.

In turn, that Puritan and other laws legislating and enforcing morality on civil society are intrinsically irrational or eventually ineffective is what Pareto implies above and even "moralist" Durkheim explicitly suggests and predicts. Durkheim does by recognizing that legal norms and sanctions cannot "awake" individuals' moral sensitiveness operating according to a sociological, non-legal law and sanction of personal, yet socially conditioned, freedom, conscience, and responsibility. As Simmel puts it, morality has "no other sanction" and law than the individual's "conscience", because the "means of moral regulation" include "persuasion, education, and enlightenment" distinguishing it from other "forms of social control" (Ruonavaara 1997), rather than coercion and oppression.

Alternatively, Pareto, Durkheim, and Simmel imply that legislating and thus enforcing morality is functionally equivalent to, and so as ineffective and irrational in the long run as, coercively imposing a "true" religion on civil society and awakening humans' religious "soul", or reviving what Weber calls the "ghost of dead religious beliefs". As known, the latter is not only, as Hume, Voltaire, and other Enlightenment figures suggest, a logical non sequitur. It is a supreme lesson from the religious history of Western and other societies, including the Dark Middle Ages, the Reformation, and Catholic-Protestant wars (Dombrowski 2001). In sum, both forms of coercive imposition are inherently irrational or counterproductive in that, as Tönnies explicitly states, the modern Western state realized that "dead morality and religion cannot be revived by coercion" and even education, thus "hardly a direct concern" of governmental action.

However, Pareto would comment that Calvinism, notably Puritanism, has never, from Calvin's Geneva to Prohibition and the "war on drugs", reached or adopted but rather rejected or attacked this realization that reviving and imposing the old morality and religion by formal laws and coercion is eventually ineffective, and thus irrational, in modern civil society. In this sense, Puritan irrational (including "dumb") laws in America legislating morality are the paradigmatic exemplar of what Mannheim calls "invalid", "antiquated", "inapplicable" legal norms expressing an "erroneously founded set of moral axioms". They meet his definition of an ethical code as "invalid" if it comprises norms, with which humans "cannot comply", or when their "unethical" action cannot be attributed to and explained by their "personal transgressions, but rather the "compulsion of an erroneously founded set of moral axioms."[40] Prohibition and its vestiges or replays in the "dry" South and beyond (Utah), the "war on drugs", and other temperance wars dramatically exemplify and confirm such norms and their effects. They indicate that it is Puritan laws that are invalid ("dumb") by imposing morality, not humans behaving "all too human" as Biblical sinners ("who has not sinned") rather than, as dictated, saints, angels, or total ascetics.

In sum, what Pareto prophetically identified as Puritan-grounded and sanctified laws and institutions coercively enforcing morality, thus moral fascism, in America are irrational or even, as many Americans experience and call them, downright "dumb", on at least two accounts. First, they are on the account of destroying or subverting civil society and political democracy through generating and, as a sort of insult to injury, rationalizing "gross abuses" of "malignant" power. Second, they are self-defeating and ineffective, thus irrational, by failing to attain their original aim of moral purity or hypocritical morality, while reproducing or aggravating a myriad of social pathologies, including organized (and disorganized) crime and violent criminals, as distinguished from mostly non-violent human sinners (e.g., alcohol and drug users) as the initial target. To that extent, from Cromwell and Winthrop et al. to their "reborn" evangelical descendants, Puritans have typically acted or appeared to others, as kinds of, to invert a famous expression (Sen

---

[40] Mannheim adds that "antiquated and inapplicable norms, modes of thought and theories are likely to degenerate into ideologies whose function it is to conceal the actual meaning of conduct rather than to reveal it."

1977), "irrational fools", if not what Hume refers to as the "'reproachful appellation of 'dumb dogs'"[41] (Baldwin 2006), with respect to legislating and imposing their own "pure", hypocritical morality on, thus eliminating or perverting, civil society, in particular individual moral liberty.

*"Draconianism"*

As indicated, still another exact "proof" or pathological syndrome of Puritan moral fascism in America comprises severe, Draconian-like punishments for moral sins and vices, just as for usual crimes, and in that sense what can be denoted (lacking a better single term) as "Draconianism". In penal or criminal-justice terms, Puritan moral fascism in America is defined by the system of severe, typically Draconian punishments, including executions, for moral non-violent sins and self-inflicted or destructive vices, just as violent and property crimes committed against others.

For example, in early New England[42] the Puritan theocratic legal system, as Tocqueville observes, punished with death adultery (and "fornication") thus made into a mortal sin, as well as other sins or crimes like blasphemy, sorcery, rape, etc. (but curiously does not mention murder). Moreover, he notices that punishment by death "was never more frequently prescribed by statute" as by the Puritan law and "there was scarcely a sin which was not subject to magisterial censure". As expected, this indicates that American Puritanism was hyper-Calvinism and US Puritans were super-Calvinists with respect to lethal and non-lethal "Draconianism", or severe and often cruel punishment for sins *cum* crimes, and inhumanity overall, just as in virtually all respects. As a particular heritage or continuity, by the early 21st century, most Southern and other extremely moralistic states like Utah[43]

---

[41] Hume observes that in England Puritan clergymen "contented themselves with reading prayers and homilies to the people, commonly received the reproachful appellation of 'dumb dogs.'" At this juncture, they prefigured both Puritan "dumb laws" and anti-secular or religious and conservative, plus relatedly overly patriotic or ethnocentric, "dumbed-down" education, in historical and contemporary America.

[42] Hume also remarks that in England the "Puritanical pulpits resounded with declamations concerning the necessity of executing justice upon great delinquents"; and, one can add, that by "executing justice" these Puritans usually meant "executions", as do their "born again" US descendents in their "tough on crime" laws and policies.

[43] Weisbrod (1999:143) refers to "upholding Utah's adultery statute" during the late 1990s.

(Weisbrod 1999) continue to, alongside the federal government (the military), to criminalize adultery and pre-marital sexual activity or certain kinds of it (including prostitution) by Puritan-era or style "dumb" laws and punish transgressions of this old puritanical code. In comparative terms, Puritan America, or its "Bible Garden", remains the only Western society that criminalizes and (like the military) punishes this particular moral sin, or, as Americans call it, "cheating", and only matched by Islamic societies, excepting Turkey (despite some unsuccessful attempts at criminalizing adultery by fundamentalist Muslim forces).

In a better known historical example, Prohibition criminalized and punished alcohol consumption, as still do Southern and other "dry" states (Merton 1968) and even does the federal government for certain categories of the population (those under 21 year), though not as severely as Puritanism did similar sins. And, what Prohibition did with respect to alcohol consumption, the subsequent "war on drugs" has done and does for drug use and possession (Reuters 2005). Yet, it has carried this Puritanical criminalization and punishment of vices and sins even further in scope and intensity to its ultimate consequences, including mass ever-growing imprisonment and (potential) executions for "free market enterprise" or profit-making in chemical substances.

Generally, Puritan moral fascism criminalizes virtually all kinds of moral sins and vices. It thus enforces its moralistic irrational (including "dumb") laws, and inflicts severe punishments on the sinful via a myriad of never-ending temperance wars against "sin and vice" in America, old and new ones, from "Salem with witches" to Prohibition to the "war on drugs". In so doing, it seeks to transform human sinners, thus potentially all humans (minus Puritan saints-masters), in criminals and punishes them accordingly, invariably harshly. For instance, early Puritanism by criminalizing adultery transformed adulterers or "cheaters" in New England and beyond, if any (e.g., Wesley and other early Methodists as "womanizers" in various accusations or rumors, cf., Baldwin 2006) from "good Christians" (Harley 1996) into mortal sinners, just as other sinful or ungodly humans in "witches", hence punished or threatened with death. And, so still do many Southern states, and, for that matter, most Islamic countries (excluding Turkey), albeit with less severe punishments short of Puritan-style executions, cruelty, and torture.

And, according to this Puritan law and its vestiges, many past and living US Presidents should be executed or somehow sanctioned for their documented and admitted sins of adultery. This category of sinners-as-criminals comprises an even large number of, especially puritanical ultra-conservative, Congressmen and other "godly" and "holier than thou" politicians from the "Bible Garden" and beyond committing such "ungodly" sins leading or not to divorces, and perhaps half (based on surveys and the equivalent divorce rate) of all married Americas self-confessing to or believed "cheating" on their spouses, during recent times.

Now, a separate chapter, if not book, would be needed to mention those Puritan-inspired US religious conservatives from the "Bible Belt" and beyond committing adultery and related sexual sins (prostitution, pornography, premarital sexuality, etc.) and even violent crimes (rapes, assaults, sex with minors). But the publicly admitted, repented, and forgiven adultery case of a former disgraced (but not for this moral sin) Speaker of the House from the "Bible Belt" is particularly revealing. First, it indicates and confirms again what Hume and Weber identified as the "pure hypocrisy" of Puritans and their evangelical descendents or disciples in the "Bible Belt" and America overall with respect to sexual and other moral sins, and virtually everything else. Second, it shows what has been observed as Calvinist illiberality in the sense of demanding for and granting moral and other freedom and thus (as the person in question did) forgiveness for sin like adultery to oneself, and yet denying them to others, a variation on the theme of Anarchy or license for Puritan masters, Leviathan or tyranny for non-Puritans. Third, it indicates that Puritan-rooted anti-adultery, like other, "dumb" laws in the "Bible Belt" are both irrational or ineffective and selectively non-enforced or discriminatory. For they neither prevented adultery in this case nor were enforced to punish what they proscribe as a sin-as-crime in this region, instead of the perpetrator being promptly given on request by "reborn" Puritan evangelicals forgiveness and compassion. Finally, one wonders what these and other Puritan-inspired "rigid extremists" like Reagan et al. would have experienced and thought if they lived and thus committed their adulteries in the "shining city upon a hill" of their role model Winthrop punishing such sexual sins with no less than cruel death. Probably, if subjected to such punishment, they would have experienced the "shining city" as the Inquisition-style darkness, and themselves as heretics or "witches", thus had "second thoughts". Yet, these "reborn" Puritan evangelicals deny to others what they demand for and grant to themselves—the freedom of choice between virtue and sin, and forgiveness and compassion for "all too human" sins, including adultery, still criminalized and punished, as via "dumb laws" in the "Bible Belt", when perpetrated by non-evangelicals.

Like virtually all other legal norms in New England and their ramifications in the South, such Puritan anti-adultery laws specifically deny and/or overlook the original implied Christian principle of forgiveness for this particular and related sins (the Biblical "who has not sinned" passage), which is perhaps why many Americans call them "dumb" and others "non-Christian". These laws simply criminalize and punish with Draconian harshness what original Christianity, including Catholicism, defined as a sin, but not (judging from the cited Biblical passage) crime, at least not an offense to be punished with death. If so, then to use Sorokin's term "Christian" brotherly love to describe Puritanism, including Winthrop et al., is a flagrant non sequitur for those writing the Biblical passage and a "cruel joke" not worth the paper on which it was written for the victims punished, notably those executed in New England and beyond (Baldwin 2006), due to its laws criminalizing such sins. This particular instance reaffirms American Puritanism's stature as Weber's "unexampled" tyranny, in particular as "unprecedented" inhumanity and the "most distant" aberration from the ideal-typical ethic of brotherhood within Christianity and even world religions (Symonds and Pudsey 2006).

Sociologically, anti-adultery and other laws criminalizing sins epitomize and reveal Puritanism's intolerance of and impatience with human weakness, mistakes, and imperfections or "impurities" within civil society. They thus indicate its disdain, disregard, and misanthropy or hatred (Symonds and Pudsey 2006) of humans to be totally controlled, oppressed, and eventually sacrificed, literally or figuratively, to the God of Calvinism. In a way, they show that, following Calvinism, Puritanism did and still does not tolerate humans as *humans* or brothers mistreated or depreciated as "others" (Schluchter 1981; also, Edgell et al. 2006), including actual or potential sinners but not necessarily (as the Bible passage implies) criminals. It instead forces humans to become saints or angels (e.g., monks) and in that sense non-or quasi-human, with their Puritan masters acting as if they were super-humans. This is what J. S. Mill means identifying Puritans' "fanatical" moral and other intolerance assuming, as some sociologists (Bauman 2001) suggest, evermore pathological, "sadistic" forms by modern Puritan-based moral fascism in America.

Then, puritanical Prohibition, criminalizing a chemical substance, alchemically converted alcohol consumers, thus the vast majority of

Americans, from "good" citizens and Christians or "regular guys", including free-market entrepreneurs, into actual criminals. This criminalization prohibited what was supposed in original Christianity, both Catholicism and the Orthodox Church, to be an element of the sacrament of the "body and blood of Jesus Christ" (Elwood 1999), the "transubstantiation of bread and wine into Christ's flesh and blood" (Mentzer 2007).

In the process and in accordance with the logic of any prohibitions of sins or pleasures (as the Biblical "forbidden apple" metaphor implies), Prohibition regenerated "bad guys" or the "real McCoys" a la Al Capone and Mafia, inventing a new form of organized crime and various other pathological unintended consequences (Merton 1968; Simon 1976). On this account, Prohibition is particularly interesting case in that it turned out to be an ultimately irrational, self-defeating, and grotesque or immature, almost childish puritanical endeavor to enforce morality by no less than constitutional law and thus government coercion. It was in a sense anti-Christian because of violating one of the two basic "Eucharistic elements" in original Christianity, Christ" "last supper" (Elwood 1999) of bread and wine (not to mention its widely documented health benefits), if not even non-Calvinist in the sense of original Calvinism[44] (Heller 1986; Mentzer 2007). This holds true of various vestiges or local replicas of Prohibition, such as no-alcohol "dry" zones in the "Bible Garden" and its equivalents (Utah), the appreciably increased federal legal limit (from 18 to 21 year) for alcohol consumption, etc. On this account, by analogy to the caste system in India, Prohibition is formally "gone with the wind", but substantively survives in civil society, specifically in Puritan moral fascism, first and foremost,

---

[44] Heller (1986:116) recounts that in 1534 (Poitiers, France) "Calvin for the first time organized an evangelical supper called a "manducation". This ceremony led by someone chosen from the assembled company was marked by a vernacular reading from the Gospel followed by a distribution of bread and wine [sic]." In turn, Elwood (1999:168) cites a French Calvinist author (Theodore Beza at Poissy) that "Christ's body 'is as far removed from the bread and wine as is heaven from earth.'" If so, Prohibition was non-Calvinist in the first sense, and truly Calvinist in the second. And, if the first is correct, this is one of those rare cases in which American Puritanism deviates from Calvinism, but in an opposite, coercive, and non-democratic, direction to that conventionally assumed by most US analysts. By doing it effectively functions as "hyper-Calvinism" and US Puritans act as "super-Calvinists" in the sense of surpassing Calvinism and Calvinists in virtue of even criminalizing one element of Christ's Eucharist. Also, Mentzer (2007:340) suggests that France Calvinism's "celebration of the Lord's Supper" (the Eucharist) involved a 'sacral, symbolic, and communal meal" with people joining in "receiving the bread and wine", while in the liturgy of fasting they joined in "renouncing temporarily eating and drinking."

in the "Bible Garden" and other "hot-red" states and Pareto's perpetually puritanical, intrusive federal government.

In sum, Prohibition was both supremely sociologically irrational with respect to free civil society and theologically contradictory in relation to original Christianity. It affirmed that Puritan moralistic tyranny was a species (*pace* Weber) of Calvinist religious irrationalism (Grossman 2006; Harley 1996) and even, as a secondary point, a reversal of traditional Christian values or, as in this case, symbols (wine). In both respects, Prohibition was, after "Salem with witches" and Calvin's Geneva before in a historical sequence, the prime candidate for being "inducted" into the Puritan "hall of infamy" of criminalizing and punishing human sins and vices, though less severely (e.g., "just" life in prison) than its Puritan-Calvinist model or precedent.

At this juncture, Hume in his sarcastic comment on the clams of Puritans as if "Jesus was Puritan" implies that the latter was not so in moral terms, as contemporary "revisionists" also argue (the Magdalena episode), thus counter-factually subjected to their laws criminalizing and punishing with death or otherwise adultery and "fornication." This is a moment of Dostoevsky's hypothetical scenario of an established theocratic church proscribing and eventually killing its own God. Also, if Jesus lived in or the God of Christianity visited "in person" America during Prohibition he would have likely been imprisoned (conceivably, for life for repeated offenses) or otherwise punished for his sin of drinking wine on his "last supper", just, if he were under 21 year old in the 1980s-2000s, especially severe in the "Bible Belt". This is all hypothetical or metaphorical, but it has the function to illustrate that American Puritanism, including "reborn" evangelicalism, is just Calvinism and Christianity "gone mad", thus perverted or reversed. In particular, wine-drinking (so "sinful") Christ, like non-Puritan and non-Protestant Christians (including Catholics), would have experienced the "Bible Belt", either as the "southern way of religion" (Boles 1999) and reality or the design and recipe for America, as a "Christian" name for Puritan moral fascism or moralistic tyranny.

In addition, some sociologists and economists (Friedman 1997; Reuter 2005) would also nominate the subsequent neo-Puritan "war on drugs", as a heir apparent and even amplification of Prohibition in respect of other "ungodly" chemical substances, for this status on the account of its ever greater scope and intensity of criminalizing and punishing moral sin and vice in America. If anything, this new temperance war is even more intransigent in criminalizing and harsher in punishing these specific sins or vices (the use, possession, production, and marketing, of drugs) turned into "drug war crimes" (Reuter 2005) than Prohibition ever was (despite its provision of life sentences for repeated violations). Like Prohibition and other temperance wars, this new war converts non-violent drug possessors and users from sinners and addicts, thus medical patients, and "regular" Americans or "good Christians" at some historical points (as before the 1930s) into "criminals" subjected to severe punishment, including life-long imprisonment and potentially death (for production and marketing). Like these wars, in the process it reproduces more criminal "Al Capones" or "real McCoys" and Mafias, thus organized and disorganized crime.

This latest and perhaps the most dramatic episode of perennial Puritan temperance wars in America indicate that Puritan-inspired moralistic repression, and thus moral fascism, has intensified and escalated or revived, rather than vanished or weakened, since Prohibition. It also indicates that such repression has become more, not less, severe, cruel and inhumane in punishing human sins and sinners. If anything epitomizes and symbolizes Puritan anti-humanism, including inhumanity, thus moral fascism, in contemporary post-Prohibition America, then it is, first and foremost, the neo-conservative "war on drugs." This holds true on the account of its unrivaled, among modern Western societies, intransigence in criminalizing and its Draconian severity in punishing, including imprisoning for life and potentially executing, nonviolent sinful offenses and offenders (Reuter 2005).

In comparative terms, the "war on drugs" is the single strongest "proof" and syndrome of Puritan moral fascism and its anti-humanism and inhumanity in contemporary America. It is in that it treats and punishes sinful drug users (let alone producers and traders) as actual criminals rather than, as in most other Western societies, addicts and thus mental patients needing medical assistance and advice, instead of harsh punishment like long and permanent a la "three strikes and you are out" imprisonment. In this sense, the new puritanical "war on drugs" is not only the more morbid, or less "fun" but equally grotesque, heir apparent of Prohibition (Friedman 1997). It is a near-reenactment of proto-Puritan "Salem with witches" in moral terms at least, as well as a functional equivalent of Iran's theocratic wars against sins and vices (Bauman 1997; Mansbach 2006; Van Dyke 1995), if not fascist, including the Nazi, campaigns against "immorality", "degenerate" humans and art, and "corruption" (Bourdieu and Haacke 1995) in interwar Europe.

And, like virtually all Puritan temperance wars, including witch-trials and Prohibition, the "war on drugs" with its unrivaled severity is the exemplar of Mannheim's surgeon performing "splendid" operation and Keynes' cure curing the disease of drug production, marketing, and consumption by eventually killing the "patient" of a free civil society, or throwing away the desired "baby" of individual moral freedom with the "dirty water" of moral sin and vice. Overall, temperance wars confirm that Puritan moral fascism or "reborn" fundamentalism in America is the type of solution to moral sins and human vices that promises to solve the "agony" of individual choices by "abolishing the choice itself" (Bauman 2001). Thus, its "allure" eventually turns out to be "fatal attraction" for human freedom and eventually, as via the death penalty, life.

In general, contemporary sociological analyses register and emphasize what is described as the Draconian severity of the contemporary Puritan-based neoconservative criminal justice system in America in punishing not just violent and serious crimes like murders, but also moral sins or non-violent offenses and misdemeanors. In this view, such severity makes this criminal justice system a "unique anomaly" among contemporary Western and other democratic societies during the early 21st century (Pager 2003). If anything, what is "fascist" about Puritan moralistic tyranny, thus makes it moral fascism, in America is that, like in Nazism and Islamic and other religious fundamentalism, sinners and other non-conformists are punished with "Draconian severity" (Patell 2001).

As expected, a cited exemplary case of this Draconian severity is the "war on drugs" as the ever-growing element and operation of a "tough on crime" criminal justice, notably penal, system and the crucial subtype of Puritanical temperance wars in contemporary America. Recall, about two thirds of almost 2.5 million federal and other US inmates during the 2000s are non-violent drug offenders and in that sense moral sinners (Becky and Western 2004) or prisoners of ethical conscience typically sentenced to long prison terms and even life imprisonment for their sins and vices (mostly marihuana use and possession). This penal harshness is especially due to "three strikes" laws passed by most US states, including "liberal" California (Akerlof 2002; Erikson and Parent 2007), carried away by the "get-tough-on-crime" paranoia, like the "frenzy" (Pager 2003) of mass imprisonment and executions of both guilty and innocent, and temperance or culture wars, incited by "born again" fundamentalism since the 1980s.

As noticed, while most Western and other democratic societies attempt to medically cure and socially rehabilitate such drug sins and sinners, Puritan moral fascism in America severely punishes and otherwise mistreats them with unrivaled brutality, cruelty, and inhumanity via the "war on drugs" and related "tough on crime" temperance wars. If anything, such a striking and ever-growing difference between the "war on drugs" in America and its more "humane" (Reuter 2005) alternatives in Western societies epitomizes and reaffirms what has been evident since the rise of Calvinism, notably Puritanism. This is that Puritanism was anti-humanist or inhumane, or more anti-human and inhumane, including un-brotherly (Symonds and Pudsey 2006), than other Protestantism such as Lutheranism and Anglicanism, Catholicism and Orthodox Christianity, as the religious and cultural legacies of these societies (Inglehart and Baker 2000), and equally as or analogously to Islam (Mansbach 2006).

Overall, it reaffirms what Weber and Tawney noted a century ago, that Puritanism and Calvinism generally effectively reversed original or traditional Christian ethical values, notably understanding, caritas, compassion, and forgiveness for sins, and is thus anti-Christian and anti-human in this respect. Evidently, it is in particular American Puritanism that continues to do so, via the "war on drugs" and its Draconian severity perverting and thus destroying Christian and any understanding, compassion, forgiveness, and related humanist values. Hence, the difference between the "war on drugs" in America and its more humane Western alternatives dramatically, and tragically for those Americans harshly punished for drug offenses, expresses the profound antinomy between Puritan moral fascism and liberal-secular civil society/political democracy.

To that extent, Puritan moral fascism in virtue of its Draconian "war on drugs" and other temperance wars effectively situates or forces America outside Western, if not even Christian in the sense of Weber and Tawney, civilization. Conversely, it brings the Puritan nation closer to non-Western or third-world, notably Islamic, authoritarian states than European societies (minus semi-theocratic Poland and, of course, the Vatican Church) (Inglehart 2004). In particular, it is only Puritan moral fascism in America and Islamic theocracy in Iran, Saudi Arabia, and similar Muslim countries that primarily treat and punish non-violent drug and alcohol users and other moral sinners as criminals rather than, as in most Western societies, first and foremost, addicts and medical patients. This reaffirms American Puritanism's and fundamentalist Islam's "elective affinity" in militant anti-humanism and inhumanity (Mansbach 2006; Turner 2002), including Draconian punishment, notably executions, for sins-crimes (Jacobs et al. 2005).

Moreover, it is only or primarily the two (plus such ultra-Catholic countries like Poland) that persist in temperance wars overall and Draconian punishments for drug-war and other moral sins, while by contrast most Western and other modern democratic societies have largely ended or moderated such activities (Inglehart 2004). For instance, among contemporary Western and other societies only Puritan moral fascism in America and Islamic theocracies like Iran and Saudi Arabia (plus North Korea, China and other dictatorships) imprison for life and even execute non-violent drug offenders[45] (users and traders) and otherwise criminalize and severely punish moral sins and sinners (e.g., alcohol use, adultery, prostitution, etc.). In particular, the Southern "Bible Garden" and Iran, Saudi Arabia, and other Islamic theocratic societies are virtually the only cases in the modern world criminalizing alcohol use and more (the second) or less (the first) severely punishing violators. They thus exemplify their observed functional equivalence in a Draconian penal, including the death penalty, system and the proto-totalitarian destruction of a free civil society overall (Bauman 1997). Notably, among contemporary Western societies, only Puritan moral fascism in America has established extremely harsh "three strikes" laws criminalizing and severely punishing nonviolent drug and even any other moral offenses, not to mention crimes, with life-long imprisonment inflicted on what are often minor drug-war and other crimes (e.g., repeated possession of small amounts of marihuana). If the description "Draconian severity" in reference to the US Puritanical criminal justice system, in particular its "war on drugs", looks hyperbolic, at least it applies to "three strikes" laws and their strikingly harsh and comparatively unrivaled punishment of nonviolent drug and similar temperance "crimes".

In general, "three strikes" laws, passed and applied in most US states, criminalize and punish with life imprisonment drug-related and other sins or vices as well as various commonly viewed minor non-violent crimes (e.g., petty theft, "bounced" checks, etc.) or misdemeanors.

---

[45] For instance, drug trade became potentially a federal capital offense in America under neo-conservatism during the 1990s, and Iran effectively punishes with death the marketing and even possession (of certain amounts) of drugs.

They thus epitomize Puritan Draconian severity and in extension moral fascism. They are a sort of Puritan "Draconianism", thus moral fascism in action or on rampage in America, alongside executions for sins or crimes, as a hyper-Draconian punishment.

In comparative terms, like Puritan moral fascism and its Draconian severity overall, these three strikes and you are out" laws and life-long punishments for drug and similar nonviolent sins make America, namely the federal government and those states with such legal norms, really exceptional. More specifically, they make it both the "laughing stock" of the world[46] (Hill 2002; Wagner 1997), including modern European societies and Canada where nothing of sorts exists, and a serious abomination of or morbid deviation from Western and global liberal-secular civil society and modernity (Inglehart 2004). In a sense, they provide the legal script for an American Puritan-rooted mixed comedy and tragedy in the eyes of the world and many Americans, notably those millions of drug-war and other moral sinners experiencing for themselves the "sword" of these laws. Hence, like virtually all other Puritan moralistic legal norms, "three strikes" laws are profoundly irrational (or, as many Americans call them, "dumb"). They are so in destroying or subverting individual moral liberty, thus free civil society, and in being eventually ineffective or counterproductive in legislating morality, as indicated by the admitted failures in the "war on drugs", not to mention alcohol prohibitions and restrictions. Moreover, if any Puritan and other moralistic laws are irrational ("dumb") and their punishments Draconian at all in contemporary America, then this holds true, first and foremost, of these particular legal norms and sanctions.

Essentially, "three strikes" laws have proven irrational and Draconian, because they have not succeeded to reestablish—and as Durkheim and Tönnies predict, hardly ever will—"dead" puritanical morality in society. In the process they have denied and undermined individual moral liberty and choice, as evident in the "war in drugs", conjoined with obstinate or recurring alcohol prohibitions or restrictions. Negatively, they have not really eradicated sin and vice, or crime, as their declared

---

[46] For instance, the *Economist* cites George Bernard Shaw's definition of some 19th century Puritan moralistic practices ("Comstockery") as "the world's standing joke at the expense of the United States" and comments that "it is hardly a joke for the people who are caught in its tentacles. There are enough real problems for America's law-enforcement officials to worry about."

aim. Rather, they have admittedly only reclassified certain categories of humans (Friedman 1997) like drug and alcohol users into sinners or new "witches" and thus criminals, and then filled with them the penal system beyond capacity and recognition. For instance, in California despite its "three strikes and you're out" law, its prisons reportedly operate at full or beyond capacity and crime has "not stopped" (Akerlof 2002). In this account, such laws with their outcomes represent an exemplar of what economists call "large negative externalities" or social, including even economic, costs from incarceration offsetting the short-term benefits from "deterring criminal activity through tougher incarceration policies" (Akerlof 2002). In short, in California and other states the harsh and mandatory three-strikes sentencing law has failed more or less dismally to reduce or control crime (Erikson and Parent 2007).

Consequently, "three strikes" Draconian laws and punishments in California and other parts of America tend to pervert civil society as the realm of individual moral and other freedom into a massive open prison or monastic order. Simply, these laws and sanctions have recreated a metaphorical "Salem with witches" in the face of drug-war and other sinners *cum* criminals and thus threaten to ultimately destroy a free civil society in a typical Puritan inverted Schumpeterian uncreative destruction. Hence, on the account of their life-long punishment for sins and other non-violent crimes, "three strikes" laws, as applied in the "war on drugs" and other temperance wars, are the paradigmatic exemplar and emblem of Puritan-style Draconian severity, thus moral fascism in America. Those millions of drug-war and other sinners *cum* criminals imprisoned either in long terms or for life—and consequently whose lives have been effectively destroyed or dramatically perturbed as the result of these "dumb" laws—are the witnesses of or rather human victims at altar of this Draconian severity and moral fascism.

In general, to describe the contemporary US Puritan-rooted criminal justice system in terms of Draconian severity is to imply that it is irrational both in the sense of destroying or restricting individual moral freedom and being self-defeating in imposing morality by coercion. Government Draconian severity in the penal system is a form of legal irrationalism, primitivism, or extremism through a sort of hyper-emotional, vengeful ("eye-for-eye"), and primitive, over-reaction, due to what Durkheim would call the irrational misfit or imbalance between crime and punishment. Hence, this redefines and reveals Puritan and similar theocratic (especially Islamic) criminal justice systems as legally irrational, primitive, or extreme. And since, as he suggests, it is the rational fit or balance of crime and punishment that precisely defines legal rationalism and justice, Draconian severity renders the Puritan and cognate (including Islamic) criminal justice system intrinsically unjust or unfair. In this sense, it is more accurately considered and described as a sort of *criminal* and *injustice* system. It is "criminal" in, as Popper (1973) suggests, the sense of committing official crimes, including murders, against humans for their sins made into crimes, as a form of state terrorism. It is "injustice" in Durkheim's sense of a misfit between crime and punishment, exemplified by drug-war "crimes" and their disproportionately severe punishments via "three strikes" and related laws. In particular, it is criminal for a government to methodically execute innocent people for imputed moral sins or crimes, as reportedly witnessed in America under neo-conservatism, as a sort of institutionalized crime, and even to punish them out of any proportion with their actual offenses (nonviolent drug use, minor theft, "bounced" checks, etc.).

In sum, penal primitivism or extremism make Puritan moral fascism a sort of what Weber would call an abomination of Durkheim's sociological rule—and even elemental common sense or basic human decency—of legal justice that punishment should "fit" crime. In that sense, it is a criminal *injustice* system. This is only "just" because the "criminal justice system", including its death-penalty subsystem, in America has typically been and remains by the 21st century the product and instrument of Puritanism's crusade against "sin" and "ungodliness", as embodied by the Puritan vice-police state or "policeman" (Merril 1945) and couched in arch-conservative "law and order" (Dahrendorf 1979) and neo-conservative "tough on crime" slogans. If the arch-Puritan legal-penal code's "overriding purpose" was eradicating and harshly punishing "all sin" and "ungodliness" both redefined and punished as crime, and forcing "repentance" from the malefactors, through the judiciary (Dayton 1999), then the neoconservative "tough on crime" criminal justice system has not substantively advanced beyond this original or primitive stage. Alternatively, the criminal justice system in America hardly ever functioned as secular, normal Durkheimian legal mechanism of fitting or balancing crime and punishment, independent of moral-religious or ideological and political considerations, as found in modern Western societies.

In a way, it is an irrational expectation or hyper-optimistic illusion to expect and hope that Puritan and other moral fascism and Calvinist theocracy as a whole, by its own nature of totalitarian destruction and disregard of human life and dignity, in America and beyond would generate, sustain, and rationalize a system of true criminal *justice* in Durkheim's sense of a fit of crime and punishment. At least, those millions of Americans punished in a Draconian manner for moral sins as well as petty nonviolent crimes have, to cite the master novelist-sociologist Balzac (Hirschman 1977; Mallard 2005), "lost illusions" about "justice" in the Puritan-style "criminal justice system" in America. They are more than two millions presently imprisoned mostly for "drug war" crimes and five millions on probation for these and similar offenses (Uggen and Manza 2002). Simply, legal "justice" applied to humans is a sort of luxury or nuisance that Puritan and any moral fascism and Calvinist and other theocracy in America "cannot afford." This holds true of justice in relation to sacrificing humans for the glory of God and a Divinely-commanded crusade on human "depravity" and "ungodliness", thus for "higher" than life causes as what Adam Smith would call "necessary goods" and neo-classical economists "opportunity costs" (foregone profitable alternatives).

The defining element and instrument of Puritan moral fascism and Calvinist theocracy in general is crusade or "holy" war in the broadest sense (including its Islamic equivalent jihad) of a perpetual warfare against the "sinful" and "ungodly" within society, via "tough on crime" laws, and other "infidel" societies by "preemptive" wars. These crusades in principle rule out or in reality destroy any notion and practice, while retaining the hypocritical semblance or rhetoric, of legal-penal justice. In Clausewitz's words, "holy" war within society and against other societies is the continuation or implementation of the politics of injustice (or ersatz-justice) of Puritan moral fascism and its "criminal justice system" and Calvinist theocracy overall. After all, what is "fascist" about Puritan and any moral fascism and theocratic about Calvinist and other theocracy is precisely the destruction or perversion of legal and any social justice with respect to humans.

Conversely, the only type of "justice" that Puritan moral fascism enacts is that, to cite Cromwell, "honoring" or increasing the glory of, the God of Calvinism. Ironically, this is what none than Parsons implies admitting the reduction of humans to the means of the "purposes of God" (and one's own private ends a la Machiavelli) in Puritanism and Protestantism as a whole. One wonders what kind of justice humans can expect or hope for so long as they are reduced and eventually sacrificed to supra-human purposes (and "all too human" interests) in a

Puritan-style criminal justice system. To wit, they must be somehow punished, including physically sacrificed to the point of ritual execution, for the glory and purpose of God, because of assumed intrinsic human "depravity" and "ungodliness" a la "original sin", regardless, as the US Supreme Court itself implied in its "infamous ruling" in the 1980s (Bauman 2001), of any secular considerations of guilt and innocence. This is what many innocent Americans experienced by being admittedly imprisoned and even executed on overt or covert religious and ideological grounds (especially in the "Bible Belt" like Texas) couched in "get tough on crime" neo-conservative laws and slogans. "Justice" in the Puritan-inspired criminal justice system in America is what economists call an "impossibility theorem" (Arrow 1950), because Puritan moral fascism or Calvinist theocracy is what it *is* precisely in virtue of being deeply unjust, cruel, and inhumane to humans, except for "holier than thou" self-declared saints as the "elect" (Seaton 2006).

Hence, legal justice is a non sequitur or effectively impossible, except for hypocritical rhetoric, in a "criminal justice system" predicated on and sanctified by what Hume prophetically detected as Puritan—and other religious or ideological, including fascist—"wretched fanaticism" and primitivism ("eye for eye") seeking to eradicate "all sin" and "ungodliness" both defined and punished as crimes. This yields a corresponding prediction or expectation. Penal injustice will persist, escalate, and intensify so long as the "criminal justice system" in America continues to be founded on or inspired by Puritan and pre-Enlightenment "religious fanaticism" (Saisselin 1992), through a fanatical warfare or paranoia against human sins and "ungodliness", couched in the neo-conservative "tough on crime" rhetoric. Under this condition, injustice will prevail and range from mass and permanent or long imprisonment of moral sinners as prisoners of ethical conscience (drug users, etc.) to the execution of innocent people, yet "depraved" on the account of original sin that they must expiate, as human sacrifices for the glory of the God of Calvinism.

The above casts a dramatically different light (or rather darkness) of penal injustice and fanatical irrationalism via Draconian severity on Puritan-inspired conservative "tough on crime" (read sin and vice) laws, institutions, and practices in America, notably the "Bible Garden". In passing, this expression is a typical Puritan-style hypocritical and deceptive play of words. Even most Americans associate "Draconian" with some degree of injustice in the sense of excessive and primitive or barbarian punishment, but not "tough", seemingly "Wild-West" style, associated with "justice" as "just deserts" for crime. Since a Puritan (like Islamic) "tough on crime" penal system was originally "Draconian", as indicated by Winthrop's design of America as "Christian Sparta", and evidently remains so by the 21st century, consequently it was and continues to be unjust or unfair. It is a sort of what Weber may call the "abomination" of legal justice, especially and predictably in the "Bible Garden". For example, some Draconian punishments of non-violent sexual and similar sinners in the region have been described even by, deliberately or forced to be, extremely harsh US judges as "a grave miscarriage of justice".[47] In sum, what is "fascist" about Puritan moral fascism, like its Islamic analogue, is its original and persistent Draconian severity—the gross misfit between crime or sin and its severe punishment—and thus legal irrationalism, primitivism, or extremism, self-perpetuating the "wretched fanaticism" of Puritanism. "Fascism" in Puritan moral fascism is its methodical injustice, as witnessed in a substantive continuity and historical sequence from Salem witch-trials to the "war on drugs" and "three strikes" laws.

Overall, while not all contemporary and past penal systems with Draconian severity in a substantive sense are fascist and conservative overall but also others (including communist as in North Korea and China), fascism and its creator conservatism tends to be invariably exemplary "Draconianism", as dramatically witnessed in Nazism and American neo-conservatism. Hence, if anything, it is its intrinsic and self-perpetuating Draconian severity that causes Puritan moralistic tyranny to effectively function as or prefigure and predict moral fascism, from the 17th century to the 21st century, from Salem witch-trials to the "war on drugs" and "three strikes" laws. And, "born again"

---

[47] For example, in the US Southern state of Georgia during the 2000s, media reported that a "former high school football star who became a national symbol for the extremes of getting tough on sex offenders was ordered released from prison by a judge who called his mandatory 10-year sentence for consensual teen sex "a grave miscarriage of justice"." Such cases, including accusations and convictions for "touching" a la Orwellian crimes, are not exceptions or accidents but a rule or pattern, exemplifications of neo-conservative moral fascism or the "tyranny of Puritanism" and its Draconian harshness in the "Bible Belt" and other Puritan "red" parts of America. In a paradigmatic instance of Draconianism in the "Bible Belt", a person was sentenced to no less than 35 years in prison for "spitting" on police officer in Texas in 2008, a kind punishment unknown in Western societies but found in Islamic theocracies.

US fundamentalists, like their Puritan role models, rationalize and celebrate their Draconian severity, including the death penalty, as some kind of "tough on crime" virtue, while universally seen as a primitive or barbarian ("eye for eye") residue within Western civilization. This instance of "evil as distorted good" evokes both the Biblical passage of "not knowing what they are doing" and Hume's diagnosis of Puritan "wretched fanaticism" and description of early Puritans "as dumb-dogs". In a sense, only inverted "irrational fools" (Sen 1977) can be proud of what reasonable persons are ashamed of. This is penal primitivism or barbarism, irrationalism, and injustice via Draconian severity in the sense of cruel, degrading, or inhumane punishment traced or linked substantively to Sparta and pre-civilized societies (formally to Athens during Draco's and prior to Solon's milder code of laws). In this regard, they substantively (though not nominally) perpetuate into seeming eternity their supreme role model and hero, Winthrop and his theological design of America as "Christian Sparta" by effectively acting or looking as the "new Draco et al." more than two millennia later.

Apparently, what is a "unique anomaly" of primitive Draconian severity among modern Western and other democratic societies in the 21st century is the source of national pride and joy and comparative advantage for US Puritan-inspired neo-conservatism in a standard ethnocentric display of its glorified American exceptionalism. In short, Draconian severity and thus moral fascism has mutated into a sort of internalized or normalized pathology in American religious conservatism, from early Puritanism to "born again" evangelicalism.

In comparative terms, US "born again" religious conservatism by its "tough" laws and policies is more Draconian and punitive overall in sanctioning, just as coercive and aggressive in criminalizing, moral sins, including drug-war nonviolent offenses, than its counterparts in other Western societies, while being only rivaled by Islamic theocracies in Iran and similar societies. This is admitted by the observation that US social conservatives have always been and continue to be "much more aggressive" in enforcing "their own morality" on the political system and civil society than their "ideological compeers elsewhere" (Lipset 1996) in the Western world and even beyond (minus Poland and Islamic theocracies) by state coercion and Draconian-like sanctions. Consequently, as other analysts observe, America has historically been and largely remains an "exceedingly puritanical society", as epitomized by—compared to, for example, Sweden and even once Puritan and Victorian England—its persistent backwardness or lagging "very much in non-punitive attitudes towards atypical sexual practices"[48] (Miller 1975). In this view, overall the "anachronisms" of Puritanism, including anti-intellectual and xenophobic prejudices, have been the "principal source of irrationality and authoritarianism" in American civil society and politics.

At this juncture, what defines or characterizes moralistic fascism and authoritarianism in general is precisely the coercive and aggressive imposition of private and narrow group morality on politics and civil society specifically via, alongside law and governmental coercion generally, Draconian sanctions, including punitive attitudes and policies toward "sexual practices". To that extent, due to this unrivalled aggressiveness in imposing morality through Draconian severity in punishing immorality, moral fascism in its Puritan version is as a rule more intense and persistent or obstinate, predicted by Hume's observation of Puritans' "unreasonable obstinacy", in America than in other Western societies, except for post-communist Poland. Only Islamic theocracies like Iran, Saudi Arabia, and elsewhere are serious contestants in this "beauty contest" of primitive Draconian punishment (Bauman 1997; Mansbach 2006; Van Dyke 1995). Moreover, this Puritan "all-American" exceptional version remains the only or primary type of moral fascism within modern Western civil society (perhaps minus Poland), as implicitly indicated by the description of the US neo-conservative criminal justice system as a "unique anomaly" in the West and even beyond ushering in the 21st century. If so, then Puritan moral fascism effectively remakes the new nation what observers describe as the "last remaining primitive society" (Baudrillard 1999) within modern Western civilization.[49] Conversely, it situates the Puritan nation closer to non-Western traditional, including Islamic and Catholic theocratic, societies (Inglehart 2004). It does especially by its inner Draconian severity, including the fundamentalist-grounded and sanctified death penalty system, as the "die hard" vestige of penal primitivism or "eye for eye" barbarism that Durkheim, Mannheim, and other sociologists assumed to be the dead past, as has become in modern Western

---

[48] Miller (1975:27) adds that when the US situation of the 1970s is compared with that of Sweden during the 1960s, the "changes are much smaller".

[49] This is not necessarily a negative value-judgment, for in American "born again" evangelicalism "primitivism" often signifies Biblical "fundamentalism" or Bibliocracy as its perennial design of America partly implemented via the "Bible Belt", thus a supreme "good" and "virtue".

civilization, except for the "new nation", notably its "Bible Garden". Such a remarkable Puritan-reproduced deviation causes celebrated American exceptionalism to be anti- or non-Western, rather than, as ethnocentrically assumed (Lipset and Marks 2000), a universal "model" for other Western and virtually all societies to adopt and emulate (Beck 2000) by the Biblical "word or sword", culture or military-imperialist wars (Steinmetz 2005).

*Sadism and Masochism*

Perhaps the most pathological syndrome or exact "proof" of Puritan moral fascism represents sadism and masochism in a typical association and mutual reinforcement. In socio-psychological (specifically, psychoanalytical) terms, an integral element of Puritan moral fascism in America is the composite and mutual reinforcement between sadism and masochism (Adorno 2001). A mix of mutually reinforcing sadism and masochism, expressing socio-psychological totalitarianism or authoritarianism (Miller et al. 1987), operates as a sort of "normal pathology" or generalized anomaly of Puritan and any moral fascism (Nazism, Islamic theocracy), though not all sadistic-masochistic and totalitarian or authoritarian traits, behaviors, and personalities are fascist.

Consequently, what is "fascist" in socio-psychological terms about Puritan moral fascism is the "normal pathology" of entwined and mutually reinforcing sadism and masochism defining psychologically or pathologically all fascisms, notably Nazism. It is what sociologists identify as the sadistic-masochistic "character structure" (Fromm 1941; McLaughlin 1996), defining and expressing totalitarian personalities (Miller et al. 1987), that renders Puritan saints-masters and absolutists of all shades and times, including "born again" fundamentalists, in America moral fascists or their functional equivalents (Adorno 2001). In particular, what contemporary analysts identify as the "sadistic intolerance to cultural otherness" in American society (Bauman 2000), especially the "Bible Garden" (Bauman 1997), by these new Puritan fundamentalists makes them act and appear as or resemble moral fascists. In this account, given Puritanism's original practice and enduring legacy in this respect (Miller 1975), predictably "reborn" fundamentalism in the "Bible Garden" and beyond seized and exploited sexual mores" as one of the "more important footholds" for intolerance (Bauman 2000) of moral difference, specifically as the most salient, intense, and persistent, though not the sole, ground. Simply, if one does not really know what Puritan moral fascism in America is in a socio-psychological and general sense and whether it exists (most US religious fundamentalists would deny its existence), then its entwined sadism-masochism, notably sadistic intolerance, as its "normal pathology" provides an answer or hint.

Predictably, the composite sadism-masochism, including sadistic intolerance, of Puritan moral fascism is not random and transient but rather systematic (built-in) and permanent. It is rooted in original Calvinism, in particular early Puritanism, self-perpetuated, and even intensified in neo-Calvinism, notably American neo-Puritanism or evangelicalism (Adorno 2001). Hence, to understand better the observed sadistic intolerance by Puritan moral fascism in contemporary and historical American society (also, Lipset 1955), it is instructive to revisit original Calvinism or Puritanism and its blend and mutual reinforcement of sadism-masochism.

In a sense, Calvinism and consequently Puritanism originated and operated as a sort of entwined and mutually reinforcing sadism and masochism, including sadistic intolerance and punishment, thus moral proto-fascism in socio-psychological or socio-pathological terms. Calvin et al.'s cruel treatment and murder of their opponents and critics like Servetus and libertines were in a way the original act of Calvinist sadism, usually mixed and mutually reinforced with a degree of masochism. This was evidenced by Calvin himself (Mansbach 2006; Heller 1986) and his disciples, from his Geneva's successors to Cromwell and his "Parliament" of Saints and the first American Puritans like Winthrop et al., as typically sadistic-masochistic and thus totalitarian personalities. In turn, Winthrop et al.'s "profitable" extermination of Native Americans, as well as their "lucrative" trade in slaves (and rum), conjoined with Salem witch-trials, was a sort of collective original act of Puritan sadism, notably the sadistic intolerance to religious and other cultural difference ("heathen" religion and culture), and thus of moral fascism in America.

Social psychologists identify and emphasize the sadistic-masochistic character structure (Fromm 1941; also McLaughlin 1996) as a constitutive psychological trait or emotional basis of original Calvinism, including Puritanism, just as modern fascism, notably Nazism. In this view, the "emotional roots" of original Calvinism (and Protestantism) and modern fascism, specifically Nazism, are substantively identical in the form of a "sado-masochistic character." This is defined by (love as) "symbiotic dependence", (sacrifice as) the "utmost subordination" of the individual to "something higher", (difference as) "difference in power", (courage as) the "readiness to submit and to endure suffering", and the like (Fromm 1941). In short, the "same principle of explanation" was applied to the rise of Calvinism (and Protestantism) and fascism both explained by "sadistic and masochistic strivings". Notably, for both early Calvinists and modern fascists, "the aim of life is to sacrificed for "higher" powers", sacred or Weber's God of Calvinism in the first case, secular or the "leader or the racial community" in the second. Both were an axiomatic (text-book) expression of sado-masochism, especially sadism through what Calvinist Rousseau[50] virtually prescribes or predicts as tormenting those who are "damned" by Divine predestination. The above yields the cited inference that on the account of this mixed sadism-masochism and related elements Calvinism fulfilled the "same sociological function" for Anglo-Saxon societies as did fascism in Germany, and thus was "linked" with Nazism, rather than with, as commonly assumed, "political freedoms and economic progress" (McLaughlin 1996).

And, Calvinism did so through Puritanism that inherited and further intensified Calvinist sadism-masochism and related elements. At this juncture, Puritanism actually performed the "same sociological function", in particular that of sado-masochism and thus moral fascism, for Anglo-Saxon societies, notably America, as did Calvinism for some parts of Europe (Geneva, Holland, in part Prussia) before and fascism later, especially Nazism for Germany. As usual, Hume among the first social analysts identify or imply elements and symptoms of sadism in early Puritanism by commenting that "nothing can be more hateful than the uncharitableness of the Puritans who condemn alike to eternal torments even the most inoffensive partisans of Popery [King James]." In particular, he notices that these Puritans harbored a sort of sadistic "malevolence", with which they "endeavored to inspire" the English House of Commons that they dominated or increasingly influenced during the early 17th century (and prior to the 1640 Puritan Revolution), as well as a "restless and encroaching spirit". What Hume identified as "malevolence" Weber did as Puritan "peculiar misanthropy" or pathological hatred (Symonds and Pudsey 2006) and in consequence sadism as the malevolent, including destructive, treatment of hated

---

[50] Thus, revealing his original or residual Calvinism, Geneva-born and Calvin's partial disciple Rousseau claims that "it is impossible to live in peace with people who one believes are damned. To love them would be to hate God who punishes them. They must absolutely be either brought into the faith or tormented."

humans. Moreover, Pareto points to Calvinist-Puritan mixed and mutually reinforcing sadism and masochism by citing the Scottish Presbyterian clergy as experiencing "great delight in tormenting" themselves and others alike through equating human pleasures with sins and thus eventually crimes subjected to severe punishment, including actually or conceivably death.

Generally, the above indicates a remarkable continuity within Calvinism, in particular Puritanism, with respect to its mix and mutual reinforcement of sadism and masochism, from the 16th and 17th to the 21st century. In this respect, a substantively continuous or almost unbroken line of development connects Calvin's inhumane torture and murder of Servetus and libertines, Scottish Calvinists' "great delight in tormenting" both themselves and others, Cromwell's "cruel persecution" of Irish Catholics and his own masochistic suffering for the "Glory of God", and notably Winthrop et al.'s "profitable" extermination of "ungodly" Native Americans and Salem witch-trials with the "sadistic intolerance to cultural otherness" by contemporary Puritan moral fascism in America. Being a native French, if by any miracle of his God of Calvinism (and most Calvinists, including Puritans, believe in and ever expect miracles), Calvin resurrected from the dead and Servetus' "cries" (Nigg 1962) and visited, as did his glorified countryman Tocqueville two centuries before, America and witnessed Puritan "sadistic intolerance" during the early 21st century—he might have realized and triumphantly stated again "the more things have changed, the more they stayed the same" from his death almost five centuries ago, simply "I told you so". This even more applies to "all-American" Winthrop et al., for (if) their peculiar micro-model or symbol of sectarian sadism, oppression, and closure, "Salem with witches" has been seemingly self-perpetuated or evoked in the "sadistic intolerance to cultural otherness" by Puritan-grounded moral fascism in modern America.

While certainly it is not fair to blame or praise, as the case may be "foreign" Calvin or "all-American" Winthrop for this continuing Calvinist-Puritan "sadistic intolerance" and moral fascism overall in America five or four centuries later, the point is that this sadism is "all in the extended and long-living family" of Calvinism from the 16th to the 21st century. From its point of origin in France to its destination in America, Calvinism has displayed, as Weber would expect, "iron consistency", and even, through Puritanism, as Hume expected, "unreasonable obstinacy", in sadism mixed and "stirred" with masochism to

Table 5.1. Syndromes of Puritan moral fascism

| |
|---|
| Denial and suppression of individual freedom in morality |
| Equation of pleasures and sins with crimes |
|    equation of pleasures with sins and vices |
|    equation of sins and vices with crimes |
| Anti-humanism |
|    antagonism to secular humanism |
|    inhumanity, brutality and cruelty |
|    Legal imposition of morality |
| "Draconianism"—penal primitivism and irrationalism |
| Sadism and masochism |
| Puritan vice-police state |

form a typically sado-masochistic totalitarian "cocktail", though sadistic elements are usually stronger or more visible. (These syndromes of moral fascism are summarized in Table 5.1.)

### The Legal-Institutional Mechanism of Puritan Moral Fascism

As implied, the legal-institutional mechanism of Puritan moral fascism as the polar antithesis and destruction of a free civil society is by assumption and in reality the theocratic or religiously driven and moralistic police state. In short, it is what for the present purpose and convenience can be described as the vice-police state. In this sense, the vice-police state is established and functions as the *modus vivendi and operandi*—the institutional life ("blood") and operating mode ("tears")—of Puritan moral fascism and Calvinist theocracy overall in America, most notably the Southern "Bible Garden" and its equivalents (Utah, etc.).

### The Vice-Police State

In legal and overall institutional terms, Puritan moral fascism in America specifically operates, enforces, and expresses itself as theocratic government or a religiously grounded and extremely moralistic policing state, for simplicity called a vice-police state. The latter is understood as a type of government and legal system that is instituted and organized for a sort of permanent war on and Draconian punishment of moral vices and sins as crimes and human sinners as criminals.

The Puritan vice-police state and hence moral fascism in America are grounded in and rationalized by the designation and operation of Puritanism as "God's vice-regent" (Zaret 1989). Essentially, the self-designation and operation of Puritanism as "God's vice-regent" logically presupposes and practically necessitates the Puritan vice-police state as its logical and necessary effective mechanism or instrument, consequently moral fascism. Hence, Puritanism in virtue of its acting as "God's vice-regent" intrinsically or ultimately produces and predicts the vice-police state as a sort of "final solution" to human vices and sins and sinners and the "evil" of individual moral freedom, thus moral fascism. Conversely, the theological origin of the modern and ever-growing Puritan vice-police state, and hence moral fascism, in America is Puritanism's original mantle as "God's vice-regent." In particular, this holds true of the "Bible Garden" vice-police state evidently predicated on and sanctified by Puritanism's self-assignment and function as "God's vice-regent" in New England's "Biblical Commonwealth". Notably, the "Bible Garden" largest vice-police state and most intense moral fascism in America and Western civil society overall is modeled after or parallels New England's "most totalitarian" (Stivers 1994) Calvinist penal system and legal theocracy embodied and enforced by the "Puritan policeman" (Merrill 1945). It thus indirectly (and perhaps unknowingly) continues and further intensifies what Calvin et al. had done in Geneva before (e.g., the Servetus and libertines episodes) (Mansbach 2006).

In this sense, like in 17th century New England's "Biblical Commonwealth", Puritanism effectively continues to function as God's anti-vice agency in the 21st century "Bible Garden" and other "hot-red" regions of America via the vice-police state and Puritan moral fascism and "reborn" fundamentalism overall. This indicates that the vice-police state and thus moral fascism is intrinsic, systemic, and constant, rather than contingent, random and transient, in Puritanism owing to its claim to and its performing non-disappearing act as "God's vice-regent". If any element concerning individual moral liberty and civil society overall in Puritanism, just as in its substantive equivalent, Islam, is "genetic", built-in, or pure (apart from "pure hypocrisy"), then it is the vice-police state. Simply, the latter is in the "genes" or "instincts" of Puritans, like Islamist fundamentalists and rulers, and their evangelical descendents as self-assigned God's vice-agents.

The above yields corresponding predictions or expectations. So long as "born again" Puritans *cum* evangelicals in America (and Islamist fundamentalists) continue to claim to be and act as God's anti-vice agents and temperance-culture "warriors" ("Christian soldiers"), the vice-police state, thus moral fascism, will self-perpetuate "live and well" in America (and Muslim countries), notably the "Bible Garden" (and Iran) as the "paradise lost and found" of anti-vice and anti-sin evangelicalism (fundamentalism). Moreover, to the extent that these God's anti-vice agents increase or consolidate their predominance or influence, the vice-police state, thus moral fascism, will further expand and intensify, as precisely happened in America, notably the "Bible Garden" (and Iran), over the 1980s–2000s. Conversely, the decrease of the first will lead to the decline of the second, as witnessed in other Western societies (with some minor exceptions like ultra-Catholic post-communist Poland) during that period.

Generally, while not all fascisms consist of true vice-police, but also non- or pseudo-moralistic police, states (as exemplified by Nazism), moral fascism always does by assumption or in reality. In short, the legal-institutional mode, code, and "name" of moral fascism in general represents the vice-police state. In particular, the legal and overall institutional mode of existence and operation or enforcement of Puritan moral fascism, thus Calvinist theocracy, in America is axiomatically or practically the vice-police state and its various agencies. Hence, what is "moral" *cum* moralistic about Puritan and any other (including Catholic, Islamic and Hindu) proxy moral fascism is criminalizing and harshly punishing "vice." And, what is "fascist" or "totalitarian" is the "police state" invariably typifying fascism and totalitarianism (e.g., communism) in general. If anything, it is the vice-police state that defines the Puritan degenerative version of civil society as moral fascism in America, minimally in the "Bible Garden" and its equivalents (e.g., Utah as the supreme exemplar). So, to invert the adage about some vices attacked and punished by anti-vice Puritan and Islamic wars, if one does not know what moral fascism is in America unless seeing it, looking at the massive, pervasive, intrusive, and ever-growing vice-police apparatus, at least the "Bible Garden" (and more minimally Utah), can help to solve the dilemma.

Thus, when various analysts register and document the rise and growth of a policing state in America, especially since post-war times (McCarthyism, etc.), they effectively imply that of its vice-police version and to that extent Puritan moral fascism. As is so manifest, vice-police represent the largest and ever-growing element and activity of the police system in America, notably the "Bible Garden." Thus, the supermajority (around 80 percent in some estimates) of the subsystems and human and material resources of the police system are designed, organized for, and devoted to the obsession with and temperance wars on "vice and sin" (Wagner 1997), notably the "war on drugs" in recent times. On this account, if, as sociologists (Bauman 2001; Bourdieu 1998; Earl, McCarthy, and Soule 2003; Wacquant 2002) suggest, there is such thing as a "big" and further growing policing, in contrast to a "small" social-security, welfare (so, really "no free lunch"), state, this is primarily of a vice-police variety, at least in the Southern "Bible Garden" as the creator or epicenter of friendly or not-so-friendly moral fascism (Bonefeld 2002).

And, the size of the police force, notably vice police, in most small towns in the "Bible Belt" (e.g., Texas, etc.) and beyond is of such magnitude and scope that it seems equal or close to the total police and even armed forces of small European democratic states. Also, the (vice) police force at most Sothern and other US universities, besides being deliberately conspicuous or visible, is virtually equal in size to that of most European small or medium-size towns and even many large cities. Moreover, the (vice) police force at, of all places, universities and schools is the primarily "only or mostly in Puritan America" phenomenon within modern Western society. This reflects and perpetuates Puritanism's antagonism to academic and other intellectual freedom as well as to secular science, knowledge, and education. The (vice) police force is non-existent or invisible and minimal at universities and other academic settings in most Western societies, but apparently pervasive and maximal at those in Puritan America, which makes the latter a unique anomaly. At least for academics, notably those harshly punished for moral and intellectual sins, from Veblen to "war on terror" academic critics (Colorado, etc.), the ever-growing police force at US universities is the "proof" or syndrome of the vice-police state and Puritan moral fascism. If anything, the comparatively unrivalled magnitude, pervasiveness, and salience of the police force indicates the (re) emergence of the vice-police state and thus Puritan moral fascism in modern America, minimally the South.

Moreover, an analysis suggests that the US neo-conservative is comparatively the largest and fastest growing policing state or police-prison industry on a scale seen "never before", except for its previous forms in Nazi Germany and fascist Italy (Miliband 1969), within post-war Western society. To that extent, this forms an equivalent, Puritan-style vice-police state. Hence, Puritan moral fascism has constructed and maintained the "big, bigger, and biggest" vice-police state, making

America a true "leader" in the latter among contemporary Western societies and beyond, predictably with only Islamic theocracies being serious rivals in this respect and anti-vice wars. As expected, it has done particularly in the "Bible Garden" become the single region with the largest and fastest growing vice-police state not only in America, but the Western world and beyond, alongside Iran (or Saudi Arabia) as indicated by their identification as the two main proto-totalitarian attacks on the "evil" and "burden" of individual and other moral liberty, and thus on a free civil society.

In view of these observations and tendencies it seems hardly necessary to "prove" or establish and illustrate the following. First, Puritan moral fascism in America, like its Islamic proxy in most Muslim societies, comprises and operates as a policing state in general. Second, the latter is specifically a vice-police state, as distinguished from its other non or less anti-vice versions, as in Nazism and in part Eastern European communism. In a way, the inner logic of "fascism" in Puritan and other moral fascism necessitates, generates, and predicts the policing state, while that of "moral" *cum* moralistic makes the latter specifically the vice-police state. Conversely, the Puritan and other, notably Islamic, vice-police state constitutes an exemplary policing state in being invariably massive, pervasive, intrusive, and oppressive, just as a "sort of religious police" (Infantino 2003). In this sense, a "small" or "minimal" vice-police state and "limited" government in Puritan and other moral fascism is an inner contradiction (oxymoron) and practical non-entity, at most a standard hypocritical claim by US "reborn" neoconservatives a la Reagan et al. Simply, there is no and there can be no such thing as "small" government in Puritan and other (notably Islamic) moral fascism *cum* a "godly community" (German 1995), as no "free lunch" in predatory Calvinist capitalism. The invariant type of government in Puritan moral fascism is a "big, bigger, biggest" and, due to its irrational "dumb" laws, "dumb, dumber, dumbest" (citing a movie comedy) and even maximal vice-police state. This is shown in a long historical continuity from New England's "Biblical Commonwealth" and its "Puritan policeman" and "Salem with witches" to the Southern "Bible Garden" and its "Monkey Trials", the "war on drugs", anti-alcohol (e.g., engaging two separate police forces in some Southern states), anti-sexuality, and innumerable other never-ending or renewed temperance and culture wars.

Conversely, a "small", "minimal", and diminishing, even virtually non-existent, as in Western societies like Scandinavia, Holland,

Germany, France, and Canada, vice-police state is a defining and constitutive element of liberal-secular civil society and democracy, the poison of which are Puritan and Islamic maximal states. If anything, it is a maximal or massive, pervasive, and ever-growing vice-police as well as warfare—and correlatively, a minimal welfare or well-being—state that makes Puritan moral fascism in America, thus the latter as a whole, a "deviant case" from Western liberal-secular civil society and democracy (Inglehart 2004). In general, it is a policing state that does so (Bourdieu 1998), but the latter is invariably of a vice-police variety given the "logic" and operation of Puritanism as God's anti-vice agent. At this juncture, Puritan-rooted celebrated American exceptionalism actually manifests itself in the specific form of an exceptionally, within Western civil society and democracy, maximal vice-police, just as warfare state, thus "big" or maximal, rather than, as ethnocentrically claimed (Lipset and Marks 2000), "small" or "minimal" government.

Historically, while the Nazi and other fascist police state in interwar Europe was mostly an ideological-political (and racist) one, the Puritan policing state in America, at least the "Bible Garden", like the Islamic in Iran and elsewhere, is primarily a religiously based and sanctified vice-police type (Infantino 2003). In general, the Puritan policing state in America represents in Hobbesian terms Leviathan or Big/Bigger/Biggest Government in inhumane moralistic repression and Draconian punishment for, including "Big Brother" in legal or illegal monitoring of, sins and vices. And, these elements are paradoxically entwined and mutually reinforced with Anarchy or small/smaller/smallest government in human well-being, including material welfare and health care. Yet, this duality of Leviathan and Anarchy far from being a paradox or unique anomaly and contradiction is apparently a model of Calvinist consistency for this policing state, expressing its "normal pathology" of Orwellian "double talk" and perpetuating Puritan fanaticism.

Since a dominant and ever-growing particular element and emblem of the above policing state is religious-style vice police (Infantino 2003), the latter functions as the institutional mode of operation and enforcement of Puritan moral fascism. Recall that the religious-style vice-police state and thus moral proto-fascism in America was originally created, enforced, and embodied by the "Puritan policeman" (Merrill 1945) as a Weberian ideal-type, founded on Puritanism as putatively "God's vice-regent" and in extension Calvinism as exemplary Protestant asceticism. The preceding reveals a striking historical continuity from Puritanism as "God's vice-regent" and the "Puritan policeman", in New England's "Biblical Commonwealth" and in extension Calvin's Geneva (the mistreatment of Servetus and libertines), to the neo-conservative vice-police state in America, notably the Southern "Bible Garden" (and Utah etc.). In short, moral fascism's vice-police state is rooted in, perpetuated, and predicted by Puritanism *cum* "God's anti-vice agency and embodied or symbolized by the "Puritan policeman", past and present.

In substantive, as distinguished from formal, terms, the Puritan and other vice-police, like any policing, state functions as the legal-institutional mechanism of a sort of official, in this case, religiously grounded and sanctified and moralistic, terrorism. Puritan and other moral, like any, fascism and all totalitarianism (Arendt 1951; Bähr 2002) is essentially official, state terrorism in itself in the sociological sense of what Comte significantly describes as "violent repression" once in political power, just as counter-state, oppositional terrorism when in opposition in the form of unlawful violence against non-Puritan institutions (Gibbs 1989; Smelser and Mitchell 2002; Turk 2004). For example, Comte identifies and emphasizes "violent repression" as the characteristic tendency and practice of Calvinism and its Puritan sects when in "government" and to that extent state terrorism (also, Mansbach 2006) and implicitly counter-state terrorism through violence or "compulsive agitation" while being in fanatical opposition. Further, historical research explicitly indicates that early English and American Puritanism effectively practiced official "holy terror" (Walzer 1963) whenever establishing its local, regional, or national dominance. Conversely, as Hume implies, Puritanism committed counter-state terrorism while placed in the opposite power constellation (Anglican, Catholic, or Lutheran domination). As usual, Puritanism thereby did not "rediscover America" or "reinvent the wheel" of "holy" terror but followed and expanded and intensified what analysts identify as Calvinist explicit or implicit state and counter-state terrorism as equivalent to those in fundamentalist Islam[51] (Mansbach 2006).

---

[51] According to Mansbach (2006:106), the Calvinist Revolution and the Protestant Reformation overall "also featured terrorism and counterterrorism, warfare unrestrained by legal conventions, and transnational proselytizing of fundamentalist principles".

The above suggests that Puritan moral fascism typically represents or conducts, first, state terrorism whenever and wherever in power or governance, as witnessed in old and New England and the "Bible Belt". A paradigmatic method or symbol of Puritan state terrorism involves the simultaneous production and persecution of "witches" or "enemies", simply witch-trials both as actual practices and metaphors, spanning from New England to, via "Monkey Trials", the South to McCarthyism and "tough" on sin-crime neo-conservatism. Second, Puritan moral fascism conducts counter-state terrorism while not being in power but in anti-government opposition. This was witnessed in England during official Anglicanism (prior to the Puritan Revolution of the 1640s) and fundamentalist ("Christian") terrorist or neofascist groups opposing and attacking the reality or prospect of a liberal, secular and pluralist society (Munch 2001) in modern America (Turk 2004). Exemplars of counter-state terrorism involve vigilante violence (Jacobs et al. 2005), including lynching, by primarily fundamentalist Puritan-rooted groups in the post-bellum South (Messner et al. 2005), as well as their attacks on government institutions (Oklahoma's bombing), international events (the Atlanta Olympics), "ungodly" and "depraved" medical (abortion) facilities and personnel, and virtually on everything "under the sun" of America that they do not approve of. Alternatively, Puritan state "holy terror", like moral fascism in general, operates and is enforced through the religious-like vice-police and generally policing state, as especially found in the "Bible Garden" and its equivalents (Utah, etc.). In short, the "Puritan policeman" fighting sin and human sinners "by sword" is the enforcer and face of "holy terror" in Puritanism and its moral fascism.

*Puritan and Islamic Vice-Police States Compared*

While being a sort of relict or revival of New England's "Puritan policeman" and by implication Calvin's Geneva (due to the Servetus episode), in comparative terms, the vice-police state in America, notably the "Bible Garden", functions as the functional equivalent or analogue of the Islamic religious police in Iran, Saudi Arabia, and other theocratic societies. This statement may sound implausible or worse and thus needs to be elaborated and substantiated.

For example, God's anti-vice "born again" Puritan agents and their temperance wars in the "Bible Garden" are functional equivalents or analogues to the commissions and activities for the "Promotion of

Virtue and the Prevention of Vice" in Islamic theocracies like Iran and Saudi Arabia. For example, reportedly Saudi Arabia's religious police, controlled by the "Commission for the Promotion of Virtue and the Prevention of Vice", arrested and killed two men, one for "allegedly consuming alcohol, another for being alone with a woman not of his family", as an exemplar of religiously (Islamic) grounded and sanctified moral fascism or totalitarianism. No doubt, such things do not and conceivably cannot happen in contemporary America, including the "Bible Belt", even under "reborn" Puritanical conservatism. Still, to put them in perspective, it is useful to recall that, first, like Islam, Puritanism defined itself and acted as "God's Vice-Regent" in New England and the "Puritan policeman" also punished with death similar sins and vices, including adultery (plus blasphemy and sorcery), still a crime in many Southern states and the US military. Second, no-alcohol zones as "dry" states or counties persist in America, notably the "Bible Belt", even after the official repeal of Prohibition, with ever-new restrictions (from the 18-to-21 year national legal limit) and severe punishments for violations. So, at least in respect of the legal treatment or punishment of alcohol use and sexuality, Islamic Saudi Arabia, just as Iran, and Puritan America, at least the "Bible Belt", are less different than US "born again" religious conservatives would admit and perhaps most Americans realize.

These seemingly trivial cases are indicative and exemplify what Weber and Parsons may call an elective affinity or convergence between fundamentalist Islam and Calvinism-Puritanism, notably Islamic and Calvinist-Puritan theocracies, in terms of moral fascism or the suppression of individual liberty and choice in morality and private life. And, the differences between them are the matter of quasi-statistical "degrees of unfreedom", with Islamic theocracies being morally and otherwise more totalitarian than their American Calvinist-Puritan counterpart as the isolated island or (for US "reborn" fundamentalists) "oasis" in the ocean or desert of Western liberal-secular modernity, rather than of the substance of illiberty.

As hinted, a shared instance of the "Prevention of Vice", thus a common syndrome of a vice-police state and moral fascism in the "Bible Garden" and Iran, Saudi Arabia, and other Islamic theocratic societies is criminalizing and harshly punishing (though more by the second) alcohol consumption (let alone drug use) as a serious sin or immoral act via legal prohibitions or restrictions and government sanctions. In short, as Pareto comments, referring to Puritanism and other asceticism, their shared "ideal is a population of ascetics [drinking] no wine",[52] thus monks in a monastic order and, if they do, of sinners-criminals in an open and eventually true prison.

Moreover, as noted, the "Bible Garden" with its no-alcohol zones or "dry" states and counties (Merton 1968) and Iran (and Saudi Arabia) with its total prohibition are the two major or salient instances in the world effectively criminalizing and punishing alcohol use. Specifically, the "Bible Garden" (and its equivalents like Utah) is the only part of the Western world that does so, just as America has the highest legal limit for alcohol consumption (increased from 18 to 21 year by "reborn" fundamentalists) in the West, and Iran and other Islamic theocracies are the most strident cases among non-Western societies.

At least on the account of no-alcohol "dry" states in the "Bible Belt", Prohibition while formally repelled at the national level during the 1930s substantively continues in this region and its equivalents like Utah. Just like during Prohibition in America, so in "dry" Southern states, especially the "deep South" (Alabama, etc.), it is easier and more "godly" and "American" to buy all kinds of big deadly weapons, including military-style armored vehicles (e.g., "hammers", perhaps tanks one day?), than a "small beer" or cheap wine. Also, Prohibition in a substantive sense continues or returns in America for those under 21 year in virtue of the puritanical increase of the legal age drinking limit by three additional years from 18 as the standard or even highest threshold in Western civil societies. Just as their older counterparts during Prohibition, those younger than 21 in contemporary America cannot legally buy or drink even a "small beer" and yet can "big" guns, and commit various school and other murders, on the predictable Puritan-rooted and "Wild West" assumption that the first is more dangerous and "ungodly" for young and other Americans than the second.[53]

---

[52] Pareto asks "what do you expect from people [drinking] no wine and modestly [lowering] their eyes when they see a beautiful woman?" and answers that they "may go and become monks [yet] cannot fight and win the battle of life." Also, Hume writes that "strongly inclined himself to mirth, and wine, and sports of all kinds, [king James] apprehended their censure for his manner of life, free and disengaged. And being thus averse, from temper as well as policy, to the sect of Puritans, he was resolved, if possible, to prevent its further growth in England."

[53] The *Economist* comments that "under Prohibition people could be imprisoned for life for consuming alcohol" and adds that "Puritanism continues to stalk the country in new guises. The most dramatic example is America's new version of Prohibition—a "war on drugs" that helps explain why one in 100 American adults are in prison.

Overall, on the account of a "small beer" 21-old Americans are still children and the "oldest" in the Western world. Yet, they are adults in virtually all other accounts, from buying and using deadly weapons, to work, marrying, driving, voting, military service, etc., including those under 18 committing crimes or sins being charged, punished, and executed, as "adults" (until recently), a practice virtually unknown in other Western societies. So, in Puritan America if you are older than 18, but younger than 21, you are not mature or adult enough to even buy and consume a "small beer," yet, you may purchase and use guns as a sort of consolation prize or substitute. But, if you are under 18 and commit a crime or sin like non-violent drug offenses, then you are treated and punished, even executed, as a true adult! One is tempted to say that this "theater of absurd" or Orwellian anti-logic can only happen in America. Still, it is more accurate and fair to say it can happen "only" in Puritan conservative ("red"), as opposed to Jeffersonian, liberal ("blue"), America, thus "only" in the latter envisioned as the "Bible-Belt" or "Christian Sparta" (or "Iran") rather than as a modern Western secular and democratic society. If anything, shared alcohol prohibitions in the "dry Bible Garden" (and Prohibition before) and restrictions (21-year legal limit), alongside the constant paranoia about and crusade against sexual sins, in America render its ever-growing Puritan vice-police state functionally equivalent to that in Iran, Saudi Arabia, and other Islamic theocracies, marked by such constraints and hysterias.

As a peculiar perversity or curiosity, some states of the "Bible Garden" (e.g., Texas) are the probably only ones in the Western world that institute and engage no less than *two* separate police forces in enforcing alcohol prohibitions (in "dry" regions) or restrictions (in others), as if one were not sufficient or efficient enough, just as Iran and other Islamic theocracies mobilize multiple vice-state commissions.[54] If there is a Puritan equivalent in the "Bible Garden" and America to the "Commission for Promotion of Virtue and the Prevention of Vice" in Islamic theocracies, then it is this double pervasive and intrusive police force

---

But there are plenty of humbler examples. Schools impose zero-tolerance rules that result in expulsion for minor offences. The citizens of Texas may not buy dildos. Americans are banned from drinking until they are 21."

[54] As another curiosity, Texas is the only region in America and the West, if not the entire world, that reportedly prohibits the Encyclopedia Britannica because of its home recipe for making beer. And, of course, "it is crime to consume liquor on the premises" in accordance with Texas's "true spirit of freedom".

fighting the sin of alcohol. Overall, America's age legal limit for alcohol consumption is a proxy at a national level of such Islamic anti-vice commissions in virtue of being, first, increased (from 18 to 21 year) during "reborn" fundamentalism, second, the highest by far among Western societies, third, incongruent with the usual threshold of maturity (16–18 years) in other domains (work, marriage, driving, voting, gun ownership, criminal justice, military service), thus self-contradictory and irrational or nonsensical. Simply, "only in Puritan America" one must be 21 year old to buy Pareto's wine (so, part of Christ's "last supper") or a "small beer" (Manent 1998), but only 18 to "get a gun" and perhaps then to go on a mass killing spree in schools and beyond, serve in the military and fight in offensive wars, etc., on the apparent assumption that the first is more dangerous to civil society and humans than the latter. To that extent, such Puritan-rooted ideas and practices are more compatible and closer to Islamic and other theocracies than modern Western democratic and secular societies. Thus, "beer" or "wine"[55] (Reiland 2006) turns out to be not really "small" (Manent 1998) but bigger and more "lethal" than the biggest and deadliest "guns" in Puritan moral fascism in America, notably the "Bible Garden", unlike Western democratic societies, but like totalitarian Islamic theocracies such as Iran and Saudi Arabia.

Yet, this evident contradiction with Western civil society and democracy and conversely the compatibility with Islamic theocracy, as well as the apparent defying of elemental common sense,[56] is perfectly logical and consistent with and thus predicted by the Puritan vice-police state and Puritanism overall. It is so given that Puritanism functioned as self-designated God's anti-vice agent defining and punishing nonviolent sins as more serious and "ungodly" than violent crimes, including

---

[55] While attending a Calvinist college in America during the 1960s, Reiland (2006:47) found that students "could be expelled for having a glass of wine with our parents during Thanksgiving or Christmas." Also, he recalls that the Calvinist college "students weren't permitted to dance at the prom. Too erotic. They just sat at card tables and listened to Guy Lombardo" (Reiland 2006:46–7).

[56] The *Economist* commented, in the aftermath of a sin of prostitution committed by a New York Governor spied on by the federal government and eventually forced to resign, that the "whole affair is a crock of nonsense" in the sense that "what business is it of the federal government what [person XYZ] got up to in Room 871 of the Mayflower Hotel in Washington, DC?" In light of this case, the magazine added that "America manages to be more unbalanced than other countries. This is partly because its legal system is out of control—an unstoppable clanking machine that has lost any ability to 'draw the line' or respect 'common sense,'" a sort of luxury in the Puritan vice police-state.

murders (adultery was a mortal sin-crime in New England, but not murder, as in Tocqueville's account), as does "reborn" Puritan-inspired fundamentalism in America and fundamentalist Islam in theocracies like Iran and Saudi Arabia. Such an original, substantively equivalent definition and punishment of sins by Puritanism (and its fundamentalist revival) and Islam helps to explain the seeming puzzle or perplexing paradox, even absurdity from the stance of a modern enlightened penal system (Rutherford 1994). This is why Puritan or fundamentalist and Islamic vice-polices states define and punish nonviolent moral vices and sins like alcohol use and notably sexual immorality (adultery, "fornication", prostitution, pornography) often more severely than violent and property crimes (robbery, physical assault, theft, etc.), including often murders, as in early New England, the fundamentalist "Bible Belt" like Texas and modern Iran.

For instance, to indicate that moral, notably sexual, sins and vices are often defined and punished as more serious offenses by the Puritan, just as Islamic, vice-police state, in Texas some murderers of their adulterous wives have been acquitted, or punished as if they committed a minor traffic violation (e.g., several months of probation), on grounds of "crime of passion" against adultery as a seemingly mortal sin-crime. Most Southern states still criminalize adultery, as do virtually all Islamic countries, with the rare exception of Turkey. Apparently, this pattern of exoneration for "crimes of passion" against sexual sins is the obverse of the Puritan Draconian death penalty and penal system of "justice", Texas and "Bible Belt" style. This also applies to the finding (as reported even by some Texan hyper-conservative newspapers) that many powerful (literally, "big-gun cowboys") in Texas have never been convicted, let alone punished, for their murders, usually of powerless low-class, minority, and foreign persons. It appears that for such a criminal justice system what does matter is *who* commits a murder and related crime, and is consequently executed and otherwise punished, rather than the very acts of murders and related crimes regardless of the class, political power, ethnicity, or nationality of the perpetrators.

Needless to say, such arbitrariness, bias, or selectivity is, to paraphrase some US judges, "perversion of justice" perverting the Puritan-rooted criminal justice system into what Popper might call a truly criminal-murderous *injustice* system. Simply, it is hardly possible to witness and envision a greater penal injustice than not punishing actual murderers (and other criminals), like those "rednecks" killing with "passion" and impunity their adulterous wives and "big gun cowboys" murdering powerless persons, and alternatively executing often innocent or merely sinful people. And, both tendencies have been witnessed in the Texas and other "Bible Belt" Puritan-based death penalty system. Yet, such ultimate penal injustice is in perfect concord with the inner logic of the Puritan, as well as Islamic, vice-police state as God's anti-vice agency.

In particular, the Puritan vice-police state in America, especially the "Bible Garden" and its extensions (e.g., Utah), is functional equivalent or analogous to those in Iran and other Islamic theocracies on the account of Draconian punishments for vices or sins to the no-return point of executions. Notably, recall that sociological analyses suggest that the Puritan-rooted system of executions in contemporary America is "functionally equivalent" to those in theocratic Iran and other third-world dictatorships (e.g., China) on the account of their shared Draconian harshness in punishing sins and crimes, including both guilty and innocent sinners or criminals (Jacobs et al. 2005). Notably, the second element—the execution of innocent persons as well as non-violent sinners (sexual and drug offenders) primarily on religious, specifically shared fundamentalist, grounds—makes Puritan and Islamic death-penalty systems almost the instruments or symptoms of state terrorism (Mansbach 2006; Turner 2002). This is in the sense of government-committed or sponsored mass, routine murder defining fascism, notably Nazism (Arendt 1951; Bähr 2002).

At this juncture, in particular vice-police states in the "Bible Garden" (Texas, Virginia, Alabama, Florida, Georgia, Oklahoma, Tennessee, etc.) and in Iran and Saudi Arabia under Islamic theocracy (and communist-capitalist China) exhibit a degree of functional equivalence or convergence in respect of Draconian sanctions, including executions, for vices prohibited by Puritan moral fascism and Islam, respectively. And, these prohibitions and their punishments encompass virtually all actual and possible human vices and sins proscribed and punished as crimes in both vice-police states, in particular alcohol consumption, drug use, and, above all, sexual immorality (adultery, prostitution, pornography) or mere sexuality ("fornication").

Recall Pareto observes that in America, Puritan fanatical anti-alcoholic religious groups are "ready to kill a person only to keep him healthy [alcohol-free]" and comments that they thus "show less sense than the inquisition, which buried men in order to save their souls", as are, even more, those in Iran, Saudi Arabia, and other Islamic theocracies. Overall, he remarks that these moralistic groups proscribe and harshly punish not only alcohol abuses, "but even the most moderate use". He comment that "it is herein that the religious and sectarian sentiments can be decried", thus apparently anticipating Prohibition in America and its "dry" vestiges in the "Bible Garden" and elsewhere, as well as its more severe versions in Islamic theocracies. This reaffirms that the Puritan vice-police state and moral fascism in America is the type of solution to vices and sinners, including alcohol and other abuses or addictions, that throws away the "baby" of normal usage with the "dirty water" of abuse. Namely, it kills the "patient" of individual liberty while performing a "splendid" operation or "curing" the disease of a lack of morality, thus being functionally equivalent to anti-vice solutions in Islamic and other (Hindu) theocratic societies.

In spite of its unrivaled consistency and obstinacy among Western societies, the Puritan vice-police state and overall moral fascism in America, notably in the "Bible Garden, like its Islamic version, has been and is likely to be ineffective in its wars on and pathological in its obsession with sin and vice. This is indicated by the dismal failure of Prohibition (Friedman 1997; Merton 1968; Simon 1976) and apparently of the war on drugs (Hill 2002; Reuter 2005) and related temperance or culture wars through Draconian "three strikes" laws and punishments (Akerlof 2002; Erikson and Parent 2007) by most US states and the Federal Government.

As Simmel, Tönnies, Weber, and Durkheim all suggest, the individual's morality's only law and sanction is ethical conscience, thus "dead" moral rules and religions, implicitly Puritan-style "dumb" laws, cannot be revived by government coercion (and non-coercive "spirituality"), considered to be a non-democratic and self-defeating non sequitur. Yet, evidently the creators and guardians of the Puritan vice-police state and moral fascism in America methodically deny or overlook this ethical axiom or true Parsonian consensus within modern Western civil society and act accordingly, in a flagrant deviation from the latter and in substantive equivalence with those in Islamic theocracies Iran and Saudi Arabia. For "reborn" Puritan-inspired evangelicals in America and Islamic fundamentalists (and perhaps orthodox Catholics and Hindus) are the only two major religious and political groups in the modern world (Inglehart 2004) continuing to deny that individual morality's only law and sanction is ethical conscience, and to claim that "dead" morals and religions or their respective "dumb" laws *can* and must be revived by government coercion, including Draconian punishment for their transgressions. In particular, the "Bible Belt" and theocratic Iran are the two major instances that deny the first axiom and practice the second non sequitur, epitomizing their shared position of proto-totalitarian destructions of human liberty and life (Bauman 1997), as well as their anti-Western or anti-liberal attributes in this respect.

In another expected example, Pareto's diagnosis and prediction that religious groups in America are "ready to kill a person only to keep him healthy" holds true a fortiori of sexual vices defined as even more serious, a sort of mortal sins and crimes, subjected to harsher punishments in both Puritan and Islamic vice-police states. As noted, such a common treatment is consistent with the definition and sanction of non-violent sexual sins ("fornication", adultery, prostitution, pornography, etc.) as more serious or "ungodly" than not only alcohol use, but virtually all other violent and non-violent crimes (including often murder) in both Puritanism and fundamentalist Islam as respective God's anti-vice agents or commissioners. In a way, Puritanism and Islam by acting as God's anti-vice agents predestine their respective vice-police states to seek, find, and punish what they imagine and want to see, primarily nonviolent sexual and similar vices and sinners like alcohol and drug use and users, and crimes proper secondarily or not all, notably not those committed by Puritan and Islamic theocratic masters or "saints". No wonder, the largest and ever-growing category of the imprisoned in modern Puritan and Islamic vice-police states in America *and* Iran and Saudi Arabia are human sinners, thus effectively innocent prisoners of conscience in an ethical and political sense, and victims of or sacrifices to moral fascism. This is exemplified by nonviolent drug and other, especially sexual, moral offenders accounting for almost two thirds of the exploding US prison population, rather than ordinary, violent criminals, during "tough" on sin-crime Puritan-style neo-conservative laws and practices. As an effect of Puritanism and Islam both claiming to be and acting as God's anti-vice agents, another shared element of Puritan and Islamic vice-police states and thus a syndrome of their moral fascism is criminalizing sexual sins or simply sexuality via legal prohibitions and Draconian punishments.

Recall, adultery was not only criminalized, but even punished with death by the "Puritan policeman" in New England, as is still, minus the death penalty, in most states of the "Bible Garden" and reinstituted in the US military, just as in Iran and other Islamic theocracies and societies (except for Turkey, despite its Muslim-based government's attempts at re-criminalizing during the 2000s). As with alcohol consumption, the "Bible Garden" and Iran and other Islamic theocracies are the only or major instances of criminalizing and punishing (more harshly by the second) adultery in the world; more precisely, the first is the only such case within Western civil society and democracy, the second the strictest cases among non-Western developing societies.[57] Also, the Puritan vice-police state in America and its Islamic version in Iran are the probably two most aggressive, pervasive, intrusive, and repressive major states in prohibiting or restricting and harshly punishing other nonviolent sexual vices and sins, old (prostitution, premarital sexuality) and new (pornography,[58] Internet indecency, etc.), in the modern world, the first within Western civil society, and the second among non-Western societies. In addition and connection to alcohol and drug use, at least such shared and comparatively unparalleled Draconian punishments as well as prohibitions or restrictions of sexual sins and simply sexuality render Puritan and Islamic vice-police states functionally equivalent or analogous.

Generally, the Puritan vice-police state in America, especially the "Bible Garden", tends to function as the functional equivalent or analogue of Islamic, including Iranian, religious police in terms of their comparatively greatest scope, magnitude, and "growth". These, notably that of the "Bible Garden" and of Iran, are probably the two major largest, fastest "growing" vice-police and punitive states, including prison and death-penalty "industries" (alongside North Korea and China), in global civil society and polity ushering in the 21st century. Specifically, the Puritan vice-police punitive (Miller 1975) state in America, notably

---

[57] To preempt moralistic accusations, this is neither a defense nor condemnation, valuation generally, of adultery and other moral vices, for only human actors as free and responsible moral agents can decide what is "right" and "wrong" for themselves. It is a statement of fact that Western liberal-secular societies do not criminalize and punish this and similar sins, while Puritan and Islamic vice-police states or "moral fascisms" do, nothing more, nothing less.

[58] As a functionally equivalent case of moral fascism in Islam, for example, its theocratic parliament "voted in favor of a bill that could lead to the death penalty for persons convicted of working in the production of pornographic movies" on Islamic grounds (the "corruptor of the world", an expression taken from the Quran). Similarly, some US states, especially in the "Bible Belt" (Florida, etc.) and the "Wild West" (Nevada), punish "promotion" of certain kinds of pornography with almost equivalent Draconian severity, such as long sentences and even life in prison. In addition, in 2007 the US Federal government sentenced a person no less than 170 years in prison for making pornography. Also, such "Bible Belt" states as Texas sentence persons on no less than 20 or so years in prison for "failing to comply with sex offender registration." Evidently, such things can and do only happen in Islamic Iran and Puritan America among modern societies.

the evangelical South, represents, as has traditionally been, the largest and fastest "growing" anti-sin, anti-vice, and penal "machine" (Mumford 1970) within contemporary Western civil society and democracy. This is indicated or approximated by a variety of indicators or estimates, including the size and growth of police force[59] (Levitt 1997) and material resources, the number of sinners *cum* criminals imprisoned, executed, and otherwise punished, like *nonviolent* drug-war (Reuter 2005) and sexual offenders as prisoners of temperance or ethical conscience, and so on. In turn, the Iranian (alongside Saudi) variant of the vice-police state holds the equivalent rank among Islamic and other non-Western societies (excepting China and North Korea).

For instance, the Puritan vice-police in America is the biggest and fastest-growing in the Western and entire world. It is on the account of the largest and growing number of imprisoned sinners-criminals, especially nonviolent drug and sexual offenders (e.g., marihuana and cocaine users, prostitution, pornography, etc.) due to Draconian "three strikes" laws, comprising almost two thirds of the nearly 2.5 million prisoners, among Western and other societies, more than, say, post-communist Russia, and even China with its much larger potentially "sinful" population. At least, these comparatively and historically, except for the Nazi penal system, unrivalled numbers of nonviolent drug-war, sexual, and other temperance-wars "criminals", as effectively prisoners of moral conscience and sins-as-crimes, are the human proofs, faces, and victims of the Puritan vice-police state in America as really, to cite Reagan et al., "we are the best" (Baudrillard 1999) or "No 1" in the Western and entire world. To that extent, this Puritan version is substantively equivalent to those vice police states in Iran, Saudi Arabia, and other Islamic theocracies.[60] And, only its Islamic counterparts and enemies in Iran (plus China) can substantively or proportionally (e.g., as rates of incarceration of moral sinners as criminals) equal or emulate such performances of the US Puritan vice-police state as the perennial Western "over-performer".

At this juncture, owing to such functional equivalence, the Puritan vice-police and thus moral fascism in America reveals itself, like its

---

[59] Levitt (1997) finds that in America the growth in the size of police forces is "disproportionally concentrated in mayoral and gubernatorial election years", primarily by "reborn" religious and political conservatives.

[60] Sen's inverted "irrational fools" are proud of what—that is, being "American" or "German" and "Islamic", on the account of a "tough on crime" vice-police state—others in Western civil society are ashamed or embarrassed of.

Draconian penal system, as a "unique anomaly" (Pager 2003) within the context of Western civil society and democracy at the start of the 21st century and compatible with non-Western theocratic and other dictatorships like Iran and China. If anything, this Puritan-generated and rationalized "unique anomaly" causes modern America to belong to or resemble less Western liberal-secular civil society, democracy, and civilization as a whole than non-Western societies, as comparative sociological studies suggest (Inglehart 2004). In a way, what distinguishes Western liberal-secular civil society and civilization from its non-Western, notably Islamic, counterparts is, as Weber and others imply, precisely the lack of or the minimal vice-police state, thus no moral fascism. This expresses Western liberalism, secularism, and rationalism versus the Oriental opposites (as exemplified by the European Union's opposing and effectively blocking Turkey's government attempt at criminalizing adultery in the 2000s). In this respect, the massive, pervasive, and ever-growing Puritan vice-police state in America, at the minimum the "Bible Garden", functions as an irrational, unreasonable—as do all policing states in general—"unique anomaly" from, and as what Weber may call the destructive abomination of, Occidental liberal-secular and rationalist civil society and civilization. Instead, it does as a later-day vestige or revival of "Oriental despotism" couched in or sweetened by Puritan Americanism.

Yet, this "unique anomaly" turns out to become the "normal pathology" or pathological normalcy of Puritan moral fascism given the inner "logic" and function of Puritanism as God's supreme anti-vice agent and "holy warrior". What is anomalous or pathological—a massive vice-police state and Draconian punishments for vices and sins— within Western liberal-secular civil society and civilization is instead perfectly regular or normal in American Puritanism, just as in fundamentalist Islam, notably the "Bible Garden" and Iran. And, so long as American "reborn" fundamentalism continues to claim to be or act as God's anti-vice regent, it will perpetuate and expand the Puritan vice-police state, thus moral fascism, as a "unique anomaly" within Western civil society, and a functional equivalent of those in Iran and other Islamic theocracies. To that extent, as Puritanism did in the past, it will remake America closer to, in Weber's words, the Orient and "Oriental despotism", traditionalism, and irrationalism than to the Occident and "Occidental" liberalism, secularism, and rationalism.

Minimally, vice-police states in America, especially the "Bible Garden", and in Iranian and other Islamic theocracies function as functional equivalents or analogues on the account of these being probably the two major exceptions to or deviations from the prevalent modern global trends to a liberal-secular civil society and democracy (Inglehart and Baker 2000). Specifically, the Puritan vice-police state and "born again" fundamentalism generally remake America (along with post-communist Poland as the "new comer" in this sense) the most salient exception to or a "deviant case" from these trends in Western civil society. And, its Islamic substitute renders Iran such a deviation in general, given that such liberalizing tendencies are also observed in many non-Western under-developed societies, excluding Islamic and most Catholic South-American countries (Inglehart 2004). In short, both vice-police states represent the most salient or manifest deviant cases from Western and global civil society and democracy during the early 21st century.

If so, then this kind of deviation from Western societies, alternatively of convergence with Iran and other Islamic theocracies, resurfaces as genuine, or exemplifies, Puritan-rooted and celebrated American exceptionalism, rather than, as usually assumed, "exceptional" democracy, liberty, and individualism (Lipset and Marks 2000). On this assumption, one wonders how to attain "democracy, liberty, and individualism" in and reconcile them with a Puritan vice-police state as, like any policing states, their antithesis or subversion, and Calvinist theocracy overall. In essence, this Parsonian goal-attainment, thus celebrated American exceptionalism defined by it, is an illogical non sequitur or "impossibility theorem" impossible to realize in reality within the framework or against the background of a self-perpetuating and ever-growing Puritan vice-police state. In sum, by being the most prominent or visible deviations from modern liberal-secular civil society, just as the biggest and fastest-growing anti-sin penal "industries", Puritan and Islamic vice-police states in America and Iran and similar theocracies objectively display a functional equivalence or affinity (Turner 2002), while otherwise (not always) being biter enemies. They indicate that totalitarian, in this case theocratic, polar opposites may well "attract each other".

Further, Puritan and Islamic vice-police states in America and Iran and other Muslim societies function as functional equivalents or analogues in virtue of their overt or tacit alliance against individual moral freedom and thus liberal-secular civil society and democracy, in spite of their initial and pervasive enmity apparently superseded in facing their major common enemy. This is witnessed by their united stand (alongside the Vatican Church) against individual moral freedom at various international conferences about civil liberties and human rights (e.g., family planning, etc.) during the 1990s–2000s to the point of becoming the major obstacles to reaching common decisions and even single-handedly or rather jointly blocking what was often a global consensus on these issues. Coincidentally or not, the joint operation as two major impediments to global liberal-secular society parallels the world's perception, as indicated by various surveys, of US and Iranian policing and warfare states as the first and second gravest danger, respectively to peace and stability.

At this point, the prevailing global trends to liberal-secular civil society and democracy, including individual moral and other freedom, operate as the efficient cause or agent provocateur for the "holy alliance" between Puritan and Islamic vice-police states (and the Vatican state). In that sense, their functional equivalence almost, at least temporarily, erases and neutralizes their other differences and intense hostilities. If anything, their open or secret allying against global liberal-secular civil society and democracy, notably individual moral liberty and privacy at the international scene and other occasions, makes Puritan and Islamic vice-police states operate as functionally equivalent or analogous. At the minimum, this holds for those of the "Bible Garden" and Iranian theocracy in virtue of their tacit alliance or objective equivalence as belonging to the same category of proto-totalitarian "solutions" to the condemned "evil" and burden" of individual and other moral freedom, thus to liberal-secular civil society. Now, the "Bible Belt" and Iranian theocracy are different, even antagonistic, "Christian" versus "Islamic" 'solutions" in this respect. Yet, they are still totalitarian or theocratic and in that sense functional equivalents or substitutes, as are consequently their vice-police states, at least from the prism of liberal-secular civil society, notably individual moral liberty. From this angle, these differences and thus those between their vice-police states are the matter of pseudo-statistical "degrees of unfreedom", with the first being statistically less unfree, rather than the substance of totalitarian, notably theocratic, illiberty. If both vice-police states "solve" the "agony" of moral choice by eliminating freedom itself, thus cure the disease by killing the patient, then they are functionally equivalent in design or outcome. Arguably, it is completely irrelevant to "dead patients" who and why "killed" them, though American and Iranian fundamentalists extol and excel themselves as "native" executors.

In turn, the above is a dimension of or in accordance with the substantive equivalence or convergence and affinity between Calvinism, including Puritanism, and Islam with respect to moralistic theocracy and thus moral fascism. This is indicated by the "evident" commonalities or parallels between Calvinists and Islamists in their "demands for austerity"[61] (Mansbach 2006; also, Friedland 2001; Mulyadi 2006; Van Dyke 1995). For instance, Weber identifies a common theocratic outcome observing that radical Calvinism inner-worldly asceticism attained a "similar solution" as Islam to the "problem of the relation between religion and politics."[62] Specifically, like Islam, Calvinism "represented as God's will the power over the sinful world, for the purpose of controlling it, by religious virtuosi belonging to the pure church", as Calvin et al. in Geneva and beyond, reaching, via their Puritan disciples, early and contemporary America. Notably, Weber notes that this solution was "fundamental in the theocracy of New England" in principle and especially in practice, suggesting that American Puritanism *cum* Calvinism in the new world was "similar" to Islam in moralistic tyranny or moral proto-fascism. In retrospect, this remark is striking and even prophetic in light of the observations of such and related affinities between America during Puritanical religious neo-conservatism and Islamic theocracies (Turner 2002), the evangelical "Bible Garden" and theocratic Iran (Bauman 1997).

In sum, the preceding suggests that, first, the institutional mechanism or penal machine of Puritan moral fascism as the poison of a free civil society is a vice-police state as its specific case of policing states or oppressive, punitive governments. Second, it indicates that the Puritan vice-police state in America is rooted in, predicted, and rationalized by Puritanism self-proclaimed as God's anti-vice, anti-sin agency. Third, it

---

[61] Mansbach (2006:112) adds that in Calvin's Geneva "taverns were banned temporarily, and gambling was forbidden much as Afghanistan's Taliban banned all outward shows of luxury and entertainment during their reign." Further, he remarks that from 1545, Calvinist officials "began visiting private homes to determine citizens' moral rectitude, and, like Iran's and Saudi Arabia's religious police, reported any offenses", as well as criticisms of Calvin, the improper dress of women, etc. (Mansbach 2006:112). Also, Mulyadi (2006:195) suggests that "the rise of Muslim puritans within the early Islamic reformist movement [e.g., in Indonesia] resembles ascetic Protestantism, particularly Calvinism".

[62] In terms of major dramatis personae, Weber comments that Calvin and Muhammad "each of whom [was] convinced that the certainty of one's own mission in the world came not from any personal perfection but from his situation in the world and from god's will".

Table 5.2.  Elements of the Puritan vice-police state

---
God's vice-agency
Maximal anti-vice police (and warfare) force vs. minimal well-being ("welfare") state
Moralistic terrorism
    state moralistic terrorism: "holy" official terror against "sinful" and "ungodly"
    counter-state moralistic terrorism: "holy" anti-liberal, anti-secular terror when not in government
Functional equivalent of Islamic vice-religious police and system of executions

---

suggests that such a Puritan state during the 2000s functions in many respects (e.g., mass incarceration and potential or actual executions for drug and related moral sins *cum* crimes) as functionally equivalent or analogous to those in Islamic theocracies and other dictatorships, expressing the long affinity of Puritanism and in extension Calvinism with Islam. (Table 5.2. summarizes the elements of the Puritan vice-police state.)

### *From a Free Private Sphere to a Coercive Monastic Order*

Puritan moral fascism in America tends to transform civil society, like polity, into a monastic order of Calvinist saints by the intransigent denial and the systematic elimination of individual freedom in morality and private life, including a vice-police state as its legal-institutional mode. In general, as a corollary of Puritan moral fascism and its vice-police state, free civil society in the sense of Parsons' societal community or Habermas' life-world, as the realm of Jefferson's principle of "life and pursuit of happiness", becomes, like liberal democracy, eventually a sort of non-entity or degenerates within Calvinist Bibliocracy.

Specifically, Puritan moral fascism converts civil society or social life in an overarching monastery to the effect that, as Calvinism commanded, "everyone must now be a monk for life" through its "radical elimination of any distinction" between the ethics of priests and of laymen (Munch 1981). In so doing, it perpetuates or reenacts in America what Calvinism attempted and realized initially in Europe. This is recreating civil society, as well as politics, after the model of the "discipline of the monastery"[63] (Gorski 1993), thus effectively eliminating it as the sphere of individual moral and other liberty. In this sense, Puritan moral fascism recreates or redesigns America if not after the model, then after the image of a monastic order governed by the "new ethics and practices" of strict discipline unleashed by Calvinist disciplinary revolutions in Europe (Loveman 2005; also, Gorski 2003). Hence, Jefferson's liberal principle of "life and pursuit of happiness" becomes, in Weber's words, methodical sanctification, including extreme asceticism or austerity to the pathological point of, as Pareto remarks, tormenting[64] oneself and others, thus mixed and mutually reinforcing sadism-masochism, within Calvinist Bibliocracy.

The above yields corresponding inferences, such as, first, Puritan moral fascism causes civil society to become a monastic order, thus effectively disappear as defined. In consequence, Puritan saints-masters coerce humans to be life-long monks and ascetics in general. Second, as a corollary, these saints pervert Jefferson's pursuit of happiness into Winthrop- or Calvin-style avoidance of pleasure *cum* sin and thus crime[65] and "ungodly", and alternatively into an almost sadistic-masochistic life of torment inflicted on oneself and especially on others. In short, Puritan moral fascism perverts America from the "land" of happiness/freedom into a "house of pain." This is a predictable outcome or realistic possibility, for Puritanism has acted and been described as the "haunting fear" that humans, including Americans, "may be happy" (Mencken 1982).

Puritan moral fascism transforms civil society into a monastic order and thus effectively eliminates or perverts it as the sphere of individual moral and other civic liberties. Consequently, Puritan saints-masters force humans to become or act as subservient monks or ascetics in

---

[63] Gorski (1993:265) adds that Calvinism enforced "ethic of social discipline charging the elect with disciplining the political community as a whole" and "collective organization". Calvinism was unique in employing surveillance as a technique of mass political organization. [It] provided channel through which the discipline of the monastery entered the political world."

[64] Pareto registers that "certain men experience great delight in tormenting themselves and others", specifically citing Calvinists in Scotland (the "Scotch Presbyterian clergy"). He adds that "according to their code, "all the natural affections, all the pleasures of society, all the pastimes, all the guy instincts of the human heart were so many sins" and comments that "long before, the monks had carried this kind of insanity to the utmost limit."

[65] Thus, Pareto comments that "pleasure and crime were synonyms in the monastic [and Calvinist-Puritan] idiom" and they still are to our modern ascetics".

general during their lives. For instance, Weber cites Calvinism's commandment "You think you have escaped from the monastery, but every-one must now be a monk throughout his life". In general, he suggests that Calvinism, specifically its strict asceticism, was ("in principle") "identical" to medieval monasticism. He adds that in particular, this "active self-control", as the end of the "rational monastic virtues everywhere", was the "most important practical ideal" of Puritanism. Weber concludes that Calvinism generally, Puritanism particularly, has carried the "rational form of asceticism" in the form of "methodical" action "from the monastery into the world." This is what also Pareto implies by observing that "long before, the monks had carried this kind of [Puritan] insanity to the utmost limit", which means that Puritanism and Calvinism overall has only extended these practices from the monastery into civil society as a whole. For example, he observes that "pleasure and crime were synonyms" both in the monastic and Puritan order and remain to "modern ascetics". This signifies that Puritanism has not invented, but just expanded this criminalization of human pleasures from the monastery into all civil society.

Second, Puritan moral fascism transforms the pursuit of happiness into a sort of Calvin-style avoidance or rejection of human pleasure and joy in secular civil society, as distinguished from what Weber calls the world beyond. Alternatively, it often effectively perverts the pursuit of happiness in civil society into what appears as the societal "house [and economy] of pain" both inflicted on sinful humans and self-inflicted, or, in Pareto's words, of tormenting oneself and especially others for, as Americans say, "the fun of it" and/or Parsons' higher "purposes of God." In this respect, Puritan moral fascism effectively transforms the life-world of the pursuit of happiness into one of methodical sadistic-masochistic pursuits, thus the opposite and destruction of life itself. It does via pain, torment, torture, and eventually individual and collective death in accordance with the nihilistic, judgment day scenario of American "reborn" evangelicalism, as shown or heralded by the collective suicides or apocalyptic visions of evangelical sects and cults in America. In sum, it eradicates or buries the pursuit of happiness, notably "ungodly" human pleasure, as a constituent of liberal-secular civil society, in Mises' "peace of the cemetery" as expressed or heralded by "dead-like", "sleepy" small "ghost-towns" in the "Bible Garden".

Simply, Puritan moral fascism makes life for most humans "hell in this world" (Tawney 1962), just as in the world beyond given Calvinism's proto-oligarchic, exclusive doctrine of predestination as the "double decree" of election of a few for heaven as "heavenly" oligarchy or "spiritual aristocracy" and eternal damnation of the rest. In turn, this Calvinist doctrine serves as the sacred, theological ground and rationalization for Puritan moral fascism's hellish treatment or image of humans in civil society. As the primary moment, Puritan moral fascism signifies the destruction of a free civil society and human liberty and life in the image of "hell in this world." As a subsidiary point, the doctrine of predestination is in stark contrast and opposition to original Christianity, including Catholicism, as what Weber calls the universalistic religion of salvation in theory "for all", including moral sinners (albeit not heretics) through what Calvinism condemned and eliminated as the very "human" cycle of sin, repentance, confession, and forgiveness (and "renewed sin"). Alternatively, it is in an affinity with Islam as, in his view, a non-universalistic (or even not a genuine) religion of salvation.

In sum, Puritan moral fascism is the anti-liberal and anti-secular "hell" of civil society. Secondarily and relatedly, Calvinism, as the exclusionary, non-universalistic religion of salvation in "heaven", is anti-Christian in reversing original universalistic Christianity with its (in Weber's words) human and understanding "Father in Heaven", while resembling more Islam on this and related accounts. Hence, most humans or non-Puritans likely experience Puritan moral, like any, fascism as extremely or supremely immoral in the fundamental sense of its extreme inhumanity. Relatedly, they experience Calvin's oligarchic doctrine of predestination, dividing humans into only a few saved and most damned and thus, as he (and his partial disciple Rousseau) proposed, to be tormented or persecuted, as "morally repugnant," as when Franklin renounced his father's Calvinism viewing its "rejection of good works" as the conventional Christian means of attaining salvation, as hostile to morality. At this juncture, Puritan moral fascism is, like oligarchic politics and other outcomes in Puritanism and Calvinism overall, theologically grounded in, sanctified, and predicted by Calvin's doctrine of predestination as the theology of "heavenly" oligarchy and thus of proto-fascism (Fromm 1941; McLaughlin 1996).

And, Puritan moral fascism subverts Jefferson's principle of human "life and pursuit of happiness" into its sadistic-masochistic and ultimately deadly opposite on the grounds of what Calvinism, notably Puritanism, condemns and attacks as, in Weber's words, the "temptation and corruption of the flesh". This leads to and rationalizes, as seen, equating human pleasures with sins and thus crimes. Hence, Calvinism's, notably Puritanism's equation of human pleasures to sins and crimes generates, predicts, and rationalizes this mutation of the "pursuit of happiness" in avoidance or rejection of pleasure, and conversely into inflicting and seeking pain or tormenting others and oneself by Puritan moral fascism in America. Some economists observe that modern America experiences a "strange irony of fate" in that its "Puritanical rejection of pleasure as the ultimate aim of life" has eventuated in a "preference system", with money making acting as the "main challenge", and "effortless, pleasureless comfort" as the "main reward" (Scitovsky 1972).

Further, most humans are probably not true saints or divines in the sense of Puritanism (as admitted in the Biblical "who has not sinned" passage), simply "no angels" (Somers 1998), and thus cannot willingly endure living as like monks or total ascetics for their entire lives. As a result, they eventually experience the monastic order in which they are forced by Puritan moral fascism via its destruction of liberal-secular civil society as a massive open prison system in the image of Bentham's *Panopticon* and Orwell's "Big Brother" intrusion. They feel the "unbearable lightness" of Puritan existence in the sense that even Puritans are "no angels", as admittedly witnessed in New England under Puritanism[66] (Seaton 2006; also, Baldwin 2006; Harley 1996).

Many humans such as the millions of Americans imprisoned for moral sins and vices like nonviolent drug, sexual, and related offenses, thus prisoners of ethical conscience, experience this Puritan monastic order effectively as a closed or true prison, including eventually (as for "free trade" in drugs, some sexual offenses) the death-penalty, system, often for the rest of their life. This is due to Draconian punishments (e.g., "three strikes" laws) and their enforcement by the massive, pervasive, and ever-growing vice-police state in the "Bible Garden" and beyond. Specifically, for actual or potential human "sinners" redefined and harshly punished as criminals by moral fascism, the latter operates as an open or true prison system. In turn, for those genuine or more likely, given Puritan perennial "pure hypocrisy", what Hume calls pretended "saints" or "divines" and "angels", it remains a medieval-style

---

[66] For instance, Seaton (2006:197) admits that in New England "even the most devoted [Puritans] deviated from the logic of Puritan theory", especially Puritanism's "admittedly old-fashioned" dichotomies casting humans in paired terms, such as nature-grace, reason-will, darkness-light, etc.

monastic order, "paradise lost and found" on earth. So, what is a "godly" place a la the medieval Christian monastery for Hume's hypocritical "saints"[67] and monks by choice is instead an open or true prison for other humans forced to make "virtue out of necessity" or else, including life-long imprisonment ("three strikes" laws for sins or petty crimes) and potential or actual executions (drug "free enterprise", etc.). Thus, human "saints" and "sinners" redefine and construct the Puritan and other monastic-style human order, as the degenerate form of civil society, in opposite terms, as "heaven and hell," respectively. This exemplifies the Thomas sociological principle of social definitions of the situation or reality (Merton 1995) with respect to moral fascism and Calvinist theocracy as a whole in America.

As hinted, the "Bible Garden" constitutes the paradigmatic exemplar of the experience, definition, or vision of the Puritan subversion of liberal-secular civil society into a medieval-style monastic order and moral fascism overall as a "godly" or "faith-based" society, simply "heaven" in America. Conversely, the Puritan-inspired Draconian penal, including death-penalty, system or "industry" is such an exemplar or approximation of its experience, definition, and expectation as an open or true prison system by actual or potential human sinners, which could conceivably comprise most Americans in reality or prospect. This is how those almost 10 millions Americans technically imprisoned or otherwise punished (e.g., probation), primarily for moral sins and vices like drug use and similar nonviolent sinful offenses, experience, redefine, or construct the Puritan monastic order and moral fascism overall and its perversion of a free civil society. They simply experience it as a societal prison and thus what Tawney calls in reference to Puritanism "hell in this world" in a sort of perpetual or multiple punishment for sins-crimes, including the denial of elemental civil and political liberties and rights after their formal release, from voting (Uggen and Manza 2002) to employment, schooling, and housing. More minimally, this holds true of the "qualified" majority (two thirds) of those 2.5 millions of US prisoners during the 2000s. Thus, imprisoned for nonviolent moral sins, for these sinners-prisoners this Puritan order operates as a true prison, sometimes for life owing to

---

[67] Durkheim predicts that in a "community of saints in an exemplary and perfect monastery crime[s] as such would be unknown but faults that appear venial to ordinary persons will arouse the same scandal as does normal crime in ordinary consciences."

"three strikes" laws and other Draconian punishments, while for those actually or likely executed it does as the literal "peace of the cemetery." As a corollary, Weber-Pareto's monks in the Puritan societal monastic order are, in virtue of being confined to it without their choice, thus denied individual moral freedom, effectively potential or real prisoners, and only a few true or pretended "saints", "angels", and ascetics freely choosing their confinement and self-repression, like self-inflicted torment and masochistic punishment.

In a way, the Puritan monastic-like order and thus moral fascism in America, by reducing humans to unwilling monks and virtual or actual prisoners, treats them as subhumans. It ushers in an Orwellian world or rather descends into a proto-Calvinist society of total and permanent control, repression, surveillance, and primitive Draconian punishment in the image of Bentham's *Panopticon*. It thus fully realizes in America during the 21st century what Calvinism attempted and yet only partly realized in Europe (e.g., Holland and to a lesser extent Germany) five or four centuries before. This is recreating society and polity after the model of the medieval Christian monastic order through "new" Calvinist methods, including proto-Orwellian, increasingly "high-tech" surveillance and control. In particular, Puritan moral fascism in America seems supreme or consummate in what Calvinism was, as sociological analyses suggest, "unique", in "employing surveillance as the technique" of social-political organization and a "channel through which the discipline of the monastery entered" both civil society and politics (Gorski 1993). This confirms that American Puritanism functions as hyper-Calvinism and its adherents act as super-Calvinists, with respect to surveillance after the model of Bentham's *Panopticon* or in the image of Orwell's "Big Brother's watching". Puritanism also does through various other methods and techniques of subverting liberal-secular civil society into a medieval-like coercive monastic order, thus an open or real prison system for most humans.

### *Global Moral Fascism—Pan-American "Manifest Destiny"?*

In accordance with the combined, essentially equivalent Calvinist-theocratic or fundamentalist and fascist or totalitarian "logic" and aim of expansion and escalation, Puritan moral fascism in America tends to expand and escalate beyond the new nation to the entire world. Predictably, the global expansion of Puritan moral fascism proceeds in the form of or rather the claim to a new, historically unprecedented "empire of liberty" as America's "Divinely" ordained mission a la "manifest destiny" in history and the instrument to "save" the world from itself, especially from its sins, vices, "degeneracy", "corruption", and "ungodliness". In particular, in recent times this process involves the expansion of Puritan moral fascism through what analysts identify as the new imperialism (Steinmetz 2005; also, Smelser and Mitchell 2002) and militarism, including imperial wars. Notably, global offensive and permanent war acts, to paraphrase Clausewitz, both as the continuation and expansion of Puritan moral fascism within society "by other means" like military aggression and imperial conquest. Simply, Puritan moral fascism expands from America to the world not only by "word" (e.g., evangelical missions) but also by "sword", just as does its substantive equivalent, Islamic theocracy, thus a new crusade and jihad, respectively (Mansbach 2006; Turner 2002).

In retrospect, Puritan moral fascism's global, military expansion expresses nationalism, militancy, and expansionism as characteristic of Calvinism, notably Puritanism. First, Calvinism, especially Puritanism, formed the exemplar of a nationalistic religion and ideology, or the major source of religious nationalisms (Friedland 2001) in America and other Protestant societies, in particular what Merton (1939) calls American nativism or simply Americanism (Lipset 1996). For instance, for Dutch Calvinism Holland was "the new Israel", thus God's "chosen instrument" for establishing his "kingdom on earth" and spreading his message, as the "community argument of predestination" (Frijhoff 2002). English-American Calvinism or Puritanism redefined England and especially America in strikingly identical terms—a "promised land" or the "new Jerusalem" (Dunn and Woodard 1996) with Divinely ordained "manifest destiny" to establish "God's Kingdom on Earth" and thus rule and save the "ungodly" and "impure" world from itself. Hence, Calvinism via Puritanism effectively founded and sanctified as "godly" what analysts describe as the American civil religion (Beck 2000; Munch 2001) or a religious-like creed of superior and universal values and institutions (Lipset 1955). It thus did Americanism, including nativism and xenophobia, initially and for long anti-Catholicism[68] (Archer 2001; Lipset 1955; Merton 1939), or what Pareto calls jingoism.

---

[68] Archer (2001:280) remarks that during the 19th century and later anti-Catholic nativist movements, as composed of those proudly "born in the USA, more or less "overlapped" with evangelicalism. In this view, "to sectarian [Protestantism] Catholicism

Concerning militancy and expansionism, Calvinism, including Puritanism, was a design and methodical practice of religious revolution and "holy" war. Thus, Weber observes that the "concept of a religious revolution" was most consistent with inner-worldly asceticism focused on the "holy orders of God's commandments within the world" and within Christianity this was primarily "true" of Calvinism that stipulated that the defense of the "faith" against its enemies ("tyranny") by the "use of force" must be a "religious obligation".[69] He cites as an exemplar "the unconquerable Cromwellian army" during the 1640s English Puritan Revolution and Cromwell's ensuing "holy wars" or crusades against "infidels" (Goldstone 1986; Gorski 2000), including, as Simmel observes, the "cruel suppression" of the Irish and other Catholics. The above reveals yet another affinity or convergence between Calvinism, notably Puritanism, and Islam in terms of both religious revolution within society and aggressive "holy" wars against other religions and societies (Mansbach 2006). Weber remarks that those religions conducting "wars of missionary enterprise" and their "derivative sects" imposed the "duty of religious revolution for the cause of faith", citing Calvinism and Islam, including Puritan and Islamic sectarian groups, as exemplars. Also, contemporary sociologists observe and emphasize an "elective affinity" between jihads in radical Islam and crusades in American "reborn" Puritan evangelicalism (Turner 2002).

Consequently, global Puritan moral fascism and in extension Calvinist theocracy perhaps promises to become the "destiny" not only of America but the world as a whole, with virtually all societies "fated" or forced through "holy" wars to embrace its American version as the "model of a universal civilization" (Beck 2000). It hence attains the initial and perennial aim of Calvinism, "God's Kingdom on Earth". Specifically, it seeks to expand Calvin's *civitas Dei* from 16th century Geneva and implicitly the medieval *respublica Christiana* to 21st century America and the world via Winthrop's 17th century "Biblical Garden."

---

was not just another Christian denomination, it was an international, authoritarian conspiracy—perhaps even the work of the anti-Christ—which posed a threat to America's culture and values not unlike that which Communism was deemed to pose in the twentieth century" (Archer 2001:280).

[69] Weber adds that for Calvin, however, "defense might be undertaken only at the initiative of the status authorities, corresponding with the character of an institutional church."

Yet, Puritan moral fascism may turn out to be what Weber may call the "adverse fate" of the world, including America itself. It may so through and due to judgment-day nihilism intrinsic to "gloomy" Calvinism, notably Puritanism as super-Calvinism in "doom and gloom" pessimism and ultimately apocalyptic self-destruction a la Armageddon. In particular, Puritan moral fascism may prove to be the "adverse fate" of the world or humanity, including America, due to global military and other self-destruction via Puritan-style permanent and offensive "holy" wars against "ungodliness" and moral sin. This is indicated by various global surveys[70] identifying US Puritan-style neoconservatism as the main and growing threat, via its offensive wars, to world peace and thus, given the ever more "nigh-tech" weapons of mass destruction, including nuclear arms, the survival of humanity, including America itself in a typical MAD scenario (Habermas 2001; Schelling 2006). After all, the very Biblical passage about the risk of being killed by one's own sword if one chooses to use it predicts or admonishes about such a self-destructive outcome. Yet, US typically nationalist, bellicose, and militarist "reborn" evangelicals behave as though this rule of their "holy book" did not apply to them as "exceptional", and instead plan, conduct, and sanctify as "godly" offensive wars on the "ungodly" world, just as contradict or neglect the "who has not sinned" section.

On the account of its apocalyptic nihilism and ultimate ("logical"?) destruction of the "ungodly" world, Puritan moral fascism and in extension Calvinist theocracy may well prove to become the "destiny" of America in a fatal form. This is the form of what Weber might call America's "adverse fate" via nihilistic self-destruction or judgment-day apocalypse by a global Puritan-style "holy" offensive ("preemptive") war on the "evil" world. If so, America's Calvinist "destiny" would instead become its "nemesis" through Puritan moral fascism and its expansion in and destruction of the world. This would be an ultimate irony or the supreme American tragedy, rather than, as in Tocqueville's

---

[70] For instance, according to the Harris Interactive survey in 2007 "more Europeans see the United States as a threat to global stability than Iran and North Korea combined." In particular, 32 percent in five major European countries and more or less loyal American allies, Britain, France, Germany, Italy and Spain, identified America as the "biggest threat" to stability and peace, as did 11 percent Americans themselves seemingly fearful of what their self-declared evangelical and bellicose or militarist, "Wild West" style, 'shoot-first-ask-questions-later" and "big-stick" government can do to the world and thus ultimately themselves.

and usual meaning, a sort of happy-ending of living "happily ever after" in freedom and "Christian love", thus a free civil society.

In essence, Puritan moral fascism and in extension Calvinist (plus Islamic) theocracy would likely *rather* destroy than embrace an "immoral" and "ungodly" world, including America itself (e.g., "blue" or any regions not a "Bible Garden"), in the form of a liberal-secular civil society and democracy. It would rather "exorcise" sinners, "infidels", and "witches" to "save" them from themselves than "live and let them live" in civil society and beyond. Hence, Puritan moral fascism would rather commit collective suicide for the "glory of God" via an offensive global, including nuclear (Schelling 2006), "holy" war or crusade against the "sinful" and "infidels" than continue to exist in the midst of an increasingly "immoral" and "ungodly" liberal-secular society. This is what various apocalyptic fundamentalist sects and cults in historical and contemporary America have precisely done, attempted, and thus prefigured for a larger scale: the "delirium" of total annihilation as the final path to Calvinist salvation (Adorno 2001). Such an outcome would be the ultimate or "logical" disappearing act of the Puritan uncreative destruction of liberal-secular civil society and eventually human life and humanity, transforming Puritanism from America's "happy destiny" to its "adverse fate" or nemesis.

For instance, a "born again" evangelical US President was threatening or implying the Third World War against "evil" countries (e.g., immediately Iran, perhaps ultimately China and Russia) through nuclear weapons. In response, some politicians questioned the "mental health" of the "commander in chief" and in extension of most Americans typically supporting such "preemptive" wars against "evil" countries. Still, this was perhaps just another symptom of the typical evangelical "method of madness" (Smith 2000) or Puritan-rooted religious fanaticism and nihilism—as detected by Hume long ago—of which "holy war" or crusade and ultimate (self) destruction become a (patho) logical outcome. Simply, if it is the problem of "mental health", it is induced by religious rather than psychological factors, by fanatical and militant Puritanism, not personality traits, reflecting the syndrome of crusaders or "holy" warriors (who can otherwise be mentally healthy or sane), not necessarily of madmen or insanity in a proper sense. Puritan and any religious, including Islamic, fanaticism and militancy, notably crusade and jihad (Turner 2002), make humans, notably ruling groups, what Keynes calls "madmen in authority" or, as the observation about the US fundamentalist President implies, mentally problematic. After all, Puritanism, with what Hume calls its "wretched fanaticism" and "holy" war against "infidels" (Goldstone 1986; Gorski 2000), was in itself a system and syndrome of religiously induced societal madness, as is perhaps any act of or claim to "purism", "absolutism", pure "methodism", or "perfectionism". And, it evidently remains via "reborn" evangelicalism in America. In a way, the nihilistic tendency of Puritan moral fascism and Calvinist theocracy as a whole, in the form of total Judgment-Day annihilation as the path to "salvation" cannot be emphasized enough and never underestimated with impunity (so, I invite the reader to pause and think of it and its potential MAD outcomes for both the "evil" world and ultimately America itself).

CHAPTER SIX

# CULTURAL SYSTEM OF CALVINIST BIBLIOCRACY

## *Theocratic Culture*

### *Culture as Theocratic Religion*

The intrinsic cultural logic and integral element or subsystem of Calvinist evangelical theocracy as a total social system in America is a theocratic culture in general, religion in particular. This is the cultural system in which secular culture, ranging from the arts to philosophy and to science, education, and technology, is subverted, subordinated, and eventually sacrificed to "higher" and "greater than life" Calvinist-as-Puritan entities and purposes. Notably, these causes are Divinity and Providential design, theocratic domination within society, and a global permanent "holy" war against other "ungodly" and "evil" cultures and societies.

In this sense, secular culture, artistic and intellectual alike, in Calvinist theocracy reaches a condition that can be diagnosed and predicted only as what Weber and medieval scholastics may call *caput mortuum* ("presumed dead"). This is the condition after the model or image of medievalism in which all secular culture was reduced to the "servant" of theology, religion, and theocracy (official Catholicism or the Vatican Church in Western Europe) and thus effectively vanished or subverted, which precisely defined the Middle Ages as "Dark" in cultural and related terms. In virtue of the *caput mortuum* terminal condition of secular culture, Calvinist Bibliocracy effectively continues and perpetuates medieval theocracy (the *respublica Christiana*) and thus in cultural terms the Dark Middle Ages in which, as Pareto remarks, all cultures, including "every discourse", "assumed the form of the Christian religion".

The cultural system of Calvinist theocracy in America and elsewhere is by assumption or in reality religiously grounded, sanctified, and dominated culture. Human culture is transformed into its opposite, thus effectively self-eliminated or perverted, as are liberal-secular civil society, political democracy, and economy into their theocratic opposites. Simply, Calvinist theocracy's cultural logic and system is axiomatically theocratic culture, thus a sort of anti-culture, including anti-art and anti-science or anti-knowledge, in the proper secular meaning of the Renaissance and the Enlightenment respectively. In this sense, secular culture, like a free civil society, democratic polity, and economy, is effectively sacrificed, as are ultimately humans, to (as Weber and other sociologists suggest), an extremely inhuman Calvinist theology (the doctrine of predestination), religion, and theocracy, just as they were to its prior condemned and attacked Catholic version (the Vatican Church) during medieval times.

Secular cultures and humans become sacrifices for the glory of what Weber[1] describes as the God of Calvinism commanding various forms of human sacrifice, which prima facie reflects barbarism or even "savagery"[2] (Berry 1997). They are sacrificed to an absolutely transcendental, "omnipotent" (Heller 1986) force. Moreover, they are sacrifices to, as none than one of his "great men of Puritanism" (Milton[3]) implies, a merciless or inhumane entity compared to the traditional Christian "Father in heaven", in his words, "so human and understanding", or "simultaneously judging and merciful" (Habermas 1996). This Calvinist entity entails an oligarchic or aristocratic dimension in the sense of positive predestination or election of "only a few" and damnation of most humans. At this juncture, the question may arise as to "what kind of God?" (Reiland 2006) cultures and humans are sacrificed or subordinated to. The answer is implied in the question: to the God of Calvinism as a sort of "Oriental despot" and generally "too willful and capricious" (Artz 1998), rather than a true Christian (or Leibniz's) "loving God" (Fitzpatrick 1999). At the minimum, they are, as Parsons (1967) implies, sacrificed or subordinated to the "purposes" of (in Weber's expression) the "Calvinist God of absolute unsearchableness of His motives by any human standard" (also, Bendix 1977). Thus, contemporary Weberian

---

[1] Weber comments that Calvinism tended to "tear the individual away from the closed ties with which he is bound to this world. The world exists to serve the glorification of God and for that purpose alone" (cf., also Bendix 1977).

[2] Berry (1997:181) invokes the view of the Scottish Enlightenment, notably Hume, that savagery can be expressed not only in infanticide or cannibalism but also in "worshipping suitably fiercesome gods who demand sacrifices or self-mutilation", including by implication the God of Calvinism.

[3] This is implicit in John Milton's cited view about the doctrine of predestination: "though I may be sent to Hell for it, such a [Calvinist] God will never command my respect." As known, Milton rejected Calvinism because of its doctrine of predestination as the major dogma of its theodicy and theology overall, just as did Franklin later.

sociologists suggest that Calvinism, notably Puritanism, extorts "a high price" by producing or commanding "an atrophy of natural feeling in men's cultural and personal life" (Bendix 1965), and consequently produces the atrophic state and eventual death of what Weber calls emotional and secular culture.

The cultural system of Calvinist Bibliocracy in America, notably the "Bible Garden", is specifically theocratic theology and religion of which, like polity and civil society, all secular culture is an instrument, appendix, or subordinate in the manner of or analogy with the Dark Middle Ages. Such a theocratic status of culture encompasses all of its elements, spanning from morals, customs, traditions and conventions to art, philosophy, and ideology and to science, knowledge, education, and technology. Just as human actors as economic agents are the servants of Calvinist saints-masters in the economy subverted in a master-servant economic system, so secular culture is reduced to the servant of the "true" reformed theology, religion, and church, and humans as cultural creatures serve and are subordinated to its Divinely predestined rulers. In short, this is a culture and society that "serves" (Beck 2000) religion and theocracy, in this case the despotic and oligarchic God of Calvinism and his putative predestined agents with Divine Rights to rule, and in that sense a proto- or neo-feudal master-servant system.

In this sense, secular culture, like a democratic polity and a free civil society, intrinsically is or ultimately becomes a non-entity within Calvinist Bibliocracy in America, just as was within the medieval Catholic theocracy in Europe, which is what Weber's Latin medievalist expression *caput mortuum* ("death's head") precisely signifies. Essentially, there is no such thing as secular culture, like civil society as the private sphere of moral and other freedom, that is independent of and separate from theocratic theology, religion, and church, in Calvinist Bibliocracy, just as "no free lunch" or caritas and generosity in its master-servant, inhumane economic system. In sum, Calvinist, like any (especially Islamic), theocracy is by theological design the intrinsic antithesis and in social reality acts as the eventual destruction of secular-liberal culture, just as polity and civil society, perverted and reduced into a terminal condition or vegetative state. In short, it is hostile and destructive to a human culture in which art, science, and literature via "expanding intellectual inquiry" have a "central role" (Berman 2000).

*Anti-Aesthetic Culture*

In particular, Calvinist Bibliocracy is the theological antithesis and the theocratic destruction of aesthetic, artistic secular culture as "emotional" or "sensual" and (so) condemned as "depraved", "sinful", "too human" or "ungodly", and optimistic or hopeful about humans. It eliminates and substitutes aesthetic culture with its non-emotional or non-sensual, "pure", "godly", moralistic, and pessimistic ("original sin") ersatz or bogus antipode reflecting anti-artistic, anti-emotional, anti-human, and "gloomy" Calvinism, notably Puritanism. Hence, in artistic terms the inner cultural logic and the constitutive subsystem of Calvinist Bibliocracy as a total social system is theocratic anti-artistic or anti-aesthetic culture and in that sense anti- or in-culture (Baudrillard 1999) in an aesthetic sense, notably in that of the Renaissance.

Calvinist Bibliocracy, in a first act, theologically condemns aesthetic secular culture as "ungodly" and "impure." In a second act, it theocratically destroys culture and substitutes it with its opposite, after the model or image of the Dark Middle Ages when theology, religion, and theocracy was the cultural and societal master and the rest of society as the servant or appendage. On this, like other, economic, political, and civic, accounts, Calvinist Bibliocracy originally, as in Calvin's Geneva, Holland, and old and New England, was basically the reenactment and even further reinforcement of medieval theocracy (the *respublica Christiana*) defined in these terms by the status of artistic and other secular culture as the servant of theology, religion, and church. And, it has operated so since and remained such up to 21st century America, as witnessed by the "Bible Garden." This entails the latter's antagonism to and attempted destruction or subversion of aesthetic and all secular culture, including art, as well as science and education condemned and attacked as "ungodly" (evolutionary biology, stem-cell research, critical social theory, etc.) and even substituted by "no schooling" at all as "better" than it non-religious type (Darnell and Sherkat 1997; Martin 2002) that, like secularism, contradicts the "Puritan ideal of strict moral education" (Fehler 2005).

In general, virtually all theocracies and perhaps religions are axiomatically antagonistic and destructive to artistic and other secular culture, and alternatively an opposite, "aesthetic" type of theocracy is an internal contradiction or an empirical rarity. At the minimum, they are the systems or "religions of restraint" (Bell 1977) in relation to artistic and all secular culture or life. Yet, it is in particular Calvinist-Puritan

Bibliocracy and generally Calvinism, notably Puritanism, that is vehemently anti-artistic and anti-cultural in secular terms, even more so than any other theocracies in Protestantism and Christianity overall (e.g., traditional Christian Orthodoxy and Catholicism) and other world religions (except for theocratic Islam and Hinduism).

Weber identifies and emphasizes Calvinism's theological antithesis to and its theocratic elimination of any aesthetic secular or emotional culture that does not directly or indirectly serve and glorify the Calvinist religion, theology, and theocracy, consequently its extreme inhumanity. In particular, he suggests that Puritanism followed and even reinforced Calvinism in this respect in adopting an "entirely negative attitude" to "all the sensuous and emotional elements in culture", or a "fundamental antagonism to sensuous culture of all kinds," notably the arts. In short, Puritanism tends to anathematize "all activities" turning humans away from the Calvinist God (Bendix 1965) in the image an "Oriental despot", with art and all secular culture as a major threat or suspect in this respect. Puritanism considers aesthetic culture to be suspect for its appeal to human "sensuality" and thus humanity (Bendix 1965), revealing Puritan anti-humanism.

Consequently, emotional or aesthetic secular culture, simply human art, in the form and sense of the artistic and, in Parsons' (1967) words, "humanistic" Renaissance becomes a non-entity, at most an alien element or non-invited "guest" within Calvinist Bibliocracy. This is what Pareto suggests in observing that Calvinism, via its anti-artistic, anti-secular, and anti-humanist or "disciplinary" revolutions (Gorski 2003; Loveman 2005), and even the Protestant Reformation overall, "halted" the Renaissance in North Europe in contrast to "refined and skeptical Italy".[4] He implies that in artistic and humanistic terms the Calvinist revolution was effectively counter-revolution in outcome. It was an adverse reaction to and reversal of the Renaissance seeking to restore the medieval status of art and all culture as the servant of religion and theocracy, simply the anti-Renaissance. Parsons (1967) evokes Pareto, registering just a "few points" of agreement (e.g., the "negative valuation" of ritual) and by implication many levels of disagreement between early Calvinist Puritans and the "men of the humanistic Renaissance",

---

[4] In general, Pareto states that the Protestant Reformation "began among the rough people of the North where Christian religion sentiment was more alive, while it made few proselytes in refined and skeptical Italy."

and, one can add, between their respective contemporary heirs and proxies, especially in America.

Pareto and Parsons both suggest that by assumption and in reality, the artistic, humanistic Renaissance and anti-artistic, anti-humanistic Calvinism and Puritanism, in particular Calvinist theocracies, were initially in Europe as opposite or distant as "heaven and earth" (in the sense of difference, and not evaluation). And, they have remained so ever since, up to the 21st century in America, notably its "Bible Garden". On this account, Calvinism, Calvinist theocracy in particular, was and remains a type of anti-Renaissance in terms of aesthetic secular culture or art and humanism overall. And, Calvinist theocracy functions as the anti-Renaissance and generally anti-aesthetic because, as Weber implies, it is anti-humanistic and anti-secular, even extremely inhumane, just as its anti-aesthetics sustains and reinforces its anti-humanism, including its anti-secularism, as the basis. By contrast, as Comte, Simmel, Weber, Pareto, and Parsons imply, the Renaissance was paradigmatically an artistic revival in virtue of reviving (classical) humanism[5] and secularism, just as its aesthetic dimension sustained and reinforced its humanistic and secular sources. In sum, if the "humanism of the Renaissance" (Byrne 1997) and its values and legacies suggest that aesthetic pursuits represent a "truly universal aspect of human nature" (Berry 1997), then Calvinist, especially Puritan, theocracy in America acts as an antithesis and destruction of this artistic and humanistic universalism.

*Anti-Rationalistic Culture*

Calvinist Bibliocracy is also the theological antithesis and theocratic destruction of intellectual or rationalist secular culture, including physical and social science, knowledge, education, and philosophy. It condemns and methodically attacks and destroys such culture as "blasphemous", "heretic", "ungodly", "infidel", and the like ("un-Christian"). It does so conjointly with its antagonism to and suppression of non-religious aesthetics in an apparently total "method in the madness" of anti-culture nihilism. Likewise, Calvinist theocracy tends to substitute rationalist or intellectual culture by its anti-rationalist or anti-intellectual ersatz variant in the form of "godly" or "faith-based" ("Christian") science, education, philosophy, even medicine and technology, just

---

[5] As known and Byrne (1997:7) remarks, the "humanism of the Renaissance had greatly admired the political, scientific, cultural and artistic achievements of ancient Greece and Rome".

as politics and government. Such a substitution and thus effective elimination of rationalist culture expresses Calvinist, notably Puritan, anti-intellectualism and anti-rationalism in a secular and cultural, as distinguished from theological and economic, sense. In sum, in intellectual, rationalist terms, the cultural logic and subsystem of Calvinist Bibliocracy as a social system is theocratic anti-intellectual and anti-rationalist, including anti-scientific, culture.

On this account, Calvinist Bibliocracy in America, notably in its new "Bible Garden", is culturally a social system and design of theocratic anti-intellectualism and anti-rationalism, in particular anti-scientism, in a secular sense. It operates or appears as the methodical antagonism and nihilism toward secular intellectualism that is, as neo-classical economist Francis Edgeworth suggests (referring to abstract theory), "despised as useless" and to cultural—not to be confused (as Weber admonishes) with economic or capitalist—rationalism, including its scientific form, denounced as "ungodly" or "blasphemous" ("un-Christian"). In particular, Calvinist Bibliocracy is the design and system of theocratic anti-scientism in opposition to scientism[6] (Habermas 1971) in the sense and shape of Weber-Merton's vocation, ethos, and application of rational secular science, method, and knowledge. This is epitomized by its "eternal" theological condemnation of and systematic theocratic attack on scientific biology because of its "un-Biblical" evolutionism (Martin 2002) and more recently embryonic stem cell research. It is also by its recent denouncing of climate science, due to its "ungodly", "un-American," or "anti-capitalist" diagnosis of global warming[7] (Nordhaus 2007), as well as its old and new assaults on the critical social sciences and scientists as "blasphemous"

---

[6] Habermas (1971:5) defines "Scientism" as "science's belief in itself [to] identify knowledge with science." Further, he suggests that "positivism stands and falls with the principle of scientism [i.e.,] that the meaning of knowledge is defined by what the sciences do can thus be adequately explained through the methodological analysis of scientific procedures" (Habermas 1971:69).

[7] Nordhaus (2007:686) comments that "no two places on earth are further apart on global warming policies than the White House and 10 Downing Street [the UK government]", citing the US President's opposition to "binding constraints on greenhouse gas emissions" (the Kyoto Protocol). Also, for example, during 2007 media reported that world leaders attempted at the first UN climate summit "to put new urgency into global talks to reduce global-warming emissions", yet the US "godly" neoconservative "administration showed no sign, however, that it would reverse its stand against mandatory emission cuts endorsed by 175 other nations". (Eventually, being in complete isolation and under overwhelming world and even American public opinion requesting such a move, the US government did make this reversal or concession at another conference, yet only to deny or qualify it after the fact in the long-standing Puritan tradition of

and "infidels" to be restrained and punished severely for their dissenting views as "blasphemy" (Bendix 1970; Bourdieu and Haacke 1995; Coats 1967). For example, US "reborn" fundamentalists' attack on climate science's thesis and evidence of global warming and stem-cell research is substantively equivalent to that by medieval theologians and theocrats, including inquisitors, on Copernicus' "ungodly" heliocentric astronomical theory. In a way, it is remarkable and even incredible, yet predictable, that US religious conservatives would make "ungodly" and politicize even this branch and research of natural science at the start of the 21st century, which confirms Puritan-based evangelical anti-scientism and anti-rationalism.[8]

Consequently, intellectual or rationalist secular culture, including science, knowledge, education, and philosophy, in the specific form and sense of the Enlightenment intrinsically is or eventually becomes a non-entity in Calvinist Bibliocracy. At most, it is subverted and abused for Parsons' "purposes of God" and of theocratic mastery, in this theocracy and Calvinism generally, Puritanism particularly. Hence, Calvinist theocracy is a type of counter- or pre-Enlightenment, just as by contrast the Enlightenment was anti- or non-Calvinist (Artz 1998; Bremer 1995; Byrne 1997), with respect to intellectual or rationalist and all non-religious culture, just as secularism, rationalism, humanism, and liberalism.

*Secular Culture versus Theocratic Religion*

In cultural terms, Calvinist Bibliocracy functions as the Puritan destruction or subversion of secular artistic and intellectual culture through replacing the latter by or submitting it to religion, theology, and theocracy in America. At the minimum, this holds true of the "Bible Garden" (if) still considered a regional phenomenon limited to the "new" evangelical South and other ("hot-red") regions growing in both population and political-cultural influence and even becoming the "not-so-silent" moral and societal majority, distinguished from less theocratic and fundamentalist or more liberal-secular ("blue") parts, in America. Yet, this minimum may well become a sort of maximum or rather

---

sanctimony and "permanent denial".) In particular, the US "born again" President "didn't take part in the day's sessions, which drew more than 80 national leaders."

[8] A "Bible Belt" governor attacked the 2000 Presidential candidate, proponent of measures to slow down global warming, and a Nobel peace laureate in words almost not fit to print (the latter's mouth being the "biggest source of pollution"!).

Pareto-like optimum for Southern "born again" evangelicals so long as the observed recent tendencies continue, as they attempt and hope and dream. Notably, this is the tendency of American politics, culture, and society as a whole toward "heading South" and being placed in the theocratic and fundamentalist or anti-secular, as well as anti-rationalist, including anti-scientific, "shadow of Dixie" (Cochran 2001), moving to "Dixieland", in the 1980s–2000s.

In a sense, the cultural logic, subsystem, and outcome of Calvinist Bibliocracy can be described as "secular culture is (eventually) dead, long live theocratic religion" in America, at least the "Bible Garden" (even more Utah as formally outside, but substantively part, of it). At this juncture, what culturally self-defines not only this region but America as a whole after the design of Calvinist Bibliocracy is the Bible as the sole or main "culture", artistic and intellectual alike, both art and science, knowledge, or education. For instance, some "reborn" US religious conservatives proclaim with apparent pride and joy that in American history the Bible was the "only common culture" (Bloom 1988), including by implication the arts and science alike, in contrast to what they disdain as secular, artistic, and intellectualist Europe, particularly France. In particular, they imply that it has been and remains the "only common or valid science" for US evangelicals, old and new, as indicated by their adoption and coercive imposition of creationism and its "intelligent-design" derivatives as an absolute in biology against "ungodly" evolutionism (Martin 2002) as a "just a theory". They do so in spite or precisely because of what Pareto calls the "scientific errors of the Bible" in relation to the physical and social sciences, and Voltaire its "contradictions" and "childish absurdities" (Artz 1998), including "uncomfortable discrepancies" between its different parts, "factual claims" conflicting with "mounting evidence", and sections appearing as "myth or fable", explained away by invoking its "Divine origin" or revelation rather than a "document with a history" (Byrne 1997). Not surprisingly, alongside the replacement of "Christian" geocentric by scientific astronomy, the "historical veracity of the biblical account of creation", maintained in both Catholicism and especially Protestantism, was contradicted and eventually replaced by the "steady rise" of such sciences as biology and geology in Europe since the 17th century[9] (Byrne 1997).

---

[9] Byrne (1997:11) cites the case of Isaac de la Peyrère who in 1655 "argued on scientific grounds that Adam could not be literally considered the first man [and] suffered much the same fate as Galileo."

In short, such sciences made "increasingly evident" that the Bible had "limitations" as the "source of historical accuracy and scientific knowledge" (Byrne 1997).

In retrospect, in a standard display of ethnocentrism or what Weber would call the "mere confession of ignorance" of history, US "born again" Calvinist evangelicals overlook or deny that the "Bible as the only common culture" is not really American superior exceptionalism. For the Bible had been, as Pareto suggests, the "only common culture" in the old Europe during the Dark Middle Ages, centuries before Tocqueville's first Puritans redesigned and recreated their Bibliocracy as a "Biblical Garden" (Gould 1996) in the "new exceptional nation" (Lipset 1996). In particular, evangelicals overlook or deny that the Bible was the "only common" and "valid" discourse and science for medievalist Catholic theologians or scholastics. This was indicated by their adoption and imposition through the "holy" Inquisition of geocentric (the "sun-revolves-around-earth" or "flat-earth") against heretic scientific heliocentric theory in astronomy, as an exemplary and ever since universally admitted case of Pareto's "scientific errors" and Voltaire's "childish absurdities in the Bible." And, this particular instance paradigmatically exemplified the Dark Middle Ages' principle that everything in conflict with "Christian truth" must be "rejected and condemned", as Copernicus, Galileo, Bruno, and other scientists-heretics realized[10] (Byrne 1997). Also, US "reborn" fundamentalists neglect or deny even more vehemently that precisely the status of the Bible as the common or dominant "culture", including, as Pareto suggests by "scientific errors", ersatz or bogus science, singularly defined medieval times as the "Dark Middle Ages." It did by substituting secular, notably classical, culture, science, and philosophy, consequently submerged, and vanished (literally, as were "pagan" books and libraries, burned at the stake) almost without trace, in theology, religion, and medieval Biblical theocracy.

At this juncture, the anti-rationalist, including, as Pareto implies, anti-scientific, status of the Bible as the "only common culture", notably sole "valid science", in Calvinist Bibliocracy and fundamentalism in America is not new and exceptional, a *cause célèbre* of American

---

[10] Byrne (1997:10–1) observes that "when Galileo Galilei was condemned by the Pope in 1633 for holding the view of Copernicus that the earth revolved around the sun, a gap was opened between religion and science which was to be exacerbated in the Enlightenment."

exceptionalism in an invidious distinction from Europe. It is rather a relict of medieval Europe or the Dark Middle Ages hence effectively resurrected from the dead past in the new Puritan nation, especially its "Biblical Gardens" like Winthrop's New England and the evangelical South as exemplified and symbolized by "Salem with witches" and "Monkey Trials", respectively. And, these examples and symbols indicate that the effects of such a status are anything but exceptional or novel ("better"), rather essentially déjà vu in the "new" Calvinist Bibliocracy as compared with the old despised Catholic theocracy—the theocratic destruction or perversion of secular culture, including science and philosophy. In a way, the ultimate outcome of the status of the Bible as the "only common culture", including "valid science", in the Calvinist Bibliocracy involved "Salem with witches" and "Monkey Trials", as historical instances or sociological metaphors of anti-rationalism, notably anti-scientism, including anti-evolutionism, just as the Inquisition and its "holy" attack on scientific astronomy in the Catholic theocracy. Hence, the anti-scientific treatment of Biblical creationism as the "only valid" biological "science" versus "ungodly" evolutionism by fundamentalism appears as a historical vestige or déjà vu replica in another scientific field of the medieval status of "godly" geocentric, against heliocentric, theory as the sole "true" astronomy. They thus share a theological antagonism to and the theocratic destruction of secular science and all culture. At this juncture, various anti-evolutionary and other anti-scientific and anti-rationalist "Monkey Trials" in the "Bible Garden" and beyond reappear as replays or relicts of the Inquisition's trials against astronomy, just as "Salem with witches" was a Puritan reenactment of medieval primitive witch-trials and beliefs[11] (Byrne 1997; Harley 1996). And, both instances of

---

[11] Byrne (1997:17-8) observes that belief in "witches" "is as old as the human race", but it was during the late Middle Ages that "there developed the notion that the power of the witch was due to her having made a pact with the Devil". In particular, he suggests that the persecution of witches during the 16-17th centuries "had its roots deep in mediaeval Europe's abhorrence of heresy and the propaganda of the heresy-hunters, and it was fed by the disruption of the religious wars which followed the Reformation" (Byrne 1997:18). Byrne (1997:18) adds that "Catholics, Calvinists and Lutherans alike persecuted witches, thinking that they were thereby preventing the devil's work; that they were hardly at the same time doing the work of the Christian God seems only to have occurred to a few. Their enthusiasm for the truth resulted in the deaths of tens of thousands of innocent people." Notably, he registers the "decline and virtual disappearance of the belief in "witches" which marked the century from about 1650 onwards" (Byrne 1997:17) and consequently their persecution in the "old" Europe. Yet, this was apparently not the case in the "new world", for the belief in and persecution of "witches"

anti-scientism and anti-rationalism were eventually caused, explained, and sanctified by the theocratic, evangelical status of the Bible as the "only common" culture and discourse, notably the sole "valid science".

Moreover, Calvinist Bibliocracy or Puritan-rooted fundamentalism in America has been more consistent and obstinate in anti-scientism and anti-rationalism than even what Comte calls the "most degenerate Catholicism" or the Vatican Church. The latter has abandoned not only, like Protestantism and other world religions, medievalist geocentric theory but, unlike Protestant fundamentalism, at least in part, Biblical creationism as the only valid biological "science" and recognized or just resigned to evolutionism (with certain qualifications). In retrospect, this would not surprise Weber and Hume, given their respective diagnoses of Calvinist "iron consistency" and Puritan "unreasonable obstinacy". In prospect, it shows that Calvinist Bibliocracy through Puritan-rooted evangelicalism will likely remain in the 21st century as antagonistic and ultimately destructive to secular science and other culture as was the medieval Vatican theocracy with its Inquisition, and even more than contemporary Catholicism and any branch of Christianity.[12] At least, the continuing attacks on evolutionism, including recently on stem-cell research, and the perennial (including "intelligent design") revivals of creationism as the "true" biological science justify the proposition "secular culture is (eventually) dead, long live theocratic religion" within Calvinist Bibliocracy in America, minimally the evangelical South, in contrast to Catholicism and non-Calvinist liberal or mainline, moderate American and other Protestantism (Hout et al. 2002; Martin 2002).

In sum, the above religious-conservative statement as well as the apparent desideratum that the Bible was and shall be the "only common culture", including "valid science" in Puritan America is both false and true. It is false in overlooking that the "holy writ" had also been such culture in medieval Christian Europe, a status eventually leading to or sanctifying anti-scientism and anti-rationalism epitomized and symbolized by the Inquisition's war on scientific astronomy. It is true in

---

continued via Puritan witch-trials in New England during the late 17th century climaxing in the Salem hysteria (Gould 1996; Harley 1996) of 1692. At least, "witches" confirm that American Puritanism was even more superstitious or irrational, primitive or backward, and atavistic or anachronistic (Miller 1975) than any European religion, including Catholicism, Lutheranism, and even its own parent Calvinism.

[12] In turn, alongside Protestant fundamentalism in America, fundamentalist Islam is, as expected, the only or main other world religion rejecting biological evolutionism.

correctly diagnosing and predicted that it has remained so, especially the "only valid science", in the "new nation" after the design of Calvinist Bibliocracy *cum* the "Bible Garden", while increasingly devoid of such status in the "old world", including post-medieval Catholicism (the Vatican Church) in part. And, it is false again in overlooking or denying that such a status also generated and/or sanctified anti-scientism and anti-rationalism, analogously epitomized and symbolized by "Salem with witches" and "Monkey Trials" in the above two "Biblical Gardens".

In essence, the image or outcome of Calvinist-as-Puritan theocracy in America is a sort of cultural nothingness or emptiness in virtue of destroying or perverting secular artistic and intellectual culture, both art and science or education, beyond a shadow of doubt and recognition. Perhaps nothing more accurately or vividly represent such cultural nothingness or emptiness in Puritan theocracy than the image and metaphor of a culture desert or Sahara and wilderness or the "Wild West" (Hill 2002). Thus, some observers depict contemporary America, especially the Southwest, as cultural, not just physical, "desert" and "wilderness", thus anti-culture in the shape of "death of culture" (Baudrillard 1999) in the sense of the Renaissance and the Enlightenment, as primarily the outcome of survived or revived Puritanism. Other analysts adopt the image of the Hobbesian anti-social state of nature (Munch 1994) and its special case, the "Wild West" (Hill 2002), for describing Puritan-style culture and society, including politics, in America. In particular, critics object that the "new South" turned into a "Bible Garden" is as culturally sterile as "Sahara desert" due to being recreated and ruled by what is called evangelical "Methodist and Baptist" anti-cultural, notably anti-artistic, "barbarism" (Mencken 1982).

If the preceding is correct, then Calvinism via Puritanism and other Protestant sects and cults (Mormonism, etc.) may have transformed natural desert[13] (McCann 2000) or "wilderness" (Munch 2001) in human society or civilization (e.g., Utah, Nevada) in a striking technological achievement. And yet, in the process it rendered America itself a cultural desert or wilderness in its own right, thus "de-civilizing" or returning the "new nation" to the "wild state" of anti-culture (Baudrillard 1999). In this account, it may have created the "first new nation" (Lipset

---

[13] McCann (2000:12) remarks that "although the Mormons build what seems an Edenic community in the Utah desert, that order depends on an "omniscient and omnipresent" system of enforcement that denies personal freedom and gives rise to rapacity and terror."

1969) but recreated or sustained it, in some descriptions, as the "only remaining primitive" (Baudrillard 1999) or the most traditional society in cultural, including moral and religious (Inglehart 2004), terms among modern Western cultures and societies.

Such cultural Puritan-rooted primitivism or traditionalism persists in conjunction and perhaps mutual reinforcement with what sociological analyses identify as political-democratic "backwardness" (Amenta and Halfmann 2000), notably in social policy or a welfare state (Quadagno 1999), traced primarily to the legacy of Puritanism (Hudson and Coukos 2005) with its lack of caritas and compassion (Tiryakian 2002). Curiously, some US religious conservatives admit that Americans look like "natural savages" (*sic*) in relation to Europeans and their early school lives are "spiritually empty" (Bloom 1988). Yet, most conservatives reproduce, extol, and rationalize this admitted savagery" and "spiritual emptiness" as what classical economists Smith, Ricardo, and Mill might call America's "comparative advantage" or superior cultural virtue and exceptionalism in the global "division of labor." These "new Puritans" invidiously distinguish such "new" exceptionalism from the "old world" despised and condemned as overly "cultural", especially artistic and intellectualistic, hence "useless", as well as "secular" and "liberal", as "ungodly" vices (Gould 1996). The above provides an additional instance in which only Sen's inverted, "irrational fools" like US Puritan, just as Islamic, fundamentalists, are proud of what would make most others in Western and other cultures embarrassed. This is cultural primitivism and irrationalism in opposition to intellectualism and rationalism exemplified by "embarrassing Monkey Trials" (Boles 1999) in the sense of anti-science attacks.

### The Puritan "Culture of Death"?

Further, the cultural system of Calvinist theocracy is ultimately what can be either literally or figuratively considered the "culture of death" or anti-life. In that sense, it is effectively anti-culture, given that the essence of culture is precisely promoting, sustaining, and celebrating, not destroying, undermining, and depreciating, human life, dignity, and happiness in Jefferson's Enlightenment-based secular sense ("in this world"). This constitutes the theocratic culture of depreciation, subordination, and ultimately sacrifice of individual humans and their life, dignity, and happiness to "greater than life" anti- and supra-human

Divine, joined with collective national ("patriotic") and self-destructive, causes and entities. A paradigmatic instance of such causes involves the "glory of God" blended with anti-liberal culture wars within-society and nihilistic "holy" war on "evil" and "ungodly" societies. In a sense, Calvinist theocracy's cultural system amounts to a "culture of death" against liberal-secular society condemned as one of "untrue" life and "false" happiness, as US Puritan apologists[14] imply (Seaton 2006; also, German 1995).

Alternatively, the cultural system of Calvinist theocracy represents a sort of culture of anti-life, including anti-pleasure to the point of what some analysts call the "masochistic ecstasy of pain" or "moral masochism" identified in ascetic cults, sects, and religions like Puritanism, as well as contemporary fascism, notably Nazism (Woodard 1938). And, it does so in virtue of what Weber identifies as the "destruction of spontaneous, impulsive enjoyment" and ultimately human life in Calvinism, especially Puritanism. In this sense, Calvinist theocracy is a lifeless, including joyless (Scitovsky 1972) or even painful, culture, just as economy and society overall. Hence, it is a far cry from and an actual contradiction to and an eventual elimination of what US "reborn" evangelicals, as typical in view of Puritan perennial hypocrisy, hypocritically declare and extol as the "culture of life" and the "right to life" in reference to their denials and suppression of the freedom of choice in a particular segment of the private sphere.

---

[14] For instance, in a eulogy to Puritan theocracy in America, Seaton (2006:196) argues that Calvinism, notably American Puritanism had "truths about man", notably death, that "liberalism ignores or obscures." Arguably, in Calvinist-Puritan language, "Covenant" was "not the Declaration's 'consent'", but instead expresses the "weighty view that sinful "natural man" stands in permanent need of the disciplining fraternal communities of church and state", including by implication being executed by these powers (Seaton 2006:196). Notably, for Puritanism, "life was on loan as an unmerited gift of the Creator; it had to be cared for and then tendered to its Owner and Master" (Seaton 2006:197–8). In particular, according to this eulogy, "fallen" bourgeois-liberal man "resented and resisted death's power over life, when he sought immortality here below in various ways" and (so) the Puritans' "gravest concerns" are about the "defects of the human will" prompting humans to "deeply unrealistic illusions and desires" (Seaton 2006:198). It infers that for Puritanism the "deepest division in mankind is that of "the unredeemed"—and thus implicitly condemned to dead both in this and the other world—and "the elect" (Seaton 2006:198) in accordance with the Calvinist dogma of predestination. In addition, German (1995:978) approvingly cites similar theological statements by New England's Puritans, namely that the " "emanation of his own infinite fullness," not the happiness of humankind, is the "ultimate end of the creation" ", that "true virtue must chiefly consist in love to God", etc.

Now, according to this new Puritan "logic" of "born again" US evangelicals, both their systematic use or fervent support of the death penalty for sins and crimes, including executions of innocent people, *and* their denial of freedom of choice in intimate life belong to the "culture of life". They see *no* contradiction between their death-penalty use or advocacy for those "proudly born in the USA" (let alone foreigners) committing mortal sins and/or crimes and their defense of the "right to life" for the unborn. (And, if they claim that the latter are actually born, they need to change by 9 months their own birth certificates to be consistent.) As usual, what is seeming "logic" in Puritanism turns out to be a self-contradiction or rather original and perpetual Puritan "pure hypocrisy", in this case, defending the "right to life" for some ("unborn"), and denying that very right to others ("born") by executing them, in an apparent Orwellian double-thinking and world. Within modern Western society, it is difficult to find or imagine a more manifest and stronger self-contradiction, self-deception, duplicity, or hypocrisy than US "reborn" Calvinists' mix of the death penalty for sins-crimes, guilty and (often) innocent persons, with the "pro-life" stance on birth control. From another prism, however, this duality turns out to reflect Calvinist "iron consistency", including Puritan "unreasonable obstinacy", a "method in the madness" of the destruction of liberty, choice, and life. For US "reborn" Calvinists' "pro-life" rhetoric in practice translates into the denial and destruction of individual liberty and choice in morality and private life (individuals' freedom and right to own their own bodies, just as property), thus being perfectly consistent with their unapologetic ("good conscience") and sadistic (cheerful) use and advocacy of the death penalty for both moral sins and crimes, guilty and (often) innocent alike.

### *Indicators ("Symptoms") of the Puritan "Culture of Death"*

Indicators of the Calvinist-as-Puritan "culture of death" or rather the "anti-culture of anti-life", including joylessness and pain, in America are numerous, manifest, and salient. Of course, the most frequent, manifest, and salient indicator is the death penalty inflicted by Puritan saints-masters in America on humans for their sins-crimes. An indirect or potential indicator involves related Draconian punishments such as life-long and otherwise lengthy imprisonment for such sinful and other offenses in virtue of causing or exacerbating various social pathologies. These pathologies range from prisons providing the "breeding ground for future crime [and sin]"[15] (Akerlof 2002), including potentially capital offenses (e.g., murders, rape, drug trade, etc.), to suicides. In light of the widespread use and fanatical support of the death penalty by Puritans and their vestiges and/or revivals in America, from New England's "Biblical Commonwealth" to the Southern "Bible Garden" (e.g., Texas, Alabama, Georgia, Tennessee, Florida, etc.), to claim that, as US "reborn" evangelicals do, theirs is the "culture of life" is a supreme, fascist-like cynicism and Orwellian double-talk, compounded with Hume's classically detected and exposed Puritan paradigmatic hypocrisy (Bremer 1995) and "wild" or "wretched fanaticism".

Substantively, the death penalty and generally the Draconian criminal (in)justice system in America operates as an indicator and element of the Puritan "culture of death", thus a broad cultural and sociological rather than merely a narrow legal and technical phenomenon, in several respects. First, it does by representing the vestige or revival of the death penalty and generally proto-Draconian penal system in New England under Puritanism. Recall Tocqueville's striking and prophetic observation that punishment by death was "never more frequently prescribed by statute" than by his first Puritans like Winthrop et al. in 17th century New England, identifying a deadly, Draconian penal system in general. It is striking and prophetic in that among modern Western societies punishment by death is "never more frequently prescribed" by law and especially applied by penal institutions than is by the Puritan-rooted judicial system in America.

Generally, Tocqueville identifies a truly theocratic Draconian penal system or lethal legal theocracy. He does in his observation that the Puritan legislator renders "attendance on divine service compulsory, and goes so far as to visit with severe punishment, and even with death, Christians who chose to worship God according to a ritual differing from his own", according to the law "whosoever shall worship any other God than the Lord shall surely be put to death" (also, Dayton 1999). And, Tocqueville comments that in so doing the "new" American Puritan legislator suffered from a kind of historical amnesia in the sense of "entirely forgetting the great principles of religious toleration that he had himself demanded in Europe", specifically England under official Anglicanism.

---

[15] Akerlof (2002:427) comments that "prison itself is a school for countercultural identity, and thus the breeding ground for future crime".

Second and as a corollary, the death penalty system in (most of) America is an indicator and element of the Puritan "culture of death" due to being religiously grounded and sanctified, specifically by fundamentalism and sectarianism. Most US "born again" fundamentalists in the "Bible Garden" (e.g., Texas[16]) and beyond systematically apply and fervently advocate the death penalty on primarily religious grounds, typically invoking the Biblical ("eye-for-eye", "blood shed", etc.) passages as the supreme basis and sanctification, as did their Puritan ancestors and role models in New England, and do their Islamic enemies invoking the Koran for their equivalent or harsher Draconian punishments. For instance, this is also what Tocqueville suggests in observing that punishment by death and generally Draconian penal legislation in Puritan New England displays "striking marks of a narrow, sectarian spirit" and "religious passions". And evidently, such a Puritan "sectarian spirit" and "religious passions" overall continue to drive and rationalize US "reborn" fundamentalists' methodical and sanctimonious (unapologetic) use and advocacy of the death penalty not only for egregious crimes like cruel, serial murders. They also growingly use and advocate punishment with death for moral sins and vices (e.g., drug marketing as a Federal capital offense), especially in their "Bible Garden" (some sexual offenses in Texas), just as their forebears did in New England (adultery, blasphemy, sorcery, etc.).

Such laws and sanctifications of the death penalty and generally Draconian punishment by the Biblical texts define and describe the ultra-religious South (notably, Texas), if not all America, as a "Bible Belt" or legal Bibliocracy. This indicates that New England Puritan theocracy has effectively self-perpetuated from the 17th to the 21st century as well as converged with Islamic theocracies also defined by legislating and sanctifying such practices by the Koran. Of course, the above Biblical commandment is applied only in the case of Americans' "sheddeth blood", not that of non-Americans, especially

---

[16] For instance, the *Economist* comments that many US neo-conservatives use and support the death penalty "for religious reasons" a la "eye-for-eye" retribution, citing a Texas state prosecutor who invokes the Biblical "Whoso sheddeth man's blood, by man shall his blood be shed" as "pretty compelling" for capital punishment. And, since the Texas legislature passed in 2007 a law punishing with the death penalty also certain crimes in which "blood is not shed" like non-murders (e.g., sexual offenses), no doubt its "godly" prosecutors will find "good" religious reasons for such punishment in the Bible, just as their Islamic counterparts do for their equivalent laws and punishments in the Koran.

those thousands of civilians, including children, killed by the US military during the "war on terror" in Iraq, Afghanistan, and elsewhere. As usual in theocracies and dictatorships, what is murder and are murderers deserving the equivalent punishment in the first case are "heroism" and "war heroes" meriting various rewards, including wealth, prestige, and political power (Presidency, government, Congress, etc.) in the second.

Third and as a corollary of the above two, the death penalty system in America is on the account of its primitive or barbarian residues an indicator and element of the Puritan "culture of death". This is what Tocqueville implies by observing that "the legislation of a rude and half-civilized people was thus applied to an enlightened and moral community" by his first Puritans in America. Seemingly, "the legislation of a rude and half-civilized people" pertains to that of primitive Biblical as well as pre-Christian communities, including Sparta and its Draconian legal system (formally originating in Athens during Draco). This was implicit in Winthrop's vision and creation of America as "Christian Sparta" and in that sense "Draconianism". In turn, by an "enlightened and moral community" Tocqueville apparently refers to a culture and society in the age of Enlightenment, as represented in this case by post-Calvinist Franklin relinquishing[17] his father's Calvinism because of its inhumanity or immorality (Byrne 1997). Such a community is thus incompatible with the "legislation of a rude and half-civilized people", including the death penalty or Draconian punishment for moral sins-crimes. Further, Comte states that Calvinism returns to the "period of the primitive Church" and even offers for as a cultural model the "most barbarous and dangerous part of the Scriptures—that which relates to the Hebrew antiquity".

Fourth, the death penalty system in America is an indicator and element of the Puritan "culture of death", because it is typically discriminatory in terms of social stratification, notably class and power (as well as gender and to a lesser extent race). As well-known, the vast majority of those effectively or expected to be executed by the US death penalty

---

[17] Echoing Weber's portrayal, however, Johnson (2003) comments that "Franklin's desire, if not his method, was shaped by the moral absolutists railing relentlessly from the pulpits in their Boston churches for self-sacrifice and a surrender of the self to the will of God [i.e.] the strict tenets of Puritanism." Also, Merton (1968:92) in a near-Veblenian sarcastic manner states that "Franklin demonstrated that God clearly "wants us to tipple" " and cites this demonstration as an instance of the Calvinist (or Christian) theological "argument from design".

system are persons of low class, power and status, or economically poor and politically powerless (as well as men and racial minorities). Typically, the system, other things equal, is more likely to execute or punish in a Draconian manner (e.g., imprison to lengthy sentences and life) low class, power, and status persons (as well as men, minorities, and foreign nationals or immigrants), than their stratification opposites (and women, the majority group, and native-born Americans) even for identical or comparable crimes like murders, etc. It thus effectively functions as the criminal *injustice* system and reflects and perpetuates the Puritan "culture of death" as part of Calvinist theocracy.

In particular, on the basic level of life and death (or imprisonment), foreign nationals and immigrants really risk their lives and freedom or take their chances in America under "reborn" religious conservatism. Other things equal, they are more likely to be executed and imprisoned (including for life), as have been in the past and are in the present, for factual or fabricated sins-crimes by the Draconian "tough on crime" neo-conservative penal system in America than other Western societies all of them abolishing executions and having less harsh and "more humane" legal systems (Reuter 2005). Overall, non-Americans face a "double jeopardy" to their lives and personal freedom in neo-conservative America. First, it is the Draconian Puritan-based death and penal system executing and otherwise punishing for moral sins, let alone crimes. Second and related, it is ascriptive Americanism (King 1999; Turner 2002) or anti-foreign, anti-immigrant institutional, including judicial, bias and discrimination (denials of welfare benefits and habeas corpus, etc.). Judicial anti-foreign bias and discrimination appear so intense that one gets the impression as though the mortal sin or crime of non-Americans were the failure to be "proudly born in the USA", more than anything else. Comparatively, non-Americans face a higher level of legal-penal risk or uncertainty, or the lower of judicial fairness or protection, in America during neo-conservatism than in any modern democratic society. This is because the Draconian-Puritan "jeopardy" is non-existent or weak in Europe, including even Calvinist Holland and once-Puritan England, and other democracies (Canada, Australia), though the anti-foreign or anti-immigrant hazard more or less still remains in most of them (Beck 2000). For most non-Americans and immigrants (legal and illegal) under the US Puritan-inspired criminal justice system, the glorified conservative "rule of law", including the Constitutional principle of equal judicial protection, due process or habeas corpus, is hardly worth the paper on which it is written.

In addition, even if unjustly accused and imprisoned in Western and Eastern European societies, foreign, just as domestic, nationals can hope for some form of trans-national protection (the European Court, etc.), while in America they are virtually helpless being at the merci of the Puritan-rooted judicial system rejecting and disdaining any international rules and conventions (viz., the World Court and the Geneva Convention) as "un-American". For instance, even some Kurdish terrorist leaders in Turkey were spared from execution due to the intervention of such trans-European legal institutions, including the European Union, while those non-Americans (and Americans) on death row and imprisoned for life have no such second-level protection or last resort in America under its Puritan-rooted Draconian and ethnocentric penal system. And, of course, this system hardly ever shows any merci for non-Americans and often Americans, given Puritanism's admittedly "merciless" (Tawney 1962) practices and intrinsic lack of compassion and caritas (Tiryakian 2002) through its reversal of original or traditional Christian values.

Fifth, the death penalty system is an indicator of the Puritan "culture of death" in virtue of executing not only guilty but also often innocent persons. If anything, even if abstracting from the above indicators, executing innocent persons, as reported and admitted by various officials (e.g., a former Illinois governor) for the death penalty system in America, in particular the "Bible Garden" (Texas, etc.), is the ultimate proof or syndrome of the "culture of death" as well as of state terrorism in the sense of government-sponsored unlawful murder and legal injustice overall. In particular, these executions are such a syndrome since (if) those innocent persons executed are usually human sacrifices to the God of Calvinist Puritanism couched in neo-conservative "tough" on crime-sin laws and policies. The latter in their apparent paranoia or excesses effectively erase the legal boundary between innocence and guilt, or effectively pervert the principle of "presumed innocent" into the "presumed guilty" opposite. Recall, the conservative US Supreme Court ruled (in 1992) that no less than an accused person "may be innocent", yet "could still be executed" if the judicial trial was "properly conducted and constitutionally correct" (Bauman 1997) via "due process." It is a ruling perpetuating what Weber calls Puritan "hard legalism" or legalistic and hypocritical morality, and about which Homans' (1961) "true" Christians may only say "Amen". It is an old (Roman) rule or proverb that when the innocent are executed or punished overall, everyone else in society (minus its masters) is in danger and forced into an open-ended death row and open prison overall. In spite or because of that ultimate risk US Puritan fundamentalists continue to methodically apply or fanatically support, as do most Americans in a self-inflicted hazard, the death penalty, perpetuating and rationalizing the "culture of death". After all, what defines the "culture of death" or state terrorism (e.g., Nazism) is precisely the fact that everyone (except for its masters or saints), either guilty for sins-crimes or innocent, can be executed.

Sixth, the death penalty system in America is an indicator and element of the Puritan "culture of death" in comparative terms in that it represents an exception or aberration among modern Western democracies. The death and overall penal system with its Draconian harshness in America is regularly identified as a "unique anomaly" among these and other democratic societies ushering in the 21 century (Pager 2003). As known, Puritan America, including the Federal government and the vast majority of the states, continues to be virtually the only Western society that applies the death penalty, and thus a salient deviant case in this respect. Moreover, sociological studies suggest that in its operation the US death penalty system is "functionally equivalent" to those in third-world authoritarian states like theocratic Iran as well as communist China[18] (Jacobs et al. 2005). In sum, on these six accounts, the death penalty system in America is an indicator and element of the Puritan "culture of death", just as a government-committed murder and in that sense state terrorism and legal injustice.

An additional related indicator and element of the "culture of death" is a sort of collective death penalty or execution through the extermination of the "ungodly" and "enemies" from the "godly" society or the exorcism of "evil" (Satan) and its emanations, "witches" by witch-trials. Such a practice transforms society into what Tawney (1962) calls a Puritan "hell in this world" for "infidels"—non-Puritans among Protestants and Christians, non-Christians among religious believers, and genuine non-believers not belonging to organized religion—or deadly "Salem" for "witches". Recall, its original act or blueprint was the Calvinist proposed "extermination" of non-evangelicals (papists, libertines, secularists, etc.) for the "holy" purpose of establishing the

---

[18] Jacobs et al. (2005:675) adopt the view that "US execution frequencies are equivalent to those in authoritarian states such as China or Iran".

"evangelical religion" (Heller 1986). Its model was found in Winthrop et al.'s "Godly" solution to the "ungodliness" and "impurity" of Native Americans and other "infidels" and "witches" (Gould 1996; Munch 2001). The collective execution or extermination of "infidels" in Calvinist theocracy operates as a sort of "holy" war within society and against itself, as witnessed in a remarkably continuous line from Calvin's France and Geneva and Holland under Calvinism to Cromwell-Winthrop's "Biblical" Commonwealths and to the Southern "Bible Garden".

In Clausewitz's terms, such a collective execution or "holy" war functions as the logical continuation or escalation of the "politics" of the death penalty for individual humans as sinners equated with criminals by other or identical "means" like lethal force extended from executing persons to exterminating out-groups in society. Alternatively, the "politics" of the death penalty against sinners eventuates in and predicts the collective execution or extermination of "infidels", just as the second reproduces and reinforces the first via feed-back effects, in Calvinist and perhaps any totalitarian (particularly Islamic) theocracy. Furthermore, the collective execution or extermination of "infidels" is probably even a more manifest, salient, and stronger indicator and element of the Calvinist (and Islamic) "culture of death" than the death penalty against persons in virtue of its comprehensive scope encompassing all kinds of "infidel" out-*groups*, not just "sinful" or "ungodly" individuals, within society and eventually the world.

Still another and the most pervasive indicator of Puritan "culture of death" in America is the celebrated, by religious fundamentalists and political conservatives, gun culture. The latter is by assumption and in reality the "culture" of death and violence. It is epitomized and symbolized by, but not limited to, the "Wild West" (Hill 2002) cultural mentality, practice, and image of inhumanity, including brutality and cruelty, as well as "rational" profit-making on those "wanted dead or alive", a seeming sequel of Puritans' profitable extermination of Native Americans.

The fundamentalist "gun culture" in America through its "Wild West" and other, notably Southern "Bible Garden", forms and symbols, descends into a Hobbesian anti-social or barbarian state of nature. To that extent, it effectively operates as anti-culture in the sense of culture as a peaceful, basically humane social condition sustaining and enhancing human life, dignity, and autonomy. In particular, a self-perpetuating syndrome or déjà vu revival of the "Wild West" gun and in extension

Calvinist[19] (Clemens 2007) death "culture" in America involves the "concealed weapons" laws in Southwestern and virtually all states (except for only Illinois and Wisconsin) permitting and tacitly encouraging people to carry and use almost cowboy-style deadly guns outside of their homes or in public (e.g., Texas), including those serving alcohol (viz., Arizona, Oklahoma, etc.). For example, a new law in Texas permits and implicitly encourages people to publicly use concealed weapons beyond their homes against attackers or intruders, including by implication any subjectively defined or perceived dangerous and suspicious persons. The law thus effectively gives and rationalizes the "license to kill" potentially everyone in a Hobbesian-like scenario of everyone being in war with and ultimately killing everyone else or the "Wild West" tradition of "shooting first, asking questions later". As a hyperconservative newspaper in the "lone star state" admitted, the law solidifies or revives Texas's long reputation "as a shoot-first-ask-questions-later place, dating back to its frontier days". If so, then not much has changed in this region from the "Wild Wild West" times (and movie) to the early 21st century.

As contemporary sociologists observe in reference to these and related practices in America, society runs the risk of "destroying" its own liberties, if it is composed of individual expected or believing that they will be able to "police" others' activities for their protection by means of the "firepower" on their own weapons, because everybody comes to "fear everybody else" (Munch 19940). Such a society is considered "close to Hobbes's state of nature" (Munch 1994), thus primitivism and barbarism rather than, as neo-conservatives ethnocentrically claim, a "universal model" (Lipset and Marks 2000) for *modern* Western civilization. Other analysts describe such a society after the model or image of the "Wild West" (Hill 2002) that hence reasserts itself as more than a metaphor or Hollywood-style invention, celebration (John Wayne), and

---

[19] Clemens (2007:539), suggests that in America Calvinism or evangelicalism "served as the matrix for the development of national social movements in the early 19th century", as urbanization and modernization overall "had strained the traditional forms of social organization, particularly the linking of religious and political authority in the 'covenanted village.'" According to this account, "orthodox Calvinist denominations [focused] on missions to the newly settled regions in the western territories [to become] a force in their own right, providing vehicles for contestation of orthodox authority but also interacting with diverse waves of revivals that introduced a popular, emotional, confessional style (Clemens 2007:539). Notably, the Calvinist "key innovation was the linking of personal sin with national problems such as temperance, moral reform, and slavery" (Clemens 2007:539).

mere exaggeration (the "Wild Wild West" movie). At this juncture, the "Wild West" and the "Bible Belt" alike are defined (as even a US President implied) by a mix of "religion and guns."

In sum, the gun culture in America is the syndrome of the Puritan "culture of death" in virtue of reproducing, expanding, and celebrating deadly weapons. Even if (as conservatives claim) they "do not kill" by themselves, these lethal weapons are actually or potentially can be used by humans against *humans* in a Hobbesian-like world of *homo homini lupus* and universal "war of everyone against everyone", and are not children's toys (though they are often used as such indicating a supreme gun-culture perversion) or even knives.[20] Given the "iron law" of a universal direct or indirect link between the amount of weapons and the rate of death or violent crime across US states (e.g., Texas vs. Vermont) and modern societies (Europe, Great Britain, Japan), it is admittedly simplistically but still realistically to say "no deadly guns, no death or violence", at least not on the scale historically and presently observed in America, especially in the "Bible Garden" and the "Wild West" (Jacobs et al. 2005; Messner et al. 2005).

Predictably, in comparative-historical terms, America's Puritan-rooted "Bible Garden" and "Wild West" culture of guns and ultimately death or violence is unparalleled within modern Western society and even the world as a whole, just as perhaps historically unprecedented during post-medieval modernity. For instance, comparative analyses identify contemporary America as the "most heavily armed" society not just, as expected, among modern Western societies, but also in the entire world in that its citizens possess almost one third of all firearms and purchase more than half [sic!] of newly manufactured guns globally each year.[21] If so, this is a society that owns almost seven times and

---

[20] Philadelphia's Police Commissioner reportedly stated in 2007, in the aftermath of a deadly attack on armored car guards, the following: "Every other country has the same problems we have. The one problem they didn't have is our gun [culture]. A robbery with a knife or a baseball bat, somebody might have been injured. A robbery with a gun, somebody's killed." Also, in light of a series of deadly shootings at US universities and high schools during the 2000s, one wonders as to how many more American students and teachers have to be killed by persons freely acquiring guns for religious-political neoconservatives and others in Congress and beyond to realize the need of sensible and effective gun control preventing or minimizing such massacres, while not affecting the supposed constitutional "right to bear arms".

[21] The Geneva-based Graduate Institute of International Studies reports in its Small Arms Survey 2007 that America has 90 guns per 100 citizens, which makes it the "most heavily armed society in the world". According to its report, US citizens possess 270 million of 875 million firearms in the world and "about 4.5 million of the 8 million new

purchases ten times more deadly weapons than its share of the global population (around 5 percent) warrants and predicts. This statistically defines and reveals America, at least the "Bible Garden" or the "Wild West" (and even more minimally, Texas), as the foremost culture of guns and by implication of death in the world during the 21st century. Moreover, the "Bible Garden" and "Wild West" culture of guns, death, and violence in America is not only by its sheer quantity of weapons the largest ("Number One") in the Western and entire world. It is in its actual operation the most intense, persistent, and celebrated or sanctified on fundamentalist ("eye for eye") religious as well as constitutional grounds (the conservative self-serving interpretation of the Constitution in terms of the individual "right to bear arms").

Apparently it seems as if US "reborn" fundamentalists and other neo-conservatives were ready to sacrifice, in an asymptotic trend of logical escalation, millions of Americans, by letting them massacre each other by deadly guns, to the conservative dogma of the "right to bear arms", reaffirming what Hume prophetically diagnosed as Puritan "wild" and "wretched" fanaticism. So, if Hume were to witness these massacres and Puritan-rooted fundamentalism's perpetuation and rationalization of them via perpetuating and rationalizing the gun culture in America, he would have simply said "I told you so, but you did not pay attention" almost three centuries ago.

Yet another, the most comprehensive indicator and element of the Puritan "culture of death" in America spanning beyond the domestic "godly" society involves global and permanent "holy" wars against "infidel" and "evil" or "inferior" cultures and societies. In spite or rather because of their "godly" goals, crusade-like wars seek and result in methodical torture[22] (Einolf 2007), death, and destruction by evermore efficient "high-tech" weapons of mass destruction, including not unrealistically collective suicide and self-destruction in accordance

---

guns manufactured worldwide each year are purchased in the United States." Overall, it is reported that "there is roughly one firearm for every seven people worldwide. Without the United States, though, this drops to about one firearm per 10 people."

[22] For example, in 2007 a letter signed by about 260 doctors from 16 countries stated that the US medical establishment has "turned a blind eye to the abuse of military medicine at the Guantanamo Bay prison." Reportedly, "health care workers in the US military seem to have put their loyalty to the state above their duty to care for patients—and American regulatory bodies have done nothing to remedy the situation". Simply, as the letter accused, "the attitude of the US medical establishment appears to be one of "See no evil, hear no evil, speak no evil" ".

with Puritan apocalyptic judgment-day nihilism in the form or image of Armageddon (Adorno 2001). In this respect, the cultural system of Calvinist theocracy in America eventuates into the "culture of global death", including, as Mises (1966) warns (let alone the Biblical sword passage), both the "holy" aggressor and the "evil" enemy in a MAD scenario (Habermas 2001), and in that sense ultimate, world anti-culture. And, to paraphrase Clausewitz's definition of war, the "culture of global death" via and due to a "holy" war is the continuation of the "culture of individual death" through executions for sins-crimes by "other means", notably ever more destructive "high-tech" weapons of mass destruction, including nuclear arms (Schelling 2006), or identical ones overall, simply physical violence and aggression. In Puritan Bibliocracy, like fascism, the destruction or depreciation of life in the world by aggressive wars is the logical extension or ultimate outcome of destroying or depreciating it home via the death penalty and other Draconian punishment, as is militarism one of totalitarianism or the reverse of democracy[23] (Kurzman and Leahey 2004).

As a corollary of the above, the cultural dimension of America's "destiny" in Calvinist theocracy is the subversion of secular culture to the "culture of death" and generally its reduction to a *caput mortuum* or vegetative desert-like state beyond recognition by being devoured by or dissolved in theology, religion, and theocratic church. In short, America's Calvinist cultural "destiny" is "presumed dead" secular culture, notably decaying or neglected art, and attacked, subverted, and abused science and education for "godly" causes. Alternatively, it is anti-secular, religious culture, including the theocratic "culture of death" via executions for sins-crimes, the extermination and persecution of the "ungodly" and "witches", a Hobbesian state of nature and gun violence, and a global "holy war" on the "evil" world. In either case, America's Calvinist cultural "destiny" is anti- or quasi-culture in a humanistic sense, the *inverse* of secular aesthetic culture in the meaning of the artistic-humanistic Renaissance, and intellectual and rationalist culture in that of the liberal-rationalistic Enlightenment, discussed next.

---

[23] Generally, Kurzman and Leahey (2004) find that militarization is "associated with a lesser likelihood" democratization in contemporary societies.

## The Adverse Fate of Aesthetic Culture in Calvinist Theocracy

### The Anti-Renaissance and Anti-Humanism

As mentioned, in terms of aesthetic secular culture and humanism, Calvinist theocracy is a type of anti-Renaissance and generally anti-artistic and anti-humanistic. It is so in the sense and form of a theocratic or religious antithesis and reversal of the artistic and humanistic Renaissance and secular art and humanism in general. Calvinist theocracy and Calvinism as a whole is the anti-Renaissance in a double sense and form, first, its historical hostility to and counterattack on the Renaissance as an artistic movement during the 16th century, second, its persistent antagonism to Renaissance-based and other secular art and humanism overall ever since, up to the 21st century. In short, it is the anti-Renaissance both in a particular historical and a general substantive sense.

In comparative and historical terms, Calvinist theocracy and Calvinism overall is more a type of anti-Renaissance and anti-artistic and anti-humanistic generally than are other theocracies and denominations in Protestantism and other Christianity, including Lutheranism, Anglicanism, and Catholicism, and world religions. As regards these latter, a predictable exception is Islamic theocracy or fundamentalist Islam (and perhaps Hinduism) as the only or main rival in this sense. In particular, within Calvinism and thus Protestantism and Christianity, Puritan theocracies and Puritanism overall are the most totalitarian, intense, and obstinate anti-Renaissance, hence anti-artistic and anti-humanistic, theocracy and branch. In short, if, as Pareto suggests, there is such thing as an anti-Renaissance in both senses within Protestantism, then it is, first and foremost, Calvinism and its theocracy, notably Puritanism and its theocracies.

First, Calvinist theocracy and Calvinism, especially Puritan theocracies and Puritanism, constitute the primary and perhaps the only consistent and persistent (obstinate) type of anti-Renaissance in a general substantive sense within Protestantism and Christianity as a whole. Calvinism, notably Puritanism, does so in that it intrinsically entails anti-artistic and other anti-cultural antagonism and ultimately generates and perpetuates coercion, repression, and decay in art and all secular culture. For example, Comte suggests that Calvinism (or "Protestantism" not differentiating its branches) is characterized by "unfavorableness to Art" and by implication all secular culture, including even positive or rational science. Also, Weber specifically observes that in Calvinism there is "no spontaneous enjoyment of art and life" due to its strict asceticism as "identical" to monasticism. This eventuates in and predicts a sort of Puritan "joyless" aesthetic culture and economy, as observed especially in America (Scitovsky 1972).

In particular, Hume suggests that within the "extended family" of Calvinism, especially Puritanism was typified by "no spontaneous enjoyment of art and life". In essence, Hume depicts English and by implication American Puritanism as anti-artistic or anti-aesthetic as well as anti-scientific, anti-intellectual, irrational, illiberal, and anti-cultural overall, or even barbarian and in that sense anti-life, and "positively" as fanatical and hypocritical. For example, he registers that prior to the civil wars, specifically the Puritan 1640s Revolution, in England "learning and the fine arts were favored at court, and a good taste began to prevail in the nation." Yet, following this Revolution what he calls "wretched fanaticism" reportedly "so much infected" Puritanism (the "parliamentary party"), including Cromwell described as "a barbarian",[24] and "was no less destructive of [artistic] taste and science, than of all law and order". Hume adds that "gayety and wit were proscribed; human learning despised; freedom of inquiry detested; cant and hypocrisy alone encouraged" by the ruling Puritans in England as well as New England (Gould 1996).

To that extent, early Puritanism was an exemplary type of anti-Renaissance, as well as of counter- or more precisely pre-Enlightenment, in a general substantive sense. It was an antithesis of what precisely defines the Renaissance, just as the Enlightenment. This includes, in Hume's words, "fine arts", "good taste", "gayety and wit", "human learning", "science", and "freedom of inquiry", or, as in Simmel's account, "knowledge", "intellectual interests", and "humanism".[25] In this respect, Puritanism was the anti-Renaissance long after the Renaissance itself as a historical movement (the late 15th century), just as the pre-Enlightenment prior to the Enlightenment (the 17th–18th centuries)

---

[24] Hume adds that "Cromwell, though himself a barbarian was not insensible to literary merit. That poet [Waller] always said, that the protector himself was not so wholly illiterate as was commonly imagined."

[25] Simmel states that the Renaissance's Humanism "embraced the poor scholar and the monk, the powerful General and the brilliant Duchess in a single framework of intellectual interests. Criteria derived from knowledge came to serve as the basis of social differentiation and group-formation".

and the counter-Enlightenment afterwards. Consequently, Puritan theocracy in America was ands remains the exemplary anti-Renaissance, just as the counter-Enlightenment, in a general substantive sense of its antagonism to, attack on, and suppression of Renaissance-rooted, as well as Enlightenment-based, ideas, values, and legacies.

Second, Calvinism and its theocracy, notably Puritanism, initially represented and acted as the main and the strongest type of anti-Renaissance in a particular historical sense within Protestantism and Christianity as a whole. It did so, as noted, by its adverse reaction to and even attempted reversal of the Renaissance as a specific historical movement and period preceding Calvinism and the Protestant Reformation in general for about half a century. Remember, Pareto notes that the Renaissance "only too soon was halted by the Protestant Reformation", particularly by implication by the disciplinary Calvinist Revolutions, in Northern Europe. While, like Comte, not differentiating between the Lutheran and Calvinist phases of the Protestant Reformation, he implies that this especially applies to Calvinism as the Second, "Calvinist Reformation" (Morck et al. 2005), and its disciplinary revolutions (Gorski 2003) in Holland and, through the Puritan Revolution and emigration, in England and America. In the new nation, actually the Renaissance never happened or came due the "preventive" measures by anti-artistic Puritanism, hence Puritan theocracy and theocrats like Winthrop et al. found virtually nothing artistic to attack and stop.

As typical, Puritanism embraced and further expanded and reinforced Calvinism's initial antagonism to the Renaissance, acting as super-Calvinism in anti-Renaissance and anti-artistic ideas and practices. For example, recollect Parsons' (1967) remark that their "negative valuation of ritual" was just one of the "few points" at which his Puritan forebears and the "men of the humanistic Renaissance" would agree. This is subject to the historical qualification that the first acted in 17th century old and New England, and the second in 15th century Europe, notably Italy. This confirms that Puritanism was not original even in this respect, but merely followed what had emerged in an artistic, humanistic, and thus largely secular movement well before its birth within the post-Renaissance family of Calvinism. Also, Parsons' "humanistic" to describe the Renaissance implies a sort of disagreement or contrast in the sense that early Puritans disagreed with or opposed its secular humanism, "intellectual interests", and "knowledge".

In particular, what Calvinism proposed and partly attempted, Puritanism implemented and expanded in that it vehemently assaulted "Renaissance experimentation" in the "arts of self-decoration" and dress (Walzer 1963; also, Turner 2002), in favor of austere cloths, materials, and colors, typically, as Edgeworth remarks, black-white perhaps unwittingly mirroring the Puritan admittedly Manichean world-view (Seaton 2006). At least, this peculiar example reveals Puritans as super-Calvinists in the anti-Renaissance by doing or completing to, as Tocqueville remarks for those in New England, the "most frivolous details", what Calvin et al. only envisioned or started (Garrard 2003; Mansbach 2006)—dictating what and how people should dress, decorate, and the like. For example, as an expression of the Puritan hostility to Renaissance-style self-decoration or dress, American Puritans reenacted medieval-style sumptuary laws in New England (Gould 1996), even while those, like witch-beliefs and trials (Byrne 1997; Harley 1996), in Europe were revoked or weakened; so much for their building a "new nation" versus the "old world". In sum, if religious conservatism in Europe and America arose in adverse reaction to the "idealism of the Renaissance" (Dunn and Woodard 1996), then this especially applied to European Calvinism and its child, American Puritanism.

Generally, at this juncture, judging by Calvinism's adverse reaction to and consequently Puritanism's hostility to the Renaissance, the latter acted as a sort of agent provocateur in artistic and humanistic terms of Calvinist Revolutions, if not, as Pareto suggests, of the entire Protestant Reformation, just as traditional "too lax" Catholicism (and early Lutheranism) did so as a causal or precipitating factor in a theological and moral-religious sense. At least, that is how Calvinism and later Puritanism "defined" or socially "constructed" the Renaissance. It did by attempting and succeeding, if Pareto is correct, to halt it, as in parts of Europe, minimally (as Hume and Weber suggest) England, or prevent it from spreading beyond the "old world", as happened in Puritan America. Pareto's remark suggests that the Renaissance precipitated, even if not directly causing, the Calvinist Revolutions. If so, it did by giving them a secondary artistic source and rationale—"ungodly" humanistic art and self-decoration—in addition and connection to the primary theological, moral-religious cause and justification ("anti-Christ", "too lax" Catholicism and even similarly defined Lutheranism).

Subsequently the Renaissance provided a sort of additional *raison d'être* for Puritanism, or another "good reason" for its continual existence and thus the extension and perpetuation of Calvinism and religious conservatism overall in England and America, just as, in conjunction, did the Enlightenment and its political expression the French Revolution. While it is simplistic to state "*no* Renaissance, as well as Enlightenment and French Revolution, no problem", *no* Calvinism, including Puritanism, and religious conservatism in general, but this is what some US neo-conservatives precisely propose[26] (Dunn and Woodard 1996).

In sum, Calvinism was a paradigmatic instance of the anti-Renaissance in Protestantism and all Christianity originally and directly by attacking and partly reversing the Renaissance, just as, notably via Puritanism, subsequently and indirectly by opposing and suppressing its artistic and humanistic ideas, values, and legacies. Consequently, in artistic terms Calvinist theocracy acted as the anti-Renaissance initially in a specific historical meaning of an adverse reaction to the prior Renaissance, and subsequently or eventually, via its Puritan extension in America, in a general substantive sense of an antithesis to Renaissance-based values and influences. Hence, it remains the anti-Renaissance long after the Renaissance ended in Europe and "did not happen," like Sombart's socialism (Lipset and Marks 2000), in or has never really "come to America".

## *The Anti-Renaissance and Anti-Humanism Initiated*

Curiously, given his "Puritan heritage" (Alexander 1983), it is none than Parsons that probably unwittingly identifies or implies by his expression "the humanistic Renaissance" the main source and rationale for Calvinist theocracy and Puritanism functioning as the anti-Renaissance in the sense of artistic and all cultural antagonism. Evidently, this is the antithesis to "humanistic" and in that sense being anti-humanistic in a secular sense.

By assumption and in reality, Calvinist Bibliocracy's intrinsic antagonism to and eventual destruction of aesthetic and other secular *human* culture is founded on and sanctified by the glorification of transcendental supra-human causes and the condemnation or devaluation of

---

[26] Dunn and Woodard (1996:78) state that "without the challenges posed by the Renaissance, the Enlightenment, the French Revolution, and utopian ideologies, there would be no articulate modern conservatism", in particular its religious version, notably American neoconservatism staunchly and proudly standing in the tradition of Puritanism.

humans and their emotions and creations as "ungodly," "sinful," or "depraved." This expresses profound anti-humanism. In this sense, anti-humanism or abhorrence for secular humanism (Van Dyke 1995) characterizing Calvinism and other religious conservatism generates, perpetuates, and predicts culture antagonism and nihilism in Calvinist and perhaps any theocracy. In essence, Calvinist cultural nihilism is the product or integral element of what Weber identifies as the "destruction of spontaneous, impulsive enjoyment" and life by Calvinism through its "harsh" and "gloomy" theological doctrine and theocratic system or design, notably by even harsher and gloomier Puritanism embodied by what Hume identifies as the "gloomy spirit of the Puritans" in England and America. Calvinist theocracy is antagonistic and destructive to aesthetic and other secular culture because Calvinism, notably Puritanism, is anti-humanistic, or inhumane, brutal or cruel, just as is, as Weber suggests, anti-emotional and, in Parsons' words, "unsentimental". In particular, it is, as Parsons implicitly admits, the anti-Renaissance because the Renaissance was humanistic, and alternatively in virtue of itself being anti-humanistic. In short, "Renaissance humanism" (Byrne 1997) acted as the agent provocateur of Calvinist-Puritan anti-humanism and consequently antagonism to art as a *human* activity, creation, and sensual or aesthetic pleasure.

Thus, Comte states that the fact that "all emancipation of the human mind" has become "more repugnant" to official Calvinism and even Protestantism as a whole, as well as its Puritan sects than to the "most degenerate" Catholicism causes and explains an artistic and anti-cultural outcome. This is what he identifies as the suppression and retrogression of artistic and other secular culture in Calvinist or Protestant, societies compared with others, in particular Catholic countries such as Renaissance Italy and France, in post-Reformation Europe. In short, he finds that national "aesthetic tendencies" were already impeded by Protestantism, notably Calvinism[27] due to its theological repugnance to humanism as well as to scientific rationalism or positivism. Notably, Comte implies that the underlying reason why Calvinism, notably Puritanism, is anti-artistic is that the development of science, industry, and (fine) art operated as the "principal, though latent" historical cause

---

[27] At this and most other junctures, Comte does not explicitly distinguish Calvinism or Puritanism from other Protestantism like Lutheranism and Anglicanism, which makes his insights somewhat too generic and imprecise.

of the "irretrievable decline of the theological and military [feudal] system." Calvinism attempted and succeeded to restore or expand and reinforce this old system, from Calvin's Geneva and Holland to, via Puritanism, England and New England.

Also, Weber suggests that what theologically grounds and sanctifies the "fundamental antagonism to sensuous culture of all kinds" in Calvinism, notably Puritanism, is transcendental anti-humanism or theological repugnance to secular humanism in the sense of human liberty, well-being, dignity, "authentic self-realization" and autonomy (Habermas 1996). This "higher" anti-humanism is manifested in Calvinism's "harsh doctrines" of the absolute transcendence and omnipotence of God, epitomizing Calvinist theodicy and theology overall, and the "corruption of everything pertaining to the flesh", even extreme inhumanity or brutality (Birnbaum 1953). In particular, Weber links its hostility to "emotional elements in culture" to the fact that emotion was originally "quite foreign" to Calvinism because of Calvin's devaluation and dismissal of all human, including even religious, emotions and feelings.

This devaluation reached the point of considering "everything emotional to be illusory" and an admittedly extreme "kind of Christian pessimism" (Heller 1986) condemning humans as fundamentally "evil" and manifesting an intense, even perhaps unrivaled hatred of humanity[28] (Fromm 1941). Predictably, this anti-humanistic hatred was grounded in and rationalized by Calvin's dogma of predestination, with its harsh condemnation of most humankind to "hell and damnation" for the high cause of affirming the "sovereignty of God's power" (Mansbach 2006). In a stark contrast within otherwise pessimistic and ascetic Protestantism, Calvin incarnated anti-emotional, "gloomy", and in that sense anti-human strict asceticism, and Luther did what Weber calls emotionalism and mysticism.

As expected, in Weber's account, Puritanism inherited and in the process reinforced and expanded Calvin's anti-human asceticism and the "Calvinistic idea of the depravity of the flesh" anathematizing and

---

[28] Fromm (1941) suggests that both Calvin and Luther "personally, belonged to the ranks of the greatest haters among the leading figures of history [and] their doctrines were colored by this hostility and could only appeal to a group itself driven by an intense repressed hostility." In his view, the "most striking expression of this hostility is found in their concept of God, especially in Calvin's doctrine" (Fromm 1941; also Mansbach 2006).

suppressing "every purely emotional" human actions and relations by the "suspicion of idolatry of the flesh". In particular, he notes that both adopting and intensifying Calvinism, Puritanism *cum* a "religion of virtuosi" relinquished the "universalism of love" or the universal ethic of brotherhood, thus by implication original Christianity (if) so defined (Sorokin 1970). Puritanism instead harnessed all activities and humans in this life into "serving God's will" (and "testing one's state of grace"). Recall, Weber suggests that due to its "unbrotherliness" Puritanism ceased to be a "genuine religion of salvation" defined by brotherliness" to the point of becoming the "most distant" deviation from and showing an "extreme contrast" to the ideal-type of brotherly ethics[29] (Symonds and Pudsey 2006). Also, remember the observation that Puritanism forced "an atrophy of natural feeling" in cultural and personal life (Bendix 1965), thus an atrophic or *caput mortuum* aesthetic and all secular culture.

Akin to Weber, Parsons (1967) implies Puritan anti-humanism identifying Puritanism's and in extension Calvinism's "devaluation" of a person's "attachment to his fellows", notably the tendency for reducing them to "impersonal, unsentimental" terms, by considering other humans in terms of their instrumentality in the service of the "purposes of God" and one's "own ends". In doing so, Parsons perhaps unwittingly goes further than Weber and Comte in identifying not just, as their did, Puritan Calvinist-rooted transcendental anti-humanism or theological repugnance for secular humanism, manifested in considering humans as the extrinsic means to the "purposes of God", not as ends in themselves in Kant's sense or in their intrinsic worth. He also identifies or implies what can be described as non-transcendental ("not-so-high") or secular

---

[29] Commenting on Weber, Symonds and Pudsey (2006:138) suggest that [Puritanism operates "without regard to the person," relinquishing "direct, personal love and care in the name of allegiance to God." They add that for Weber, this Calvinist "impersonality is a logical consequence of the Puritan conceptualization of predestination: God's plan cannot be known or doubted; those in need should not be helped as this would seem to question God's creation of the order of the world; those in need would seem to deserve their suffering since through labor there is always the opportunity to develop God's bounty; and to be in needful suffering and not laboring in the world would indicate damnation, which no action on this earth can, nor should try to, alter" (Symonds and Pudsey 2006:138-9). Moreover, they infer that Puritan "brotherliness" is so "impersonal, mainly exclusive" and thus its "internal logic pushes it to a position of extreme contrast with the ideal-type" (Symonds and Pudsey 2006). In short, it is "sect brotherliness" in the form of "requirement of care only for those "brothers" in the faith" as against the "universalism of the church" (Symonds and Pudsey 2006:137).

anti-humanism in the form of Machiavellianism and admittedly Benthamite utilitarianism overall (Mayway 1984), analogously expressed in considering humans as the effective means to one's "own ends", thus outside of Kant's "kingdom of ends" (Habermas 2001).

In sum, Parsons serendipitously rediscovers what Weber and especially Comte intimated. This is a composite of transcendental, "godly" *and* of Machiavellian, utilitarian anti-humanism, thus a dual violation of or "double jeopardy" to Kantian or humanistic ethics, in Puritanism and Calvinism as a whole. Yet, Parsons does not explicitly describe and explicate the reduction of humans to Divine and secular ends as dual (or any) anti-humanism, thus as an anti-Kantian procedure. Instead, he extols theological individualism (individuals' "immediacy to God") within Puritanism, which suggests that his Puritan heritage has effectively neutralized his declared "Kantian core" (Munch 1981). In passing, it is striking how a self-defined Kantian sociologist like Parsons could overlook or gloss over such manifest and flagrant, and not just single but dual, Puritan violation of Kant's deontology or ethic. This includes Kant's principle of "never" treating humans as merely the means to other ends (Angel 1994), no matter how "sacred" or "noble", but rather as ends in themselves, as expressed in his statement that every human being "exists as an end in himself and not merely as a means to be arbitrarily used by this or that will." Apparently, his Puritan heritage prevented Parsons from fully realizing that Puritanism violated Kantian and other deontology's categorical imperative of acting toward "every person as an end, and not merely as a means" (Angel 1994), and thus, to paraphrase, make your actions a general rule and yourself a "role model" for others to follow and emulate. Another sociological study also shows that because Calvinism depreciated and disdained human emotions as "chimerical", Puritanism consequently "turned outward" and became "anti-sensuous and anti-spontaneous in the extreme" to the point of "methodical, ruthless" brutality (Birnbaum 1953). This exemplified Puritanism's extreme anti-humanism in full action acting as the ultimate source of its antagonism to and destruction of secular aesthetic and other culture.[30]

---

[30] Birnbaum (1953:141) comments that Puritans' "brutality reminds us of Freud [i.e.,] the harshness of the psychological discipline imposed by western culture", with apparent reference to Calvinism and Christianity overall.

## The Anti-Renaissance Generalized and Perpetuated

As implied, in the "extended family" of Calvinist theocracies or Calvinism Puritan theocracy or Puritanism especially functions as the anti-Renaissance in a general substantive sense of the initial antithesis and the ultimate reversal of Renaissance-based artistic and humanistic values and legacies. If anything, in respect of the anti-Renaissance and anti-art overall Puritanism has invariably been and remains hyper-Calvinism, and Puritans super-Calvinists consummating what Calvin et al. initiated, suppressing or disfiguring "ungodly" art and other sensual and secular humanistic culture. For instance, Voltaire's plays and even some of Rousseau's books had been proscribed and burned[31] in Switzerland's "Calvinist cantons" (Byrne 1997), including Geneva, and Calvinists (including Rousseau) attacked modern theatre for, like all secular art, "corrupting" morals (Garrard 2003). Puritanism inherited and further intensified and expanded this initial anti-artistic antagonism in Calvinism. For example, following Calvinism's ban of theatre in Geneva, which its "proud citizen", Calvinist Rousseau praised as a "wisely" action against "corrupting books" and "destructive vices" (Garrard 2003), early Puritans condemned and banned this art form, including Shakespeare's works, at a larger societal scale, in England and New England (Walzer 1963). As usually, Puritanism in doing so did not "reinvent the wheel" or "rediscover America" but only intensified and escalated what its parent Calvinism had done before and established as a model or pattern of action for its disciples as well as derivatives. Apparently, even in seemingly frivolous or trivial anti-artistic particulars like hostility to theatre and related secular art (music, dance, decoration), Puritanism was totally "parasitic" on Calvinism, as was with respect to "deadly" serious theological matters like the doctrine of predestination, with its (in Weber's words) "terrible seriousness" and "extreme inhumanity."

Thus, what original Calvinism revealed and attempted yet eventually failed in Europe, with certain minor and partial exceptions (Geneva,

---

[31] Garrard (2003:114) comments that "in a letter to Voltaire in 1760, Rousseau accused him of "ruining" [by his plays] his beloved Geneva—the "anti-Paris"—incontrovertible proof of which came shortly afterward when his native city banned and burned both *The Social Contract* and *Emile*." And, in response, Rousseau relinquished his "proud citizen of Geneva" self-description and thus his Calvinism "forever" (second time).

Holland), its derivative Puritanism more fully displayed and succeeded in England and especially America, notably the "Bible Garden." This is artistic and other cultural antagonism, nihilism, repression, and decay, thus the anti-Renaissance. Instances abound and are well-known or even legendary, but still instructive to mention in order to exemplify the anti-artistic and generally anti-humanistic (including anti-amusement or "anti-fun") logic, operation, and outcome of Puritanism and its theocracy.

For instance, Hume registers that in the English Parliament, the dominant Puritans passed "a bill for the reverent observance of Sunday, which they termed the Sabbath, and the depriving the people of those amusements which they were accustomed to take on that day."[32] He cites the case of "festivals, which, in other nations and ages, are partly dedicated to public worship, partly to mirth and society, were here totally appropriated to the offices of [Puritanism], and served to nourish those sullen and gloomy contemplations to which the people were, of themselves, so unfortunately subject."[33] What Hume observed for English Puritans, Tocqueville did for their American counterparts and descendents. For illustration, Tocqueville observes that their "strictly Puritanical origin", combined with their "exclusively commercial habits" and "even the country they inhabit", tend to "divert" Americans from the "pursuit of science, literature, and the arts."

Following and evoking Hume, J. S. Mill provides a sort of global or comparative picture of Puritan theocracy with respect to its strong anti-artistic and related tendencies and practices, as witnessed in Great Britain and New England. Thus, he remarks that "wherever the Puritans have been sufficiently powerful, as in New England, and in Great Britain at the time of the [Holy] Commonwealth, they have endeavored, with considerable success, to put down all public, and nearly all private, amusements: especially music, dancing, public games, or other assemblages for purposes of diversion, and the theatre." Notably he suggests that what actuate these anti-artistic practices are the "religious and moral sentiments" of Puritans ("the stricter Calvinists and Methodists")

---

[32] Hume comments that this was "a Judaical observance of the Sunday, chiefly by means of the Puritans [thus] the people, under color of religion, were, contrary to former practice debarred such sports, and recreations as contributed both to their health and their amusement."

[33] Hume adds that before the Puritan Revolution, the "king imagined, that it would be easy to infuse cheerfulness into this dark spirit of devotion", seen as characteristic of religion overall, Puritanism in particular.

as "intrusively pious members" of society with "fanatical intolerance." Similarly, his successor Marshall notes that Puritans were "hostile to all lighter" thoughts and amusements, thus "took little joy" in society, "shunned public amusements," and held attitudes "hostile to art." The seeming outcome is what contemporary analysts (Scitovsky 1972) denote a Puritan-based "joyless", and in that sense effectively lifeless, culture and economy, especially in America.

In turn, following on or evoking Hume's cited example and even words, Weber cites the instance of the "fanatical opposition of the Puritans to the ordinances of the King, permitting certain popular amusements on Sunday outside of Church hours by law", and observes that this fanaticism was driven by their "resentment against the intentional diversion from the ordered life of the saint." Weber provides two additional instances by remarking that, first, "in the pictorial arts Puritanism perhaps did not find very much to suppress." Second, in his view "very striking is the decline from what seemed to be a promising musical beginning (England's part in the history of music was by no means unimportant) to that absolute musical vacuum which we find typical of the Anglo-Saxon peoples later, and even today."

As a particular curiosity, he cites "the Puritan town government [that] closed the theatre at Stratford-on-Avon while Shakespeare was still alive and residing there in his last years," thus perhaps did what Calvin et al. in Geneva (excluding the ban of Voltaire's plays), Holland, and Prussia had never done before. This reaffirms that Puritans have typically been super-Calvinists at least in anti-artistic antagonism and suppression. Weber comments that Shakespeare's "hatred and contempt of the Puritans appear on every occasion" and may well have commented on their Calvinist "iron consistency" or, with Hume, their "unreasonable obstinacy" if visited America yet again almost a century later and witnessed the following event. As proximate déjà vu of the 17th century Puritan town government, about three centuries later (in 1996) New Hampshire's schools "removed" Shakespeare's play *Twelfth Night* from the curriculum (Hull 1999). This Puritanical act would have hardly surprised Weber and Hume, just as Shakespeare himself. Yet, it confirms that some things virtually never change—or as Calvin might say, the "more they change the more they stay the same" substantively— in Puritanism and its vestiges, in this case, its hostility to and suppression of "ungodly" and "immoral" art and other secular culture. Hence, this and various similar acts are not isolated accidents, random errors, or exceptions. Rather, they exemplify a general rule, persistent pattern, and "method in the madness" of anti-artistic and anti-humanistic Puritan theocracy or, as in this specific case, its vestiges and reflexes in America.

In comparative terms, prohibiting or condemning Shakespeare's and various other artistic works as "indecent", "ungodly", "liberal", and similar anti-artistic acts can and does happen "only in America" after the model or image of Puritan theocracy within contemporary Western secular culture, just as in Islamic theocracies among third-world countries, as well as Nazism and other fascism in interwar Europe[34] (Hull 1999). In contemporary terminology, they can happen only in a society after the design of a "Bible Garden" in a sociological, as distinguished from geographic, sense penetrating or surviving not only in the ultra-conservative ("hot-red") South but even what is supposed to be the liberal-secular ("blue") Northeast ("live free or die" Puritan-founded New Hampshire). Alternatively, it does not or cannot in most liberal-secular cultures and societies, especially Western Europe (e.g., the European Union[35]), as suggested by some observations contrasting artistic freedom and creativity in the latter with the "Bible Belt" suppression and retrogression of art and other secular culture on "godly" and "morality" grounds.

*Indicators of Puritan Anti-Artistic Antagonism*

Instances and indicators abound concerning the anti-artistic antagonism, repression, and eventual retrogression, or what Weber would call the "adverse fate" or atrophy (Bendix 1965), at least the "peculiar status"[36] (Saisselin 1992), of the arts in Calvinist theocracy as America's societal "destiny". An instance of such "adverse fate" or atrophy of the arts is their public and private depreciation, negligence, and hence

---

[34] Hull (1999:49–50) registers the Nazis' "mass book-burnings in an attempt to destroy the work of Jewish and liberal thinkers and writers" in Germany over the 1930s as well as that "books suspected of containing communist propaganda [were] burned in US information libraries abroad, and many of these libraries [were] closed" during McCarthyism.

[35] For example, during the 2000s some of its officials stated that "the European Union is not a bible belt, we believe in freedom of expression and artistic creativity", in reference to America and its Southern region. This implies that art and all secular culture cannot really survive or flourish in a "Bible Belt", while US fundamentalists condemn and dismiss Europe for such freedom and creativity as "ungodly", "immoral", and too "secular" or "liberal" overall.

[36] Saisselin (1992:3) registers the "peculiar status of art in the United States, as something divorced from experience", simply as being in "museums."

decay in America primarily as the legacy of Puritanism and its anti-artistic ideas, institutions, and practices. Observations show that Puritanism with its anti-artistic preconceptions, and in extension Calvinism, continues to over-determine or predestine the striking neglect and decline, including government's financial and other depreciation, of the arts in modern America, just as it did in Great Britain and New England.

Thus, analysts observe that Americans' "very modest enjoyment" of the arts represents "part and parcel" of their "modest enjoyment of life" (Scitovsky 1972) primarily as the legacy of Puritanism. Particularly the US government's "miserly attitude" to the arts is identified as the "integral part of a larger collective preference system", specifically society and its "Puritan attitude" (Scitovsky 1972). In short, Puritanism primarily or even single-handedly is instrumental in the "neglect of the arts" (Scitovsky 1972) in America. As observed, Americans, while "smile condescendingly" over the "prejudices" of 18th century Puritan America such as its moralistic disapproval of the theatre and "wasting" time and money on the arts (and sports), their behavior remains "governed by those prejudices" as "no smiling matter" (Scitovsky 1972). Perhaps what best demonstrates America's Calvinist-as-Puritan "destiny", that is over-determination or path-dependence, in cultural, specifically artistic, terms, is the observation that Americans continue to be "governed" by Puritanism and its anti-artistic and related "prejudices". Apparently, Puritan and in extension Calvinist anti-artistic, like most others, prejudices and anachronisms have not yet been "overwhelmed" (Miller 1975), but self-perpetuated and even expanded, as from New England to the South, in modern America.

In comparative terms, the Puritan-rooted depreciation, neglect, and consequent decay of aesthetic and related secular culture in America typically reaches a level that is unrivaled among contemporary Western cultures and societies, including even proto-Calvinist Holland and once-Puritan Great Britain. In turn, it is only rivaled by or comparable to that in Islamic anti-artistic theocracies. In particular, the "adverse fate" or atrophy, if not death, of the arts in the Southern "Bible Garden" as Mencken's anti-cultural "Sahara desert" is historically unprecedented and comparatively unparalleled within modern Western culture. It is only equaled or emulated by that in Iranian and other Islamic theocracies as its substantive proto-totalitarian equivalents or analogues (Bauman 1997). Notably, the US government's "miserly attitude" towards the arts, while with a precedent or model in New England's

Puritan theocratic state, is without a parallel or proxy among contemporary Western governments, as indicated by the comparative figures of public spending on art (see below). Alternatively, it is probably only matched by that of Islamic theocracies and other third-world dictatorships.

Another, corollary instance and indicator of the "adverse fate" or atrophy of the arts in/by Puritan theocracy is the decay or regression of (educated) artistic tastes and practices in America, including the "new" American "godly" (and "pop") art and culture. The latter substitutes for and attacks the disdained "old" European "high art and culture", including, as seen, Shakespeare's and other "ungodly" and "immoral" works.[37] In a sense, Puritan theocracy or its vestige in America tends to transform the educated taste or preference for the "high" ("elitist") and secular arts—as embodied by the Enlightenment "man of taste" making "aesthetic judgment" versus "economic man" (Saisselin 1992)—into a distaste for them and their ramifications in culture. Conversely, it perverts them into uneducated tastes or "revealed preferences" for secular arts' "godly" and moralizing (and people's) ersatz or bogus substitutes premised on "Calvinistic sermon about the temptations of the soul, carnal corruption, the desecration of innocence, and about the purifying power of guilt and remorse"[38] (Johnson 2003). Thus, the Puritan moralistic degeneration of aesthetic culture in America effectively causes the end of "art for the sake of the art", or as Western and other societies have known it since the Renaissance and classic Greek civilization, barbarically (nearly) destroyed as "pagan" by the Christian "Dark Middle Ages."

---

[37] While *de gustibus non est disputandum* or one does not dispute tastes (Stigler and Becker 1977) in general, including the "particular "difficulty" of aesthetic judgment" (Cascardi 1999), hardly anyone, except for US "reborn" anti-artistic Puritans, would deny that, for example, Shakespeare's proscribed *Twelfth Night* as well as De Vinci's or Beethoven's works reflect more educated artistic tastes than their "godly" and pop-art literary, painting, and musical ersatz-substitutes ("Christian" art) in America. In short, the first class of artworks or "great art" elicits "claims of [educated] taste" (Cascardi 1999); the second does those of uneducated tastes.

[38] Johnson (2003) suggests that "an intrinsically American moralistic obsession with the ideas of innate depravity" in artistic culture and life overall is rooted in Puritanism with its Manichean "spiritual schism", such that the "convenience of having an identifiable evil facilitates the curative [moralistic] notion of art." He cites the view that "Puritanistic, Calvinistic concepts of evil and sin poisoned most American Dreams [thus] there was never a natural innocence." Also, Johnson (2003) interprets the American Revolution as unleashing a "particularly American version of moral perfection, grown from the seeds of early Puritanism."

In this connection, some analysts suggest that the fear of "Americanization" in the sense of a process of artistic-cultural expansion whereby "uneducated tastes" are expanded to the world is "well founded" (Scitovsky 1972). On this account, what sociologists observe and most other, developed and developing, societies experience or perceive as, Puritan-rooted "cultural imperialism" (Smelser and Mitchell 2002) functions accordingly and the "spiritual" complement of the "new" American conservative-driven military imperialism (Steinmetz 2005). In a sense, it effectively expands the evolutionary regression or downgrading of educated artistic tastes into more primitive forms, ultimately the suppression or decay of "high" art and other secular culture, from America to the world as a whole. Puritan "cultural imperialism" thus tends to expand from America to the world its transformation of the educated taste for the "high" and secular arts into a distaste for them and uneducated tastes for their "godly" and moralizing ersatz substitutes, thus its termination of "art for the sake of the art". In sum, it seeks to extend the "adverse fate" or atrophy of "high" secular art from America's national to global anti-artistic "destiny" via cultural imperialism driven and justified by "jingoistic, Reagan era" super-patriotism[39] (Johnson 2003).

In retrospect, the above indicates a striking, yet expected historical continuity from what Hume identified as Puritan "wretched fanaticism" that was "destructive of taste and science" alike in old and New England during the 16th–17th centuries to Puritan-rooted "uneducated tastes" in contemporary America. At this juncture, the religious "fanaticism" of Puritanism represents the extant historical source of these "uneducated tastes"—rather than, as it might seem, the lack of education in itself—just as Puritan anti-artistic "prejudices", still shape the public and private neglect, continuing depreciation, and the resulting decay of the arts, in America. (While higher education is linked with weaker

---

[39] Johnson (2003) adds that another "great American moralistic mythmaker" was Reagan, with his "myths of small town, cherry-pie America'". In this view, "Reagan was never as cynical as his handlers; he believed his own rhetoric [or] bombastic sloganeering. All-American longing for a return to Edenic purity [involves] black and white Manichean camps of goodness and evil. [For] a jingoistic, Reagan era superpatriot, the dangers [are] that trinity of American scourges: sex, drugs, and rock'n'roll" (Johnson 2003). Johnson (2003) comments: "straight talking, living, shooting, from the heart —the "Heartland," [i.e.] the politically convenient idea of Middle America, that nevernever land envisioned by Charlton Heston, Ronald Reagan, and the Daughters of the American Revolution. No urban complexity, sophistication, affection, or inexplicable anomie."

fanaticism and intolerance in religion and lower religiosity overall, many educated persons in America, notably the "Bible Garden", appear religiously fanatical and intolerant, as well as highly religious, including fundamentalist or evangelical.)

Still another, quantitative indicator of the "adverse fate" or atrophy of aesthetic culture in Calvinist theocracy is the lowest public spending on the arts ("high" and "low") in America compared to contemporary Western cultures. The magnitude of the differential between Puritan America and other Western cultures is so large and dramatic that it conveys the impression as if art became a sort of luxury that the wealthiest nation or government in the world cannot (just as, perhaps related, universal health care and the elimination of poverty) afford. Comparative data show that the total public or governmental expenditure (per capita) on the arts in America is ten times (not 10 percent) or so lower than in other contemporary Western cultures like Germany, France, and Canada, and five times than in once-Puritan Great Britain, as during the 1980s–1990s (Throsby 1994). In particular, as a ratio of total public spending the government expenditure on the arts in America is ten or more times lower than in Germany and France and seven and eight times than in Canada and Great Britain, respectively. Also, as a percent of GNP it is ten or so times lower in America than in Germany, France, and Canada, and seven times than in Great Britain. This striking and persistent difference between America and other Western societies is just a public financial or fiscal facet and outcome of what Hume and contemporary analysts identify and emphasize as Puritan anti-artistic and other "fanaticism" and prejudices, notably US government's "miserly attitude" to the arts as the integral element of a "collective preference system" inherited from Puritanism (Scitovsky 1972). In short, the US government's Puritan-based "miserly attitude" to the arts generates and predicts an equivalent level of expenditure on them, "low, lower", lowest" among modern Western cultures.

As a corollary of the above, aesthetic anti-culture in the sense of the anti-Renaissance substantively understood is the anti-artistic and overall anti-humanistic dimension of America's "destiny" in Calvinist theocracy. It is America's Calvinist anti-artistic "destiny" in the form of the "adverse fate" or atrophy of the arts or "high" aesthetic culture depreciated, neglected, and decayed as "ungodly" and "immoral", as well as luxury that cannot be afforded or nuisance to be avoided, in the last Puritan nation. Calvinism proves to be America's anti-artistic "destiny" in that what Weber identifies as the Calvinist ascetic or generalized

Table 6.1. Attributes of the cultural system of Calvinist theocracy—anti-aesthetic culture

*Anti-Renaissance*
Historical hostility to and attack on the Renaissance as an artistic movement
Persistent antagonism to Renaissance-based and other secular art and humanism
Indicators of anti-artistic antagonism
    public and private depreciation, neglect, and decay of the arts
    regression of educated artistic tastes and practices
    lowest public spending on the arts among Western cultures

monastic principle of "no spontaneous enjoyment of art and life" engenders, predicts, and rationalizes an equivalent Puritan joyless and lifeless, and to that extent anti-human culture (and economy). It thus does a sort of aesthetic, just as intellectual or rationalist anti-culture or emptiness, discussed next. (Table 6.1 summarizes the anti-Renaissance attributes of Calvinist theocracy's cultural system.)

*The Adverse Fate of Intellectual Culture in Calvinist Theocracy*

*The Counter-Enlightenment*

In addition and connection to being the anti-Renaissance or anti-artistic and anti-humanistic, in cultural, specifically intellectual, terms Calvinist theocracy in America is a type of counter-Enlightenment and anti-intellectual and anti-rationalist, as well as anti-secular and anti-liberal, in general. It is such in the ways, means, and meaning of a theocratic and other religious antithesis and reversal of the intellectual and rationalist Enlightenment and intellectualism and rationalism (including scientism), as well as secularism, pluralism, and liberalism, in general. Thus, Calvinist theocracy and Calvinism overall is the counter-Enlightenment in a dual meaning and way. First, it is on the account of its historical opposition to and assault on the Enlightenment as a particular intellectual and rationalistic movement and process in 17th and especially 18th century Western Europe, notably France, with certain ramifications or reflections in America (Byrne 1997; Patell 2001). Second, it is in virtue of its continual hostility to and culture wars against Enlightenment-based intellectualism and rationalism, just as secularism and liberalism, in America and beyond since those times, up to the 21st century. In sum, it is the counter-Enlightenment, just as the anti-Renaissance, both in particular or historical and general or substantive terms, as elaborated next.

First, Calvinist theocracy in America was the counter-Enlightenment in the particular sense and form of its historical hostility and revolt or "holy" war against the Enlightenment as a concrete intellectual and rationalist, just as secular-liberal democratic, movement in Western Europe, especially France, and to a lesser extent America (Jefferson et al.) during the 17th and particularly 18th century. For instance, Mises (1957) implies that during the late 18th century and later the old Calvinist as well as other (Catholic) churches represented religious and theocratic revolt against "reason and freedom" and thus the anti-Enlightenment, given that, as Weber states, all human liberties and rights "find their ultimate justification in the belief of the Enlightenment in the workings of individual reason." In a similar sociological account, Calvinist, just as other medieval-based (Catholic) religious, orthodoxy waged a "holy" war in the form of a "mindless defensive battle" (Habermas 2001) against the 18th century Enlightenment on the grounds of its secularism, liberalism, and rationalism, thus acting as the virulent anti-Enlightenment.

For example, Calvin's theological and theocratic successors in Geneva (e.g., Vernet, etc.) denounced the French philosophical Enlightenment as "false" on the ground of its "indifference, deism and the subversion of Christianity"[40] (Sorkin 2005). At least, most Calvinist and other religious conservatives were and remain "skeptical" about whether the Enlightenment was a "good thing (Dombrowski 2001) in virtue of not being "grounded in and supported by religion" and thus representing the path to "destruction, immorality, and depravity", and the "dissolution and ruin" of culture and all society (cited in Schmidt 1996). In another

---

[40] However, Sorkin (2005:286) suggests that in Vernet's view, "no fundamental or insuperable divide" existed between "Christianity and Enlightenment" and even that the latter was "compatible with faith." Presumably, Vernet appropriated "key Enlightenment ideas to rearticulate and renew belief" by the notion of "reasonable belief," involving a balance between "reason and revelation" (natural religion) and liberty of conscience and toleration based in "natural law" (Sorkin 2005:300; also, VanDrunen 2006). He infers that Vernet demonstrated the "compatibility of Enlightenment and belief" (Sorkin 2005:305), but apparently by "Enlightenment" does not mean the specific, notably French, 18th century philosophical Enlightenment that Calvinism assailed as the "false" one of "indifference, deism and the subversion of Christianity".

example, in J. S. Mill-Weber's accounts, a particular, moralistic revival and emotional intensification of Calvinism, specifically English Puritanism, designated as "Methodism"—a designation as non-pretentious or non-ambitious as "perfectionism"—arose in direct or indirect revolt against the Enlightenment (and Anglicanism déjà vu) during the late 18th century. While "Methodism" has moderated its anti-Enlightenment and anti-liberalism overall since, most Calvinist branches and revivals or survivals in America and beyond (e.g., Baptism and related sects and cults) retained, intensified and expanded such antagonism. In these accounts, "Methodism" arose as a peculiar species of Calvinist inner revivalism (German 1995) revolting against the Enlightenment and its secularism and liberalism, climaxing (alongside Baptism) through the Great Awakenings in America, while challenging for "Christian" dominance admittedly petrified Calvinism in New England (Baldwin 2006). And, the anti-Enlightenment nihilism of Puritanism and Calvinism overall, just as official Catholicism (Burns 1990), was part of religious-political conservatism's opposition to, alongside the "idealism" of the Renaissance, the "flawed vision" of the secular Enlightenment challenging "sacred" traditional society and culminating in the French Revolution's "freedom of form and spirit" and the "mistaken promises" of liberal utopian ideologies (Dunn and Woodard 1996).

In general, Calvinist and other (e.g., Catholic) religious conservatism in Europe as well as America revived or reinvented itself by arising and acting as the counter-Enlightenment (Nisbet 1966) during the late 18th and early 19th century and has, with minor modifications, continued to do since, through the 21st century. At this juncture, the admittedly "embarrassing Monkey Trial" (Boles 1999) by fundamentalism against evolutionary biology in the "Bible Garden" (Tennessee) of the 1920s can be cited as an exemplary case or symptom of the Puritan original and persistent counter-Enlightenment in America, and so can its various subsequent replays and proxies during the 1980s–2000s. These Puritan replicas or vestiges indicate a pattern or method, not an accident or randomness, in attacks on this and virtually all secular science, knowledge, and education as a threat to sacred and political authority (Darnell and Sherkat 1997; Martin 2002). It attacks most social sciences, theories, and methods, particularly theoretical, critical sociology[41]

---

[41] Bourdieu and Haacke (1995:55) comment that the "very existence of social science is unbearable" in authoritarian, including implicitly theocratic, societies. In their

(Bendix 1970; Bourdieu and Haacke 1995), and usually apologetic economics (Coats 1967; Samuelson 1994), just as climate science due to its "ungodly" or "un-American" global warming theory, as well as embryonic stem cell research, recently.

Second, as the above suggests, Calvinist theocracy in America has continued to act as the counter-Enlightenment in the general and substantive sense of its persistent antagonism to and "culture wars" against Enlightenment-based and other intellectualism and rationalism, as well as secularism and liberalism, since the late 18th century through "Monkey Trials" as a generic term for anti-rationalist or anti-science attacks during the 20th and 21st centuries. Namely, it has done so in virtue of Puritan anti-intellectualism and cultural anti-rationalism, notably anti-scientism, or antagonism toward and repression and decay in intellectual and rationalist secular culture, as witnessed in American Puritanism's "backlash against Cartesian rationalism"[42] (Johnson 2003). Essentially, Calvinist theocracy continues to be, like Calvinism and its revivals as a whole, the consistent and obstinate counter-Enlightenment, because it persists in its antagonism and militant revolt against the intellectual and rationalist, including scientific, legacy of the Enlightenment long after the latter nominally ended as a historical movement, just as the anti-Renaissance even if the Renaissance did not happen or come to the new nation. In sum, it is hostile to and attacks Enlightenment cultural values lying at the "heart" of Western civilization, such as "disinterested pursuit of the truth", "cultivation of art", "commitment to critical thinking", just as democracy (Berman 2000).

Evidently, what Weber and Hume identified as Calvinist "iron" consistency" or Puritan "unreasonable obstinacy" has been especially enduring and effective with respect to the counter-Enlightenment in a substantive general sense. This entails opposing and attacking the cultural as well as political heritage of the Enlightenment, including that of once "Parisian" Jefferson as the prime (Patell 2001), albeit atypical (Archer 2001), representative of the latter in America.[43] In this sense,

---

view, particularly "all authoritarian regimes have suppressed sociology from the outset. What they want is an applied sociology that can help manage conflicts and contradictions and rationalize domination" (Bourdieu and Haacke 1995:55).

[42] For instance, Johnson (2003) observes that American Puritan Romantics arose as a "backlash against Cartesian rationalism" and the like.

[43] Clark (1999:69) remarks that in post-Jefferson antebellum America the "force of universalist enlightenment thought waned" and Calvinist evangelicalism or revivalism *cum* "Christian egalitarianism" reasserted itself. And yet, the observation that the

Calvinist theocracy and in extension Puritan-based religious conservatism in America remains substantively the counter-Enlightenment in the 21st century as was historically during the late 18th and early 19th centuries (Nisbet 1966) in the aftermath of and adverse reaction to the Enlightenment. If some things never change—or the "more they change the more they stay the same"—in Calvinist theocracy and Puritan religious conservatism overall in America, this is, at the minimum, its counter-Enlightenment and thus anti-intellectualism, anti-rationalism, as well as anti-secularism and anti-liberalism, like its anti-Renaissance or anti-artistic and anti-humanist antagonism.[44] In sum, Calvinist theocracy constitutes the counter-Enlightenment substantively in intellectual, ideational terms, and the anti-Renaissance in a substantive artistic, humanistic sense.

*The Counter-Enlightenment as the Dark Middle Ages Déjà Vu*

Alternatively, Calvinist theocracy in America, just as Calvinism in general, including Puritanism, originates and functions as a sort of revival or perpetuation of the Dark Middle Ages, medieval irrationalism as well as theocracy. Thus, Tawney (1962) notices that Calvinism, Puritanism in particular, perpetuated and further intensified the "medieval idea of a Church-civilization" of both "doctrinal purity" and "social righteousness", simply a society as the union of "Church and State in one", hence theocracy precisely defined by such a fusion of sacred and secular power. Also, contemporary sociologists observe that the original aim of the Protestant Reformation, including the Calvinist Revolution, was reestablishing a "'purer' medieval socio-political and religious order" (Eisenstadt 1965), and in that sense remaking the Dark Middle Ages evermore "darker", not "modernizing", in particular liberalizing and democratizing, society.

For instance, recall that Calvinist Geneva due to its theocratic model was considered or described as the "Rome of Protestantism" and Calvin

---

"Christian doctrine of equality of souls did not make all Christians political democrats" (Linton 2001;18) also applied to Calvinists and other Protestants in America. This is a moment that Parsons (1967) overlooked in extolling Calvinist or Protestant theological egalitarianism or individualism, in the sense of all individuals' "immediacy" to God, as conducive to and even determinative of egalitarian and liberal democracy.

[44] At this juncture, medieval scholastics might say "nothing new under the sun", and British Anglican kings, the "old king of anti-Enlightenment is dead, long live the new king of counter-Enlightenment", in Calvinist theocracy.

as "the Pope of the Protestants" (Mansbach 2006; Sorkin 2005), thus perpetuating and further intensifying, darkening the Dark Middle Ages. In a historical sequence, then Holland's late 16th century Calvinist theocracy was painted in "tones of dark foreboding" (Kaplan 2002). Subsequently, Calvinism attempted to restore the medieval theocratic *Respublica Christiana* in the early 17th century Germany (Nischan 1994) though it eventually failed, and via Puritanism temporarily succeeded in England (Elwood 1999) and enduringly in New England. And, American Puritanism aimed to create a "new Jerusalem", a living community of saints" recreating America as a "self-conscious religious experiment" akin to that of Christendom in the Dark Middle Ages (Stivers 1994; also, Dunn and Woodard 1996).

For instance, that Calvinism retrieved or perpetuated medievalism is what none than Durkheim intimates by stating that "liberal philosophy has had as its precursors heretics of all kinds whom the secular arm rightly [sic!] punished" for their freedom and independence of thought by the Inquisition during the Dark Middle Ages. Notably, he adds that secular power "has continued to do so up to the present day", including by implication Calvinist and Catholic theocracies or state churches by some vestige or proxy, respectively, of the medieval Inquisition. To exemplify such an implication, in 17th century New England's "Biblical Commonwealth", the judicial system (magistrate) had a "religious duty to punish heresy," plus idolatry and apostasy, through the so-called "bloody tenet of persecution" advocated and implemented by "almost all Puritans" (Coffey 1998), including even those supposedly defending religious tolerance and freedom, as Roger Williams, the "famous dissenter", admitted and complained[45] (Dayton 1999). For example, one of those supposed or pretended Puritan defenders of tolerance and freedom of conscience (e.g., Ames) in New England admittedly argued in favor of the significant overlap of the "jurisdictional boundaries of

---

[45] Dayton (1999:29) observes that Roger Williams in 1644 "declared it a "monstrous paradox" that in the Puritan colonies "Gods children should persecute Gods children." " Admittedly, though the founders of these Puritan colonies (Massachusetts, Connecticut, New Haven), "protested that there was no established religion in their jurisdictions, their statutes and practices made clear that anyone who publicly challenged the reigning congregational orthodoxy would be either reclaimed or banished through] enforcing consensus among inhabitants on matters of doctrine and worship [or] 'true religion' " (Dayton 1999:29). In particular, Massachusetts's *Body of Liberties* of 1641, as "influential for all Puritan colonies", "perfectly expressed the blinkered view of the founders on the concept of liberty" (Dayton 1999:29).

ministers and magistrates" stating that "the chief care of the magistrate ought to be that he promote true religion and repress impiety" or heresy on the theocratic equation of civil magistrates and "divine ministers" (Davis 2005). Further, recall that New England's authorities punished a religious dissenter as a heretic precisely one year (1834) after the official "disestablishment" of its Puritan theocracy (Hull 1999).

Such practices affirmed that the formal separation of church and state was and is not a necessary and sufficient condition of the substantive differentiation between religion and politics or culture, thus for religious and political freedom. Also, recall what Durkheim was almost about to witness (dying a few years earlier) but virtually predicted. This was the "Monkey Trial" of biological evolution theory in the "Bible Garden", as a paradigmatic exemplar of condemning and punishing the "freedom and independence of thought" as impiety, heresy, or blasphemy by secular power, though not so harsh as the "holy Inquisition" but equally grotesque in retrospect.

Further, Simmel observes that Calvinism and Protestantism overall does not have "any real heretics" or dissenters in contrast to Catholicism, and, one can, as Weber implies, add, like fundamentalist Islam and by implication fascism, notably Nazism. Simmel hence implies that Calvinist (and Islamic) theocracy has been more efficient in punishing and suppressing heretics or dissenters, just as has Nazism, than even the medieval Vatican Church. It thus expressed what Weber identifies as Calvinism's "most absolutely unbearable" church control of individuals that "could possibly exist" and its "unprecedented" and "extreme" inhumanity, including cruelty and brutality, notably Puritanism's "unexampled" tyranny and, as Hume implies, sheer barbarity.

Specifically, in stating that Calvinism, including Puritanism, has no, or rather attempts to extirpate, real heretics, Simmel perhaps (should have) had in mind, alongside Calvin et al.'s execution and persecution of libertines and other dissenters (Servetus, etc.) in Geneva, certain Calvinist synods and their decisions against heresy or dissent during the 16th and 17th centuries. Predictably, the most likely and "qualified" candidate is the late 16th century Calvinist synod in Paris and its decision that evangelicalism could only be established through the "extermination" of non-Calvinists like Papists and libertines (Heller 1986). Evidently, to those French and other Calvinists attending the Paris Synod the most effective and "simplest" solution to the problem of theological heresy as well as secular political dissent was exterminating non-Calvinist or non-evangelical "infidels", just as is, mutatis mutandis, the ideal or ultimate one for US "born again" evangelicals, as well as Islamic fundamentalists. Another candidate was the Calvinist Synod of Dort (Holland) of the early 17th century (1618–19), which condemned the dissenting (Arminian) view that Divine predestination or grace might be "resisted" and that humans played some part, via proxy "good works", in their own "salvation"[46] (Byrne 1997; also, Sorkin 2005). If the first Synod was a sort of declaration of a "holy" war against non-Calvinists as external "enemies", the second was a condemnation of any form of internal doctrinal heresy or dissent within Calvinism as well as an expression of Calvinist transcendental or theological anti-humanism by reaffirming what Weber describes as the extremely inhuman and harsh doctrine of predestination.

In general, like other main Protestant and Christian denominations, Calvinism attempted to eradicate or stifle theological and political dissents. At most, as did the Reformation, it tried to create the "possibility" for doctrinal dissent "in the name of the gospel" or "Christian truth" (Byrne 1997) rather than as a true religious and civil liberty, thus a sort of ersatz-dissent or, in Simmel's words, a "compensatory substitute" for the freedom and "independence of thought". Yet, as Simmel implies, Calvinism eradicated heresy or dissent more consistently, effectively, and vigorously than its rivals like Catholicism, Lutheranism, and Anglicanism as "relatively weak" in spite of the "subjugation" of Catholics

---

[46] Byrne (1997:13) adds that "in England this theological conflict over grace came to have important political overtones. In 1646 the English Parliament, through the Westminster Confession, adopted the ruling of the Synod of Dort and thus turned the Church of England in a more orthodox Calvinist direction; monarchists, however, tended in the main to be Arminians and the theological difference came to be one of the marks which distinguished the monarchist from the Calvinist republican." A "more orthodox Calvinist direction" refers to Puritanism. Puritanism, while initially a movement within the Church of England, temporarily supplanted the latter and ruled the English Parliament during the 1640s–60, thus including the Westminster Confession, following the victorious Puritan Revolution against Anglicanism and the Monarchy. For instance, Weber cites the Westminster Confession of 1647" (sic!) as one of those Calvinist Synods, along with Dordrecht in 1618, during the 17th century making the elevation of the doctrine of predestination "to canonical authority the central purpose of their work". He suggests that the Westminster Confession turned Puritanism (not Anglicanism) in a "more orthodox Calvinist direction" in observing that "the schism in the English Church became irrevocable under James I after the Crown and the Puritans came to differ dogmatically over just this doctrine", with the first rejecting it and the second adopting it. However, Weber fails to mention that the Puritan Westminster Confession and other 17th century synods (Dordrecht) occurred almost a century after the Calvinist Synod in France of 1559 proposing the establishment of Calvinism via the "extermination" of non-evangelicals and effectively canonizing the doctrine of predestination (Heller 1986).

and internal dissenters in England (Byrne 1997). For instance, in Geneva during his theocratic governance, Calvin's "vigorous assault on dissent" was victorious and his theological and political authority remained "unchallenged"[47] through executions, plus imprisonments and banishments, of dissenters as heretics, including the most prominent dissenter, Servetus "burned at the stake"[48] (Mansbach 2006). In this account, Calvin's Geneva tolerated, like subsequent Puritan and Islamic theocracies, "neither heresy nor apostasy" and exerted "ideological monopoly over citizens' behavior" (Mansbach 2006). Following their master, Calvin's main successors in Geneva (e.g., Vernet) admittedly did not advocate toleration for non-Calvinists like Catholics, "let alone Jews" (Sorkin 2005) and other non-Christians.

In particular, Simmel implies the primary reason why English Puritanism had no "real heretics", in this case "out-dissenters", or was more efficient in suppressing them than medieval Catholicism. It was Puritanism's "cruel suppression", or extermination and displacement, of the Irish Catholics, the "victims of draconian penal laws" (also, under Anglicanism before and after, Byrne 1997), and other out-groups (in part Anglicans) in the aftermath of its transiently victorious revolution of the 1640s. The general reason consisted in that following Calvinism, Puritanism defined itself and acted as a "crusade", especially against Popery as a foreign treat (Goldstone 1986). Recall, as the self-proclaimed "Lord of the Domain", Cromwell's political actions were effectively violent, militant "holy" wars (Gorski 2000) against Catholic and other "infidels" as heretics or dissenters. The latter were therefore presented with a "rational choice", like (as Weber implies) in Islam, just as in Nazism. This is either extermination as the Puritan Pareto-style optimum *or* subjugation, conversion, and displacement as the "second best" or "charitable" solution to their "ungodliness". Also, Scotland under Calvinist Presbyterianism's official rule had "less scope" for religious dissent (Byrne 1997) in the late 17th century following the defeat of Cromwell's Puritans and the restoration of Anglicanism and the monarchy (in 1660), just as the anti-Catholic, proxy-Calvinist (and Dutch-originated) "Glorious Revolution"[49] (of 1688), in England.

---

[47] For instance, Mansbach (2006:112) suggests a dissenter in Geneva, Jacques Gouet, "beheaded in 1547 for speaking against Calvin's doctrines, could expect little mercy", just as Servetus "burned at the stake".

[48] For illustration, in 1552, a "city ordinance decreed that Calvin's [*Institutes*] was a "holy doctrine which no man might speak against" (Mansbach 2006:112-3).

[49] Byrne (1997:33) notes that following the Toleration Act of 1689 Puritans or Protestant Nonconformists "were treated lightly", but "Catholics continued to suffer

By analogy, Simmel might imply that the primary reason why American Puritanism had no "real heretics"—or was more efficient in their suppression than had been Catholicism—was the methodical use of "ecclesiastical power against suspected heretics" (German 1995), as done by the Calvinist Congregational Church in New England (also, Baldwin 2006; Davis 2005). For instance, New England's Puritan colonies had codes of law, as exemplified by Massachusetts's *Body of Liberties* (1641), authorizing the government via magistrates to apply the death penalty and other severe punishments, including whipping (*sic*) and banishment, for "crimes of religious belief" (Dayton 1999). At this juncture, Massachusetts' *Body of Liberties*, admittedly expressing the Puritans' "blinkered" cynical and hypocritical view on religious and other freedom (Dayton 1999), was not worth the paper on which it was written for the non-Puritans, especially Quakers, Catholics, and Native Americans, even internal dissenters adhering to "Calvinist beliefs" and belonging to the "Puritan fold" (but rejecting, say, infant baptism). This is what that "famous" and banished dissenter and potentially "real heretic", Williams implied complaining that "God's children should persecute God's children" in Puritan New England was a "monstrous paradox".

At most, this and other persons formed or belonged to a small circle of dissenters or "real heretics" within early American Puritanism and in extension Calvinism. Admittedly, only "few voices" within American Puritanism followed Williams in redefining religious liberty from the Puritan "freedom to exercise all the ordinances of God," "according to the rules of scripture", and to accept "Calvinist tenets" into the liberty and "multiplicity of denominations", or a "vision of many faiths coexisting in peaceful harmony" in America and beyond during the 17th century (Dayton 1999). Prima facie, the freedom and heterogeneity of beliefs within Puritanism, so long as "all" members adopt "Calvinist tenets" and act as "Calvinists" (e.g., dissenting Baptists) accepting the "validity of the orthodox Puritan churches",[50] was admittedly the

---

under the rule of law". Also, Champion (1999:18) suggests that "the compromise of the 1689 toleration was a successful attempt to stave off the threat of James II's alternative of a much more radical liberty of conscience. Christian consciences of a Unitarian or Catholic commitment would have to wait until the early decades of the nineteenth century to gain full rights of citizenship."

[50] Dayton (1999:33) cites the excommunication of Anne Eaton, a Baptist dissenter (and the Governor's wife) in 17th century New England, who argued that a "heterogeneity of believers could exist within the Puritan fold, as long as all church members

reversal, if not mockery, of religious liberty, pluralism, and competition in America, celebrated and invidiously distinguished from "state churches" in Europe by US rational-choice theorists of religion. It was a sort of ersatz, cynical, or hypocritical freedom analogous to the "freedom" of thought and movement within Bentham's *Panopticon* or a totally monitored and controlled neo-conservative prison system in America (or the Nazi camps), the elimination or perversion of religious liberty.

In sum, Puritans, once seizing the "reins of government" in early America, faced the "problem" (Dayton 1999) of heretics or dissenters both within and outside the Calvinist family, and apparently solved it efficiently—or more so than official Catholic and Anglican churches— by executing or banishing them. As Mises (1957) states, "nothing could be less compatible with true religion than the ruthless persecution of dissenters and the horrors of religious crusades and wars", which particularly applies to Calvin's "true" Reformed Church and its persecutions and "holy" war against heretics and "infidels". While self-evident, this needs to be reiterated and emphasized in light of these Calvinist original and, via "born again" fundamentalism, persistent tendencies toward "ruthless persecution of dissenters" and religious wars used and claimed, like in Islam, as the "holy" instrument to establish "true" religion and "godly" society (Turner 2002).

In retrospect, the preceding indicates and confirms what has been intimated before. First, on the account of its unprecedented efficiency in eradicating heretics or dissenters, Calvinism, Puritanism in particular, was a sort of super-medievalism by, if Simmel is correct, succeeding in what medieval Catholicism with its "Holy Inquisition" had eventually failed or only dreamed of. Evidently, the Calvinist ideal of a "purer" medieval social order than that created by Catholicism included as its defining element a sort of totalistic "purity" from religious heresy, thus complete "purification" of heretics or dissenters and sinners. So did consequently that of Puritanism. This thus defines or reveals itself as "purism" from blasphemy or dissent (plus sin and vice), purifying

---

accepted Calvinist tenets." In this account, aiming to remain within the "Puritan fold", Eaton, like most New England Baptists, argued for a "very limited notion of religious liberty", and not for a "multiplicity of denominations" or abolishing the "laws requiring all residents to attend church" and a "tax system by which everyone paid to support the orthodox churches" (Dayton (1999:39). Thus, these "Baptists presented themselves as Calvinists who did not deny the validity of the orthodox Puritan churches", with Eaton's "prior Calvinist credentials" as an exemplar (Dayton (1999:40).

impure religion (and immorality) by reestablishing and claiming to be what it considers the "pure church" or rather, in Weber's words, the "pure sect" of Calvinism. Second, on this very account, Calvinism, in particular Puritanism, originated and functioned as the substantive equivalent or counterpart of fundamentalist Islam, as the only or main contestant in the efficient and violent elimination of heretics or religious dissenters. Third, on the same basis, Calvinism, particularly Puritanism, functioned as proto-fascism, thus prefigured fascism, notably Nazism as the probably supreme, though non-theocratic, instance of such effective elimination of dissenters and dissent.

As hinted, some version or proxy of the medieval Inquisition was an ultimate "proof" or syndrome that Calvinist theocracy originated and functioned as a revival or perpetuation of the Dark Middle Ages. Hence, as Simmel, Weber, and other sociologists imply, this intimates the reason why, Calvinist, notably Puritan, theocracy solved the problem of heretics or dissenters more efficiently than did its disdained Catholic predecessors. It did because its Inquisition-style practices against theological heresy and any dissent were more consistent, methodical, obstinate, and thus effective than even the Roman "Holy Inquisition" in accordance with Calvinism's "iron consistency" and Puritanism's "obstinacy". In essence, Calvinist theocracy initially reestablished and has subsequently maintained a version or proxy of the Inquisition as an effective instrument to reestablish a "purer" medieval cultural and social order, hence an ultimate tool to resurrect from the dead past, as in the wake of the Renaissance, the Dark Middle Ages.

Weber remarks in Europe and America alike "Calvinistic theocracy" or "State Churches" enacted the "ecclesiastical supervision of the life of the individual" that "almost amounted to an inquisition" against the "liberation of individual powers", including both theological heresy and secular cultural and political dissent. Moreover, Tawney (1962) observes that early Calvinism in Europe, in particular Puritanism in old and New England, imposed an "inquisitorial discipline" and consequently functioned as a sort of "iron medievalism" déjà vu, just as was (self) described as "iron Protestantism". For instance, in Holland under official Calvinism, from the stance and experience of out-groups and its opponents, the Calvinist Church "merely" substituted the old Holy (Spanish) Inquisition with a "new Genevan one" through its violent attempts to "suppress" Catholicism and even Protestantism like Lutheranism (Kaplan 2002). And, the "new Genevan" Inquisition was predictably Calvin's original creation or design in 16th century Geneva following his failure to reestablish it in France, exemplified in his Inquisition-style trial and cruel execution (burning at the stake) of his critic Servetus and other libertines or dissenters for heresy.

Calvin thus provided a prototype or venerable precedent for subsequent Calvinist, in particular Puritan, corresponding practices (Mansbach 2006), from, in addition to Holland under official Calvinism, post-Calvin Geneva (Sorkin 2005) to the 21st century "Bible Garden". Recall, they include Calvin's successors' (e.g., Vernet's) denial of toleration to Catholics and other non-Calvinists and, in their Puritan forms, Cromwell's "holy" wars against "infidels", Winthrop et al.'s witch-trials and near-extermination of Native Americans in their "Biblical Commonwealth", fundamentalist "Monkey Trials" in the "Bible Garden", as well as puritanical culture wars and "tough on crime" laws and policies, notably the death penalty and penal system, in America. Historical research indicates that Calvin's accusation and capital punishment of Servetus for heresy provided "a model of a Protestant heretic trial" that was no different from the "methods of the medieval Inquisition", with the "victorious" Calvinist (and Protestant) Reformation being, like the Catholic Church, not able or willing to resist the "temptations of power"[51] (Nigg 1962). Moreover, another study suggests that his key role in the "capture and execution of the Spanish physician and amateur theologian" Servetus (in 1553) has influenced the historical "judgment of Calvin" more than any other event, even overshadowing his other activities and continuously embarrassing his "modern admirers" (Ozment 1980).

*Counter-Enlightenment in Religious and Cultural Intolerance*

In addition, Calvinist theocracy and Calvinism, in particular Puritanism, represent the counter- or pre-Enlightenment in virtue of religious and other cultural, just as joint political and ideological, intolerance. In essence, Calvinist, like any, theocracy practices and generates religious and other cultural, like political-ideological, intolerance. It operates as the counter- or pre-Enlightenment given that the Enlightenment became a paradigmatic exemplar of tolerance in religion and culture as well as politics and society. For instance, Weber observes that Calvinism,

---

[51] Nigg (1962:328) comments that "the execution of Servetus did not really bolster the strength of the Geneva Reformation. [Rather] it gravely compromised Calvinism and put into the hands of the Catholics, to whom Calvin wanted to demonstrate his Christian orthodoxy, the very best weapon for the persecution of the Huguenots, who were nothing but heretics in their eyes."

including Puritanism, adopts the "principle of the freedom of conscience" only for its members, but not for others (in exact contrast to consistent Quakerism that "rejects any attempt to compel those who are not Quakers or Baptists to act as if they belonged" to it) (also Baltzell 1979).

This implies that Calvinism aims at monopolizing the freedom of conscience for itself, while denying it to non-Calvinists and non-Puritans, especially non-Protestants (Catholics) and non-Christians both condemned and persecuted as "infidels". And, in doing so Calvinism, in particular Puritanism, adopted the Enlightenment principle of the freedom of conscience in order to effectively destroy it, just as interwar fascism, including Nazism, tactically embraced liberal democracy (free elections) to eventually eliminate it. Needless to say, the freedom of conscience and liberty in general does not make sense if it is only granted to oneself and denied to others (Kaplan 2002), as Calvinism, especially Puritanism in England and New England (Champion 1999; Dayton 1999), did. Particularly, Weber suggests that what he calls "blissful bigotry" (and "blissful ignorance") is "usually ascribed to the typical Puritan, inner-worldly asceticism."

In view of Weber's observation about Calvinism's, notably Puritanism's, monopolizing of the freedom of conscience for itself and denying it to others, the "logic", as Hume might have critically commented, appears to be the following. Namely, "we Calvinists-Puritans are free to exercise the freedom of conscience and practice our religion, but you are not to practice yours, because ours is true and yours false, so you either conform to the only faith and church, or *else*". The "else" involves conversion and subjugation as the "second best" solution *or* extermination and destruction as the Pareto-like optimum for Calvinism, especially Puritanism. To indicate the Calvinist-Islamic affinity or convergence (Mansbach 2006), the same monopolistic "logic" of religious intolerance is characteristic for fundamentalist Islam which (as Weber implies) presents via its jihad "infidels" with the choice of conversion and subjugation *or* extermination. And, like in Calvinism, particularly Puritanism, the exterminating solution is typically a long-run optimum and the former the "second best" short-term option in radical Islam. This was exemplified by the Islamic Ottoman Empire's brutal treatment of orthodox and other Christians ("infidels") from the medieval Byzantine Church[52] (Kuran 2004) to the early 20th century

---

[52] Seemingly nostalgically, Kuran (2004:76) states that "when the Turkish Sultan Mehmet II conquered the last remnants of Byzantium in 1453 and declared Istanbul

(e.g., the mass murder or even, in most views, genocide, of Christian Armenians by the Turkish Muslim government).

This is what has been described as the Calvinist-Puritan illiberal syndrome of religious and other cultural intolerance or anti-liberalism in religion and culture overall. For Calvinism in Holland and elsewhere, including Puritanism in old and New England, its self-celebrated love of religious and other cultural and political liberty—and when *not* in political power and cultural dominance—hardly ever translated into "liberality" as the willingness for granting others the freedom one demands for oneself[53] (Kaplan 2002). This freedom was instead characteristic of the Enlightenment (Kaplan 2002), exemplified by Voltaire's advocacy of tolerance in religion and all society as the "Enlightenment's greatest champion of religious toleration" (Fitzpatrick 1999), and of liberalism overall.

As usual, Calvin provided the model or precedent for such Calvinist, including Puritan, illiberality and anti-liberalism. He did by anathematizing and persecuting, to the no-return point of murdering, those advocating and promoting religious and other cultural tolerance and liberty as libertines[54] (Ozment 1980), as epitomized by his admittedly "illiberal handling" of a libertine or dissident, Servetus (Davis 2005). En passant, "libertines" was a negative and derogatory term used by Calvinism, including American Puritanism (Gould 1996), just as by official Catholicism, and equivalent to the pejorative meaning of "liberals" (the "L-word") in contemporary America due to "reborn" fundamentalism. At this juncture, US "born again" fundamentalists' attacks on those defending and enhancing religious and other cultural tolerance and liberty or dissenters as "liberals" are the déjà vu replicas or echoes of Calvin's and Winthrop et al.'s on "libertines" or dissidents. In this respect, to paraphrase a postwar phrase about Keynesianism (De Long 2000), "we US fundamentalists are all Calvinists" or heirs apparent of Calvin. For example, after his hometown and extolled "model" of

---

the new capital of his expanding empire, he had the largest, best-supplied and technologically most sophisticated army in Europe."

[53] Referring to historian Robert Fruin, Kaplan (2002:18) cites the "way the Dutch ruled their colonies" and adds that one "might well have cited the Reformation as another example".

[54] Ozment (1980: 368–9) cites the case of Jacques Gruet "whom Calvin considered a Libertine, had written letters critical of the Consistory and [also] petitioned the Catholic king of France to intervene in the political and religious affairs of Geneva. With Calvin's concurrence he was beheaded for treason."

government, the Geneva city-state had proven "less tolerant", even to his own ideas and works, than "anticipated", its proud citizen, Calvinist Rousseau (Sorkin 2005) essentially traced this "intolerance back to Calvin himself" (Byrne 1997; Garrard 2003) and his lack of tolerance of libertines and any dissenters. In Rousseau's words, Calvin as a "theologian" displayed a complex of "superiority" and was "outraged that anyone disputes it with him" (on Rousseau's relationship to Calvinism and the Enlightenment, cf., Garrard 2003). In particular, Rousseau himself temporarily converting into Catholicism might have added that post-Calvin Geneva's official (Vernet) intolerance of non-Protestants like Catholics and non-Christians (Jews, etc.) (Sorkin 2005) could be traced back to Calvin's virulent anti-Catholicism.

At this point, Calvin's theological intolerance of and outrage against libertines and other dissenters prefigured and perhaps inspired and predicted (Mansbach 2006), directly or indirectly, via Winthrop et al. (e.g., John Cotton,[55] cf., Davis 2005; Harley 1996), that of US contemporary fundamentalists toward "liberals" or religious and cultural Other (Edgell et al. 2006; Habermas et al. 1998). Perhaps, contemporary US fundamentalists' admitted intolerance to and exclusion of "liberals" and other out-groups (Smith 2000) cannot be directly traced back to Calvin and his outrage and attacks against "libertines" but only indirectly, through his Puritan disciples like Winthrop et al. and their "austere Calvinism" and "exclusionary Puritanism" (Symonds and Pudsey 2006). Still, what is relevant is that a pattern of continuity and consistency is evident within the Calvinist framework. Intolerance, like anti- or pre-liberalism in general, is not random and transient but systematic and persistent, a kind of "method in the madness", within Calvinism, from Calvin and his heirs to "reborn" US fundamentalists via Winthrop et al.,

---

[55] Davis (2005:336) describes John Cotton "as senator of a Calvinist tendency to prefer social and religious uniformity to liberty of conscience" and contrast him with Roger Williams, "patron saint of the American commitment to freedom of conscience [yet] also a product of Calvinism". He infers that Calvinism "has been of many voices on the question of freedom of conscience" producing both Williams and Baxter, "two Puritans with very different perspectives" (Davis 2005:354). However, this statement seemingly overlooks that it was established Calvinism that banished Roger Williams from Massachusetts in 1635 precisely for his espousal of "religious toleration" (Hull 1999:45). Hence, this event indicates that Roger Williams was a dissenter ("heretic") from, not a product of, Calvinism. Accordingly, if Williams' is "more liberal doctrine of freedom of conscience" (Davis 2005:354) than that of "conventional" Puritans like Ames, this is because of his dissent ("heresy") from, and not conformity with, Calvinism.

Geneva's model-theocratic state to the "Bible Garden" through New England's "Biblical Commonwealth". While it may not be fully accurate or fair to trace US fundamentalists' (e.g., Baptists') intolerance and exclusion of Other to their "father" Calvin (Hinson 1997) or Winthrop et al., it is "all in the extended family" of strict Calvinism, including "exclusionary Puritanism". Even if US "reborn" evangelicals are less intolerant and exclusive (Smith 2000) than were Calvin et al. aiming to establish evangelicalism by exterminating non-evangelicals, this is the matter of statistical-like degrees of intolerance and exclusion or unfreedom rather than of substance in the same "family".

Predictably, Puritanism, including its American transplant, has inherited and reinforced and expanded Calvinism's religious, moral, and other cultural intolerance after the model of Calvin's intolerant theocratic rule in Geneva (Mansbach 2006). This is exemplified by most of Weber's "great men" of Puritanism, excluding post-Calvinist Franklin (Byrne 1997; Johnson 2003), from Winthrop and Cromwell to their contemporaries and descendents[56] (Baxter, Cotton, in part Ames in Davis 2005). Indicative instances are New England's Puritan leaders' "policy of intolerance" and the opposition to the "language of individual rights" and the "formal policy of toleration" in England in the aftermath of the "Glorious Revolution" of 1689 (Dayton[57] 1999).

Recall that Mill identifies the "fanatical" religious, moral and other intolerance of early Puritans in Great Britain as well as New England yielding "European Enlightenment theories about degeneracy in the New World" (Gould 1996). Also, some contemporary sociologists detect the "sadistic intolerance to cultural otherness" (Bauman 2000) in contemporary America, notably the Southern "Bible Garden" (Bauman 1997). To that extent, Puritan "fanatical" intolerance in old and New

---

[56] Davis (2005) cites prominent Puritans like Baxter and Cotton as exemplars of Calvinism's religious intolerance or its denial of freedom of conscience to non-Calvinists. Also, he invokes Ames, described as a "conventional Puritan" in New England, as exemplifying "some of the best and worst" of Calvinism, namely "vacillating between a respect for the integrity of conscience (thus anticipating Williams)" and a conservatism that awards preference to revelation and conventional conceptions of political order, even at the expense of freedom for conscience" (Davis 2005:336).

[57] Dayton 1999:40) suggests that in New England during the 1680s the "laity embraced a slightly expanded notion of tribe whereas nearly all clergy remained bitterly opposed to the language of individual rights and the formal policy of toleration that was imposed on them by the king and parliament in the wake of the Glorious Revolution. Yet Puritan ministers after the settlement of the 1680s treated Baptists, Quakers, and Anglicans with as much contempt as they could muster."

England's "Biblical Commonwealths" anticipates, if not inspires, evangelical "sadistic" intolerance in the "Bible Belt", and conversely, the second perpetuates and reinforces or evokes the first. And, the descriptions "fanatical" and "sadistic" suggest that Puritanism and its revival via fundamentalism operates as hyper-Calvinism and Puritans act as super-Calvinists in respect of religious and generally cultural intolerance, as in most respects.

Moreover, Calvinism's (and Islam's) monopolistic appropriation of the principle of the freedom of conscience only for its adherents and allies (Kaplan 2002; Sorkin 2005; also, Davis 2005), while denying it to non-Calvinists (and non-Muslims), is an aggravated symptom of what Weber calls the "childlikeness",[58] and other early sociologists like Comte and Spencer deem the "childish" character, of religious beliefs and feelings (Lemert 1999). Yet, as Durkheim may say, such claims are a "very serious thing", as is, in his opposite description, religion, notably what Weber describes as the "terrible seriousness" of Calvinism and its dogma of predestination. As Americans would say, such respective claims to and denials of religious freedom and tolerance rationalized by the Calvinist "logic" of intolerance would be "funny" if they were not actually made seriously and even fanatically and eventually deadly, as through the religiously grounded death penalty and penal system, as well as aggressive "holy" wars on "evil".

Calvinist theocracy and Calvinism in general therefore effectively denies and eliminates what Weber describes as "an inalienable" human personal right versus "any power", including political and religious ("hierocratic"). He comments that such freedom of conscience could be the "oldest" and even the "most basic" human liberty and right in virtue of incorporating "all ethically conditioned action and guarantees freedom from compulsion", particularly state power. Notably, he suggests that the "ultimate justification" of "all" of these human liberties and rights lies in the Enlightenment's confidence in the "workings of individual reason". The denial of religious tolerance and freedom to "infidels" reaffirms the fundamental contradiction and tension between Calvinism, including Puritanism, especially its Bibliocracy, and the

---

[58] In an Enlightenment-mode, Einstein also denoted religion or belief in God an "incarnation of the most childish superstitions." In his words, "the word God is for me nothing more than the expression and product of human weaknesses, the Bible a collection of honorable, but still primitive legends which are nevertheless pretty childish."

Enlightenment in Europe (Artz 1998; Garrard 2003) and America (Bremer 1995; Gould[59] 1996), though to a lesser extent in view of the weakness or derivative nature of Enlightenment ideas (Archer 2001; Byrne 1997) in the "new nation." It thereby perpetuated and further expanded, as happened in Puritan America, the conflict between the Enlightenment and the Dark Middle Ages, notably medieval Catholic and Protestant theocracies, characterized by intolerance and unfreedom in religion and intellectual and artistic culture subverted into the servant of theology.

The denial reveals Calvinism, notably Puritanism, as the pre- and counter-Enlightenment alike in religious tolerance and freedom. The Calvinist "pre- Enlightenment" is exemplified by the existence of what Weber considers theocratic Calvinism, including Baptism with its "strictest Bibliocracy", in 16th century Europe and later America, thus prior to the Enlightenment. The Calvinist counter-Enlightenment is indicated by the rise of what Weber calls neo-Calvinism in Geneva (represented by Vernet, cf., Sorkin 2005) and Holland (Hiemstra[60] 2005) in adverse reaction to the Enlightenment and liberalism in general during the 18th–19th centuries, including Methodism as the Puritan emotional, initially anti-Enlightenment (and anti-Anglican), revival in England over the late 18th century (Baldwin 2006).

Generally, Calvinist and other (e.g., Catholic, Islamic) religious conservatism during the 19th century and beyond continued to reinvent itself and act as a counter-Enlightenment (Nisbet 1966) by its "holy" war or "mindless" battle (Habermas 2001) against the Enlightenment and its principle and institution of religious tolerance, pluralism, and liberty (Dombrowski 2001), that is, liberalism, secularism, rationalism, and modernism.[61] Consequently, in virtue of being a pre- and counter-Enlightenment alike in religious and other cultural intolerance, Calvinist theocracy and conservatism was both pre- and anti-liberal,

---

[59] Gould (1996:29) comments that "conservative nationalists" in colonial and post-revolutionary New England "dissolved the whole issue of Puritan intolerance within the larger solvent of "those times of ignorance" ".

[60] For example, Hiemstra (2005:160) registers that in 19th century Holland neo-Calvinism (Kuyper) "developed the idea of a pluriform public order in order to counter the hegemony" of secularism and liberalism, as part of the 18th century Enlightenment, within Dutch public schools.

[61] Johnson (2003) registers and laments "America's rejection of modernism" primarily due to Puritanism and in extension Calvinism. Similarly, Seaton (2006:197) describes and celebrates American Puritanism as a "synthesis and a distinctive version of premodern articulations" of humans and culture.

thus pre- and anti-modernity, pre-liberalism before and anti-liberalism following modern liberalism. Calvinist pre-liberalism and pre-modernity in general was manifested in Calvin's, later ruling Calvinists' and Winthrop et al.'s intolerance, persecution, and execution of libertines in Geneva, Holland, and New England, respectively, and anti-liberalism and anti-modernity generally in their descendants' corresponding intolerant and inhuman practices against liberals and moderns, especially and increasingly in America. In turn, since libertines and even (as Durkheim suggests) medieval heretics were "precursors" of liberals or liberal philosophy, thus the heralds of the Enlightenment, just as the Renaissance was its artistic prelude, Calvinist theocracy's counter-Enlightenment and anti-liberalism via religious and other intolerance perpetuates and expands from Europe to America a long-standing tradition of the Dark Middle Ages (and earlier times). In short, it was really "nothing new under the sun".

In sum, it seems as if not much substantively changed from Calvin's intolerant treatment and murdering of libertines through Mill's English-American Puritans' "fanatical" religious and other cultural intolerance of "infidels" to "born again" US fundamentalists' "sadistic intolerance" to "ungodly" and so "un-American" liberals, secularists, and others culturally different (Bauman 2000). While certainly many things have changed in formal or nominal terms (discourse, names, etc.) in Calvinism since Calvin et al.'s admittedly "illiberal" treatment of libertines or dissenters, Calvinist theocracy has revealed a remarkable substantive continuity in intolerance or exclusion, in a historical sequence from 16th century Geneva's *civitas Dei* to 21st century America's "godly" culture and society (Edgell et al. 2006). In short, Calvinism and its evangelical theocracy was and remains, via its Puritan version in America, a counter-Enlightenment and thus anti-liberalism with respect to religious and other cultural tolerance and freedom subverted into its opposite.

*Counter-Enlightenment in Intolerance in Comparative Perspective*

Further, in comparative terms, Calvinism, and Calvinist theocracy in particular, was and remains, via Puritanism and its resurrected Bibliocracy in America, what Weber would describe as the staunchest counter-Enlightenment and thus anti-liberalism in this sense. It was in virtue of being the most intolerant branch and theocratic realization of Protestantism and Christianity generally, and predictably only matched and emulated by fundamentalist Islam among world religions. At this juncture, Weber's identified "iron consistency" of Calvinism operated and manifested itself as the most consistent religious and other cultural intolerance in Protestantism and Christianity. In particular, this holds true of Puritanism, as Hume suggests on various occasions, and implicit in its self-definition or description as "iron Protestantism" (Tawney 1962) and of its adherents as Protestant (or anti-Catholic) fanatics, the "hotter sort" of Protestants (Gorski 2000).

Thus, Comte implies that Calvinist theocracy is more intolerant in religious and other terms than its Catholic adversary stating that "all emancipation of the human mind became more repugnant" to official Calvinism (and Protestantism) and its Puritan sects than to the "most degenerate" Catholicism. Significantly, he observes that Calvinism indulges in consistent and systematic intolerance in that it commits "violent repression" against other religious ideas and groups whenever it is in government or power, thus when it established theocracy. Being a French, he certainly knew and might have invoked as the supreme act of religious intolerance and projected violent repression, Calvinism's "logical" conclusion in 16th century France (the 1559 Synod in Paris) that its evangelicalism could only be established by the "extermination" of non-Calvinists, including Catholics, libertines, and secularists.

In turn, Simmel explicitly states that Calvinism (or Protestantism overall) often conducts "much greater dogmatic intolerance" than does Catholicism. He perhaps had in mind the French Calvinist Synod's decision, or conversely, the 1598 Edict of Nantes granting Calvinists in France the "status of a protected religious minority within an officially Catholic society" (Elwood 1999), or "some measure of toleration to French Protestants" (Fitzpatrick 1999). By contrast, Calvinism, from Calvin's Geneva and the French Calvinist Synod to Calvinist-ruled Holland and through Puritanism to Cromwell's old and Winthrop's New England, consistently refused to grant to Catholicism (and even in part Lutheranism and Quakerism) what it had demanded for itself and granted in France and later Germany, namely the "status of a protected religious minority within an officially *Calvinist* society" and "some measure of toleration.

Thus, in Geneva under Calvin's rule citizens were forced to "renounce Catholicism", as well as "non-biblical" names for their children, and generally their attendance at sermons was "mandatory" and were punished or threatened with imprisonment for the "failure to attend" (Mansbach 2006). Moreover, in this account, Calvin et al., as self-proclaimed

Divinely ordained leaders, were as "intolerant and fanatical" as contemporary Islamic fundamentalists and terrorists (Osama bin Laden) (Mansbach 2006). Further, Calvin's successors (Vernet, etc.) in Geneva admittedly denied toleration, and thus granting the status of a protected religious minority, to Catholics and other non-Protestants, let alone non-Christians (Sorkin 2005). Also, in Holland ruled by Calvinism Catholicism was not granted nor even approached the "status of a protected religious minority within an officially Calvinist society" until the late 18th century, under the primary impetus of the Enlightenment and its new, liberal principle of religious tolerance and pluralism as universal liberty in religion (Fitzpatrick 1999; Kaplan 2002; yet see Davis[62] 2005), two centuries after Calvinists gained protection in Catholic France and Lutheran Germany. Moreover, Calvin's heirs admittedly encountered in Holland "a militant, intolerant Calvinism" (Sorkin 2005) surpassing even that in Geneva as the "Rome of Protestantism".

English-American Puritanism functioned as hyper-Calvinism and its adherents acted as super-Calvinists in respect of religious intolerance and antagonism to Catholicism, or anti-Catholicism (notably, anti-Popery), as Hume classically recounted. This is indicated by what Merton (1939) and other sociologists identify as Puritan original and

---

[62] Davis (2005:335) objects that the "doctrine of freedom of conscience is still widely and popularly held to be a product of the allegedly atheistic mood of the Enlightenment and to owe very little to religion. Certainly few contemporary human rights advocates expect to find historical antecedents for [it] in [Calvinism]. [Supposedly] classical Calvinism bred intolerance, and numerous historical examples from Geneva to Puritan Massachusetts seem to bear out this judgment. Despite its reputation, however, Calvinism harbors just as much propensity for defending the integrity of a free conscience as it does for fearing such freedom." In this view, "Calvin himself symbolized the uncertainty surrounding freedom of conscience [viz.,] his overtures of mutual toleration to German Lutherans and his illiberal handling of the dissident Servetus indicates" (Davis 2005:336). This overlooks that Calvin and his heirs (Vernet, etc.) denied tolerance for virtually all other religions, including non-Protestants like Catholics, let alone non-Christians and atheists, thus their toleration of Lutherans was an exception, not a rule. Still, Davis (2005:336) claims that there is a "stereotype" of early Calvinists specifically American Puritans, as intolerant toward the basic right of conscience, which "cannot hold in light of legitimate ambiguity [so] positive potential, on the subject of freedom of conscience" in Calvinism, including Puritanism. For example, he contends that the Puritan Ames "reveals some raw historical ingredients for a liberal freedom of conscience", and yet admits that "possibilities exist only within the larger context of the Puritan's deference to the "superior" manifestations of divine law in Scripture and civil institutions" (Davis 2005:353). Admittedly, Ames "construes civil and biblical authority so extensively as to threaten the freedom of any belief at odds with those communal standards" (Davis 2005:353).

persistent anti-Catholic[63] (Reiland 2006) and other nativist, anti-foreign sentiments, ideas, and practices spanning from the 17th century to the 19th and 20th–21st centuries. These anti-Catholic continuities span from New England's official Puritanism (Davis 2005) to evangelicalism and sectarianism in contemporary America, notably Southern Calvinist-inspired Baptism (Hinson 1997) and allied sects and cults. All of them share virulent anti-Catholicism (notably, anti-Popery) a la Calvin et al. (Sorkin 2005) and sanctify this antagonism as a "crusade for Christ and Scripture" condemning Catholicism as "non-Christian" (and the Pope as "anti-Christ").

Also, Weber suggests that Calvinism, including Puritanism, tends to be more religiously intolerant or less tolerant than Lutheranism and Catholicism by observing that "if they are strong enough, neither the Catholic nor the (old) Lutheran Church and, all the more so, the Calvinist and Baptist old church recognize freedom of conscience for *others*." His "strong enough" evokes Comte-Mill's observations of Puritans' tendency to suppress the arts and amusements wherever and whenever "powerful enough", as in Cromwell-Winthrop's "Holy Commonwealths". in general, they all suggest and predict that, to cite Acton's famous statement, "absolute power corrupts absolutely" Calvinism, including Puritanism, and more so than either Lutheranism or Catholicism, through denying religious tolerance and freedom to non-members and out groups.

Evidently, Calvinist disciplinary revolution, and perhaps the Protestant Reformation as a whole, despite its opposite claims, by practicing religious and other intolerance, coercion and wars (Mansbach 2006) was even more incapable or unwilling of resisting the temptation and thus corruption of absolute or dominant power (Nigg 1962) than had been official Catholicism and Lutheranism before. At the minimum, Calvin et al., like Luther, acted or appeared as "dogmatic and intolerant" as the medieval Catholic Church (Dombrowski 2001), and not more "liberal" and tolerant, contrary to what they claimed and often supposed in the literature[64] (Davis 2005; Sorkin 2005). Calvinism in

---

[63] Reiland (2006:47) relates the following story from a Calvinist college in America he attended during the 1960s: "Some kid pointed me out as a "papist." It meant that I supported "Romanism" [or] the Vatican instead of the US It was like I'd stepped into the Thirty Years War, but I'd never heard of that either."

[64] Davis (2005:348) admits that New England's "conventional" Puritans like Ames denied that non-Christians are to be "extended freedom of conscience at all, given that their consciences err in a fundamental way by contesting or ignoring the moral author

Geneva and beyond, like Lutheranism, reestablished theocratic rule that was admittedly as "repressive of individual differences as the old Roman orthodoxy" (McLaren and Coward 1999). This Calvinist "reformed" intolerance targeted not only Roman Catholics but also other Protestant reformers taking "different roads", not to mention non-Christians and non-believers as "entirely outside the bounds of tolerance"[65] (McLaren and Coward 1999).

Weber comments that theocratic, both Catholic and Protestant, churches are not able to act in a different way because of their "institutional commitment" to safeguarding individual salvation, or, as with Calvinism, to protecting the "glory of God." Notably, he thus implies and perhaps predicts that the lack of religious and other cultural tolerance and freedom for *others* is, by being Divinely ordained and sanctified, intrinsic to Calvinism, including Baptism, just as is to official Catholicism for other reasons. This has proven prophetic especially for Calvinist Baptism given its "sadistic intolerance" to religious and cultural otherness, including "sexual mores" (Bauman 2000) and secularism (Edgell et al. 2006) alike, on "godly" evangelical grounds in America, notably the "Bible Garden."

In particular, Weber notes that religious toleration "was least strong" precisely in those societies "dominated by Puritanism", specifically "Puritan old or New England" and identifies the Puritans' "ethical mistrust" of non-Puritans, especially foreigners, including foreign bankers and other businessmen. This mistrust reflects what Merton (1939) denotes Puritan-rooted nativism, of which anti-Catholic sentiment is an early and particular dimension. This nativism is the species of religiously grounded nationalism, especially prevalent in Calvinist

---

ity of Christian Scripture". This denial explicitly applied to native Americans condemned and persecuted as "heathen" as well as non-believers, but implicitly to Catholics also openly or tacitly denounced as "non-Christian" by most early American Puritans, just as by modern Calvinist evangelicals like Southern Baptists and related sects and cults (Mormons, etc.) in America. Overall, Davis (2005:349) suggests that Ames's Puritan "exaltation of the Bible as the pinnacle expression of moral law threatens the freedom of conscience only when this standard extends beyond [persons] and communities to empower civil authorities to forcibly coerce compliance from a "deviant" conscience", including Catholic and/or "non-Christian". And, yet admittedly "this is exactly what Ames recommends" (Davis 2005:349), thus affectively eliminating freedom of conscience or religious tolerance for Catholics and other non-Puritans *cum* "non-Christians".

[65] McLaren and Coward (1999:2) comment that this Calvinist and overall Protestant pattern "is all too common. Religious groups who have been victims of repression by the state and orthodox religion have not been free of intolerance themselves".

societies like America as the "new Israel" with Divinely ordained "manifest destiny", just as Islamic countries, and not in those more liberal or secular (e.g., France) (Friedland 2001). Weber might comment that this minimal religious and ethical tolerance in Puritan-dominated societies was expected in view of the Calvinist inner "logic" and "iron consistence" of intolerance and repression, and surprising only to those like Parsons et al. extolling Puritanism and its, in Hume's expression, "pretensions" to theological individualism, pluralism, and freedom. In sum, Weber's and other observations confirm, first, that Calvinism was "iron" Protestantism in religious as well as other intolerance and coercion by being more intolerant than Lutheranism and Catholicism; second, that Puritanism was hyper-Calvinism and Puritans super-Calvinists in this and related respects.

Hence, as a rule, religious and cultural tolerance, pluralism, and freedom have, if ever, been established, promoted, and sustained in historically Calvinist and Puritan societies, this has almost invariably been *not* because but in spite of and opposition by Calvinism and Puritanism. By analogy, this applies to tolerance and freedom in Catholic and Islamic societies: *not* because but in spite and opposition of Catholicism and Islam, with Italy and Turkey as respective salient examples. This holds true of a historical Calvinist sequence that runs from Calvin's France and Geneva and Holland under Calvinism and Germany during its "Calvinization" to old and New England and contemporary America, notably the "Bible Garden".

*Instances of Religious Tolerance and Freedom in Calvinist Societies— Despite Calvinism*

The case of Holland seems particularly instructive and indicative in this respect. Thus, Holland has become or is often considered a sort of model society in terms of religious and other cultural, including moral and ethnic, tolerance, pluralism, and freedom. And, because historically it was and nominally still remains a Calvinist society (Tubergen et al. 2005), at first glance one can assume that this remarkable outcome and image has occurred precisely because of Calvinism. Yet, historical and sociological research clearly and unambiguously indicates that this country has evolved in a religiously and otherwise tolerant, pluralist, and liberal society in spite and even, especially in early periods, opposition of rather than due to Calvinism as an official church from its founding. Seemingly, this represents a paradox or puzzle, but actually confirms what has been identified as the Calvinist rule or historical pattern of religious intolerance and coercion.

According to historical research, the "central paradox" of the early Dutch Republic was the "existence of a confessionally pluralistic society with an official intolerant Calvinist Church" excluding and discriminating against Catholics, as well as even other Protestants like Lutherans, and vehemently opposing "any official status for Catholicism" (Hsia 2002). Yet, sociologically this was not really paradoxical. It instead exemplified the sociological rule or historical pattern that religious pluralism, tolerance, and freedom, as Comte, Simmel, and Weber imply, are likely to exist not because but in spite of Calvinism, given its inner "logic" of intolerance and coercion on the grounds of the glory of God. Conversely, it would be an illogical paradox or contradiction to assume that religious pluralism, freedom, and tolerance existed and persisted in this and other Western societies because, not in spite of, Calvinism, which is contradicted by its "logic" and practice alike.

The observed "juxtaposition of Calvinist hegemony and religious toleration" (Hsia 2002) in Holland effectively operated as a contradiction or disjuncture, rather than a Weberian elective affinity or intimate connection, thus logical and expected, not paradoxical and unexpected, in light of Calvinism's "logic" and "iron consistency" of intolerance. In this account, the official Calvinist, "Reformed" Church exercised "far greater political pressure" and attained a "more repressive hegemony" over religious minorities like Catholics and in part Lutherans outside of Amsterdam (Hsia 2002), for instance, and logically (thus not paradoxically) or consequently religious tolerance, pluralism, and freedom were weaker in these regions.[66] No wonder, some supposedly "enlightened" Calvinists (Vernet) considered official Calvinism in Holland to be even more "militant, intolerant" than that in post-Calvin Geneva (Sorkin 2005).

Further, another historical study proposes that the interlinked outlawing of Catholicism and the elevating of Calvinism to the rank of the "official faith" of the Dutch Republic in 1573–81 involved the "decisive 'rejection of toleration'" (Kaplan 2002). In this view, the "true test" of tolerance in Holland and other Calvinist societies was toleration of those dissenters ("radicals") completely breaking with conventional

---

[66] Hsia (2002:6) adds that in Holland Catholics "were excluded from guild membership and citizenship until the 18th century."

Christianity (e.g., deists or atheists like Spinoza) and, as the result, enjoying "scant freedom of expression" and often suffering "direct persecution" rather than of competing Protestant and Christian churches (Kaplan 2002). Of these, the Catholic church was not tolerated and outlawed anyway. Alternatively, it was primarily the Enlightenment that advocated and caused a "genuine tolerance" in the modern sense of religious freedom and pluralism to prevail during the late 18th century[67] (Kaplan 2002).

To that extent, the instance of Calvinist Holland confirms that Calvinism was at most pre- Enlightenment and deeply inconsistent with, rather than compatible with and even prefiguring, the Enlightenment with regard to religious tolerance, pluralism, freedom, and related respects. Conversely, it reaffirms that the Enlightenment substantively superseded and replaced, rather than continued and realized what Calvinism had initiated, wanted, or "promised" in this respect. Notably, the above observation suggests that it was the Enlightenment and thus liberalism, and not Calvinism, that acted as the primary source and inspiration of religious tolerance, freedom, and pluralism in Holland, just as virtually everywhere else in Europe and beyond, from France, Germany, and England to Jeffersonian America (Patell 2001). In sum, Enlightenment-based liberalism or pluralism proved a prime mover of religious freedom and tolerance, rather than Calvinism, as well as Lutheranism and Catholicism (Dombrowski 2001), in Western societies.

At most and exceptionally, a modicum of religious tolerance, pluralism, and freedom in early Holland was a sort of "virtue" made out of necessity and expedience or just "lesser evil" for ruling Calvinism than a ruinous all-out religious war, as witnessed earlier between Huguenots and Catholics, in which the Calvinists were defeated, in late 16th century France and elsewhere. Historical research indicates that as long as Holland's Calvinist theocracy cum a "socio-Christian order" was safe and non-threatened, "even militant Calvinists" could tolerate "certain differences of opinion" (Frijhoff 2002) perhaps having in mind the "adverse fate" of their brothers aiming at "extermination" of non-Calvinists and libertines in France.

---

[67] Kaplan (2002:25) adds that "until the Enlightenment to tolerate something meant merely to 'souffrir' [suffer], or grudgingly concede its existence [not] religious freedom."

Typically, ruling Calvinism in Holland, like France and Geneva, opposed and repressed religious tolerance, pluralism, and freedom, via its coercive imposition and harsh punishment of theological and other dissent. For instance, the strict Calvinists practiced or demanded a "severe repression" of all the forms or manifestations of Catholicism in public and private alike, though even they hardly ever dared to attack the "fundamental law of freedom of individual conscience" instituted and defended by the secular political authorities and non-Calvinists like Lutherans[68] (Frijhoff 2002). In regional terms, Calvinists reportedly succeeded in imposing and applying the "principle of forced Calvinisation" in South Holland, and nationally self-perpetuated themselves as the "only legally recognised confession"[69] as the "true Reformed Christian religion" (Frijhoff 2002), while other religious confessions were outlawed, as with Catholicism, or had "semi-public worship" like Lutheranism. Not surprisingly, as super-Calvinists the English Puritans in exile to Holland before and after England's 1640s Puritan Revolution glorified the Dutch Republic, due to its "dominant Calvinist Church", as a "Protestant paradise" (Frijhoff 2002; also, Sprunger 1982) and a model for their own republics in the form of official Puritan churches in Great Britain and New England. The study infers that a "permanent tension" existed between the "figure of unity" around the Calvinist Church (and its "secular derivatives") and the "model of religious toleration" (Frijhoff 2002), affirming that tolerance was *not* Calvinism's outcome but its opposite or an alien element.

Also, a historical analysis finds evidence contradicting the view that the Dutch Republic was a sort of "haven in a heartless world" for its non-Calvinist populations (Prak 2002). In this account, the "rule" was that only Calvinists were permitted to become citizens in Holland to the effect that those wanting to do so were forced to profess of the "true" Christian Religion and thus adhere to the "only" Reformed Church (Prak 2002). In class terms, Calvinist middle classes in Holland especially practiced "religious bigotry", while the elites preventing the

---

[68] Frijhoff (2002:36) reports another instance exemplifying Calvinism's persecution of libertines or secularists, including atheists, in Holland, indicating Calvinist pre- and anti-liberalism: "In 1669, a Spinozist [atheist] was condemned to an unusually severe and cruel punishment on account of his "blasphemous speeches" ".

[69] Frijhoff (2002:40) add that "as soon as the [1648 Westphalia] Peace was signed, [Calvinism] made one last effort to ensure for itself the status of a State Church" of Holland, more precisely the Netherlands.

"systematic harassment" of non-Calvinists or non-Protestants beyond the sphere of religion[70] (Prak 2002).

In sum, Holland provides a paradigmatic exemplar and confirmation of the sociological rule or historical pattern that religious and cultural tolerance, pluralism, and freedom originated and have existed in historically Calvinist and Puritan societies in spite and even opposition, not because, of Calvinism and Puritanism, but primarily due to the Enlightenment and liberalism. While perhaps the most salient or "paradoxical", Calvinist Holland is not the only case, as shown by Germany, Great Britain, and America. Like Holland, post-Reformation Germany, specifically Prussia, provides an illuminating case of emerging religious toleration, pluralism, and freedom not as the outcome of, but in contradiction with and opposition by, Calvinism and its attempted expansion and dominance in this Lutheran (and Catholic) country. Historical research shows that religious toleration and pluralistic confessionalism rather than Calvinization prevailed and were established in Germany during the early 17th century in spite, and not because, of and rejection by Calvinism (Nischan 1994).

As typical, Puritanism inherited, reinforced, and expanded Calvinist religious and other cultural intolerance to the point of becoming and acting as hyper-Calvinism and Puritans as super-Calvinists in this and related respects. Moreover, if this description of Puritanism and Puritans is true or plausible at all, it is so with respect to such intolerance of other religions, moral values, cultures, and societies, alongside "vigorous hypocrisy". As usual, Hume provides a detailed and suggestive historical "proof" and picture of Puritan religious and other intolerance, repression, and related attributes and practices in England and beyond. For example, he remarks that the "religious Puritans murmured at this tolerating measure of the king [James toward Catholics]" and "ungracious at court [is] the character of a Puritan". In particular, Hume recounts that the Puritan parliament rejected "any intention to relax the golden reins of discipline or to grant any toleration; [Puritans] called [liberty of conscience] a toleration for soul-murder".[71] Further,

---

[70] Prak (2002:164–8) cites the cases of Arnhem that in 1666 reaffirmed "not to admit any Catholics, nor Lutherans [even], as citizens" and of Zwolle where religion "was really the only reason why people were refused citizenship status" and the Reformed Church "filed a petition for the exclusion of Catholics."

[71] Hume adds that the Puritans "openly challenged the superiority, and even menaced the established [Anglican] church with that persecution which they afterwards exercised against her with such severity."

he counterfactually predicted what had actually happened: "The Puritanical parliament, having at length subdued their sovereign, would no doubt, as soon as they had consolidated their authority, extend their ambitious enterprises to Ireland, and make the Catholics in that kingdom feel the same furious persecution, to which their brethren in England were at present exposed." Notably, Hume observes that "one principal ground of that enmity which the Puritans professed against [the prince of Ireland] was this tacit toleration [of Catholics]. The [Puritan] parliament, even when unprovoked, had ever menaced the Papists with the most rigid restraint, if not a total extirpation". Predictably, Hume's exemplar is Cromwell depicted as actuated by "his bigoted prejudices; as no human mind ever contained so strange a mixture of sagacity and absurdity as that of this extraordinary personage".[72] Also, recall Weber's observation about Puritanism's "blissful bigotry" in general.

In addition, a contemporary sociological analysis confirms or echoes Hume and Weber. It suggests that at the "heart of Puritanism" was a "coercive, intolerant politics of moral reform" in accordance with its theocratic conception that "public enforcement of piety and social discipline" represented the way (by the elect) of honoring God (Zaret 1989). Consequently, Puritanism is found to have minimal (if any) significance for "liberal-democratic principles of tolerance and voluntarism" and instead "authoritarian implications" by coercively imposing a theocratic "Holy Commonwealth" in which, as its rulers and laws (of "liberty of conscience") commanded that "there may be no toleration of any other religion" (Zaret 1989). On this account, Puritan laws of "liberty of conscience", as in New England, were really what Weber may call "pure hypocrisy" and not worth the paper on which they were written for most non-Puritans (Dayton 1999).

In this account, in Puritanism at most occasional calls for toleration were a "concession to necessity" resulting from "sectarian conflicts among the godly" rather than a "principled call for full religious liberty" (Zaret 1989). In particular, religious, cultural, and political intolerance

---

[72] Hume cites Cromwell's Swedish alliance that, "though much contrary to the interests of England, he had contracted merely from his zeal for Protestantism." Hume adds that "as the Spaniards were much more Papists than the French, were much more exposed to the old Puritanical hatred [Cromwell] hoped that a holy and meritorious war with such idolaters could not fail of protection from Heaven". This perhaps prefigures US Puritan-inspired neo-conservative global as well as culture wars as a pretended "mission from God".

and radicalism via a "coercive, intolerant" politics in Puritanism (and other religion) were reportedly "inevitable" in virtue of its rejection of human reason in "favor of unbridled revelation" (Zaret 1989; also, Davis 2005). This thus manifested what other analysts describe (*pace* Weber and Parsons) as Calvinist "religious irrationalism" (Grossman 2006), in particular, the "irrationality" of Puritan and other Protestant sectarianism (Zaret 1989).

In sum, in Hume's classical and subsequent sociological accounts, early Puritans were extremely intolerant Calvinist "sectaries" initially driven and ultimately blinded by "bigotry and fanaticism". Hume anticipated Mill's diagnosis of the "fanatical" religious, moral, and other intolerance of English-American Puritans, who thus effectively acted as super-Calvinists in this respect, as well as Weber's of their "blissful bigotry". Hume's "sectaries" have continued to do so by the early 21st century, as indicated by the observation of the "sadistic intolerance" (Bauman 2000) to religious and other cultural difference by "born again" fundamentalists in America.

*Counter-Enlightenment in Cultural Anti-Rationalism*

In general, Calvinist theocracy constitutes the counter- or pre-Enlightenment in virtue of cultural anti-rationalism, including anti-intellectualism and anti-scientism, conjoined with pessimism. As noted, Calvinism, in particular Puritanism, represents or entails cultural anti- and pre-rationalism, as epitomized in the "Calvinist mistrust of the powers of human reason" (Byrne 1997), including anti-intellectualism and anti-scientism. To that extent, it acts as a counter- or pre-Enlightenment versus or in contrast to the Enlightenment as the axiomatic model and paradigmatic exemplar of rationalism, intellectualism, and scientism, as well as optimism.[73]

Like religious conservatism in general, Calvinism, including Puritanism, represents what Mannheim identifies as traditionalistic, namely medievalist or feudal-rooted, anti-rationalism, for it tends to descend into "complete irrationalism",[74] especially in cultural, including intellectual, scientific, philosophical, and theoretical terms,

---

[73] This holds true in spite of Calvinism being, if Weber is correct, economic or capitalist rationalism is not necessarily connected with non-economic, including political-legal and cultural, rationalisms, as he emphasizes.

[74] Mannheim (1936:121) remarks that religious and other conservatism "is essentially the expression of a feudal tradition".

as distinguished from the economic or capitalist a la Weber and Parsons. In a similar sociological account criticizing Weber's thesis of Calvinist capitalist rationalism, Calvinism is considered the species of religious and cultural irrationalism because of its "irrational" theological doctrines (shared with Lutheranism) such as the dogma of "predestined salvation" (Grossman 2006). A paradigmatic exemplar of Calvinism's, specifically Puritanism's, fall into "complete irrationalism" involves notorious witch-trials, premised on the irrational and medieval-based belief in the existence of witches (Byrne 1997), in 17th century Puritan-ruled New England (Harley 1996). Another instance involves their sequels or proxies such as anti-rational and embarrassing "Monkey Trials" against biological and other "ungodly" science in the "Bible Belt" (Boles 1999) and beyond in America, up to the early 21st century.

In passing, while Weber proposes and emphasizes the economic or capitalist and political rationalism of Calvinism, he implies its non-economic, including cultural, irrationalism. While a seeming contradiction, he recognizes and even insists that various, economic and non-economic, forms of rationalism or societal rationalization are not necessarily connected, but often in tension and contradiction, with each other. Calvinist non-economic and overall irrationalism is implicit in his observation that "both inner-worldly asceticism" like Calvinism and mysticism "ultimately condemn the social world to absolute meaninglessness, or at least they hold that God's aims concerning the social world are utterly incomprehensible". He adds that the "rationalism of religious and organic [universalistic] doctrines of society cannot stand up under this [Calvinist and mystical] idea; for [the first] seeks to comprehend the world as an at least relatively rational cosmos in spite of all its wickedness; the world is held to bear at least traces of the divine plan of salvation." Weber infers that "for the absolute charisma of virtuoso religiosity", epitomized by Calvinism and its Puritanism (Symonds and Pudsey 2006), this relativization *cum* rationalization "is indeed objectionable and estranged from the holy." This reveals Calvinist-Puritan social anti-rationalism, despite assumed economic rationalism in an affinity with the "spirit of capitalism."

Indicators and instances of Calvinist and other religiously grounded cultural irrationalism or anti-rationalism are multiple, intertwined, and mutually reinforcing. They comprise anti-intellectualism, anti-philosophical and anti-theoretical tendencies, anti-scientism, and the like, combined with and rationalized by what Weber and other analysts identify as the gloomy "moral pessimism of Calvinism"[75] (Byrne 1997) and consequently Puritanism. Generally, a sociological analysis suggests that Calvinism, in particular Puritanism, alleged the "corruption of reason and its limited role" in religion, thus rejecting human reasoning in favor of "unbridled revelation", and resulting in religious and other cultural and political intolerance and radicalism (Zaret 1989). In this view, alternatively a liberal, Enlightenment-based rationalistic and "optimistic appraisal" of humans and society substituted for Calvinist, including Puritan, anti-rational and "pessimistic doctrines" crucial to Puritanism's "godly politics", that is, for its idea of "corruption of reason and humanity's abject dependence on divine grace"[76] (Zaret 1989).

An indicator, syndrome, or instance of Calvinist and other religiously grounded cultural irrationalism comprises anti-intellectualism in secular, as distinguished from theological, terms. If, as Weber observes, in Lutheranism (post-Luther) "the dominant interest is the struggle against intellectualist rationalism" as well as political liberalism, this holds true even more of both early and later Calvinism that continued and further reinforced this Lutheran anti-intellectualism and anti-rationalism overall. This is in part implied in Weber's remark that "pastoral influences were dominant in Lutheranism and early Calvinism" and hence by implication anti-intellectualism and anti-rationalism in both. On this account, like other religious conservatism, Calvinism constitutes the antithesis of what Mannheim describes as Enlightenment-grounded liberal (or "bourgeois") intellectualism or liberalism that "strives to conquer a sphere completely purged of irrationalism" with "undaunted optimism" versus, in Weber's words, the Calvinist "gloomy" and extremely inhumane theology a la the doctrine of predestination. In particular, what Weber describes as "disillusioned and pessimistically inclined" as well as by implication anti-intellectualist and anti-liberal Puritanism revealed "such a striking contrast to the quite different spectacles through which the Enlightenment later looked upon men".[77]

---

[75] Byrne (1997:125) adds that Calvinism's moral pessimism is expressed in that "as only a few are truly Christian (Calvin's elite), the vast majority of human beings find themselves together in their intellectual and moral failure."

[76] Zaret (1989:175) adds that "in the world of the Enlightenment the union of morality and utility [contains] no religious veneer", in contrast to Benthamite utilitarianism.

[77] More precisely, Weber refers to that "disillusioned and pessimistically inclined individualism which can even to-day be identified in the national characters and the institutions of the peoples with a Puritan past, in such a striking contrast to the quite different spectacles through which the Enlightenment later looked upon men."

Hence, as typical, Puritanism, especially its American version and its evangelical revival, functions as hyper-Calvinism and US Puritans act as super-Calvinists in anti-intellectualism and cultural irrationalism overall as well as "gloom and doom" pessimism. At the minimum, if not Calvinism as a whole, at least American Puritanism and Puritans are the paradigmatic exemplar and emanations of anti-intellectualism and cultural irrationalism within religious conservatism. In consequence, Puritan Bibliocracy in America, from New England's to the Southern "Biblical Garden", has operated as the most anti-intellectual, thus culturally anti-rational, just as the most anti-artistic and totalitarian (Munch 2001; Stivers 1994), Calvinist-Protestant and any Christian theocracy, equaled or emulated only by past and present Islamic theocracies.

Thus, historical research indicates that the Enlightenment or the Age of Reason during the 18th century was "strongly opposed" by American Puritanism as the theocratic or officially established Calvinist Congregational Church in New England[78] (Foerster 1962; also, Archer 2001; Baldwin 2006). Furthermore, the Enlightenment's even "more formidable opponent" was the "counter-offensive of the Revivalist movement" (Foerster 1962) of Puritanism, specifically the Puritan-inspired evangelical Great Awakenings expressing "Calvinist revivalism" (German 1995) during the 18th and early 19th century. Admittedly, these movements were the counter-offensive against the Enlightenment and in stark contrast to its American representatives living in Paris: Paine's "acid rationalism", Franklin's "serene common sense"[79] (Foerster 1962), and above all Jefferson's liberalism and secularism (Archer 2001; German 1995).

Alternatively, these Calvinist revivals were irrational, "emotional explosions" punctuated by "visions and trances" ("weeping and swooning"), and embraced "especially among the lower classes and at the

---

[78] Foerster (1962:26) adds that while the Age of Reason "was spreading, from the second decade to the end of the eighteenth century, the two leading orthodox churches—the Congregational (Calvinist) and the Anglican—were well entrenched, though weakening by deist infiltration and attrition."

[79] Byrne (1997:48) comments that Franklin, while being the American ambassador to Paris, "quickly moved away from the Calvinism in which he was raised, thinking (like many of his contemporaries) that its rejection of good works was inimical to morality." Also, recall Weber's remarks that whenever Methodists like Wesley "attacked the emphasis on works of his time, it was only to revive the old Puritan doctrine that works are not the cause, but only the means of knowing one's state of grace, and even this only when they are performed solely for the glory of God."

frontier" (Foerster 1962). For example, the first Great Awakening of the 1730s was seen as driven by "atavistic", including anti-capitalist, thus anti-rationalist impulses seeking to resurrect those religious bonds integrating the old "Puritan community" (German 1995) via an "eruption of Protestant enthusiasm" (Byrne 1997). In this account, the driving or active force of the First, as well as the Second, Great Awakening was neo-Calvinism (the New Divinity) as a "version of Calvinism" with "theological grounds for conversionist preaching"[80] (German 1995) and thus Calvinist revivalism, mixed with anti-optimism versus the "prevalent psychological optimism" of the Enlightenment (Hume). Hence, this revival originated and epitomized, and the Second Awakening of the 1800s escalated, what analysts call the "drama" between fundamental "American Enlightenment ideals" and "revivalist Christianity" or Calvinist revivalism (Byrne 1997). Moreover, the "drama" has been continuously replayed in America to "this day" through various political and cultural conflicts, including separation of church and state (the issue of prayer in schools), the relation of science and "revealed truth" (evolutionism versus creationism), as if almost nothing had substantively changed in the system or design of Calvinist theocracy since the 1730s–1800s (Byrne 1997).

Recall that the aggregate outcome of these Calvinist anti-Enlightenment and generally anti-rationalistic revivals was that by the early 19th century, Presbyterians, Methodists, Baptists, and other revived Puritans succeeded to establish "Protestant evangelicalism as the dominant religion of America" (Foerster 1962). Of course, this happened most dramatically in the South converted from an Anglican region into a neo-Puritan "Bible Garden" (Boles 1999) subjected to Mencken's (1982) Baptist-Methodist "barbarism". Hence, through the anti-Enlightenment Great Awakenings, these "atavistic" American Puritans (likely unknowingly) fulfilled the 16th century French Calvinist Synod's imperative and achieved what Calvinists had failed to realize in Europe (minus Geneva and Holland). This was establishing pre- and then anti-Enlightenment Protestant evangelicalism as predominant in society (Heller 1986; Mansbach 2006), with or without what Calvinism envisioned and practiced, in particular via Puritanism in old and New

---

[80] German (1995:967) adds that "supporters of the [Great] awakening formed the New Light movement, which dominated the religious and political life of New England in the decades leading up to the Revolution" and of which an "intellectual expression" was the New Divinity with its revivalist "version of Calvinism".

England. Recall, this Calvinist vision was the "extermination" of non-evangelicals, including Native Americans, Catholics, Anglicans and other non-Calvinist Protestants (e.g., Quakers), secularists, and any "ungodly" out-groups (Smith 2000).

In general, Calvinist theocracy anathematizes and attacks secular intellectualism and cultural rationalism on the grounds of the latter being "too human", thus "evil", "depraved", or suspect on its own right, and "ungodly". Hence, its anti-intellectualism and cultural irrationalism (Grossman 2006) mirrors Calvinism's intrinsic hostility and distrust for *human* intellect and reason condemned as "evil", "corrupt", and "dangerous" and thus subordinated and eventually sacrificed to Divine "intelligent design." Alternatively, it expresses the Calvinist repugnance or abhorrence for secular humanism shared with other religious conservatism (Van Dyke 1995). In sum, Calvinist theocracy purges *human* from, thus actually vanquishes, secular intellectualism and cultural rationalism, and injects "Divine" to and sanctifies anti-intellectualism and cultural or non-economic (even if not necessarily economic) irrationalism.

Another syndrome of Calvinist cultural anti-rationalism involves anti-philosophical and anti-theoretical tendencies also shared with other religious conservatism. Comte observes that fully or partly Calvinist countries like Holland, Germany, and especially England, "the political triumph" of Calvinism (and Protestantism) effected neutralizing "philosophical emancipation" linking its social organization with the "conservative system." Consequently, he infers that "all emancipation of the human mind" became "more repugnant" to theocratic or official Calvinism (Protestantism) perpetrating "violent repression" and its Puritan sects in "compulsive agitation" (when not in government) than to even the "most degenerate Catholicism". This indicates that these anti-philosophical tendencies expressed and reproduced Calvinist anti-humanism through its repugnance to secular humanism.

Calvinism, especially Puritanism, reveals its anti-theoretical tendencies across the entire realm of secular intellectual culture, including philosophy, science, and education. It does so by (as Edgeworth implies) condemning or dismissing abstract and generalizing theory "despised as useless" in spite or precisely because of that the latter satisfies "a legitimate curiosity" and is integral to liberal education and culture. Like all religious and cultural conservatism, Calvinism, especially Puritanism, shows, in Mannheim's words, "no predisposition towards theorizing" and concerns itself not with ideas, but instead with "practical control" of culture and all society.[81] Mannheim suggests that the underlying reason and justification for this anti-theoretical tendency is that Calvinism and all religious conservatism regards culture and society as "part of a natural world-order", notably as Divinely preordained, that "consequently presents no problems" to be questioned and solved by theorizing and any intellectual or other activity.

In Calvin's words, society is a *civitas Dei* instituted, as in 16th century Geneva under the "Calvinist form of theocratic government"[82] (Byrne 1997), for the "glory of God" and endured by humans even when it is a medieval-style tyranny (Heller 1986). This consequently makes any theorizing or methodical thinking about, by likely questioning or revealing, as in the proverbial emperor with no cloths, such a Divine social order "ungodly", thus blasphemous to be punished accordingly, or at best superfluous and useless to be avoided as waste of time and energy. To invert Marx's (in)famous remark about philosophers, the point and function of theologians and similar "godly" intellectuals in a Calvinist theocracy is *not* to contemplate or theorize about the social world, but to perpetuate and glorify—and do not dare to change, as by definition futile and impossible—it as "Divinely ordained" and thus eternal.

Alternatively, Calvinist theocracy and Calvinism as a whole condemns or suspects the theorizing or contemplating about—because of its actual or potential questioning of—the social world as "ungodly", dangerous, or threatening (Habermas 1989) to this Divinely ordained order. Theorizing thus becomes a sort of sociological and even theological heresy or blasphemy, or (as Edgeworth suggests) idle speculation at most in Calvinist theocracy. This helps to explain why Calvinist, like other, theocracies condemn, suppress, and severely punish theoretical dissent and dissenters, social and theological alike, as "ungodly" blasphemy and heretics, and also dismiss or disdain theorizing overall

---

[81] Mannheim (1936:229) adds that this conservative anti-theoretical tendency "is in accord with the fact [view] that human beings do not theorise about the actual situations in which they live as long as they are well adjusted to them." He comments that while originally "not concerned with ideas", conservatism was "forced" into this "arena of conflict" by its opponent, liberalism (Mannheim 1936:231).

[82] Byrne (1997:185) remarks that "in Rousseau's home and model state, Geneva, where the Calvinist form of theocratic government existed in an at times uneasy relationship with the liberating Protestant emphasis on the purity of the gospel and the inviolability of the individual conscience" or what Parsons extols as individuals' immediacy to God."

as idleness, in a long historical sequence and continuity from Calvin's *civitas Dei* in 16th century Geneva to the "Bible Garden" in 21st century America.

Yet, the above entails an apparent logical-empirical contradiction. If the Calvinist *civitas Dei* is by definition unchangeable by human intervention, then theoretical dissent and theorizing overall by *humans* are inconsequent to this Divinely ordained order, so need not be condemned as "ungodly" blasphemy and punished as mortal offense with death and Draconian harshness in general, as was initially. For example, Calvin proclaimed and treated his *civitas Dei* in Geneva as Divinely ordained, thus axiomatically unchangeable by humans, yet condemned, repressed, and punished their theoretical or theological dissent and theorizing overall as blasphemy to the point of executing dissenters as heretics, as exemplified by the beheading of libertines, as well as the burning of Servetus. Thereby, Calvin set the model and precedent for subsequent ideas and practices in Calvinism, specifically instituting and declaring Calvinist Biblical theocracies as Divinely ordained and thus eternal and impervious to human intervention. Yet, these theocracies condemned and punished theoretical, both secular and theological, dissent or theorizing overall by humans as dangerous to these orders and "ungodly," thus contradicting elemental logic and implicitly their own Divinity. For to define such "idle speculation" and "useless" theorists as a danger to what the God of Calvinism created for eternity is to self-contradict and even mistrust Providential "Intelligent Design"!

This is essentially the pattern of Calvinist theocratic masters' acting since Calvin, from official Calvinism in Holland to "born again" ruling fundamentalists in the "Bible Garden", via Cromwell and Winthrop et al. in old and New England's "Holy Commonwealths". For example, Cromwell instituted and declared a la Calvin the Puritan "Holy Commonwealth" in England as Divinely ordained, thus humanly unalterable and himself as the "Lord of the Domain", and yet attacked and expunged theoretical, political, and theological dissent and human dissenters as dangerous "infidels" through crusades (Goldstone 1986; Gorski 2000). Induced by their "austere Calvinism" Winthrop and his followers displayed an almost identical pattern of action before and after. They did by instituting and proclaiming their "Biblical Commonwealth" in New England as a God's Kingdom on Earth beyond human power or intervention (Seaton 2006), yet punishing by cruel death theoretical dissent as blasphemy (a deadly sin-crime) and dissenters as "witches." They hence self-contradicted the unchangeable "shining city upon a hill", thus Divine immutable ordinance, by a society as sectarian, irrational Salem threatened by powerless humans redefined and exorcised as "witches" (Harley 1996), what Weber says an "impossible contradiction."

Similarly, Puritans' "born again" descendents in America deliberately follow and even expand Winthrop's and implicitly Calvin's model by reestablishing or projecting their "Bible Garden" as Providential Design and thus eternal or millennial for humans. Yet, they condemn, suppress, and punish dissent and dissenters as blasphemy (though not punishable with death) and "ungodly" and thus "un-American" through culture and other, including global military, wars. For instance, while doing the first they at the same time denounce and attack theoretical science, knowledge, and secular education overall as a mortal threat to both sacred and political authority (Darnell and Sherkat 1997) and hence to be substituted by their religious opposites or substitutes and even *no* (and home) schooling as "better" in an evangelical theocracy. And yet, if the "Bible Garden", like any Calvinist evangelical theocracy, is "Divinely" ordained, thus immutable with respect to mere humans ("little guys"), one wonders why and how *human* secular theorizing or thinking, knowledge, and schooling, including higher education despite its global expansion in contemporary society (Schofer and Meyer 2005), can logically or actually pose a mortal danger to such a Divine, eternal order.[83] Simply, how finite humans can undo by words and even deeds what the infinite God of Calvinism created for eternity?—only Calvin and his Puritan followers like US evangelicals can answer the question and resolve Weber's "impossible contradiction."

In sum, on this account Calvinism, notably Puritanism, has exhibited since Calvin "iron consistency", though in a sense different from that Weber identified. This is "consistency" in a self-contradiction between defining Calvinist theocracy as "Divinely ordained" beyond human power, while proscribing and suppressing the theorizing, notably theoretical dissent, by humans as dangerous to this order and thus

---

[83] This is a logical derivation from the premise, not an empirical proposition or generalization. It is so given that Calvinist, like other, theocracies in Europe and America have been historically mutable or transient due to human intervention—"come and gone"—as witnessed by New England's "Biblical Commonwealth", though the "Bible Belt" apparently aims to be an exception, alongside the Vatican Church as well as Islamic theocracy.

Divinity—yet, an "impossible contradiction". This turns out to be paradoxically Calvinist "iron consistency" in inconsistency or illogicality and intellectual irrationality. Either as an inner contradiction or "iron consistency", Calvinist theocracy, like all religious conservatism, is antitheoretical, because it is instituted and self-defined as part of a "natural", notably unchangeable and eternal Divine, order. For this order axiomatically rules out and practically suppresses or discourages any theorizing about, as potential questioning of, what the God of Calvinism created for eternity and humans cannot, thus do not dare to, change in accordance with the "what God has done, humans shall not undo" commandment.

Another, corollary indicator of Calvinist cultural anti-rationalism includes anti-scientism in the sense of an antithesis of what contemporary sociologists call scientism (Habermas 1971) as a particular scientific dimension of rationalism and intellectualism. Calvinist and all religious anti-scientism is defined and manifested by anti-scientific theological "godly" ideas and their realization in equivalent theocratic practices and institutions. These anti-scientific practices are implied in Calvinism's anti-philosophical and especially anti-theoretical tendencies, as its anti-theorizing tendency is particularly strong in science, notably the social sciences. On this account, Calvinist, especially Puritan, theocracy acts as the overt or covert opposite and suppression of scientific, to be distinguished from economic or capitalist, rationalism (Goldstone 2000; Martin 2002; Zaret 1989), theoretical science, knowledge, and method in particular. In Comte's terms, it does as the theological negation and the theocratic destruction of scientific (and philosophical) positivism, particularly theoretical positive social science (sociology), method, and knowledge.

In particular, Calvinist theocracy, notably its Puritan version in America, has been hostile to and distrustful of what Comte considers theoretical or fundamental science and knowledge, social and natural, as a sort of true "forbidden apple." Instead, it embraces, like religious and political conservatism as a whole, including its extreme product fascism, as Mannheim remarks, non-theoretical ("empirical", "pragmatic") knowledge establishing and maintaining "practical control", specifically theocratic rule within society and a total "holy" war of extermination and conquest against other "ungodly" cultures and societies. Thus, Calvinist theocracy consistently rejects or suspects Comte's principle of (to restate it) "from fundamental science and theoretical knowledge comes prediction." And it perverts "from prediction comes liberal-democratic, human action" into "here comes" theocratic control and world military domination in a mutual relation and reinforcement. Now, as contemporary sociologists imply, Calvinist theocracy in America could and can, just as did Nazism, destroy scientism and cultural rationalism generally only "at a psychological cost of regressions" (Habermas 1975), ultimately into barbarism or primitivism.

And, it is Comte himself that among the first social scientists identifies and emphasizes Calvinist anti-scientism and anti-positivism or anti-rationalism overall. Thus, he observes that Calvinism (and Protestantism) is, in addition to its anti-artistic attributes, characterized by "anti-scientific tendencies" due to its "incorporation" with government power and the "repugnance" of Calvinist and other theology to the "spread of the positive spirit" in Europe, especially England via Puritanism.[84] He infers that Calvinism (and Protestantism overall) is pervaded by "dangerous inertia" toward adopting scientific positivism, notably positive and theoretical social and other science, method, and knowledge. Sociological research confirms or echoes Comte's insights. A sociological analysis shows that, while Calvinism in the 17th century might have engendered "scientific rationalists" as in Holland, by the 18th century the cultural dominance of "Calvinist orthodoxy" generated "widespread public opposition to aspects of the new science", including even medicine (smallpox inoculation), with its orthodox elite becoming "fearful of heresy among the laity" (Goldstone 2000; also, Hiemstra 2005). Another sociological analysis suggests that Puritanism with its "social radicalism" developed as a "charismatic revolt against those worldly institutions", such as growingly secular universities, alongside the "ungodly" state and law and "impure" church, that were anathematized and attacked as "impediments to the creation of a holy commonwealth" (Zaret 1989).

As a Calvinist irrational, anti-scientific vestige, US evangelicals oppose or distrust certain kinds of vaccination and other medical procedures and medicines, as if nothing really changed from the 18th century to the 21st century. For instance, media reported in 2008 that "measles cases in the US are at the highest level in more than a decade, with nearly half of those involving children whose parents rejected vaccination [mainly] for religious [or ideological] reasons." No wonder,

---

[84] For example, Comte uses the term "irrational [national] exclusiveness" in reference to England.

some parents, members of evangelical sects and cults in America, during the 2000s reportedly left their children die of curable diseases (e.g., diabetes) in expectation that Weber's "God of Calvinism" would cure them rather than seeking, and even refusing, secular medical assistance. Such bizarre cases confirm over and over that Calvinist theocracy or evangelicalism overall in America is supreme nihilism, destructive to the lives and freedoms of non-Calvinists or non-evangelicals *and* ultimately self-destructive literally devouring its own children in the image of Hobbes' sea-monster Leviathan.

What Comte implies his predecessor Hume explicitly proposes. This is that Puritanism was hyper-Calvinism and Puritans super-Calvinists with respect to "anti-scientific tendencies" and "dangerous inertia" concerning scientific rationalism, like in virtually all respects. Recall Hume does so by observing that early English Puritanism was so "much infected" by "wretched fanaticism" that was "destructive" of science, just as artistic taste and law and order, making "human learning despised; freedom of inquiry detested" by its adherents. Similarly, he identifies "Puritanical absurdities" and observes that in England it was in "vain attempted to convince the Puritans by argument"[85] and in that sense science, philosophy, and rational methods overall.

Also, a sociological study reports an episode of "wretched fanaticism" in that none than Hume's illustrious predecessor John Locke reportedly saw in 1656 a young "Puritan fanatic" (Nayler) riding a "donkey into Bristol" and claiming to be the messiah (Zaret 1989). Perhaps in view of such instances of religious fanaticism even Locke— a Puritan[86] (Kloppenberg 1998) and more "godly" and religiously intolerant of non-Christians, non-believers, and Catholics (Byrne 1997) than "ungodly" Hume—admits that "there is absolutely no such thing

---

[85] Hume adds that "the religious zeal of the puritans was not so easily restrained; and it inspired a courage which no human motive was able to surmount." He also provides the following example: "In 1573, a Puritan, being persuaded that it was meritorious to kill such as opposed the truth of the gospel ran into the streets, and wounded [a] famous sea captain."

[86] Kloppenberg (1998:25) refers to the "sober Puritanism of Locke". However, Walzer (1963: 67) objects that "the faith of the Puritan saints" and the "tolerant reasonableness" of liberals like Locke "had very little in common". Also, Zaret (1989:173) suggests that, with his "appeal to reason" in religion as a "means for attacking" the irrationality of] sectarianism", Locke rejected the Puritan idea that "political institutions have a divine mandate." Notably, Zaret (1989:175) cites Locke's statement that "there is absolutely no such thing [as] a Christian commonwealth", which is precisely what Puritanism and Calvinism overall intended to establish.

[as] a Christian commonwealth" (Zaret 1989) as the supreme ideal of Puritanism and all Calvinism. The model was the medieval *respublica Christiana* reestablished by Calvin et al. in Europe and America.

Hume might have added that such anti-scientific fanaticism and absurdities "infected" equally and perhaps even more subsequently those Puritans moving from England to the "new world" and, if he lived through the 2000s, their "reborn" evangelical descendents. In his context, this rendered American Puritanism and its revival via evangelicalism as "destructive" of science and learning (and artistic taste) as its English ancestor. As known, Puritans' failure to establish a "coercive moral regime" in England prompted them to institute it beyond (Zaret 1989), as in New England, thus bringing their old anti-scientific fanaticism and absurdities to the new world.

Hume might have cited "Salem with witches" in New England as the exemplary case and symbol (the "mother") of all Puritan "wretched fanaticism" and anti-scientific "absurdities" or irrational prejudices, and in extension of Calvinist anti-scientism and cultural anti-rationalism. While Salem's witch-trials are admittedly "unique" irrational phenomena in Anglo-American history and law, they reflected Puritanism and its fanaticism and in extension Calvinism as the "dominant religious ideology", Calvinist demonology obsessing with "Satan's powers" more than other Protestantism and Christianity[87] (Harley 1996). While in post-Puritan Restoration England, for example, non-Calvinist (Anglican) physicians accounted for "demonic phenomena" with reference to "disease or fraud", medieval-rooted "Calvinist demonology" was irrationally obsessed with "Satan's powers" reigning supreme in New England (Harley 1996). No wonder, the Quakers in New England were the "most vociferous opponents" of the Puritan witch-trials by comparing their own persecutions with the "prosecution of witches" (Harley 1996). To that extent, with their basis in the irrational belief in witches and their cruel effect of the "capital crime of witchcraft", New England's witch-trials

---

[87] Harley (1996) comments that "since Calvinists focused more closely on the reading of God's providence than other Christians did, this was the context for their discussion of Satan's powers", in particular the "capital crime of witchcraft" by what he cites as "Special Providences of God towards his New-England people." He also cites the ruling Puritans' declarations of "Prodigious Witchcrafts, Diabolical Possessions, Remarkable Judgements upon noted Sinners", including Cotton Mather's of "A dreadful Knot of Witches in the Country" and his unrepentant claim that "justice being so far, executed among us". For example, Mather reportedly "did not lose his belief in witchcraft", just as the equally "unrepentant" Lieutenant-Governor Stoughton (Harley 1996).

represented the true (patho) logical outcomes of Calvinism's cultural irrationalism, notably Puritanism's fanaticism, a sort of Calvinist-Puritan, "normal pathology". This holds true, with certain qualifications, of such vestiges or proxies of the Puritan witch-trials as "Monkey Trials" against scientific rationalism in the "Bible Belt". At the minimum, these two related beliefs and practices, universally considered fanatical, superstitious, or irrational, reveal Calvinism, specifically Puritanism, as the species of Mannheim's "complete irrationalism" in cultural terms, even if being (as in Weber-Parsons' accounts) an exemplar or spiritual source of economic rationalism a la the "spirit of capitalism" (yet cf., Alexander 1998; Delacroix and Nielsen 2001; Grossman 2006). In sum, at least "Salem with witches" as an actual event and the symbol of an irrational sectarian society presents Puritanism and Calvinism overall as religious fanaticism and cultural irrationalism, though, charitably interpreted a la Weber, not economic (yet the Calvinist Great Awakenings are depicted as "anti-capitalist" in German 1995).

Similarly, various vestiges or proxies of Salem's witch-trials such as the "Monkey Trial" against biological science as the concrete historical episode in the post-bellum South would have hardly surprised Hume and might be cited as the candidate for the "second best" and neo-Puritan or evangelical paradigmatic example of the "wretched fanaticism" of Puritanism and in extension the "religious irrationalism" of Calvinism. This curious, although less lethal and more grotesque episode exemplifies and reaffirms the remarkable sociological continuity from New England's "Biblical Commonwealth" to the Southern "Bible Garden" with respect to cultural irrationalism, including religious fanaticism and superstition. This would likely prompt Hume to exclaim "I told you so" if he visited by any miracle (of course, an "impossibility theorem" denied to him by Puritanism given his skepticism to religion and this lack of a belief in Puritan miracles) America over the 2000s. By analogy to Salem's witch-trials, Southern "Monkey Trials" in the sense and form of consistent methodical attacks on and subversions of science, including but not confined to evolutionary biology, and secular knowledge, method, and education (Martin 2002) qualify as Hume's most obstinate case of Puritan evangelical "fanaticism" and anti-scientific "absurdities", thus anti-scientism and irrationalism in the extended Calvinist family. Hume might identify the most general, enduring, and drastic "proof" or pathological syndrome in this sense in American fundamentalism's "Divine revelation" that even *no* science, knowledge, or education, not to mention religious home-schooling found and growing in the "Bible

Garden", is "better"—a sort of genuinely "blissful ignorance" (Wacquant 2002)—than their secular forms anathematized and attacked as "ungodly" and threats to sacred and political powers (Darnell and Sherkat 1997). This leads to Calvinist scientific irrationalism or anti-scientific nihilism, as elaborated next.

*Counter-Enlightenment in Anti-Scientific Nihilism*

As a corollary, Calvinist theocracy and Calvinism overall, including Puritanism, represents the ultimate counter-Enlightenment on the account of anti-scientific antagonism, repression, and decay in America. In particular, Calvinist theocracy in America intrinsically harbors hostility to and systematically practices repression of academic freedom as one of the principles and legacies of the Enlightenment. For example, some analyses suggest that "genuine academic freedom" in Puritan America has "never" represented the rule but, by implication, an exception, with social and other scientists being the "principal victims of attacks" (Coats 1967).

These attacks on academic freedom have been typically (though not solely) the acts of Calvinist and related conservative forces placing science at the "list of threats to Christian orthodoxy"[88] (Fehler 2005), since their adverse reaction to the American, Jefferson-Franklin-Madison's rendition or approximation of the Enlightenment (Patell 2001), via "Monkey Trials" and McCarthyism and continuing through the 21st century. Through its attacks on academic and other freedom Calvinist theocracy methodically targets and seeks to discredit a major principle and legacy of the Enlightenment and liberal rationalism generally[89] (Bendix 1970). Like other theocracies, it condemns, attacks, and eventually eliminates academic freedom as the license for "ungodly" and "un-American, or heretical and dissenting ideas and activities, thus as "evil" and "depraved", at most a luxury or idle superfluity that Calvinist theocracy and America "cannot afford" without the high cost

---

[88] Fehler (2005:139) observes that in the 19th century America Calvinists aimed that the "religious community reclaim a sense of authority in an age of science." Overall, he suggests that "science had clearly joined the list of threats to Christian orthodoxy that included industrialism and professionalism" (Fehler 2005:140).

[89] Bendix (1970:95) comments that "we are all familiar with outside attacks of religious and political fundamentalists upon the inherent radicalism of free inquiry". Also, he suggests that "the liberal principle of academic freedom is a vantage point of considerable promise for sociological theory however precarious it may be politically. The scholarly responsibilities are consonant with a liberal position" (Bendix 1970:95).

of "ungodliness" and dissent. At least, this antagonism or suspicion to an Enlightenment-based value and institution reproduces Calvinist theocracy's cultural system as the model or exemplary counter-Enlightenment.

Moreover, academic freedom is a sort of supreme "evil" or enemy for Calvinist and any theocracies because of its fusion of "academic" or "intellectual", thus including knowledge and science, with "freedom", not just human liberty but that in generating and diffusing "ungodly" and "un-American" ideas and values, the true "forbidden apple". It is a sort of "double jeopardy" for this and other theocracies in that it expresses not one, but two elements of the Enlightenment. These elements are, first, rationalism, including intellectualism and scientism in the meaning of secular academic research, method, and knowledge, and second, liberalism understood as the principle and social system of universal human liberty. Conversely, academic freedom is a dual danger in that it supersedes and challenges both anti-rationalism, including anti-intellectualism and anti-scientism, and anti-liberalism as the rejection of the principle and system of liberty, as characteristic for Calvinist and other theocracies. Hence, Calvinist theocracy condemns, attacks, and ultimately destroys academic and all intellectual freedom on double grounds: first, because the latter is "academic" and "intellectual" manifesting cultural, notably scientific, rationalism, and second, because it is "freedom" expressing the liberal ideal and system.

At this point, the dual composite of anti-rationalism, notably anti-intellectualism and anti-scientism, and of anti-liberalism causes, sanctifies, and predicts such antagonism and nihilism to academic freedom in Calvinist and other theocracy. Simply, considering both human reason *and* liberty "ungodly", notably denouncing or distrusting free knowledge or science as a real or proxy "forbidden apple", leads to condemning and attacking academic freedom and converting the free intellectual world, including academia, into a metaphorical "Salem with scientists *cum* witches." Recall, Calvinist theocracy was part of what Mises (1957) identifies as revolt against both human reason and liberty represented by the Enlightenment or of religious conservatism's "mindless" war (Habermas 2001) against the latter and secular liberalism overall. Thus, its persistent attacks on academic freedom in America are the special effects, cases, or survivals of its overall revolt against human reason and liberty. This puts such Puritan and other fundamentalist attacks on academic freedom in America in a proper perspective, thus endows them with an inner logic of anti-rationalism and anti-liberalism, and makes and predicts them as a sort of "method in the madness", not as random and transient.

In consequence, Calvinist theocracy in America generates and perpetuates intellectual decay, a sort of "poverty of philosophy" in a broad sense. At most, it results in and sustains what Comte and Mill would call respectively social statics and a "stationary state" in intellectual (like artistic) culture, including secular science, knowledge, and education, in historical and modern America, at least its "Biblical Commonwealths" from New England to the evangelical South. Further, such a condition of stagnation assumes or approaches the image of Mises' expression the "peace of the cemetery", especially in the "Bible Garden" and its evangelical and pseudo-evangelical extensions (Montana, Idaho, Nebraska, Utah, etc.). Mises' expression is particularly applicable to the Southern and other "Bible Garden" on the account of being Mencken's cultural "Sahara desert" or a "nightmarish world" (as Utah is described by McCann 2000) in intellectual as well as artistic terms, plus to Iran, Saudi Arabia, and other Islamic theocracies.

In comparative terms, various observations suggest that intellectual, like artistic, culture is less advanced, dynamic, and rich in Puritan America than in most other Western societies. In a way, they indicate a sort of American Puritan-reproduced backwardness or exceptionalism in terms of intellectual, and even more artistic, culture, just as, often related, political democracy and progressive social policy (Amenta et al. 2001), a welfare state (Quadagno 1999), labor and similar human rights or industrial democracy (Flanagan 1999; Nickell 1997), and other respects. Recall, comparative sociological analyses identify Puritan America as a "deviant case" deviating far away from the global process of cultural, including scientific, rationalism, and liberalism and moving again toward religious irrationalism, traditionalism, and anti-liberalism during the late 20th and early 21st century (Inglehart and Baker 2000; Inglehart 2004). Predictably, they reveal it as the most salient and persisting deviation within modern Western culture and society (along with Catholic Ireland and especially Poland) and the world, together with Islamic theocracies or societies and other developing (e.g., Latin American) countries (Inglehart 2004; also Byrne[90] 1997). Moreover, on

---

[90] Byrne (1997:27–8) remarks that in "contemporary Western countries (with some exceptions such as the United States, Poland and Ireland) the arguments and debates of the state and the church overlap to a less significant degree than they did centuries or even decades ago and where religion plays a much reduced role in public life".

the account of such Puritan-induced deviation and backwardness in both intellectual and especially artistic culture, observers describe not complimentary contemporary America as "the last remaining primitive society" (Baudrillard 1999), at least among modern Western societies, primarily due to its Puritan and in extension Calvinist legacy.

In particular, analysts observe that, primarily because of its Puritan origins and legacies, today's America is deprived from—or for "reborn" anti-intellectual fundamentalists "blessed" by lacking—the "kind of intellectual scene" found in France and Europe[91] (Munch 2001). To that extent, this observation indicates some degree of under-development or stagnation of intellectual culture in Puritan America at least by comparison with the old, despised Europe. In turn, what Europe's "intellectual scene" is to that of America, the latter, excluding the "Bible Belt", is overall to those of Iran and other Islamic theocracies and societies (minus Turkey)—that is, more dynamic, advanced, richer, and freer. Yet, these and other "third-world" countries are not the references for comparison that Americans would like to, and most sociologists do, use, instead comparing, if ever, the country with the other parts of the Western world.

Further, this under-development of intellectual culture often escalates in or perpetuates a kind of Puritan-rooted (including "Wild West") anti-intellectualism that is unparalleled in scope and intensity among contemporary European and other Western societies (Australia, Canada,[92] etc.). It is a common observation, perception, and perhaps

---

[91] The *Economist* comments that Washington, DC "has traditionally been an unbalanced city when it comes to the life of the mind. It has great national monuments, from the Smithsonian museums to the Library of Congress. But day-to-day cultural life can be thin. It attracts some of the country's best brains. But far too much of the city's intellectual life is devoted to the minutiae of the political process. Dinner table conversation can all too easily turn to budget reconciliation or social security."

[92] Hiemstra (2005) suggests that neo-Calvinism, acts as the main anti-scientific and rationalist as well as anti-liberals force by opposing liberal education and liberalism overall in modern Canada, as during the post-war period. In his view, Canada's "liberals wanted churches to limit their focus to happiness in the next life and to stay out of public affairs [and] the state to focus on happiness in this world and to keep out of religious beliefs and ecclesiastical affairs (Hiemstra 2005:148–52), with schools generating and propagating "rational Enlightenment values as the means [of] progress", while Canadian Protestant churches were "polarized between moralistic Methodism and secularizing modernism." In turn, Neo-Calvinists, emigrating from Holland, promoted their "idiosyncratic ideas of Christian schooling" (plus politics, economics, and media), thus in "opposition to prevailing liberal and secular thinking" that religion is "private and limited to devotional practices", along with "neutral rational schooling" and public schools "were thus unsuitable for neo-Calvinists" (Hiemstra 2005:153–5). Hiemstra

stereotype, but probably not totally false, that Puritan America has historically been and still remains the most anti-intellectual or the least intellectual culture and society within the Western world and even beyond. And, it is this anti-intellectualism or minimal intellectualism—especially pervasive in American politics and civil society, and in part higher education and science—that ultimately causes and explains, just as reflects, why the "new nation" does not have the "kind of intellectual scene" existing in France and most other European societies, thus cultural backwardness or decay. On this account, Calvinist theocracy in America effectively operates as the most pervasive, persistent, and intense counter-Enlightenment among Western societies. Anti-intellectualism is the axiomatic antithesis of the Enlightenment as essentially a kind of intellectualism, and both the cause and syndrome of intellectual and other cultural decay overall.

Calvinist theocracy and Calvinism overall, including Puritanism, represents the ultimate counter-Enlightenment in particular on the account of anti-scientific antagonism, nihilism, and decay, as well as manipulation and abuse, in America. In essence, it does through its theocratic subversion and exploitation alike of science, knowledge, education, and technology for the glory of the "God of Calvinism" via totalitarian rule within society and "holy" war against other, "ungodly" and "evil" societies. In this respect, the Calvinist, like all religious, including Catholic and Islamic, counter-Enlightenment functions as a sort of return to the Dark Middle Ages, notably medieval theocracy in society and "holy" permanent wars against other societies.

In particular, Calvinist theocracy involves the Puritan manipulation[93] and exploitation of science, education and technology in America for theocratic and imperialistic purposes. It thus harnesses science,

---

(2005:156–7) that neo-Calvinists "retreated from public schools to develop independent schools" as "authentically Christian and free of inappropriate government direction and control" by turning down free public education in "favour of starting Christian schools", so that the "recurring emphasis of neo-Calvinist schools was to operate out of an integrally biblical perspective". Conversely, Neo-Calvinists "rejected the liberal idea of a state-dominated school system" as well as the "individualism central to the liberal idea of Canadian society" Hiemstra (2005:161–3). Hiemstra (2005:163) concludes that "since the neo-Calvinists believed that everyone operates out of one or another religiously defined world view, there is no recourse in public life to a common rational foundation as a basis for co-operation", thus implying anti-rationalism.

[93] For instance, like on previous occasions during the 2000s, in 2007 more than US 12,000 scientists signed a statement criticizing the neoconservative administration for "manipulating" climate science, specifically the theory and evidence of global warming, and various other sciences, including medicine, no less.

knowledge, education, and technology in the service of human subjugation and ultimately violent death, not, as it claims and most Americans believe, liberation and life. First, it places them in the service of the Divine design of America as a "Biblical Garden", as indicated by evolutionism, embryonic stem-cell research, climate science (global warming), critical social sciences, and virtually all other secular science (including medicine), knowledge, and education reduced and eventually sacrificed to the efficient means for higher causes. These include Parsons' "purposes of God" and theocracy through "Monkey Trials" as actual events and a generic metaphor for anti-scientism. Calvinist theocracy transforms science and knowledge into what Weber calls theodicy involving, in Parsons' words, an endeavor to "demonstrate the goodness of God",[94] and eventually a "high-tech" instrument of theocracy. In Parsons' words, in this theocracy, like others, scientific theories and facts are only important if they "demonstrate the goodness of God" and the "godliness" of Puritan theocratic rule and rulers.

Second, Calvinist theocracy puts science, knowledge, education, and technology in the function or service of a permanent holy war or crusade against what it construes as the "evil", "ungodly", and "unfree" world and the resulting first-ever "empire of liberty" (thus) as a sort of ultimate end of history. This is witnessed by sacrificing or harnessing and exploiting scientific and technological progress, including scientists themselves, for the "higher cause" of aggressive nationalism, militarism, and imperialism. In particular, such exploitation proceeds through the invention and actual or experimental use of ever-more advanced "high-tech" weapons of mass destruction, particularly "new generations" of and the threat of using nuclear arms (Schelling 2006). These are used or threatened to use against constantly reproduced "foreign enemies", in the manner of reproducing domestic "witches" or "un-American" persons, notably non-believers (Edgell et al. 2006), in a sectarian[95] or exclusionary (Symonds and Pudsey 2006) culture and society in the image of "Salem".

---

[94] Parsons (1967:6) admits that the function of science or the importance of scientific facts is not to "demonstrate the goodness of God" or theodicy, thus indirectly questioning or "controlling for" his "Puritan heritage".

[95] Following on Weber's views, Symonds and Pudsey (2006:137) state that "a much more limited form of brotherly love was developed within [Calvinism] when the idea of universal suffering was abandoned and boundaries for group membership were instead placed around proof of one's state of grace. This Protestant form of brotherliness might be termed "sect brotherliness, "as it is usually based on a requirement of care only for those "brothers" in the faith as against the universalism of the "church".

Calvinist theocracy in America hence transforms science, knowledge, and technology into the efficient instruments of global subjugation, military conquest, and imperial domination, rather than liberation, prosperity, and progress. It seeks to "export" domestic theocratic control and repression to the world, as done during the 1980s–2000s by "evangelical" US Presidents a la Reagan et al. (For a recent book is entitled "Evangelical President" with reference to the 2000–2008 incumbent.) Cynics may comment that "exporting" Puritan-rooted control, repression, and indoctrination ("brain washing") from America to the world as a whole by US "evangelical" Presidents and their "holy" wars and Hollywood movies has been the "most competitive" export of American Calvinist capitalism. They may add that this is so given the low competitiveness of most economic goods (cars, electronics, foods, etc.), as indicated by large trade deficits and the humiliating decline of the dollar (supposed to, yet failing in the long-run to, increase exports because they are just too uncompetitive by price-quality ratios in the global market) to what American expatriates and others experience as an almost worthless piece of paper[96] in the 2000s.

Given the potentially MAD outcome of "godly" militarism and imperialism, notably a "holy" war on the "evil" world involving "high-tech" nuclear weapons of mass destruction (Habermas 2001; Schelling 2006), this theocracy is likely to finally accomplish what no previous Calvinist and any theocracies and other totalitarian systems (Nazism, communism) have ever fully accomplished. Namely, it effectively converts science and technology not only from human creations into anti- and supra-human instruments, as do all theocracies. It perverts them as the means of humans' liberation and life into the lethal weapons of global self-destruction and death after the "intelligent design" or image of evangelical judgment-day annihilation *cum* salvation (Adorno 2001) via nuclear Armageddon or otherwise (e.g., opposing actions on global warming).

If this outcome eventually materializes, Puritan theocracy in America will be the first in human history to fulfill Calvinism's original and evangelicalism's eternal dream of destroying "ungodly" human civilization, and restoring, as Hume and Comte imply, "godly" barbarism and

---

[96] For instance, it was reported that even prostitutes in Brazil during 2008 would not accept dollars as a payment for their services, thus adding a sort of insult to the injury of the precipitous decline of the value of the dollar (though recovering somewhat in the second part of the year after years of sustaining decline).

primitivism *cum* Biblicism from the ashes of this nuclear or other judgment-day as the supposed new beginning of the coming of "God's Kingdom of Earth". Never mind that in the process it will likely also destroy the "new nation" and thus transforms the "Bible Garden" into "Biblical fire and flood" (by nuclear weapons perhaps combined with global warming). This is in perfect accordance with the expected MAD outcome of a theocratic "holy" war on the "evil" world by high-tech weapons of mass destruction like "nukes" in spite or because of the almost universal repulsion or taboo against using them. As regards the latter, some US analysts (Schelling 2006) suggest that the "widespread taboo against nuclear weapons and its inhibition on their use" is in the "American interest". Conversely, US neo-conservative government's proclamation of its "continued dependence" on nuclear weapons, including its Puritan self-righteous "readiness" for using them in "preemptive" strikes against "enemies", and its supposed need for "new" nuclear capacities and tests should be evaluated in view of the "corrosive effect on a nearly universal attitude [as] cultivated through universal abstinence of 60 years" (Schelling 2006).

On this account, the control and use of science and technology, notably nuclear and other high-tech weapons of mass destruction, by US "reborn" evangelicals and other conservatives (Eisenhower, Goldwater, Reagan et al.) pose an equivalent long-run risk to human civilization and survival as that by Islamic theocrats and terrorists, neo-Nazis and other neo-fascists, even admittedly greater as compared with "ungodly" defunct communism[97] (Schelling 2006). For instance, some analysts

---

[97] Schelling (2006:930) cites the following Eisenhower's statement: "In any combat where these things can be used on strictly military targets and for strictly military purposes, I see no reason why [nuclear weapons] shouldn't be used just exactly as you would use a bullet or anything else". Remarking that that "gases were not used" in WW II Schelling (2006:932) comments that Eisenhower's argument "could have applied: "In any combat where these gases can be used on strictly military targets and for strictly military purposes, I see no reason why they shouldn't be used just exactly as you would use a bullet or anything else." But as Supreme Commander of the Allied Expeditionary Forces, General Eisenhower, as far as we know, never proposed any such policy." Schelling (2006:932) infers that he (and his secretary of state) "urge[d] doing for nuclear weapons what Eisenhower apparently never thought of doing for gas in the European theater." In addition, Eisenhower's argument was adopted and even reinforced by US extreme neoconservatives like Goldwater and Reagan, as witnessed by their infamous plans or treats ("jokes"?) for using nuclear weapons against the "evil empire" of the Soviet Union. In turn, in Schelling's (2006:933) view, "that the Soviets had absorbed this nuclear inhibition was dramatically demonstrated during their protracted campaign in Afghanistan. I never read or heard public discussion about the possibility that the Soviet Union might shatter the tradition of nonuse to avoid a costly and humiliating

suggest that US ruling conservatives (the Eisenhower administration) during the 1950s seriously contemplated engaging in a nuclear war (against China and the Soviet Union) and thus potentially generating a MAD outcome for America itself (at least in the second case) in the belief that "somehow or other we must manage to remove the taboo from the use of these weapons" (cited in Schelling 2006). Most US "reborn" evangelicals or neo-conservatives have overtly or covertly persisted in seeking to remove the taboo, exemplified by Goldwater's admittedly "mad" plans or treats, Reagan's infamous public "jokes", and another President's "not rule out" statements about using nuclear weapons against the "evil empire" and the "axis of evil" during the Cold War and the "war on terror", respectively. For instance, the neo-conservative "godly" US Senate rejected (in 1999), with a Puritan-style self-righteousness and its aggressive nationalism and disdain for international rules and obligations, the Comprehensive Test Ban Treaty, ratified by almost 200 countries, in spite or perhaps because of its potential for enhancing the "nearly universal revulsion against nuclear weapons" (Schelling 2006).

In a way, their control and use of science and technology, notably nuclear weapons, pose the ultimate risk, because Puritan evangelicals once in power typically become or act as what Keynes calls "madmen in authority". The latter generates the equivalent risk for human society, including America itself as the "Bible Garden", of putting science and technology, including (but not confined to) nuclear and other high-teach weapons of mass destruction, in their control. And, this Puritan "madness in authority" is not only due to Acton's law of absolutely corrupting and eventually "mad" (Bourdieu 2000) absolute power, as in the case of "not so godly" Nazism and other non-theocratic totalitarianism (e.g., "ungodly" communism) as well. It is also due to what Hume identified and emphasized as Puritan "wretched fanaticism" in religious terms, just like in the case of medieval Catholic and past and present Islamic and other typically fanatical theocrats.

---

defeat in that primitive country" in contrast to Eisenhower and other US conservatives. Further, he comments that "not many of us in the 1950s or 1960s would have thought that were the Soviet Union to engage in war, and lose a war, in Afghanistan it would behave there as if nuclear weapons did not exist. We can be grateful to them for behaving that way in Afghanistan, adding one more to the list of bloody wars in which nuclear weapons were not used" (Schelling 2006:934).

The above indicates the "double jeopardy" and generally the "clear and present danger" of science and technology, notably high-tech weapons of mass destruction, being controlled and used by US Puritan evangelicals. Their duality of political power and religious fanaticism tends to make them dual "madmen in authority" or "double agents" of a nihilistic MAD outcome in the form or image of nuclear (perhaps mixed with global-warming) judgment-day Armageddon. This evangelical (like Islamic) duality of "mad" political power and religious fanaticism and the resulting nihilistic control and abuse of science and technology, notably "high-tech" weapons, can be underestimated or "forgotten" only at one's own peril, virtually never with impunity. This is what "witches", "ungodly", and other "un-American" persons found for themselves in Puritan America, from Salem through "Monkey Trials" to McCarthyism and culture wars, let alone foreign "infidels" and "enemies" in a sequence from Native Americans to the "axis of evil".

In sum, Calvinist theocracy in America reduces intellectual culture in the form of science, knowledge, education, and technology to the instruments of, first, theodicy *cum* demonstrating God's "goodness" and "purposes", and of divinely ordained theocracy, second, of militarism and imperialism via a "holy" war against the "ungodly" world and imperial dominance. To that extent, this, like any, theocracy effectively ends intellectual culture, notably science, as one has known it since the Enlightenment and before (ancient Greece and Rome), thus acting as anti-scientific "terminator". Simply, the tools of rational science and technology when given to or seized by US Puritan theocracy become irrational gadgets, notably self-destructive weapons, thus actually

Table 6.2. Attributes of the cultural system of Calvinist theocracy—anti-rationalist culture

*Counter-enlightenment*
   Historical opposition to and assault on the Enlightenment as an intellectual movement
   Continual hostility and wars against Enlightenment-based intellectualism and rationalism
   Indicators of counter-Enlightenment
     religious and cultural intolerance
     cultural anti-rationalism, including anti-intellectualism
     anti-scientific nihilism

CULTURAL SYSTEM OF CALVINIST BIBLIOCRACY         495

destroyed or perverted, as if they were placed in what Pareto calls a "cage for the insane" driven in this case by the "madness" of absolute political power *and* religious fanaticism.

As a corollary of anti-scientific nihilism, then intellectual anti-culture in the sense of the counter-Enlightenment becomes the intellectual or philosophical aspect of America's "destiny" in Calvinist theocracy. Consequently, it is America's Calvinist intellectual "destiny", or anti-intellectual "adverse fate" in view of the original and persistent anti-intellectualism, including theocratic "no science is better than secular science" anti-scientism, in the "Puritan nation". (The counter-Enlightenment attributes of the cultural system of Calvinist theocracy are summarized in Table 6.2.)

CHAPTER SEVEN

CALVINISM RECONSIDERED

*Reconsidering Calvinism*

A fuller sociological reconsideration of Calvinism is in order to better understand Tocqueville's Puritan "destiny" of America. It is also so for better understanding America's genesis and past, at least in conventional wisdom, especially conservative reconstructions of the history of the "new nation" (Seaton 2006), favoring Calvinist to other Protestant, including Anglican, "Pilgrims" (in the sense of settlers) and settlements, not to mention their prior and later Catholic counterparts.

In a sense, the thesis of America's Calvinist-as-Puritan "destiny" stands or falls with the argument and demonstration that Puritanism constitutes and functions as the offspring or subtype of Calvinism in particular, not just, as commonly viewed, of Protestantism in general. In other words, Tocqueville's implied equation[1] (Alexander 1998) of America's "destiny" with its Calvinist social predestination through its Puritan over-determination hinges on what Weber suggests as the substantive equivalence and Sombart as a kind of tautological identity between Puritanism and Calvinism. Perhaps for many Americans, especially US religious conservatives, it is more disputable and implausible to consider Puritanism to be Calvinism sociologically and theologically (plus geographically) emigrating from the "old" to the "new world" via England than considering America to be Tocqueville's "puritanical nation", with a Puritan "destiny", path-dependence, or heritage. The latter is more or less established in the sociological literature (Inglehart 2004; Lipset 1996; Munch 2001) and celebrated in America, notably by conservatism.

This necessitates and warrants to "rediscover" and reconsider what Tocqueville (just as Weber and Sombart) probably considered paradigmatic or axiomatic and was likely well-known to his first Puritans and

---

[1] This term is used by analogy to "Weber's equation of the spirit of capitalism with 17th and 18th century English entrepreneurs [yet] widely disputed" (Alexander 1998:171).

early Calvinists, but somewhat obscured, ignored, and negated by their descendants, including their liberal admirers (e.g., Hartz 1963). This is the intimate relationship of "all-American" Puritanism, consequently America's Puritan "destiny", to European Calvinism in comparative and historical perspective. This is a sociological "rediscovery" or reconsideration of Calvinism and Puritanism. It is a reanalysis of their nature, structure, and operation as social phenomena, rather than a historical account, as their history is well-known and its details beyond the scope of this work, or better than their sociology ("iron law"). In short, it is an attempt at and a contribution to the comparative sociology, not the history, of Calvinism and Puritanism.

Recall, Calvinism originated as French Protestantism or France's Reformation during the mid and late 16th century initially following, and yet increasingly differing from, its original Lutheran form (Elwood 1999; Foerster 1962; Heller 1986; Hsia and Nierop 2002; Mentzer 2007; Nischan 1994). Thus, Jean (not John) Calvin was the "French Protestant Reformer" (Foerster 1962) later moving to exile in Geneva during the early and mid 16th century. In turn, Puritanism was English-American Calvinism, or Calvinist, as distinguished from and usually opposed to Lutheran, Anglican, and other, Protestantism spreading from Europe, specifically France, to and then dominating in England temporarily and America enduringly. In short, Puritanism was, as Weber and Mises put it, an "Anglo-Saxon" extension of European Calvinism in England and America (Dahrendorf 1959).

*From Calvinism to Puritanism and Back*

In essence, Puritanism originated, functioned, and remained through its various survivals and revivals as English-American Calvinism, or Calvinist, as distinguished from Lutheran, Anglican, and other, Protestantism moving from Europe to and operating in England and notably America. In particular, Puritanism in colonial America, especially in New England was "early American Calvinism" (German 1995), and conversely, the second was (named) the first.

For illustration, Weber considers and describes Puritanism as the "Calvinistic movement in England" initially and transiently and in America subsequently and enduringly. Contemporary analysts echo Weber observing that Puritanism was the "English Calvinist dissenting" movement arising within, yet rebelling against, officially established Anglicanism, purporting to "purify" the Anglican Church along the "Reformed" lines of Calvinism (Sprunger 1982). In this account, a "balanced combination of doctrinal Calvinist theology" (including Calvin's theodicy *cum* Divine omnipotence and absolute transcendence), notably the doctrine of predestination, with "intense personal piety" provided the "essence" of Puritanism. Especially, Weber identifies and emphasizes the "role of a particular interpretation of Calvinism" for early English and American capitalists (Dahrendorf 1959) under the "new" name of Puritanism, as exemplified by Franklin, due to his "strict Calvinistic father", described as one of the "great men of Puritanism."

In this sense, Weber and other sociologists establish a sort of substantive equivalence of Calvinism and Puritanism. The first was evidently the original or the whole, and the second the derivative, if not the "carbon-copy", or the part, with some formal secondary differences mostly around historical, geographical, and personal rather than crucial sociological (and theological) lines, as the matter of degree and quantity, not substance and quality (see Appendix). Curiously, US Puritan-inspired, usually nativist religious conservatives establish or imply such a Calvinist-Puritan substantive equivalence. Arguably, America's founding values and social institutions were shaped by Calvinism in the derivative form of Puritanism as the "dominant political and intellectual force" during colonial and revolutionary times (Dunn and Woodard 1996), though most of US conservatives invidiously treat the second as "all-American", "native", or "original".

Moreover, Weber's colleague Sombart states that Calvinism "is only Puritanism" and conversely, thus establishing a kind of equation or tautological identity between the two. In turn, Weber, like Hume and Mill, not to mention Calvin himself, may object that it is more historically accurate to state that Puritanism "is only Calvinism", given that the latter preceded and ramified or evolved in the former in certain settings beyond its point of origin in Europe. This holds true, unless "Puritanism" in Sombart's statement is, as frequently, understood in the general meaning of "purism"—"pure" church and purist asceticism, or moral absolutism, austerity, and restraint—characterizing virtually all world religions and churches (Bell 1977; Sorokin 1970), preceding Calvinism as well as Protestantism and Christianity. It is in this sense that Puritanism was and remained, as Mises (1966) echoing Weber puts it, "Anglo-Saxon", the English-American species or derivative specifically of European Calvinism, not just Protestantism and Christianity. At this juncture, Puritanism emerged and remained as "only" Calvinist in Sombart-Weber's sense in that, as contemporary sociologists suggest, Calvinism fulfilled the "same sociological function" for Anglo-Saxon societies (McLaughlin 1996) as did Lutheranism and Protestantism overall (as well as fascism) in European societies, including Germany. Thus, the uncertainty and anxiety of predestination *cum* election or damnation—whether one is of the elect versus the damned—directed the "development of Calvinism after Calvin in a Puritan direction" (Birnbaum 1953) in Anglo-Saxon societies.

At the minimum, Puritanism, even if, as its adherents and descendents claim or imply, not being "only" Calvinism in Sombart's sense, was more influenced, inspired, and shaped by the latter than was by Lutheranism and in extension the latter's substitute in England, Anglicanism (though it arose and initially functioned within the Anglican Church that it eventually attacked and temporarily supplanted, just as it deposed the Monarchy, via the 1640s Puritan Revolution). Thus, a sociological analysis indicates that "Puritan sects and denominations" in England and America followed Calvinism rather than Lutheranism in seeking a "truly reciprocal penetration of religious ethics and the world" (Munch 1981) by mastering the latter, and in other respects.

To return to Tocqueville and emphasize—given most Americans' likely unawareness and many US nativist conservatives' denial or disguise of—what he did not state but certainly knew well. This was the fact that his first Puritans were the English-American members of a global network, the "brothers" within an international brotherhood, the "children" of an extended family of Calvinists in the post-Reformation Western world. Simply, they were Calvinist, not just any, Protestants moving to and acting in England and America from Europe as their original home, in the sense not only of geography or emigration. They were also and more relevantly in the sense of sociology or social ideals, practices and institutions, as well as of theology (religious doctrine, belief, and organization). In sum, Puritans in both England and America were born and raised as Weber's strict Calvinists or "Calvinist Puritans", distinguished from the non-Calvinist, such as, in his words, the "Pharisees (i.e., Puritans)" (also, Sorkin 2005).

A case in point involved Puritan Presbyterians described as "Scottish Calvinists", just as Huguenots were the French embodiments of Calvinism and thus their precedents.[2] Also, English Puritans were basically Calvinists at least in virtue of what Hume significantly

---

[2] However, according to Weber, "the Scottish nobility, like the British and the French, completely dropped out from the Calvinist religion in which it had originally played a considerable role."

identified as their "communication with Calvin, and the other reformers who followed the discipline and worship of Geneva", noting, and thus anticipating Weber, that Calvinist Huguenots "so much resembled the Puritans in discipline and worship, in religion and politics".[3] Specifically, Hume considered and described the latter as sectarian Calvinists (the "sect of Puritans") by observing that these "sectaries were [so] called on account of their pretending to a superior purity of worship and discipline", and yet "whose principles appear so frivolous, and habits so ridiculous," thus followed mostly by "persons of weak understandings [sic!]."

Hume might have commented that such Puritans claims to religious and moral "purity" or "pure church" were as credible or serious, and conversely frivolous or ludicrous, as those to "perfection." In a way, "Puritanism" or "Puritans" as a name or claim is a functional equivalent of "Perfectionism" or "Perfectionists," evidently alongside what Keynes calls "purism". This is what Weber implies by describing "Puritanism" as a "highly ambiguous word" for an "ascetic movement" within Calvinism and Protestantism. Counterfactually, if "Puritanism" or "Puritans" were instead designated "Perfectionism" or "Perfectionists", not many even then would, just as do now, take such designations and claims seriously and subjected them to mild reprobation or ridicule. For, as Calvinists are the first to contend or admit, no humans are, but only the "God of Calvinism", perfect and in that sense "pure" in moral and any sense. Yet, by appropriating the term "Puritanism" or "Puritans" they contradicted their own denial of perfection and "purity" to humans, overlooking that no human is perfect and "pure", thus sounding pretentious, if not ridiculous, at least to Hume and non-Puritans as he implies by the word Puritan "pretensions". Still, "Puritanism" or "Puritans" for long took itself or themselves and even were taken by many others as credible and serious in their claims to moral purity (and "pure church") and perfection. And, when these claims turned out to be impossible "pretensions" and even, as Hume and Weber suggest, mere hypocrisies, "Puritanism" or "Puritans" ceased to be taken seriously even by itself or themselves and became a sort of extinct species as a name, though not as an idea and legacy perpetuated or revived in American fundamentalist Protestantism. This helps to explain why even in America,

---

[3] Hume adds that the "Puritanical sect had indeed gone so far, that a book of discipline was secretly subscribed by above five hundred clergymen; and the Presbyterian government thereby established in the midst of the church."

including New England, no "Puritanism" and "Puritans" exist anymore. To claim or self-designate "Puritanism" or "Puritans" is equivalent to claiming or self-designating "Perfectionism" or "Perfectionists", "Purism" and "Purists", having zero or minimal credibility and seriousness. In Weber's words, these claims are as (in)credible as the claim of the Pharisees, a claimed "aristocracy with respect to salvation which stood in contrast to the godless Jews", to be "Puritans"—as proto-typical hypocrisy. In this sense, his equation "the Pharisees (i.e., [non-Calvinist] Puritans)" can be restated as the Calvinist "Puritans, that is, Pharisees."

In general, Puritanism in England and America comprised "various cross-currents of though and opinion", but crucially all these multiple Puritanisms were "generally Calvinist in tone" and had a "certain continuity" since the late 16th and early 17th century[4] (Kearney 1965). Thus, the earliest Puritans were simply "Puritanical English Calvinists" arising and acting within the "larger structure of the Church of England" and whose ideological loyalty was primarily devoted to the "international Calvinist movement" (Sprunger 1982). Similarly, Tocqueville's first and later American Puritans were "Calvinists" (Bremer 1995), notably "stodgy Orthodox Calvinists" (Gould 1996) reflecting the nature of Puritanism in America as "early American Calvinism" (German 1995). Notably, Calvinism admittedly was at "the core of New England Puritanism" (Bremer 1995) in theological and sociological terms, or religious doctrines and beliefs and social institutions and practices, alike.

The above indicates that Puritanism was not only "iron" (Tawney 1962) Protestantism, and Puritans the "hotter sort" of Protestants (Gorski 2000), as usually considered, which is an imprecise, overly general definition for the present analysis. Further, Puritanism was specifically Calvinism, and Puritans were Calvinists, moving geographically or sociologically from Europe to and operating and dominating in England temporarily and America enduringly. This holds true of Puritanism, just as by analogy Calvinism and Calvinists are not just any but, as self-defined particular, notably radical, Protestantism and Protestants, the second form and embodiments of the Protestant

---

[4] Kearney (1965:107) specifies Puritanism's "continuity" or "growing circle of discontent both within and without the Established [Anglican] Church from the 1560s onwards" to Cromwell's times (the 1640–60s) and later on, including by implication Methodism as a Puritan revival in adverse reaction to the Enlightenment and liberalism overall during the late 18th century.

Reformation and Reformers carried to its "final" stage and realization via Calvin's Reformed Church. In England and America a "uniquely Anglo-American variety of Calvinist Puritanism" (Hudson and Coukos 2005) epitomizes European Calvinism and hence what Weber calls ascetic Protestantism, in contrast to its non-ascetic branches, Lutheranism and Anglicanism.

In particular, Puritanism is considered sectarian Calvinism and Protestantism overall, or Calvinist and generally Protestant sectarianism. This is what Weber implies observing that "only one" of "ascetic" Protestant groups is "not a sect, but a church in the sociological meaning" of a religious, hierocratic institution, Calvinism, as does Comte[5] though not explicitly distinguishing the latter and Puritanism. In Weber's view, Puritanism as a sect "adheres to the ideal of the *pure ecclesia* (hence the name 'Puritans'), the *visible* community of saints, from whose midst the black sheep are removed so that they will not offend God's eyes". (*Pure ecclesia* indicates that nevertheless Puritanism continues to claim or, as Hume would say, pretend to be a "pure church" rather than a sect.) Notably, he observes that Puritan sects' "major domicile" was and remains America, initially New England (Munch 1981). Also, recall his observation that in America's Puritan sects the "intensity of indoctrination and the impact of exclusion are much more effective than any authoritarian ecclesiastic discipline," thus by implication Calvinism (and Catholicism and Orthodox Christianity) as "church". This reaffirms that American Puritanism was hyper-Calvinism in this and virtually all respects.

At this juncture, it is not precise enough to consider Puritanism as what Weber himself calls Protestant sectarianism (Lipset 1996) or sectarian Protestantism, as usually done, but to specify this Puritan attribute of "sect" or an exclusive group of belief and morality, in relation to Calvinism as "church" or religious institution. As sociological analyses suggest, "Puritan sects" emerged and existed "only in Calvinism" (Munch 1981), and not within Lutheranism and other non-Calvinist Protestantism (despite their subversive rise and existence within Anglicanism temporarily deposed and almost destroyed by them

---

[5] Comte refers to "primitive Protestantism" or Lutheranism and by implication Calvinism in contrast to its "more advanced sects", thus implicitly Puritanism via explicitly Presbyterianism. In another interpretation, he classifies even Calvinism under these "advanced sects" by distinguishing Lutheranism thus understood (and Episcopalism) from the "Presbyterian or Calvinist" branches of Protestantism.

in England and America, especially the "old" South). Specifically, it was only or primarily French Calvinism, but not German Lutheranism, as the Second and First Protestant Reformation respectively, that resulted in "Puritan sectarianism" in England and then America (Heller 1986).

## *Calvinism's Genesis Revisited*

If Puritanism is essentially English-American sectarian Calvinism, then understanding fully the second and its genesis, nature and effects helps understand and explain the first, thus America's Puritan "destiny" or legacy. And conversely, it is difficult to fully comprehend and account for the latter without taking account of these Calvinist origins or connections, as some US religious conservatives (e.g., Dunn and Woodard 1996) implicitly admit (but do not analyze or elaborate).

As regards its genesis, it is instructive to acknowledge and remember that Calvinism was conceived and originated as French Protestantism or France's Reformation during the early 16th century (Elwood 1999; Garrard 2003; Heller 1986; Mentzer 2007) initially following, and yet increasingly differing from and opposing, even in Germany itself (Nischan 1994), its original Lutheran version. In geographic terms, Calvinism was originally Protestantism or the Reformed Church "born in France" in contrast and eventual contradiction with Lutheranism as "produced" in Germany. If instead of Anglicanism attacked, as Hume describes in vivid details, by Puritans as retaining many Catholic ("Roman") ideas and practices, Puritanism was the "true English Reformation" (Tawney 1962) or religious Revolution (Goldstone 1986; Gorski 2000), especially during the early 17th century, then Calvinism was so for France and later the French-speaking cantons of Switzerland like Geneva for the most of the 16th century. In this respect, the "true English Reformation", including the 1640s actual Puritan Revolution, was Act II or a sequel of the Calvinist Reformation in France a century or so before (the 1530s), not of the Lutheran Reformation in Germany instead paralleled or evoked by Anglicanism. Conversely, Calvinism in genesis and action was Act I of or prelude to the birth and revolt of Puritanism. In sum, initially Calvinism was the "French Reformation" (Heller 1986) and later became the "Genevan creed" (Nischan 1994), following Calvin's exile from France to Swiss Geneva, hence transformed into the paramount "Calvinist city" (Byrne 1997) from the early 16th century.

Hence, in revisiting and condensing the historical genesis and development of Calvinism the following sociological and other moments are particularly salient for the present analysis and the comparative sociology of Calvinist-Puritan Protestantism. First and foremost, the "emergence of French Calvinism" (Heller 1986) signaled 16th century France's Protestant Reformation by definition or axiomatically, yet often obscured, blurred, or "forgotten", especially by non-French analysts and others, including even Weber himself and other German sociologists or historians, for a variety of religious, political, and related (e.g., nationalist) reasons. Curiously, Weber and many other German authors hardly ever mention that Calvinism was France's Protestantism or Reformation, just as Lutheranism was Germany's, and that Calvin was French, but invoke Switzerland or Geneva. This is unsurprisingly given the ever-increasing nationalism, seemingly infecting even such seminal social scientists, in Germany before and after WW I, as implied and even witnessed by Parsons. Yet, in (not) doing so, they leave the false impression to uninformed readers as if Calvinism was Switzerland's Protestantism or Reformation and Calvin "Genevan", and perhaps by implication "almost" German like (but less than) Lutheranism and Luther, as do, for that matter, their English-American counterparts by renaming Calvin from "Jean" into "John" (a common tendency to give English names to non-English persons). Needless to say, they both overlook or forget that Calvin was writing in French as well as Latin, born in a small obscure town in France, Noyon, as well as went to exile in French-speaking Geneva in Switzerland. But such are apparently the "perversities" of nationalism or patriotism and ethnocentrism overall for what Weber himself classically advocated to be value-free, including by implication non-nationalist, sociology and other social science.

For instance, the history of Calvinism starts with its "genesis in seven provincial centres" (Heller 1986) in France during the 1530s, in addition to and association with Swiss Geneva later on, following Calvin's exile. This may be redundant to state for most readers, but when reading the existing sociological and other literature since Weber the impression is as if Calvinism and Calvin were anything but the "French" Protestant Reformation and "reformer" (e.g., "Swiss", "German", "Dutch", and even as "John" "English" or "American"?).

As a corollary, Calvinism operated as the "Second" and, as it claimed, "true" and "final" Protestant Reformation in France and beyond, including, as it attempted and failed in, Germany (Nischan 1994), initially building on and eventually deviating from and even assaulting and displacing the First Lutheran version, as in Geneva, Holland, and in part Prussia (Gorski 2003). In Comte's words, Calvinism emerged as "more advanced", as distinguished from and opposed to Lutheranism as "primitive", Protestantism in historical, though not necessarily theological as well as sociological, terms. In particular, ironically French Calvinism arose and acted as "a more militant Protestant movement" (Heller 1986) than had Lutheranism before and cognate early and contemporaneous Protestantism in Europe, including Germany (Nischan 1994), Holland (Hsia and Nierop 2002) and, through Anglicanism, England (Gorski 2000).

Third, originally the Calvinist "Second" Protestant Reformation was as, and perhaps even more, dominated and shaped by a "great" historical personality as had been the Lutheran First Reformation and, if Weber is correct, virtually all religious movements in history founded and ruled by charismatic leaders and prophets (e.g., Buddha, Christ, Mohammed) or charisma as the "authoritarian principle" of legitimation of power in contrast to legal-rational authority in liberal-democratic or secular societies (Lenski 1994). This is what also even Calvinist-born Rousseau[6] implies in his description of Calvin as "undoubtedly a great man", yet "in the end [only] a man, and what is worse, a theologian", with "all the pride of a genius who feels his superiority" over humans (also, Byrne 1997; Garrard 2003).

Thus, Calvin, born and raised, of all places, in a small, obscure provincial town in France, less than 100 km north of (less than 1 hour by train from) of Paris (Noyon,[7] population of about 14,000 in 2008), initiated or contributed to the "development of French Protestantism"

---

[6] Garrard (2003) emphasizes Rousseau's "Calvinist background in Geneva", with its "strong tradition" of Rousseau-style civil religion or what himself called and extolled as "a kind of Theocracy". For example, Rousseau extolled the "rough Spartan manliness of Geneva" and even praised its Calvinists *cum* Spartans for "wisely" banning the modern theater (Garrard 2003). In this view, Sparta provided Rousseau "with his political ideal", who urged that Calvin's Genevans "should follow the example of the authoritarian Spartans rather than the democratic Athenians" (Garrard 2003:112). In a curious episode, Rousseau "was outraged; he feared that the theater would debase the morals of his innocent compatriots and that Voltaire 'would cause a revolution'" in Geneva glorified as the "anti-Paris" (Garrard 2003:113-4). And yet, his own beloved and glorified Calvinist city "banned and burned both *The Social Contract* and *Emile*, which caused Rousseau to renounce his "Genevan citizenship 'forever'" (Garrard 2003:114).

[7] The house in Noyon in which Calvin was born has become and remains "Musée Jean Calvin."

from the 1530s such that his influence was prominent even before his 1536 exile from France to French-speaking Geneva, by establishing an "extensive network of personal ties" in his hometown and beyond, including Paris and (old) Orleans (Heller 1986). Moreover, reportedly from the 1540s Calvin succeeded not just to "master the popular reformation in France" but also to transform it into the "basis of an effective religious and political movement". In this account, through his "intellectual and political leadership", Calvin developed and expanded nascent French Protestantism from a "subterranean and fragmented movement of reformation" into a "cohesive force" posing a serious challenge to the established "ecclesiastical and political order"[8] (Heller 1986). For instance, by 1545 Calvin established his charismatic, authoritarian "leadership of the evangelical movement in France as well as elsewhere" acting as the "head of the French Reformation" and beyond by "force of his example", his "organizing powers", and the "clarity of his theological teaching" (Heller 1986).

Calvin thereby objectively prefigured or anticipated and likely subjectively influenced or inspired what Weber calls the "great men of Puritanism", charismatic or not, including, on his list, Baxter, Milton, Cromwell, and Wesley in England, and Winthrop, Franklin and (implicitly) others (e.g., Adams, Ames, Davenport, etc., cf., Baldwin 2006; Davis 2005; Dunn and Woodard 1996) in America. In sum, Calvin reinvented and redirected French Protestantism in a definite, increasingly non-Lutheran ("non-primitive" in Comte's word) direction to develop into what has come to be termed after his name as "Calvinism" or the "Reformed Church" in Europe and then England (and Scotland) and America, though usually renamed as "Puritanism".

Fourth, Calvinism's social-economic, specifically class, bases, and appeals initially were varied, ranging from aristocratic to low middle classes, while gradually, as seen, the aristocracy became a dominant group, especially in 16th century France. Thus, historical research indicates that Calvin's theology (including his theodicy of Divine omnipotence), with its blend of rigid social-political "conservatism" and "ecclesiastical radicalism" appealed to low-middle classes and aristocrats (craftsmen and notables), the result being the "union of the mass of evangelical artisans with the Protestant elite" (Heller 1986) exerting

---

[8] Heller (1986:111) adds that "from exile in Geneva, Calvin was able gradually to gain moral and intellectual ascendancy over the French Reformation".

dominance. As regards the second class, Weber observes that the French, Scottish, and English nobility "originally played a considerable role" in the rise and expansion of Calvinism (but he hardly ever mentions its genesis in France), though it subsequently, as since the 17th century, "completely dropped out" from it. Thus, Weber implies that Calvinism consequently became mostly a bourgeois or capitalist movement, just as it did via Puritanism in England and America (Dahrendorf 1959; German 1995; Moore 1993).

Historical research also indicates that, in part contradicting Weber, in France Calvinism's social-class bases while "overlapping" did not "fit exactly" modern capitalism, in virtue of its appealing more to "skilled petty producers" with their "violently hostile" anti-capitalist outlook than to capitalists, though making certain concessions" to the capitalist economy[9] (Heller 1986). Moreover, in this view, Calvinism in France turned out to be an "abortive bourgeois movement" or revolution because its material basis or mode of production was "only partially" differentiated from feudalism (Heller 1986), thus what Weber would call "economic traditionalism", as during the 16th century and even later (Grossman 2006). And, recall that this economic backwardness or weakness found its political expression in Calvinism's subordination to the aristocracy in France, and yet in "complete accord with Calvin's belief in the inviolability of the secular order" (Heller 1986), including medieval-style theocratic tyranny and feudal servitude.

In sum, Calvinism's genesis was, first, as French Protestantism during the 16th century; second, as a corollary, as the "Second" Protestant Reformation; third, founded and dominated by a Weberian (pseudo-)charismatic authoritarian religious leader; and fourth, socially based on and appealing initially to social groups like aristocratic and low-middle classes, while being eventually dominated by the aristocracy, as before the 17th century. And, following Calvin's death in exile in Geneva, Calvinism from France expanded to parts of Western Europe (Holland, Prussia), and then beyond to England and America among "English-speaking people" (Sprunger 1982) to be renamed as "Puritanism", where in literally all cases and respects it proved more influential and successful, even triumphant, than in his French homeland.

---

[9] In Heller's (1986:255) view, artisans in particular established the "anti-feudal character of early French Calvinism alongside Puritan sectarianism" in England, yet subsequently (willingly) subjected to the dominance of the feudal nobility.

## The Dual Story of Calvinism: From an Abysmal Failure in the "Old World" to a Fateful Triumph in the "New Nation"

Calvinism eventually failed to attain its Weberian mastery of the world in its native land France and most of Europe, excluding, alongside the town of Geneva (Garrard 2003; Mansbach 2006), in part Holland (Munch 1981; Hsia and Nierop 2002; Sprunger 1982; Tubergen et al. 2005) and Germany, more specifically and temporarily Prussia (Billings and Scott 1994; Gorski 2003) or Brandenburg (Nischan 1994). And yet, it became victorious and successful overall in the form of Puritanism in initially non-Calvinist settings like England albeit partly and transiently, and above all in America almost totally and enduringly attaining its virtually total and permanent mastery of the world or society from the 17th to the early 21st century (with some qualifications).

This is a well-established historical moment for most readers. Yet, what is sociologically relevant is that Calvinism failed in the old world where it originated, notably in its homeland, for the substantively identical societal reasons it succeeded and triumphed (Davis 2005; German 1995; Seaton 2006) in the "new nation", just as partly and temporarily in England. The principal (though not exclusive) societal reason for this duality of a European failure and an American triumph (German 1995) was Calvinism's theological design and social system of medieval-style theocracy, specifically what Weber identifies as Calvinist Bibliocracy. The following elaborates on and substantiates this crucial sociological point in a comparative-historical context, but is not another history of the commonly known "rise and fall"—or rather conversely—of Calvinism in France and Europe and via Puritanism in England and America.

In general, Calvinism proved abortive or a failure in its homeland, France, in contrast to Lutheranism and its victory or success in (most of) Germany[10] (Foucault 1996), in one of those rare and striking cases of religious movements and leaders or prophets failing in their own home (thus confirming an ancient Roman adage), while succeeding or triumphing beyond. First and foremost, as initially French Protestantism or the "Second" Reformation in France, Calvinism suffered a failure to attain its total mastery of the world in a sociological sense of "mundane

---

[10] Foucault (1996:389) suggests that the Protestant Reformation in general "did not have in France the fullness and success it knew in Germany".

affairs" or establish its religious and societal dominance in its homeland, including Calvin's own obscure provincial hometown near Paris. In short, Calvin's own "Reformed Church" failed to substantively and enduringly, as distinguished from formally and transiently, "reform" France in theological and sociological, religious and secular, terms. Recall historical research indicates that Calvinism in France during the 16th century proved to be an "abortive" religious and societal reform or rather revolution due to being "economically and politically immature" (Heller 1986), or backward and even irrational (Grossman 2006), specifically (based on) a sort of late or post-feudalism rather than modern Weberian capitalism, political liberalism, and secularism.

In political terms, this implies that Calvinism was "abortive" and "immature" because it was deeply imbed in and inspired by pre-liberal, pre-democratic medievalism (Eisenstadt 1965), crucially the medieval *respublica Christiana* (Nischan 1994) as the ideal, rather than, as often assumed, ushering in liberal-democratic modernity. In sum, Calvinism failed in France because it attempted to restore the Dark Middle Ages by reestablishing and "purifying" the medieval theocracy *cum* "godly society", and not to usher in or herald the liberal-secular Enlightenment (Artz 1998; Byrne 1997; Garrard 2003).

As comparative sociological analyses suggest, originally the Calvinist (just as Lutheran) Reformation instead of being a liberal-democratic and modernizing movement operated as the exact opposite seeking to reestablish a "purer" medieval societal and religious system (Eisenstadt 1965). This thus expressed Calvinism's basic sociological continuity with medievalism and its theocracy and in part theology[11] (VanDrunen 2006). To that extent, Calvinism originated and acted as an anti-liberal and anti-modern phenomenon in virtue of, as even Weber concedes, being "directly hostile" to modernity or "the whole aspect of modern life". This included modern liberalism and hence, given that the latter is, as Mannheim puts it, inherently rationalistic due to the Enlightenment, rationalism or rationalization (Grossman 2006). Notably, Calvinism did so on the account of its Spartan-style austere or

---

[11] VanDrunen (2006:144) suggests that "there was considerable continuity between the Reformers and their medieval predecessors regarding natural law", as they both "coordinated natural law and Biblical morality." In particular, following his medieval predecessors, Calvin reaffirmed their "identification of the Decalogue as a summary of the natural law and it became standard fare in later Reformed theology" (VanDrunen (2006:156).

ascetic (Garrard 2003) and disciplinary, thus repressive and authoritarian, revolutions (Gorski 2003; Loveman 2005).

Specifically, Calvinism developed as anti-modernism and anti-liberalism by arising as a religious counter-revolution via restoration of theocratic medievalism, especially the *respublica Christiana* and ancient traditionalism, exemplified in 16th century Europe by Geneva's *civitas dei* and "rough Spartan manliness" extolled by its proud "citizen"[12] Rousseau (Garrard 2003). Calvinist restorationism was also epitomized on a larger scale in 17th century America by its "stodgy" (Gould 1996) Calvinists' (Winthrop et al.'s) design and designation of Puritan-ruled New England and the "new nation" as the medievalist "godly" community (German 1995; Stivers 1994) and no less than "Christian Sparta" (Kloppenberg 1998), after Calvin's Geneva equivalent model or precedent of the *civitas dei* and "rough Spartan manliness". This Spartan equivalence of Geneva and New England confirms that early American Puritans were completely unoriginal or parasitic in relation to Calvin et al., near totally dependent on "austere Calvinism." It makes one wonder if they could design and imagine New England and America as a whole as something else than just as a mere extended replica or proxy and echo of Geneva as local "Christian Sparta" in Europe.

Alternatively, original Calvinism, notably American Puritanism, operated as a religious and social anti-liberal "primitivism and restorationism" (Coffey 1998) in that it did *not* aim to restore "liberal Athens" but instead "austere Sparta" (Garrard 2003). Alternatively, Enlightenment-based liberals like Hume considered ancient Sparta a "completely inappropriate model for modern civilization" (Garrard 2003) and preferred "liberal Athens". This illustrates the deep gulf or incompatibility between liberal democracy, classical and modern alike, and Calvinism, notably Puritanism.

In this account, generally Calvinism's "original political impulse" (like Lutheranism's) was "totalistic" in virtue of totally controlling and

---

[12] Byrne (1997:184) adds that it is "worth noting Rousseau's bitter disappointment when the Small Council of Geneva (the highest ruling body) condemned *Emile* and *The Social Contract*. The city-state which Rousseau had admired as a model of good government had shown itself somewhat less tolerant than he had anticipated". Also, Garrard (2003:2) registers that the appearance of Rousseau's two works provoked "censure from authorities" in "Calvinist Geneva", just as "Catholic Paris". For instance, the "Small Council of Rousseau's native city [Geneva] denounced *Emile* as a book that "destroys the Christian religion and all revelation" and ordered that it be destroyed with *The Social Contract* as "reckless, scandalous, impious"" (Garrard 2003:70).

constraining "autonomous activities" in the economy and politics alike, rather than liberal-democratic (Eisenstadt 1965). And apparently, this Calvinist "original political impulse" failed to fully materialize and expresses itself at least in 16th century France, while succeeding and even completely triumphing in subsequent periods and other societies. Most notably, Calvinism attained such a triumph (German 1995) in 17th century and later America through Puritanism to produce and self-perpetuate one of the probably most striking ironies or perversities (Merton 1968; also, Boudon 1982) of Western and world history.

Therefore, Calvinism's eventual defeat in France and in extension Europe (except for Geneva locally and Holland nationally) was not only or mainly military in a domestic religious war, as usually assumed in focusing on the Calvinist Huguenots (Sprunger 1982) defeated by the monarchic and Catholic forces during the late 16th century. It was also and primarily a general sociological defeat in the sense of the Calvinist "abortive" attempt at its economic and political total mastery of society, as well as a theological one in its failing to displace Catholicism as the hegemonic and official religion of the French *ancien regime* which Tocqueville, incidentally, analyzed and partly glorified (Parsons[13] 1937). For example, the French monarchy battled and ultimately defeated the Calvinist Huguenots, starting with the "siege of La Rochelle by Louis XIII" and culminating in the "outlawing of the Protestant church [Calvinism] by Louis XIV"[14] (Acemoglu et al. 2005). Yet, this defeat and its outcome was the military as well as legal aspect of Calvinism's general character as an "abortive" (Heller 1986) movement and its failed attempt to become a dominant social and religious force in post-Reformation France. The military defeat of the Huguenots as a "perpetual minority" (Sprunger 1982) in France only put the "nail in the coffin" of Calvinism, as the latter had perhaps been, as Weber and medieval scholastics would put it, *caput mortuum* or marginal in social and theological terms well before these religious wars, if not from its very birth, in Calvin's own obscure French hometown.

---

[13] Parsons (1937:xiii–iv) comments that Tocqueville "represented the anxious nostalgia of the Ancien Regime" and adds that "indeed, Tocqueville was the apologist of a fully aristocratic society."

[14] Acemoglu et al. (2005:568) add that "early Atlantic activity enriched some merchant groups, in particular the protestant Huguenots" in France. Of course, the "protestant Huguenots" were not just any Protestants (e.g., Lutherans, etc.), but specifically and obstinately "Calvinist" ones, French Calvinists.

Counter-factually, Calvinism's chances of attaining its total "mastery of the world" in France against the dominant social background of Catholicism and the official Catholic Church (plus the Lutheran Reformation as its militant déjà vu), as well as the humanistic and secular Renaissance, were as great as in late medieval Italy characterized by these attributes—nearly minimal. This is what Pareto implies in remarking that the Protestant Reformation (apparently referring to Lutheranism) "began among the rough people of the North where Christian religion sentiment was more alive, while it made few proselytes in refined and skeptical Italy". Yet, Calvinists would and did admonish "never say never", as in their vocabulary, especially that of their English-American incarnates, Puritans, "failure" or "defeat" did and does not exist in spite or because of their "abortive" movement in France and most of Europe. No wonder, Hume classically attributed "unreasonable obstinacy" in face of repeated failures to Calvinist Puritans.

Further, in substantive sociological terms it was not the royal army that defeated or put the "nail in the coffin" of Calvinism and its Huguenots in France during the late 16th century. It was rather the 17th–18th century French Enlightenment as the essentially anti-Calvinist as well as anti-Catholic and generally secular, liberal, and rationalistic intellectual revolution (Delanty 2000; Garrard 2003). En passant, in theological terms, Calvinism failed to become a dominant religious doctrine or official "Reformed Church" in France probably because Catholicism was stronger than it had hoped for and remained hegemonic in theology and society alike in spite or perhaps because of the Protestant Reformation, in contrast to Germany during the early 16th century as well as Holland and England under "Roman" Anglicanism later. And, it also failed in Germany, including Prussia, later for analogous reasons, namely it underestimated the strength and influence of Lutheranism in both German theology and society.

Now, from the prism of the Enlightenment and liberalism, Calvinism, like Catholicism, was a vestige or attempted revival of medieval ideas, institutions, and times, simply the Dark Middle Ages (Artz 1998; Dombrowski 2001; Habermas 2001). At least, the Enlightenment's displacement and discredit of Calvinism, just as of Catholicism, as a relevant social force in France and beyond, including Holland eventually (Kaplan 2002), was the final sociological act or reenactment of the military defeat of the Huguenots and most other Calvinists in Europe (e.g., Germany), as well as, *cum* Puritans, in England (though not Scotland).

Conversely, such defeats were Act 1 or the prelude of this social failure. For illustration, recall, like in France, in officially Calvinist Holland during the 18th century the Enlightenment, in virtue of its concept of "genuine" tolerance in religion as religious liberty, prevailed over official Calvinism and its prior "rejection of toleration" and practice of intolerance and persecution for freedom of expression (Kaplan 2002). This was a universal pattern of the Enlightenment in relation to Calvinism, as well as official Catholicism, in 18th century Europe and, via Puritanism, England and America due to Jefferson's Enlightenment-inspired liberal ideas (Patell 2001).

In sum, Calvinism proved to be ultimately "abortive" as the claimed "Second" and final Reformation or "true" and "only" Protestantism in France. Judging from sociological and other analyses, it did in virtue of being politically primitive and, contrary to Weberian conventional wisdom, economically backward[15] or immature (Grossman 2006; Heller 1986), medievalist or theocratic in political and social terms (Nischan 1994), as well as late or pseudo-feudalist and just partly capitalist in economic respect. In essence, Calvinism became a sociological "failure" in France and Europe overall because it was (perceived) closer to the Dark Middle Ages and even austere Sparta than to the Enlightenment, to medievalism than to liberalism (Walzer 1963). Yet, it was a triumph (German 1995) and "over-achiever" in America and transiently England precisely for the same reason, notably its design for a "purer" medievalist illiberal order.

In a way, what was socially defined or constructed as and eventually proved a fatal defect or "curse" for Calvinism in France and most of, notably post-Enlightenment, Europe as a whole became a sort of supreme perfection or Divine "blessing" in America in one of those remarkable perversities or ironic twists of comparative social history and geography. To condense what has been argued and demonstrated previously, Calvinism ultimately proved a kind of monumental sociological "failure" and "outcast" in France and Europe in general since the Enlightenment, yet the genesis and "destiny" of America via Puritanism, primarily in virtue of its social system or design of medieval-like Bibliocracy, the *respublica Christiana*. In short, medieval Bibliocracy

---

[15] Contradicting Weber, Grossman (2006:205) suggests that Calvinism was the "religion of the threatened" middle *non*-capitalist strata engaged in "backward, small-scale craft production" and their "doctrine of self-justification."

turned out to be the nemesis or euthanasia of Calvinism in France and the "old world" as whole, yet the elixir or the formula for its eternal life in the "new nation." And, a greater sociological irony or perversity is difficult to imagine or find in French-American and generally Western post-medieval, modern history. As a related secondary point, stridently anti-Catholic Calvinism[16] proved a theological "failure" and outcast in France and most of Europe (minus Geneva and Holland), because it underestimated and "miscalculated" the strength and influence of official Catholicism, earlier Protestantism like Lutheranism in Germany and Anglicanism in England.

Next, following Catholic France, Calvinism eventually proved to be both a sociological and theological failure in early Lutheran Germany, specifically in 17th century Prussia. In a way, Calvinism's eventual failure or defeat in France not only preceded but also perhaps prefigured or anticipated that in Germany and most of Europe, with some exceptions like Geneva and Holland. Generally, like in France, in Germany Calvinism represented or claimed to be the "Second" and last, "true", Protestant Reformation, claiming that the "First" Lutheran Reformation was not complete, sufficient, and "genuine." In particular, Calvinism in Germany, like France, probably failed socially, to attain its total mastery of the world, primarily because of its medieval political backwardness, notably theocratic primitivism or absolutism via "godly" politics, as epitomized by its institutional practice and ideal of medieval-style theocracy and/or absolute tyranny. Also, it did so theologically, to establish itself as the absolute doctrine and the official Reformed Church—as had in French-speaking Geneva and Holland—through complete "Calvinization", because of its underestimating and miscalculating of the strength, pervasiveness, and influence of German Lutheranism, like French Catholicism, in theology and society alike.

First and foremost, Calvinism extended from France to Germany its social system, as effectively established in Swiss Geneva and later with

---

[16] For instance, the so-called "World Evangelical Alliance", established in England 1846 and globalized during the 1950s, s a sort of global informal neo-Calvinism and its last meeting in France (Toulouse, August 2007) evoked, if not reenacted, the late 16th century French Calvinist Synod (Paris 1559) concluding that evangelicalism could be established only by the extermination of non-evangelicals. While not being formally or explicitly Calvinist, WEA perpetuates or evokes Calvinism, including Puritanism, in various respects, from anti-Catholicism to anti-artistic and moral repression. For instance, its official history states that WEA "protested against the "Papacy and Popery" " while 'attacking organised games and amusements'" during the 19th century.

some modifications in Holland, and its theological design of the medievalist *republica Christiana*. Negatively, it opposed through its political absolutism the transformation of the medieval *republica Christiana* into a "system of independent principalities and states" (Nischan 1994), a trend in which religious pluralism or confessional coexistence (confessionalism) "converged" with state-formation in Germany and Europe overall. To that extent, Calvinism proved to be a sociological "failure" in Germany, like France, because it evidently failed, or in retrospect was "predestined" to fail, to stop or reverse this long-term process toward religious tolerance, liberty, and pluralism, as championed by the Enlightenment and liberalism (Dombrowski 2001; Kaplan 2002), and away from intolerance and absolutism as its typifying elements. Generally, in Germany Calvinism failed sociologically and theologically because (apart from being defined as "foreign") of its joint societal and theological "absolutist tendencies" that were "inherent" in the Calvinist Second Reformation (Nischan 1994) or disciplinary revolution (Clemens 2007; Gorski 2003; Loveman 2005), "second" indicating a "further fragmentation within Protestantism" itself (Byrne 1997).

For example, historical research shows that in Prussia (the Brandenburg principality) during the period of 1600–1630 the Calvinist Reformation failed largely due to its failure to find "sufficient support beyond the ruling elite" (the Hohenzollern court). Thus, it could not prevail in what Simmel also called the "confessional struggles" about Calvin's doctrine of predestination, between Lutherans and Calvinists[17] (Nischan 1994). In this account, the Second Reformation in Germany eventually failed to attain its "initial objective—the country's complete calvinization" (Nischan 1994) through its disciplinary revolution. This holds true, though with some unintended side-effects and reluctant tactical concessions like more "toleration" (plus diplomatic initiative) and less "governmental absolutism" than usually assumed for Prussia admittedly known "mostly for its authoritarianism and militarism, not for its toleration and constitutionalism" (Nischan 1994). For illustration, while "still" expecting or hoping for the state (Brandenburg's) "eventual calvinization",[18] its Calvinist rulers, in a variation on the

---

[17] Nischan (1994:239) adds that since the 1586 Calvinist Colloquy of Montbéliard in France, the doctrine of predestination "had become a major issue dividing the two confessions."

[18] For instance, Nischan (1994:245) cites the Prussian rulers' "original plan to staff Frankfurt's theological faculty exclusively with Calvinists."

theme of making a virtue of necessity, conceded the "coexistence of the Reformed court and Lutheran popular churches" (Nischan 1994), as the reality, though continuing to exclude Catholics.[19]

Hence, like in France, Geneva, and Holland, and, via Puritanism, England and America later, these Calvinist side-effects, concessions, or adjustments in Germany were the kinds of exceptions confirming rather than contradicting the "rule" or what Michels may call the "iron law" of Calvinism and absolutism or intolerance, including theocracy as its religious expression and outcome. They confirm what has been observed as a Calvinist rule or "law" before, during, and after the attempted "Calvinization" of Lutheran-Catholic Germany. This is that religious coexistence, tolerance, freedom, and pluralism, including Calvinist, Lutheran and Catholic multi-confessionalism, were established and sustained in Germany and elsewhere in *spite* rather than because of Calvinism and its disciplinary revolution, as even more paradigmatically witnessed in Holland, as well as, through Puritanism, in England and America.

To summarize, as it previously did in France, Calvinism ultimately failed as the putative "Second", definitive Protestant Reformation or "truly" Reformed Church in Germany. And, it did so in Germany for the essentially identical reasons it had been "abortive" in France. It failed sociologically because of its social and political primitivism as medieval absolutism epitomized by its system or design of theocracy; and theologically because of its miscalculation of German Lutheranism's theological and popular religious influence. In a way, it was unrealistic or over-optimistic, if not insolent, by Calvinists to attempt the "Second Reformation" and claim a "truly" Reformed Church via "Calvinization" in Germany as the home of Protestantism and Luther, almost like attempting to "Calvinize" the Vatican and its Popes. Yet, this historical episode far from being random and isolated reveals what Hume, Weber, and other sociologists consider the pattern of methodical recklessness, including extreme obstinacy, zeal, fervor and fanaticism, in Calvinism and Puritanism. These known historical facts are highly relevant for a comparative sociological analysis, because they reveal or confirm the rule, pattern, or "iron law" of Calvinism, including Puritanism, and

---

[19] Nischan (1994:245) concludes that "since they failed to win popular support and the Hohenzollern rulers were too weak to impose their court religion, the original goals of the Second Reformation—the Mark's complete calvinization—had to be adjusted to the given confessional and political realities".

absolutism, notably absolutist medieval-style theocracy as the central organizing concept and thesis of this work.

They are also in indicating or intimating that Calvinism failed abysmally, to become even a sort of "bad name" or nuisance, in France, Germany, and the "old world" on the same grounds that it succeeded triumphantly in America to the point of becoming its "destiny" and genesis—medieval-style Bibliocracy. An exception was Calvinism's success and dominance in the form of becoming the official "true Reformed Church" in Holland during the late 16th century (alongside the Swiss town of Geneva following Calvin's exile from France in 1536). It attained its perennial ideal of total mastery of the world or society through and following what Weber describes as the "ecclesiastic revolution of the strict Calvinists in the Netherlands during the 1580s", where, like in Scotland, Calvinism instantly assumed the power of a "predominant religion" (Sprunger 1982) and an official, state church (Hsia and Nierop 2002).

Yet, even the exceptional Dutch case confirms the rule or "iron law" of Calvinism in relation to absolutism or monism. This is that religious tolerance, pluralism, and freedom were established or promoted in modern Holland not because but precisely in spite and opposition of the Calvinist revolution and ensuing theocratic dominance or project (Clemens[20] 2007; Hsia and Nierop 2002). In this account, its success in Holland is better described as a case of "rise and decline" of Calvinism in the sense of its initial triumph to become an official religion and its ultimate demise, discredit, and dilution (Kaplan 2002; Tubergen et al. 2005), including its merger with Lutheranism,[21] as the system and design of absolutist medieval-style theocracy.

In dramatic contrast to its protracted "abortive" birth and eventual defeat in France and its subsequent failure in Germany and most of Western Europe overall, with the local and transient exceptions of Geneva and Holland, Calvinism's long journey via Puritanism to England and especially America can be described as resounding success or triumphant (not Pyrrhic) victory. Alternatively, Calvinism succeeded

---

[20] Clemens (2007:534) comments that through "disciplinary technologies" Calvinism in Holland "created conditions under which two formerly separate concerns—for salvation and for the health of the state—were joined in novel ways, creating new opportunities for the expansion of state enterprises," thus operating as effective theocracies.

[21] Holland's main Calvinist and Lutheran churches reportedly merged during the 2000s, while Dutch Catholics have become the largest single religious group (30 percent) in the meanwhile (cf., also Tubergen et al. 2005).

or triumphed through Puritanism in England and especially America on the essentially identical grounds that it initially or ultimately failed in Europe, in particular the social system and theological design of medieval-style Bibliocracy as Calvinist, "Christian" theocracy. This indicates the salient "role of a particular interpretation of Calvinism" (Dahrendorf 1959) in the form of Puritanism not only, as assumed in Weberian sociology (for a critique, cf., Fromm 1941; McLaughlin 1996; also, Alexander 1998; Cohen 1980; Grossman 2006; MacKinnon 1988), for early English and American capitalism, but also for what Weber significantly identifies and describes as Calvinist Bibliocracy in England and notably America. For example, Calvinist Bibliocracy assumed the form of a "Holy Commonwealth" in England temporarily (the 1640s–60s) following the anti-Anglican, anti-monarchical Puritan Revolution (Goldstone 1991; Gorski 2000) and a "Biblical Commonwealth" in New England more lastingly (the 1630s–1830s) and completely, established and maintained by Tocqueville's first Puritans.

Thus, renamed English Puritans in England Calvinists dethroned and executed the king and transiently eliminated the monarchy (Elwood 1999) via a victorious Calvinist disciplinary revolution (Loveman 2005) or rather counter-revolution. Then, they instituted their own version of theocratic "godly" republic under what Comte calls the reign of Saints (Cromwell et al.) after the model and image of the medieval *respublica Christiana* (Nischan 1994) or feudal tyranny (Heller 1986). Recall "Puritanical English Calvinists" arose and initially operated, as in Hume's classical account, as a sectarian movement within, yet eventually against, the "larger structure of the Church of England" (Sprunger 1982). It thus did as a subversive radical Calvinist element ("Trojan horse") within Anglicanism's religious infrastructure that was "dissolved, dismantled, and destroyed" by Puritanism (Champion 1999). Furthermore, as Tocqueville's first Puritans in New England and eventually America, Calvinists similarly displaced, executed, and abolished ("civilized") any "ungodly" and "impure" non-Calvinist forces (Native Americans, Catholics, Quakers, etc.). And, in the process they created and sustained the probably longest and the most totalitarian Calvinist theocracy (Munch 2001; Stivers 1994) or Bibliocracy as exemplified and symbolized by "Salem with and without witches." In sum, Calvinist Bibliocracy in America such as New England's "Biblical Commonwealth" lasted for full two centuries—and, as a historical curiosity, preceded—that in England, Cromwell's "Holy Commonwealth" lasting only for about two decades.

On this account, Calvinists were in the long run even more successful and triumphant, a sort of "over-achievers", in America than in England, let alone France, Germany, and Europe overall (perhaps minus Geneva and Holland). It is in this respect and at such a historical juncture that Calvinists appear and act as America's genesis and "destiny" alike, although in the slightly, "cosmetically" changed face and with the new English name of Tocqueville's first Puritans and subsequently other sectarian Protestants. Conversely, this reaffirms that it is not entirely precise and sufficient (though not inaccurate) to state, as Tocqueville, Weber, and other analysts do, that America's "destiny" or genesis is entailed in the first Puritans, for, as they certainly knew, these were substantively Calvinists just moving and acting beyond France, notably in the "new world."

The preceding indicates that, as in England partly and temporarily, in America Calvinism triumphed almost completely and enduringly by means or virtue of the "traditional dominance and prestige" of Puritanism and other sectarian Protestantism in American history and society (Jenness 2004; also, Gusfield[22] 1963; Lipset 1996; Munch 2001). Conversely, the historical predominance and social prestige of Puritanism and sectarian or fundamentalist Protestantism overall expressed and thus self-perpetuated Calvinism's fateful "triumph" (German 1995) in and "predestination" of American history and society, America's Calvinist genesis and "destiny". After all, Puritanism substantively originated and functioned as what Weber denotes Calvinist sectarianism, that is, a "sect" within Calvinism as a "church" or "hierocratic institution", though with underlying sectarian tendencies and outcomes. Alternatively, the underlying cause and explanation why Puritanism emerged and acted as "sect" within the Calvinist "church" was that its parent, Calvinism had sectarian potentials inherent to the exclusionary or non-universalistic and inhumane doctrine of predestination *cum* salvation of a few chosen and damnation, thus eventual exclusion and even extermination of, most humans.

---

[22] For instance, Gusfield (1963:7) suggests that the passage of the Eighteenth Amendment in America "was the high point of the struggle to assert the public dominance of old middle-class values. It established the victory of Protestant over Catholic, rural over urban, tradition over modernity, the middle class over both the lower and upper strata." Notably, he cites this case as "a prime example of criminalization as a function" of symbolic politics or symbolic crusade (Gusfield 1963:151), Puritan-style culture or temperance wars in America (Wagner 1997).

Hence, in spite or rather because of their initially victorious revolution dethroning and executing an "ungodly" king and temporarily abolishing the monarchy, displacing Anglicanism, and establishing a "purer" theocratic medieval-style "republic", Calvinists as English Puritans did not succeed to become England's "destiny" (though perhaps did in Scotland). Analogously, as Veblen's "late-comers" compared to both Anglicans and Catholics, they were not England's genesis despite their claims to represent "authentic" English religion and law against "foreign treats" like "papists" (Goldstone 1991; Gorski 2000). In a way, Calvinism failed to attain total societal mastery in England (even if not Scotland) because of what Weber calls the "abortive" rule of Cromwell's theocratic "Parliament of Saints" and thus the eventually failed English Puritan Revolution, as an instance of Calvinist disciplinary counter-revolutions as restorations of medievalist or other primitive theocracy and in part ancient Sparta and its discipline.

By contrast, by founding and perpetuating the longest and the most totalitarian Calvinist theocracy after the perennial model of the medieval *respublica Christiana*—rechristened the "Biblical Commonwealth" and symbolized by "Salem with witches"—Calvinists through their agents the first American Puritans became the genesis and, if Tocqueville is correct, "destiny" of America. This is probably the reason why Tocqueville identified America's, but not England's (or even Scotland) and other Western country's, "destiny", as well as genesis, in Puritanism and thus by implication Calvinism. And, this is the reason why this work applies Calvinism's concept of predestination via the Puritan over-determination primarily to America, secondarily or not at all to England and other more or less historically Calvinist societies in the "old Europe" in which Calvinists failed on the same basis or for the identical cause they triumphed in the "new world". Calvinism's historical path in and social predestination of Western societies can be represented in the following stages (Table 7.1).

*Summary of Calvinism's Path: The Birth, Decline, and Rebirth*

Evidently, Calvinism's geographic and historical trajectory proceeded from its failure in the total mastery of the social world in 16th century France and the rest of Europe, with local and partial exceptions (Geneva, Holland, and Prussia) to its triumph in 17th century England (and Scotland) and especially America. While Calvinism eventually failed in its very homeland France and most of Europe (excluding Geneva and

Table 7.1. Calvinism's historical path in and social "predestination" of Western societies

*Calvinist stages and outcomes*

Stage 1. Calvinism's genesis and original failure
    [a] → France, the homeland of Jean Calvin during the 1520s–30s
    [b] → the "abortive" French Protestant Reformation during the 1530–80s

Stage 2. Calvinism's first expansion and success
    [a] → Swiss Geneva: the first Calvinist theocracy (Bibliocracy) established and ruled by Calvin in exile during the 1530s
    [b] → Holland: triumph over Catholicism and the second Calvinist theocracy (the official "true Reformed Church") during the 1580s.

Stage 3. Calvinism's further expansion and failure déjà vu
    [a] → Germany, especially Prussia: the failed "Second" German Reformation against Lutheranism during the 1620s
    [b] → the rest of Europe: mostly failed "Second" Reformations against Lutheranism and Catholicism during the 17th and 18th century

Stage 4. Calvinism's expansion, derivation and triumph via Puritanism
    [a] → England during the late 16th and early 17th century: the temporary theocratic "republic" (the 1640s–60s) through the eventually "abortive" Revolution against Anglicanism (and monarchy)
    [b] → America during the 1620s–30s: the most enduring and totalitarian Calvinist Bibliocracy (the "Biblical Commonwealth", the 1620s–1830s) via emigration, conquest, persecution and extermination ("Salem with and without witches").

Stage 5: Calvinism's eclipse and discredit by modern liberalism and secularism
    [a] *caput mortuum* (almost dead) ← the Enlightenment in France and Europe, including England (Locke, Hume) via Puritanism during the 18th–19th century
    [b] partial and transient decline via Puritanism ← the Enlightenment (Jefferson, Madison) in revolutionary America (e.g., the "disestablishment" of New England's Puritan theocracy in 1833)

Stage 6: Calvinism's anti-liberal counter-reaction, partial rebirth from the "dead" and "second death"

Table 7.1. Continued

[a] counter-reaction in Europe → neo-Calvinism, Holland in the 19th century, and fascism, Germany, etc. in the 1920s–30s (also, formation and expansion of the neo-Calvinist "World Evangelical Alliance").
[b] rebirth in America → neo-Puritanism or Protestant fundamentalism and sectarianism and neo-fascism ("Christian" militia) during the 1980s–2000s
[c] "second death" ← global liberalization and secularization or the "new Enlightenment" in Europe and most of the democratic world versus neo-Calvinist anti-liberalism and anti-secularism or the "new anti-Enlightenment" in America (plus Catholic and Islamic ones in the Vatican, Poland, Iran, etc.) during the 2000s

*Note:*
→ causal path or historical movement from the left to the right.
← causal path or historical movement from the right to the left.

Holland), it became victorious via Puritanism in initially non-Calvinist societal settings like England partly and transiently (more successfully in Scotland) and America almost completely and permanently.

Recall, as French Protestantism or France's Reformation Calvinism proved an "abortive" revolution because of its societal primitivism, including economic backwardness or immaturity *cum* late feudalism (Grossman 2006; Heller 1986), notably its medievalism manifested in its obsession with the medieval theocracy, as was also in the rest of Europe, as exemplified by its failure of complete Calvinization in Germany (Nischan 1994). In turn, Calvinism as Puritanism was initially triumphant in England (and Scotland) through, first, as Hume classically recounts, attaining majority in the Parliament (House of Commons) and then by the victorious Puritan Revolution of the 1640s. However, its triumph proved temporary and partial even in England (though perhaps not in Scotland). For the Calvinist Revolution eventually turned out, like those in France and Germany, "abortive", an outcome overlooked or downplayed in the sociological and economic literature since Marx linking it with the conquest of "free competition" (also, Goldstone 1991; Gorski 2000; Moore 1993). Thus, while/if "the role of a particular interpretation of Calvinism for early English capitalists" (Dahrendorf 1959) through Puritanism was prominent in Weber's and even seemingly Marx's context, its religious-political stature suffered a major decline and discredit following the restoration of the Anglican Church's official status and the Monarchy. While as Puritans in England, Calvinists dethroned and killed a monarch (Champion 1999) and temporarily dispensed with the monarchy, their English Revolution proved ultimately "abortive" like their disciplinary revolutions in Europe, notably Catholic France and Lutheran Germany (Prussia).

And, in New England and eventually America, notably the "awaken" South, Calvinists rechristened as "all-American" Puritans, while did not have to depose and execute an "ungodly" king and abolish a monarchy, established and maintained their long totalitarian rule through a legal theocracy (Munch 2001; Stivers 1994) for two centuries, from the 17th to the 19th century (Baldwin 2006; Davis 2005). It was in New England and its "Biblical Commonwealth" that Calvinists realized their perennial vision or, as Comte puts it, old dream of evangelical theocracy as "Divinely" ordained more completely and enduringly than virtually anywhere else before or after, including Calvin's France and Geneva, Germany, and Holland (and Scotland) where they had not attained the point of Winthrop et al.'s absolute rule (Hsia and Nierop 2002). This is what is suggested by describing New England's Puritanism and its "Biblical Commonwealth" as the "most totalitarian" (Stivers 1994) subtype of Calvinism and Calvinist theocracy, thus more so than those in France, Geneva, Germany (and Scotland), and Holland with its official "Reformed Church" (tempered by secular power and countervailing Lutheranism and in part Catholicism).

The failure of Calvinism was by assumption a failed design and endeavor of "Divinely" ordained theocracy and its total mastery of the world overall by abortive disciplinary revolutions, in respective societies, including France, Germany and, via Puritanism, eventually Great Britain (except for Scotland). And, contrary to "rational expectations", such a theocratic failure in these societies hardly ever dissuaded and gave Calvinists "food for thought" that their theocracy, thus total mastery of the world, might *not* be as "Divinely" ordained as they claimed, for if it were it would have been instituted all by itself, by Providential Design. Rather, it induced them to persist and attempt to triumph elsewhere, notably as Tocqueville's first Puritans in the "new nation". It reaffirmed Weber's Calvinist "iron consistency" in the form of Hume's

Puritan "unreasonable obstinacy", yet triumphant, thus "reasonable" in this case, in the face of repeated failures or defeats, as in most of Europe. Conversely, the triumph of Calvinism via Puritanism in America was axiomatically the victory of a social system or theological design of its "Divine" theocracy—rather than, as usually assumed, democracy and secularism—and its total mastery of the world through a victorious disciplinary revolution. This is what Comte suggests in his observation that the initial "political triumph" of Calvinism (and Protestantism) in England, Holland and in part Germany effectively neutralized the "tendency to philosophical emancipation" by its connection with the "conservative" social system.

If these considerations are correct, Calvinism's ultimate failure at its home France and the rest of Europe (excepting Geneva locally and Holland decreasingly), and its triumph and heritage via Puritanism in distant foreign lands like America enduringly and England temporarily created one of the greatest ironies, perversities, and mysteries in modern Western history. In a way, this is perhaps the "mother" of all ironies or mysteries[23] of history and the present: French Calvinism, notably its Biblical theocracy, acting as America's "destiny" or predestination via Puritanism's over-determination of the latter and its "Bible Commonwealth". In sum, this is a dual historical story or sociological outcome. On one hand, it is what Weber might call Calvinism's "adverse fate" or "predicament" at home through its generally failed societal predestination of the "old world." On the other hand, it is Calvinism's fateful triumph or fortune outside its home via the Puritan over-determination of the "new nation." At this point, it appears that the "God (church) and King (state) of Calvinism is *caput mortuum* (presumed dead) in Europe, long live and well the God and King of Calvinism in America via Puritan Divines and Masters."

### The Spirit and Heritage of Calvinism Reconsidered

To better understand America's Calvinist societal, as distinguished from Divinely ordained or "manifest, "destiny," thus its present and future, requires more fully understanding the spirit, or nature and

---

[23] "Mystery" is applicable so long as most Americans are unaware of and, if they were, would be likely astounded and displeased by, the extant underlying French-Calvinist origins or links of the Puritan "first new nation".

operation, of Calvinism after its genesis as a sociological and historical phenomenon (as differentiated from deciphering the Design of and Predestination by the God of Calvinism). Conversely, without understanding the second it is difficult to understand or make sense of the first. This "destiny" may remain an incomprehensive accident, perversity, or mystery of history, or a sort of "freak of nature" (e.g., geography, climate, etc.), rather than Michels' like "iron" sociological law of Calvinism and its societal predestination or mastery of societies, while itself claiming to be predestined by Divine Providence as the "chosen" and master force in society.

## "What is in the Name" (of Calvinism)?

The preceding intimates the essence and meaning of Calvinism, including Puritanism, and by implication America's Calvinist-as-Puritan "destiny". Still, the question of "what is in the name" of Calvin et al. perhaps needs to be addressed more explicitly and completely precisely for the purpose of better understanding their "predestination" of the "new nation" via the first Puritans. Simply, answering "what is in the name" of Calvinism will disclose and perhaps predict what is in the "store" for America and its Calvinist "destiny". Calvinism and in consequence Puritanism is or claims to be a special brand of Protestantism and Christianity, by invidiously distinguishing itself from and even opposing other Protestant and Christian branches, including Lutheranism (as well as Anglicanism) and Catholicism. Specifically, "what is in the name" of Calvinism and consequently Puritanism is, first, orthodox or conservative, second, extreme or radical, third, disciplinary and repressive, in addition and connection to, as seen, fourth, fundamentalist and theocratic Protestantism. Alternatively, Calvinism's sociological, as well as theological, "name" is Protestant orthodoxy or conservatism, extremism or radicalism, discipline and repression, as well as fundamentalism and theocracy discussed earlier.

### Orthodox, Conservative Protestantism

Calvinism and consequently Puritanism is typically orthodox or conservative, distinguished from liberal, Protestantism, or alternatively Protestant orthodoxy or conservatism, as Simmel, Weber, and other sociologists suggest. Simmel observes that due to the "confessional controversies", centered around the predestination doctrine, between Lutherans and Calvinists ("Reformed"), Protestantism split into a "liberal and orthodox party", Lutheranism and Calvinism, respectively, and thus lost its "unity," even self-replicating the "conflict with the enemy". After all, Simmel's use of "Reformed" and implicitly "Reformation" in reference to Calvinism—but not curiously to Lutheranism as what Comte calls "primitive Protestantism"[24]—implies that he regards the first as the orthodox or conservative Protestant branch. Thus, Simmel actually adopted Calvinism's self-description of or claim to the true and only Reformed Church or Protestant Reformation and in that sense orthodox or conservative Protestantism. In a similar vein, Weber considers Calvinism, including Puritanism as its sectarian ramification, orthodox or conservative, as well as radical and ascetic, branch of Protestantism, as compared to Lutheranism and its English analogue Anglicanism considered, if not truly unorthodox or liberal, then more moderate (also, Munch 2001). He typically describes Calvinism and Calvinists as "strict", including Calvin's "strict" and "harsh" theological doctrine of predestination, and to that extent orthodox or conservative (rigid or stringent) Protestantism and Protestants.

In particular, Weber emphasizes that Calvinism, including Puritanism, originated and operated as orthodox or ascetic Protestantism in that only Calvinists and Puritans aimed to and succeeded to fulfill the Protestant Reformation's original moral commandment: "you think you have escaped from the monastery, but everyone must now be a monk throughout his life." As he puts it, in Calvinism and Puritanism, but not in Lutheranism and Anglicanism, "every Christian had to be a monk all his life" as the orthodox, primitive ideal of Protestantism, if not Christianity. He infers that the "methodical quality of ethical conduct" into which humans were forced by "Calvinism as distinct from

---

[24] Comte implies that Protestantism overall is conservative or orthodox itself in identifying its "dangerous inertia" and contending that the Protestant, both Lutheran and Calvinist, "revolution produced no innovation". According to Comte, the Protestant (Lutheran) "revolution produced no innovation, in regard to discipline, ecclesiastical orders or dogma [so Luther's] success was mainly due to the ripeness of the time". For instance, his argues that Protestantism's dogma of free inquiry was a "mere sanction of the pre-existing state" in most Christian nations. Also, he maintains that national "aesthetic tendencies were already checked by Protestantism" with its "unfavorableness to Art" and even "anti-scientific tendencies." He suggests that these anti-artistic and anti-scientific tendencies are due to the "incorporation of Protestantism with the government [and also] the repugnance of theology to the spread of the positive spirit [and] irrational [national] exclusiveness [English]." Also, he argues that Catholicism and monarchical systems were "more favorable to Art" than Protestantism and aristocratic regimes.

Lutheranism" generated a "thoroughgoing Christianization" of all social life in the sense of universal asceticism or monasticism and oppression in society.[25]

Also, contemporary sociologists observe that "only" Calvinism in France, Geneva, and Holland and its Puritan sects in England and America attained the "radical elimination" of a distinction between the ethic for priests and the ethic for laymen (Munch 1981), in opposition to Lutheranism (and Catholicism). Prima facie, such elimination rendered Calvinism, including Puritanism, orthodox, as well as radical Protestantism, given that the Protestant Reformation sought a "stronger ethical penetration of the world" (Munch 1981), while the failure to fully attain this original aim made Lutheranism less ascetic or more moderate. Calvinism's "radical elimination" of a distinction between the ethics for priests and for others is another expression for eliminating the boundaries between, as Weber suggests, the monastery and society, monks and other humans, as the orthodox, original Protestant ideal, yet not attained by Lutheranism. And, this Lutheran "failure" provided the rationale for the "Second Reformation" through Calvinist, including Puritan, disciplinary revolutions inspired by austere Sparta (Garrard 2003).

Alternatively, the Protestant Reformation's initial aim of a "stronger ethical penetration of the world" is just another way to restate its commandment "you think you have escaped from the monastery, but everyone must now be a monk throughout his life". Since this commandment was fully fulfilled or methodically pursued only in Calvinism, including Puritanism, the latter became effectively or appeared as orthodox or conservative Protestantism. This holds true of Calvinism at least in ascetic terms in contrast to Lutheranism evolving from a "primitive" and anti-liberal, proto-conservative Protestant type to an almost non-orthodox or non-conservative, in part liberal,[26] one in moral terms, or

---

[25] Weber adds that Calvinists accused Lutherans for a "virtual reluctance to becoming holy", just as the latter did the former for their "unfree servitude to the law" and arrogance.

[26] Weber remarks that "in modern Lutheranism (for this was not the position of Luther himself) the dominant interest is the struggle against intellectualist rationalism and against political liberalism", but apparently what was "modern Lutheranism" a century ago is not today, as shown by prevalent liberal-secular Lutheran tendencies in Germany and Scandinavia as "post-Christian" societies in moral-cultural and other terms (Inglehart 2004), as well as in America (despite some "evangelical" Lutheran denominations).

non-ascetic, moderate, and mainstream Protestantism in Europe such as Germany and Scandinavia and America (Hout et al.; Martin 2002; Munch 2001).

Hence, Calvinism is Simmel's "orthodox party" or conservative type in the sense of what Weber describes as ascetic and thus "true" Protestantism, as exemplified and symbolized by the above commandment of the Protestant Reformation. Alternatively, it is at least as self-conscious ascetic or austere Protestantism that Calvinism, including Puritanism, represents the orthodox or conservative Protestant type. In turn, Lutheranism is Simmel's "liberal party" in virtue of being, together with Anglicanism, as in Weber's and other sociological accounts (Munch 1981; Nischan 1994), non- or least ascetic (and so not "true"?) Protestantism, thus failing to fulfill the original Protestant moral commandment of universal and permanent monastic-style asceticism in society. No doubt, this is an ironic twist or seeming paradox, because Lutheranism was precisely original Protestantism or the first Reformation, thus presumably orthodox, conservative, and Calvinism, including Puritanism, derivative or the second, hence supposedly, as often is described, "liberal" or "modernist"[27] (Mayway 1984).

In formal terms, Lutheranism as "primitive" Protestantism, the First Reformation is and can claim to be orthodox or conservative. And yet, in a substantive sense Calvinism, in spite or because of being or claiming to be the "Second Reformation", has assumed or given the mantle of Protestant and even Christian "orthodoxy"[28] or conservatism. At least, in its substantive self-definition and Goffman's style "presentation of self" in society, Calvinism represents and operates as orthodox Protestantism, the "true" and "only" Reformed Church. This happened in 16th century Holland (Hsia and Nierop 2002), and almost France before, and virtually always and everywhere Calvinism established its total mastery of society, from Calvin's Geneva to, via Puritanism, Winthrop-Cromwell's "Holy Commonwealths" and beyond.

---

[27] Harley (1996) refers to the liberal Calvinists of the Brattle Street Church group" in New England, but suggests that these were an extremely small minority within early American Calvinism as largely anti-liberal or conservative as well as anti-rational, as witnessed by the conduct of key Calvinist figures (the Matters, etc.) during Salem's Puritan witch-trials.
[28] For instance, Nigg (1962:328–9) remarks that by the "execution of Servetus" for heresy and similar acts "Calvin wanted to demonstrate his Christian orthodoxy" to the Catholic Church.

Calvinism is an orthodox type of Protestantism and religion in the sense of a general substantive or sociological definition of religious orthodoxy as Divinely sanctified moralistic absolutism and theocratic fundamentalism (Mansbach 2006). It is in the sense of the worldview that the ultimate source of moral rules is God and legal codes must positively express "absolute and timeless divine law" (Davis and Robinson 2006). Using these criteria, especially the second defining and identifying legal theocracy, Calvinism functions or qualifies probably more than does Lutheranism as orthodox Protestantism and perhaps Christianity overall, though both, like Catholicism and the Christian Orthodox Church, share theological, doctrinal orthodoxy.[29]

To better understand such an apparent irony, paradox, or contradiction of a "younger" member of the extended Protestant family becoming or claiming to be orthodox or conservative compared with the oldest or the parent, it is useful to reconsider that Calvinism as the "Second Reformation" attacked, as in Germany and elsewhere, Lutheranism as the first Reformation. (In passing, Weber and other sociologists suggest that in many respects early and later Lutheranism, including Anglicanism, was and remained closer to Catholicism than to Calvinism, which highlights and perhaps justifies the latter's claim to orthodox Protestantism or Protestant orthodoxy.) Calvinism did so primarily (not solely) on the ground that Lutheranism retained too many elements of Catholicism or not being anti-Catholic enough, thus not "true" Protestantism, an attribute and designation self-appropriated by Calvinists. This happened first in France (Elwood 1999; Heller 1986; Mentzer 2007) and Geneva (Sorkin 2005; VanDrunen 2006), then in Holland (Hsia and Nierop 2002), Germany (Nischan 1994), and Europe overall (Gorski 2003). A cited exemplar involved the French Calvinists' (Huguenots') cries of "Kill all the [Catholic] priests" (Elwood 1999). They apparently followed Calvin as an "implacable foe of Catholicism" (Mansbach 2006) and every other religion (minus Lutheranism?, cf., Davis 2005) and group in virtue being one of the most intense "haters" (Fromm 1941; Mansbach 2006) of humans.

Predictably, Puritanism in England adopted and further escalated this Calvinist original pattern and method by attacking, as Hume

---

[29] Davis and Robinson (2006:169) distinguish "doctrinal orthodoxy" in Protestantism and Christianity overall—defined as "belief in the specific tenets of a faith tradition (e.g., the existence of heaven and hell, the divinity of Jesus)"—from orthodoxy as "a broad theological orientation toward the locus of moral authority."

recounted in detail, and temporarily supplanting and discrediting Anglicanism for its imputed "Catholicism" and "religious indifferentism" (Byrne 1997), thus not "true" Protestantism (as it did in Scotland even more successfully in the long run). Also expected, it did so subsequently in America through its attack on and eventual displacement of Episcopalism on these and related grounds ("foreign", British religion), especially in the old South via the Puritan-incited Great Awakenings (e.g., Jonathan Edwards, etc.) (Byrne 1997) and following the American Revolution.

Alternatively, like Calvinism in Europe, Puritanism claimed to represent and function as the "true" and "only" Reformed Church and in that sense orthodox Protestantism in England and America in an invidious distinction from Anglicanism (Episcopalism) accused as still practicing the "Roman religion". For example, Hume registered that Puritanism claimed that, as the Church of England (like Catholicism) relapsed into "idolatry", it remained the "only true religion" and in that sense orthodox Protestantism and (so?) Christianity, while describing such Puritan claims as "delusions". More precisely, Puritanism constituted or claimed to be orthodox, true Calvinism, or Calvinist (thus "Christian") orthodoxy. Especially, American Puritanism constituted "Calvinist orthodoxy"[30] (Clark 1999) and its members and leaders acted and looked as "stodgy orthodox Calvinists" (Gould 1996). This was evidenced by "the orthodox Calvinist clergy" or "orthodox Congregational" (Fehler 2005) ministers in America during the early and mid 19th century[31] and before, especially in New England (Baldwin 2006).

The above was also partly implicit in the self-definition or perception of Puritanism as "iron Protestantism" as the metallic image of theological and other orthodoxy or rigidity, and of Puritans as the "hotter sort" (Gorski 2000) of Protestants, as another physical imaginary of being orthodox, conservative or, as Hume[32] classically described them,

---

[30] Clark (1999:64) suggests that the "struggle against Calvinist orthodoxy expressed itself in a revision or rejection of traditional sources of religious authority" 19th century antebellum America. In particular, during these times liberal Protestant "reformers commonly criticized [Calvinist] religious institutions as "undemocratic"" or "authoritarian religious power" (Clark 1999:65–6).

[31] Fehler (2005:147) observes that Calvinist orthodoxy in America, embodied by the "Congregational clergymen of New England", during was "challenged on many fronts", particularly by liberalism (as well as religious populism), the 19th century.

[32] Hume points to the "rigid tenets of [the Puritan] sect". For example, he adds that "to show how rigid the English, chiefly the Puritans, were become [e.g.], a bill was introduced into the house of commons for the more strict observance of the Sunday,

rigid and uncompromising, as well as, overly zealous, fanatical, and extreme generally. Contemporary Puritans or rather their evangelical descendents in America continue to be (self) defined and perceived in such and related terms. Some analysts describe US "born again" Puritan-inspired neo-conservatives like Reaganites (e.g., Reagan's admiration for Winthrop) as "rigid and uncompromising extremists" (Blomberg and Harrington 2000), in that sense orthodox, "hotter" Protestants, though "orthodox" may sound as an understatement, if not compliment, in relation to "extremism." This reveals an apparent continuity from what Hume detected as the "rigid tenets" of early Puritan "sectaries" to "born again" US evangelicals or religious conservatives.

In sum, at least its negative "Catholic" imputation to Lutheranism (plus Anglicanism) and its positive pretension to being the "true" and "only" Reformed Church redefine Calvinism and consequently Puritanism as orthodox or conservative Protestantism, as Protestant orthodoxy or conservatism. And, the fact that virtually every Protestant denomination or sect made and makes such claims does not affect (diminish) the posture or stature of Calvinism as the "true" Reformed Church and to that extent orthodox or conservative Protestantism. In spite or because of being merely the "Second Reformation", Calvinism, including Puritanism, originated and established itself as, or is considered in the literature and beyond, orthodox or conservative as well as radical or fundamentalist, thus anti-liberal, Protestantism. It is in relation to its "primitive" or original type, Lutheranism, as well as Anglicanism, becoming more liberal or moderate. For instance, in America Calvinism via Puritanism and its own survivals or evangelical revivals (e.g., Baptism and its allies) has established itself and is described in the sociological literature and society, as fundamentalist or conservative and in that sense orthodox Protestantism, as distinguished from and opposed to its liberal, moderate, or mainline branches, like Lutheranism and Anglicanism (Hout et al. 2001; Martin 2002). An indicative historical instance was the Calvinist "conservative clergy" (Fehler 2005) and/or "orthodox" undemocratic authority[33] (Clark 1999) in New England and America during the 19th century.

---

which they affected to the Sabbath. One Shepherd opposed this bill, objected to the appellation of Sabbath as Puritanical, defended dancing by the example of David, and seems even to have justified sports on that day."

[33] Clark (1999:62) adds that liberal Protestantism's struggles, including the "assertion of the right of private judgment", against Calvinist "orthodox authority" during the 19th century "signaled an end to the reign of Calvinism" in America.

Calvinism is, first and foremost, strict or rigid social-political conservatism. This is to be distinguished from, and is not necessarily associated with, theological conservatism or orthodoxy in religious doctrine, as official Catholicism is self-defined and considered, just as the Orthodox Christian Church in Christianity, and often Lutheranism within Protestantism. Tawney (1962) observes that the "first characteristic" of Calvinism, including Puritanism, is its "conservatism" in societal, notably moral and cultural, terms, indicating how little, if anything, has changed in the "presentation of social ethics of the Christian faith" since medieval and earlier times.

Predictably, Calvin as an arch-conservative, specifically medieval-style traditionalist, set the model and tone of rigid societal, including economic, political and cultural conservatism in Calvinism, including Puritanism, combined with theological and religious radicalism in the form of extreme anti-Catholicism and even anti-Lutheranism. Historical research shows that Calvin blended his radical anti-Catholic and in part anti-Lutheran Protestant theology with a "thick underlay of social and political conservatism" (Heller 1986). Consequently, ruling groups in France and beyond expected and found in Calvin an "upholder of social and political order", in particular medievalism, notably medieval theocracy or despotism overall and feudalism (recall it was still the early 16th century). In this account, Calvin fused his "conservative view of society" with an "equally conservative theory" of religion advocating obedience to "established secular authority" and dictating "submission to the new ministerial order"[34] (Heller 1986), predictably to the Calvinist theocracy via the "only true" Reformed Church that he established in Geneva and later his followers expanded to Holland (and in part Prussia). The study concludes that Calvin's was a dual, social-religious Machiavellian-like strategy of reassuring the monarchy, seigneurs, and notables in France of the "essential conservatism of his secular goals" and seeking "radical reform in the realm of religion" (Heller 1986). Calvin's principal successors in theocratic Geneva (e.g., Vernet, Beza) inherited and loyally perpetuated his original strict social and political conservatism[35] (Sorkin 2005), with minor modifications (VanDrunen 2006).

---

[34] Heller (1986:136) adds that "at no point does Calvin support change in the order of politics or society. In this realm change was always viewed as exceptional and never legitimate if based on popular will. Calvin confines his radicalism to the spiritual realm".

[35] In a laudatory study, Sorkin (2005:291) admits that Vernet was an "apologist for the status quo" who understood theocratic practices, and not correct theological

Negatively, as noted, Calvinism was strident anti- and pre-liberalism, including anti-secularism, anti-pluralism, and anti-humanism, as the obverse side of its strict conservatism. In its self-description Calvinism, like official Catholicism, originally acted as an opponent of what it condemned and attacked as "libertinism" as the older name or precursor of liberalism, namely "libertine" secularism, religious tolerance and pluralism, and humanism. Calvin et al. executed various "libertines" in Geneva for their blasphemy as well as advocacy of religious tolerance and freedom of conscience (Ozmend 1980), and his successors (e.g., Vernet) loyally continued this original Calvinist hostility and contempt for "libertinism"[36] (Sorkin 2005). Also, recall Weber's implied observation that the struggle against social liberalism and rationalism was the "dominant interest" in original and subsequent Calvinism, just as in post-Luther Lutheranism. Particularly pertinent is his observation that if "strong enough" Calvinism (e.g., Baptism) did not recognize freedom of conscience for *others* and even more so than the old Lutheranism and Catholicism.

Subsequent historical studies confirm Weber's observations about Calvinism and its anti- or pre-liberalism, notably its illiberality in the sense of denying to others what it demands for itself, religious freedom

---

doctrines (e.g., predestination), as a "Christian's primary concern." Admittedly, Vernet adopted conservatism in politics in emphasizing that "mankind's weak and corrupt nature required obedience" instead of the "exercise of liberty" and even claiming that a "people that governs itself is the least free and the most unhappy of all peoples [sic!]" (Sorkin 2005:297–8). In this account, Vernet revealed a conservative ("republican") preference for "hierarchy over democratic participation", making order a "synonym for submission to authority" and reducing liberty to "nominal sovereignty", so treating freedom and submission as "synonymous", on the holy grounds that subordination was as "essential to Christianity as to society", which expresses a "conservative, state-centered politics" (Sorkin 2005:299–300). Sorkin (2005:301) concludes that Vernet showed "profound abhorrence of democracy and liberty" in favor of his "eager embrace of subordination" and conservative "patrician politics" overall. In turn, VanDrunen (2006:143–6) suggests that some Calvinists like Beza as Calvin's "virtual successor" in Geneva "stepped beyond the rather strict obedience that Calvin commended toward civil authority and advocated various degrees of civil disobedience and even revolution" using natural law (understood as the "law of God inscribed upon the heart and known through conscience"). And, following Calvin, they all were "committed to the authority of Scripture" (VanDrunen 2006:150), not only in theology but also in politics and society, thus theocrats and by implication political-social conservatives *cum* evangelicals (Heller 1986).

[36] Sorkin (2005:304) refers to Vernet's view that during the 16th century the "great Reformers" like Calvin "steered between the extremes of libertinism and Epicureanism" on one hand and the "public superstition of the Roman Church", between the "age-old evils" of libertine "impiety (indifference) and "superstition" (manifested in Catholicism).

(Kaplan 2002; Nischan 1994). Calvinism transmitted its anti- and pre-liberalism, including its anti-secularism, anti-pluralism, and anti-humanism to first England and then America via Puritanism. The latter inherited and even further escalated and intensified these Calvinist original anti-liberal tendencies, initially in the form of Puritan antagonism to and attack on "libertinism" (Gould 1996). For instance, in 18th and 19th century New England, liberalism (including capitalism) and Calvinism entailed "different" and often "contradictory values", with neo-Calvinist (New Divinity) theocrats condemning Jefferson as a secular equivalent of the "wicked king Jeroboam" (German 1995; also, Baldwin 2006). Admittedly, post-revolutionary Calvinism in America did not adopt a "liberal" culture and democratic political system, and did not legitimize "cultural pluralism, egalitarian democracy, or progressive optimism about the human condition" (German 1995). Instead, it maintained, solidified, and expanded Calvin et al.'s original illiberal, non-democratic, and anti-humanistic doctrines of human moral "depravity"[37] (Mentzer 2007; Sorkin 2005).

Alternatively, nascent political liberalism in Great Britain, notably the foremost liberal Hume and even in part Puritan Locke rejected Puritanism's Calvinist old ideal and practice of theocratic "godly" politics by means of a medievalist "Christian commonwealth"[38] (Zaret 1989). The same holds of early political liberalism in America, as epitomized by Jefferson-Madison's rejection of the Puritan design of America as illiberal or austere "Christian Sparta" (Kloppenberg 1998), rather than "liberal Athens" (Garrard 2003), seemingly escalating Geneva's theocracy and "Spartan" discipline. Overall, during post-revolutionary times Calvinist theocracy and orthodoxy in America was reportedly challenged on "many fronts", especially by liberalism (and populism), and eventually "lost ground" to these and related countervailing forces[39] (Fehler 2005).

---

[37] German (1995:994) adds that following the American Revolution Calvinist intellectuals (Edwards, etc.) "were already turning their attention from America's political and economic life to its soul", as a sort of rationalization for their anti-liberalism, notably theocratic anti-secularism grounded on Calvin's "doctrine of human depravity".

[38] Zaret (1989:163) comments that liberal-democratic ideology, exemplified by Locke, in England "was not a secular extension" of Puritan ideas but "developed explicitly against the application of these beliefs to politics rejecting the claim" that politics and religion are "inseparable". In this view, Locke's and other liberal-democratic ideology, notably by implication that of Hume, was simply a negative "response to the radicalism" of Puritanism.

[39] Specifically, according to Fehler (2005:147) US Calvinists like the "Congregational clergymen" of New England "lost ground" to "professionalism and materialism", as well

As a particular dimension or close correlate of its societal conservatism (and theological orthodoxy), just as its anti-liberalism, Calvinism, including Puritanism, is absolutist or monistic, as distinguished from and often opposed to non-absolutist or pluralist and liberal, Protestantism. Calvinism and in consequence Puritanism constitutes and operates as Protestant absolutism and monism, and alternatively anti-relativism or anti-pluralism and anti-liberalism overall in society, including religion and culture and politics. The above reintroduces what has been described as Michels' style "iron" law of Calvinism, including Puritanism, as intrinsic absolutism or monism, and conversely anti-relativism[40] and anti-pluralism. This appears as a near-universal sociological rule operating virtually anywhere and always Calvinists originated and ruled, from France and Geneva to Germany and Holland, and *cum* Puritans to England and America.

Predictably, the theological rationale for Calvinism's sociological "law" of absolutism or monism in society is its nature and operation as, or its claim to being, orthodox Protestantism. Its strong claim to being the true Reformed Church (Hsia and Nierop 2002) grounds and rationalizes Calvinism acting and ultimately establishing itself as the "only" official church, reformed or un-reformed. This precisely happened whenever and wherever Calvinists attained social dominance, from Calvin's Geneva and Holland to, via Puritanism, England (temporarily) and America (New England). Hence, the "true Reformed Church" claim is the underlying theological foundation and sanctification of what Weber identifies as Calvinist state churches or theocracies, specifically Bibliocracy, established, as he suggests, virtually everywhere and whenever Calvinism became dominant, as in Geneva, Holland, and, through Puritanism, Great Britain and New England.

In essence, Calvinism's spirit of or rather its claim to being orthodox "true" Protestantism ultimately generates, explains, and predicts Calvinist theocracy in the form of the only officially recognized Reformed and any other Church in society, expressing and realizing its societal (and theological) absolutism and monism. If any absolutism, monism,

---

as "populist" Methodist, Baptist, and other religious movements" as during the Great Awakenings (also, Baldwin 2006). Yet, German (1995) describes these revivalist movements or awakenings as basically the particular expressions of "Calvinist revivalism".

[40] For instance, a "born again" Calvinist (Methodist) US President publicly stated that America should "reject this dictatorship of relativism and embrace a culture of justice and truth" *cum* religious absolutism and monism.

or anti-pluralism is actually or potentially, intrinsically or ultimately, logically or empirically, totalitarianism (Dahrendorf 1959; Habermas 2001; Infantino 2003; Mises 1966), then Calvinism as absolutistic, monistic, or anti-pluralist Protestantism objectively entails or produces totalitarian elements or outcomes, though in the form of "holy" theocracy as the "true" and "only" religion and church in society. And, this absolutism has evidently yielded corresponding theocratic implications for America's Calvinist "destiny" or "predestination" through its Puritan over-determination, as elaborated previously.

*Extreme, Radical Protestantism*

Calvinism and hence Puritanism is extreme, radical, including militant or violent, Protestantism, as distinguished from and opposed to Protestantism's moderate and liberal, particularly non-militant and non-violent, branches such as (if Hume, Simmel, Weber, and other sociologists are correct), Lutheranism (Munch 1981), Anglicanism (Munch 2001), and Quakerism (Martin 2002). Alternatively, given Calvin's original extreme or radical ideas and practices (the killing of Servetus, "libertines", and related activities in Geneva), Calvinism is paradigmatic Protestant extremism or radicalism, notably violence, militancy, and militarism. Thus, Calvinism is "more radical" or extreme than Lutheranism (Mansbach 2006), as is Puritanism more than Anglicanism. As a syndrome of radicalism, Calvin surpassed Luther in postulating and establishing "theocratic authority"[41] (Mansbach 2006). In general, historical research shows that Calvin and subsequent Calvinism help to explain the "emergence of the new forms of radicalism" in politics and society disturbing the "peace of early modern Europe" (Elwood 1999).

At this juncture, readers may wonder whether and how, if ever, Calvinism, including Puritanism, reconciled its radicalism with its conservatism, as apparently contradictory elements. This is evidently a question for and that Calvin, as well as his Puritan disciples Cromwell and Winthrop, would probably and implicitly did in his (their) theological writings and theocratic practices answer the best. Calvin's own

---

[41] Mansbach (2006:109) adds that Lutheran Zwingli also went beyond Luther in "theocratic authority" and that his post-Luther fundamentalism "influenced the theocratic inclinations of strict versions of Protestantism in Puritan New England [and French Huguenot], and it continues to influence evangelical US Protestants."

answer would be that Calvinism, including Puritanism, combined theological radicalism or radical change in the realm of theology and religion with sociological conservatism or the preservation of the existing social order as Divinely ordained, thus that this combination is not necessarily contradictory in its context. In short, both Calvinist theological radicalism and sociological conservatism are just different forms of extremism, and no contradiction exists. Overall, in Calvinism and other world religions and ideologies, "strict" conservatism or orthodoxy, including absolutism or monism, a la the "true" and "only" church or ideology is typically a particular form of extremism, as is radicalism in the usual sense. Simply, both Calvinist (and other) "strict" conservatism and radicalism express ("load on") extremism; conversely, the second is epitomized or operationalized by the first. This seemingly paradoxical mixture of conservatism and radicalism is manifested (and resolved) by Calvinist-Puritan (and other) conservative counter-revolutions.

First, Calvinism is Protestant societal extremism or radicalism in constituting an extreme or radical species of ascetic Protestantism. At the minimum, Calvinism operates as extremism or radicalism in virtue of its extreme, strict[42] asceticism or austerity[43] (Frijhoff 2002). Puritanism inherited, intensified, and escalated this Calvinist asceticism by acting as an ever-more extreme "child" than its "parent" in this and related respects, notably more austere and totalitarian, as evidenced by its American variant (Munch 2001; Stivers 1994). Of secondary importance, Calvinism, including Puritanism, is theological extremism or radicalism, particularly extreme or radical anti-Catholicism, as

---

[42] Weber remarks that "an ascetic control of this world [was] characteristic of Calvinism. It is no accident that inner-worldly asceticism reached its most consistent development in the Calvinist god of absolute unsearchableness of His motives by any human standard. He adds that Calvinism and other ascetic Protestantism "made even smaller concessions to the realities of sensuality" than Judaism through the "strict rejection of all things of the flesh". In general, he observes that ascetic Protestantism included "Calvinist and Baptist Puritans, Mennonites, Methodists and Pietists" and "drew the core of its following from the middle and lower ranks of the citizen". Also, citing Sombart, Rettig and Pasamanick (1961:22) suggest that ascetic Protestantism, specifically Calvinism in the 16th century and Puritanism in the 17th century were lower middle-class movements because its "moral rigidity also serves the function of expressing resentment against the higher classes."

[43] Frijhoff (2002:49) registers that "Dutch Calvinism" was characterized by "austerity", combined with theological, and not social or secular, individualism, its "tendency to be shut in on itself, its fundamental sense of [religious] equality, and its eschatological certitude of being elected".

Hume, Weber, and other analysts suggest (Elwood 1999; Grossman 2006; Heller 1986; Mansbach 2006).

Notably, Calvinism represents extremism or radicalism on the account of its militancy and violence, including militarism and religious war or crusade. Historical research indicates that Calvinism's "growing militancy" and "widespread popular unrest" were inspired and incited by "Calvinist extremists" in France[44] (Heller 1986). Also, recall the Calvinist "cries of "Kill all the [Catholic] priests" in France. Notably, while failing in France, in Holland Calvinism operated as a "set of organizational and political strategies" whereby "disciplined" and "militant" religious minorities attempted and succeeded to seize political power (Gorski 1993). In another similar, yet less successful attempt, the "introduction of Calvinism" into some areas in Germany (e.g., Prussia) involved "armed violence and iconoclastic riots", manifesting "militant Calvinist policy or Calvinist militancy" (Nischan 1994).

In light of the above, Weber typically describes Calvinism and Calvinists as "radical", in particular as the (Reformed) "Church militant" as well as extremely ascetic, and in that degree and sense extreme or non-moderate Protestantism and Protestants, as distinguished from more moderate, including less ascetic, Lutheranism and Anglicanism. For example, he observes that original European Calvinists and their sectarian derivatives ("the first Swiss and South German Baptists") conceived the "Biblical way of life" and thus practiced what he calls Bibliocracy with "radicalism" compared to that of extreme medieval monasticism (e.g., Saint Francis), that is, as a "sharp break with all the enjoyment of life", after the model of the Apostles.

Notably, Weber identifies and emphasizes militancy and militarism in Calvinism in that the latter acts as the "Church militant" through "holy" (or "just") war or crusade as the supposed instrument to realize God's commandment to "tame the world of sin, for His glory."[45] In this

---

[44] Heller (1986:237) remarks that a "Calvinist synod at Chalons-sur-la-Saone concluded that the evangelical religion could not be established without the extermination [sic!] of papists, parlementaires and nobility. Such incitement led to attacks on aristocratic chateaux by rural folk". In turn, Mentzer (2007:341) notes that the "first national synod [of the Calvinist Church of France] convened clandestinely at Paris in 1559".

[45] Weber states that "when salvation aristocracies are charged by the command of their God to tame the world of sin, for His glory, they give birth to the "crusader." Such was the case in Calvinism and, in a different form, in Islamism." He adds that "at the same time, however, salvation aristocracies separate "holy" or "just" wars from other, purely secular, and therefore profoundly devalued, wars. The just war is engaged in for

context, while contrasting it with Lutheranism described as rejecting crusade, Weber compares Calvinism to Islamism with respect to "holy" war, implying Calvinist-Islamic elective affinities or convergence in terms of militarism and militancy in general (Mansbach 2006; Turner 2002). Echoing Weber a subsequent study describes Geneva's "radical Calvinists" (French refugees) under Calvin and their instrumentality in returning "Calvinist fundamentalism" to their homeland as "starkly similar" to Muslim militants in a "variety of settings pitting Muslims against non-Muslims"[46] (Mansbach 2006), especially Christians, from Afghanistan to Bosnia, Kosovo, and Macedonia. And, in all these cases militant Islamists were supported and even incited, as in the last three, as "freedom fighters" by the US "godly" government. Furthermore, some sociologists explicitly suggest that contemporary Calvinist-rooted fundamentalism in America and Islamism exhibit an affinity in "holy" war, crusade and jihad respectively, or what is called "jihadic politics" and thus political and other radicalism or extremism (Turner 2002).

As noted, another syndrome of Calvinist radicalism was that the "radical elimination of any distinction" between the ethics for priests and for others, so a "stronger ethical penetration" of society as the Reformation's original goal and rationale, was attained "only in Calvinism" in 16th century France, Geneva, and Holland and "Puritan sects and denominations" in 17th century England and America, but not in Lutheranism (Munch 1981), as "primitive" Protestantism, and Anglicanism (Munch 2001). In this account, another less manifest, related element of radicalism and, contrary to conventional wisdom, anti-individualism or collectivism was the "tight binding of the individual to the group by its approval" (Munch 1981). This collectivism was especially attained within American Puritanism with its

---

the sake of executing God's commandment, or for the sake of faith, which [so] always means a war of religion. Therefore, salvation aristocracies reject the compulsion to participate in those wars of the political authorities which are not clearly established as holy wars corresponding to God's will [i.e.,] wars not affirmed by one's own conscience." For instance, he cites the "victorious army of Cromwell's Saints" as acting "in this way when it took a stand against compulsory military service", and comments that Lutheranism "has taken the very opposite stand. It has rejected the crusade" generally "active resistance against any secular coercion in matters of faith".

[46] Mansbach (2006:113) infers that generally "fundamentalism is not unique to Islam and can be seen today in evangelical Christianity", plus Orthodox Judaism, and even the revival of Hinduism in India.

"communitarian impulse"[47] (Dayton 1999), which reinvented and intensified Calvinism with its manifest or latent collectivist tendencies[48] (Mentzer 2007). It exemplified the general pattern of the Puritan "child" or disciple in America surpassing the Calvinist "father" or master in Europe in virtually all respects, notably "holy" Bibliocracy.

Predictably, Puritanism inherited, further reinforced, and escalated Calvinist extremism or radicalism (Goldstone 1986; Zaret 1989), including militancy and militarism. It did to the point of, as Hume classically observed, fanaticism, violence, brutality, cruelty, and inhumanity via "holy" terror and wars against the "impure" and "infidels" (Gorski 2000) in England (Walzer 1963; Zaret 1989) and America (Munch 2001; Stivers 1994). For illustration, Hume describes early Puritans as "violent Protestants" who were in particular prone to bring their antagonism to the "utmost extremity" against the Roman Church, and infers that the "extreme rage" against Popery became a "sure characteristic of Puritanism". The latter hence followed and reinforced Calvin et al.'s initial strict and militant anti-Catholicism or anti-Popery (Sorkin 2005). Further, Hume states that the "plague" of Puritanism in England was so "violent" that it resulted in a war in which they attacked and executed the king (Elwood 1999), while alerting to Puritans' "wild fanaticism", and "noise and fury, cant and hypocrisy".[49]

Also, Weber identifies and emphasizes Puritanism's militant and violent tendencies and outcomes grounded in its attribute as the non-universalistic or non-genuine religion of salvation ("particularism of grace") and as extreme asceticism, and sanctified by its belied in the "fixed and revealed commandments" of an omnipotent, "quite

---

[47] Dayton (1999:29–30) that the "communitarian impulse" was "central" to New England's Puritan leaders to the effect that the "right to worship freely would extend only to those who cleaved to the ministers" and magistrates" conception of godly, scriptural rules".

[48] For instance, Mentzer (2007:340) finds that in early French Calvinism "fasting was less an individual act than [in] medieval Christians. The accent was on the collectivity [i.e.] the "body" of believers. [Like] the Reformed celebration of the Lord's Supper—a sacral, symbolic, and communal meal—the fast was a shared liturgical event that served to define membership in the community of the faithful. In the Eucharist people joined in receiving the bread and wine; in the liturgy of the fast, they [did] in renouncing temporarily eating and drinking."

[49] Hume adds that the Puritans "as moved by the spirit, they displayed their pious zeal in prayers and exhortations, and raised their own enthusiasm, as well as that of their audience, to the highest pitch, from that social contagion which has so mighty an influence on holy fervors, and from the mutual emulation which arose in those trials of religious eloquence." He concludes that their assemblies were "dangerous societies."

incomprehensible" God of Calvinism. Thus, he states that Puritanism understands "God's will" as signifying that (to paraphrase) "thou shall impose" his commandments on the "creatural world by the means of this world", that is, violence and "ethical barbarism". They included war, as the instrument or barrier resisting the "obligation of brotherliness in the interest of God's 'cause' ", and alternatively reproducing unbrotherliness (Symonds and Pudsey[50] 2006) and inhumanity, including cruelty and brutality. Specifically, he suggests that such violence or "ethical barbarism" in Puritanism, like Calvinism overall and Islamism, typically assumes the form of religious war or the "obligation to crusade" and jihad, as exemplified and realized by "genuine Puritan revolutions" and their "counterparts" in Islamic and other versions. Puritanism, like Calvinism overall and Islamism, does so on the grounds of opposition of an "absolute and divine" natural law to the "creaturely, wicked, and empirical orders of the world" and thus a religious obligation that "thou shall realize" this divine law by "holy" war or violence in accordance with the rule "one must obey God rather than men".

Evoking Hume and Weber, subsequent historical studies identify Puritans" radicalism, militancy, and "fanaticism of Calvinist godliness" (Walzer 1963) in England as well as America. A cognate sociological account suggests that Puritanism was characterized by political and social radicalism in virtue of its "sectarian attempts" to create a theocracy ("Holy Commonwealth") by applying Calvinist theological doctrines to politics and society (Zaret 1989). In this account, the radicalism of Puritanism, as an "inevitable" result of its rejection of human reason "in favor of unbridled revelation", operated as a "charismatic revolt" against all social institutions, including the previous (Catholic or Lutheran) church, law and the state, and universities, that were viewed as the "impediments to the creation" of theocracy (Zaret 1989). Alternatively, liberal-democratic ideology, including even Puritan Locke (let alone anti-Puritan Hume), rejected the social radicalism of Puritanism and in extension of Calvinism and Protestantism as a whole (Zaret 1989). In particular, sociological analyses emphasize that

---

[50] Referring to Weber, Symonds and Pudsey (2006:137) remarks that "although the Protestant sects will put up certain barriers, there is also a universal aspect to Protestant brotherliness in the obvious sense that we are all God's children and that [beyond the American model] systematic charities were organized for those not capable of work, such as orphans and cripples. So, in terms of the ideal-type, Protestantism is both exclusive and universal unevenly, with the major tendency moving against universality."

Puritanism was "politically radical", a specie of radicalism culminating and epitomized in the English Puritan Revolution of the 1640s (Goldstone 1986; Moore 1993) and its precedent New England's "Biblical Commonwealth" under Winthrop's rule since the 1630s and its ramifications such as the Great Awakenings of the 1740s–1800s reflecting Calvinist revivalism, in America.

As noted, Calvinism originated and functioned as the "Second Reformation" formally or declaratively and as a religious-political revolution or rather counter-revolution substantively. By assumption, Calvinism was societal extremism[51] in the sense of radicalism in virtue of being what Comte describes (in reference to Protestantism in general) as the "first general phase of the revolutionary philosophy". In particular, the Calvinist "Second Reformation," or more than the Lutheran, was not just a reform in the strict sense (thus a misnomer) in theology, religion, and society, producing a "Reformed Church". It was rather, in Comte's words, "revolution", though he adds that it "produced no innovation" in theological (dogma, discipline, religious order) and sociological terms, notably class structure and political freedom, compared to previous societies and times, such as medievalism and traditional Christianity (e.g., Catholicism). If Comte is right, then this gives an

---

[51] Weber comments that the character of Calvinism "differs from that of all other churches, Catholic, Lutheran and Islamic. The basic dogma of strict Calvinism, the doctrine of predestination, makes it impossible for the church to administer sacraments [with] any significance for eternal salvation. The elect need no church for their own sake. By no means does the church exist for the salvation of souls and the sinners" community of love; its sole purpose is the augmentation of God's glory and honor, thus a cold Divine reason of state." In his view, "predestination is a "belief of virtuosi, who alone can accept the thought of the everlasting "double decree." But as this doctrine continued to flow into the routine of everyday living and into the religion of the masses, its gloomy severeness became more and more intolerable." He adds that "the "determination of earthly life and the predestination of other-worldly life have been established from the eternity. The damned might well complain about their sinfulness imposed by predestination, if animals could complain that they had not been created human beings [per] Calvinism. Calvinism involved the "combination of faith in absolutely valid norms with absolute determinism and the complete transcendentality of God [as] a product of great genius." For example, he remarks that in contrast to Catholicism, for Calvinist Puritans (like Jews, the Holy Scripture "is a binding law, which the individual must know and interpret correctly." In turn, Heller (1986:114) suggests that "it was Calvin above all who fully worked out the religious implications of the concept of God's omnipotent will expressed through revelation." Similarly, Elwood (1999:9) observes that French Calvinism "offered more than a simple championing of God's transcendence [and] rejection of Catholic affirmations of the embodiment of God and the sacred in physical media, events, and institutions [but] revolutionary ways of conceiving of [divine] power".

interesting and unexpected twist to Calvinism as a paradigmatic "revolutionary philosophy" within Protestantism and to the Calvinist Reformation as the paradigmatic case of a Protestant and generally religious "revolution", thus theological and social "innovation".

Specifically, the above makes Calvinism operate and appear as counter-revolutionary or reactionary and the Calvinist, Second Reformation as a counter-revolution or reaction. This holds true if the lack of substantial theological or sociological innovations defines counter-revolutions or the inverse (i.e., "un-creative destructions") of what Schumpeter analyzes as the revolutionary process of "creative destruction" defined instead by societal, notably economic, inventions, as elaborated below. And, if revolution is considered the expression and form of radicalism strictly speaking, counter-revolution or reaction is one of extremism in the broad sense, specifically what Comte[52] denotes as "retrograde" or reactionary and extreme conservatism within Calvinism and perhaps generally. Either revolutionary or counter-revolutionary, that is a revolution or counter-revolution, Calvinism represents radicalism, as in the first case, or extremism, as in the second. Moreover, in a sociological account, Calvinist movements were the "first revolutionary parties", and with its "radical ethic of social discipline", original Calvinism prefigured the "program of revolutionary republicanism" in countries like France and via Puritanism America (Gorski 1993).

In comparative-historical terms, while originally extreme or radical, especially militant, in France Calvinism became ever more subsequently and in non-French societal settings, notably via Puritanism and in Anglo-Saxon societies. Historical research indicates that while original "Calvinist militancy" was eventually undermined within the French religious and social setting, it acted as a "potent source of revolutionary energy" in other settings, including Holland and Great Britain and by implication America (Elwood 1999), ranging from "various degrees of civil disobedience" to "revolution" (VanDrunen 2006). In this account, Calvinism in Scotland acted as the catalyst in the "revolt against the regency of Mary of Guise", while providing "symbolic and conceptual support for the deposition of Mary Stuart" (Elwood 1999). Calvinists in Holland overturned the Spanish rule and instituted

---

[52] In general, Comte observes that "with every new uprising" of social difficulties, the "retrograde school" proposes the restoration of the "old political system" as "the only certain and universal remedy", which is both diagnostic and prophetic of religious reactionary conservatism, including Calvinism.

a theocratic "republic", and, of course, in England they dethroned and killed the king, transiently abolishing the monarchy.[53] Calvinists-as-American Puritans transferred and intensified this initial "Calvinist militancy" and "revolutionary energy" to New England against corresponding "evil" and "ungodly" forces (Native Americans, Quakers, etc.) and eventually the rest of America, notably the "old" South, via the Great Awakenings (Baldwin 2006; German 1995).

However, as hinted, a "considerable irony" or contradiction obtains in an "association of revolutionary politics" with Calvin as an extremely "politically conservative" figure (Elwood 1999; also, Heller 1986). Reportedly, Calvin and other key "Reformed" figures had no intention of contributing to "social revolution" and thus radical change in society. Instead, they confined the impact of their "Reformation" within the "specifically religious or 'spiritual' " realm (Elwood 1999; Heller 1986), as did his disciples in Geneva (e.g., Vernet[54]) (Sorkin 2005), with secondary exceptions to his demand of "strict obedience" to political authority (VanDrunen 2006).

An apparent solution to that above "considerable irony" or inner contradiction was that Calvinism, including Puritanism, adopted both revolutionary or radical protest politics *and* strict political conservatism in the function of attaining its "holy" purpose of total mastery of society in the form of "Divinely ordained" theocracy. Specifically, revolutionary and overall radical protest politics, including both genuine

---

[53] French Calvinists gained the "status of a protected religious minority within an officially Catholic society [by] accepting the Edict of Nantes of 1598" (Elwood 1999:171). According to Elwood (1999:5) Calvinism effected in Reformation France "a semiotic revolution—a revolution that created a conceptual framework for the new, revolutionary modes of social and political thought and activity that convulsed European societies at the dawn of the modern age". Similarly, Fitzpatrick (1999:47–8) suggests that the Edict of Nantes "afforded some measure of toleration to French Protestants" and that its revocation in 1685 "created a situation far worse than the existing one of limited toleration." Also, Mentzer (2007:348) registers the "revocation of the Edict of Nantes and the proscription of Protestantism in 1685."

[54] Sorkin (2005:286) remarks that Calvin's successor in Geneva Vernet helped to "restore Rousseau to Calvinism". Also, Garrard (2003:1) specifically notices that Rousseau went back to his native city in 1754 to be "readmitted to the Calvinist Church and to have his Genevan citizenship restored." And to reveal his restoration to Calvinism and his original "Calvinist background" (Garrard 2003:72) in Geneva, Rousseau proposed punishing with death those who did not provide public proof of their belief in the civil religion ("the existence of an omnipotent, intelligent, benevolent divinity that foresees and provides"), within his republican "Theocracy" or "Theocratic Government" in which to "serve the State is to serve its tutelary God".

revolution and "various degrees of civil disobedience", acted as the most effective strategy and instrument of (re)establishing its Divine theocracy as "domination over the sinful world" by Calvinist saints. Alternatively, they did as the strategy and means of destroying non-Calvinist (Catholic, Lutheran, Anglican, Native American or pagan) institutions, powers, and ideas and their liberal-secular versions like the Renaissance and the Enlightenment.

Conversely, strict political and other conservatism was the necessary and effective means of petrifying or perpetuating Calvinist theocracy and domination once established, as in Geneva, Holland, and, via Puritanism, Scotland, old and New England, against countervailing religious and secular forces. In light of such dual imperatives, for Calvin et al. no great irony, mystery, or self-contradiction existed between their revolutionary politics *and* political conservatism. Rather, both were logical and effective strategies and instruments a la Machiavellianism in the service of Divine design, as are for their heirs, fundamentalist Protestants in America, as well as Islamic fundamentalists (Mansbach 2006; Turner 2002) and fascists in Europe (McLaughlin 1996).

*Disciplinarian, Repressive, and Hyper-Ascetic Protestantism*

Calvinism is disciplinarian and repressive Protestantism, distinguished from and opposed to its non-disciplinarian, non-repressive, and liberal versions like, in Weber's and other sociological accounts, Lutheranism, Anglicanism, and others (Quakerism, etc.). In short, Calvinism, including Puritanism, is the epitome and face of Protestant disciplinarianism, repression, and social control, as well as asceticism overall.

For instance, Comte suggests that Calvinism, including Puritan Presbyterianism as its extension into Scotland[55] (Berry 1997; Gorski 2003),

---

[55] Berry (1997:12–3) notes that "after much struggle and bloodshed, and after the accession of William and Mary [invited by anti-Catholic Anglicans from Calvinist-ruled Holland], the 1690 Settlement established Presbyterianism as the officially sanctioned form of Church government [in Scotland] and subscription to the tenets of the Westminster Confession was made the test of orthodoxy." He adds that "six years later this was put into fateful effect with the execution of a nineteen-year-old student Thomas Aikenhead for blasphemy (even after he had recanted of his alleged view that theology was 'a rapsidie of faigned and ill invented Nonsense' " (Berry (1997:13). Berry (1997:13) adds that the Union with England in 1707 "should have confirmed the Church's position since the retention of Presbyterianism was one of the articles of the Treaty", though "gradually as the new century advanced the rigours of Calvinist theology lessened" such that from the 1730s on within Presbyterianism "there was a divergence between

practices "violent repression" and is thus "best suited to opposition," and alternatively unsuited or unfit for government in contrast with Lutheranism and Episcopalism. He hence anticipates what Weber identifies as the "unexampled tyranny" of Calvinist Puritanism. Further, Comte argues that, while in Catholicism "simply a consequence of its modern disorganization", the "forcible repression" of religious and all social freedom[56] is "inherent in the very nature" of Calvinism (and Protestantism), and invariably occurred as soon as Calvinists seized power, including Puritan sects from the moment temporal powers "passed into their hands for however a short time". Arguably, Calvinism grants "entire impunity to private oppression", except for a "few temporal rules generally framed and always applied by the oppressors themselves", in the face of Calvinist theocrats. Particularly, Comte cites "civilizing the enslaved" as the "excuse" for slavery[57] in Calvinism. This apparently refers to American Puritanism's attempt to "civilize" *cum* enslave and exterminate Native Americans in New England (Gould 1996; Munch 2001) and similar practices (after the Great Awakenings) against these and other "ungodly" and "inferior" groups (Mexicans, etc.) in the South and the "Wild West" (Clemens 2007). As known, these Puritan "civilizing" processes were driven and sanctified by the theological concept of America's Divine "manifest destiny."

Subsequent sociological analyses validate Comte by identifying Calvinism's, in particular Puritanism's, "almost military" and "inquisitorial" discipline, mixed with its "remorseless and violent rigors" and "iron

---

those who held fast to what they regarded as authoritative Calvinist doctrine and those who took a more "rational" or less scriptural approach and who emphasised social obligations at least as much as personal salvation".

[56] At most, for Comte in Calvinism and Protestantism overall free inquiry is "restrained within the limits of the Christian theology". Moreover, in his view, both Calvinism and Lutheranism were as "hostile to mental liberty [and progress] as Catholicism."

[57] Comte adds that both Calvinism and Lutheranism were "sanctioning the political subservience that was only implicit among Catholic peoples [thus] the servile transformation". Further, he argues that both are "yet even more hostile to progress [than Catholicism] and [have] been instituted from the beginning for perpetual subjection". Arguably, Protestantism overall by elevating its subjection to temporal power "into principle could not but be retrograde", just as Catholicism. In particular, he remarks that Protestantism overall "has nowhere, and least of all in England shown itself averse to the spirit of caste, which it has even attempted to restore". He refers to what he calls the "inherent nullity of Protestantism appeared in the impotence of its puny authorities to protect the lower classes". In his view, Protestantism is associated with "aristocratic" and Catholicism with "monarchical" rule.

collectivism" (Tawney 1962)—rather than, as Parsons et al. suppose, individualism—or strict "collective organization" (Gorski 1993). A sociological study suggests that Calvinism was more disciplinarian, repressive, and thus authoritarian than Catholicism and other Protestantism like Lutheranism and Anglicanism, as were consequently Calvinist societies Holland, England, and Scotland relative to Catholic and Lutheran countries[58] (Gorski 2003).

In a way, as Weber and contemporary sociologists imply (Gorski 2003; Munch 1981), Calvinism and in consequence Puritanism is disciplinarian, repressive, and authoritarian overall in virtue of being ascetic, as well as orthodox, absolutist, and radical, Protestantism.[59] For what defines Calvinist and other extreme asceticism or austerity, as well as orthodoxy, absolutism, and radicalism, is strict discipline, severe repression, and total control to the point of, as Calvin et al. command, and Simmel, Pareto and Sorokin observe, humiliation[60] (Mentzer 2007) and torture or torment of oneself and others alike, thus sado-masochism. Conversely, Calvinism's genesis and methodical operation as extremely ascetic, as well as orthodox or conservative, absolutist, radical and fundamentalist, Protestantism generates, explains, and thus predicts its exemplary Protestant disciplinarianism, control, repression, and authoritarianism or even proto-totalitarianism overall, including fascism (Adorno 2001; McLaughlin 1996), as its definite syndromes and outcomes.

---

[58] Moreover, Gorski (2003:xvi) argues that "what "steam did for the modern economy, [Calvinist] discipline did for the modern polity", specifically the absolute or authoritarian state.

[59] Weber remarks that the French "Huguenot and Scottish nobility later stopped fighting for Calvinism, and everywhere the further development of ascetic Protestantism became the concern of the citizen middle classes."

[60] For example, Mentzer (2007:331) registers the public "day of fast and humiliation" among Calvinists in France, the Netherlands and Scotland, as well as English Puritans as an "eminent expression" of Calvinist and Puritan piety. In this account, within Calvinism the fast "possessed a strong disciplinary element: moral failure necessitated contrition and reform of behavior" (Mentzer 2007:331). Predictably, Calvinism made attendance at fasting "obligatory, and failure to participate was treated as a moral fault, subject to consistorial discipline and censure" (Mentzer 2007:341). Notably, Mentzer (2007:335) cites Calvin's statement that fasting is "useful for subduing the flesh, or testifying our humiliation [and] an auxiliary to prayer", and alternatively that "with a full stomach our mind is not so lifted up to God", even that life is a "sort of perpetual fasting". Mentzer (2007:336) comments that for Calvin "restraint in the consumption of food and sobriety with respect to drink were always commendable Christian virtues", and, notably a "means for maintaining discipline". He concludes that Calvin et al. "emphasized sacred transcendence" as against Catholic insistence on "God's constant, close presence [e.g.,] the transubstantiation of bread and wine into Christ's flesh and blood" (Mentzer 2007:339; also, Elwood 1999).

The point is that Calvinist, including Puritan, strict discipline, total control, and severe repression, including humiliation, sadism-masochism, and cruel and inhuman treatment, are not random or contingent and transient, as often assumed. They are rather intrinsic, systematic, and permanent to Calvinism, notably Puritanism, as self-defined supreme ascetic, austere, and strict Protestantism, simply "genetic" or "built-in". As Weber implies about original Calvinism and its sectarian Puritan derivatives (e.g., Baptism, Methodism), they all emerge and operate as the "methodical" doctrine and practice of sanctification, some sort of "method in the madness" (Smith 2000) of extreme control, discipline, repression, and asceticism overall. In his view, extreme and systematic inner-worldly asceticism[61] by the "methodical mastering" of one's own and eventually others' behavior in social life, thus by implication mixed sadism and masochism (Adorno 2001; Fromm 1941; Mansbach 2006; McLaughlin 1996), "included, above all, ascetic Protestantism", specifically Calvinism and consequently Puritanism.

An historical model and image of Calvinist, especially Puritan military-style discipline, control, repression, and asceticism overall, including self-humiliation or self-abnegation, was ancient Sparta as the pre-Christian exemplar and symbol of these attributes. Remember, Calvin and his successors modeled French-speaking Geneva after "austere Sparta" as the ideal rather than "liberal Athens", the "authoritarian" Spartans rather than the "democratic" Athenians (the "anti-Paris"), while Enlightenment liberals like Hume rejected the Spartan as a "completely inappropriate model for modern civilization" (Garrard 2003). Also, recall Tocqueville's first Puritans, Winthrop et al., designed and created and their descendents persisted (Samuel Adams, etc.) in recreating Puritan America as what they called no less than "Christian Sparta". As with Calvin's Geneva Spartan model, the latter was a theological design and social system only to be rejected or tempered by Enlightenment-based liberal-democratic figures like, alongside Hume, Jefferson and Madison during and after the Revolution, two centuries after its establishment (Kloppenberg 1998). On this account, American Puritanism was no more than ascetic, austere Calvinism (Kloppenberg 1998) expanded beyond France and Geneva, and Winthrop et al. just Calvin's loyal "children" or agents in the "new nation".

---

[61] Weber adds that Calvinism introduced the "idea of the necessity of proving one's faith in worldly activity [as] it gave religiously inclined people a positive incentive to asceticism."

The historical perversity of Calvinist Sparta indicates that Calvinism, including American Puritanism, did *not* find medieval theocracy and its harsh monastic discipline, repression, and asceticism (including the Inquisition), and even the very first austere Christian communities and times, to be disciplinary, repressive, and ascetic *enough* for its purpose and taste. Instead, it went back to pre-Christian, thus, in an inner contradiction, "pagan" or "heathen"[62] (Fehler 2005; VanDrunen 2006), societies and times to rediscover austere, authoritarian Sparta as its model or image! This exemplifies Calvinist-Puritan, primitivism, incorporating medievalism or Christian fundamentalism (Mansbach 2006) *and* pre-Christian antiquity and anti-humanism, including no less than what Hume and Comte identify as "barbarism",[63] in respect of extreme discipline, (self) humiliation, repression, asceticism, and related respects.

Remember, the Calvinist Second Reformation (Morck et al. 2005) was not just a reform or "improvement" in terms of religious and societal discipline, repression, and asceticism (and theology) within Protestantism and Christianity. It was essentially a disciplinary, repressive, and ascetic revolution, and thus radical social change (Clemens 2007; Gorski 2003; Loveman 2005; Nischan 1994). Perhaps Comte's "primitive Protestantism" or the Protestant Reformation proper can (as he, Weber and, other sociologists suggest) be described in such terms, as indicated by its initial commandment of everyone becoming a monk (and priest). Yet, Calvinism apparently did not find the first Protestant Reformation and thus in extension initial Lutheranism, sufficiently disciplinary, repressive, and ascetic for its purpose and taste. Arguably, this perceived Lutheran insufficiency in discipline, repression, and asceticism overall provided the putative ground and rationale for the Calvinist Second and "final" Reformation, thus the "true" Reformed Church, just as that of medieval Catholicism did for Lutheranism and its Reformation.

---

[62] VanDrunen (2006:164) remarks that Calvinist theorists post-Calvin (e.g., Beza) used "appeals to heathen writings" or the "wisdom of pagan antiquity", which contradicts anti-paganism in Calvinism and Christianity overall. This is what in turn Fehler (2005:137) explicitly suggests by stating that early Calvinists and other Protestants, including American Puritans, "may have objected to blending Christianity with pagan philosophy", as America's "orthodox Calvinists", following their predecessors in Geneva, also attempted during the 19th century.

[63] This pre-Christian primitivism, including "Spartanism", alongside its observed reversal of Christianity's traditional values like compassion, forgiveness and humanism overall, makes some analysts, including Hume, Comte, and in part Weber, wonder if or deny that Calvinism, particularly Puritanism, is truly, at it claims, "Christian."

For example, Calvin, after failing in his native France, reintroduced the "new system" of both ecclesiastic and societal Spartan-style discipline at Geneva (Heller 1986). And, his successors perpetuated this disciplinary innovation (Garrard 2003; Sorkin 2005) and even extended it to Holland, Scotland and England (Gorski 2003; Murdock[64] 2005), and eventually America (Davis 2005). In short, Calvinist disciplinary revolutions unleashed the "new ethics and practices of self-discipline" (Loveman 2005) and repression through constructing and enforcing "disciplinary technologies"[65] (Clemens 2007) in Europe and beyond.

For illustration, Calvinist theocratic churches first in France and then Western Europe overall aimed at disciplining the faithful centering on the human body, by restraining humans" sexuality, regulating their marriages, prohibiting "games and dancing", eliminating "extravagant dress and makeup", suppressing carnivals and similar events, and dissuading people from the "excesses" of eating and drinking, including fasting as a act of collective denial of food and drink[66] (Mentzer 2007). Simply, Calvinism in Europe disciplined, controlled, and repressed the "human body both physically and spiritually" (Mentzer 2007). And, Puritanism in England and America inherited and even further intensified this Calvinist discipline, control, and repression often reaching the point of medieval-like superstition or irrationalism.[67]

---

[64] In a review of Gorski's (2003) book on Calvinism, Murdock (2005) cites what he calls "one striking example" of Calvinist moral discipline and repression in Holland. This is the ""drowning cell" in the Amsterdam house of discipline for beggars and vagrants. Those inmates who refused to undertake forced labour or who rebelled against the institution's strict moral code could find themselves in a room which steadily filled with water. "Patients" could only empty the room by furiously pumping out water, which was intended to cure their laziness" (Murdock 2005:146). Coincidentally or not, the Calvinist "drowning cell" for disciplining the lazy is strikingly similar to "water-boarding" used by the US neoconservative government as an "enhanced" interrogation technique (yet widely seen as torture) against "enemies" in its Puritan-style "holy" war on the "axis of evil" (Turner 2002).

[65] Clemens (2007:534) suggests that "the Protestant Reformation, and Calvinism in particular, created new orientations among believers who then constructed disciplinary technologies that could elicit believer-like behavior, even from reprobates."

[66] Mentzer (2007:333-4) comments this Calvinist "puritanical notion of proper Christian comportment meant a constant struggle to govern and direct the body" of all believers. For instance, he notes that French and other European Calvinists, including English Puritans, "collectively denied their real bodies food and drink" (Mentzer (2007:360) through fasting in contrast to the latter as a more "individual act" among medieval Christians.

[67] For instance, Mentzer (2007:357) finds that Puritans in England, "much as their French Reformed co-religionists, valued the practice" of fasting and related forms of disciplining humans and their bodies, yet irrational or unusual "were the fasts that

In consequence, recall Calvinist societies in early modern Europe, including, alongside France's Huguenot sections, Calvin's Geneva, the Netherlands, Scotland, England (temporarily), and Prussia were "more disciplined" and repressive ("orderly") than Catholic, Lutheran, and Anglican countries or regions (Gorski 2003), as was Puritan America, especially New England (Munch 2001).

At this juncture, the Calvinist Second Reformation acted as not merely a disciplinary, repressive, and ascetic revolution. For the Lutheran First Reformation was so as well, at least initially and generally compared with Catholicism and its perceived lack or laxity in this respect as, in Weber's and other sociological accounts, the identified cause or rationale for the rise of Protestantism before Calvinism. The Calvinist Second Reformation was a hyper-disciplinary, repressive, and ascetic revolution, or super-revolution in discipline, repression, and asceticism within Protestantism and Christianity. This is implied in his sociological definition of Calvinism, including Puritanism, as truly ascetic Protestantism in contrast to Lutheranism and Anglicanism defined instead as non- or least ascetic Protestant types.

At this point, Calvinism, including Puritanism, and their revolutions are more accurately or completely considered and described as *hyper* ascetic and disciplinary, and Lutheranism and Anglicanism as under ascetic and disciplinary, Protestantism. This holds true since all Protestant types and reforms were almost axiomatically (the Reformation's design) more or less ascetic and disciplinary, compared to supposedly non-ascetic, undisciplined, or "lax" Catholicism. In short, Calvinism involved super- and non-Calvinism under-regulation and control with respect to moral discipline and asceticism (Heckathorn 1990). Arguably, the Protestant Reformation in its initial design erupted as a hyper-disciplinary, repressive, and ascetic revolution making human society an expanded monastery, or original Protestantism intended to become Sorokin's socio-cultural "ideational" super-system of inflexible discipline, repression, and asceticism. If this is correct, Calvinism could plausibly and did effectively claim to be the "true Reformed Church", and thus Simmel's "orthodox party," in contrast to Lutheranism seen as failing to fully realize, hence not "true" to, this original Protestant

---

some English Puritans held to exorcise demons" from young people. Mentzer (2007:358) also registers the "astonishing persistence" of such irrational medieval traditions in Calvinist (Reformed) congregations in Scotland, though fasting in them followed or paralleled the "French Reformed experience".

design or, as Comte put it, dream. This consequently applies to Puritanism as the "true English Reformation" (Tawney 1962) in relation to Anglicanism.

The Calvinist-Puritan operated in design or effect as an illiberal counter-revolution or reaction in the sense of the restoration of medievalist monastic, and even Spartan (Garrard 2003), discipline, repression or authoritarianism, and asceticism. This is a far cry from the picture of the Puritan as liberal-bourgeois revolution (Moore 1993) whereby (as Marx put it) free competition was "conquered" in England, ushering in political liberalism and democracy, modern capitalism, and scientific and technological advances (Merton 1968; yet, Becker 1984; Goldstone 2000; Mallard[68] 2005). Thus, Comte argues that the Calvinist and Protestant revolution generated "no innovation, in regard to discipline, ecclesiastical orders or dogma", just as with respect to political freedom or subjection and class structure (caste), compared with medievalism and traditional Christianity. On this account, he usually describes Calvinism and Protestantism in general as "retrograde" and to that extent counter-revolutionary or reactionary.

The very term the Calvinist "Second Reformation" or "Reformed Church", though its theological and social outcomes might be revolutionary as unintended consequences, implies a design and praxis of counter-revolution or reaction. It does in the form of restoring or redeeming the Christian "golden past" or Biblical "paradise lost" from existing "evil" and "ungodly" non-Calvinist powers such as Catholicism (France and Holland), even in part Lutheranism (Germany) rather than revolution proper in Schumpeter's sense of simultaneously destroying the old order and creating the new or innovation, in short "creative destruction". In this respect, the "Second Reformation" or "Reformed Church" really better defines or describes Calvinism's genesis and character in substantive terms than disciplinary and ascetic, let alone proto-liberal "revolution". Alternatively, "disciplinary revolution" is, if not inaccurate, imprecise or misleading to describe Calvinism and its "Second Reformation". For (if) the latter did not invent substantively any new discipline, but only it restored, albeit reinforced, the old, including that of Christian medieval monasticism and asceticism, lost in "lax" official Catholicism, and even pre-Christian Sparta as perhaps the first

---

[68] In implied contrast to Marxian and related economic explanations, Mallard (2005:1006) remarks that the Puritan revolution in England and elsewhere was not "purely driven by technological changes."

"revolution" in this respect within Western civilization and the Calvinist-Puritan ideal. This was exemplified by Calvin's modeling of Geneva as "austere Sparta" and then, via social contagion, Winthrop's semi-grotesque design of America as "Christian Sparta".

Moreover, the Calvinist "Second Reformation" was also a counter-revolution in the form of universalizing (Walzer 1963) these medievalist (Mentzer 2007) and various other pre-modern, including Spartan (Garrard 2003), elements and times. This was indicated by its reinforcement and its attempted fulfillment of the First Reformation's original commandment (paraphrasing) "thou shall now be monks for their lives". At least from the stance of the Enlightenment and liberalism in general, the Calvinist "Second Reformation" *cum* a hyper-disciplinary, repressive, and ascetic revolution was a revival and even extension of the Dark Middle Ages" and in part Sparta's severe moral discipline, repression, authoritarianism, and monastic asceticism from the dead past. Hence, it was a counter-revolution, just as had been, at least in Weber's account (also, Eisenstadt 1965; Mansbach 2006), the Protestant Reformation proper due to its original design of human society as a super-monastery and of humans as life-long monks.

Calvinism by its Second Reformation set the pattern or model for virtually all subsequent Calvinist, including Puritan, revolutions as counter-revolutions. This is the pattern of restorations and extensions of dead, past institutions and practices, invariably medieval (monastic) discipline, repression, asceticism, and theocracy in the form of hyper-disciplinary, repressive, and ascetic Bibliocracy, and even their pre-medieval forms, as epitomized by Calvin et al.'s and American Puritanism's ideal of "Christian Sparta". Namely, they proved to be counter-revolutions in being theocratic restorations and fundamentalist revivals overall by restoring and further expanding and intensifying medieval Bibliocracy as the Calvinist-Puritan "golden past" or "paradise lost." In turn, Calvinist counter-revolutions or restorations express and materialize Calvinism's genesis and character as strict and extreme societal conservatism or conservative extremism. Conversely, the second generates and predicts the first.

In general, Calvinist-Puritan putative revolutions function in their design or outcome as counter-revolutions, because they are backward- rather than forward-looking, centered on the past, not the future, in Mannheim's words, anti-utopias, not utopias. In Schumpeter's terms, these disciplinary, repressive, and ascetic revolutions act as counter-revolutions in virtue of being the almost polar opposite of "creative destruction" as the process of destroying the old and creating new social (including economic) structures within modern society (capitalism). Instead, they represent a sort of "un-creative destruction" by destroying existing, pre- or non-Calvinist-Puritan social structures, yet without really creating new, "liberal", or "modernist" ones, or substantial institutional inventions. Instead, they restore and universalize, with minor modifications, those from a defined "golden past" or "paradise lost", namely monastic and theocratic medievalism and even Spartan and other pre-medievalism. Comte precisely intimates this moment observing that Calvinist and generally Protestant revolutions engendered "no innovation" with respect to discipline, church, or dogma in relation to medieval and prior Christian societies and periods.

In addition to the "Second Reformation" in France as the point of origin and model, this pattern of uncreative destruction through restoration was witnessed in virtually all subsequent Calvinist disciplinary and generally ascetic revolutions, from Geneva, Holland, and Prussia to, through their Puritan versions, in England (the 1640s–60s) and America (the Great Awakenings of the 1740s–1800s, etc.). For instance, sociological analyses (Goldstone 1986, 1991) show that the Calvinist *cum* Puritan Revolution in England resisted and attacked all political and other societal "innovations" in favor of restoring medievalism via a "defense of traditional English ways" (e.g., the "ancient" constitution). Alternatively, it attempted to destroy, and temporarily abolished or deposed, Anglican as well as monarchical institutions through a "crusade" against non-Calvinist, notably Catholic, forces[69] (also, Elwood 1999; Gorski 2000; Zaret 1989).

On this account, it effectively operated or qualified as a counter-revolution in the form of restoration or uncreative destruction rather than genuine revolution in Schumpeter's sense of creative destruction as the simultaneous process of destroying the existing societal system and of innovation (his preferred term is "invention") by creating new social, including economic and political, structures. At the minimum, the English Puritan Revolution proceeded as an anti- or pre-liberal (Zaret 1989) disciplinary counter-revolution rather than, as Marx and

---

[69] Goldstone (1986:295) suggests that "Puritanism developed a revolutionary appeal [because it] was a crusade—against corruption, Catholicism and popery—offered as a panacea. [It] was thus more an amalgamation of English Protestant nationalism; a defense of traditional English ways; and an attack on all [policy] innovations than a purely religious phenomenon."

contemporary sociologists assume, liberal-democratic, bourgeois "revolution" (Moore 1993), just as Calvinism, including Puritanism, did not create, usher in, or was not liberalism, particularly secularism and pluralism. In a sense, just as the original Calvinist revolution in Europe, the Puritan in England was an attempt at revival of the pre-liberal Dark Middle Ages, notably the medieval theocracy, not at ushering in the liberal-secular and rationalist Enlightenment only to be fully ushered in by anti-Puritan (and anti-religious) Hume et al. in Scotland and Great Britain overall (Berry 1997). In Tocqueville's terms, English-American Puritanism emerged from the "midst of an ancient feudal society" such as medieval, old England and then attempted to restore it as the "golden past" (Goldstone 1986) via counter-revolutions as cases of adverse reaction (and selection).

For instance, like the English Puritan Revolution of which they were a sort of replica or reflex, the evangelical Great Awakenings in America proved essentially counter-revolutions. They did in virtue of being the "counter-offensive" (Foerster 1962) or revival of Puritanism and thus Calvinism against nascent liberalism, secularism, and rationalism (Fehler 2005), notably the Age of Reason or the Enlightenment (Byrne 1997), during the 18th–19th centuries. They proved to be the counter-revolutionary movements and instruments of Calvinism, with their evangelicalism expressed and realized in "revivalism" (Clark 1999). They were the ultimate manifestations of Calvinist revivalism (German 1995) or Puritan restorationism (Coffey 1998), fulfilling Calvin's and Winthrop's vision or dream of a "cohesive, stable, and religious society" (Baldwin 2006). For instance, the first Great Awakening of the 1730s (led and personified by Puritan Jonathan Edwards) was regarded as deriving from an "atavistic, anticapitalist impulse" (German 1995) in the form of what was Hume's nightmare scenario, an "eruption of Protestant enthusiasm"[70] flourishing mostly among the "rural poor" (Byrne 1997) and to that extent counter-revolutionary or reactionary as well as anti-rationalistic. This holds true of the second Great Awakening of the 1800s as the sequel of the first and more successful

---

[70] Byrne (1997:52) adds that Edwards" and other revivalist Puritans" emphasis on personal commitment and inward faith demonstrated through vibrant outward expression was one of the aspects of religion which the cool detachment of the Enlightenment ideal found most repugnant; here, if more evidence was needed, was another clear example of Hume's contention that human beings are governed by their passions much more than by their reason."

by resulting in the definitive "triumph" of evangelical religion in America[71] (Baldwin 2006) by expanding Calvinism *cum* Puritanism from New England to the "new nation" as a whole, notably the South turned from a not so godly" Anglican region into a "Bible Belt".

In essence, both proved Puritan counter-revolutions attempting to reestablish and expand Calvinist theocracy from New England to all America. They did in accordance with Calvinism's premise that a "widespread" religious, specifically evangelical, revival was the only effective way and means to fulfill Calvin-Winthrop's dream or vision of a theocratic, "cohesive, stable, and religious" society (Baldwin 2006). Still another moment indicated that the celebrated Great Awakenings were Calvinist counter-revolutions and offensives in America against emerging liberalism, secularism and rationalism, notably the Enlightenment. It was the moment that New England and other Calvinists (Presbyterians, Baptists, Methodists) acted as the major strategists, protagonists, and supporters (German 1995), or "wholehearted participants" (Baldwin 2006) in both evangelical revivals.

And, this original "drama" or battle between Calvinist theocratic revivalism or "revivalist Christianity" and "fundamental American Enlightenment ideals" admittedly continues to be reenacted in modern America in various political and cultural conflicts, including the issue of separation of church and state, and the relation of science and religion (Byrne 1997). Also, comparative sociological studies find that historically Puritan societies like America and in part the Great Britain (the "English-speaking zone") hold less "secular-rational" or more traditionalist and conservative social values than the non-Puritan (the "Protestant Europe zone"), as do Catholic (the "Latin-American zone") and Islamic countries (Inglehart and Baker 2000).

In sum, virtually all Calvinist revolutions were extremely disciplinary, repressive, and ascetic counter-revolutions as restorations. They were

---

[71] Baldwin (2006:97) states that evangelical religion, as expressed in the Second Great Awakening, "provided just the kind of religious and moral energy" that ruling Calvinists in New England "feared would be sorely lacking if disestablishment and voluntarism destroyed the established religious culture." While recounting their distrust toward the early Methodists in New England, Baldwin (2006:97) admits that both they and Calvinists held that " "the "vision of a cohesive, stable, and religious society" could only be achieved [via] a widespread religious revival", in fact an original Calvinist principle that Methodism and other evangelicalism (Baptism) in America apparently embraced. Baldwin (2006:106) also admits that Calvinists were "wholehearted participants in the evangelical revival" of the 19th century marking the "triumph" of evangelical religion (and "voluntarism" or rather sectarianism) in America.

Table 7.2.  Main characteristics of Calvinism

Religious orthodoxy and social conservatism
  medievalism
Anti-liberalism
  anti-secularism
  anti-pluralism
  anti-humanism
Absolutism and monism
  anti-relativism
Extremism and radicalism
  militancy and violence, including militarism and religious war
  counter-Revolution
Disciplinarianism and asceticism
  strict discipline
  repression
Fundamentalism and theocracy
  evangelicalism
  Bibliocracy

"uncreative destructions" by, rather than creating new structures, reviving from the "dead past" and even intensifying and universalizing medieval-style Bibliocracy as Calvinism's original, perennial ideal, while destroying virtually everything else, including non-theocratic institutions and "ungodly" humans, in the process. In this sense, they were restorations of the anti- or pre-liberal Dark Middle Ages, not creations or inventions, nor even anticipations, of the liberal-secular Enlightenment. They were theocratic and fundamentalist revivals, simply revivalist and thus counter-revolutionary or reactionary, as exemplified both by Calvin's original "Second Reformation" in France and its Puritan sequels the "Great Awakenings" in America. Hence, at this juncture theocracy, specifically Bibliocracy, and fundamentalism reaffirms and reappears as the defining and central element of America's Calvinist "destiny" or "predestination" via Puritanism. (Table 7.2. provides a summary of the main characteristics of Calvinism.)

### *Calvinism Reinvented and Reinforced: Reenter Puritanism*

English-American Puritanism basically reinvented and further expanded and reinforced these properties and outcomes of French-European Calvinism. As noted, Puritanism originated and operated as a kind of hyper-Calvinism, Calvinism ever-more "turned mad" (Bourdieu 2000) or "gone wild" (Habermas 2001) in respect of conservatism, radicalism, including violence and militarism, repression, authoritarianism, asceticism, as well as fundamentalism and evangelical theocracy in Great Britain and especially in America. Notably, recall American Puritanism was the most conservative or retrograde, extreme (or radical), absolutist, repressive, and totalitarian subtype of Calvinism (Gould 1996; Munch 2001; Stivers 1994) and thus hyper-Calvinism, and US Puritans were super-Calvinists and, as they claimed, "supermen" overall. Admittedly, in America Calvinist rigid religious and political conservatism prevailed in the "colonial period among the Puritans" (Dunn and Woodard 1996). Simply, American Puritanism was a kind of metastasizing, escalating, and intensifying Calvinism eventually reaching the "cancer stage" (McMurtry 1999) of self-destructive and deadly theocracy (Salem, etc.). It was "strict, stricter, strictest", including "totalistic, more totalitarian and most totalitarian" (Stivers 1994), or "absolute, more absolute, most absolute" and "harsh, harsher, harshest" (Munch 2001), and "dumb, dumber, dumbest" ("dumb" Puritan laws persisting in the "Bible Belt" and beyond) Calvinism. It was from the stance of non-Puritanism and non-Calvinism, notably liberalism, secularism and rationalism, simply the Enlightenment.

In particular, recall the Puritan Bibliocracy in early America such as New England's "Biblical Commonwealth" was the "most totalitarian" as well as enduring subtype of Calvinist theocracy ever established since Calvin's original theocratic experiment of the *civitas Dei* in Geneva. Thus, Weber implies that what he calls the Puritan "theocracy of New England" was the supreme or consummate case and realization of theocratic and radical Calvinism. Recall his observation that "under Winthrop's leadership" Massachusetts would permit the "settlement of gentlemen in, even an upper house with a hereditary nobility" only if potential candidates showed adherence to the Church. He adds that Puritan-ruled Massachusetts and in extension New England stayed closed for the sake of Church discipline" during and long after Winthrop's rule (Davis 2005; Munch 2001), as to non-Puritans (e.g., Quakers), let alone non-Protestants (Catholics) and non-Christians (Native Americans), all of them condemned, persecuted, and often executed for their "ungodliness". Elaborating on Weber, Tawney (1962) registers that in early America the "theocracy of Massachusetts" was "merciless" to both religious freedom and economic "license." Admittedly, Puritanism overall was hostile to toleration in religion and individualism in favor of its "iron collectivism" and "almost inquisitorial discipline" in society. A subsequent sociological study also shows that in early America, Puritanism established legal theocracy defining its criminal justice system "almost word for word from the Old Testament" (Stivers 1994). This provides a model for "born again" evangelicalism to ground and sanctify the penal, notably death-penalty, system in the "Bible Belt" by the Biblical principles of punishment ("eye for eye", "who shed blood"), revealing a remarkable continuity and Hume's detected Puritan obstinacy from the 17th to the 21st century. In sum, American Puritanism reinvented itself and functioned as the "most totalitarian form of Calvinism", searching for and imposing a "rigorous moral discipline" to substitute for an unsatisfactory "minimalistic morality" in earlier Christianity, especially Catholicism (Stivers 1994).

American Puritanism apparently rediscovered such moral discipline not only in Christian medievalism like monasticism but also in pre-Christian times and pre-medievalism, reaffirming Puritan primitivism or fundamentalism in moral and related terms. Thus, virtually imitating or emulating Calvin's Geneva as "austere Sparta" and the "anti-Paris" (Garrard 2003), American Puritanism pursued and even implemented the ideal of America as a "Christian Sparta" via "Puritan millennialism" in the North (Kloppenberg 1998), specifically New England. On the account of this historical primitivism, American Puritanism functioned as hyper-Calvinism and Winthrop et al. as super-Calvinists doing what and succeeding where Calvinism and Calvin had dreamed about but had never done or succeeded before in Europe. This is extending ancient, pre-Christian (or "pagan") austere, authoritarian Sparta from a model for only a Calvinist-ruled city (Geneva) to the ideal or design for an entire society or a Puritan "new nation".

In this sense, American Puritanism revealed itself as supremely primitive, anachronistic, austere, despotic, and inhuman, and Winthrop et al. as "world champions" in these respects, in the "extended family" of Calvinism and Calvin. This holds true insofar as Sparta originally was, versus liberal-democratic Athens, and still remains the paradigmatic exemplar and symbol of primitivism, anachronism, austerity, despotism, and inhumanity, including extreme discipline, moral repression, and cruelty. If American Puritanism was, as its apologists (Seaton 2006) claim and is frequently believed, truly democratic, liberal, and humanistic, it would have preferred Athens and its democracy, proto-liberalism (Garrard 2003; Infantino 2003), and humanism as the model for America. Simply, it would have designed and created America as "Christian

Athens", as in a way Jefferson, Madison, Franklin, and other liberal-democratic figures did or attempted by reconciling religion and democracy (Byrne 1997; Kloppenberg 1998), and not as "Christian" austere and authoritarian Sparta. No wonder, these US founders rejected the Puritan design and creation of America as "Christian Sparta", thus implicitly following Hume's rejection of the latter as a "completely inappropriate model for modern civilization" (Garrard 2003).

American Puritanism's original design as well as act of creation of America as "Christian Sparta" rather than as "Christian Athens" revealed clearly and unambiguously its anti- or pre-liberal, undemocratic, and primitive nature or aims, a strikingly manifest and salient moment yet overlooked or downplayed by US conservative sociologists and denied by "born again" Puritan fundamentalists. In retrospect, it is really remarkable and striking that even during the early 17th century or late medievalism that a Christian and any religious or political group like American Puritanism would choose as its model for human society a pre-Christian case dating about 20th centuries ago like ancient Sparta! Yet, this surprise evaporates or diminishes if one recalls that in doing so American Puritanism only adopted and expanded original Calvinism's blueprint and remolding of Geneva as austere, authoritarian Sparta (Garrard 2003), and thus it did not really "discover America" or "reinvent the wheel" in this respect.

The obvious question for Winthrop et al. and their descendents and admirers is simply why should "Christian [despotic, primitive] Sparta" rather than "Christian [democratic, proto-modernist] Athens" be the design of America insofar as the "new nation" is the "chosen land" of liberty, democracy, and modernity? (Lipset and Marks 2000). No rationalization of this prima facie irrational social choice can change the fact that Puritanism chose and methodically pursued despotism, repression, primitivism, and anti-humanism rather than democracy, liberty, modernity, and humanism. It did so by designing and essentially creating America, initially New England, after the model and image of ascetic-despotic Sparta rather than of liberal-democratic Athens, at least during the 17th–18th centuries until the American Revolution and its aftermath[72] (Fehler 2005). If anything, it is this striking Puritan

---

[72] Fehler (2005:134–7) suggests that during the 19th century orthodox Calvinism in America embraced Athens (and to a lesser extent Rome) and classical culture overall because of its "ability to unify a society" as a "cultural, political, and artistic ideal on which the young American republic should model itself" in the belief that the "young

*original* choice that made and still apparently makes American Puritanism hyper-Calvinism and hence totalitarianism, and revealed and reveals its members as super-Calvinists and thus totalitarians.

As a corollary, Calvinism endows America's destiny via Puritanism with corresponding intertwined and mutually reinforcing elements in conjunction with and revolving around the main and permanent element of theocracy as sociologically a total, and politically totalitarian, social system. These are, first, rigid conservatism or traditionalism and anti-liberalism; second, extremism, including violence, militancy, militarism, nationalism, and expansionism, third, strict discipline, repression, authoritarianism, and asceticism, fourth, theocratic fundamentalism, and related elements, such as anti-egalitarianism, anti-humanism, anti-secularism, anti-rationalism, and the like.

## Appendix: "Differences" between Calvinism and Puritanism Revisited

This appendix summarizes and reconsiders the supposed differences between French-European Calvinism and its Anglo-American transplant Puritanism. As argued, these are not primary or substantive, but rather mostly secondary or formal, differences ("differences").

For instance, a certain actual or potential "difference" between Calvinism and Puritanism is along the dimension of church-sect, with the first being presumably church, and the second a sect, as Weber and other sociologists (Munch 1981) suggest. However, originally Calvinism was, as seen, implicitly sectarian Protestantism, and Puritanism consequently Calvinist sectarianism. This is what Weber indicates by his expression "Calvinism and the other Puritan sects" as well as observation that even when and where the Reformed Church becomes a "universal organization" it continues to condition membership "on a contractual entry into some particular association" like Puritan sects in England and America (viz., Independents, Congregationalists, Presbyterians, Baptists, Methodists). He also notes that Calvinism resembles

---

republic was in constant peril of moral decline". In particular, it extolled Aristotle as "the most pious of all the heathen" in that an understanding of his ideas "would inform a distinctly American Christian humanism" (Fehler 2005:137). Fehler 2005:138) comments that orthodox Calvinism through the "cult of classicism" was "eager to reestablish their influence that had largely diminished in the wake of the American Revolution". In his view, "though the Calvinists no longer exerted an especially strong influence over their country, they could still demonstrate the importance of their role as moral legislators" (Fehler 2005:139). In theological terms, he comments that Protestants during the Reformation and the early Puritans "may have objected to blending Christianity with pagan philosophy [as] necessary to establishing republican Christianity in the new nation", notably that the "ancient civilizations lacked one element of greatness, Christian revelation" and that the ancients "lived before Christian revelation" (Fehler 2005:134–8).

these Puritan sects on the account of its "aristocratic [oligarchic] charismatic principle of predestination" and the "degradation of office charisma" by the command that (to paraphrase) "thou shall" perform the "elimination of those visibly condemned by God" as the holy "task of every member", thus strongly reinforcing the "importance" of the sect or congregation "vis-à-vis any office". At this juncture, he cites as an exemplar "the ecclesiastic revolution of the strict Calvinists in the Netherlands during the 1580s." Also, a sociological study shows that more than baptism, as in traditional Christianity, including Catholicism, was required to become a "member of the Reformed Church" in the Netherlands (Pollmann 2002) and in extension a Dutch citizen during Calvinist theocratic rule since the late 16th century. Consequently, only those making a "formal declaration of their faith" could be accepted as members by the notorious (Mansbach 2006) "consistory" of the Calvinist Church, thus form the "membership of the Reformed Churches" (Pollmann 2002).

In turn, even Puritanism considers and designates itself as a "pure church" (*pure ecclesia*) and, as Weber remarks, "hence the name 'Puritans'". This was paradigmatically exemplified by the official Congregational, yet substantively Calvinist (Baldwin 2006; Foerster 1962; German 1995), "Church" in early America. For example, Hume in his classical history of the "spectre" of Puritanism observes that the early English Puritans represented a sect "secretly" lurking in the Anglican church, and yet claimed to be the "only pure church; that their principles and practices ought to be established by law; and that no others ought to be tolerated",[73] which identifies the Puritan original blueprint of legal theocracy and intolerance.

Specifically, Puritanism tends to be a sect while being in what Hume, Comte and Weber identify as fanatical opposition, Simmel as protest, and Mises as revolt against non-Puritan powers, institutions, and values (Catholicism, Anglicanism, Lutheranism, liberalism, secularism, etc.), thus demanding freedom and tolerance for itself from them. Yet, it acts as a "church" or an established religious, typically theocratic institution such as Cromwell's Divine Parliament and New England's Congregational "Church" whenever and wherever it seizes government or, as Mill remarks, power. Puritanism eventually eliminates liberty and tolerance, or what it had self-righteously demanded for itself as a sect, as Hume[74] and Tocqueville classically observe and other

---

[73] Hume significantly comments that in view of such Puritan claims and aims "it may be questioned, therefore, whether the administration at this time could with propriety deserve the appellation of persecutors with regard to the Puritans [sic!]." Also, he notes that the "religious Puritans murmured at this tolerating measure of the king" James toward English Catholics, thus following Calvinists in Holland, Germany and elsewhere in Europe who opposed toleration for Catholicism.

[74] Hume admits that "so absolute, indeed, was the authority of the crown, that the precious spark of liberty had been kindled, and was preserved, by the Puritans alone; and it was to this sect, whose principles appear so frivolous, and habits so ridiculous, that the English owe the whole freedom of their constitution." However, he suggests that when in governance or power they effectively eliminate religious liberty and tolerance by their claim to be the "only pure church" and establishing their doctrines and

sociological studies suggest (Gorski 2000; Zaret 1989). The identical pattern of behavior is observed in Mormonism as sociologically, albeit not theologically, neo- or quasi-Puritanism in America: a sect while in opposition or minority, as in most US regions and beyond, yet a church or theocratic institution whenever in power or majority, as witnessed in Utah[75] (Weisbrod 1999).

Another actual or potential "difference" between Calvinism and Puritanism concerns the theological doctrine of predestination, as a non-sociological and non-scientific matter in the strict sense, so a few remarks will suffice. Calvinism's doctrine of predestination was adopted and restated by early Puritanism, officially by the Puritan English Parliament, through the 1647 Westminster Confession cited by Weber,[76] as a clear theocratic act endowing the "theological conflict over grace" with "important political overtones" (Byrne 1997; also, German 1995). Subsequently, the doctrine was relaxed and even abandoned in its pure form by neo-Puritanism or Puritan-based evangelicalism driven by perpetual revivalism (Clark 1999), especially in America from the 18th to the 21st century, like Baptism and Methodism. Thus, Weber notes that the dogma

---

practices "by law", while tolerating "no others". He implies that this precisely happened under Cromwell's "Holy Commonwealth" following the temporarily victorious Puritan Revolution as well as New England's "Biblical Commonwealth". As regards the latter, Tocqueville remarks that Puritanism "entirely forgetting the great principles of religious toleration that [it] had himself demanded in Europe, makes attendance on divine service compulsory, and goes so far as to visit with severe punishment, and even with death, Christians who chose to worship God according to a ritual differing from his own." At least, this is proof or exemplar of Puritanism's duality or duplicity of demanding freedom and tolerance for itself as a sect and of unfreedom and intolerance when being an official church.

[75] Weisbrod (1999:145) suggests that when established or a majority, as in Utah, Mormonism proclaims that its "particular values should be adopted as universal" via imposition and thus acts as a theocratic church (Mode I). And yet, when in the opposite situation, as in most US states, Mormonism "seeks to make room for its own values within a larger system", thus acting as a sect (Mode II).

[76] Weber cites the following Westminster Confession's evident adoption or rendition of the Calvinist doctrine of predestination: "By the decree of God, for the manifestation of His glory, some men and angels are predestinated unto everlasting life, and others foreordained to everlasting death". Or in more detail, it declared that "those of mankind that are predestinated unto life, God before the foundation of the world was laid, according to His eternal and immutable purpose, and the secret counsel and good pleasure of His will, hath chosen in Christ unto everlasting glory, out of His mere free grace and love, without any foresight of faith or good works, or perseverance in either of them, or any other thing in the creature as conditions, or causes moving Him thereunto, and all to the praise of His glorious grace." Weber comments that in respect of the doctrine of predestination the Westminster Confession "is simply repeated by both Independent [Puritan] and Baptist creeds". Also, German (1995:980) registers that the Westminster Confession was "adopted by English Calvinists in 1643 [sic!] and then "endorsed by New England Congregationalists in the Cambridge Platform of 1648." For instance, he invokes New England's younger Puritan Edwards publishing a "lengthy treatise against universal salvation" (German 1995:984). Still, German (1995:970) suggests that "17th century American Puritans blunted the doctrine of predestination by teaching that sinners could prepare themselves for salvation [sic!]"

of predestination was "rejected" by, for instance, Baptism first and then Methodism. As regards the latter, he observes that Methodism showed "indifference to or repudiation of the dogmatic basis of Calvinistic asceticism" and formed "a religious basis for ascetic conduct after the doctrine of predestination had been given up" in favor of it opposite or mitigation, Arminian theology[77] (Baldwin 2006). The latter was traced to the Dutch dissident Calvinist theologian Jakob Arminius, and condemned as "Roman" by Calvinism (the Synod of Dort 1618–19) and then Puritanism (the Westminster Confession) (Byrne 1997; Sorkin 2005).

Yet, in spite of formally abandoning the Calvinist doctrine of predestination, Methodism as well as Baptism substantively functioned as though in accordance with or produced outcomes equivalent to those generated by the doctrine. Namely, Methodist and Baptist leaders in America, especially the South after the Great Awakenings, acted as if they were Weber's "predestined aristocracy of salvation", thus of society, while substituting what he calls the absolute "certainty of salvation" (*certitido salutis*) or the "serene confidence" in Divine grace for the "sullen worry" of original Calvinists in Europe. In this sense, paradoxically Methodists and Baptists effectively intensified the formally abandoned Calvinist doctrine of predestination or rather its outcomes, by injecting it with the categorical self-righteous "certainty" or "confidence" of "their *own* salvation" and conversely damnation of others. Simply, they substituted for the God of Calvinism in deciding who are "saved" or elected (themselves) and who are "damned"[78] (all others) (Baldwin 2006).

Namely, both original Calvinists and neo-Puritan Methodists, as well as Baptists, acted as if they were positively predestined or saved, and all others damned, with the difference that the first were uncertain (modest), the second certain or confident (immodest) in this respect. This is what Weber implies ironically observing that in Methodism (as exemplified by Wesley[79] and his "anti-Calvinistic faction") "the self-confidence of the righteous man" in

---

[77] Baldwin (2006:94) observes that early Methodists in New England "were attacked for their Arminian theology" rejecting or mitigating the Calvinist doctrine of predestination. In this view, Methodist Arminian theology "was as odious" to American Calvinists as the Methodists" excessive emotionalism, expressing the "doctrinal differences" between their Arminianism and the "established Calvinism of New England" (Baldwin 2006:103). In sum, for these Calvinists, the Methodist Arminian emphasis on "human initiative amounted to [salvation] by works" (Baldwin 2006:103), a supreme theological heresy in Calvinism, for which, Servetus, for instance, was burned at the stake by Calvin et al. in Geneva. In turn, Byrne (1997:13) describes Arminianism as "Calvinists leaning back somewhat towards Roman Catholicism."

[78] This is in part implicit in Baldwin's (2006:103) observation that "opponents claimed that the Methodist scheme of salvation set aside God's grace because it made salvation depend on man's choice, thereby making the individual indebted to himself, and not to God", in this case "man's choice" practically signified that of Methodists or rather their leaders.

[79] Baldwin (2006:107) registers "Wesley's public opposition to the American Revolution" as well as accusations of "sexual impropriety" against him during the "early years of his traveling ministry."

salvation attained "untold heights, an emotional intensification of the Puritan type" and by implication the Calvinist doctrine of predestination. After all, as Weber observes, many Methodists and other neo-Puritans have remained "adherents of the doctrine of predestination" and "always" contended that they did *not* really differ from the established Calvinist Church, as in New England (Baldwin 2006), "in doctrine, but only in religious practice."[80] And, contemporary Baptism in America, notably the South, has reportedly experienced "a resurgence" of the Calvinistic doctrine (Hinson 1997) of predestination or "unconditional election" and theology overall, resulting in the "Calvinizing of Southern Baptists", during recent times, just as most early Baptists in Puritan-ruled New England declared themselves as "Calvinists" (Dayton 1999).

In turn, like subsequent Puritanism, what Weber calls neo-Calvinism, as in Holland, "no longer dared to maintain the pure doctrine of predestined grace" or predestination from proto- or original Calvinism (also, Gorski[81] 2003; Hiem-stra 2005). Moreover, despite "Calvinist scholastic dogmatism" even some of Calvin's own successors in Geneva (Vernet) admittedly relinquished or tempered the doctrine of predestination by adopting none than its original theological nemesis or mitigation, Arminian theology[82] (Sorkin 2005). Hence, on this account, neo-Puritanism such as Baptism and Methodism in America actually followed on or paralleled neo-Calvinism, just as early Puritanism did original Calvinism in fully adopting its doctrine of predestination (e.g., the Westminster Confession). To that extent, no essential theological difference effectively exists between Calvinism and Puritanism, including between neo-Calvinism and neo-Puritanism, in respect of the doctrine of predestination or salvation, despite certain secondary divergences. In a way the doctrine of predestination was, as Weber suggests, "never completely eliminated" from Calvinism and in consequence Puritanism, but "only altered its form", as in neo-Calvinism and consequently

---

[80] Weber adds that "for those Methodists who were adherents of the doctrine of predestination, the *certitido salutis* appeared in the "immediate feeling of grace and perfection instead of the consciousness of grace which grew out of ascetic conduct in continual proof of faith", as in early Calvinism.

[81] Gorski (2003:170) remarks that while being "weak or absent in the soteriology of the first generation of Protestant Reformers", notably Calvin's doctrine of predestination, the emphasis on "ethical behaviour became increasingly prominent in the thinking of second generation Protestants" (e.g., Spener). Also, Murdock (2005:147) comments that within Calvinism, "there was a significant distinction between the reception of ideas about predestination in much of the Reformed world and the particular Puritan [and Dutch] precisionist understanding of the connection between ethical conduct and signs of election." In turn, echoing Weber Hiemstra (2005:146) remarks that in the 19th century Kuyper and other Dutch Calvinists updated the "Calvinist idea of God's sovereign care of creation in order to address a rapidly modernizing culture" and registers Kuyper's "willingness to reform Calvinism when it appeared wrong or antiquated" resulting in "neo-Calvinism".

[82] Sorkin (2005:288) comments that Arminian theology "had softened the doctrines of predestination and the elect by introducing the role of free will and [hypothetically] the possibility of universal grace". Thus, Vernet rendered Arminianism the "public creed of Geneva" against "Calvinist scholastic dogmatism" (Sorkin 2005:289–91).

neo-Puritanism, as exemplified by American Southern Baptism's reaffirmation of "unconditional election" and related Calvinist "points".

And, from a sociological standpoint, it is completely immaterial whether Calvinism and Puritanism, including their modern revivals or survivals like Baptism and Methodism, adopt or not the doctrine of predestination and any other theological dogma about what Weber calls the world beyond. What is sociologically relevant is whether Calvinism and Puritanism, regardless of embracing or not such theological dogmas, tend to eventually make human life, as Tawney put it, "hell in this world" through Biblical theocracy, like Southern Baptism and in part Methodism in the South and beyond via the design for a "Bible Belt." To paraphrase Mencken (1982), a prime sociological moment is that the US South *cum* a "Bible Belt" is ruled by Baptist and Methodist theocratic evangelicalism ("barbarism"), no matter whether or not Baptism and Methodism adopt the Calvinist doctrine of predestination to sanctify their dominance.

Another difference" between Calvinism and Puritanism pertains to the role of emotion or sentiment in religious and other human behavior. Presumably, Calvinism represents a supreme anti- or non-emotional religion in contrast to Puritanism (and Pietism), especially neo-Puritanism (Methodism, Baptism, other evangelical sects or cults), as a sort of religious hyper-emotionalism. Yet, like in the case of the doctrine of predestination, hardly any substantive differences existed between original Calvinism and early Puritanism with respect to the role of human emotions in religion and society. Both were the exact opposite of what Weber calls religious emotionalism, or, to use Parsons" (1937) word, "unsentimental." In Weber's view, Calvinists, notably Calvin, devalued and dismissed religious and all human emotions or feelings in considering "everything emotional to be illusory", which made emotion "originally quite foreign to Calvinism". For example, while Luther embraced "mysticism and emotionalism", Calvin adopted and intensified asceticism as the exact opposite. Confirming or evoking Weber, contemporary historical research suggests that most Calvinist practices (the quarterly celebration of the "Lord's Supper") in France were "relatively unemotional", just as the "buildings for French Reformed worship" were unaesthetic or "plain and unadorned" (Mentzer 2007), and in extension, via Puritanism, in Scotland and England.

Also, in Weber's account, Puritanism showed an "entirely negative attitude" to "all the sensuous and emotional elements in culture", or "fundamental antagonism to sensuous culture of all kinds", following Calvinism and its "harsh doctrines of the absolute" transcendence of God and the "corruption of everything pertaining to the flesh" as the theological-moralistic rationale. In short, Puritanism, like Calvinism and other radical asceticism, enabled and forced humans to act against their emotions via what Weber denotes the "destruction of spontaneous, impulsive enjoyment". And, by embracing and intensifying the "Calvinistic idea of the depravity of the flesh"[83] (Mentzer 2007;

---

[83] Mentzer (2007:348–54) indicates that for Calvinists the "great disasters" that they ("Reformed Christians") "had suffered in France" (viz., the "revocation of the Edict of

also, Johnson 2003), Puritanism, like all extreme asceticism, stigmatized "every purely emotional" personal relations by the "suspicion of idolatry of the flesh".

Also, recall neo-Puritanism such as Southern Baptism in America during the 19th century and later embraced and even intensified the notion of human "total depravity" as one the "five points of Calvinism"[84] (Hinson 1997). In addition, elaborating on Weber Parsons (1937) admits that Puritanism involved the "devaluation" of an individual's "attachment to his fellows". Admittedly, it did "above all, the tendency" for reducing humans to "impersonal, unsentimental terms" and considering them for their "usefulness, ultimately to the purposes of God, more immediately to his own ends", rather (or less) than from the "point of their value in themselves". As mentioned, this observation by a major US sociologist with a "Puritan heritage" (Alexander 1983) admits not only to Calvinist anti-emotionalism ("unsentimental") and transcendental anti-humanism ("purposes of God"), but also to a sort of Machiavellianism and utilitarianism ("his own ends") overall within Puritanism (Mayway 1984). In sum, original Puritanism followed and intensified Calvinism's depreciation or dismissal of human emotions or feelings as "chimerical" and consequently "turned outward" (Birnbaum 1953), ultimately to total mastery of the world, in a "methodical, ruthless way" and by "brutality".[85] With respect to anti-emotionalism, like most others, Puritanism is really English-American Calvinism just further intensified, and Puritans Anglo-Saxon Calvinists become evermore anti- or non-emotional.[86]

By contrast to Calvinism and Puritanism, neo-Puritanism, like Methodism and Baptism, is what Weber calls religious hyper-emotionalism, as is, in part even quasi- or neo-Calvinism (e.g., eventually Lutheran Pietism). While

---

Nantes and the proscription of Protestantism in 1685") were the "product of people's moral depravity", as well as their "irreverence, indifference, blasphemy, insolence, and sacrilege", thus of "God's terrible anger". Also, Johnson (2003) suggests that the "intrinsically American moralistic obsession with the ideas of innate depravity" is rooted in Puritanism and in extension Calvinism.

[84] Hinson (1997) adds that during the first half century years after the founding of the Southern Baptist Convention in 1845, the "denomination elected presidents who mostly adhered to the "five points of Calvinism", such as "Total depravity, Unconditional election, Limited atonement, Irresistible grace, Perseverance of the saints". And, in his view, "contemporary SBC Calvinists regard themselves as inerrantists and denominational conservatives" (Hinson 1997). Also, in response to the charges that Calvinism is ""logically antimissionary," robs persons of responsibility for their conduct, and is marked by intolerance, divisiveness, and haughtiness", Hinson (1997) cites some prominent Baptists" defense that the Southern Baptist Convention, "which has become one of the greatest missionary-sending agencies in history, was rocked in the cradle of Calvinism."

[85] Birnbaum (1953:138–9) adds that the pride of being one is of the "elect", "which denied to external agencies the obligation or right to intervene in the earthy life of the individual [source of anti-welfare bias], combined with the concept of the inner isolation of the believer to produce Puritan independence and brutality.

[86] For example, Fehler (2005:143) observes that during the 19th century US Puritan or "orthodox Congregational" and Presbyterian ministers favored "emotionally moderated sermons".

original Calvinism, thus Puritanism, "greatly prized the control of affect", neo-Puritanism or Protestant evangelicalism, exemplified by Baptism and Methodism, constituted or was linked with "emotional religion" with its usual appeal to a "ruder class than the middling sort" that early Calvinists and Puritans favored (Urdank 1991). Thus, neo-Puritanism, especially in America, emerged as a revolt against "worldliness and skepticism", notably rationalism or the Age of Reason, through the "emotional explosions" of evangelical revivals, including "visions and trances", "weeping and swooning", observed "especially among the lower classes and at the frontier" (Foerster 1962). Simply, Baptism revived and Methodism originated as "poor man's Calvinism", infused with such hyper-emotionalism, as distinguished from Calvin-Winthrop's aristocratic and "cold" Calvinism.

As paradigmatic cases, the Great Awakenings of the 1740s–1800s were mass Protestant, specifically Puritan, evangelical-revivalist movements which caused "highly emotional waves of religious frenzy" to overwhelm America, notably the South (Archer 2001). Such "emotional explosions" of Calvinist revivals or "religious frenzy" were, however, "originally quite foreign" to Calvinism and Puritanism, and probably would have bewildered (but likely approved by) Calvin and Winthrop belonging to the opposite, "cold" side of emotionalism. Thus, Baptism represented an emotional and moralistic revival or reinforcement of Calvinism and Puritanism by pursuing, as in Weber's account, "complete conquest of the power of sin" and condemning the "godlessness" and "depravity" of humans (excepting of course Baptists) "even more harshly" than did original Calvinists. He observes that Baptism is a sort of "hysterical" religion or rather sect in virtue of its "idea of expectant waiting for the Spirit to descend", revelation, and "rebirth" replacing or mitigating the Calvinist dogma of predestination. On the account of its "hysterical" emotionalism, Baptism and generally Baptist-linked Protestant sectarianism in America can be considered and described as non-Calvinism and thus non-Puritanism. However, in moral terms, Baptism developed in and remains a sort of revived or reinforced Calvinism and thus Puritanism in that, as Weber remarks, Baptist hyper-emotional and "strict" morality in practice followed the "path" of the "Calvinistic ethic", notably Calvin et al.'s "doctrine of human depravity" (German 1995; Sorkin 2005).

Also, Methodism originated and remained as hyper-emotionalism, thus non-Calvinism or non-Puritanism in this respect, yet also as revivalist moralism and to that extent neo-Calvinism and neo-Puritanism. In Weber's words, Methodism arose as the "emotional intensification"[87] of English Puritanism and hence Calvinism, and the methodical pursuit of "sinless perfection" for the aim of reaching the absolute certitude of salvation (*salutis*). Methodism thus

---

[87] Weber adds that in early Methodism "the self-confidence of the righteous man reached untold heights" within even English Puritanism and in extension Calvinism. In his view, for early Methodists attaining "sinless perfection" or sanctification "finally guarantees the *certainty of salvation* and substitutes a serene confidence for the sullen worry of the Calvinist."

developed as "an emotional but still ascetic type" of Calvinist religion, as a seemingly contradictory complex, if emotionalism and methodical asceticism, as he implies, are mutually exclusive, joined with its "repudiation" of or "indifference" to the "dogmatic basis of Calvinistic asceticism" like the strict dogma of predestination. In essence, as Mill implies, Methodism was another (after Baptism), specifically parallel counter- or post-Enlightenment—minimally, "untouched"[88] (Byrne 1997) by or "unimpressed" with the Enlightenment—in the form of systematic moralistic revival *and* a hyper-emotional reinvention of originally moralistic, anti-emotional Calvinism and Puritanism. Thus, Weber observes that Methodism assumed a "strongly emotional character, especially in America", involving an "emotional struggle of such intensity" as resulting in the "most terrible ecstasies" usually occurring in American public meetings. He identifies what he calls the "often definitely pathological [*sic*] character of Methodist emotionalism", emulating the "hysterical" attributes of Baptism[89] (Baldwin 2006). In view of such "pathological" hyper-emotionalism, like hysterical Baptism before and afterwards, Methodism can be deemed and called non-Calvinism, thus non-Puritanism, as axiomatic anti-emotionalism within Protestantism and Christianity.

However, like Baptism, Methodism originated and in part remained a kind of revived or adapted Calvinism, thus Puritanism, in moral-ascetic and most other terms, minus emotionalism and predestination. This is what the very term aims or indicates, that is, what Weber describes as the *methodical* doctrine and practice of sanctification via "sinless perfection" or "freedom from sin". Still, it may, as he implies, seem difficult[90] to reconcile moralistic "methodism" or ascetic rationalism *and* hyper-emotionalism as, in his view, axiomatic irrationalism, unless one assumes or identifies a sort of "method in the hyper-emotional madness", including, in his words, public and "terrible ecstasies", as associated with Protestant evangelicalism in America (Smith 2000). Weber infers that the "fundamentally Calvinistic character of its religious feeling here remained decisive" in Methodism, despite its hyper-emotionalism and its rejection of the dogma of predestination, since its "emotional excitement took the form of enthusiasm which was only occasionally, but then powerfully stirred, but which by no means destroyed" the moralist-ascetic pattern of behavior in Calvinism and consequently Puritanism. For illustration, early Methodists in America, including New England, demonstrated Calvinist, specifically Puritan-style, "moral earnestness" which, in the long-standing

---

[88] According to Byrne (1997:31), the "revivalism of the Methodists in England (like Pietism in Germany) "ran parallel to" and was "largely untouched" by the Enlightenment.

[89] Baldwin (2006:112–3) complains that for opponents, including New England's established Calvinists *cum* Puritans, "hysterical affection is often mistaken for devotion" in American Methodism, for instance, "those who had been struck by the Spirit staggered around or fell down kicking and screaming".

[90] Thus, Weber observes that this "emotional religion [Methodism] entered into a peculiar alliance, containing no small inherent difficulties, with the ascetic ethics which had for good and all been stamped with rationality by Puritanism" and thus ultimately by Calvinism.

tradition of Calvinism and Puritanism, Methodism tried to impose on others[91] (Baldwin 2006), just as did and still does Baptism (Hinson 1997).

And, neo-Calvinism in some degree or form no longer seems to maintain, but instead relaxes or modifies its pure and simple anti-emotionalism, by analogy and perhaps connection to the dogma of predestination. This is at least indicated by what Weber denotes as the "purely emotional form of Pietism." He describes Pietism in some respects—the "connection between predestination and the doctrine of proof" or the certainty of salvation—as a "development of Calvin's original doctrines" and often a "fundamental" part of, though later splitting from, the Calvinist movement" in Europe (Holland, Germany) and England to become "Lutheran"[92] (Gorski 2003) and a "more benign expressions of religious belief" (Byrne 1997). In Weber's account, the "Pietism of the Continent of Europe", in particular Germany and Holland, and the "Methodism of the Anglo-Saxon peoples", including America, alike were late Calvinist or Puritan secondary movements. They both "revived" anti-emotional Calvinism and Puritanism with a high dose of emotionalism as a psychological ("feel good") medicine to its perceived crisis. At this juncture, neo-Puritanism epitomized by Methodism and Baptism appears as hardly different from neo-Calvinism, including Pietism, in terms of Weber's religious emotionalism, just as original Puritanism was not from Calvinism in anti-emotionalism.

An additional sociological most relevant "difference" between Calvinism and Puritanism relates to the issue of unfreedom and authoritarianism versus liberty and democracy in society. Presumably, Calvinism was illiberal, anti-secular, undemocratic, and, also because, European, but Puritanism liberal, secular, democratic, and, due to being, English-American, the original and continuing source of liberty and democracy in America and in part England. For example, some US analysts argue that Puritanism was the liberal "movement of Locke from the Old World" to the New, not the illiberal "movement of Calvin" and the "depravations of Europe" (Hartz 1963). Arguably, because of its "fragmentation" in America, Puritanism "detached" from the "European past" and then elevated itself to the "rank of a national absolute" in liberal-secular and democratic, rather than, as Calvinism tried in Europe, opposite, terms (Hartz 1963).

This is an instance of the "liberal mythology" (Gould 1996) or "naïve assumptions" (Coffey 1998) and "speculative explanations" (Zaret 1996) of "all-American" Puritanism as the source of liberty and democracy in America in an invidious ethnocentric distinction from European Calvinism, as well as Lutheranism, and Anglicanism, not to mention Catholicism. Yet, recall that

---

[91] For example, Baldwin (2006:111) notes that that early American Methodists "eschewed swearing, gambling, card playing, and dancing, and they pressed others to do likewise". Overall, he proposes that the Methodists played a "central role" in the evangelical revival in which established Calvinists "were wholehearted participants" (Baldwin 2006:109).

[92] Also, Weber describes Pietism as the "penetration" of Calvinism, including the doctrine of predestination and asceticism, into the "non-Calvinist" denominations. Gorski (2003) uses the expression "Lutheran Pietism" and suggests that it was "heavily influenced" by English Puritanism.

some other writers suggest that in America, just as in post-Reformation Europe, the value of freedom was linked to Calvinism and its doctrines of predestination and "human sin" (Means 1966), including their Puritan extensions or applications. In this view, "democratic values and institutions" flourished in the "new nation" due to none than its "Calvinist heritage" (Kloppenberg 1998; also, Dunn and Woodard 1996).

It seems logically a non sequitur and historically incorrect to admit that Calvinism was illiberal, anti-secular, and undemocratic, even downright "depraved", in Europe and then to argue that it miraculously by a Divine miracle (or perhaps due to a larger geographic space and milder weather?) became, through admittedly *Calvinist* Puritanism, in particular the established Congregational Calvinist Church (Foerster 1962; German 1995), an exact opposite. Presumably, this is the source of liberty and secular democracy in America. This argument is logically so self-contradictory and empirically invalid as is analogous (Merton 1939) to arguing or implying that, as US fascists (e.g., "Christian" neo-Nazis) do, that fascism supposedly transformed itself from totalitarian in Europe to "libertarian" when coming to America, again due to "fragmentation" and certain Divine or natural miracles in the "new world".

As the matter of fact, if there is any relevant difference in this respect between European Calvinism and "all-American" Puritanism, it is exactly opposite to what is argued by these US analysts and claimed by conservative and other politicians in America. As argued and shown before, the difference is that Puritanism reinvents, reinforces, and surpasses rather than deviates from or mitigates Calvinism in its original anti-liberalism, anti-secularism, and authoritarianism, or simply un-freedom. Recall, sociological analyses identify early Puritanism in America such as New England as actually the most totalitarian (Stivers 1994) rather than supposedly "libertarian" Calvinism and in extension Protestantism. Hence, the "difference" is simply that "all-American" Puritanism has been even more "totalitarian" or anti-liberal and repressive, notably theocratic, than European Calvinism had even been or rather had an opportunity to be. This is so given the latter's discredit and counteracting by the Enlightenment and liberalism, as well as by moderate Lutheranism, Anglicanism, and in part Catholicism, in Europe like France, Holland, Germany, and England, or more so than in America (Munch 2001). It is for such a reason and in this sense that American Puritanism has always been just a sort of super-Calvinism, more Calvinist than Calvinism itself, perhaps in accordance with the observed "pattern" of disciples and converts becoming "more Catholic than the Pope"[93] (Lipset 1955). Negatively, for the same reason, it is not trans-Calvinist liberalism and secularism, thus the source

---

[93] Most Christians and others in Europe are perplexed or bemused, as the case may be, by US fundamentalists" (e.g., Baptists') and perhaps most Americans' claims to be more or "only true" Christian, as well as that the "new nation" is more fundamentalist and religious (celebrated in Lipset 1996) than the "old world" where Christianity was precisely invented and/or institutionalized long before the discovery of America. Yet, this seems a generalization of the "pattern of the convert becoming more Catholic than the Pope". In a seeming unrealistic or grotesque extension of this pattern, "politically

of freedom and secular democracy in America, which contradicts the "liberal mythology," "naïve assumptions", and "speculative explanations" of Puritanism in relation to liberty and democracy.

Hence, Puritanism has been and remained via perennial Puritan revivals and survivals "quite the [illiberal and anti-secular] movement of Calvin" from France (Geneva) to America, not the liberal and secular "movement of Locke from the Old World" to the "new nation." It is merely Calvinism evermore "turned mad" or "gone wild" in the sense of extreme anti-liberalism and thus totalitarianism beyond its point of origin, as in the "new world" where it found what it had demanded and was denied in France and Europe overall. This was the unrestrained license to theocratic rule and mass murder after the model or image of Calvin et al.'s murdering of Servetus and "libertines" for heresy, yet couched in and sanctified as "freedom of religion". To that extent, to differentiate Calvinism as "European" or "foreign" expressing "the depravations of Europe" and Puritanism as "American" or "native" endowing America with or reflecting its "purity" and "innocence" is but a typical Veblenian invidious distinction and what Weber calls (about the concept of "national character") the "mere confession of ignorance", the ethnocentric fallacy of Puritan-rooted religious nationalism (Fried-land 2001; also, Calhoun 1993). In sum, Calvinism and Puritanism as a theological parent and child, master and disciple respectively, do not substantively or appreciably differ with respect to unfreedom or authoritarianism, liberty and democracy, with both being in essence authoritarian or illiberal and anti-democratic religious and social systems. And, if they differ at all, as in quasi-statistical degrees of unfreedom, the Puritan child tends to be evermore anti-liberal, totalitarian, and lethal than the Calvinist father. They thus differ in an opposite sense and direction to what the view of "liberal-democratic" American Puritanism suggests and US (and English-Scottish) Puritans and their descendents claim.

Conceivably, some other "differences" in addition to those above (listed in Table 7.3) between Calvinism and Puritanism could be identified. Yet, as the aforesaid suggests, they are mostly formal, terminological and theological, analogous to those between an original and a derivative, rather than substantive, significant or sociological for the present purpose.

Table 7.3. "Differences" between Calvinism and Puritanism

Church vs. sect
The doctrine of predestination
Role of emotion
Unfreedom and authoritarianism vs. liberty and democracy
Others?

---

incorrect" comedians may comment that if a life is discovered on some new planets like Mars, only "Martians" will be more "Christian" or "godly" than US "reborn" fundamentalists.

# CHAPTER EIGHT

# CONCLUSIONS

## *"Destinies" of Human Societies*

The idea of destiny or fate can be applied to analyze and predict the evolution of modern nations or societies. This yields the concept of national or societal destiny or fate, as distinguished from individual destinies. Hence, this is a sociological, thus scientific and collective, not a theological or transcendental and individual, concept. In this sense, destiny or fate as applied to societies is a synonym, analogy, or metaphor for societal determination or codetermination (not determinism) in respect of certain social determinants, in this case Calvinism, including Puritanism, in Europe and America. It is also synonymous and analogous with related ideas such as what Weber calls, referring to Calvinism, mastery of the world and contemporary sociologists (Inglehart and Baker 2000) term historical path-dependence, societal legacy or heritage, impact, influence, function, or role with respect to such social factors. In this sense, the concept of societal destiny or fate can be adopted and considered as scientifically useful and legitimate for analyzing and predicting the evolution of modern societies, including Europe and America in connection with Calvinism. If so, there *is* perhaps such thing as the destiny of nations or societies, as demonstrated by America in relation to Calvinism through Puritanism.

In particular, Weber while analyzing Calvinism in relation to capitalism and modernity provides sociological usefulness and legitimacy to the concept of national destiny or societal fate with respect to contemporary Western societies. Thus, he observes that the "most fateful force in our modern life" is capitalism to the effect that the "fate of our times is characterized by rationalization and intellectualization and, above all by the disenchantment of the world", as capitalist processes and outcomes. In general, he adopts such expressions as the "community of political destiny", "the destiny of religions", and the like. Also, Comte employs the expression "collective destinies of mankind" through the "march of one unbroken sequence" from its "primitive theological" to its "transient metaphysical" and to its "final positive" stage. And, his French contemporary Tocqueville gives sociological usefulness and legitimacy to the concept with respect to American society by explicitly using the expression "the destiny of America".

At the minimum, Weber, Comte, and Tocqueville imply that the concept of societal destiny in a strict sociological meaning—that is, social codetermination or path-dependence—thus devoid of theological and religious connotations, is not, as it might seem at first glance, metaphysical or fatalistic and unscientific, but can be used at least as an analogy or metaphor in scientific analysis and discourse. This also applies to contemporary sociologists (e.g., Habermas 2001) defining the modern nation as a "pre-political community of shared destiny" and using the term "fate" in respect of contemporary developed and underdeveloped societies (Bendix 1984).

By analogy to its general meaning of predestination and/or predetermination, the idea of destiny or fate when specifically applied to societies or nations implies societal predestination or codetermination, involving multiple determinants, not a single one. And, it is Calvinism itself that is the exemplary case of the idea of predestination or predetermination within Protestantism and Christianity and even among world religions (alongside, in part, Islam, as Weber implies), though in a theological or non-sociological, thus non-scientific sense. Still, the latter can serve as an instructive analogy and metaphor for its sociological and scientific meaning and form.

Hence, Calvinism's doctrine of predestination or predetermination (terms distinguished but also sometimes used interchangeably by Weber and others) can be usefully and legitimately applied to analyzing the long-term evolution or path-dependence of modern societies, including Europe and America. Weber states that it is in Calvinism that "the idea of the determinism or predestination from all eternity of both human life on this earth and human fate in the world beyond comes in its strongest possible expression". This implies the ideas of "predetermination" understood, in Weber's view, as "applied to fate in this world, not in the next" or the "religious determination of life-conduct" *and* of "predestination" in the sense of "human fate in the world beyond".[1]

---

[1] Weber distinguishes the doctrine of predestination with its "terrible seriousness", almost exclusively attributed to Calvinism, from that of "predetermination" or determinism associated with other world religions like Islam. Thus, he remarks that the "Mohammedan idea was that of predetermination, not predestination, and was applied to fate in this world, not in the next. In consequence, the most important thing, the proof of the believer in predestination, played no part in Islam", unlike in Calvinism

The second idea posits transcendental or Divine predestination—that is, salvation and damnation—by the God of Calvinism of humans predetermining their "fate in the world beyond", as a theological, thus non-sociological or non-scientific problem.

This applies to the transcendental predestination, more precisely predetermination in Weber's sense ("applied to fate in this world"), by Calvinist as well as non-Calvinist divinities of supra-individual categories like certain social groups and whole nations or societies as God's "chosen people" and the like. A paradigmatic case is the idea of America as God's "chosen nation" and "promised land" with "manifest destiny" or "Divine mission" in the world according to Puritan religious nationalism (Friedland 2001) and the resulting civil religion of Americanism (Lipset 1996). In Comte's terms, the transcendental predestination or predetermination of societies and groups is a theological or metaphysical rather than a positive or rational problem, thus within the province of theology and metaphysics (and ideology and politics), not science, specifically sociology.

Scientific sociology has no objective empirical ways of validating or "falsifying" the assumption or claim that a society is God's "chosen people" or "promised land". Virtually all human societies or groups, from the smallest barbarian tribes visited by anthropologists to the largest past and present empires, each has, as Weber suggests, claimed God's predestination *cum* election, and thus Divine Right to its mastery of others supposedly denied Providential favor. This historically has been and remains the "recipe for disaster" in the form of intermittent, brutal, and ultimately self-destructive wars of religion, thus extermination, between those societies or groups making claims to Divine Choice. They range from inter-tribal and pre-Christian constant religious battles to Christian (Catholic and Protestant) crusades domestically and globally and Islamic anti-Christian jihads, the last two continuing in various relics through the early 21st century (Turner 2002). In Hobbesian words, this has been a formula and practice of permanent "war of everyone against everyone else" in societal or collective terms, thus a return to the pre-social state of nature or barbarian anarchy.

---

and its English offspring Puritanism. He adds that "all the great men of Puritanism (in the broadest sense) took their departure from this doctrine, whose terrible seriousness deeply influenced their youthful development [from ] Milton [to] Baxter, and, still later, the free-thinker Franklin".

578                           CHAPTER EIGHT

In game-theoretic terms, it is a zero-sum game in which relative gains and losses are eventually balanced in the image of an accounting balance-sheet (or income statement).

Yet, apparently "reborn" US Puritan and Islamic fundamentalists refuse to learn from or overlook this Hobbesian history and zero-sum scenario by persisting in their claims to be God's "chosen people" with Divine Mission and Right to rule the world by ultimately destroying it, via some modern versions of crusades and jihads, respectively, against "infidels" and the "impure". At this juncture, to paraphrase Clausewitz's famous definition of war, Puritan and Islamic "holy" wars against the "evil" world are the continuation of the politics of "God's "chosen nation" or "Providential destiny" by "other means", including military aggression, conquest, and terrorism (domestic and global).

In the present context, sociology and other social sciences cannot prove or disapprove, confirm or disconfirm, whether America and any Western or other society[2] (England, Germany, France, Italy, Russia, Holland,[3] India, China, Japan, etc.) has a "manifest destiny" in the sense of transcendental predestination *cum* election and Divine mission, thus the right to rule the world, any more than a few humans are "saved" and most others "damned", as Calvinism postulates by its oligarchic or aristocratic doctrine of predestination. Simply, it cannot, as Weber would say, provide comfort or cause discomfort to those societies or groups, just as individuals, making and holding these claims or beliefs which, as Merton (1968) puts it, are "notoriously subject to error". This is because such societal or collective as well as individual self-claims to favorable Divine predestination, like religion and theology, are the articles of faith or conviction, and not proofs or empirical data, in Weber's words, value judgments, not factual statements, thus outside of the realm of sociology and other social science. In general terms, unlike

---

[2] For instance, Pareto comments in the wake of WW I that "patriotism has risen to new heights and is assuming the form of religion—in Germany [in] the "German God", in England through *imperialism*, in France through *nationalism*, and in the [USA] through *jingoism*, etc."

[3] Frijhoff (2002:51) observes that ruling Calvinism as its State Church claimed that Holland *cum* the "new Israel was the instrument that God had recently chosen to realise his kingdom on earth and spread his message." Needless to say, Calvinism made such claims to the "new Israel" (or Jerusalem) déjà vu through Puritanism about England and notably America. In passing, even theologically non-Calvinist, yet sociologically—in the sense of moralistic theocracy—Calvinist, Mormonism claimed such a status in Brigham Young's proclamation of "the exodus of the nation of the only true Israel from these United States" (cited in Weisbrod 1999:148).

theology, sociology cannot validate or invalidate such beliefs, values, and claims, because they define, in Comte's words, a theological primitive rather than a positive-rational modern age or society, notably a military-theocratic *ancien regime*, not liberal-secular and pacifist democracy and modernity defined instead by scientific and educational rationalism (Schofer and Meyer 2005).

Comte and Spencer, like most early sociologists, including Durkheim and Weber, argued and predicted that the theological age, a military-theocratic society in particular, was or would be the "dead past" in the form and image of the Dark Middle Ages. It would be displaced by the positive-rational, peaceful industrial and liberal-democratic social system, in Western civilization via societal rationalization, liberalization, and differentiation (Alexander and Colomy 1990), including pacification and secularization, exemplified by the Enlightenment. Despite sociology's anti-rationalist and anti-secular detractors, this classical sociological thesis and prediction of rationalism and liberalism, including secularism, has proven remarkably valid for most modern Western societies ushering in the 21st century (Inglehart and Baker 2000), as indicated by the "reality of a liberal and pluralist society" (Munch 2001), with the salient and persisting exception of America as a striking "deviant case" (Inglehart 2004; also, Byrne 1997).

As regards the latter, for instance, more Americans and all US fundamentalist Protestants, reportedly believe in Biblical creationism than adopt Darwinian evolutionism—though ironically or contradictorily hold some version of social Darwinism a la "natural selection" or "survival of the fittest" in society, notably the economy—on the grounds that evolution is an "untrue", at best "unproven" biological theory versus God's revealed "truth." Also, the vast majority (70 percent) of Americans and virtually all US fundamentalists believe in the existence of the "Devil" and implicitly "witches" compared with only a fraction of Europeans (11 percent of Danes and 19 percent of the French) (Glaeser 2004), hence opposing science that contradicts such beliefs as irrational superstitions. This holds true, with certain modifications, of their belief in religious and other conservative adverse alternatives to various condemned "ungodly" and "un-American" scientific practices and theories, from stem-cell research to global warming, as recent, almost bizarre and self-destructive instances of Puritan fundamentalism's long-standing antagonism to science and secular knowledge in America.

What is sociologically pertinent is not whether biological evolutionism (and creationism); stem-cell research, and global warming are valid theories, or the "Devil" and "witches" exist, as specific concerns for biology, medicine, climate science, or chemistry, as is if the earth revolves around the sun for astronomy, not for sociology. Rather, what is relevant in sociological terms is that prevalent anti-evolutionary beliefs in creationism, let alone in the "Devil" and "witches", as well as anti-global-warming conservatism, like those in medieval "godly" astronomy ("the sun revolves around the earth"), express an "irrational choice" or "revealed preference" for religion, theology, and theocracy, particularly Biblical inerrancy and Bibliocracy, against science and rationalism. It is contrary to what Comte, Spencer, and Weber expected, and yet (like "Satan" or "witches") "only" in America versus the "old" Europe.

On the account of the finding that most Americans when given a choice would choose religion and theology over science and other rational-secular values (Inglehart 2004), notably that fundamentalist Protestants believe that no knowledge or education is "better" than its secular form (Darnell and Sherkat 1997), "evangelical America" (Smith 2000) seems closer to Comte's theological-theocratic and Spencer's military than positive and pacifist age and society. Thus, it appears closer to the Dark Middle Ages than the liberal Enlightenment, in proof of the celebrated exceptional failure of the liberalization, secularization, and rationalization thesis (Lipset 1996) in the "first new nation" (Calhoun 1993). At least, in the Western world the unparalleled tenacity of the medieval superstitious belief in the "Devil" and "witches" versus science contradicting such beliefs renders the "new nation" descend into the irrational Dark Middle Ages rather than continue the rationalist Enlightenment, thus even older than the "old world". In a way, the belief in the "Devil" and/or his supposed associates "witches" is the foremost vestige and symbol of the Dark Middle Ages, a sort of the "mother" of all superstitions and irrationalities (Byrne 1997), a superstition largely eradicated in modern society, with the striking exception of the "new nation" (and Islamic theocracies). This and related irrational beliefs and practices hence reveal celebrated American exceptionalism as exceptional "godly" irrationalism within modern Western society.

Predictably, US "reborn" conservatives extol and exploit a la Machiavellianism the "all-American" propensity for religious "solutions" to non-religious problems (Jepperson 2002) by forcing Americans to choose "either faith or else science" on virtually all occasions, from human genesis to "Satan" and "witches" to health (stem-cell research, etc.) and private life, democracy and politics, education and culture. In this respect, America was and remains a "self-conscious religious experiment" analogous to that of "Christendom in the Middle Ages" (Stivers 1994). This may seem irrelevant or tangential to the present question, until and unless one realizes, as posited and shown in this work, that Calvinism is primarily (albeit not only) determinative, via Puritanism and fundamentalist Protestantism, of this remarkable, ever-renewing, and celebrated American exceptionalism to and striking deviation from Western rationalism, secularism, and liberalism, while reviving and revoking theocratic medievalism. (Recall, seven of ten persons in modern Puritan America believe in Satan and/or "witches" and only one in Lutheran Denmark.) At least in this sense, Calvinism acts or qualifies as Tocqueville's "destiny" of America at the start of and perhaps throughout the third millennium.

In any event, sociology cannot validate or invalidate "Divine destiny" or "chosen people" beliefs, values, or claims, because they define the Dark Middle Ages in which all culture was the servant or addendum of religion, not the Enlightenment as the origin and champion of modern science, including sociology, education, and rationalism (Delanty 2000). And yet, sociological analysis can confirm or disconfirm whether America has a "destiny", as Tocqueville suggests, in Calvinism through Puritanism as an instance of what Weber calls "concrete structures of social action", specifically non-economic institutions or religious factors, which is a non-theological problematic (Smelser 1997) for sociology and all social science. This work has thus adopted and applied Tocqueville's sociological meaning of America's "destiny", its historical and empirical "over-determination" (Alexander 1998) by Puritanism rather than its transcendental, Providential predestination by the God of Calvinism or in the sense of the Calvinist main theological doctrine as a non-sociological and non-scientific matter.

The above is important to emphasize and reiterate because when, or if, some US neo-conservative sociologists (e.g., Lipset 1996; Lipset and Marks 2000) enthuse about America's "chosen nation", "manifest destiny", "Divine mission", or "promised land" they effectively leave the domain of sociology and social science overall and move into that of theology and religion, including religiously grounded and sanctified nationalism (Friedland 2001) and ethnocentrism *cum* Americanism or civil religion (Beck 200; Munch 2001). In Weber's words, in doing so they effectively pervert sociology and science from the vocation involving facts or factual statements into the profession of personal values or value judgments ("patriotism", etc.) that contaminate and eventually poison what is supposed to be an objective scientific analysis treating societal subjects as Durkheimian data or "things", not sacred entities that humans cannot examine and question. They sacrifice sociology or science to the God of Calvinism endowing America with a "Divinely inspired"[4] (Weisbrod 1999) ("manifest") destiny", thus "Divine Right" to "save" the "ungodly", "corrupt" world from itself by eventually destroying it via a global permanent "holy war" on "evil" in accordance with Puritan apocalyptic Judgment Day nihilism in a "delirium of self-annihilation" *cum* Calvinist salvation (Adorno 2001). To claim that the *God* of Calvinism endows America with a "manifest destiny" via collective predestination *cum* election, just as predestining a few as "elected" and most humans as "damned", is a paradigmatically theological and contradictory doctrine combining and conflating the "community argument" of "chosen people" with the "theological argument of predestination [of individuals]"[5] (Frijhoff 2002).

As regards this theological contradiction, arguing that the God of Calvinism endows America with a "manifest destiny" via collective predestination versus other nations or societies deprived of Divine favor is actually or potentially self-contradictory, just as a déjà vu variation on the primitive or tribal theme of a "chosen people" and ethnocentric or nationalist (Friedland 2001), thus factually or possibly militaristic and imperialist (Steinmetz 2005). This is because or if *not* all individuals and groups can by assumption be or are in reality predestined ("elected") even in a nation endowed with "manifest destiny" ("election"). By assumption, non-Calvinists or non-Puritans, and both many Christians and all non-Christians, cannot be "chosen" or "saved" in a narrowly constituted, essentially sectarian Puritan society after the image of "Salem with witches" (Putnam 2000), yet hypocritically called "Christian America" (Smith 2000) due to US evangelicals monopolizing the only true "Christians" status and denying it to others (Catholics, mainline Protestants, etc.). This necessitates and rationalizes in the

---

[4] Weisbrod (1999:139) remarks that, like Calvinist evangelicals, even Mormons, originally seeking (as Brigham Young stated) a "move out of the United States", regarded America and its Constitution as "divinely inspired."

[5] Frijhoff (2002:51) remarks that in Calvinism's claim to Holland as the "new Israel" and the "instrument" of God the "community argument here joined the theological argument of predestination, which also implied a certainty of being saved [plus] an obligation to sanctification."

"logic" of Calvinism or Puritanism their exorcism, at best exclusion (Edgell et al. 2006), from this paradise of "manifest destiny", as shown by old and New England's Puritan persecutions, extermination, and "holy" wars against "infidels", from Irish Catholics ("Papists") to Native Americans, Quakers, and "Salem with witches".[6]

The idea of America's "manifest destiny" or Divine mission bestowed by the God of Calvinism is self-contradicting, because it cannot by definition and does not in reality include all Americans, like non-Puritan Christians and non-Christians, but only Calvinist Puritans and other Protestant sectarians and fundamentalists, and among them primarily their masters a la Winthrop et al. and their evangelical heirs. In short, it is a Calvinist, religious version of the "impossibility theorem". It is so in the sense that, as Weber puts it, the "basic dogma of strict Calvinism", the exclusionary or oligarchic and inhumane doctrine of predestination, "makes it impossible" for every human to reach, just as for the church to administer, "eternal salvation" limited to "only a few" become spiritual aristocrats and eventually political oligarchs or theocrats. Alternatively, it can only be made "consistent" and possible through creating a totally Puritan *cum* "Christian" America by "purifying" the latter not only from "impure" non-Christians, not to mention non-believers and agnostics as supremely "un-American" enemies (Edgell et al. 2006), but also from Christian non-Puritans (Catholics, Anglicans, Lutherans, etc.), as attempted at various historical points, from anti-Indian "purifications", anti-Quaker persecutions, and Salem's witch-hunts to the evangelical "Bible Belt" and its "Monkey Trials".

In addition to and conjunction with this contradiction, the Divine "destiny" idea is, first, a remnant of "chosen people" primitivism or tribalism, and second, a religious source and sanctification of nationalism, militarism, and imperialism. Arguing that the "God" of Calvinism or any religion bestows on America and other "superior" nations (e.g., England, Germany, France) such "destiny" or Divine mission and right to "save" the "evil" world is a theological (and ideological) doctrine, thus

---

[6] And, even when promising universal inclusion a la Jefferson's "liberty and justice for all", in history and reality the "Puritan nation" of "manifest destiny" has typically confined those "elected" or "saved" to a certain religious and ethnic-racial group, as a rule proverbial WASP as self-claimed "true" or "only" Americans, at least in the past, albeit with various subsequent adaptations or mitigations like the 2008 Presidential election. For example, Munch (2001:232) observes that "the conservative interpretation takes the constitution to maintain the understanding of American citizenship in terms of white Protestant men of Anglo-Saxon origin".

outside of the proper scope and method of sociology and science overall, despite US (and before English, German and French) conservative sociologists' embrace and espousal of such "holy" arguments (Dunn and Woodard 1996; German 1995; Lipset and Marks 2000; Seaton 2006).

Hence, the combined and conflated "chosen people" claims and the theological doctrine of predestination is a dual argument which theology only can and does "prove" and develop (and resolve its contradiction), but sociology and other science cannot and does not. Conversely, a sociological thesis that only sociology and other social science, but not theology, can confirm or disconfirm and elaborate is that Calvinism, while itself (its members) claiming to be predestined by God, represents America's "destiny" in Tocqueville's sense via its societal and empirical (not theological) predestination or what Weber may call its predetermination of the "new nation".

The above reintroduces the general concept of empirical social predestination of societies or nations as a sociological, thus non-theological problematic. Recall, it conceives and signifies societal codetermination in the form and sense of determination of society by multiple social determinants, one of which is primary and the others secondary, however, as well as historical path-dependence, mastery of the world in Weber's meaning, heritage, survival, function, and the like. An obvious exemplar and illustration of the concept of social predestination is American society's observed over-determination by or path-dependence (Inglehart and Baker 2000) on Calvinism through Puritanism. In Weber's words, the concept in this context specifically means predestination as applied to collective "fate in this world, not in the next," thus predetermination in and of society or determining "human life on this earth." In particular, it is an equivalent of what he calls "religious determination of life-conduct", analogous to, but different from, Divine predestination in the "world beyond."

Hence, the concept of societal predestination applies Calvinism and its major theological dogma to analyzing itself, specifically its sociological determination of or historical and present influence in modern societies like Europe and America. Rather than analyzing Calvinists as theologically predestined ("elected") by the God of Calvinism, it analyzes Calvinists themselves as sociologically predetermining, specifically mastering, these societies, notably America. It is important to make and keep the distinction between theological and sociological predestination in Calvinism and generally religion. In the first,

Calvinists or their leaders are predestined by their God as the "chosen people" or the "elect" group (or, as with their Puritan "children", sect). In the second, they, in virtue of or by a claim to such transcendental predestination, predestine, notably mastering, societies. In sum, in theological predestination, Calvinism (its adherents) is a "dependent variable" or an effect of sacred power, in the sociological, an independent variable or determinant itself of the "world of mundane affairs". In the first, Calvinism is the servant and "tool" of Divinity, in the second, the master and factor of human society, in accordance with Weber's identified Calvinist total mastery of the social (and physical and geographical) world.

### The "Wealth and Destiny of Nations"

Identifying and implicitly predicting America's "destiny" in Calvinist Puritanism, Tocqueville, by generalizing this observation, implied that the "destinies" of Western and other societies were primarily (but certainly not solely) determined and predicted by religious forces, generally what Weber calls ideal or spiritual, as contrasted with material or economic, values and interests. In turn, prior and seemingly unrelated to Tocqueville's identification and prediction of America's Puritan "destiny", Adam Smith ushered in modern economic science with his *Wealth of Nations*. The latter is formally pertinent in that it inspired the second part of the title of this work (while substituting "societies" for "nations") and in that sense relates to Tocqueville's *Democracy in America* inspiring the first.

However, the *Wealth of Nations* is substantively pertinent to the present analysis and argument, thus related to Tocqueville's concept of national destiny, mostly negatively, as what *not* to do in identifying, analyzing, and explaining such destines or fates of societies. This holds true insofar as Smith's work assumes or implies that economic factors determine and predict the destiny or happiness of societies—that is, "all you need to be predestined *cum* saved or happy is riches"—committing the fallacy of economism, the economy's determinism of society. Also, this applies to, for example, of Ricardo's and Mill's *Principles of Political Economy*, Marx's *Capital*, Sombart's *Quintessence of Capitalism*, Schumpeter's *Capitalism, Socialism and Democracy*, and other cognate (e.g., Braudel's *Civilization and Capitalism*) or ideologically opposite works (viz., Mises' *Human Action*, Hayek's *Economic*

*Freedom*, Friedman's *Capitalism and Freedom*). They commit or imply the fallacy of economic determinism and reductionism, including, as committed by orthodox economics, market absolutism or "fundamentalism" (Barber 1995; Hodgson 1999; Stiglitz 2002).

Conversely, Weber's *Economy and Society* both in its title and analysis avoids and even counteracts economic determinism or materialism, as do Comte's, Durkheim's, Simmel's, Pareto's, Parsons', and other pertinent sociological works[7] (Aron 1998). As Weber implies, it is *not* the economy—Smith's wealth or Marx's capital—that simply, unconditionally, and totally determines and predicts the destiny or fate of society as a whole. Rather, it is often conversely, as suggested by his sociological and historical analysis of the impact of social non-economic forces, like Protestantism, notably Calvinism,[8] and other world religions, on modern capitalism.[9] In his terms, societal predestination or codetermination thus involves the "degree of elective affinity between concrete structures of social action and concrete forms of economic organization", simply society and economy. An exemplary case is his thesis and comparative analysis of the "degree of elective affinity" between religion and economy, specifically Calvinism and modern industrial ("bourgeois") capitalism in Western societies.

The preceding suggests the need for avoiding and overcoming economism or economic determinism, including market absolutism, in analyzing the sociological "destiny" of nations or societies, from Smith,

---

[7] Aron (1998:5) comments that Durkheim, Pareto, and Weber transcended a "strictly economic interpretation of human motivations" (and behaviorism) and are "unanimous in their rejection of external or materialistic explanations as well as of rationalizing and economic explanations of human behavior." He adds that this is reason why Parsons authored *Structure of Social Action* "whose sole purpose was to show the affinity between" them (Aron 1998:5).

[8] Referring to Weber, Kaufman (2004:336) comments that the "transformation of Calvinist theology into the "spirit of capitalism" is only one such example of the power of endogenous cultural change". His answer to the question of "how exactly it was that Calvinist Christians constructed a new repertoire of economic action out of their struggles with "salvation anxiety" is that Calvin "crafted the doctrine, but his followers "made" capitalism".

[9] Weber considers and describes capitalism as the "most fateful force in our modern life" thus seemingly continuing Marx's as well as, from the opposite theoretical position, Menger's and the Austrian economic school's capitalist determinism. Yet, Weber, unlike Marx and Austrian marginalism, treats even "fateful capitalism", like the economy in general, as in part determined or dependent rather than only a determining or independent variable in relation to Protestantism or religion and society overall. At least, that is what his analysis in *the Protestant Ethnic and the Spirit of Capitalism* attempts to do, just as the title suggests.

Ricardo, Mill, and Marx to neoclassical marginalism to contemporary "libertarian" economics (Austrian and Chicago Schools, etc.). This signifies that Smith-Ricardo-Mill's wealth, Marx's capital or productive forces, as well as Mises-Hayek-Schumpeter's free-market capitalism, in short economic factors are not solely or even primarily determinative of the "destiny" of nations or the "fate" of societies, including Spengler's "rise and decline of the West". No simple equation exists and can be established between Smith-Marx's wealth or capital of nations and Tocqueville-Weber's national destinies, as between Mises-Schumpeter-Hayek's capitalism and liberal democracy, or free-markets in particular and societal liberty in general.

No simple equation or association exists between the wealth and "destiny" of nations because of the salient and countervailing action of religious and other non-economic forces in determining or predicting such national or societal destinies. The founding religion and other social forces are equally important as, if nor even more than, simply Smith's wealth and Marx's productive forces, including modern capitalism and free markets, as Durkheim, Weber, and other sociologists posit and show (Munch 2001). A comparative sociological analysis indicates that global social-cultural change is "path dependent", rather than simply determined by economic development, in that "the broad cultural heritage" of a society—Protestant, Roman Catholic, Orthodox, Confucian, or communist—impresses an enduring "imprint on values" and institutions despite modernization in the economy, technology, and politics (Inglehart and Baker 2000).

For instance, Puritan America is commonly deemed or described as the wealthiest and the most modern nation economically or technologically but in cultural, notably moral-religious, and related non-economic terms continues to be considered or depicted as what some observers call the "last remaining primitive", traditional, or conservative, society (Baudrillard 1999) among contemporary Western societies. In virtue of this cultural and other non-economic, including in part political, backwardness (Amenta et al. 2001), it remains a sort of Western analogue to poor and developing or backward (Bendix 1984) hyper-religious societies, including Catholic South America and Poland (and in part Ireland), and Islamic countries (Inglehart 2004; also, Byrne 1997; Friedland 2002; Munch 2001).

Thus, a comparative sociological analysis finds that Puritan America is one of the two "striking deviant cases" (the second being Catholic Ireland) among modern Western societies from the processes of secularization, liberalization, and rationalization in virtue of exhibiting a "much more religious outlook" than its economic development would predict (Inglehart 2004). According to such findings, America is "not a prototype of cultural modernization" that other societies should follow, as Parsons et al. contended, but rather a "deviant case", with a "much more traditional value system than any other advanced industrial society" (Inglehart 2004). Notably, on the traditionalism versus secularism dimension modern America is reportedly ranked "far below" other advanced Western societies, having levels of religiosity, church attendance, and nationalism ("national pride") that are "comparable" to those in certain "developing", in particular Islamic and Latin American, countries (Inglehart 2004). These findings reveal the "phenomenon of American Exceptionalism" (Inglehart 2004) in its true nature and light as exceptional religious fundamentalism or traditionalism and nationalism, not, as claimed by US "born again" conservatives and over-patriotic sociologists (Lipset and Marks 2000), superior "libertarianism" and democracy. For example, Sweden, Australia, and even once-Calvinist and now Calvinist-Lutheran-Catholic Holland, are found to come closer to the "cutting edge of cultural change" than Puritan America[10] (Inglehart 2004).

If not America as a whole, a paradigmatic case is its "Bible Garden" usually identified as a functional equivalent or analogue of Islamic Iran by virtue of their shared proto-totalitarian "solutions" to the "burden" of individual liberty or the "agony" of personal choice through abolishing the liberty or choice itself (Bauman 1997, 2001; Friedland 2002; Van Dyke 1995). Recall this striking functional equivalence includes their shared system of executions and other Draconian punishments for sins-crimes (Jacobs et al. 2005), despite their drastic economic differences in the "wealth of nations", capitalism, and free markets. Generally, modern America is observed to constitute a society "simultaneously unusually" economic or hyper-capitalist and "yet also unusually" religiously "determined" in the sense of over-Puritan, politically "molded" and communally "structured, just as "individualistic and

---

[10] Inglehart (2004:18) adds that "though church attendance remains relatively high in Poland and Ireland (and the United States, to a lesser degree), it has fallen drastically in most of the historically Catholic countries of both Western and Eastern Europe; and it has fallen even more drastically in most of the historically Protestant societies—to the point where some observers now speak of the Nordic countries as post-Christian societies."

conformist" (Munch 2001) alike. In sum, it is a society of "incomparable contradictions", in which capitalism and theocratic religion, as well as the "political struggle for power" and "communal association", have all reached the extreme point (Munch 2001).

A number of proofs or symptoms show that contrary to the "wealth of nations" argument Calvinism via Puritanism is America's "destiny" or primary determinant, rather or more than capitalism and free markets; and it is so in disjuncture from and contradiction (Munch 2001), not in a Weberian "intimate connection" or "elective affinity", with the capitalist economy. One symptom is that the vast and ever-growing majority (two thirds) of the US prison population during the 2000s are moral sinners or (substantively) innocent prisoners of ethical conscience, simply "impure" non-violent offenders, like those committing drug-war and related sins (Reuter 2005), not, as many Americans are led to believe by the puritanical highly efficient apparatus of "brainwashing", hardened criminals committing violent crimes against property and persons, or murderers.

Another, more specific and direct proof or symptom in this respect is that many "free enterprise" capitalists are imprisoned and even effectively or potentially can be executed on the account of marketing "immoral" or "indecent" (Friedman 1997; Merton 1968) commodities and services (drugs, alcohol, sex toys, prostitution, residual Sunday prohibitions, television, movie and Internet content, etc.). These would-be-capitalists conform with Weber's spirit of capitalism, yet violating Puritan moralist absolutism and theocratic fundamentalism, punished typically with Draconian harshness out of any proportion with their "crimes". Hence, they are subjected to substantive injustice and in that sense a sort of state terrorism precisely devoid of any penal justice, after the model or image of Puritanism's "holy" terror against "sin" (Walzer 1963; Zaret 1989). (This applies a fortiori to those innocent persons executed or otherwise severely punished for fabricated murders or sexual offenses like rapes in the "tough on crime" neo-conservative paranoia.) As a corollary, Calvin's and directly Winthrop's theocratic dream has or will come true through neo-conservative Draconian "tough" laws and punishments, including the death penalty, and culture wars against non-violent sins and vices redefined and severely punished as crimes (the "war on drugs", sexuality, Internet control, etc.), but not or less than that of Franklin as Weber's epitome of the American spirit of capitalism, let alone the liberal-democratic ideals of Jefferson and Madison.

Overall, what analysts identify as the persistent and ever-growing "obsession with vice and sin" to the pathological point of anti-sin paranoia in America (Wagner 1997) indicates that it is the old Calvinism via Puritanism that continues to be the "destiny" of the "new nation" rather (or more) than modern capitalism and free markets. And, it does so in disassociation from or contradiction and tension, not, as assumed following Weber by Parsons et al., association, with modern capitalism and free markets. It is illustrated by the Draconian punishment and potential execution of what are economically "capitalist" entrepreneurs in certain "chemical substances" (Friedman 1997) or human services that Puritan moral fascism criminalizes as "immoral" and "ungodly", with alcohol and especially sexual sins or mere sexuality (even among consenting adults) as perennial paradigmatic cases, and various (non-medical and medical alike) drugs as the more recent case.

For instance, in addition and connection to prohibited drug entrepreneurs, perhaps nothing more vividly ("graphically") or grotesquely illustrates America's Calvinist *cum* Puritan "destiny"—in disjuncture from and contradiction with capitalism and free markets—than those poor "free-enterprise" women in Texas, Oklahoma, and the "Bible Belt" overall imprisoned or otherwise punished for selling and even buying (or using) sex toys or more than a certain legally prescribed amount of them (e.g., 4–6). An even more obvious and perennial instance involve those would-be capitalists producing, marketing, and even consuming alcohol during Prohibition, as well as in its vestiges in Southern "dry" states.

Another more comprehensive and perhaps oldest set of practices also indicates America's "destiny" in Calvinism in tension with and even suspension of capitalism in that it comprises various residual or proxy Sunday prohibitions of virtually any economic and other activity (including work, sale of goods and services, etc.) not devoted to the "glory of God" (church service, etc.), in Southern and most other US states, including once Puritan New England. A more recent "high-tech" exemplar is the US neoconservative government ban on Internet (online) gambling during the 2000s to the point of agreeing to compensate some countries affected (the European Union, Japan and Canada) for violating WTO rules of "free and fair trade" rather than revoking, let alone repenting, this action, exhibiting or evoking Puritan moralistic intransigence. With some exceptions, most US states prohibit gambling in any form, with many from the "Bible Belt" prohibiting even public lottery. At least, such cases confirm and reveal that whenever in contradiction or friction Puritanism typically overcomes capitalism, thus the God of Calvinism defeats "Mammon" in America—Winthrop et al. "beat" Franklin and Jefferson, thus Calvin does Adam Smith, if not every day, then most of the time.

### The Calvinist-Capitalist Elective Affinity in the "New Nation": Theocratic Capitalism?

On this account, Calvinism usually prevails via Puritanism over the spirit of capitalism and, of course, liberal-secular democracy, thus Calvin and Winthrop et al. over Franklin and Jefferson. And, it does if and when such contradictions or tensions (Munch 2001) occur between Puritan "morality" or "godliness" and frequently economic freedoms as well as invariably moral and other civil liberties. For instance, Prohibition and its revivals or vestiges through "dry" zones in the "Bible Belt" and beyond (e.g., Utah, Kansas) are, as Merton (1968) suggests, the perennial, and the war on drugs, as some US conservative economists admit (Friedman 1997), the most radical and dramatic, "proof" or syndrome of this prevalent pattern or "method in the madness".

Simply, if Smith's "wealth of nations" or Franklin's spirit of capitalism, not to mention Jefferson's ideal of democracy, were stronger than Calvin-Winthrop's (in retrospect) "ghost" of theocratic coercion and moralistic absolutism, these and other past and continuing temperance wars would have not happened, or at least not in the form, scope, and severity they did and do. These supposedly impossible wars span from national Prohibition by no less than a constitutional amendment to the "war on drugs" generating the unparalleled prison population explosion and various social pathologies, including future crime precisely due to imprisonment for sin (Akerlof 2002). In sum, when in contradiction and tension, as is frequently (Munch 2001), the God of Calvinism or Biblical theocracy typically, with certain variations and exceptions, overwhelms or defeats the glorified "Mammon" (Bellamy 1999) of capitalism or free markets, let alone the "Satan" of "ungodly" and "un-American" liberal-secular democracy or liberalism, in America. At least, Calvinism and its theocracy is or can be harnessed against capitalism[11] (German 1995) and *a fortiori* political liberalism, because of their different and often opposite values.

---

[11] German (1995:969) recognizes that Calvinism and capitalism, as well as liberalism, entail different and even "contradictory values". Specifically, he suggests that in America (18th century New England) "Calvinism could be enlisted *against* capitalism", even though there was the "triumph of Calvinism *and* capitalism".

At this point, America's Calvinist "destiny" economically manifests itself as theocratic, opposed to liberal-secular, capitalism in which "theocratic" typically dominates "capitalism", let alone liberalism. In short, it does as "faith-based" capitalism or capitalist Biblical theocracy—"capitalist" yet "theocracy" *cum* Bibliocracy, "free" enterprise and markets but still in a "Bible Garden". Figuratively, non-theocratic or non-evangelical and non-religious persons in America are less likely to become prominent Congressmen and Presidents (including Governors, etc.), in "faith-based" capitalism than is Marshall's monkey to retype Shakespeare's collected works or "a blindfolded chimpanzee" playing with the *Wall Street Journal* to select a portfolio that would perform just as well as that of economists (Malkiel 2003). Historically and comparatively, they are less likely to do so than the likelihood of Sorokin's future "sensate" or "earthly" Popes as well as of moderately religious or "liberal" presidents in Iranian and other Islamic theocracies and societies (as confirmed even in the 2008 Presidential election of another President of "faith"). In a way, Jefferson, Madison, Franklin, and other "not so godly" Americans would have less chance to become (again or the first time) Presidents in this theocratic "godly" capitalism and polity than heretics Copernicus, Galileo, and De Vinci to be rehabilitated, if not canonized, by the Vatican Church, and moderate Muslims to be elected to political positions in Islamic theocracies. In sum, America's destiny or story is the "triumph" of both Calvinism and capitalism (German 1995), thus of a mix of Calvinist theocracy with a capitalist economy. In this sense, this is the precisely triumph and thus "destiny" of theocratic capitalism, or capitalist, as distinguished from non-capitalist, including feudal and other traditional, theocracy.

At this point, Weber's "elective affinity" between Calvinism and capitalism effectively operates or reappears in America as one between Calvinist theocracy *cum* Puritan Bibliocracy and a capitalist, free-market economy, which frequently, however, involves various frictions, tensions, or contradictions, thus "disaffinity", between the two. This is a logical consequence of Weber's analysis, albeit he did not explicitly pursue it. If Calvinism is inherently theocratic by decreeing Biblical theocracy as "Divinely" ordained, the Calvinist-capitalist affinity inexorably assumes an equivalent form, that between Bibliocracy and capitalism, the "Bible Garden" and "free enterprise" (as epitomized by the "God and free markets" Christian Coalition of the 1980s). Yet, Calvinist Bibliocracy and capitalism can come in certain frictions or contradictions and in these "disaffinities" the God of Calvinism typically (of course, not always) prevails over "Mammon" in Puritan America, rather than, as he implied,[12] conversely.

In general, Weber's is a case of an elective affinity between a theocratic religion and the capitalist economy. Yet, this turns out often into a disaffinity between the two, given, as Weber himself intimates (in *Economy and Society*), the inherent or eventual contradictions, oppositions, or frictions between virtually all world religions, including even original Calvinism, and modern capitalism, "God" and "Mammon", religious faith and wealth overall. Alternatively, the point is that the elective affinity between Calvinism and capitalism is *not* one, as commonly assumed, between Calvinist political democracy and the capitalist economy, for the reasons stated above. Namely, as Weber implies, if theocracy and tyranny overall (Heller 1986) is "Divinely" ordained in Calvinism, then political, especially liberal-secular, democracy and society is alternatively, so to speak, "Divinely damned" or "ungodly", thus effectively precluded from entering in the elective affinity with modern capitalism, simply a non sequitur. In sum, the curious composite of "capitalist theocracy" or theocratic "faith-based" capitalism" as America's Calvinist economic "destiny" indicates that Weber's affinity between Calvinism and capitalism proves to be one between theocracy, and not liberal-secular democracy, and the capitalist economy, often turning into a mutual disaffection or tension in which Calvin's omnipotent God defeats Mammon if not always, then most of the time.

However, it is also necessary to avoid and overcome the opposite temptation of what Weber would call the "spiritualistic" or idealistic fallacy and other non-economic mono-causal explanations of the "destiny" of modern nations and societies, including America. Alternatively, founding religion is not the only factor, but one among multiple social factors in the "rise and decline" of Western and other societies like America. In Weber's terms, the "destinies" of nations or societies are codetermined and co-predicted by both Tocqueville's religious and Smith-Marx's secular social factors, their religion and their wealth or capital, or by ideal and material, spiritual and economic, values and interests, and not exclusively by either category.

---

[12] For illustration, Weber comments that even in Puritan America "the pursuit of wealth, stripped of its religious and ethical meaning, tends to become associated with purely mundane passions, which often actually give it the character of sport."

Hence, this reintroduces the notion and method of multiple societal determination, what Weber calls codetermination and Veblen cumulative causation, involving various determinants, as distinguished from single-cause determinism and explanation, in analyzing the "destiny" of modern societies, including America. In turn, as noted, within this set and conjoined process of determination some factor(s) is/are still more important and primary, and the others less so and secondary. And, Calvinism, while certainly not the only determinant, belongs to those primary determinants of America's "destiny" and genesis in the form of "all-American" Puritanism, in addition to and conjunction with those of a non-religious nature in the strict sense as usually identified in the sociological and other literature (capitalism, free markets, natural resources, mass immigration, geographic space, expansion and wars, technology, political revolution, etc.).

For the purpose of analysis, this work has treated these non-religious determinants as "control variables" or what Parsons calls residual factors. It has done by analogy to Weber's treatment of Calvinism as not the sole determinant but belonging to the primary codeterminants or correlates of modern capitalism, alongside non-Calvinist forces such as (in his *General Economic History*) monetary calculation or accounting, freedom of the market, rational science and technology, rational law and state, including bureaucratic administration, commercialization of economic life, including speculation, formally free labor, societal rationalization, etc.

*The Supreme Historical Irony? The Calvinist "French Connection" to America*

This work has identified certain "ironies of sociology, history, and geography", specifically the irony that Calvinism originated in the "old world" and yet has since become the "destiny" of the "new nation". Calvinism was not only formally "born" in, but substantively the oldest part of, the "old" Europe, 16th century Reformation France. In substantive terms, Calvinism constituted the oldest Protestantism on the account of being the most primitive, traditionalist, conservative, orthodox, fundamentalist, and theocratic Protestant type, as Comte Simmel, Weber, and other sociologists imply. In particular, as Hume and other analysts suggest, Puritanism was the most conservative or fundamentalist, sectarian, and theocratic or totalitarian Calvinism (Munch 2001;

Stivers 1994) and consequently the oldest or the most primitive Protestantism (Goldstone 1991; Hudson and Coukos 2005) in this sense. Yet, America is commonly considered and celebrated as the first new, the newest or youngest Western nation (Lipset 1969; Lipset and Marks 2000).

The above stark contrast between Calvinism or Puritanism and America then yields what is apparently a supreme instance of social ironies and paradoxes, if not what Merton (1968) calls perversities. This is the irony or paradox, if not perversity, of the substantively oldest, the most primitive, and traditional type of religion, ethic, and culture (i.e., Protestantism) within the post-Reformation West (Munch 2001) predestining or over-determining the historically newest and youngest and the most technologically modern and dynamic Western society—Calvinism's societal predestination, via Puritanism's historical over-determination, of America.

A related geographic and historical irony or paradox is that a "foreign" French-born complex of religious values and institutions like Calvinism has become America's "destiny" and genesis albeit via and disguised as "all-American" Puritanism. On a lighter note, then it is more than "French fries" that US Puritan-inspired nativist neo-conservatives need to rename if they want to validate their claim to or maintain their self-delusion of native Puritanism and Protestant conservatism (Lipset 1996) overall as America's genesis and "destiny" opposed to and purified from "foreign", notably "old European", elements. For attaining that purpose, they likely need to rename "French unfreedom Calvinism" into American "freedom Calvinism", as through their notion of "all-American" Puritanism removing or obscuring its Calvinist, foreign "un-American" parentage, in an Orwellian attempt at reconstructing post-Reformation (and previous) Western history and civilization. For instance, if Calvinism was "a belief system" that foreigners imposed on the Dutch people during the 16th century (Kaplan 2002), specifically the French or "Genevan creed (Nischan 1994), then it was also "foreign" to America, even if through supposedly but consequently anything but "native" Puritanism, as was Catholicism condemned, despised, and attacked for the same reason.

Now, one might object that it is not needed to emphasize that French-made Calvinism was "foreign" to America, just as to Holland, England, and Germany, so Puritanism less "native" or "American" than commonly supposed, because this holds true of Catholicism, Anglicanism, and Lutheranism. This objection overlooks that America has never defined itself in terms of a Catholic "destiny", nation, or identity since both its Puritan genesis and its revolutionary birth and that, relatedly, Catholicism has been a minor social force compared to Protestantism, in particular Puritanism, in American history and society, despite some recent changes. Moreover, it has almost invariably defined itself in terms of anti-Catholic "destiny" or identity, as during Puritanism with its vehement Calvinist anti-Catholicism (Merton 1939) inherited, though disguised, by contemporary sectarian Protestantism (Lipset 1996), at least in the "Bible Belt". As known, early Puritanism, claiming to be truly "native" and "American", condemned and attacked Catholicism ("Papists") as the supreme "foreign" and so "evil" epitome and symbol of the "old" and "depraved" Europe, as does contemporary sectarian Protestantism (like Baptism and related sects) explicitly or implicitly. Thus, "foreign" Catholicism has been and remains the key (though not the only) ground for nativism or anti-foreign nationalism (Friedland 2001) in Puritanism and other sectarian Protestantism in America, from the 17th to the 21st century.

The aforesaid of Catholicism holds true, with some qualifications, of Anglicanism and Lutheranism by comparison with Puritanism in America. Anglicanism has not been America's "destiny" or identity, excluding the pre-revolutionary Episcopalian South, in the same manner or degree as Puritanism, though historically may have been its actual genesis given the Anglican migration preceding the Puritans, a moment curiously ignored or almost hidden in the literature and common discourse celebrating only the second as the "Pilgrims" or the "first" (Seaton 2006). Thus, the Anglican Pilgrims in the general sense of "explorers", "adventurers", "colonizers", or "founders" (even if for, as Weber notes, economic rather than religious reasons) and settlements preceded those of the Puritans by almost two decades (Virginia in 1607 compared to New England in the 1620s). And yet, it is the Puritans that are conventionally considered, described, and glorified, especially by US Puritan-inspired conservatives, as "the Pilgrims", thus the pre-revolutionary "fathers" of America (Seaton 2006), but not non-Puritan Protestants, let alone Columbus et al. as condemned Catholic "Papists".

This conservative reconstruction of American and Western history is apparently false, an Orwellian historical falsification and manipulation for political purposes, "proving" the Puritan genesis, thus present and future "heart and soul", simply "destiny" of America. It is so whatever its reasons and rationalizations, such as Anglicanism as "foreign" associated with the British Empire and, via its imputed "Catholic" residues, the "old" Europe, plus less ascetic, "Christian" than Puritanism as "native", anti-British or anti-royal, and "pure" moralistic Christianity. And, most US religious conservatives overlook or deny that their Puritan heroes and role models were theologically, sociologically, and often geographically none than French-European Calvinists, just as condemned Catholics were "Roman Papists", thus both religious groups were "born and raised" in the "old world" and to that extent "foreign".

The aforesaid holds good even more of Lutheranism, a less salient and manifest religious factor in American history and society than Anglicanism, let alone Puritanism and in extension Calvinism. Furthermore, like Catholicism before and after, Anglicanism was attacked and effectively supplanted as "foreign" through the Puritan Great Awakenings, notably following the Revolution, in the South transformed into a Calvinist "Bible Belt", while Lutheranism, of which the Anglican Church was an English ramification or analogue, has hardly ever been prominent or visible on a scale comparable with Calvinism in America since its genesis. Evidently, French Calvinism was defined and remained in America, through and by Puritanism as its loyal disciple or agent, as not only less "foreign" than Roman Catholicism, German Lutheranism, and English Anglicanism, but "native" and truly "American"; and yet, as Merton (1968) might say, such are the perversities of the "social logic" in Calvinist American and general Western history. (One wonders what conservative Americans would think and do if they somehow miraculously realized or recognized that "all-American" Puritanism as their "destiny" was French Calvinism theologically, sociologically, and often geographically—as the complex of ideas, institutions and persons—moving from France and Geneva to America via England, as did Catholicism from Rome, Lutheranism from Germany, and Anglicanism from England. Politically incorrect comedians in America would predict renaming "French" into "freedom" or "American" in the expression "French Calvinism" judging by a grotesque precedent set by US puritanical "freedom fries" neo-conservatives.)

Further, for non-Calvinists, "the devil" was the very "originator" of Calvinism (cited in Nischan 1994) in the face of Calvin, as perceived in Germany and partly Holland, just as in his native France. This was not only because of Calvin's role in killing Servetus and libertines for blasphemy and other brutal personal acts, but his theological doctrines, notably the extremely inhumane, exclusionary, or anti-universal, oligarchic doctrine of predestination. If so, then this also holds true of his theological followers within Puritanism. At this point, the latter effectively functioned as an English-American agent or instrument of spreading the "devil" of Calvinism via Calvinization, thus a Calvinist "Trojan horse", in America and in part England. It was a process eventually failing in the old world, including France, Germany, and in part modern Holland, and yet fully and enduringly triumphing in the "new nation".

Even if instead an angel or any embodiment of human good rather than the "devil" were the "originator" of Calvinism and redefined Calvin accordingly (Sorkin 2005), this still does not change the fact that his own creation became the "destiny" of a society he did not even know or envision, not of his homeland and its neighbors, as he had intended and practically attempted. Regardless of being either the "devil" or an "angel" (value-laden terms to be avoided anyway), Calvin himself would have likely considered and described the above moment as the probably most unexpected outcome and serendipitous discovery in post-Reformation Western history and society if he, "born again" (by analogy to his US descendants' claims to religious rebirth) by a miracle of his God of Calvinism, visited America during Tocqueville's time and the 2000s, and then went back to his homeland France, his adopted home Geneva, and proto-Calvinist Holland. He would have found at his serendipitous chagrin and delight respectively, thus established the following dual diagnosis. The God of Calvinism in the sense of primitive evangelical theocracy is for all intents and purposes *caput mortuum* (dead) in his very home and the old Europe overall, yet very much "alive and well", in fact perpetually revived and perfected, in the new nation that he never saw or even envisaged, during the early 21st century.

For European Calvinists and their "children" or agents American Puritans, such a duality likely represents the most unexpected triumphal outcome and serendipitous discovery—a sort of "rediscovery of America" more than five centuries after it was discovered, notably a Hollywood-style "happy-end" in the new, exceptional nation in virtue of its Calvinist *cum* Puritan "destiny". Thus, for most ordinary, including, as often (self) described, Puritan-style "God-fearing", "Bible-thumping", ignorant, "gun-totting", culture-warring, and super-patriotic-crusading Americans, it is the "best kept secret" and thus a sort of ultimate "shock". For non-Calvinists and non-Puritans and from the stance of liberal-secular democracy and modernity, this, specifically the triumph of Calvinism (German 1995) and its design of Biblical theocracy in America, is perhaps the most dramatic case of what Merton (1968) calls the "perversities of social logic", specifically in post-Reformation Western society and history. And for others, including value-neutral sociologists and other social scientists, it is probably the most striking and salient instance of sociological and historical-geographic ironies or paradoxes within Weber's Occident, if not all the modern world.

The preceding yields a sort of epilogue déjà vu—substantively, "nothing new under the sun of Calvinism", from France 1559 to America 2009. The original act within the "extended family" of Calvinism, and implication of Tocqueville's America's "destiny" in its offspring Puritanism, was probably the decision of the Calvinist Synod in, of all places, Paris, France in 1559 for establishing the "evangelical religion" through the extermination and persecution of non-evangelicals as the only efficient and feasible method for that "holy" purpose. And, the final act involves the ways and means of Calvinist-inspired "born again" evangelicalism (Southern Baptism and allied sects and cults) in America, notably the "Bible Belt", during the 2000s through the original method of, to cite its methodical-fanatical exponents, "persecute [and exterminate] non-evangelicals and the ungodly. Let them perish and let [their] children be fatherless, and [their wives] widow[s]." And, this is the only relevant (to use a movie title) "French connection" between pre-modern and pre-Enlightenment Paris and the modern and anti-Enlightenment "Bible Belt" as the axiomatic "anti-Paris", just as was Geneva under Calvin's and subsequent Calvinist rule (Garrard 2003).

Most strikingly and controversially, the preceding rediscovers that virtually (not literally) everything that is negative and destructive to human liberty, well-being, and life, simply "evil as distorted good" in American history and society from the 17th to the 21st century emanates in one way or another from Calvinism via Puritanism as its "destiny" or main determinant and heritage. Conversely, virtually everything that is positive and constructive to human liberty, well-being, and life in American history and society during this period derives in some ways from (to use Ross' word) the "antidote" to Calvinism through Puritanism as the "poison". While seemingly simplistic and "shocking" to most Americans, this somewhat serendipitous "rediscovery," as is within Tocqueville's context, is the true "diagnosis" of America's Calvinist-as-Puritan "destiny." To finish on a lighter note, Americans can hence plausibly "blame the French", notably Paris, as the creator and home of Calvinism, for their Calvinist "destiny" (not just for "French fries", etc.).

Or perhaps Tocqueville was incorrect—America's "destiny" is *not* really embodied in the first Puritans and thus original Calvinists, Winthrop and in extension Calvin. Rather, it may well be incarnated in their opposites or countervailing forces such as Jefferson and Madison and their rejection of the Puritan design or dream of America as "Christian" austere, authoritarian Sparta as an extension of Calvin's Spartan Geneva in favor of its paradigmatic antipode, liberal-democratic "Athens" through and following the American Revolution. Hence, just as its true "genesis" was not the Puritan establishment of New England as a colony within the British Empire but the anti-British Revolution, its "destiny" may not be Calvinist Biblical theocracy as a "Divinely" ordained total/totalitarian social system. Instead, it may be the latter's polar opposite, Jeffersonian liberal-secular democracy and society. Or perhaps it is both in a certain paradoxical combination or coexistence and mutual contradiction or tension. This is yet another story beyond the scope of this work for other analyses and analysts.

Lastly, perhaps the idea of America's and any other society's "destiny" in either Calvinist theocracy or liberal democracy—or else both in a blend and friction—is implausible by implying a sort of unacceptable societal fatalism or determinism, just as that of an individual's fate, thus should be discarded as fatalistic or overly deterministic. And, this is yet another story also beyond this work's confines and for other analyses and analysts.

# REFERENCES

Acemoglu, Daron. 2005. "Constitutions, Politics, and Economics: A Review Essay on Persson and Tabellini's The Economic Effects of Constitutions." *Journal of Economic Literature* 43:1025–1048.
Acemoglu, Daron, Simon Johnson, James Robinson, and Pierre Yared. 2005. "The Rise of Europe: Atlantic Trade, Institutional Change, and Economic Growth." *American Economic Review* 95:546–579.
Adorno, Theodor. 2001. *The Stars Down to Earth and Other Essays in the Irrational in Culture*. New York: Routledge.
Akerlof, George. 2002. "Behavioral Macroeconomics and Macroeconomic Behavior." *American Economic Review* 92:411–433.
——. 2007. "The Missing Motivation in Macroeconomics." *American Economic Review* 97:5–36.
Alderson, Arthur and François Nielsen. 2002. "Globalization and the Great U-Turn: Income Inequality Trends in 16 OECD Countries." *American Journal of Sociology* 107:1244–1299.
Alexander, Jeffrey. 1983. *Theoretical Logic in Sociology*. Berkeley: University of California Press.
——. 1998. *Neofunctionalism and After*. Oxford: Blackwell Publishers.
——. 2001. "Theorizing the Modes of Incorporation: Assimilation, Hyphenation, and Multiculturalism as Varieties of Civil Participation." *Sociological Theory* 19:237–249.
Alexander, Jeffrey and Paul Colomy (eds.). 1990. *Differentiation Theory and Social Change*. New York: Columbia University Press.
Almeida, Paul. 2003. "Opportunity Organizations and Threat-Induced Contention: Protest Waves in Authoritarian Settings." *American Journal of Sociology* 109: 345–400.
Amenta, Edwin, Chris Bonastia and Neal Caren. 2001. "US Social Policy In Comparative and Historical Perspective: Concepts, Images, Arguments, and Research Strategies." *Annual Review of Sociology* 27:213–234.
Amenta, Edwin and Drew Halfmann. 2000. "Wage Wars: Institutional Politics, WPA Wages, and the Struggle for U.S. Social Policy." *American Sociological Review* 65:506–528.
Angel, Leonard. 1994. *Enlightenment East and West*. Albany: State University of New York Press.
Archer, Robin. 2001. "Secularism And Sectarianism in India and the West: What Are the Real Lessons of American History?" *Economy and Society* 30.273–287.
Arendt, Hannah. 1951. *The Origins of Totalitarianism*. New York: Harcourt Brace Jovanovich.
Aron, Raymond. 1998. *Main Currents in Sociological Thought*. New Brunswick: Transaction Publishers.
Arrow, Kenneth. 1950. "A Difficulty in the Concept of Social Welfare." *Journal of Political Economy* 58:328–346.
——. 1994. "Methodological Individualism and Social Knowledge. *American Economic Review* 84:1–9.
Artz, Frederick. 1998. *The Enlightenment in France*. Kent: Kent State University Press.
Ashton, Robert. 1965. "Puritanism and Progress." *The Economic History Review* 17:579–587.

Bähr, Peter. 2002. "Identifying the Unprecedented: Hannah Arendt, Totalitarianism, and the Critique of Sociology." *American Sociological Review* 67:804–831.
Baldwin Eric. 2006. "'The Devil Begins to Roar': Opposition to Early Methodists in New England." *Church History* 75:94–119.
Baltzell, Digby. 1979. *Puritan Boston and Quaker Philadelphia.* New York: Free Press.
Barber, Bernard. 1995. "All Economies Are 'Embedded': The Career of a Concept, and Beyond. *Social Research* 62:387–413.
Barnes, Barry. 2000. *Understanding Agency.* London Sage Publications.
Basker, Emek. 2007. "The Causes and Consequences of Wal-Mart's Growth." *Journal of Economic Perspectives* 21:177–198.
Bateson, Gregori. 1979. *Mind and Nature.* New York: Dutton.
Baudrillard, Jean. 1999. *America.* London: Verso.
Bauman, Zygmunt. 1997. *Postmodernity and its Discontents.* New York: New York University Press.
——. 2000. *Community.* Cambridge: Polity Press.
——. 2001. *The Individualized Society.* Cambridge: Polity Press.
Bebchuk, Lucian and Jesse Fried. 2003. "Executive Compensation as an Agency Problem." *Journal of Economic Perspectives* 17:71–92.
Beck, Ulrich. 2000. *The Brave New World of Work.* Cambridge: Polity Press.
——. 2002. "The Cosmopolitan Society and its Enemies." *Theory, Culture and Society* 19:17–44.
Becker, George. 1984. "Pietism and Science: A Critique of Robert Merton's Hypothesis." *American Journal of Sociology* 89:1065–1090.
Becky, Pettit and Bruce Western. 2004. "Mass Imprisonment and the Life Course: Race and Class Inequality in U.S. Incarceration." *American Sociological Review* 69:151–169.
Beiner, Ronald. 1992. *What's the Matter with Liberalism?* Berkeley: University of California Press.
Bellamy, Richard. 1999. *Liberalism and Pluralism.* New York: Routledge.
Bell, Daniel. 1977. "The Return of the Sacred? The Argument on the Future of Religion." *British Journal of Sociology* 28:419–449.
——. (ed.) 2002. *The Radical Right.* New Brunswick: Transaction Publishers.
Benabou, Roland. 2000. "Unequal Societies: Income Distribution and the Social Contract." *American Economic Review* 90:96–129.
Bendix, Reinhard. 1965. "Max Weber and Jakob Burckhardt." *American Sociological Review* 30:176–184.
——. 1970. *Embattled Reason.* New York: Oxford University Press.
——. 1977. *Max Weber.* Berkeley: University of California Press.
——. 1984. *Force, Fate and Freedom.* Berkeley: University of California Press.
Berman, Morris. 2000. *The Twilight of American Culture.* New York W. W. Norton.
Berry, Christopher. 1997. *Social Theory of the Scottish Enlightenment.* Edinburgh: Edinburgh University Press.
Binmore, Ken. 2001. "The Breakdown of Social Contracts," in Durlauf Steven and Peyton Young, eds., *Social Dynamics.* Cambridge: MIT Press, pp. 213–236.
Bird, Colin. 1999. *The Myth of Liberal Individualism.* New York: Cambridge University Press.
Birnbaum, N. 1953. "Conflicting Interpretations of the Rise of Capitalism: Marx and Weber." *British Journal of Sociology* 4:125–141.
Bjorkland, Anders and Markus Janti. 1997. "Intergenerational Income Mobility in Sweden Compared to the U.S." *American Economic Review* 87:1009–1032.
Blinkhorn, Martin. 2003. *Fascists and Conservatives.* London: Taylor & Francis.
Blomberg, Brock and Joseph Harrington. 2000. "A Theory of Rigid Extremists and Flexible Moderates with an Application to the U.S. Congress." *American Economic Review* 90:605–620.

Bloom, Allan. 1988. *The Closing of the American Mind*. New York: Simon and Schuster.
Boles, John. 1999. The Southern Way of Religion. *Virginia Quarterly Review* 75:226–247.
Bollen, Kenneth. 1990. "Political Democracy: Conceptual and Measurement Traps." *Studies in Comparative International Development* 25:7–25.
Bollen, Kenneth and Pamela Paxton. 1998. "Detection and Determination of Bias in Subjective Measures." *American Sociological Review* 63:465–478.
Boettke, Peter. 1995. "The Road to Serfdom Revisited: Government Failure in the Argument Against Socialism." *Eastern Economic Journal* 21:7–26.
Bonefeld, Werner. 2002. "Review of Golsan, Richard, *Fascism's Return, Scandal, Revision, and Ideology since 1980s*." *Capital & Class* 77:145–147.
Boudon, Raymond. 1982. *The Unintended Consequences of Social Action*. New York: St. Martin's Press.
Bourdieu, Pierre. 1988. *Outline of a Theory of Practice*. Cambridge: Cambridge University Press.
———. 1998. *Acts of Resistance*. New York: Free Press.
———. 2000. *Pascalian Meditations*. Stanford: Stanford University Press.
Bourdieu, Pierre and Hans Haacke. 1995. *Free Exchange*. Stanford: Stanford University Press.
Bowles, Samuel. 1998. "Endogenous Preferences: The Cultural Consequences of Markets and Other Economic Institutions." *Journal of Economic Literature* 36:75–111.
Breen, Richard and Jan Jonsson. 2005. "Inequality of Opportunity in Comparative Perspective: Recent Research on Educational Attainment and Social Mobility." *Annual Review of Sociology* 31:223–243.
Bremer Francis. 1995. *The Puritan Experiment*. Hanover: University Press of New England.
Brooks, Clem. 2000. "Civil Rights Liberalism and the Suppression of a Republican Political Realignment in the US, 1972 to 1996." *American Sociological Review* 65:483–505.
Brooks, Clem and Jeff Manza. 1997. "The Social and Ideological Bases of Middle-Class Political Realignment in the U.S., 1972–1992." *American Sociological Review* 62:191–208.
Brouwer, Steve. 1998. *Authoritarian Democracy*. New York: Henry Holt and Co.
Buchanan, James. 1991. *The Economics and the Ethics of Constitutional Order*. Ann Arbor: University of Michigan Press.
Budros, Art. 2004. "Social Shocks and Slave Social Mobility: Manumission in Brunswick County, Virginia, 1782–1862." *American Journal of Sociology* 110:539–579.
Burns, Gene. 1990. "The Politics of Ideology: The Papal Struggle with Liberalism." *American Journal of Sociology* 95:1123–1252.
Byrne, James. 1997. *Religion and the Enlightenment*. Louisville: Westminster John Knox Press.
Caldwell, Bruce. 1997. "Hayek and Socialism." *Journal of Economic Literature* 35:1856–1890.
Calhoun, Arthur. 1925. "Social Development." *Social Forces* 4:43–56.
Calhoun, Craig. 1993. "Nationalism and Ethnicity." *Annual Review of Sociology* 19:211–239.
Carter, Dan. 1996. *From George Wallace to Newt Gingrich*. Baton Rouge: Louisiana State University Press.
Cascardi, Anthony. 1999. *Consequences of Enlightenment*. New York: Cambridge University Press.
Champion, Justin. 1999. "Willing to Suffer: Law and Religious Conscience in Seventeenth-Century England," in John McLaren and Harold Coward, eds., *Religious*

*Conscience, The State, And The Law*. Albany: State University of New York, pp. 13–28.

Chaves, Mark. 1999. "Religious Congregations and Welfare Reform: Who Will Take Advantage of 'Charitable Choice'?" *American Sociological Review* 64:836–847.

Clark, Elizabeth. 1999. "Speech for the Soul: Religion, Conscience, and Free Speech in Antebellum America," in John McLaren and Harold Coward, eds., *Religious Conscience, The State, And The Law*. Albany: State University of New York, pp. 62–76.

Clemens Elisabeth. 2007. "Toward a Historicized Sociology: Theorizing Events, Processes, and Emergence." *Annual Review of Sociology* 33:527–49.

Coats, A. W. 1967. "Sociological Aspects of British Economic Thought." *Journal of Political Economy* 75:706–729.

Cochran, Augustus. 2001. *Democracy Heading South*. Lawrence: University Press of Kansas.

Coffey, John. 1998. "Puritanism and Liberty Revisited: The Case for Toleration in the English Revolution." *The Historical Journal* 41:961–985.

Cohen, Daniel. 2003. *Our Modern Times*. Cambridge: MIT Press.

Cohen, Jere. 1980. "Rational Capitalism in Renaissance Italy." *American Journal of Sociology* 85:1340–1355.

Collins, Randall. 1975. *Conflict Sociology*. New York: Academic Press.

——. 1997. "An Asian Route to Capitalism: Religious Economy and the Origin of Self-Transforming Growth in Japan." *American Sociological Review* 62:843–865.

——. 2000. "The Sociology of Philosophies: A Precis." *Philosophy of the Social Sciences* 30:157–201.

Dagger, Richard. 1997. *Civic Virtues: Rights, Citizenship, and Republican Liberalism*. New York: Oxford University Press.

Dahrendorf, Ralph. 1959. *Class and Class Conflict in Industrial Society*. Stanford: Stanford University Press.

——. 1979. *Life Chances*. Chicago: Chicago University Press.

Darnell, Alfred and Darren Sherkat. 1997. "The Impact of Protestant Fundamentalism on Educational Attainment." *American Sociological Review* 62:306–315.

Davis, James. 2005. "William Ames's Calvinist Ambiguity over Freedom of Conscience." *Journal of Religious Ethics* 33, 335–355.

Davis, Nancy and Robert Robinson. 2006. "The Egalitarian Face of Islamic Orthodoxy: Support for Islamic Law and Economic Justice in Seven Muslim-Majority Nations." *American Sociological Review* 71:167–190.

Dayton, Cornelia. 1999. "Excommunicating the Governor's Wife: Religious Dissent in the Puritan Colonies before the Era of Rights Consciousness," in John McLaren and Harold Coward, eds., *Religious Conscience, the State, and the Law*. Albany: State University of New York, pp. 29–45.

Delacroix, Jacques and François Nielsen. 2001. "The Beloved Myth: Protestantism and the Rise of Industrial Capitalism in Nineteenth-Century Europe." *Social Forces* 80:509–553.

Delanty, Gerard. 2000. "The Foundations of Social Theory: Origins and Trajectories," in Bryan Turner, ed., *The Blackwell Companion to Social Theory*. Malden: Blackwell, pp. 21–46.

De Long, Bradford. 2000. "The Triumph of Monetarism?" *Journal of Economic Perspectives* 14:83–94.

Desai, Mihir. 2005. "The Degradation of Reported Corporate Profits." *Journal of Economic Perspectives* 19:171–192.

Deutsch, Kenneth and Walter Soffer (eds.). 1987. *The Crisis of Liberal Democracy*. Albany: State University of New York Press.

Dombrowski, Daniel. 2001. *Rawls and Religion*. New York: State University of New York Press.

Dunn, Charles and David Woodard. 1996. *The Conservative Tradition in America.* Lanham: Rowan & Littlefield.
Earl, Jennifer, John McCarthy, and Sarah Soule. 2003. "Protest Under Fire? Explaining the Policing of Protest." *American Sociological Review* 68:581–606.
Edgell, Penny, Joseph Gerteis and Douglas Hartmann 2006. "Atheists as Other: Moral Boundaries and Cultural Membership in American Society." *American Sociological Review* 71:211–234.
Einolf, Christopher. 2007. "The Fall and Rise of Torture: A Comparative and Historical Analysis." *Sociological Theory* 25:101–121.
Eisenstadt, Shmuel. 1965. "Transformation of Social Political, and Cultural Orders in Modernization." *American Sociological Review* 30:659–673.
Eliasoph, Nina and Paul Lichterman. 2003. "Culture in Interaction." *American Journal of Sociology* 108:735–794.
Elwood, Christopher. 1999. *The Body Broken.* New York: Oxford University Press.
Emerson, Michael and David Hartman. 2006. "The Rise of Religious Fundamentalism." *Annual Review of Sociology* 32:123–141.
Erikson, Emily and Joseph Parent. 2007. "Central Authority and Order." *Sociological Theory* 25:245–267.
Erikson, Robert and John Goldtrope. 2002. "Intergenerational Inequality: A Sociological Perspective." *Journal of Economic Perspectives* 16:31–44.
Esping-Andersen, Gosta. 1994. "Welfare States and the Economy," in Neil Smelser and Richard Swedberg, eds., *The Handbook of Economic Sociology.* Princeton: Princeton University, pp. 711–732.
Fehler, Brian. 2005. "Classicism and the Church: Nineteenth-Century Calvinism and the Rhetoric of Oratorical Culture." *Rhetoric Review* 24:133–149.
Fishback, Price. 1998. "Operations of Unfettered Labor Markets: Exit and Voice in American Labor Markets at the Turn of the Century." *Journal of Economic Literature* 36:722–765.
Fischer, Stanley. 2003. "Globalization and Its Challenges." *American Economic Review* 93:1–30.
Fitzpatrick, Martin. 1999. "Enlightenment and Conscience," in John McLaren and Harold Coward, eds., *Religious Conscience, the State, and the Law.* Albany: State University of New York Press, pp. 46–61.
Flanagan, Robert. 1999. "Macroeconomic Performance and Collective Bargaining: An International Perspective." *Journal of Economic Literature* 37:1150–1175.
Fligstein, Neil. 2001. *The Architecture of Markets.* Princeton: Princeton University Press.
Foerster, Norman. 1962. *Image of America.* Notre Dame: University of Notre Dame Press.
Foucault, Michel. 1996. "What is Critique?" in James Schmidt, ed., *What is Enlightenment?* Berkeley: University of California Press, pp. 382–398.
Fourcade, Marion and Kieran Healy. 2007. "Moral Views of Market Society." *Annual Review of Sociology* 33:285–311.
Frank, Robert and Philip Cook. 1995. *The Winner-Take-All Society.* New York: Free Press.
Fritchman, Stephen. 1944. *Men of Liberty.* Boston: Beacon Press.
Friedland, Roger. 2001. "Religious Nationalism and the Problem of Collective Representation." *Annual Review of Sociology* 27:25–52.
——. 2002. "Money, Sex, and God: The Erotic Logic of Religious Nationalism." *Sociological Theory* 20:381–425.
Friedman, Milton. 1997. "Economics of Crime." *Journal of Economic Perspectives* 11:194.
Friedman, Milton and Rose Friedman. 1982. *Capitalism and Freedom.* Chicago: University of Chicago Press.

Frijhoff, Willem. 2002. "Religious Toleration in the United Provinces: From 'Case' To 'Model'," in Hsia Po-chia and Henk van Nierop, eds., *Calvinism and Religious Toleration in the Dutch Golden Age*. New York: Cambridge University Press, pp. 27–53.
Fromm, Erich. 1941. *Escape from Freedom*. New York: Holt, Rinehart and Winston.
Fulton, John. 1954. *Michael Servetus Humanist and Martyr*. New York: Herbert Reichner.
Fung, Archon. 2003. "Associations and Democracy: Between Theories, Hopes, and Realities." *Annual Review of Sociology* 29:515–539.
Garrard, Graeme. 2003. *Rousseau's Counter-Enlightenment*. Albany: State University of New York Press.
Garry, Patrick. 1992. *Liberalism and American Identity*. Kent: Kent State University Press.
Gelernter, David. 2005. "Americanism–and its Enemies." *Commentary* 119:41–48.
German, James. 1995. "The Social Utility of Wicked Self-Love: Calvinism, Capitalism, and Public Policy in Revolutionary New England." *Journal of American History* 82:965–998.
Ghent, W. J. 1902. *Our Benevolent Feudalism*. New York: Macmillan.
Gibbs, Jack. 1989. "Conceptualization of Terrorism." *American Sociological Review* 54:329–340.
Giddens, Anthony. 1979. *Central Problems in Social Theory*. Berkeley: University of California Press.
——. 1984. *The Constitution of Society*. Berkeley: University of California Press.
——. 1998. *The Third Way*. Malden. Blackwell Publishers.
——. 2000. *The Third Way and its Critics*. London: Polity Press.
Glaeser, Edward. 2004. "Psychology and the Market." *American Economic Review* 94:408–413.
Goldberg, Chad. 2001. "Social Citizenship and A Reconstructed Tocqueville." *American Sociological Review* 66:289–315.
Goldstone, John. 1986. "State Breakdown in the English Revolution: A New Synthesis." *American Journal of Sociology* 92:257–322.
——. 1991. "Revolution and Rebellion in the Early Modern World." Berkeley: University of California Press.
——. 2000. "The Rise of the West—or Not? A Revision to Socio-economic History." *Sociological Theory* 18:175–194.
Gorski, Philip. 1993. "The Protestant Ethic Revisited: Disciplinary Revolution and State Formation in Holland and Prussia." *American Journal of Sociology* 99:265–316.
——. 2000. "The Mosaic Moment: An Early Modernist Critique of Modernist Theories of Nationalism." *American Journal of Sociology* 105:1428–1468.
——. 2003. *The Disciplinary Revolution*. Chicago: University of Chicago Press.
Gould, Philip. 1996. *Covenant and Republic*. New York: Cambridge University Press.
Gouldner, Alvin. 1970. *The Coming Crisis of Western Sociology*. New York: Avon.
Greeley, Andrew and Michael Hout. 1999. "Americans' Increasing Belief in Life After Death: Religious Competition and Acculturation." *American Sociological Review* 64:813–836.
Gross, Bertram. 1980. *Friendly Fascism*. Boston: South End Press.
Grossman, Henryk. 2006. "The Beginnings of Capitalism and the New Mass Morality." *Journal of Classical Sociology* 6:201–213.
Gusfield, Joseph. 1963. *Symbolic Crusade*. Urbana: University of Illinois Press.
Habermas, Jürgen. 1971. *Knowledge and Human Interests*. Boston: Beacon Press.
——. 1975. *Legitimation Crisis*. Boston: Beacon Press.
——. 1989. *The New Conservatism*. Cambridge: MIT Press.
——. 1996. "The Unity of Reason in the Diversity of its Voices," in James Schmidt (ed.). *What is Enlightenment?* Berkeley: University of California Press, pp. 399–425.
——. 2001. *The Postnational Constellation*. Cambridge: MIT Press.

Habermas, Jürgen, Ciaran Cronin and Pablo De Greiff. 1998. *The Inclusion of the Other.* Cambridge: MIT Press.
Hallett, Tim. 2003. "Symbolic Power and Organizational Culture." *Sociological Theory* 21:128–149.
Harley, David. 1996. "Explaining Salem: Calvinist Psychology and the Diagnosis of...." *American Historical Review* 101:306–330.
Hartz, Louis. 1963. "American Historiography and Comparative Analysis: Further Reflections." *Comparative Studies in Society and History* 5:365–377.
Hayek, Friedrich. 1960. *The Constitution of Liberty.* South Bend: Gateway Editions.
Heale, M. J. 1998. "Review of Dan Carter, *The Politics of Rage.*" *Journal of American Studies* 32:134–135.
Heckathorn, Douglas. 1990. "Collective Sanctions and Compliance Norms: A Formal Theory of Group-Mediated Social Control." *American Sociological Review* 55:366–384.
Heineman, Kenneth. 1998. *God is a Conservative.* New York: New York University Press.
Heller, Henry. 1986. *The Conquest of Poverty.* Leiden: Brill.
Hiemstra, John. 2005. "Calvinist Pluriformity Challenges Liberal Assimilation: A Novel Case for Publicly Funding Alberta's Private Schools, 1953–1967." *Journal of Canadian Studies* 39:146–173.
Hill, Steven. 2002. *Fixing Elections.* New York: Routledge.
Hinchman, Lewis. 1984. *Hegel's Critique of the Enlightenment.* Gainesville: University Presses of Florida.
Hinson, Keith. 1997. "Calvinism Resurging Among SBC's Young Elites." *Christianity Today* 41:86–87.
Hirschman, Albert. 1977. *The Passions and the Interests.* Princeton: Princeton University Press.
——. 1993. "Exit, Voice, and the Fate of the German Democratic Republic: An Essay in Conceptual History." *World Politics* 45:173–203.
Hodgson, Geoffrey. 1999. *Economics and Utopia.* New York: Routledge.
Holton, R. J. 1987. "The Idea of Crisis in Modern Society." *British Journal of Sociology* 38:502–520.
Homans, George. 1961. *Social Behavior.* New York: Harcourt, Brace & World.
Hout, Michael and Claude Fischer. 2002. "Why More Americans Have No Religious Preference: Politics and Generations." *American Sociological Review* 67:165–190.
Hout, Michael, Andrew Greeley and Melissa Wilde. 2001. "The Demographic Imperative in Religious Change in the United States." *American Journal of Sociology* 107:468–510.
Hsia Po-chia and Henk van Nierop (eds.). 2002. *Calvinism and Religious Toleration in the Dutch Golden Age.* New York: Cambridge University Press.
Hsia, R. Po-Chia. 2002. "Introduction," in Hsia R. Po-chia and Henk van Nierop, eds., *Calvinism and Religious Toleration in the Dutch Golden Age.* New York: Cambridge University Press, pp. 1–7.
Hudson, Kenneth and Andrea Coukos. 2005. "The Dark Side of the Protestant Ethic: A Comparative Analysis of Welfare Reform." *Sociological Theory* 23:1–24.
Hull, Mary. 1999. *Censorship in America.* Boulder: NetLibrary.
Infantino, Lorenzo. 2003. *Ignorance and Liberty.* New York: Routledge.
Inglehart, Ronald and Wayne Baker. 2000. "Modernization, Cultural Change and the Persistence of Traditional Values." *American Sociological Review* 65:19–51.
Inglehart, Ronald (ed.). 2004. *Human Beliefs and Values.* México: Siglo XXI.
Ingram, Paul and Karen Clay. 2000. "The Choice-Within-Constraints New Institutionalism and Implications for Sociology." *Annual Review of Sociology* 26:525–546.
Jacobs, David, Jason Carmichael and Stephanie Kent. 2005. "Vigilantism, Current Racial Threat, and Death Sentences." *American Sociological Review* 70:656–677.

Jenness, Valerie. 2004. "Explaining Criminalization: From Demography and Status Politics to Globalization and Modernization." *Annual Review of Sociology* 29:147–171.
Jepperson, Ronald. 2002. "Political Modernities: Disentangling Two Underlying Dimensions of Institutional Differentiation." *Sociological Theory* 20:61–85.
Johnson, Jeff. 2003. "Pervert in the Pulpit: The Puritanical Impulse in the Films of David Lynch." *Journal of Film & Video* 55:3–14.
Kaplan, Benjamin. 2002. "'Dutch' Religious Tolerance: Celebration and Revision," in Hsia Po-chia and Henk van Nierop, eds., *Calvinism and Religious Toleration in the Dutch Golden Age*. New York: Cambridge University Press, pp. 8–27.
Kaufman, Jason. 2004. "Endogenous Explanation in the Sociology of Culture. *Annual Review of Sociology* 30:335–357.
Kearney, H. F. 1965. "Puritanism and Science: Problems of Definition." *Past and Present* 31:104–110.
Kenshur, Oscar. 1993. *Dilemmas of Enlightenment*. Berkeley: University of California Press.
King, Desmond. 1999. *In the Name of Liberalism*. New York: Oxford University Press.
Kiser, Edgar. 1999. "Comparing Varieties of Agency Theory in Economics, Political Science, and Sociology: An Illustration from State Policy Implementation." *Sociological Theory* 17:146–170.
Kloppenberg, James. 1998. The *Virtues of Liberalism*. New York: Oxford University Press.
Korpi, Walter and Joakim Palme. 1998. "The Paradox of Redistribution and Strategies of Equality: Welfare State Institutions, Inequality and Poverty in the Western Countries." *American Sociological Review* 63:661–687.
Kuran, Timur. 2004. "Why the Middle East is Economically Underdeveloped: Historical Mechanisms of Institutional Stagnation." *Journal of Economic Perspectives* 18:71–90.
Kurzman, Charles and Erin Leahey. 2004. "Intellectuals and Democratization, 1905–1912 and 1989–1996." *American Journal of Sociology* 109:937–986.
Kurzman Charles, Chelise Anderson, Clinton Key, Youn Ok Lee, Mairead Moloney, Alexis Silver, and Maria W. Van Ryn. 2007. "Celebrity Status." *Sociological Theory* 25:347–367.
Lane, Robert. 2000. *The Loss of Happiness in Market Democracies*. New Haven: Yale University Press.
Lee, Cheol-Sung. 2005. "Income Inequality, Democracy, and Public Sector Size." *American Sociological Review* 70:158–181.
Lehmann, Jennifer. 1995. "The Question of Caste in Modern Society: Durkheim's Contradictory Theories of Race, Class and Sex." *American Sociological Review* 60:566–585.
Lemert, Charles. 1999. "The Might Have Been and Could Be of Religion in Social Theory." *Sociological Theory* 17:240–263.
Lemieux, Pierre. *Smoking and Liberty*. Montreal: Varia. 1997.
Lenski, Gerhard. 1984. *Power and Privilege*. Chapel Hill: University of North Carolina Press.
——. 1994. "Societal Taxonomies: Mapping the Social Universe." *Annual Review of Sociology* 20:1–26.
Levitt, Steven. 1996. "How Do Senators Vote? Disentangling the Role of Voter Preferences, Party Affiliation, and Senator Ideology." *American Economic Review* 86:424–441.
Linton, Marisa. 2001. *The Politics of Virtue in Enlightenment France*. New York: Palgrave.
Lipset, Seymour. 1955. "The Radical Right: A Problem for American Democracy." *The British Journal of Sociology* 6:176–209.
——. 1969. *Revolution and Counterrevolution*. London: Heineman.
——. 1996. *American Exceptionalism*. New York: Norton.
Lipset, Seymour and Gary Marks. 2000. *It Didn't Happen Here*. Norton.

Lipset, Martin and Earl Raab. 1978. *The Politics of Unreason*. Chicago: University of Chicago Press.
Loveman, Mara. 2005. "The Modern State and the Primitive Accumulation of Symbolic Power." *American Journal of Sociology* 110:1651–1683.
Lucas, Robert. 2000. "Some Macroeconomics for the 21st Century." *Journal of Economic Perspectives* 14:159–168.
MacKinnon, Malcolm. 1988. "Weber's Exploration of Calvinism: The Undiscovered Provenance of Capitalism." *British Journal of Sociology* 39:178–210.
Malkiel, Burton. 2003. "The Efficient Market Hypothesis and Its Critics." *Journal of Economic Perspectives* 17:59–82.
Mallard, Grégoire. 2005. "Interpreters of the Literary Canon and Their Technical Instruments: The Case of Balzac Criticism." *American Sociological Review* 70:992–1010.
Manent, Pierre. 1998. *Modern Liberty and Its Discontents*. Lanham: Rowman & Littlefield Publishers.
Mannheim, Karl. 1936. *Ideology and Utopia*. New York: Harcourt.
——. 1967. *Essays on the Sociology of Culture*. London: Routledge & Kegan Paul.
Mansbach, Richard. 2006. "Calvinism as a Precedent for Islamic Radicalism." *Brown Journal of World Affairs* 12:103–115.
Manza, Jeff and Clem Brooks. 1997. "The Religious Factor in US Presidential Elections, 1960–1992." *American Journal of Sociology* 103:38–81.
Markoff, John. 1997. "Peasants Help Destroy an Old Regime and Defy a New One: Some Lessons from (and for) the Study of Social Movements." *American Journal of Sociology* 102:1113–1142.
Martin, John. 1998. "Authoritative Knowledge and Heteronomy in Classical Sociological Theory." *Sociological Theory* 16:99–130.
——. 2002. "Power, Authority, and the Constraint of Belief Systems." *American Journal of Sociology* 107:861–904.
Mayway, Leon. 1984. "In Defense of Modernity: Talcott Parsons and the Utilitarian Tradition." *American Journal of Sociology* 89:1273–1305.
McCann, Sean. 2000. *Gumshoe America*. Durham: Duke University Press.
McCleary, Paul. 2002. "Book Review–Gross Bertram, Friendly Fascism." *Social Policy* 32:60–65.
McLaren, John and Harold Coward (eds.). 1999. *Religious Conscience, the State, and the Law*. Albany: State University of New York Press.
McLaughlin, Neil. 1996. "Nazism, Nationalism, and the Sociology of Emotions: Escape from Freedom Revisited." *Sociological Theory* 14:241–261.
McMurtry, John. 1999. *The Cancer Stage of Capitalism*. London: Pluto Press.
Means, Richard. 1966. "Protestantism and Economic Institutions: Auxiliary Theories to Weber's Protestant Ethic." *Social Forces* 44:372–381.
Mencken H. L. 1982. *A Mencken Chrestomathy*. New York: Vintage Books.
Mentzer, Raymond. 2007. "Fasting, Piety, and Political Anxiety among French Reformed Protestants." *Church History* 76:330–362.
Merrill, Louis. 1945. "The Puritan Policeman." *American Sociological Review* 10:766–776.
Merton, Robert. 1939. "Review of Ray Billington, *The Protestant Crusade, 1800–1860*." *American Sociological Review* 4:436–438.
——. 1968. *Social Theory and Social Structure*. New York: Free Press.
——. 1995. "The Thomas Theorem and the Matthew Effect." *Social Forces* 74:379–422.
Messner, Steven, Robert Baller and Matthew Zevenbergen. 2005. "The Legacy of Lynching and Southern Homicide." *American Sociological Review* 70:633–655.
Miller, Joanne, Kazimierz Slomczynski and Melvin Kohn. 1987. "Authoritarianism as Worldview and Intellectual Process." *American Journal of Sociology* 93:442–444.
Miller, Michael. 1975. "Notes on Neo-Capitalism." *Theory and Society* 2:1–35.
Miliband, Ralph. 1969. *The State in Capitalist Society*. New York: Basic Books.

Mises, Ludwig von. 1950. *Socialism*. New Haven: Yale University Press.
———. 1957. *Theory and History*. New Haven: Yale University Press.
———. 1966. *Human Action*. Chicago: Henry Regnery.
Mitchell, Joshua. 1995. "Locke's Muted Calvinism, Book Review of 'John Locke: Resistance, Religion and Responsibility,' by John Marshall." *Review of Politics* 57:734–736.
Moisseroon, Jean-Yves. 2002. "Money Without Exchange: Theoretical Reconsiderations," In Adaman Fikret and Pat Devine, eds., *Economy And Society*. Montréal: Black Rose Books, pp. 134–149.
Moore, Barrington. 1993. *Social Origins of Dictatorship and Democracy*. Boston: Beacon Press.
Mouw, Ted and Michael Sobel. 2001. "Culture Wars and Opinion Polarization: The Case of Abortion." *American Journal of Sociology* 106:913–943.
Morck, Randall, Daniel Wolfenzon and Bernard Yeung. 2005. "Corporate Governance, Economic Entrenchment, and Growth." *Journal of Economic Literature* 43: 655–720.
Mulyadi, Sukidi. 2006. "Max Weber's Remarks on Islam: The Protestant Ethic Among Muslim Puritans." *Islam & Christian-Muslim Relations* 17:195–205.
Mumford, Lewis. 1970. *Myth of the Machine*. V. 2. New York: Harcourt Brace Jovanovich.
Munch, Richard. 1981. "Talcott Parsons and the Theory of Action." *American Journal of Sociology* 86:709–739.
———. 1994. *Sociological Theory*. Chicago: Nelson-Hall Publishers.
———. 2001. *The Ethics of Modernity*. Lanham: Rowman & Littlefield.
Murdock, Graeme. 2005. "Review of Philip Gorski, *The Disciplinary Revolution*." *European History Quarterly* 35:144–147.
Myles, John. 1994. "Comparative Studies in Class Structure." *Annual Review of Sociology* 20:103–124.
Myrdal, Gunnar. 1953. *The Political Element in the Development of Economic Theory*. London: Routledge and Kegan Paul.
The New Schaff-Herzog *Encyclopedia of Religious Knowledge*. 1977. Grand Rapids: Baker Book House.
Nickell, Stephen. 1997. "Unemployment and Labor Market Rigidities: Europe versus North America." *Journal of Economic Perspectives* 11:55–74.
Niggle, Christopher. 1998. "Equality, Democracy, Institutions, and Growth." *Journal of Economic Issues* 32:523–531.
Nigg, Walter. 1962. *The Heretics*. New York: Alfred A. Knopf.
Nisbet, Robert. 1952. "Conservatism and Sociology." *American Journal of Sociology* 58:167–175.
———. 1966. *The Sociological Tradition*. New York: Basic Books.
Nischan, Bodo. 1994. *Prince, People, and Confession*. Philadelphia: University of Pennsylvania Press.
Nordhaus, William. 2007. "A Review of the Stern Review on the Economics of Climate Change." *Journal of Economic Literature* 45:686–702.
Orren, Karen. 1991. *Belated Feudalism*. New York: Cambridge University Press.
———. 1994. "Institutions, Antinomies, and Influences in Labor Governance." *Law and Social Inquiry* 19:187–193.
Ozment, Steven. 1980. *The Age of Reform (1250–1550)*. New Haven: Yale University Press.
Pager, Devah. 2003. "The Mark of a Criminal Record." *American Journal of Sociology* 108:937–975.
Pampel, Fred. 1998. "National Context, Social Change and Sex Differences in Suicide Rates." *American Sociological Review* 63:744–758.
Parsons, Talcott. 1937. *The Structure of Social Action*. New York: McGraw-Hill.
———. 1951. *The Social System*. New York: Free Press.

———. 1967. *Sociological Theory and Modern Society*. New York: Free Press.
Patell, Cyrus. 2001. *Negative Liberties*. Durham: Duke University Press.
Perrone, Luca. 1984. "Positional Power, Strikes, and Wages." *American Sociological Review* 49:412–426.
Perrucci, Robert and Earl Wysong. 2008. *The New Class Society*. Lanham: Rowman & Littlefield.
Phelps, Edmund. 2007. "Macroeconomics for a Modern Economy." *American Economic Review* 97:543–561.
Piketty Thomas and Emmanuel Saez. 2006. "The Evolution of Top Incomes." *American Economic Review* 96:200–205.
Plotke, David. 2002. "Introduction," in Daniel Bell, ed., The *Radical Right*. New Brunswick: Transaction Publishers, pp. vi–lxxvi.
Pollmann, Judith. 2002. "The Bond of Christian Piety: The Individual Practice of Tolerance and Intolerance in the Dutch Republic," in Hsia Po-chia and Henk van Nierop, eds., *Calvinism and Religious Toleration in the Dutch Golden Age*. New York: Cambridge University Press, pp. 53–71.
Popper, Karl. 1973. *The Open Society and Its Enemies*. Vol. 2. London: Routledge and Kegan Paul.
Prak, Maarten. 2002. "The Politics of Intolerance: Citizenship and Religion in the Dutch Republic (Seventeenth to Eighteenth Centuries)," in Hsia Po-chia and Henk van Nierop, eds., *Calvinism and Religious Toleration in the Dutch Golden Age*. New York: Cambridge University Press, pp. 159–178.
Pryor, Frederic. 2002. *The Future of U.S. Capitalism*. New York: Cambridge University Press.
Putnam, Robert. 2000. *Bowling Alone*. New York: Simon & Schuster.
Putterman, Louis, John Roemer and Joaquim Silvestre. 1998. "Does Egalitarianism Have a Future?" *Journal of Economic Literature* 36:861–902.
Quadagno, Jill. 1999. "Creating a Capital Investment Welfare State: The New American Exceptionalism." *American Sociological Review* 64:1–11.
Reiland, Ralph. 2006. Fat Cats, Calvin, and the Poor. *Humanist* 66:46–47.
Reinhardt, Uwe. 2000. "Health Care for the Aging Baby Boom: Lessons from Abroad." *Journal of Economic Perspectives* 14:71–83.
Rettig, Salomon and Benjamin Pasamanick. 1961. "Moral Value Structure and Social Class." *Sociometry* 24:21–35.
Reuter, Peter. 2005. "Review of Jeffrey Miron, *Drug War Crimes*." *Journal of Economic Literature* 43:1075–1077.
Rutherford, Andrew. 1994. "Crime Control as Industry: Towards Gulags, Western Style?" *British Journal of Criminology* 34:391–392.
Samuelson, Paul. 1994. "The Classical Classical Fallacy." *Journal of Economic Literature* 32:620–639.
Schelling, Thomas. 2006. "An Astonishing Sixty Years: The Legacy of Hiroshima." *American Economic Review* 96:929–937.
Saisselin, Rémy. 1992. The *Enlightenment against the Baroque*. Berkeley: University of California Press.
Schmidt, James (ed.). 1996. *What Is Enlightenment?*. Berkeley: University of California Press.
Schofer, Evan and John Meyer. 2005. "The Worldwide Expansion of Higher Education in the Twentieth Century." *American Sociological Review* 70:898–920.
Schuparra, Kurt. 1998. *Triumph of the Right*. Armonk: M.E. Sharpe.
Schutz, Eric. 2001. *Markets and Power*. Armonk: M.E. Sharpe.
Scitovsky, Tibor. 1972. "What's Wrong with the Arts Is What's Wrong with Society." *American Economic Review* 62:62–69.
Seaton, Paul. 2006. "Wrestling with Gods and Men: Wilson Carey McWilliams on the Puritans." *Perspectives on Political Science* 35:195–199.

Seed, John. 2005. "The Spectre of Puritanism: Forgetting the Seventeenth Century in David Hume's History of England." *Social History* 30:444–462.
Sen, Amartya. 1977. "Rational Fools: A Critique of the Behavioral Foundations of Economic Theory." *Philosophy and Public Affairs* 6:317–44.
Simon, Herbert. 1976. *Administrative Behavior*. New York: Free Press.
Simon, Julia. 1995. *Mass Enlightenment*. Albany: State University of New York Press.
Singh, Robert (ed.). 2002. *American Politics and Society Today*. Malden: Blackwell Publishers.
Schluchter, Wolfgang. 1981. *The Rise of Western Rationalism*. Berkeley: University of California Press.
Smeeding, Timothy. 2006. "Poor People in Rich Nations: The United States in Comparative Perspective." *Journal of Economic Perspectives* 20:69–90.
Smelser, Neil. 1997. *Problematics of Sociology*. University of California Press.
Smelser, Neil and Faith Mitchell. 2002. *Terrorism*. Washington: National Academies Press.
Smith, Christian. 2000. *Christian America?* Berkeley: University of California Press.
Solon, Gary. 2002. "Cross-Country Differences in Intergenerational Earnings Mobility." *Journal of Economic Perspectives* 16:59–66.
Somers, Margaret. 1998. "We're No Angels: Realism, Rational Choice, and Rationality in Social Science." *American Journal of Sociology* 104:722–784.
Sorkin, David. 2005. "Geneva's Enlightened Orthodoxy: The Middle Way of Jacob Vernet (1698–1789)." *Church History* 74:286–305.
Sorokin, Pitirim. 1959. *Social and Cultural Mobility*. Glencoe: Free Press
——. 1970. *Social & Cultural Dynamics*. Boston: Porter Sargent Publisher.
Sprunger, Keith. 1982. *Dutch Puritanism*. Leiden: Brill Academic Publishers.
Steinfeld, Robert. 2001. *Coercion, Contract, and Free Labor in the Nineteenth Century*. Cambridge: Cambridge University Press.
Steinmetz, George. 2005. "Return to Empire: The New US Imperialism in Comparative Historical Perspective." *Sociological Theory* 23:339–367.
Stigler, George and Gary Becker. 1977. "*De Gustibus Non Est Disputandum.*" *American Economic Review* 67:76–90.
Stiglitz, Joseph. 2002. "Information and the Change in the Paradigm in Economics." *American Economic Review* 92:460–501.
Stivers, Richard. 1994. *The Culture of Cynicism*. Cambridge: Blackwell.
Symonds, Michael and Jason Pudsey. 2006. "The Forms of Brotherly Love in Max Weber's Sociology of Religion." *Sociological Theory* 24:133–149.
Tawney, Richard. 1962. *Religion and the Rise of Capitalism*. New York: Harcourt.
Temin, Peter. 2006. "The Economy of the Early Roman Empire." *Journal of Economic Perspectives* 20:133–151.
Terchek, Ronald. 1997. *Republican Paradoxes and Liberal Anxieties*. Lanham Rowman & Littlefield.
Throsby, David. 1994. "The Production and Consumption of the Arts: A View of Cultural Economics." *Journal of Economic Literature* 32:1–29.
Tiryakian, Edward. 1975. "Neither Marx nor Durkheim ... Perhaps Weber." *American Journal of Sociology* 81:1–33.
——. 2002. "Review of Richard Munch, *The Ethics of Modernity*." *American Journal of Sociology* 107:1629–1631.
Trey, George. 1998. *Solidarity and Difference*. Albany: State University of New York Press.
Trigilia, Carlo. 2002. *Economic Sociology*. Malden: Blackwell Publishers.
Tubergen, Frank van, Manfred te Grotenhuis and Wout Ultee. 2005. "Denomination, Religious Context, and Suicide: Neo-Durkheimian Multilevel Explanations Tested with Individual and Contextual Data." *American Journal of Sociology* 111:797–823.
Turk, Austin. 2004. "Sociology of Terrorism. *Annual Review of Sociology* 29:271–286.

Turner, Bryan. 2002. "Sovereignty and Emergency: Political Theology, Islam and American Conservatism." *Theory, Culture & Society* 19:103–119.

Uggen, Christopher and Jeff Manza. 2002. "Democratic Contraction? Political Consequences of Felon Disenfranchisement in the United States." *American Sociological Review* 67:777–803.

Urdank, Albion. 1991. "Religion and Reproduction among English Dissenters: Gloucestershire Baptists in the Demographic Revolution." *Comparative Studies in Society and History* 33:511–527.

VanDrunen, David. 2006. "The Use of Natural Law in Early Calvinist Resistance Theory." *Journal of Law & Religion* 21:143–167.

Van Dyke, Vernon. 1995. *Ideology and Political Choice*. Chatham: Chatham House.

Vergunst, Noël. 1998. *The Institutional Dynamics of Consensus and Conflict*. Amsterdam: Vrije University Press.

Wacquant, Loýc. 2002. "Scrutinizing the Street: Poverty, Morality, and the Pitfalls of Urban Ethnography." *American Journal of Sociology* 107:1468–1532.

Wagner, David. 1997. *The New Temperance*. Boulder: Westview Press.

Wall, Steven. 1998. *Liberalism, Perfectionism And Restraint*. New York: Cambridge University Press.

Wallace, Michael, Larry Griffin and Beth Rubin. 1989. "The Positional Power of American Labor, 1963–1977." *American Sociological Review* 54:197–214.

Walzer, Michael. 1963. "Puritanism as a Revolutionary Ideology." *History and Theory* 3:59–90.

Weisbach, Michael. 2007. "Optimal Executive Compensation versus Managerial Power: A Review of Lucian Bebchuk and Jesse Fried's *Pay without Performance*." *Journal of Economic Literature* 45:419–428.

Weisbrod, Carol. 1999. "The Law and Reconstituted Christianity: The Case of the Mormons," In John McLaren and Harold Coward, eds., *Religious Conscience, The State, And The Law*. Albany: State University of New York, pp. 136–153.

White, Michelle. 2007. "Bankruptcy Reform and Credit Cards." *Journal of Economic Perspectives* 21:175–199.

Woodard, James. 1938. "The Relation of Personality Structure to the Structure of Culture." *American Sociological Review* 3:637–651.

Wolff, Edward. 2002. *Top Heavy*. New York: New Press.

Wuthnow, Robert. 1998. *After Heaven*. Berkeley: University of California Press.

You, Jong-sung and Sanjeev Khagram. 2005. "A Comparative Study of Inequality and Corruption." *American Sociological Review* 70:136–157.

Zaret, David. 1989. "Religion and the Rise of Liberal-Democratic Ideology in 17th Century England." *American Sociological Review* 54:163–179.

——. 1996. "Petitions and the Invention of Public Opinion in the English Revolution." *American Journal of Sociology* 101:1497–1555.

# INDEX

absolutism, 37, 51–2, 56, 65, 78, 84–8, 141, 194, 243–44, 247, 254, 279–80, 286, 297, 300, 303, 305–06, 310, 395, 499, 515–18, 530, 536–38, 548, 586, 589, 591
agency, 10, 17, 28, 29, 61, 79, 87–88, 120, 185, 301, 305, 307, 311, 313–15, 322, 363, 368, 375, 383–84
AGIL model, 35, 91, 98
agnostics, 34, 131, 149–50, 154, 204–05, 290, 583
American Revolution, 15, 22–23, 24, 51, 134, 153, 208, 210, 214–15, 217–18, 236, 252, 293, 438, 535, 561, 600
Americanism, 25, 32, 54, 230, 276, 332, 380, 391, 416, 577, 581
anarchism, 141
Anglicanism, 15–16, 24, 41, 53, 61–62, 78, 97, 123, 129–30, 133–34, 153, 208, 217–18, 248, 253–54, 266, 279, 282, 299, 301, 348, 369, 413, 424, 429, 443, 448–49, 498, 500–06, 513–15, 521–22, 526–32, 539–40, 546–48, 552–53, 563, 571–72, 595, 596–97
anti-labor, 142–43, 145–46, 157–62, 169, 176–77, 179–80, 187–89, 192, 286, 313
aristocracy, 12, 93, 103, 105, 108–10, 137, 142, 146, 159, 184, 193, 222–24, 260, 261–68, 270, 273–74, 278, 281–84, 286, 288–290, 387, 502, 507–08, 565
asceticism, 14, 28, 74–75, 78–80, 104, 187, 222, 248, 261, 288, 304, 319, 368, 370, 383–86, 392, 425, 430, 454, 472, 499, 528–29, 538, 541, 546–54, 558–59, 562, 565–71
authoritarianism, 79, 86, 89, 141, 143–44, 196, 208, 212, 236–40, 249, 257, 297, 303, 357–58, 516, 548, 553, 554, 559, 562, 571–73
autocracy, 177

Baptism, 5, 39, 43–44, 74–78, 83, 134, 153, 203, 242, 266, 272, 274, 279, 285, 295, 443, 459, 463–64, 532, 534, 549, 557, 564–71, 596, 599
barbarism, 45–46, 220, 316, 329, 356–57, 398, 409, 420, 475, 481, 491, 542, 550, 567

Bible Belt (*see* Bible Garden)
Bible Garden, 43, 55, 220, 250, 254, 265, 280, 283, 291–95, 301, 307, 316, 336, 341–45, 354, 358, 362–69, 371–80, 382–83, 386–89, 394, 399–400, 402–09, 413–14, 417, 419, 421–22, 434, 436–37, 440, 443, 453, 457, 464–65, 475, 478–79, 484, 487, 492–93, 588, 592
Biblical Commonwealth, 14, 18, 30, 42, 52, 57–68, 70, 80, 86, 111, 113, 126, 145, 150, 159, 199, 209, 214, 250, 259, 281–83, 292–95, 301, 304, 316, 363, 366, 368, 413, 453, 457, 479, 484, 519, 521, 524, 559, 564
Biblical theocracy, 14, 18, 36, 42–44, 48, 51–55, 62, 64, 68–69, 70–78, 94–95, 106, 109, 116, 119, 135, 147, 218, 245, 294, 298, 318, 525, 567, 591–92, 598, 600
Bibliocracy, 14, 18, 41–49, 52–57, 64–70, 73–80, 86–88, 90–91, 94–97, 111, 117–19, 121, 134, 145, 152, 157, 170, 191, 294, 298, 357, 384–85, 397, 399–409, 414, 423, 428, 458–60, 474, 509, 514, 518–19, 522, 536, 539, 541, 554, 558–59, 580, 592
bourgeoisie, 108, 113, 137, 263

Calvinist Puritanism, 4, 24, 87, 91, 188, 417, 503, 547, 572
Calvinist synod, 42, 131, 241, 243, 246, 447, 539
capitalism, Calvinist 90, 92, 107, 115, 117, 125, 141, 161, 164, 169, 175–92, 276, 333, 366, 491
capitalist dictatorship, 121, 143, 179
caste system, 122, 147, 148, 151–57, 159, 162–63, 177, 181–83, 344
Catholicism, 12, 15–16, 29, 47, 66, 87, 95–97, 110, 119, 126, 133, 142, 191, 216, 235–38, 242–49, 253–57, 267, 271, 282, 290–91, 296, 308, 312, 324, 327–28, 331, 343–44, 387, 397, 405, 408–09, 427–29, 447–56, 461–68, 476, 503, 512–15, 522–34, 543, 547–48, 552–55, 560, 563–65, 571–72, 595–97
Christian Commonwealth, 46

# 616 INDEX

Christian Sparta, 60, 79, 136, 201, 228, 355–56, 372, 511, 535, 553–54, 560–561
Christianity, 16, 48–49, 64, 75, 84, 135, 202, 234, 237, 247, 261, 267–71, 288, 290, 305, 312, 323–24, 343–45, 387, 392, 401, 408, 424–28, 431–32, 442, 460–61, 467, 475, 499, 503, 526–27, 530–34, 540, 543, 550–53, 557, 560–63, 570–72, 576, 597
civil society, 31, 35–36, 67, 69–70, 89–98, 107, 138, 152, 163, 193, 200, 205, 240, 290, 297-2, 303–73, 375–91, 393–95, 398–99, 489
civilization, 47, 125, 127, 348, 356–58, 380, 392, 409, 420, 438, 444–45, 491–92, 511, 549, 554, 561, 579, 595
collective bargaining, 178, 180–81
collectivism, 234, 239, 299, 308, 540, 548, 560
Comte, Auguste 16, 18, 22–26, 29–30, 34, 44–52, 55–56, 63–64, 82, 108, 112, 125, 139, 147, 166, 205–06, 222, 259–61, 265–98, 305, 312, 324, 368, 402, 408, 415, 424–29, 431–32, 458, 461–63, 476, 480–82, 491, 503, 506–07, 519, 524–27, 543–47, 553, 555, 563, 575–80, 586, 594
Congregational Church, 5, 15, 51, 74, 118, 193, 206, 250, 252, 292, 450
conservatism, 1, 4, 11–13, 25, 35, 77, 83, 87, 108, 113, 117–18, 137, 142–48, 154, 162, 167, 175, 186–89, 196, 200, 203, 210–14, 227, 232, 238, 240, 248, 253, 256, 275–76, 283, 304, 309–10, 316–17, 330, 336, 349, 352, 355–56, 369–70, 383, 416, 427–29, 443–45, 457–77, 486, 497, 507, 526, 529, 532–38, 544–46, 554, 558–59, 562, 580, 595
constitution, 12, 79, 332, 335, 555, 563, 583
consumerism, 54
cosmopolitanism, 247
counter-Enlightenment, 69, 426, 441–45, 459–60, 485, 489, 494–95
creative destruction, 2, 162, 304, 544, 553, 555
Cromwell, Oliver 15, 19, 44–46, 52, 63, 65, 72–73, 81, 103–04, 111–13, 123, 131, 137–38, 148–53, 196–97, 206, 220, 224, 232, 245, 251, 261, 273, 281, 286, 291–92, 298, 300–01, 328, 330, 339, 353, 359, 361, 392, 419, 425, 449, 453, 461, 470, 478, 502, 507, 519, 521, 529, 537, 540, 563–64
crusade, 8, 36, 45, 135, 149, 151, 153, 229, 246, 248, 255, 259, 297, 352–53, 372, 391, 394, 422, 449, 463, 490, 520, 539, 540, 542, 555
culture wars, 69, 89–90, 162, 168, 170, 197, 228, 245, 248, 254–55, 295, 309, 316, 336, 347, 366, 376, 411, 441, 444, 470, 494, 589

Dark Middle Ages, 47, 69, 99, 133, 195, 221, 228, 241, 397, 400, 406, 407, 445–46, 452, 459–60, 489, 510, 513–14, 554, 558, 579, 580–81
death penalty, 56, 152, 176, 226, 228, 240, 256, 295, 307, 312, 317, 329, 334, 337, 349, 356, 374–75, 377–78, 412–15, 417–19, 423, 453, 458–89
*Democracy*, 1, 2, 177, 235, 257, 260, 585
democratization, 178, 215, 423
Despotism, 78
determinism, 9, 25, 31, 37, 543, 575–76, 585–86, 594, 600
disciplinary revolution, 463, 516–17, 519, 525, 553
discrimination, 131, 149–50, 153, 155, 200, 205, 268, 294–95, 416
disestablishment, 51, 53, 60, 63, 65, 140, 157, 202, 212, 215, 293, 447, 522, 557
distribution, 105, 120, 183, 186, 344
diversity, 240, 255, 276
doctrine of predestination, 102, 105, 121, 174, 262, 267–70, 272–75, 324–25, 328, 387, 398, 433, 448, 473, 499, 516, 520, 527, 543, 564–67, 571, 573, 576, 578, 584, 597
Draconianism, 340, 350, 355, 362, 415
duopoly, 180–81, 276, 283
Durkheim, Emile 13, 32, 53, 61, 90–91, 94, 164–65, 168, 241, 269–70, 272, 338, 350–53, 357, 376, 389, 446–47, 458, 460, 579, 586–87

economic democracy, 177–81
Ross, Edward 21
Egalitarianism, 181
elective affinity, 14–15
emotionalism, 75, 78, 430, 565, 567–71
empire of liberty, 32, 36, 54, 82, 164, 391, 490
Enlightenment, 4–5, 9–12, 23–24, 51, 59–61, 75, 89, 103, 112–13, 127, 133, 153, 173, 201–03, 217, 221, 236, 239–43, 248–49, 253–54, 291, 314, 338, 354, 398, 409–10, 415, 425–28, 438, 441–45, 453–62, 473–75, 485–89, 494, 502, 510–16, 522–23, 549, 554–72, 579–81, 599

INDEX 617

Enronism, 122, 146, 167-72, 192, 286
enslavement, 127-32, 136, 151, 157, 172
estate, 137, 147
European Calvinism, 2, 4, 7, 11, 15, 17, 28, 247, 301, 427, 498-99, 503, 558, 562, 571-72
evangelicalism, 24, 33, 41-48, 58, 69-70, 74-77, 83-84, 131, 150, 154, 157, 162-63, 194, 203, 205, 229, 233, 244-48, 254-55, 274, 283, 295-96, 302, 312, 325, 345, 356-57, 364, 386, 391-92, 408, 420, 444, 457, 461-63, 475, 482-83, 491, 515, 556-58, 560, 564, 567, 569-70, 599
evolutionism, 230, 403, 405, 407-08, 475, 490, 579
exceptionalism, 55-56, 67, 70, 111, 126, 139, 171, 212, 227, 231, 233-35, 238, 247, 251, 255, 289, 300, 356, 358, 367, 381, 406-07, 410, 487, 580-81
exclusion, 131-32, 149-56, 163, 165, 200, 205, 245-46, 262, 268-69, 271, 275, 278-80, 290-95, 313, 456-57, 460, 469, 503, 520, 583
expansionism, 125, 128-29, 165, 391-92, 562
extremism, 306, 327, 351-52, 355, 526, 532, 537-41, 544, 554, 562

fanaticism, 88, 292, 296, 354-56, 367, 394-95, 413, 422, 425, 435, 439-40, 471, 482-84, 493-95, 517, 541-42
feudalism, 93, 102, 104-09, 124, 136-38, 140-44, 148, 156-57, 161-62, 164, 166, 171, 182-85, 187-88, 191, 306, 508, 510, 523, 533
Franklin, Benjamin 11, 22-23, 38, 59-61, 68, 112, 129, 151, 171, 173-75, 201, 210, 223, 236, 243, 247, 252, 267-68, 271, 312, 324, 328, 332, 387, 398, 415, 457, 474-85, 499, 507, 561, 577, 589, 591-92
French Revolution, 428
functionalism, 86, 91
fundamentalism, 39, 41-45, 55, 67-70, 77-78, 113, 124, 132, 149, 154, 163, 170, 184, 210-12, 226, 233, 244, 248, 251, 279, 295-96, 314, 317, 323, 335, 347, 357-58, 363-64, 373-74, 380-81, 406-08, 414, 422, 443, 451, 458, 484, 526, 530, 540, 550, 558-60, 562, 579, 586, 588-89

Geneva, Calvinist 329, 445, 511
genocide, 128, 131, 135-36, 455
Gini index, 184

godly politics, 193, 201, 227, 229-30, 232-33, 235, 259, 277-78, 473
Great Awakenings, 17-18, 24, 30, 32-33, 53, 61-63, 68, 75, 98, 118, 123, 125, 134-35, 139, 153, 158, 196, 199, 206-07, 209, 214, 216-18, 245, 252, 265-66, 279, 282, 292-93, 443, 474-75, 484, 531, 543, 545, 547, 555-58, 565, 569
gun culture, 72, 419, 421-22

Hayek, Friedrich 96, 119, 160-62, 176, 304, 311, 314, 585, 587
hierarchy, 113, 138, 195, 215, 534
hierocracy, 63, 96
Hinduism, 88, 148, 237-38, 253, 288, 305, 401, 424, 540
Hobbes, Thomas 1, 27, 95, 297, 420, 482
holism, 30-36, 94-96
Holy Commonwealth, 18-19, 45-46, 64, 111, 113, 138, 196, 214, 261, 291, 470, 519, 542, 564
holy war, 276, 394, 423, 490, 582
Huguenots, 62, 72, 263, 453, 467, 500-01, 512-13, 530
humanism, 17, 19, 78, 112, 186, 188-90, 197, 237-38, 240, 243, 260, 307, 314, 319-20, 322-26, 328-29, 346, 349, 362, 401-02, 404, 424-26, 429-32, 441, 448, 476, 534, 550, 558, 560-62, 568
Hume, David 1, 17-18, 26-27, 45-46, 56, 64, 73, 81, 92, 103, 112, 149-50, 208, 220, 247-48, 257, 261-66, 273, 281-83, 291-92, 298, 305, 311-12, 321, 332, 340, 345, 356-57, 360-61, 371, 388-89, 394-95, 408, 413, 422-29, 434-35, 439-40, 447, 454, 461-62, 469-71, 482-84, 491-93, 499-504, 513, 519, 522-24, 530-32, 537, 541-42, 549-50, 556, 560-61, 563, 594

imperialism, 32, 54-55, 82, 239, 391, 439, 490-91, 494, 578, 583
imprisonment, 152, 176, 188, 200, 307, 319, 323, 341, 346-47, 349, 354, 389, 412, 416, 461, 591
inclusion, 111, 583
individualism, 27, 227, 235 39, 249, 252, 299-300, 308-81, 432, 445-65, 473, 489, 538, 540, 548, 560
Industrial Revolution, 138
inhumanity, 17, 172, 189, 197, 243, 262, 268, 275, 297, 302, 304, 323, 325-29, 331, 340, 343, 346, 348-49,

362, 387, 401, 415, 419, 430, 433, 447, 541–42, 560
inquisition, 194, 375, 452
intellectualism, 403, 410–41, 444–45, 471–74, 476, 480, 486, 488–89, 494
irrationalism, 115, 139, 277, 296, 314, 322, 345, 351, 354–56, 362, 380, 410, 445, 471–74, 476, 484–85, 487, 551, 570, 580
Islamism, 288, 539–40, 542

Calvin, Jean 25, 506, 522
Jefferson, Thomas 4–5, 11, 15
jihad, 8, 135, 149, 151, 246, 255, 268, 353, 391, 394, 454, 540, 542
jingoism, 25, 391, 578
John Winthrop, 5

Keynes, John M. 28, 82, 162, 185, 208, 228, 253, 333, 335, 347, 394, 493, 501

Leviathan, 82, 95, 121, 150, 159, 166, 178, 192, 256, 342, 367, 482
liberalism, 5, 9–12, 25, 39, 58–59, 65, 75, 89, 108, 111–19, 123, 138, 142–44, 162, 194–96, 201–02, 215–16, 227, 235–49, 251–57, 276, 300, 316, 380, 404, 411, 441–55, 459–60, 467–69, 473–74, 477, 486–88, 502, 510, 513–14, 522–23, 531, 534–36, 553–60, 562–63, 572–73, 579, 581, 591–92
liberalization, 123, 154, 215, 254, 523, 579–80, 588
liberal-secular democracy, 32, 54, 67, 69–72, 89, 106, 138, 158, 163, 194, 204, 211–12, 216, 221, 227–28, 230, 236, 238–40, 251–52, 255, 257–60, 262, 265, 304–05, 307, 318, 591, 593, 600
life-world, 35, 98, 297, 302–03, 384, 386
Locke, John 27, 46, 81, 112, 482, 522, 535, 542, 571, 573
Lutheranism, 5, 12–16, 25, 30, 47, 62, 75, 96–97, 105, 123, 130, 134, 195, 242, 253–54, 279, 288, 299, 305, 326, 348, 408, 424, 429, 448, 452, 461–68, 472–73, 499–500, 503–06, 513–18, 526–30, 532–34, 539–40, 546–48, 552–53, 563, 571–72, 595–97

Machiavellianism, 34–35, 173, 175, 212, 252, 432, 546, 568, 580
Madison, James 4, 11, 22–23, 59–61, 68–69, 112, 120, 201–202, 210, 236, 247, 252, 275, 277–78, 295, 485, 522, 535, 549, 561, 589, 592, 600
mafia capitalism, 122, 164, 167–171, 192
manifest destiny, 1, 3, 7, 9–10, 54, 79, 82, 128, 131–32, 187, 276, 391, 465, 547, 577–78, 581–83
markets, 54, 181, 587–92, 594
Marx, Karl 2, 22, 26, 36–38, 103, 107, 125, 128, 138, 172, 191, 222, 261, 265–66, 305, 328, 477, 523–24, 553, 555, 585–87, 593
master-servant economy, 99, 101–11, 113–14, 116, 119
mastery of the world, 11, 15, 28–29, 32–33, 35, 53–54, 57, 94–96, 102, 288, 509, 518, 525, 568, 575, 584
materialism, 39, 54, 56, 218, 535, 586
medievalism, 12, 18, 44, 108, 138, 144, 218, 241, 256, 300, 304, 321, 397, 446, 451–52, 510–11, 514, 523, 533, 543, 550, 553, 555, 558, 560–61, 581
Merton, Robert 25–26, 34, 85, 94, 107, 115, 134, 141, 168–70, 174–75, 192, 226, 230, 296, 335–36, 341, 344, 371, 376, 389, 391, 403, 415, 462, 464, 512, 553, 572, 578, 589, 591, 595–98
Methodism, 5, 75, 153, 203, 242, 266, 274, 279, 443, 459, 488, 502, 549, 557, 564–71
Michels, Robert 111, 123, 146–47, 157, 216, 222, 237, 266, 268–69, 272–73, 275, 279–81, 286–87, 517, 526, 536
militarism, 25, 32, 34, 54–55, 78, 82–83, 239, 276, 391, 423, 490–91, 494, 516, 537, 539–41, 558–59, 562, 583
Mill, John S., 26, 29, 53, 62, 64, 79, 81, 242, 298, 321, 343, 410, 434, 443, 457, 460, 463, 471, 487, 499, 563, 570, 585, 587
Mises, Ludwig 3, 96, 107, 119, 135, 160–61, 176, 244, 246, 277, 386, 423, 442, 451, 486–87, 498–99, 537, 563, 585, 587
modernism. *See* modernity
modernity, 12, 44, 124, 144, 221, 230, 233, 243, 246, 248–49, 255, 258, 350, 370, 421, 460, 510, 520, 561, 575, 579, 598
Monarchy, 248, 448, 500, 524
monasticism, 74, 187, 288, 320, 322, 386, 425, 528, 539, 553, 560
monism, 194, 244, 518, 536, 538, 558
monopolization, 147–49, 181, 289, 291, 294

INDEX 619

monopoly, 73, 122, 180–81, 272, 276–77, 449
moral fascism, 52, 59, 84–90, 98, 145, 170, 297–319, 323, 328–33, 338–41, 344–70, 373, 375–80, 383–95, 590
moralism, 51, 74, 86–87, 303, 305, 310, 315, 569
Mormonism, 49–50, 280, 409, 564, 578
multiculturalism, 240

nationalism, 17, 25, 32, 55, 78, 82, 239, 391, 464, 490, 493, 505, 555, 562, 573, 577–78, 581, 583, 588, 596
nativism, 25, 32, 126, 391, 464, 596
Nazism, 84, 86, 97, 101, 196–98, 209, 253–54, 256, 258, 299, 302, 306, 308, 310, 319, 327–28, 330–31, 337–38, 347, 355, 358–60, 364, 366, 375, 411, 418, 436, 447, 449, 452, 454, 481, 491, 493
neo-Calvinism, 59, 72, 77–78, 216, 274, 359, 459, 475, 488, 515, 523, 566, 568–69, 571
neo-conservatism, 83, 117–18, 144–46, 162
neo-Darwinism, 144, 182
neo-fascism, 86, 212, 216, 310, 314, 523
Neo-Feudalism, 142, 145
New Deal, 142–143, 162, 182, 184
nihilism, 83, 198, 233, 296, 311, 314, 393, 394, 402–03, 423, 429, 434, 443, 482, 485–86, 489, 494–95, 582

oligarchy, 12, 105, 110–11, 137, 143–44, 146, 159, 162, 166, 193, 222–24, 259–60, 264, 266–70, 272–75, 278–84, 287–90, 312, 328, 387
oligopoly, 181, 272, 276, 283
optimism, 112, 471, 473, 475, 535
Orthodox Church, 237–38, 253, 344, 530
orthodoxy, 23, 209, 215, 242, 249, 330, 442, 446, 453, 464, 481, 485, 526, 529–32, 533, 535–36, 538, 546, 548, 558

pacification, 579
Pareto, 18–19, 25, 39, 53, 90–91, 94–98, 103, 113, 128, 137–41, 149, 151, 164, 175, 187, 202–03, 215, 222, 228, 245, 261, 266, 275, 284–89, 307, 315, 319, 321–22, 333–39, 345, 361, 370–71, 375, 385, 386, 390–91, 397, 401–02, 405–06, 424, 426–27, 449, 454, 495, 513, 548, 578, 586

Paris, 4, 13, 42, 131, 173, 433, 447, 461, 474, 506–07, 510–11, 515, 539, 549, 560, 599
Parliament of Saints, 44–45, 52, 81, 193, 206, 220, 261, 264, 273, 281, 291, 521
Parsons, Talcott 4, 11, 26, 32, 39, 53, 90–94, 98, 107, 115, 118–19, 139, 152–53, 163, 173, 234–36, 238–39, 249–50, 276–77, 297, 302–03, 307–08, 314, 326, 333, 353, 370, 384, 386, 398, 401–04, 428–29, 431–32, 445, 465, 471–72, 477, 484, 490, 505, 512, 548, 567–68, 586, 588, 590, 594
path-dependence, 6, 9–10, 16, 24, 56, 59, 65, 67, 73, 135, 169, 437, 497, 575–76, 584
patrimonialism, 102, 140, 143–44
perfectionism, 305–306, 310, 395, 443
pessimism, 112, 320, 323, 393, 430, 471, 473–74
pluralism, 181, 207–08, 235, 240, 242–44, 247, 253–56, 294, 441, 451, 459, 462, 465–69, 516–18, 534–37, 556, 558
plutocracy, 34, 148, 159, 161, 178, 193, 260, 284, 286–90, 293
positivism, 403, 429, 480–81
poverty, 104–05, 120, 181–82, 186, 190, 226, 440, 487
predation, 164–67, 170–71, 220, 280
predatory capitalism, 122, 124, 163–69, 171–72, 179, 192, 366
Presbyterianism, 5, 15, 18, 65, 71, 153, 266, 279, 449, 503, 546
primitivism, 45, 122, 124–25, 136, 204, 351–52, 354–57, 362, 410, 420, 481, 492, 511, 515, 517, 523, 550, 560–61, 583
prohibition, 286, 336, 371
Protestantism, sectarian 10, 19, 140, 520, 562, 596
purism, 27–28, 51, 56, 124, 300, 302, 305–06, 310, 395, 451, 499, 501

radicalism, 12, 24, 44, 74, 78, 299, 310, 471, 473, 481, 485, 507, 526, 533, 535, 537–44, 548, 558–59
rationalism, 5, 10, 54, 240, 242, 247, 279, 300, 314, 322, 333, 352, 380, 403–04, 407–10, 429, 441–42, 444–45, 459, 471–74, 476, 480–89, 494, 510, 528, 534, 556–57, 559, 562, 569–70, 579–81
rationalization, 105, 107, 133, 155, 175, 186, 270, 305, 387, 422, 472, 510, 535, 561, 575, 579–80, 588, 594

# 620 INDEX

Reaganism, 117, 143, 177, 188
reductionism, 31–32, 586
Reformation, 3–4, 9, 12, 14, 26–28, 30, 41, 48, 65, 74, 95, 103, 115–16, 135, 138, 141, 196, 207, 241–42, 246, 271, 299–300, 305, 309, 338, 368, 401, 407, 426–27, 429, 445, 448, 453, 455, 463, 469, 498, 500, 503–10, 512–17, 522–23, 527–30, 532, 540, 543–45, 550–55, 558, 562, 572, 594–95, 598, 599
Reformed Church, 2, 12, 17, 22, 27, 47, 74, 123, 151, 193, 195, 251, 254, 262, 272, 451, 468, 503–04, 507, 510, 513, 515, 517–18, 522, 524, 527, 529, 531–33, 536, 543, 550, 553, 563
Renaissance, 197, 310, 398, 400–02, 409, 423–29, 433–34, 438, 440–45, 452, 460, 513, 546
republic, 19, 60–61, 119, 203, 235, 250–51, 261, 265, 277, 519, 521–22, 545, 561–62
revivalism, 118, 207, 209, 216, 218, 252, 265, 279, 443–44, 474–75, 536, 543, 556–57, 564, 570
robber barons, 141, 143, 145–46, 162, 182, 184–85, 266, 285–87, 293

sadism-masochism, 34, 188, 359–60, 385, 549
sanctification, 7
Schumpeter, Joseph 2, 109, 118, 129, 138, 150, 162, 201, 217, 230, 304, 308, 322, 544, 553–55, 585, 587
scientism, 39, 296, 403–04, 407–09, 441, 444, 471–72, 480–81, 483–84, 486, 490, 495
sectarianism, 27, 74, 78, 84, 109, 210, 245, 278–80, 285, 292, 299–300, 313, 414, 463, 471, 482, 503–04, 508, 520, 523, 557, 562, 569
secularism, 5, 9–11, 15, 39, 54, 75, 111, 113, 116, 118, 144, 201–02, 216, 227, 235–36, 238–40, 242, 247–48, 252–56, 279, 300, 380, 400, 402, 404, 441–45, 459, 464, 474, 510, 522–23, 525, 534–35, 556–59, 563, 572, 579, 581, 588
secularization, 154, 215, 254, 523, 579–80, 588
segregation, 153–57, 205, 211, 294, 295
servitude, 122, 124, 127, 131, 136, 143, 145, 147, 149, 152, 156–57, 177, 508, 528
Simmel, Georg 8, 45, 94, 124, 127, 129–30, 134, 149, 151–52, 199, 202, 204–05, 213, 214, 220–21, 246, 271, 276, 292, 299, 301, 304, 308, 328, 338, 376, 392, 402, 425, 447–52, 461, 466, 516, 526–27, 529, 537, 548, 552, 563, 586, 594
slavery, 93, 102, 107, 111, 122–37, 139–40, 147, 149–150, 152, 154, 156–59, 177, 181, 183, 205, 294, 309, 420
Smith, Adam 2, 353, 585, 591
social contagion, 25, 168, 170, 256, 541, 554
societal predestination, 9, 11, 14, 19, 28–29, 31, 37–48, 49, 525–26, 576, 584, 586, 595
Sombart, Werner 4, 26–28, 63, 80, 115, 276, 300, 428, 497, 499–500, 538, 585
Sorokin, Pitirim 35, 37–38, 45, 48–49, 90, 94–95, 121, 145, 148, 174, 191, 198, 203, 222, 288, 328, 343, 431, 499, 548, 552, 592
Spencer, Herbert 82, 134, 138, 164, 166, 231, 241, 458, 579–80
spiritualism, 34, 36, 39, 54

Tawney, R. H. 26, 28, 34, 42, 46–47, 50, 53, 93, 95–97, 137, 153, 191, 206, 208, 222, 234, 239, 250, 271, 275, 300–01, 308, 312, 325, 327, 348, 386, 389, 417–18, 445, 452, 461, 502, 504, 533, 548, 553, 559, 567
terrorism, 170, 232, 317–18, 337, 352, 368–69, 375, 384, 417–18, 578, 589
Thatcherism, 177
Tocqueville, Alexis 1–8, 13–14, 20–23, 30–31, 36–39, 50–52, 55–58, 64–65, 79–81, 82, 84–85, 126, 128, 138–39, 151, 172, 184, 207, 235, 249, 252, 289, 292, 313, 340, 361, 374, 393, 406, 413–15, 427, 434, 497, 500, 502, 512, 519–21, 524, 549, 556, 563–64, 575–76, 581, 584–85, 587, 593, 598–600
Tönnies, Ferdinand 124–25, 162, 171, 259, 292, 338, 350, 376
total social system, 31, 35–36, 53, 56–57, 89–95, 102, 104, 109–10, 116–17, 120–2, 134, 147, 157–59, 166, 169, 193, 297, 304, 311, 315, 397, 400
totalitarianism, 65, 84, 86, 96–98, 134, 194–96, 198, 244, 249–50, 253, 256–57, 297, 303, 305–06, 308, 310, 317, 327, 358, 364, 368, 370, 423, 493, 537, 548, 562, 573
traditionalism, 12, 45, 108, 304, 380, 410, 487, 508, 511, 562, 588
tyranny, 46, 50–52, 56, 78–82, 84–88, 95, 98, 145, 194, 208–09, 220, 241, 263,

272–73, 297–98, 302–03, 305, 308, 310–11, 316, 319, 322, 327, 342–43, 345, 347, 355, 383, 392, 447, 477, 508, 515, 519, 547, 593

union organization, 145, 178
universalism, 112, 165, 240, 247, 259–60, 269, 271–72, 275, 278–79, 322, 326, 402, 431, 490
utilitarianism, 173, 252, 432, 473, 568

Vatican Church, 66, 204, 206, 254, 257, 334, 348, 382, 398, 408–09, 447, 479, 592
Veblen, Thorstein 141, 143, 145, 162–64, 169–70, 192, 264, 284, 289, 365, 521, 594
vice-police state, 135, 170, 219, 318, 352, 362–70, 373–76, 378–81, 383–84, 388

war of extermination, 127, 129, 151–52, 164, 232, 246, 277
wealth, 2, 34, 38, 56, 103, 105–06, 120, 144, 148, 156, 164, 177, 178, 181–86, 189, 287, 415, 586–89, 591, 593
Weber, Max 2–5, 9–20, 24–39, 43–44, 47–51, 54–57, 62–65, 70–75, 78–81, 84–86, 88–90, 95–98, 102–07, 109–30, 134–41, 143–45, 147–56, 160–63, 165–66, 170–76, 188–94, 206–08, 210–12, 222–24, 237–39, 241–42, 245–48, 257, 261–74, 280–81, 283–90, 292–93, 297–302, 304–05, 308–09, 312–14, 592–94, 596, 599
welfare capitalism, 189
welfare state, 141, 171, 191, 256–57, 410, 487

xenophobia, 78, 391